Lecture Notes in Computer Science 6458

Commenced Publication in 1973
Founding and Former Series Editors:
Gerhard Goos, Juris Hartmanis, and Jan van Leeuw

Editorial Board

Printing: Mercedes-Druck, Berlin
Binding: Stein+Lehmann, Berlin

Lecture Notes in Computer Science 6498

Commenced Publication in 1973
Founding and Former Series Editors:
Gerhard Goos, Juris Hartmanis, and Jan van Leeuwen

Editorial Board

David Hutchison
Lancaster University, UK

Takeo Kanade
Carnegie Mellon University, Pittsburgh, PA, USA

Josef Kittler
University of Surrey, Guildford, UK

Jon M. Kleinberg
Cornell University, Ithaca, NY, USA

Alfred Kobsa
University of California, Irvine, CA, USA

Friedemann Mattern
ETH Zurich, Switzerland

John C. Mitchell
Stanford University, CA, USA

Moni Naor
Weizmann Institute of Science, Rehovot, Israel

Oscar Nierstrasz
University of Bern, Switzerland

C. Pandu Rangan
Indian Institute of Technology, Madras, India

Bernhard Steffen
TU Dortmund University, Germany

Madhu Sudan
Microsoft Research, Cambridge, MA, USA

Demetri Terzopoulos
University of California, Los Angeles, CA, USA

Doug Tygar
University of California, Berkeley, CA, USA

Gerhard Weikum
Max Planck Institute for Informatics, Saarbruecken, Germany

Pu-Jen Cheng   Min-Yen Kan
Wai Lam   Preslav Nakov (Eds.)

Information Retrieval Technology

6th Asia Information Retrieval
Societies Conference, AIRS 2010
Taipei, Taiwan, December 1-3, 2010
Proceedings

 Springer

Volume Editors

Pu-Jen Cheng
National Taiwan University
Department of Computer Science and Information Engineering
Taipei 10617, Taiwan R.O.C.
E-mail: pjcheng@iis.sinica.edu.tw

Min-Yen Kan
National University of Singapore
Department of Computer Science, School of Computing
Singapore 117417
E-mail: kanmy@comp.nus.edu.sg

Wai Lam
The Chinese University of Hong Kong
Department of Systems Engineering and Engineering Management
N.T., Hong Kong, China
E-mail: wlam@se.cuhk.edu.hk

Preslav Nakov
National University of Singapore
Department of Computer Science, School of Computing
Singapore 117417
E-mail: nakov@comp.nus.edu.sg

Library of Congress Control Number: 2010938622

CR Subject Classification (1998): H.3, H.4, F.2.2, I.4-5, E.1, H.2.8

LNCS Sublibrary: SL 3 – Information Systems and Application, incl. Internet/Web
and HCI

ISSN   0302-9743
ISBN-10   3-642-17186-9 Springer Berlin Heidelberg New York
ISBN-13   978-3-642-17186-4 Springer Berlin Heidelberg New York

springer.com

© Springer-Verlag Berlin Heidelberg 2010
Printed in Germany

Typesetting: Camera-ready by author, data conversion by Scientific Publishing Services, Chennai, India
Printed on acid-free paper   06/3180

Preface

The Asia Information Retrieval Societies Conference (AIRS) 2010 was the sixth conference in the AIRS series, aiming to bring together international researchers and developers to exchange new ideas and the latest results in information retrieval. The scope of the conference encompassed the theory and practice of all aspects of information retrieval in text, audio, image, video, and multimedia data.

AIRS 2010 continued the conference series that grew from the Information Retrieval with Asian Languages (IRAL) workshop series, started in 1996. It has become a mature venue for information retrieval work, finding support from the ACM Special Interest Group on Information Retrieval (SIGIR); the Association for Computational Linguistics and Chinese Language Processing (ACLCLP); ROCLING; and the Information Processing Society of Japan, Special Interest Group on Information Fundamentals and Access Technologies (IPSJ SIG-IFAT).

This year saw a sharp rise in the number of submissions over the previous year. A total of 120 papers were submitted, representing work by academics and practitioners not only from Asia, but also from Australia, Europe, North America, etc. The high quality of the work made it difficult for the dedicated program committee to decide which papers to feature at the conference. Through a double-blind reviewing process, 26 submissions (21%) were accepted as full oral papers and 31 (25%) were accepted as short posters.

The success of this conference was only possible with the support of all of the authors who submitted papers for review, the program committee members who constructively assessed the submissions, and the registered conference delegates. We thank them for their support of this conference, and for their long-term support of this Asian-centric venue for IR research and development.

For a conference to run smoothly, much behind-the-scenes work is necessary, most of which is largely unseen by the authors and delegates. We would like to thank Preslav Nakov, our publication chair, who painstakingly worked with each individual paper's authors to ensure formatting, spelling, diction, and grammar were completely error-free. We thank Lun-Wei Ku, our finance chair, who worked hard to reduce the conference registration rates. We also thank Chien-Wen Chen and Yen-Chieh Huang, our two AIRS 2010 webmasters, whose timely actions ensured that the website stay in sync with our program as it evolved. We would also like to thank Si-Chen Lee, President of the National Taiwan University, for accepting to be the honorary chair for the conference.

December 2010

Pu-Jen Cheng
Min-Yen Kan
Wai Lam

Organization

The Sixth Asia Information Retrieval Societies Conference (AIRS 2010) was organized by the National Taiwan University in cooperation with ACM SIGIR, ACLCLP, ROCLING, and IPSJ SIG-IFAT.

Steering Committee

Hsin-Hsi Chen	National Taiwan University, Taiwan
Wai Lam	The Chinese University of Hong Kong, China
Gary Geunbae Lee	Pohang University of Science and Technology, Korea
Alistair Moffat	The University of Melbourne, Australia
Hwee Tou Ng	National University of Singapore, Singapore
Tetsuya Sakai	Microsoft Research Asia, China
Dawei Song	The Robert Gordon University, UK
Masaharu Yoshioka	Hokkaido University, Japan

Advisory Board

Mun Kew Leong	National Library Board, Singapore
Sung Hyon Myaeng	Korea Advanced Institute of Science and Technology, Korea
Kam-Fai Wong	The Chinese University of Hong Kong, China

Organization Executive Committee

Honorary Conf. Chair	Si-Chen Lee President, National Taiwan University, Taiwan
Conference Chair	Pu-Jen Cheng National Taiwan University, Taiwan
Publication Chair	Preslav Nakov National University of Singapore, Singapore
PC Co-chairs	Wai Lam The Chinese University of Hong Kong, China Min-Yen Kan National University of Singapore, Singapore

Finance Chair	Lun-Wei Ku
	National Taiwan University, Taiwan
Webmasters	Chien-Wen Chen
	National Taiwan University, Taiwan
	Yen-Chieh Huang
	National Taiwan University, Taiwan

Area Chairs

Timothy Baldwin	The University of Melbourne, Australia
Atsushi Fujii	Tokyo Institute of Technology, Japan
Winston Hsu	National Taiwan University, Taiwan
Joemon Jose	University of Glasgow, UK
Tie-Yan Liu	Microsoft Research Asia, China
Tetsuya Sakai	Microsoft Research Asia, China
Kazunari Sugiyama	National University of Singapore, Singapore
Bin Wang	Chinese Academy of Sciences, China
William Webber	The University of Melbourne, Australia
Min Zhang	Tsinghua University, China
Yi Zhang	University of California, Santa Cruz, USA

Program Committee

Akiko Aizawa	National Institute of Informatics, Japan
Tomoyoshi Akiba	National Institute of Advanced Industrial Science and Technology, Japan
Enrique Alfonseca	Google Zurich, Switzerland
Sachi Arafat	University of Glasgow, UK
Ching Man Au	NTT Communication Science Labs, Japan
Jing Bai	Microsoft, USA
Timothy Baldwin	The University of Melbourne, Australia
Gosse Bouma	University of Groningen, Netherlands
Deng Cai	Zhejiang University, China
Rui Cai	Microsoft Research Asia, China
Ben Carterette	University of Delaware, USA
Enhong Chen	University of Science and Technology, China
Hsin-Hsi Chen	National Taiwan University, Taiwan
Seungjin Choi	Pohang University of Science and Technology, Korea
Shane Culpepper	RMIT University, Australia
James Curran	The University of Sydney, Australia
Rebecca Dridan	The University of Melbourne, Australia
Georges Dupret	Yahoo! Labs, USA

Atsushi Fujii	Tokyo Institute of Technology, Japan
Yong Gao	Yahoo! Beijing, China
Bo Gong	Oracle Corporation, USA
Jesse Prabawa Gozali	National University of Singapore, Singapore
Jiafeng Guo	Institute of Computing Technology, CAS, China
Cathal Gurrin	Dublin City University, Ireland
Ben Hachey	Capital Markets CRC, Australia
Kenji Hatano	Doshisha University, Japan
Daqing He	University of Pittsburgh, USA
Yin He	University of Science and Technology, China
Xiaofei He	Zhejiang University, China
Tao Hong	Zhejiang University, China
Winston Hsu	National Taiwan University, Taiwan
Xuanjing Huang	Fudan University, China
Adam Jatowt	Kyoto University, Japan
Hideo Joho	University of Tsukuba, Japan
Joemon Jose	University of Glasgow, UK
Hanmin Jung	Pohang University of Science and Technology, Korea
Noriko Kando	National Institute of Informatics, Japan
In-Su Kang	Kyungsung University, Korea
Evangelos Kanoulas	University of Sheffield, UK
Sarvnaz Karimi	NICTA, The University of Melbourne, Australia
Jaana Kekalainen	University of Tampere, Finland
Jinyoung Kim	University of Massachusetts, Amherst, USA
Jungi Kim	Pohang University of Science and Technology, Korea
Sang-Bum Kim	SK Telecom, Korea
Fuminori Kimura	Ritsumeikan University, Japan
Kazuaki Kishida	Keio University, Japan
Iraklis Klampanos	University of Glasgow, UK
Mounia Lalmas	University of Glasgow, UK
Wei Lai	Microsoft Research Asia, China
Andrew Lampert	CSIRO, Australia
Raymond Lau	City University of Hong Kong, Hong Kong
Gary Geunbae Lee	Pohang University of Science and Technology, Korea
Jong-Hyeok Lee	Pohang University of Science and Technology, Korea
Kian Chin Lee	Multimedia University, Malaysia
Hyowon Lee	Dublin City University, Ireland
Mun-Kew Leong	National Library Board, Singapore

Guoliang Li	Tsinghua University, China
Juanzi Li	Tsinghua University, China
Sujian Li	Peking University, China
Wenjie Li	The Hong Kong Polytechnic University, Hong Kong
Tie-Yan Liu	Microsoft Research Asia, China
Ting Liu	Harbin Institute of Technology, China
Yi Liu	Google Inc., USA
Yiqun Liu	Tsinghua University, China
Yue Liu	Chinese Academy of Sciences, China
Zhiyuan Liu	Tsinghua University, China
Si Luo	Purdue University, USA
Xueqiang Lv	Beijing Information Science and Technology University, China
Hao Ma	The Chinese University of Hong Kong, China
Qiang Ma	Kyoto University, Japan
Akira Maeda	Ritsumeikan University, Japan
David Martinez	NICTA, The University of Melbourne, Australia
Massimo Melucci	University of Padua, Italy
Alistair Moffat	The University of Melbourne, Australia
Tatsunori Mori	Yokohama National University, Japan
Mas Rina Mustaffa	Universiti Putra Malaysia, Malaysia
Seung-Hoon Na	National University of Singapore, Singapore
Preslav Nakov	National University of Singapore, Singapore
Hidetsugu Nanba	Hiroshima City University, Japan
Jianyun Nie	University of Montreal, Canada
Iadh Ounis	University of Glasgow, UK
Seong-Bae Park	Kyungpook National University, Korea
Will Radford	The University of Sydney, Australia
Reede Ren	University of Glasgow, UK
Ian Ruthven	University of Strathclyde, UK
Tetsuya Sakai	Microsoft Research Asia, China
Falk Scholer	RMIT University, Australia
Kazuhiro Seki	Kobe University, Japan
Yohei Seki	University of Tsukuba, Japan
Satoshi Sekine	New York University, USA
Hideki Shima	Carnegie Mellon University, USA
Toshiyuki Shimizu	Kyoto University, Japan
David Smith	University of Massachusetts, Amherst, USA
Ruihua Song	Microsoft Research Asia, China

Young-In Song   Microsoft Research Asia, China
Virach Sornlertlamvanich   NECTEC, Thailand
Mark Stevenson   Sheffield University, UK
Kazunari Sugiyama   National University of Singapore,
                                   Singapore
Bin Sun   Peking University, China
Le Sun   Chinese Academy of Sciences, China
Motofumi Suzuki   The Open University of Japan, Japan
Yu Suzuki   Nagoya University, Japan
Yee Fan Tan   National University of Singapore,
                                   Singapore
Chong Teng   Wuhan University, China
James Thom   RMIT University, Australia
Paul Thomas   CSIRO, Australia
Andew Trotman   University of Otago, New Zealand
Yuen-Hsien Tseng   National Taiwan University, Taiwan
Kiyotaka Uchimoto   National Institute of Information and
                                   Communications Technology, Japan
Takehito Utsuro   University of Tsukuba, Japan
Stephen Wan   Macquarie University, Australia
Bin Wang   Chinese Academy of Sciences, China
Jun Wang   University College London, UK
Mingwen Wang   Jiangxi Normal University, China
William Webber   The University of Melbourne, Australia
MingFang Wu   RMIT University, Australia
Yunqing Xia   Tsinghua University, China
Jun Xu   Microsoft Research Asia, China
Yinghui Xu   Ricoh, Japan
Ichiro Yamada   National Institute of Information and
                                   Communications Technology, Japan
Mikio Yamamoto   University of Tsukuba, Japan
Hongfei Yan   Peking University, China
Rong Yan   Carnegie Mellon University, USA
Patrick Ye   Monash University, Australia
Emine Yilmaz   Microsoft Research Cambridge, UK
Masaharu Yoshioka   Hokkaido University, Japan
Hwan Jo Yu   Pohang University of Science and
                                   Technology, Korea
Jinhui Yuan   Tsinghua University, China
Min Zhang   Tsinghua University, China
Yi Zhang   University of California, Santa Cruz, USA
Jin Zhao   National University of Singapore, Singapore
Jun Zhao   Chinese Academy of Sciences, China
Le Zhao   Carnegie Mellon University, USA
Zhaohui Zheng   Yahoo! Labs, USA
Tingshao Zhu   Chinese Academy of Sciences, China

Secondary Reviewers

Mathieu Blondel
Zhengguang Chen
Zhanying He
Jinha Kim
Sungchul Kim
Taehoon Kim
Youngdae Kim
Jaeyong Lee
Fangtao Li
Jiyi Li

Meladel Mistica
Joel Nothman
Sun Park
Huan Xia
Bin Xu
Dazhou Wang
Hao Wu
Lanbo Zhang
Miao Zheng

Sponsoring Institutions

National Science Council, Republic of China (Taiwan)
Ministry of Education, Republic of China (Taiwan)

Table of Contents

Poster Session

Session 4: NLP for IR – I

Session 5: Machine Learning for IR – II

Session 6: IR Models – II

Session 7: Web and QA

Session 8: Multimedia

Relevance Ranking Using Kernels

Jun Xu[1], Hang Li[1], and Chaoliang Zhong[2],[*]

[1] Microsoft Research Asia, 4F Sigma Center, No. 49 Zhichun Road, Beijing, China 100190
[2] Beijing University of Posts and Telecommunications, Beijing, China 100876
{junxu,hangli}@microsoft.com, clzhong@cn.fujitsu.com

Abstract. This paper is concerned with relevance ranking in search, particularly that using term dependency information. It proposes a novel and unified approach to relevance ranking using the kernel technique in statistical learning. In the approach, the general ranking model is defined as a kernel function of query and document representations. A number of kernel functions are proposed as specific ranking models in the paper, including BM25 Kernel, LMIR Kernel, and KL Divergence Kernel. The approach has the following advantages. (1) The (general) model can effectively represent different types of term dependency information and thus can achieve high performance. (2) The model has strong connections with existing models such as BM25 and LMIR. (3) It has solid theoretical background. (4) The model can be efficiently computed. Experimental results on web search dataset and TREC datasets show that the proposed kernel approach outperforms MRF and other baseline methods for relevance ranking.

Keywords: Information Retrieval, Relevance Ranking, Kernel.

1 Introduction

Relevance ranking is still a central issue of research in Information Retrieval. Traditionally, relevance ranking models are defined based on the bag-of-words assumption, i.e., query and document are viewed as two sets of words. These include Vector Space Model (VSM) [17], BM25 [15], and Language Models for IR (LMIR) [22].

There is a clear trend in IR recently on study of models beyond bag-of-words, particularly under the notion of term dependency or proximity, which assumes terms are dependent and takes into consideration in relevance ranking the cooccurrences of query terms in documents. For example, if the query is "machine learning book", then a document containing the phrase "machine learning" and the term "book" should be more relevant than a document in which the terms "machine", "learning", and "book" occur separately. It is obvious from the example that dependency information needs to be leveraged in relevance ranking. For instance, a model for using term dependency based on Markov Random Fields (MRF) has been proposed [11], in which the information on independent terms (unigrams), sequential terms (n-grams), and dependent terms is exploited. MRF is regarded as a state-of-the-art method for using term dependency.

In our view, an ideal ranking model using term dependency should have the following characteristics. (1) It can incorporate various types of term dependency information

---

[*] The work was conducted when Chaoliang Zhong was visiting Microsoft Research Asia.

P.-J. Cheng et al. (Eds.): AIRS 2010, LNCS 6458, pp. 1–12, 2010.
© Springer-Verlag Berlin Heidelberg 2010

to represent relevance, and thus can achieve high accuracy in ranking. (2) It has strong connections with existing models . (This is necessary, as existing models of BM25 and LMIR already perform quite well.) (3) It is based on solid theory. (4) It can be efficiently computed. Although previous work on term dependencies made progresses, further study on the problem still appears to be necessary. In this paper, we aim to conduct a comprehensive study on relevance ranking using term dependency, and to propose a general ranking model which has the advantages. Specifically this paper proposes a novel approach to relevance ranking, on the basis of String Kernel in statistical learning. It defines the relevance ranking model as a kernel function of query string and document string. The original query string and document string are mapped into vectors in a higher dimensional Hilbert Space and relevance (similarity) between the two representations is defined as dot product in the Hilbert Space.

As case studies, we introduce two kernel functions, BM25 Kernel and LMIR Kernel, and use one existing kernel function, Kullback-Leibler (KL) Divergence Kernel, in this paper. The former two are asymmetric kernel functions and the last is a symmetric kernel function. They correspond to different ways of mapping the original query and document strings to the Hilbert Space.

(1) The kernel based models can naturally represent various types of term dependency information, for example, n-grams and n-dependent-terms. Since the essence of relevance is to compare the similarity between query and document, a richer model on the similarity between query and document can then be realized with the approach and high performance in relevance ranking can be achieved. (2) BM25 Kernel and LMIR Kernel respectively include conventional BM25 model and LMIR model as special cases. (Note that many other relevance models can also be interpreted as kernel functions, for example, the traditional VSM.) Within the kernel framework, different ranking models can be easily studied and compared. (3) Kernel methods are becoming very popular in statistical learning. It is attractive because of its powerful representability. The proposed approach using kernel thus has a solid theoretical background. It bridges the gap between relevance ranking and machine learning, and provide a framework for automatically learning ranking model using kernel machines. (4) Kernel functions are essentially dot product. This enables an efficient computation in search.

The implication of the work is far beyond using term dependency. The proposed kernel-based ranking models are actually generalized versions of conventional ranking models. It provides a new view, namely kernel function, on relevance ranking.

We conducted experiments using data from a web search engine and TREC data, and found that BM25 Kernel, LMIR Kernel, and KL Kernel perform better than MRF and other bag-of-words models for relevance ranking. We conclude, therefore, that the kernel approach proposed in this paper really has advantages.

2   Related Work

Conventional Information Retrieval models such as Vector Space Model (VSM) [17], BM25 [15], and Language Models for IR (LMIR) [22] were originally proposed based on the bag-of-words assumption, which is obviously too strong, as in many cases query terms (words) are related, and their relations (dependencies) should also be considered in relevance ranking. The ranking models beyond the bag-of-words may be categorized into two groups. One approach considers the use of term dependency, specifically, it assumes that the query is composed of several units of terms (e.g., n-grams) and utilizes the occurrences of the units in the document in ranking. For example, Metzler and Croft [11] proposed using Markov Random Fields to characterize different types of term dependency relations. For other related work see [1,2,4,13]. The other approach considers the use of degree of approximate match of query to document, for example, it looks at the minimum span of the query terms appearing in the document, also referred to as proximity. Tao and Zhai [19] conducted a comprehensive study on proximity measures for relevance ranking and found that the proximity measures are useful for further improving relevance. (Also refer to [8,6].)

Kernel function characterizes a kind of similarity between two representations $k(x, y)$, where x and y denote representations. For example, String Kernel is a special type of kernel function defined on text strings, i.e., x and y are strings [5,9]. KL Divergence Kernel is a type of kernel function defined based on KL Divergence [12]. Kernel functions have been applied into several tasks in IR. In [21], the KL Divergence Kernel was used for calculating the similarity between documents given a query. In [9], a method for text classification using String Kernels was studied. In [16], a kernel function for measuring similarity between short texts was proposed. In [10], a number of String Kernel functions were surveyed.

There are two ways to create (or identify) a kernel function. The Mercer's theorem provides a sufficient and necessary condition of kernel function, that is, any continuous, symmetric, positive semi-definite function $k(x, y)$ is a kernel function. One can also define a kernel function in a constructive way, i.e., through definition of mapping function. Usually a kernel function is symmetric in the sense $k(x, y) = k(y, x)$. Asymmetric kernel functions have also been introduced, which satisfy $k(x, y) \neq k(y, x)$ [20]. Obviously asymmetric kernel functions are more general than symmetric kernel functions.

3   Kernel Approach

The essence of relevance is to compare the similarity between query and document, or the matching degree between query and document. Different ways of defining the similarity or matching degree lead to different ranking models. In this paper, we use kernel techniques in statistical learning to construct ranking models. We first give a general model, and then some specific examples.

3.1   General Model

There are three issues we need to consider when defining a ranking model: query representation, document representation, and similarity calculation between query and document representations. Here, we assume that query and document are two strings of words (terms). Such a representation can retain all the major information contained in the query and document. We then define the similarity function between the query and document as kernel function between query string and document string.

Suppose that Q is the space of queries (word strings), and $\mathcal{D}$ is the space of documents (word strings). (q, d) is a pair of query and document from Q and $\mathcal{D}$. There is a mapping function $\phi : Q \mapsto \mathcal{H}$ from the query space to the Hilbert space where $\mathcal{H}$ denotes the Hilbert Space. $\phi(q)$ then stands for the mapped vector in $\mathcal{H}$ from q. Similarly, there is a mapping function $\phi' : \mathcal{D} \mapsto \mathcal{H}$ from the document space to the Hilbert Space $\mathcal{H}$. $\phi'(d)$ then stands for the mapped vector in $\mathcal{H}$ from d. The similarity function between q and d is defined as a kernel function between q and d,

$$k(q,d) = \langle \phi(q), \phi'(d) \rangle = \sum_i \phi(q)_i \cdot \phi'(d)_i. \tag{1}$$

The kernel function is actually the dot product between vectors $\phi(q)$ and $\phi'(d)$, respectively mapped from q and d. We call the kernel function $k(q,d)$ in Eq. (1) (general) kernel-based ranking model. Note that $k(q,d)$ is an *asymmetric* function, which means $k(q,d) \neq k(d,q)$, because ϕ and ϕ' are not necessarily identical. When ϕ and ϕ' are identical, the kernel function becomes a symmetric function, i.e., $k(q,d) = k(d,q)$.

The general kernel-based ranking model can include most existing relevance ranking models such as VSM, BM25, LMIR, and even LSI [3], as will be made clearer later. For example, in VSM, the query string and the document string are mapped into vectors of tf-idf values and dot product between the vectors is calculated and used, which is a very simple example of the general ranking function in Eq. (1).

3.2   Model Construction

Let us introduce the way of creating a kernel-based ranking model. We first identify a 'type of dependent query terms' for which we care about the occurrences in documents. (For example, if the type is bigram, we decompose the query "machine learning book" into two bigrams "machine learning" and "learning book", and we look at their occurrences in documents.) Next we assume to respectively map the query string and document string into vectors of the type in a Hilbert Space. (For example, we map query and document into vectors of bigrams.) We can then construct a kernel function for the type on the basis of the mapping functions. Finally, we can define a ranking model by combining the kernel functions in different types using the properties of kernel functions (cf., Section 4.3). That is to say we actually create kernel functions.

As types, we can consider the occurrences of independent query terms in the document (unigrams), the occurrences of sequential query terms in the document (n-grams), or the occurrences of dependent query terms in the document (n-dependent-terms). Then we can create a vector of unigrams, a vector of n-grams, or a vector of n-dependent-terms in the Hilbert Space. The relation between unigrams, n-grams, and n-dependent-terms is illustrated in Fig. 1. For each type, the set of possible units (unigrams, n-grams, or n-dependent-terms) is fixed, provided that the vocabulary is fixed. We denote the set of units as $\mathcal{X}$ and each element of it x.

In this paper we give three examples of kernel-based models. They are BM25 Kernel, LMIR Kernel, and KL Kernel.

3.3   BM25 Kernel

BM25 Kernel is a generalization of conventional BM25 model using String Kernel. It has a similar form as BM25, but is more general in the sense that it can make use of term dependencies in different types. It is an asymmetric kernel function.

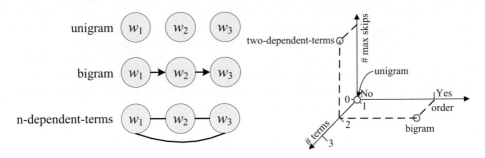

Fig. 1. Illustration of unigram, n-gram, and n-dependent-terms

Fig. 2. Three factors for term dependency

The BM25 Kernel function between query q and document d in type t is defined as

$$\text{BM25-Kernel}_t(q, d) = \langle \phi_t^{\text{BM25}}(q), \phi_t'^{\text{BM25}}(d)\rangle,$$

where $\phi_t^{\text{BM25}}(q)$ and $\phi_t'^{\text{BM25}}(d)$ are two vectors of type t in the Hilbert Space mapped from q and d. Each dimension of the vector corresponds to a unit x:

$$\phi_t^{\text{BM25}}(q)_x = \frac{(k_3 + 1) \cdot f_t(x, q)}{k_3 + f_t(x, q)} \text{ and } \phi_t'^{\text{BM25}}(d)_x = \text{IDF}_t(x) \cdot \frac{(k_1 + 1) \cdot f_t(x, d)}{k_1\left(1 - b + b\frac{f_t(d)}{avg f_t}\right) + f_t(x, d)},$$

where k_1, k_3, and b are parameters, $f_t(x, q)$ and $f_t(x, d)$ are frequencies of unit x with type t in q and d, respectively, $f_t(d)$ is total number of units with type t in document d, and $avg f_t$ is average number of units $f_t(d)$ with type t per document within the whole collection. $\text{IDF}_t(x) = \log\frac{df_t - df_t(x) + 0.5}{df_t(x) + 0.5}$ is inverse document frequency of unit x with type t, where $df_t(x)$ is number of documents in which unit x with type t occurs, and df_t is total number of documents that have units with type t. BM25 Kernel in type t becomes

$$\text{BM25-Kernel}_t(q, d) = \sum_x \text{IDF}_t(x) \times \frac{(k_3 + 1) \times f_t(x, q)}{k_3 + f_t(x, q)} \times \frac{(k_1 + 1) \times f_t(x, d)}{k_1\left(1 - b + b\frac{f_t(d)}{avg f_t}\right) + f_t(x, d)}.$$

Finally, BM25 Kernel is defined as a linear combination of kernels over all the types:

$$\text{BM25-Kernel}(q, d) = \sum_t \alpha_t \text{BM25-Kernel}_t(q, d), \ \alpha_t \geq 0. \tag{2}$$

3.4 LMIR Kernel

We employ Dirichlet smoothing as an example. Other smoothing methods can also be used. The LMIR Kernel between query q and document d in type t is defined as

$$\text{LMIR-Kernel}_t(q, d) = \langle \phi_t^{\text{LMIR}}(q), \phi_t'^{\text{LMIR}}(d)\rangle + f_t(q) \cdot \log\frac{\mu}{f_t(d) + \mu},$$

where μ is free parameter, and $\phi_t^{\text{LMIR}}(q)$ and $\phi_t'^{\text{LMIR}}(d)$ are two vectors of type t in the Hilbert Space mapped from query q and document d, respectively. Each dimension of the vector corresponds to a unit x:

$$\phi_t^{\mathtt{LMIR}}(q)_x = f_t(x, q) \text{ and } \phi_t'^{\mathtt{LMIR}}(d)_x = \log\left(1 + \frac{f_t(x, d)}{\mu P(x|t)}\right),$$

where $P(x|t)$ is probability of unit x with type t in the whole collection. $P(x|t)$ plays a similar role as inverse document frequency $\mathtt{IDF}_t(x)$ in BM25 Kernel. Combining the two, the LMIR Kernel function in type t becomes

$$\mathtt{LMIR\text{-}Kernel}_t(q, d) = \sum_x f_t(x, q) \cdot \log\left(1 + \frac{f_t(x, d)}{\mu P(x|t)}\right) + f_t(q) \cdot \log\frac{\mu}{f_t(d) + \mu}.$$

Finally, we have

$$\mathtt{LMIR\text{-}Kernel}(q, d) = \sum_t \alpha_t \mathtt{LMIR\text{-}Kernel}_t(q, d), \ \alpha_t \geq 0. \tag{3}$$

3.5   KL Kernel

In this paper, we also use the KL Divergence kernel as a specific kernel-based ranking model, referred to as KL Kernel. Unlike BM25 Kernel and LMIR Kernel, KL Kernel is a *symmetric* kernel function. Another difference is that KL Kernel represents a mapping of the query and document into a Hilbert Space with an infinite number of dimensions. KL Kernel was previously used in document similarity comparison [12], and this is the first time it is used in relevance ranking.

In KL Kernel in a type t, the query and document are represented by distributions. We define a distribution $\mathbb{P}_t(q) = (P(x_1|t, q), P(x_2|t, q), \cdots, P(x_N|t, q))$ of units x with type t in query q, where $P(x_i|t, q)$ is probability of unit x_i given type t and query q, and N is size of X. Similarly, we define a distribution $\mathbb{P}_t(d) = (P(x_1|t, d), P(x_2|t, d), \cdots, P(x_N|t, d))$ of units x with type t in document d. Then, the KL Kernel function between q and d in type t is defined as

$$\mathtt{KL\text{-}Kernel}_t(q, d) = \exp\{-D(\mathbb{P}_t(q)\|\mathbb{P}_t(d)) - D(\mathbb{P}_t(d)\|\mathbb{P}_t(q))\}.$$

Note that the kernel function represents dot product between two vectors in a Hilbert Space with infinite number of dimensions. (We can use Mercer's theorem to prove that it is a kernel function. [12]) $D(\mathbb{P}_t(q)\|\mathbb{P}_t(d))$ is the KL divergence of $\mathbb{P}_t(d)$ from $\mathbb{P}_t(q)$:

$$D(\mathbb{P}_t(q)\|\mathbb{P}_t(d)) = \sum_{i=1}^N P(x_i|t, q) \log\frac{P(x_i|t, q)}{P(x_i|t, d)}.$$

The KL Kernel function is defined as

$$\mathtt{KL\text{-}Kernel}(q, d) = \prod_t \mathtt{KL\text{-}Kernel}_t(q, d)^{\alpha_t}. \tag{4}$$

According to the properties of kernel function, $\mathtt{KL\text{-}Kernel}(q, d)$ is still a kernel. For efficiency consideration, we actually take logarithmic function of the kernel function. This will not change the ranking results.

$$\mathtt{KL\text{-}Kernel}'(q, d) = \log(\mathtt{KL\text{-}Kernel}(q, d)) = \sum_t \alpha_t \left(-D(\mathbb{P}_t(q)\|\mathbb{P}_t(d)) - D(\mathbb{P}_t(d)\|\mathbb{P}_t(q))\right).$$

Smoothing is also needed in estimation of the probability distributions in KL Kernel. In this paper we employ the Dirichlet smoothing method [22]: $P(x|t, d) = \frac{f_t(x,d)+\mu P(x|t)}{f_t(d)+\mu}$.

4   Advantages of the Kernel Approach

4.1   Representability

The kernel approach to ranking has rich representation ability. There are several orthogonal factors which one needs to consider when using term dependencies of different types. They are number of terms, order preservation, maximum number of skipping terms. Suppose that the query is "machine learning book". Number of terms indicates whether the term units we use consist of two terms or three terms, etc in documents ("machine learning" vs "machine learning book"). Order preservation means we care about the order of query terms ("machine learning" vs "learning machine") in documents. Maximum number of skipping terms includes the cases in which there are other terms occurring in between the terms in question ("machine book").

Combining the factors above can give us different types of dependencies, including some complex ones. The n-gram models belong to the cases in which different numbers of *ordered and non-skipping* terms are used. The n-dependent-terms models fall into the cases in which different numbers of *non-ordered and skipping* terms are used. The unigram model is the simplest. Fig. 2 shows the relations among the factors. Each factor is represented as one axis; the first axis corresponds to order preservation, the second maximum number of skips, and the third number of terms. It further shows the positions of different types of dependencies.

One can immediately notice that the kernel approach proposed in this paper can easily utilize the different types of term dependencies (types). In the experiments in this paper, we make use of three types: unigram, bigram, and two-dependent-terms.

4.2   Relation to Conventional Models

It is easy to verify that BM25 Kernel and LMIR Kernel respectively include conventional BM25 and LMIR models as special cases. Specifically, when the type is unigram, the kernel functions become the existing ranking models.

The kernel approach to relevance ranking proposed in this paper, thus, provides a new interpretation of many IR ranking models. These include not only BM25 and LMIR, but also VSM and even LSI. Relevance ranking models are nothing but dot product between vectors which are nonlinearly mapped from query and document.

The kernel functions (BM25 Kernel, LMIR Kernel, and KL Kernel) have similar shapes as functions of unit frequency in document (e.g., term frequency in document for the case of unigram). (Note that unit frequency in query is usually fixed to one, because queries are short.) Fig. 3 shows plots of the functions. From the figure we can see that although BM25 and LMIR were derived from different theories, they actually have similar shapes as functions of unit frequency. This can in part explain why BM25 and LMIR perform almost equally well in practice. This also strongly suggest kernel functions including KL Kernel would have similar performances in relevance ranking. As will be seen in Section 5, this is in fact true.

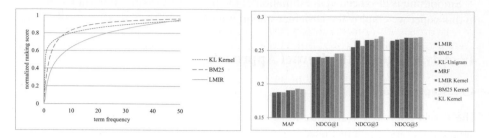

Fig. 3. KL Kernel, BM25 Kernel, and LMIR Kernel as a function of unit (term) frequency

Fig. 4. Ranking accuracies on the web search data

4.3   Theoretical Background

Another advantage of taking the kernel approach is that it has solid theoretical background. As a result, deeper understanding of the problem and broader use of the technique become possible.

For example, it is easy to verify that kernel functions have the following closure properties, which means several ways of combining kernel functions will still result in kernel functions. Let k_1 and k_2 be any two kernels. Then the function k given by

1. $k(x, y) = k_1(y, x)$;   2. $k(x, y) = k_1(x, y) + k_2(x, y)$;
3. $k(x, y) = \alpha k_1(x, y)$, for all $\alpha > 0$;   4. $k(x, y) = k_1(x, y) \cdot k_2(x, y)$

are also kernels. Note that this is true even for *asymmetric* kernel functions. That means we can create different ranking models by taking sum or product of kernel functions.

In recent years, kernel learning[18,14], which aims to learn a kernel function from training data, has been proposed. The proposed kernel approach for relevance ranking bridges the gap between information retrieval and machine learning. It provides a framework for learning optimal ranking model using machine learning. We will further investigate the problem in our future work.

4.4   Efficient Implementation

The kernel functions proposed above can be calculated efficiently. This is because kernel functions are essentially dot products and their computations only need to be performed on units which occur in query or document. (The values of the other units are just zero). For example, for $D(\mathbb{P}_t(q)\|\mathbb{P}_t(d))$ (with Dirichlet smoothing) in KL Kernel we actually only need to calculate

$$
\sum_{x: f_t(x,q)>0 \vee f_t(x,d)>0} P(x|t, q) \log \frac{P(x|t, q)}{P(x|t, d)} + \sum_{x: f_t(x,q)=0 \wedge f_t(x,d)=0} \frac{\mu P(x|t)}{\mu + f_t(q)} \log \frac{f_t(d) + \mu}{f_t(q) + \mu}
$$

$$
= \sum_{x: f_t(x,q)>0 \vee f_t(x,d)>0} P(x|t, q) \log \frac{P(x|t, q)}{P(x|t, d)} + \frac{\mu}{\mu + f_t(q)} \log \frac{f_t(d) + \mu}{f_t(q) + \mu} \sum_{x: f_t(x,q)>0 \vee f_t(x,d)>0} (1 - P(x|t)),
$$

where μ is the smoothing parameter.

5   Experiments

We conducted experiments to test the effectiveness of the proposed kernel approach, using a dataset from a web search engine and TREC data sets of OHSUMED [7] and AP. Specifically, we tested the performances of BM25 Kernel, LMIR Kernel, and KL Kernel. In the kernels, as types of term dependencies we used unigram, bigram, and two-dependent-terms. The final ranking score is defined as linear combination of the kernel function scores:

$$\text{Score} = (1 - \lambda_1 - \lambda_2) \cdot \text{kernel}_{unigram} + \lambda_1 \cdot \text{kernel}_{bigram} + \lambda_2 \cdot \text{kernel}_{two-dependent-terms},$$

where λ_1 and λ_2 are parameters. (It is still a kernel function, c.f., Section 4.3.)

BM25 and LMIR (with Dirichlet smoothing) were selected as baselines in the experiments, as representatives of bag-of-words models. We also viewed KL-Unigram as a baseline, in which only unigram is used in KL Kernel. MRF was also chosen as a baseline of using term dependencies. For MRF model the same term dependency information (unigram, bigram, and two-dependent-terms) was used for fair comparison.

We adopted mean average precision (MAP) and NDCG@N ($N = 1, 3$, and 5) as evaluation measures. The web search dataset has five levels of relevance: "Perfect", "Excellent", "Good", "Fair", and "Bad". We considered the first three as relevant when calculating MAP. The OHSUMED dataset have three levels of relevance: "definitely relevant", "partially relevant", and "not relevant". We considered "definitely relevant" and "partially relevant" as relevant when calculating MAP.

5.1   Experiments on the Web Search Dataset

In this experiment, we used the web search dataset. The dataset contains about 2.5 million web pages, and 235 long queries randomly selected from query log. Each query has at least 8 terms. The average query length is 10.25 terms. We use long queries because the paper focuses on the term dependency in search. For each query, the associated documents are labeled by several annotators. In total, there are 6,271 labeled query-document pairs. On average each query has 26.68 documents labeled.

We tested the accuracies of ranking models and obtained the results in Fig. 4. We can observe an overall trend that the kernel based ranking models perform better than the bag-of-words models and the MRF model. Specifically, the kernel-based models outperform their counterparts (for example, BM25 Kernel works better than BM25, etc). There are always kernel-based models working better than MRF in different settings.

In the experiments, we tuned two parameters λ_1 and λ_2 for each kernel function. We investigated the sensitivity of the performances with respect to the two parameters. Specifically, we changed the values of a parameter and fixed the other at its optimal value (the optimal values are $\lambda_1 = 0.4$ and $\lambda_2 = 0.1$). The performances in terms of MAP with respect to parameter values are reported in Fig. 5.

The KL kernel has another parameter μ. We also carried out experiments to investigate how this parameter impacts the performances. We changed the values of the parameter and observed the model's performances in terms of MAP. Fig. 6 shows the performance curve. We can see that there is a flat region near the optimal value ($\mu = 4.0$), which means the model's performances are not sensitive to μ.

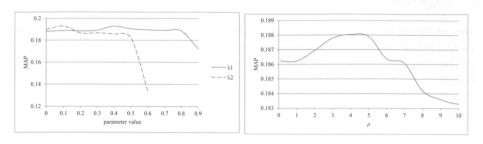

Fig. 5. Ranking accuracies of KL Kernel w.r.t. λ_1 and λ_2

Fig. 6. Ranking accuracies of KL Kernel w.r.t. μ

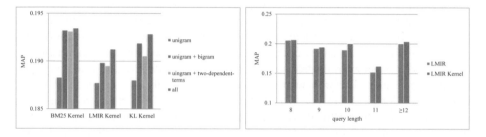

Fig. 7. BM25 Kernel, LMIR Kernel, and KL Kernel with different term dependencies

Fig. 8. Ranking accuracies of KL-Unigram and the KL Kernel by query lengths

We conducted experiments to verify how the use of term dependency information can improve ranking accuracy. Specifically, we tested the performances of BM25 Kernel (and also LMIR Kernel and KL Kernel) with unigram only, with unigram plus bigram, with unigram plus two-dependent-terms, and with unigram plus bigram and two-dependent-terms (denoted as "all"), in terms of MAP and NDCG. Fig. 7 shows the results in terms of MAP. We can see that bigram and two-dependent-terms really help to improve the ranking accuracies in terms of MAP (we observe the same tendency for the results in terms of NDCG). If they are combined together, the ranking accuracies can be further improved. This indicates that the kernel-based model really has the ability of incorporating different types of dependency information.

We also conducted experiments to investigate how KL Kernel can improve the ranking accuracies, especially on long queries. We calculated MAP (and NDCG) for KL-Unigram and KL Kernel on each query, and grouped the queries by length. Fig. 8 show the results. From the results, we can see that KL Kernel improve MAP scores when queries become longer. This indicates that the kernel-based models are more effective when queries become longer. The same tendency can be found for methods of BM25 Kernel, LMIR Kernel and for measures of NDCG.

5.2   Experiments on the OHSUMED and the AP Datasets

In this experiment, we used the OHSUMED [7] and TREC AP datasets to test the performances of the ranking models. The OHSUMED dataset consists of 348,566

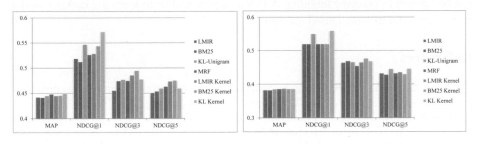

Fig. 9. Ranking accuracies on the OHSUMED   **Fig. 10.** Ranking accuracies on the AP data

documents and 106 queries. There are in total 16,140 query-document pairs upon which relevance judgments are made. The relevance judgments are either "d" (*definitely relevant*), "p" (*possibly relevant*), or "n"(*not relevant*). The AP collection contains 158,240 articles of Associated Press in 1988 and 1990. 50 queries are selected from the TREC topics (No.51 ~ No.100). Each query has a number of documents associated and they are labeled as "relevant" or "irrelevant". In total, there are 8,933 query-document pairs labeled. On average, each query has 178.66 labeled documents.

We used the Lemur toolkit[1] as our experiment platform. The datasets were indexed and queries were processed with Lemur. The experimental results are shown in Fig. 9 and Fig. 10. Again, we can see that the kernel-based models work better than the bag-of-words models and MRF. However, the improvements are smaller than those on the web search data. This is probably because the query length of data is short (on average 4.96 terms per query on OHSUMED and 3.22 terms per query on AP).

6   Conclusion

In this paper, we have studied relevance ranking models, particularly, those using term dependencies. Our work is new and unique in that we employ the kernel technique in statistical learning in the analysis and construction of ranking models. We have defined three kernel based ranking models: BM25 Kernel, LMIR Kernel, and KL Kernel. The former two are generalization of BM25 and LMIR, and the latter is a new model.

The general ranking model employed in the our approach has (1) rich representability for relevance ranking particularly for that using term dependencies (different types of term dependencies are summarized in the paper, and the kernel based ranking model can naturally represent them.), (2) strong connections with existing models, (3) solid theoretical background, and (4) efficient calculation.

Experimental results on web search data and TREC data show that (1) the kernel based ranking models outperform the conventional bag-of-words models and the MRF model using the same information, (2) the kernel functions can really effectively incorporate different types of term dependency information (from unigram to bigram and two-dependent-terms), (3) the kernel functions work particularly well for long queries.

There are several issues which need further investigations as future work. (1) The relationship between the proposed approach needs more studies. (2) Kernel functions

---

[1] http://www.lemurproject.org/

can be learned in machine learning. A future step would be to learn the ranking model by plugging it into some kernel machines.

References

1. Bai, J., Chang, Y., Cui, H., Zheng, Z., Sun, G., Li, X.: Investigation of partial query proximity in web search. In: Proc. of 17th WWW, pp. 1183–1184 (2008)
2. Büttcher, S., Clarke, C.L.A., Lushman, B.: Term proximity scoring for ad-hoc retrieval on very large text collections. In: Proc. of 29th SIGIR. pp. 621–622 (2006)
3. Deerwester, S., Dumais, S.T., Furnas, G.W., Landauer, T.K., Harshman, R.: Indexing by latent semantic analysis. J. of American Society for Information Science 41, 391–407 (1990)
4. Gao, J., Nie, J.Y., Wu, G., Cao, G.: Dependence language model for information retrieval. In: Proceedings of the 27th Annual International ACM SIGIR Conference, pp. 170–177 (2004)
5. Haussler, D.: Convolution kernels on discrete structures. Tech. rep., Dept. of Computer Science, University of California at Santa Cruz (1999)
6. Hawking, D., Thistlewaite, P.B.: Proximity operators - so near and yet so far. In: Proceedings of the 4th Text Retrieval Conference (1995)
7. Hersh, W., Buckley, C., Leone, T.J., Hickam, D.: Ohsumed: an interactive retrieval evaluation and new large test collection for research. In: Proc. of 17th SIGIR, pp. 192–201 (1994)
8. Keen, E.M.: Some aspects of proximity searching in text retrieval systems. J. Inf. Sci. 18(2), 89–98 (1992)
9. Lodhi, H., Saunders, C., Shawe-Taylor, J., Cristianini, N., Watkins, C.: Text classification using string kernels. J. Mach. Learn. Res. 2, 419–444 (2002)
10. Martins, A.: String kernels and similarity measures for information retrieval. Tech. rep., Priberam, Lisbon, Portugal (2006)
11. Metzler, D., Croft, W.B.: A markov random field model for term dependencies. In: Proceedings of the 28th Annual International ACM SIGIR Conference, pp. 472–479 (2005)
12. Moreno, P.J., Ho, P.P., Vasconcelos, N.: A kullback-leibler divergence based kernel for svm classification in multimedia applications. In: NIPS 16, MIT Press, Cambridge (2003)
13. Na, S.H., Kim, J., Kang, I.S., Lee, J.H.: Exploiting proximity feature in bigram language model for information retrieval. In: Proc. of 31st SIGIR, pp. 821–822 (2008)
14. Ong, C.S., Smola, A.J., Williamson, R.C.: Learning the kernel with hyperkernels. J. Mach. Learn. Res. 6, 1043–1071 (2005)
15. Robertson, S.E., Walker, S., Jones, S., Hancock-Beaulieu, M., Gatford, M.: Okapi at trec-3. In: Proceedings of the 3rd Text REtrieval Conference (1994)
16. Sahami, M., Heilman, T.D.: A web-based kernel function for measuring the similarity of short text snippets. In: Proc. of 15th WWW, pp. 377–386 (2006)
17. Salton, G., Wong, A., Yang, C.S.: A vector space model for automatic indexing. Commun. ACM 18(11), 613–620 (1975)
18. Sonnenburg, S., Rätsch, G., Schäfer, C., Schölkopf, B.: Large scale multiple kernel learning. J. Mach. Learn. Res. 7, 1531–1565 (2006)
19. Tao, T., Zhai, C.: An exploration of proximity measures in information retrieval. In: Proc. of 30th SIGIR, pp. 295–302 (2007)
20. Tsuda, K.: Support vector classifier with asymmetric kernel functions. In: European Symposium on Artificial Neural Networks, pp. 183–188 (1999)
21. Xie, Y., Raghavan, V.V.: Language-modeling kernel based approach for information retrieval. J. Am. Soc. Inf. Sci. Technol. 58(14), 2353–2365 (2007)
22. Zhai, C., Lafferty, J.: A study of smoothing methods for language models applied to information retrieval. ACM Trans. Inf. Syst. 22(2), 179–214 (2004)

Mining YouTube to Discover Extremist Videos, Users and Hidden Communities

Ashish Sureka, Ponnurangam Kumaraguru,
Atul Goyal, and Sidharth Chhabra*

Indraprastha Institute of Information Technology,
New Delhi - 110078
{ashish,pk,atul08015}@iiitd.ac.in, sidharth.chhabra2011@coe.dce.edu
http://www.iiitd.edu.in/~pk/precog/

Abstract. We describe a semi-automated system to assist law enforcement and intelligence agencies dealing with cyber-crime related to promotion of hate and radicalization on the Internet. The focus of this work
is on mining YouTube to discover hate videos, users and virtual hidden
communities. Finding precise information on YouTube is a challenging
task because of the huge size of the YouTube repository and a large
subscriber base. We present a solution based on data mining and social network analysis (using a variety of relationships such as friends,
subscriptions, favorites and related videos) to aid an analyst in discovering insightful and actionable information. Furthermore, we performed
a systematic study of the features and properties of the data and hidden social networks which has implications in understanding extremism
on Internet. We take a case study based approach and perform empirical
validation of the proposed hypothesis. Our approach succeeded in finding
hate videos which were validated manually.

Keywords: Information Retrieval, Hate and Extremism Detection, Security Informatics, YouTube Content Analysis, Social Network Analysis.

1   Introduction

Video-sharing websites such as YouTube have become a channel for spreading extremism and being used as a Internet based distribution platform for like-minded
people to interact, publicize and share their ideologies [5]. Due to low publication barrier (self-publishing model) and anonymity, websites such as YouTube
contains a large database of user generated content (UGC) in the form of videos
and textual comments which are malicious and racist (this is despite several
efforts by YouTube administrators to remove offensive content based on users
complaints) [1], [6]. Online extremism and hate content can have a negative
impact to the society and the prevalence of such easily accessible content (as

---

* The author is a student at DTU (Delhi Technological University). However, this work
  was performed while the author was doing his internship at IIIT-D (Indraprastha
  Institute of Information Technology, Delhi).

P.-J. Cheng et al. (Eds.): AIRS 2010, LNCS 6458, pp. 13–24, 2010.

anyone can watch online videos and does not even need to create an account) is thus a major concern to the people, government and law enforcement agencies. Solutions to counter cyber-crime related to promotion of hate and radicalization on the Internet is an area which has recently attracted a lot of research attention. The information need of a law enforcement agent or a security analyst detecting cyber-hate on YouTube (the focus of this work) is the following[1]:

1. *Videos* promoting hate and extremism
2. Influential *users* and *leaders* playing a central role in spreading such sentiments
3. Virtual *communities* and hidden social networks of people with the shared agenda and interest

Furthermore, a study of the *properties* of hate related YouTube videos, users and communities can lead to a better understanding of the problem and have implications in designing solutions to address such a problem. Finding extremist videos, users and virtual communities on YouTube is a technically challenging task due to the vastness of YouTube repository in terms of the number of videos, users and the different types of relationships between them. Keeping in mind the need to devise solutions for countering and studying cyber-hate, the *research aim* of this work is:

1. To investigate solutions to support a security analyst to extract actionable information from YouTube with respect to cyber-hate and extremism
2. To investigate the properties and features of the extremist content, users and hidden communities on YouTube

We now compare and contrast our work from closely related previous research and in context to related work list the unique contributions of this paper.

Analysis of Online Hate Videos. Reid et al. studied extremist and terrorist groups' videos and perform a content analysis of 60 jihadi videos. They analyze attributes like video types (documentary, suicide attack, propaganda, instruction), production features (special effects, subtitles) and communication approaches (audience segmentation) [11]. Adam et al. study online radicalization by analyzing dataset from a group within YouTube. They studied user-profile information, perform sentiment and lexical analysis of forum comments, apply social network analysis and derive insights on gender differences in views around jihad-promoting content on YouTube [1]. Conway et al. perform an analysis of jihadi video content on YouTube with a focus on martyr-promoting material from Iraq [6]. They studied a sample of 50 videos uploaded by 30 individual users and analyzed user profiles (categorizing users as supporters or critic), comments (total of 1443 comments by 940 separate users), demographic details (age and current location), popularity metrics (such as number of views, comments and ratings).

---

[1] Based on inputs from senior officers from law enforcement and intelligence agencies.

Analysis of Online Hate Blogs. Chau et al. present a semi-automated approach to analyze virtual hate communities in blogosphere. They analyze anti-Blacks hate groups and bloggers on Xanga which is a popular blog hosting website [4]. The similarities between the work by Chau et al. and this paper are the application of network analysis and text analytics to analyze subscription linkages and textual comments respectively. While the motivation between the two works is the same, Chau et al. analyze anti-Blacks hate groups in Blogosphere whereas we study anti-India hate groups in YouTube.

Analysis of YouTube Social Network. There are several papers on the study of YouTube video sharing community and social network analysis. Due to the limited space in the paper, we discuss a few recent and closely related work. Biel et al. study the properties and structure of YouTube social networks with a focus on analyzing the network of subscriptions (large-scale static and dynamic analysis) [2]. Santos et al. collect a representative sample of YouTube using a crawler and analyze the structural properties and social relation-ships among users, among videos, and between users and videos [12]. Mislove et al. examine data gathered from YouTube Flickr, YouTube, LiveJournal, and Orkut and presents a large-scale measurement study and analysis of the structure of multiple online social networks [9].

Research Contributions. This study is an attempt to advance the state-of-the-art in the area of *cyber-hate analysis and detection*. The study focuses on YouTube online video sharing and social networking website. In context to the related work, the specific novel contributions of this paper are:

1. A *general framework* to facilitate security analysts and intelligence agencies to identify hate and extremist content, users and hidden communities on *YouTube*. To the best of our knowledge, this paper is the first study to perform an *integrated analysis of a wide variety of user and video attributes and relationship in the context of cyber-hate in YouTube*. The study investigates popularity metrics, user and video features, network relationships such as friends, favorites/playlists and subscriptions, related video relationship and performs linguistic analysis of user comments.
2. A method to discover *hate content, users and communities* on YouTube by leveraging a variety of user-user (e.g. friends and subscriptions) and user-video (e.g. uploader and favorites/playlists) relationship using social network analysis tools and techniques.
3. We believe that it is important to study cyber-hate having a focus on different nations, religions and communities so that comparisons and references can be made to better understand the problem from different perspectives. To the best of our knowledge, this is the first *India-centric* academic research on analyzing cyber hate on a video sharing and social networking website.

The remainder of the paper is organized as follows: In Section 2, we discuss the framework that we developed to analyze the data set from YouTube, the methodology by which we collected the data set from YouTube, and the results from the data analysis that we performed on the collected data. Finally, in Section 3, we conclude the paper with usefulness of this research work.

2   Empirical Analysis

2.1   Proposed Framework

Figure 1 presents the proposed framework to analyze YouTube repository for extracting hate-promoting users, videos and communities. As shown in Figure 1, the starting point is a seed list of videos (generated manually) which is then used as a seed reference to extract more users and videos (through a process called as *bootstrapping* or *snow ball sampling* [10]). Figure 1 shows various network analysis and linguistic analysis modules to analyze several types of user and video relationships present in YouTube. Each of the component (user comment analysis using natural language processing techniques, socio-centric and ego-centric graph analysis for community discovery, network analysis based on friends and subscription relationship for uncovering additional like-minded users) illustrated in the Figure 1 is described in the following sections of the paper. As shown in Figure 1, the ultimate goal (output produced by the system) is to assist a security analyst in retrieving and visualizing relevant useful and actionable information.

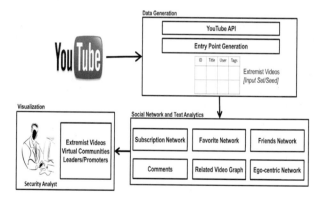

Fig. 1. The framework that we used in the analysis. We used the YouTube API to download the details of the videos, and users. We stored it in a database and ran our analytics tool on it to produce statistics and visualization.

2.2   Seed Dataset (Entry-Point)

The approach presented in this paper assumes that an entry point (seed list) is provided to the system as an input which is used as a base to uncover additional videos, users and communities. The authors of this paper with the support of six undergraduate students identified 75 YouTube videos based on a manual search. We created a list of Video IDs and the values of all other fields are

Table 1. Illustrative list of videos and selected popularity indicators in the input set (UD: Upload Date (all videos were uploaded in 2009), DS: Duration in Seconds, AR: Average Rating, NR: Number of Raters, VC: View Counts, NF: Number of Favorites, NC: Number of Comments). We have anonymized the titles of the videos, user IDs, names, and video IDs in the paper.

Title	Category	UD	DS	AR	NR	VC	NF	NC
Title 1	Film & Animation	07 Sept.	307	4.428	7	1419	2	17
Title 2	Music	01 Nov.	274	4.466	15	2992	4	32
Title 3	People & Blogs	16 June	46	3.428	98	20743	22	196
Title 4	News & Politics	13 Aug.	475	4.765	47	6117	24	95

automatically retrieved using the YouTube APIs.[2] Table 1 lists the title of the video and selected meta-data[3] for a few sample videos belonging to the input set.[4]

2.3   Video and User Properties

YouTube has two main objects: videos and users. We compute descriptive statistics of various video and user attributes belonging to the input set of videos (refer to Figure 2). Some insights that we draw from these descriptive statistics are:

1. We computed statistical measures for view counts (mean = 10640), favorites (mean = 17.05), comments (mean = 116.9), average rating (mean = 3.94) and raters (mean = 53.25).
2. The video length ranges from a minimum value of 21 seconds to a maximum value of 646 seconds. We notice that 25% of the videos have duration of less than 2 minutes (1st quartile = 124 seconds) and 50% of the videos have duration of less than 255 minutes (Median = 250 seconds). The data is right skewed as majority of the videos are less than 4.5 minutes (3rd quartile = 336.5). Our results was not different from Reid et al. – average length of videos was 6 minutes and 32 seconds [11].
3. The total numbers of favorites across all the videos are 1279. The mean value for number of favorites is 17.05. We notice that the total number of favorites for the top 5 videos is 518. This shows that there are certain videos which are very popular and are favorited by many users.
4. We found that 88% of the uploaders of videos are male and the average age is 25.4 (based on the information reported by users on their public profile). Our findings were aligned with previous studies by Adam et al. and Conway et al [1], [6].

---

[2] YouTube Data API http://code.google.com/apis/YouTube/
[3] The table displays values retrieved as of 11th May 2010.
[4] By the time we finished our analysis (June 23, 2010), we found that two of the videos were removed from YouTube because of violation of terms of service. This also confirms that the videos that we were studying are truly hate promoting videos.

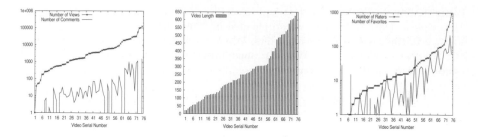

Fig. 2. Left: Presents number of views and comments for the videos in the data set; Middle: Presents video lengths of the videos in the data set; Right: Provides number of raters and number of favorites for the videos in the data set. The serial number of videos (x-axis) across the graph is not in the same order and is arranged with respect to monotonically increasing Y-axis value.

2.4 Linguistic Analysis of User Comments

We created a video-user matrix to identify users (from a set of 3037 unique users) who have commented on several videos belonging to the 75 extremist videos. Our hypothesis is that users who have actively commented (irrespective of the polarity or sentiment of the comment) on the extremist videos are potential candidates for further analysis. We identified top 12 most active users for the input set of videos and manually inspected their profile on YouTube to validate our hypothesis. We observed that 8 out of the 12 users are either active in promoting their ideologies or belong to the category of followers. We extract content-bearing words and phrases based on their presence across video comments. The extracted words and phrases consists of country and state names: India, Pakistan, Kashmir, religions: hindu, muslim, abusive phrases like: fuck you, shut up, son of a bitch and words like world, people and army. We performed an analysis of psychometric properties of users' comments using LIWC[5] (Linguistic Inquiry and Word Count) and topic discovery using LDA[6] (Latent Dirichlet Allocation) in order to gain a deeper understanding of textual messages. The output of LIWC reveal a high frequency of religious and swear words. The vocabulary size (number of unique words) of the user comments corpus was 2200 after eliminating all the stop words and symbols. We applied LDA to model documents (where all user comments for a video represents a document) as a mixture of topics where topics are distributions over words. We generated 3 topics from the comment corpus: Topic 1: miltary, dosti, succeed, jang, allaho, akabar; Topic 2: condom, viagara, penis, fuckpakigirl, hindoo, pundit; and Topic 3: mujahiddeen, hadith, jihad, saeed, kafir, destroy. Topic 2 contains terms which are more sexually abusive and derogatory, whereas Topic 3 contains words which are about terrorism and war.

---

[5] Linguistic Inquiry and Word Count (LIWC) http://www.liwc.net/
[6] Gensim Python Framework for Vector Space Modeling.

2.5   Social Network Analysis

User Network (Friends) and Related Videos. We created a set of unique userids who uploaded videos in the input set of 75 videos. A user can create a profile and invite other users to become friends. A particular user's friends list can be public or private depending on the users profile settings. If a user has not marked his or her friends list as private then the friends list can be viewed on the profile page of the respective user and can also be retrieved using the YouTube APIs. However, we notice that several users (33%) make their friend list as private and hence we were not able to retrieve friend list for such users. We created a social network graph only between the uploaders of videos belonging to our input set to test our hypothesis of the presence of a hidden virtual community and presence of influential or central users. Figure 3 (Left) is a social network graph which shows 60 unique users (derived from the input set) connected to each other using friends relationship. Only 25 of the 60 users have atleast one edge. It shows the presence of a hidden community of users having a shared interest and common agenda. Note that we are able to extract friend relationship only for those users who have marked their friend list as public and despite this restriction we observe a presence of a hidden community of users having a common interest. We compute statistical measures[7] such as betweenness centrality, closness centrality and degree to identify important and central nodes (leaders or influential users). Table 2 lists the top three userids (in decreasing order of rank) derived from computing statistical measures indicating their importance in the graph Figure 3 (Left).

Figure 3 (Right) presents a graph where each node represents a video in the input set of videos and each edge represents a related-video relationship. YouTube computes a list of related videos for each video based on the similarity of title, description, keywords and factors internal to YouTube. In the graph, two vertices are connected to each other if one video appears in the Top-25 related-video (based on the YouTube relevance ranking algorithm) list of the other video. Chatzopoulou et al. study related-video graph to understand the general characteristics and features of YouTube video [3]. We found various central videos fulfilling different purposes of hate-community for example Video ID: WV7 (maximum degree centrality) is a hate-propagating lecture by a so called "Dr." whereas Video ID: 0wm (maximum closeness centrality) shows brutalities against a section of people in India and thus incites anger. Video ID: 1rE (maximum betweeness centrality) supports terrorism and openly calls for a war.

Multiple Relations between Users. Figure 4 (Left) embodies in it all three relationships namely friends, subscription and video-shared. There is an edge from node A to node B if: A and B are *friends* and have mutually agreed to share content, A has *subscribed* to B and hence all B's updates are available to A or A has *favorited* or added a video in his playlist which has been uploaded by node B. In Figure 4 (Left), we observe that 40 out of 60 are connected through one of the three mentioned relationships. The layout in the figure has in the center the node

---

[7] Using JUNG: http://jung.sourceforge.net/

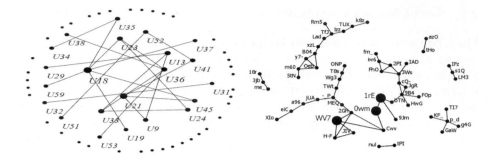

Fig. 3. Left: Social network graph (friends) between users of input set; Right: Presents the related video relationship. Only the first three characters of the video ID is shown in the figure and the central videos has been highlighted. We used SocNetV[8] and ORA[9] for creating these graphs.

Table 2. Top ranked users from social network graph in Figure 5 in terms of statistical measures indicating importance. We found some of the top 10 users are prominent in all measures. We see the user u18 in all three columns showing that he is most popular in the users that are studying.

Rank	Betweenness Centrality	Closeness Centrality	Degree
1	u18	u31	u18
2	u36	u32	u21
3	u21	u18	u36

with highest betweeness centrality and it diminishes with radius. We found that user u36 stands out as a central leader. Centrality measures namely betweeness, closeness and inverse closeness statistically indicate that the topology of the network is core periphery (alpha=2).

Ego-centric Network Graph Around Central Nodes. Figure 4 (Right) presents an ego-centric network graph[10] (where the edge represents a bidirectional relationship of friends) for a user in the top 3 rank with respect to betweenness centrality and degree. Ego-centric is a graph which is centered on a particular vertex or node drawn to pay close attention to the relationship of a particular node (understand the view of network through the eyes of the "node.") It pays close attention to relationships of that node and the community structure around it. The graph in Figure 4 is an ego-centric graph where the depth is 2 and the maximum number of friends explored for a particular node is 50 (for illustration). Our hypothesis is that users who have high centrality in the socio-centric graph of the graph can be an entry point to further identify users having common interests and views (a belief in extremism and radicalization in our specific case

---

[8] http://socnetv.sourceforge.net/
[9] http://www.casos.cs.cmu.edu/projects/ora/
[10] Drawn using Vizster http://hci.stanford.edu/jheer/projects/vizster/

study). The basic premise is that a social network and ties of a user reflects the profile and interest of the user. Hence, community of persons which have high centrality in the socio-centric graph drawn from the uploaders of the input set of videos can reveal more persons with similar agenda and beliefs. We perform a manual inspection of the YouTube activity and profile of each node connected to the ego-center of Figure 4 (Right). Our analysis reveals that the ego-center is surrounded by people of the same kind or persons having common interests. We notice that the ego-center in the graph has 37 contacts (the communities or clusters are shaded) and a manual inspection of all the profiles reveals that 31 of the 37 contacts have YouTube activity which denotes hate and extremism. Amongst the remaining 6 contacts, 2 accounts were suspended (hence we cannot make a conclusion on these accounts but according to the YouTube policy an account is suspended if it violates community guidelines and terms of use).

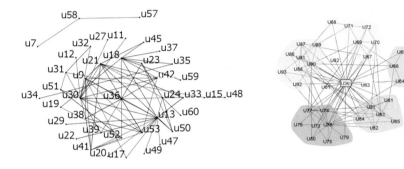

Fig. 4. Left: Social network graph (multiple relations) between users of input set. Right: Egocentric graph of an influential node (depth = 2, maximum friends = 50). The boundaries show communities that we found in the data.

Subscription Relationship Network. In contrast to friends relationship which is bidirectional, YouTube provides a unidirectional connection called as subscriptions. One user can subscribe to the videos uploaded by another user by subscribing to his channel. Unlike friends relationship, analysis of the network of users using subscription relationship is relatively unexplored in the literature. Biel et al. and Maia et al. recently studied the network of subscriptions and concluded that exploiting subscriptions relationship can offer additional insights into the patterns of users' behavior [2], [8]. Building on this, we hypothesize that additional hate-promoting users and contents can be discovered from the initial set of videos and uploaders by exploiting the subscription relationship. Our rationale is that if several users (who are already labeled as hate-promoting) subscribe to a particular user then it is highly likely that the subscribed user will share common interest. Similarly, if a user subscribes to many users in the input set of users then the subscriber is likely to have common interest with the users in the input set.

Figure 5 (Left) shows a selected portion of the subscription network for the users in the input set. The direction of arrow (since subscription relationship is a directed relationship) shows the flow of information which is opposite to the direction of subscription. The subscription network in Figure 5 (Left) reveals that some users are a major source of content provider for the users in the input set. This observation can be used to uncover additional users and community resulting in bootstrapping from the entry point. We validate our conjecture by performing a manual inspection of the profile and activity of the discovered users.

Maia et al. studied subscription relationship and interaction patterns between users in YouTube to characterize and identify user behavior [8]. We draw from Maia et al. idea of categorizing user behavior based on subscription activity and identify 10 users who have maximum number of subscriptions. These 10 users can be classified as hate-promoting content seekers. A node with high out-degree or large number of subscribers indicates a content producer. We identify 10 users who have been subscribed by the initial set of users and act as information hubs for the hate community. We identified four users who are common in both the list which can be categorized as nodes who are playing active role in both dissemination and consumption of hate content.

Favorite/Playlist Relationship Network. Figure 5 (Right) presents connections between users in the input dataset and the videos favorited/playlisted (added to their playlist) by them. Both of these action are like-video actions. Our hypothesis is that if several users (who have been tagged as hate-promoting) favorite/playlist a particular video then the likelihood of the liked video being hate-promoting is high. The rest set of arrows in the left in Figure represents edges connecting a user and a video through a favorite/playlist relationship. The second set of arrows on the right connects a video and its uploader. We found three of the top six (max. in-degree) videos had a clear hate-promoting agenda. The rest three videos were not hate-spreading (through the video content) but were sensitive as they received several hateful comments. A careful analysis of the uploaders profile reveals that four uploaders amongst the six belonged to the hate-promotion category. None of these four uploaders as well as the six

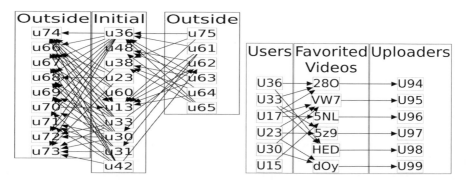

Fig. 5. Left: Shows a selected portion of the subscription network of users. One in the middle are from our data set, ones in the left and right of this figure are outside our data set; Right: Presents a connection between users in the input dataset and the videos favorited by them.

videos were present in the initial seed list of users and hence we were able to augment the list of the hate-promoters. This supports our hypothesis that favorite/playlist relationship can be exploited to bootstrap the initial set of videos and users.

Iterative Expansion of Seed List of Users and Community. Table 3 present empirical results to test the proposed hypothesis by combining three relations (friends, subscriptions and favorites) as a single relation and then expanding the user network graph from a seed list of users to identify additional like-minded users and community. The system extends the seed list of users in each iteration based on five centrality measures: in-degree, hub, information, out-degree and betweeness. We measure the precision of the system by manually validating user's profiles. The system was able to add 98 (true positive) users with an average precision of 88% in two iterations.

Table 3. Empirical results of the bootstrapping process (addition of 98 users from the initial seed list of users within 2 iterations). Abbreviations - Iter: Iteration, TP: True Positive, FP: False Positive, CD: Can't Determine, Prec: Precision, NU: New Users. Top-K represents the number videos that we took for the analysis after ranking them.

Iter	Seed	Nodes	Links	Centrality	Top-K	TP	FP	CD	Prec	NU
				Indegree	50	46	4	0	0.92	19
				Hub	50	48	2	0	0.96	23
1	60	1628	5649	Information	50	48	2	0	0.96	16
				Outdegree	50	48	2	0	0.96	16
				Betweeness	50	40	7	3	0.85	18
				Indegree	100	88	11	1	0.88	23
				Hub	100	85	13	2	0.86	36
2	106	5240	30481	Information	100	88	10	2	0.89	31
				Outdegree	100	92	7	1	0.92	25
				Betweeness	100	83	14	3	0.85	12
Avgerage Precision : 0.88					New Users (TP) Added: 98					

3   Discussion

We present an approach (based on exploiting relations between users) to retrieve hate and extremist videos, users and communities from YouTube. The proposed system was able to bootstrap from 60 (seed-list) to 158 (true positive) users in two iterations. The system was able to search 98 users automatically with a precision of 88%. The proposed approach can discover central, and influential users and videos as well as hidden communities using social network analysis techniques (using friends, subscriptions, favorites and related videos). The output shows that the proposed approach can potentially help a security analyst find what he is looking for (i.e., able to assist in solving his information need) and producing an output in a form (reports, network graphs) which is more insightful and actionable than just a flat list of videos and users.

Acknowledgments

This work was supported by a DIT (Department of Information Technology), Government of India grant. The authors would like to thank all members of PreCog research group at IIIT-Delhi.

References

1. Bermingham, A., Conway, M., McInerney, L., O'Hare, N., Smeaton, A.F.: Combining Social Network Analysis and Sentiment Analysis to Explore the Potential for Online Radicalisation. In: IEEE International Conference on Advances in Social Network Analysis and Mining, Washington, DC, USA, pp. 231–236 (2009)
2. Biel, J.: Please, Subscribe to Me! Analysing the Structure and Dynamics of the YouTube Network
3. Chatzopoulou, G., Sheng, C., Faloutsos, M.: A First Step Towards Understanding Popularity in YouTube. In: Second International Workshop on Network Scienece for Communication Networks (NetSciCom), San Diego, USA (2010)
4. Chau, M., Xu, J.: Mining Communities and their Relationships in Blogs: A Study of Online Hate Groups. Int. J. Hum.-Comput. Stud. 65(1), 57–70 (2007)
5. Chen, H., Chung, W., Qin, J., Reid, E., Sageman, M.: Uncovering the Dark Web: A Case Study of Jihad on the Web. Journal of American Society for Information Science and Technology 59(8), 1347–1359 (2008)
6. Conway, M., Mcinerney, L.: Jihadi video and Auto-radicalisation: Evidence from an Exploratory YouTube Study. In: Ortiz-Arroyo, D., Larsen, H.L., Zeng, D.D., Hicks, D., Wagner, G. (eds.) EuroIsI 2008. LNCS, vol. 5376, pp. 108–118. Springer, Heidelberg (2008)
7. Fu, T., Huang, C.-N., Chen, H.: Identification of Extremist Videos in Online Video Sharing Sites. In: ISI 2009: Proceedings of the 2009 IEEE International Conference on Intelligence and Security Informatics, Piscataway, NJ, USA, pp. 179–181. IEEE Press, Los Alamitos (2009)
8. Maia, M., Almeida, J., Almeida, V.: Identifying User Behavior in Online Social Networks. In: SocialNets 2008: Proceedings of the 1st Workshop on Social Network Systems, pp. 1–6. ACM, New York (2008)
9. Mislove, A., Marcon, M., Gummadi, K.P., Druschel, P., Bhattacharjee, B.: Measurement and Analysis of Online Social Networks. In: IMC 2007: Proceedings of the 7th ACM SIGCOMM Conference on Internet Measurement, pp. 29–42. ACM Press, New York (2007)
10. Paolillo, J.C.: Structure and Network in the YouTube Core. In: HICSS 2008: Proceedings of the Proceedings of the 41st Annual Hawaii International Conference on System Sciences, p. 156. IEEE Computer Society Press, Los Alamitos (2008)
11. Reid, E.: Analysis of Jihadi Extremist Groups Videos. Forensic Science Communications 11(3) (2009)
12. Santos, R.L.T., Rocha, B.P.S., Rezende, C.G., Loureiro, A.A.F.: Characterizing the YouTube video-sharing community

Title-Based Product Search – Exemplified in a Chinese E-commerce Portal

Chien-Wen Chen and Pu-Jen Cheng

Department of Computer Science and Information Engineering, College of Electrical Engineering and Computer Science, National Taiwan University
{r97019,pjcheng}@csie.ntu.edu.tw

Abstract. There are too many products in an on-line shopping website. We need to help buyers to find products they want in an efficient way. A keyword-based IR system seems suitable for searching products. Unfortunately, we observe from real world query logs and find that queries for product search are usually very short. What is worse, a document described a product may have lots of words of related products. It is hard for an IR system to distinguish representative terms from other noisy terms. Hence, we propose a supervised learning method to realize semantic types of each term in product document titles. Then we modify Language Model to improve the relevance of search results. Our methods have significant improvement in search result precision in real world document collection and query collections.

Keywords: Information Retrieval, Language Specific IR, Domain-specific IR, product search, E-commerce.

1 Introduction

There are too many products in an on-line shopping website. Take eBay for example, their platform sells more than 75 million kinds of products at any time [8]. We need to help buyers to find products they want in an efficient way. The two common methods are searching and browsing by categories. A keyword-based IR system seems suitable for searching products. Figure 1 shows a snapshot example of shopping.com[1] issuing a query "iphone" on June 2010.

An efficient retrieval system that can provide the most relevant ranking list of products to meet buyer's query is very important. If the retrieval system cannot provide suitable ranking list corresponding to buyers' query in an efficient way, buyers may change to other shopping platforms which therefore declines shopping platform provider's profit. Unfortunately, we observe from real world query logs and find that queries for product search are usually very short. A query for product search consists of only 1.28 English words or 3.22 Chinese characters in average. So, it is hard to realize buyer's intention. What is worse, a document describing a product may contain lots of words associating with related products. It is hard for an IR system to distinguish representative terms from other noisy terms. The retrieved products often match the keywords from query issued by buyers, but have poor relevance.

---

[1] http://www.shopping.com/

P.-J. Cheng et al. (Eds.): AIRS 2010, LNCS 6458, pp. 25–36, 2010.
© Springer-Verlag Berlin Heidelberg 2010

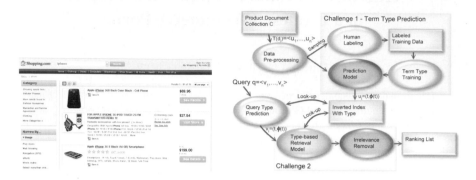

Fig. 1. A snapshot of an on-line shopping platform. (Shopping.com).

Fig. 2. System architecture

For example, when a buyer issued a query "iphone", we assume that the buyer was interested in the iphone cellphones, instead of iphone accessories such as iphone compatible batteries, leathers, or screen protectors. Unfortunately, from Fig. 1, we can see that the top two retrieved results when issuing query "iphone" are iphone accessories: black case and transmitter, instead of iphone cellphones. Accordingly, the IR system for product search needs more sophisticated methods in the hope of understanding buyers' and sellers' intentions.

We make an assumption that a buyer specifies keywords to describe products that he or she wants to buy. The buyer is interested in main products, instead of accessories. Ravi Chandra et al. also make similar assumption [3]. In this work, we observe that each term in a product document title has different semantic types in different circumstances. Hence, we propose an approach which considers not only the string of the term but also the semantic type of the term in each product document title. We apply a supervised learning method to labeling the semantic type for each term in product document title and modify the conventional Language Model to improve the relevance of search results.

The rest of this paper is organized as the following. Section 2 introduces many related works and existing approaches. Section 3 formulates this problem and defines notations in this paper. In section 4, our methods are described in detail. And in section 5, we introduce our dataset and report experiment results to verify our methods. Finally, section 6 is our conclusions and future works.

2   Related Work

Some existing works are based on logs, which are knowledge from previous buyers. On-line shopping platforms record users' browsing history, keywords for search, clicking behavior on products, or transaction records to purchase products. Methods using the history data are known as log-based solutions. Nish Parikh and Neel Sundaresan make a detailed study of eBay logs. They try to find semantic query relations and build graphs for searching or recommendation applications [7]. Also, they try to find burst events from queries [8]. Ravi Chandra et al. directly explore rules from logs for product search [3]. An association-rule-mining-liked method is proposed by them and has good performance.

Logs can also be used by collaborative filtering or recommendation systems. Using collaborative filtering techniques in e-commerce platforms has been discussed for years [9,2,10]. Raz Lin et al. integrate both information retrieval and collaborative filtering techniques for search in on-line shopping platforms. Their solution considers not only buyers' but also their neighbors' browsing history and preference profiles [5,6]. Another research group, Y.S. Kim et al., considers navigational and behavior patterns as well [4]. They also give more considerations to the products that are clicked but not purchased.

Log-based solutions may have good performance, but they also have many disadvantages. First of all, they cannot response to the market immediately. Time and adequate users are required to shape up rules from the logs. Second, log data is usually difficult to obtain due to privacy issues. Most of large scale websites have their own privacy policies. Last, using log data to change searching behavior will influence future log data. Log-based methods can only be applied once in some circumstance. For these reasons, we would like to solve this problem using only contents.

3   Problem Specification

To formalize this problem, we define a term in the first place. A **term** t can be a separate word in English, a single symbol such as punctuation marks, or characters in Chinese. Each term t has its own part of speech, denoted as $POS(t)$. We regard a product as a document with one or more terms. A **product document** d_i representing a product to be sold contains two disjoint parts: title $T(d_i)$ and description $D(d_i)$. A **title** consists of m tuples: $T(d_i) = < u_1, u_2, ..., u_m >$. A **description** consists of a set of terms: $D(d_i) = \{t_j\}$. A tuple consists of two parts: a term and a semantic type of the term. A **tuple** is defined as $u_j = < t_j, \phi(t_j) >$, where $\phi(t_j)$ is a notation representing a semantic type for term t_j. We will describe how to determine the semantic type for a term in our methodologies later. Also, a **product query** q consists of a set of tuples: $\{v_1, v_2, ..., v_n\}$.

The problem to be focused in this paper can be formulated. Given a product document collection $C = \{d_1, d_2, ..., d_k\}$ with k product documents and a query q, our objective is to rank all product documents $d_i \in C$ ordered by a scoring function $Score(q, T(d_i))$ in a decreasing order.

4   Methodology

Figure 2 is our system architecture. As defined above, given a data collection C, we have to pre-process the product documents, including storage, indexing, and Chinese word segmentation. Our methods have three main phases to solve the problem. The first phase of our method is named "term type prediction". In this phase, we aim to predict the semantic type of each term from product document titles. Using this type information, the second phase is a type-based retrieval model which retrieves relevant product documents from product document collection. And the final phase is a filter to remove irrelevant product documents in the final ranking list. The three main phases will describe in detail in the following subsections.

4.1   Term Type Prediction

Term Type Prediction in Product Document Title. In our observation for mismatched product documents, the crux of the problem we find is that the retrieval system does not understand the semantic type of each term in the product document. For instance, consider these two product document titles:

- USB Desktop Battery Charger Cradle For Nokia N97 Mini **Cellphone**
- Nokia N97 Mini Unlocked **Cellphone** Plus Free Battery

When a buyer issues a query "cellphone" and intents to buy a cellphone, these two product documents may be retrieved because of matched keywords. However, we humans can easily distinguish that the second product document is the real cellphone, but the first product document is only an accessory of cellphones. Even though both product document titles contain the same term "cellphone", the semantic type of this term are different. In the second product document, the term "cellphone" is a product, but in the first product document is not. The main product of the first product document is battery, whereas the main product of the second product document is cellphone.

Hence, our idea is to let the retrieval system to understand the semantic type of each term for each product document title. By observation from query collection in our experiments, high frequency query terms have three main kinds of types: product, brand, and model. To simplify, we aim to categorize each term into one of the four types:

- Product (P): the major sale goods.
- Brand (B): production companies or retailers.
- Model (M): the design model, usually appears in electric products. E.g. "N97", "nano", "shuffle", "X61", or "hero".
- None (N): none of above.

The objective categorizing results for the above examples are:

- USB^N Desktop^N Battery^P Charger^P Cradle^P For^N Nokia^B N98^M Mini^M Cellphone^N
- Nokia^B N97^M Mini^M Unlocked^N Cellphone^P Plus^N Free^N Battery^N

We apply a well-known supervised machine learning approach named support vector machine (SVM). We train three binary classifiers to determine each term in title: "Is a Product or not", "Is a Brand or not", and "Is a Model or not". We use about 50 features for each term in product document title. For a product document title $T(d_i) = \{u_1, u_2, ...u_m\}$, a term t_j in the tuple $u_j = < t_j, \phi(t_j) >$ has the following features:

- Part of speech features. (t_{j-1}, t_j, t_{j+1}) We observe that a term with Product type tends to be a noun term $(Pos(t_j) = Noun)$, which follows an adjective term $(Pos(t_{j-1}) = Adj.)$, or follows a non-word term $(Pos(t_{j-1}) = NotAWord)$. Brand or Model type terms are usually not written in Chinese.

- Is parentheses (t_{j-1}, t_j, t_{j+1}). Chinese sellers like to put Brand terms into parentheses. E.g. "()", "[]", "{}" or "⟨⟩".
- Is color (t_{j-1}, t_j, t_{j+1}). Color terms are usually neither Brand, Model, nor Product. E.g. "red", "gold", or "two color".
- Length of term (t_{j-1}, t_j, t_{j+1}). In multi-byte encoded languages like Chinese, this value is the number of characters, instead of number of bytes.
- Is alphabets and/or digits only (t_{j-1}, t_j, t_{j+1}). Brand or Model type terms usually consist of only alphabets or digits.
- Term frequency features (t_j). We find that Brand terms sometimes occur twice in a product document title.
- Document frequency features (t_j). A term with very high document frequency may be a useless stopword. A term with very low document frequency may be a Model term since Model terms are usually very specific.
- Location-based features (t_j). Term occurrence position is very useful. Brand terms are usually placed in the first term and Product terms are usually placed in the last term because of Chinese grammars. But there are still many exceptions.

Term Type Prediction in Query. After giving a type for each term in each product document title, we also have to give a type for each term in the query. For a query $q = \{v_1, v_2, ...v_n\}$ with n terms, we predict each type $\phi(t_j)$ for each term t_j in tuple v_j as the most likely semantic type according to the whole corpus. This method is good for some terms that have ambiguous semantic types. For example, the term "Apple" is not only a famous computer company but also a kind of fruit. But in the whole corpus, the term "Apple" is more likely to be a brand of Apple Computer Inc., instead of a fruit product. For this reason, we predict $\phi(t_j) = U$ if $P(\phi(t_j) = U|T(C)) > 50\%$ where $U \in \{Product, Brand, Model\}$. Otherwise, $\phi(t_j) = None$.

4.2   Retrieval Model

To find relevant product documents, we modify Language Model with Bayesian smoothing using Dirichlet Priors. Given a query q, we have to estimate the probability of generating q from each product document title $T(d)$. The probability $P(q|T(d))$ is the final scoring function $Score(q, T(d))$ for retrieval ranking. With Bayesian smoothing using Dirichlet Priors, we assume pseudo counts $\mu_1 P(t_i|T(C))$ for unseen terms in product document title $T(d)$.

$$P(q|T(d)) \approx \prod_1^n \left(\frac{|T(d)|}{|T(d)| + \mu_1} P(t_i|T(d)) + \frac{\mu_1}{|T(d)| + \mu_1} P(t_i|T(C)) \right) \quad (1)$$

For a query term t_q and another term t_d from product document title, we define two matching conditions: 1) Exactly matching: $t_q = t_d$ and $\phi(t_q) = \phi(t_d)$. 2) Partial matching: $t_q = t_d$. Note that the two conditions are not disjoint, a term satisfies exactly matching also satisfies partial matching. We give some pseudo count $\mu_2 P(t|T(d))$ for terms satisfying partial matching for smoothing propose, instead of restricting the exactly matching for all terms. Hence, we have:

$$P(t|T(e)) = \frac{|T(d)|}{|T(d)| + \mu_2} P_{ext}(t = u, \phi(t) = \phi(u)|e, u \in T(e)) \tag{2a}$$

$$+ \frac{\mu_2}{|T(d)| + \mu_2} P_{par}(t = u|e, u \in T(e)) \tag{2b}$$

where t is a term and e can be a product document d or the whole product document collection C. To observe the effect of this approach, take the logarithm of equation 1 and place equation 2 into it, we have:

$$log P(q|T(d)) \approx \tag{3a}$$

$$\sum_{i=1, t_i \in T(d)}^{n} log \left(\frac{|T(d)|^2 P_{ext}(t_i|T(d)) + \mu_2 |T(d)| P_{par}(t_i|T(d))}{\mu_1 |T(d)| P_{ext}(t_i|T(C)) + \mu_1 \mu_2 P_{par}(t_i|T(C))} + 1 \right) \tag{3b}$$

$$+ n \frac{\mu_1}{|T(d)| + \mu_1} \tag{3c}$$

Part (3b) is like the term frequency - inverse document frequency (TF-IDF) weighting and part (3c) can be regard as document length normalization. We can also find that a product document title with a term exactly matching another term in query will have more likelihood to be retrieved than only partial matching.

4.3 Irrelevant Removal

In the previous phases, many smoothing strategies are adopted to improve the search recall. But this also causes noises. To have a better ranking precision, we try a naive method to eliminate irrelevant product documents from the retrieved set. We make an assumption that most of top retrieved product documents are relevant. Hence, this phase aims to eliminate product documents that are not similar to the top retrieved product documents. The elimination method simply calculates an average vector from top ten retrieved product document titles, and removes product documents with cosine similarity to the average vector less than or equal to 0.5.

5 Experiments

In the experiments of term type prediction, we will show our prediction result. In the other phases, the type-based retrieval model and the irrelevant removal, we will evaluate our methods by common information retrieval evaluation criteria.

5.1 Data Collection

Our experimental datasets have two parts: the product document collection and the query collection.

Product Document Collection. The product document collection contained 984,096 product documents and was crawled from Yahoo! Taiwan Shopping platform on October, 2009. Yahoo! Taiwan Shopping is a famous shopping website in Taiwan. Each product document has about 10 columns including id, category, title, subtitle, thumbnail image, description and timestamps. In our observation, the average number of terms in all product document titles is 11.4703 and the average unique number of terms in all product document titles is 11.2823.

Table 1. Query collection

Data Source	Y! TW Shopping	Ruten Auction
Number of queries	29,537	542,824
Number of unique queries	11,314	74,765
Average query length (Chinese characters)	3.22	3.00
Average query length (English words)	1.28	1.12

Query Collection. The query collection was a set of query keywords issued to Yahoo! Taiwan Shopping and Ruten Auction Platform[2] on April 25, 26 and 27 in 2010. Ruten Auction Platform is another shopping website in Taiwan funded by PChome Online and eBay Inc. Different from Yahoo! Taiwan Shopping, products in Ruten Auction Platform were decided by various sellers like eBay, yet products in Yahoo! Taiwan Shopping were decided by inner salesmen. The query collection was collected from the logs of Web Reputation Service provided by Trend Micro Inc. A simple observation is shown in Table 1.

5.2 Term Type Prediction Evaluation

To produce training data for supervised learning, we have to sample some product to be labeled by human. We reference to the categories of the product document collection. The three main categories of products in amount are clothing accessories (17%), clothes(17%), and 3C (Computer, Communication, and Consumer Electronic) (13%). Therefore, we sample 400 product documents for each category from the three main categories. The total 1,200 product document titles are labeled by humans. We have three volunteers. A volunteer has to label one of the four types for each term in each product document title. We choose the labels with at least two agreements on type from the volunteers.

We use LibSVM [1] for SVM training. To find the best parameters γ and C for the C-Support Vector Classification and the Gaussian radial basis function, we try different parameters using a grid tool to reach the best accuracy. Using the parameters for the best accuracy, the performances including accuracy, recall, precision and F-score are shown in the left side in Table 2 (Micro View). In this classification problem, recall means the percentage of correct prediction from all true positive examples. Precision means the percentage of correct prediction from all examples which are predicted as positive. The F-score is a measurement considering both recall and precision. Note that F-score does not consider true negative examples, which are very common in this training method. This report is a micro view since we evaluate in term level. We find out that type Brand is the easiest one to predict, yet type Product and Model are good for precision but poor in terms of recall.

To avoid the problem of Chinese word segmentation, we also evaluate in a macro view. We concatenate terms by human and restrict the correct prediction to only exactly matching the concatenated section. For example, we can consider a title with four tuples

---

[2] http://www.ruten.com.tw/

Table 2. Term type prediction performance

Type	Micro View				Macro View		
	Accuracy	Recall	Precision	F-score	Recall	Precision	F-score
Product	92.80%	59.09%	79.23%	67.69%	42.83%	69.80%	53.08%
Brand	96.20%	89.67%	83.76%	86.61%	87.58%	82.78%	85.11%
Model	96.43%	62.11%	76.82%	68.69%	43.48%	67.77%	52.97%

$T(d_i) = < u_1, u_2, u_3, u_4 >$. If the ground truths of terms with Product type are u_2 and u_3, a prediction $\phi(u_1) = N, \phi(u_2) = P, \phi(u_3) = P, \phi(u_4) = N$ is correct and otherwise conditions like $\phi(u_1) = P, \phi(u_2) = P, \phi(u_3) = P, \phi(u_4) = N$ or $\phi(u_1) = N, \phi(u_2) = P, \phi(u_3) = N, \phi(u_4) = N$ are incorrect. The performances including recall, precision and F-score are available in the right side in Table 2 (Macro View). We do not report the accuracy because it is hard to define true negative conditions in macro view. In this report, the recall of Product type and Model type is very low, similar to the micro view performance.

Table 3. Feature contribution analysis

Type		NR	PAll	PN	PV	PAdv	PAdj	PNC	PNW	PTS	CLR	LEN	AD	TF	DF	LOC
Product	Accuracy	-00.00%	-01.20%	-00.10%	-00.22%	+00.03%	+00.10%	-00.00%	-00.47%	+00.01%	-00.20%	-00.95%	-00.04%	+00.04%	-00.20%	**-04.68%**
	Recall	-00.00%	+07.48%	+02.03%	+01.57%	+00.45%	+01.13%	-00.00%	**-01.13%**	+00.34%	+00.06%	+03.82%	+00.06%	+00.62%	+01.29%	+14.24%
	Precision	-00.00%	-11.96%	-02.32%	-02.79%	-00.11%	-00.06%	-00.00%	-02.97%	-00.14%	-01.72%	-09.11%	-00.39%	-00.13%	-02.58%	**-26.73%**
	F-score	-00.00%	-00.77%	+00.42%	-00.05%	+00.25%	+00.71%	-00.00%	-01.83%	+00.17%	-00.60%	-01.37%	-00.11%	+00.35%	-00.14%	**-06.50%**
Brand	Accuracy	-00.00%	-00.57%	-00.20%	-00.09%	-00.08%	-00.04%	-00.06%	-00.25%	-00.38%	-00.12%	-00.41%	-00.15%	-00.06%	-00.25%	**-01.64%**
	Recall	-00.00%	+02.73%	+00.32%	+00.37%	-00.00%	-00.10%	-00.16%	-00.73%	-00.31%	-00.42%	-00.16%	-00.10%	+00.11%	+00.26%	**-02.04%**
	Precision	-00.00%	-04.56%	-01.33%	-00.76%	-00.43%	-00.12%	-00.23%	-00.96%	-01.94%	-00.44%	-02.19%	-00.76%	-00.38%	-01.56%	**-07.51%**
	F-score	-00.00%	-01.32%	-00.57%	-00.24%	-00.23%	-00.11%	-00.20%	-00.85%	-01.19%	-00.43%	-01.26%	-00.46%	-00.16%	-00.72%	**-05.07%**
Model	Accuracy	-00.00%	-00.28%	-00.09%	-00.01%	+00.03%	+00.03%	-00.00%	-00.12%	-00.07%	-00.01%	**-00.51%**	-00.14%	+00.01%	-00.06%	-00.20%
	Recall	-00.00%	+05.69%	+00.57%	+00.23%	+00.68%	+00.57%	-00.00%	**-00.46%**	+00.79%	+00.91%	+02.16%	+02.05%	+00.68%	+02.50%	+12.97%
	Precision	-00.00%	-06.62%	-01.57%	-00.27%	-00.02%	+00.06%	-00.00%	-01.47%	-01.55%	-00.71%	-07.75%	-03.20%	-00.28%	-02.33%	**-08.54%**
	F-score	-00.00%	+00.29%	-00.30%	+00.03%	+00.41%	+00.37%	-00.00%	**-00.87%**	-00.15%	+00.26%	-02.10%	-00.12%	+00.30%	+00.51%	+02.83%

NR : Reserve all features. PAll : Remove all part of speech features. PN : Remove feature "Is noun". PV : Remove feature "Is verb".
PAdv : Remove feature "Is adverb". PAdj : Remove feature "Is adjective". PNC : Remove feature "Is not Chinese". PNW : Remove feature "Is not a word".
PTS : Remove all parentheses related features. CLR : Remove feature "Is color". LEN : Remove term length feature.
AD : Remove all alphabets or digits related features. TF : Remove all term frequency related features.
DF : Remove all document frequency related features. LOC : Remove all location-based features.

Feature Contribution Analysis. We are curious about which feature is useful during training. Accordingly, we decide to remove some features and check whether the performance is affected or not.

The percentage of change in accuracy, recall, precision, and F-score are shown in Table 3. Negative value indicates that the performance has decreased after the removal of feature or group of features and vice versa. Values that contribute the highest performance in a row are marked in bold. In this result, we can find that location-based features (LOC) have significant contributions when predicting Product or Brand. A possible reason is that sellers tend to put Product or Brand terms in the first place or the last place in a product document title. Another discovery is that term length (LEN) or "Is not a word" (PNW) features contribute a lot when predicting Model because sellers usually use one character symbols to decorate model strings.

Category of Products Prediction Performance Analysis. Finally, we observe the prediction performance in each category of products. Figure 3 shows the three main

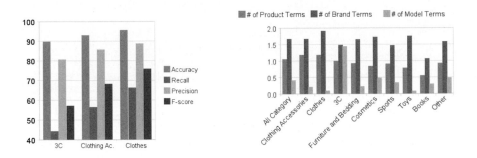

Fig. 3. Product type prediction performance in three main categories

Fig. 4. Number of terms in prediction result

categories labeled by human in advance. Clothes products are easier to predict than 3C products in terms of accuracy. We speculate that 3C products have the poorest recall due to the diversity of 3C products. 3C products contain various products and their accessories. Like the cellphone examples in section 4.1, a cellphone can have lots of possible related accessories terms together in title. So, it is hard to distinguish Product terms in 3C product titles. After applying the prediction model to all categories of products, the average number of terms in the prediction result is reported in Fig. 4. Clothes products tend to have more Brand type terms because a Chinese brand is often split into many separated terms. 3C products have more Model terms, since models usually appear in 3C products. For example, "K800i", "3310", "X61", or "U5F" are models for cellphones and laptops.

5.3 Retrieval Model Evaluation

We split the query collection into two parts: 1) High frequency queries (HFQ). The most frequent queries to be issued. 2) Random queries (RQ). Randomly sampled queries from the original list of queries. We sample 30 queries from each part for evaluation.

We compare our methods with different parameter μ_2 and some existing methods or implementations, including Vector Space Model (Apache Lucene[3]), conventional Language Model, and search results from on-line product search services for well-known Chinese shopping platforms in Taiwan. We compare with on-line product search services including Yahoo! Taiwan Shopping (YTS), Yahoo! Taiwan Portal Product Search (YPS)[4], and PChome Shopping[5] on May 2010. It is important to note that the on-line product search services have different product corpora from our methods currently used. Hence, the comparisons of on-line product search services are for reference only.

Figure 5 is an average evaluation result of HFQ and RQ dataset from query collection Ruten Auction and Yahoo Taiwan Shopping because each separated result is almost the same. LM means conventional Language Model. M_0, M_1 and M_1_F are our methods

---

[3] http://lucene.apache.org/

[4] http://tw.info.search.yahoo.com/products

[5] http://shopping.pchome.com.tw/

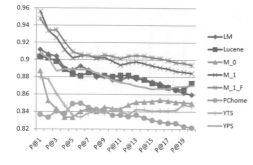
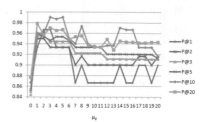
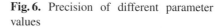

Fig. 5. Precision of Retrieval Results. (HFQ and RQ).

Fig. 6. Precision of different parameter values

with parameter $\mu_2 = 0$, $\mu_2 = 1$, and $\mu_2 = 1$ with irrelevant removal. Our methods M_1 and M_1_F are significantly different from baseline methods LM and Lucene from Student's t-test with $p-value < 0.01$ in precision at one. Compared only with baseline Lucene, M_1 and M_1_F also have significant different with $p - value < 0.05$ when measuring P@1, P@2, P@3, P@5, P@10 and P@20. In this Fig., we can see that our method with $\mu_2 = 1$ plus irrelevant removal has the best performance. Our method with $\mu_2 = 0$ causes very bad performance. Therefore, giving some pseudo counts for terms with type mismatch is necessary. Figure 5 also shows that conventional methods without considering semantic types of each term, such as Language Model and Vector Space Model (Lucene), may have worse performance.

We also try to figure out the effect of our parameter μ_2. In fig. 6, we can see that allowing only exactly matching ($\mu_2 = 0$) results in very bad performance. $\mu_2 = 1$ is much better. When μ_2 is closed to the average number of terms in product document titles $|T(d)| = 11.4703$, the performance costs down again.

5.4   An Example

Consider a query "laptop". Obviously, a buyer issuing this query tends to buy a laptop. The top ten retrieved product document titles (translated from Chinese to English by human) by Lucene are shown in the left side of Table 4. Without considering each semantic type of each term in title, even though all these ten titles have the term "Laptop", they are obviously not laptops.

On the other hand, the right side of Table 4 are product document titles retrieved by our methods. The top eight results are truly laptops and highly related to the buyer's query. In the term type prediction phase, we have predicted the term "MSI" as a Brand and "Laptop" as a Product in the first retrieved product document. The query term "laptop" is predicted as a Product type because 71.13 percent of product document titles having this term are predicted this term as Product type in the whole corpus. Therefore, the first product document gets high score because of not only term "Laptop" matching but also type Product matching.

Table 4. A search result example comparison

1. Ideastye **Laptop** Accessories Package
2. Fujitsu S6120/S6120D/S6130/S6210 **Laptop** Transformer
3. Fujitsu S2010/S2020/S2110/S2120 **Laptop** Transformer
4. Fujitsu S6000/S6010/S6120/S6110 **Laptop** Transformer
5. NU Multi-functional **Laptop** Dock
6. KINYO **Laptop** Heat Sink (NCP-001)
7. OMEGA Lightweight **Laptop** Bag
8. **Laptop** USB Cooling Plate
9. New **Laptop** RS233 Parallel Expresscard
10. Pads 10.2-inch **Laptop** Bag

1. MSI U100Plus Small **Laptop** (Black)
2. MSI U100Plus Small **Laptop** (Black)
3. MSI U100 Small **Laptop** (White)
4. MSI U100Plus Small **Laptop** (Black)
5. MSI U100Plus Small **Laptop** (N280)
6. IdeaPad S10 Magic Butterfly Long Performance Mini **Laptop** (Black)
7. IdeaPad Magic Butterfly 10-inch S10 Mini **Laptop** (Black)
8. MSI U100Plus (N280) Small **Laptop** (White)
9. ACER TravelMate 290 4050Series **Laptop** Battery
10. DELL Inspiron 300M Latitude X300 **Laptop** Battery

6   Conclusion

In this work, we firstly point out the problem of product search in current on-line shopping platforms. Next, we describe our key idea to find the semantic types of each term in product document titles and propose a supervised learning method to learn a prediction model. To find relevant products, we modify Language Model to improve the relevance of search results using the prediction model.

In the future, we can try to use the type prediction model in other applications like recommendations or user interfaces in browsing products. Also, our method may be applied to other vertical search domains such as movie search, news search, or blog search.

References

1. LIBSVM: a library for support vector machines,
   http://www.csie.ntu.edu.tw/~cjlin/libsvm
2. Gil, A., Garcíai, F.: E-Commerce Recommenders: Powerful Tools for E-business. Crossroads 10(2), 6–6 (2003)
3. Jammalamadaka, R.C., Chittar, N., Ghatare, S.: Mining Product Intention Rules from Transaction Logs of an Ecommerce Portal. In: Proceedings of the 2009 International Database Engineering and Applications Symposium, pp. 311–314. ACM, New York (2009)
4. Kim, Y.S., Yum, B.J., Song, J., Kim, S.M.: Development of a recommender system based on navigational and behavioral patterns of customers in e-commerce sites. Expert Syst. Appl. 28(2), 381–393 (2005)
5. Lin, R., Kraus, S., Tew, J.: Attaining Fast and Successful Searches in E-commerce Environments. In: Sebastiani, F. (ed.) ECIR 2003. LNCS, vol. 2633, pp. 120–134. Springer, Heidelberg (2003)
6. Lin, R., Kraus, S., Tew, J.: OSGS - A Personalized Online Store for E-commerce Environments. Inf. Retr. 7(3-4), 369–394 (2004)

7. Parikh, N., Sundaresan, N.: Inferring Semantic Query Relations from Collective User Behavior. In: Proceeding of the 17th ACM Conference on Information and Knowledge Management, pp. 349–358. ACM, New York (2008)
8. Parikh, N., Sundaresan, N.: Scalable and Near Real-Time Burst Detection from eCommerce Queries. In: Proceeding of the 14th ACM SIGKDD International Conference on Knowledge Discovery and Data Mining, pp. 972–980. ACM, New York (2008)
9. Sarwar, B., Karypis, G., Konstan, J., Riedl, J.: Analysis of Recommendation Algorithms for E-Commerce. In: Proceedings of the 2nd ACM Conference on Electronic Commerce, pp. 158–167. ACM, New York (2000)
10. Wang, H.F., Wu, C.T.: A strategy-oriented operation module for recommender systems in E-commerce. In: Proceedings of the 9th WSEAS International Conference on Applied Informatics and Communications, pp. 78–83. WSEAS Stevens Point, Wisconsin (2009)

Relevance Model Revisited: With Multiple Document Representations

Ruey-Cheng Chen, Chiung-Min Tsai, and Jieh Hsiang

National Taiwan University,
1 Roosevelt Rd. Sec. 4, Taipei 106, Taiwan
cobain@turing.csie.ntu.edu.tw,
cmtsai@mail.lis.ntu.edu.tw,
jhsiang@ntu.edu.tw

Abstract. In this work, we extended Lavrenko's relevance model [6] and adapted it to the cases where an additional layer of document representation is appropriate. With this change, we are able to aggregate heterogeneous data sources and operate the model in different granularity levels. We demonstrated this idea with two applications. In the first task, we showed the feasibility of using a carefully-selected vocabulary as the query expansion source in a language model to enhance retrieval effectiveness. The proposed query refinement model outperformed the relevance model counterpart in terms of MAP by 17.6% under rigid relevance judgment. In the second task, we established a ranking scheme in a faceted search session to sort the facets based on their corresponding relevance to the query. The result showed that our approach improved the baseline performance by roughly 100% in terms of MAP.

Keywords: Bayesian relevance model, multiple representations.

1 Introduction

Over the past few years, the abundant information on the Web along with the rise of Web users has silently changed the usual shape of information retrieval in the way we model documents. A document used to be only a collection of terms, and retrieval models were acting merely based on this piece of information to direct user to the documents that were most likely what they needed. There was also a time when user-contributed tags or human annotations were not so popular or even made available to the researchers. Today, the table has turned. We have seen many successful IR applications that made use of these external resources to improve retrieval efficiency, cases where the use of metadata items and keywords, data that surrounds the documents but is usually left outside of a formal model, could benefit the research field.

Presence of augmented contents poses a new challenge to researchers in the way retrieval is operated on top of heterogeneous data sources. One intuitive way to get over this is to mix text data from various sources into one distribution, which is a commonly-used technique in the literature. Doing so, however, might

P.-J. Cheng et al. (Eds.): AIRS 2010, LNCS 6458, pp. 37–48, 2010.

give rise to other issues since the new representation did not necessarily share the same context with the original one, making it difficult to assign weights or distribute probability masses. Recall that we have experienced the same issue when trying to mix the contents in the document title with that in the document body to create an single index; any attempt for adjusting the weight of title words might end up harming theoretical soundness.

This issue has brought our attention to the possibility of building additional layers of document representations into existing retrieval frameworks, in which we are able to aggregate information contents and to manipulate them in different granularity levels as necessary. Consider applications that could take advantage of this idea, such as facilitating cross-language information retrieval in a corpus where documents possess multiple representations over different languages [5]; receiving user queries in a general vocabulary while operating the retrieval process in another level where documents are indexed with more specific terms; or searching for named entities that are relevant to the user queries in a collection where manually-labeled, high-quality annotations were already made available at the document level.

The aforementioned thoughts have motivated our research on formal retrieval methods. In addition to the regular term set T, we look for ways to build a *secondary document representation S* into a model so as to enable simple interaction between the two layers, such as retrieving elements from one side with that of the other as the query. In mathematical terms, we want to estimate the probability $\Pr(s|t)$, given that a document d_i is indexed in two different representations T_i and S_i, where $T_i \subset T$ and $S_i \subset S$. A concrete application of this is to let the user form a query $\mathbf{q} \subset T$ and to estimate the probability $\Pr(s|\mathbf{q})$ accordingly.

To achieve our goal, in this paper we propose a generalization over the relevance models [6,5]. The original relevance model was adapted to the cases where two individual term distributions were available in the text collection. We take a Bayesian generative approach, starting from a graphical model in which documents, terms, and hyperparameters are all explicitly specified and then break down the full-blown probabilistic network to a few equations that could easily implemented at the index level.

The rest of the work is structured as follows. First, we introduce a Bayesian generative process that involves two individual term distributions in Section 2 and show that the process leads to a generalized relevance model. Then, in Section 3, we present two applications of our model. In Section 3.1, the idea of query expansion in language modeling is revisited by considering user queries in a set of terms indexed in general vocabulary and further expanding the set by collecting relevant concepts in a more specific vocabulary; the other task we introduce in Section 3.2 is about named-entity ranking, in which we use $\Pr(s|\mathbf{q})$ to sort the named entities retrieved in a facet search session and present the entities according to their relevance to the query. In each task, the corresponding evaluation benchmark is also described. We briefly summarize the related work in Section 4. Finally, we discuss a few issues arise in the development of the work and give out concluding remarks in Section 5.

2   Model

In this model, we hypothesize the existence of the two independent multinomial distributions $\tau^{(j)}$ and $\phi^{(j)}$ associated with each document d_j; we further assume that, in each document, the terms observed in the *primary* representation T_j are drawn from the first multinomial, and those in the *secondary* representation S_j drawn from the second. The advantage of making this independent assumption can be stated in two respects. First, separation of the generation processes on both sides may lead to a cleaner framework, which makes model inference a bit easier; second, we want to highlight the fact that these two terms sets do not necessarily share the same context and further simplify the dependency relations in the resulting Bayesian network.

2.1   The Generative Framework

Figure 1 shows our proposed Bayesian generative framework. Consider the collection is composed of N documents, in which each document d_j is associated with two sets of terms T_j and S_j. We refer T_j as the primary representation and S_j the secondary representation. Each document d_j possesses two multinomial distributions, denoted by $\tau^{(j)}$ and $\phi^{(j)}$, from which elements in T_j and S_j are drawn independently, respectively. The two multinomials for a document could also be understood as two independent document models $p(w|\tau^{(j)})$ and $p(w|\phi^{(j)})$ that work on two different sets of vocabularies. Two Dirichlet distributions $\{\alpha_i; i \in [1, |T|]\}$ and $\{\beta_k; k \in [1, |S|]\}$ are assumed in the model to govern the generation of these multinomials.

As suggested in the upper-half of Figure 1, the input query $\mathbf{q}$ is modeled as a set of observed terms drawn from an unknown document model x in the collection. Specifically, we assume that the query terms and the primary representation of document x are encoded in the same vocabulary. By making this assumption, we are able to match the query against all the document models and to estimate the query likelihood $\Pr(\mathbf{q}|d_j)$. This leads us to probabilistic generative methods, such as language modeling. Recall that the unknown document x is connected to another unknown variable y. The variable y represents the most probable term generated from the secondary multinomial distribution $\phi^{(x)}$.

The entire generative process can be summarized as follows:

1. For each document d_j,
    (a) $\tau^{(j)} \sim \text{Dirichlet}(\alpha_i; i \in [1, |T|])$
    (b) $\phi^{(j)} \sim \text{Dirichlet}(\beta_k; i \in [1, |S|])$
    (c) For $i \in \{1, \ldots, |T_j|\}$, $t_i \sim \text{Mult}(\tau^{(j)})$
    (d) For $k \in \{1, \ldots, |S_j|\}$, $s_k \sim \text{Mult}(\phi^{(j)})$
2. For some unknown document d_x,
    (a) For $i \in \{1, \ldots, |\mathbf{q}|\}$, $q_i \sim \text{Mult}(\tau^{(x)})$

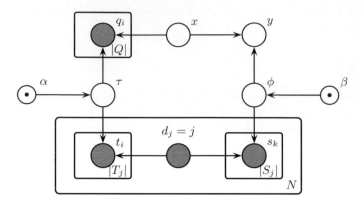

Fig. 1. The document-centric generative model is shown in the plate notation, in which shaded nodes denote observed variables. The document d_j generates two representations T_j and S_j, where each term in T_j is represented as t_i and that in S_j represented as s_j. The query terms are represented as q_i's, which are drawn from an unknown document model x; the document is associated with an unknown term $y \in S$.

2.2   Inference

The discussions have brought us to the focus of this work, which is to explicitly estimate the likelihood of one term s in the secondary term domain being triggered[1] by another set of terms in the primary term domain. This task can be framed as an optimization problem:

$$y^* = \arg\max_{y \in S} \Pr(y|\mathbf{q}, \mathbf{t}, \mathbf{d}, \mathbf{s}) \tag{1}$$

where $\mathbf{t}$ and $\mathbf{s}$ represent all the observed terms in the primary/secondary representations in the collection, respectively; $\mathbf{q}$ represents the input query and $\mathbf{d}$ denotes all the observed documents. The right-hand-side of Equation (1) can be broken down into the following form:

$$
\begin{aligned}
\Pr(y|\mathbf{q}, \mathbf{t}, \mathbf{d}, \mathbf{s}) &= \sum_{x \in [1,N]} \Pr(y|x, \mathbf{q}, \mathbf{t}, \mathbf{d}, \mathbf{s}) \Pr(x|\mathbf{q}, \mathbf{t}, \mathbf{d}, \mathbf{s}) \\
&\propto \sum_{x \in [1,N]} \left\{ \int \Pr(y|x, \phi^{(x)}) \Pr(\phi^{(x)}|d_x, \mathbf{s}_x) \mathrm{d}\phi^{(x)} \right. \\
&\qquad \left. \int \Pr(\mathbf{q}|x, \tau^{(x)}) \Pr(\tau^{(x)}|d_x, \mathbf{t}_x) \mathrm{d}\tau^{(x)} \Pr(x) \right\} \\
&= \sum_{x \in [1,N]} \frac{\beta_y + c_{y,x}}{\sum_k \beta_k + c_{k,x}} \frac{\mathcal{B}(\{\alpha_i + c_{i,x} + c_{i,q}\})}{\mathcal{B}(\{\alpha_i + c_{i,x}\})} \Pr(x) \tag{2}
\end{aligned}
$$

---

[1] We coin the term due to the lack of obvious dependency between both sides.

The last line follows the conjugacy of Dirichlet distribution, as in:

$$\Pr(\phi^{(x)}|x, y, d_x, \mathbf{s}_x) \sim \text{Dirichlet}(\{\beta_k + c_{k,x}; \forall k\})$$
$$\Pr(\tau^{(x)}|x, \mathbf{q}, d_x, \mathbf{t}_x) \sim \text{Dirichlet}(\{\alpha_i + c_{i,x}; \forall i\}).$$

Recall that $\mathcal{B}(\cdot)$ is the multinomial beta function defined by:

$$\mathcal{B}(a_1, \ldots, a_n) = \frac{\prod_i \Gamma(a_i)}{\Gamma(\sum_i a_i)}.$$

2.3   Hyperparameters

There are two particular prior distributions that we want to study in this work. Consider a prior as a vector of size $|S|$: $(\beta_1, \beta_2, \ldots, \beta_{|S|})$. The first one is the *uniform* prior:

$$(c, c, \ldots, c),$$

in which we let $\beta_k = c$ for each $k \in [1, |S|]$ and c denote some constant. The second one is called *smoothed-Dirichlet*, which is widely-used as a smoothing method in the language modeling applications for information retrieval [11]:

$$(\mu \Pr(s_1|C), \mu \Pr(s_2|C), \ldots, \mu \Pr(s_{|S|}|C)),$$

where $\Pr(s_k|C)$ denotes the probability of generating term s_k (in the secondary term domain) from the collection by viewing the entire collection as one language model; μ represents some constant.

2.4   Computational Efficiency

One interesting feature of our model is that it offers seamless integration with the language-model-based retrieval method. It comes from the fact that we could further simplify Equation (2) by assigning α as a smoothed-Dirichlet prior and $\Pr(x)$ as a uniform prior. When $\alpha_i = \mu \Pr(t_i|C)$, it can be shown that:

$$\frac{\mathcal{B}(\{\alpha_i + c_{i,x} + c_{i,q}\})}{\mathcal{B}(\{\alpha_i + c_{i,x}\})} \propto \text{L}_{\text{LM}}(\mathbf{q}|d),$$

where $\text{L}_{\text{LM}}(\mathbf{q}|d)$ denotes the query likelihood score in the language model with Dirichlet smoothing scheme. In this case, the model scores becomes:

$$\Pr(y|\mathbf{q}, \mathbf{t}, \mathbf{d}, \mathbf{s}) \propto \sum_{x \in [1,N]} \frac{\beta_y + c_{y,x}}{\sum_k \beta_k + c_{k,x}} \text{L}_{\text{LM}}(\mathbf{q}|x) \qquad (3)$$

It can be shown that the expected complexity for computing the summation is linear to the size of top-ranked documents, namely n, and the average size of secondary domain terms associated with each document, i.e., $(\sum_j |S_j|)/N$.

3   Experimental Results

In this section, we introduce two applications of our proposed framework. In the first experiment, we use a different set of terms to refine the query model so as to leverage retrieval effectiveness; in the second experiment, we showed that we were able to retrieve the named entities relevant to the user query from a database by supplying the entities as the secondary document representation. Both experiments were conducted in a general way so as to be reproduced by any follow-up research.

3.1   Query Refinement Using the Secondary Representation

The probability estimate $\Pr(y|\mathbf{q}, \mathbf{t}, \mathbf{d}, \mathbf{s})$ that we obtained from the proposed model can be seen as a *refined query model*. In other words, we employ a two-stage retrieval strategy by launching an initial retrieval run to populate a refined model, and then re-submit the model as a new query to the retrieval system. Our idea here differs from the previous efforts [6] in the use of a more specific vocabulary as the secondary representation. The major obstacle, however, for realizing such type of model-based query refinement lies in the restriction of the language modeling framework, according to which the input query should be specified as a sequence of terms. We used a technique that enabled a second-round retrieval by *realizing* the probability distribution $\Pr(y|\mathbf{q}, \mathbf{t}, \mathbf{d}, \mathbf{s})$ as a sequence of *expected terms*, in which each term s_k appears exactly $\mathrm{E}(s_k|\mathbf{q}, \mathbf{t}, \mathbf{d}, \mathbf{s})$ times. It can be shown that the technique reduces to the KL-divergence retrieval framework [10].

The benchmark corpora that we used here was the NTCIR-4 Test Collection. We considered a subtask of the NTCIR-4 CLIR Task [4]: Chinese-to-Chinese monolingual document retrieval. The dataset comprised of totally 381,681 newswire articles and 59 test topics. Only title queries were used in this experiment. Limited preprocessing steps were applied to the corpus in advance. All the punctuation marks, whitesapces, and separators were discarded and the remaining texts were send to a simple tokenizer. As a result, the output was a mixture of CJK-character bigrams and English word unigrams, which formed the primary document representations in our model and in other baseline methods. The secondary representation we chose was the top-500,000 CJK-character bigrams in the entire collection ranked by the corresponding *tf-idf* score; the candidate set was formed by excluding those bigrams occurred less than 5 times. The parameters described here were determined through experimentation.

Our model was developed from scratch in C++, and the rest of the experimental runs were established on top of the Lemur toolkit[2]. From all the retrieval methods supported by the tool, we selected `tfidf`, `okapi`, and `indri` (a language-model-based method) as the baseline methods; our own language model implementation is denoted as `lm`. Standard query expansion techniques for each method were also tested: Pseudo-relevance feedback (`PRF`) was implemented for both `tfidf` and `okapi` models, and an adaptation of Lavrenko's relevance model

---

[2] http://www.lemurproject.org

(RM) was also built into the core of Indri index; our refinement model is denoted as BRM in this experiment.

We stuck with the default parameter values for all the participant models in the regular runs; for standard query expansion, we set the number of feedback documents as 20 and the number of feedback terms as 100. The refined query was computed under the same restriction in BRM, where terms other than the top-ranked 100's were completely ignored. Recall that our model reviewed all the retrieved top-1000 documents to achieve the probability estimates. The performance is measured in terms of mean average precision and precision-at-5.

Table 1 shows the experimental result. Among all the regular runs, our language modeling implementation (lm) achieved the lowest MAP under both judgment sets; the retrieval performance was greatly improved when the refinement model (lm+BRM) was applied, achieving 0.207 for rigid relevance judgment and 0.261 for relax in terms of MAP. It turned out that the proposed query refinement model greatly enhanced the performance of relevance model counterpart in Indri (indri+RM) by 17.6% in terms of MAP. Since our proposed model can be viewed as a relaxed (or adapted) version of the original relevance model, this encouraging result partly confirmed our hypothesis that bad expansion terms could be avoided by biasing the expansion source toward a secondary document representation that possesses a cleaner, highly-discriminative vocabulary.

The overall best performance, however, still fell on the tfidf-side. The expansion run okapi+PRF achieved 0.224 under rigid and 0.270 under relax judgment set in terms of MAP. Generally, the performance for all the expansion runs can be summarized as: $okapi + PRF > tfidf + PRF > lm + BRM \gg indri + RM$. As we can see in Table 1, even though the proposed method achieved roughly comparable performance as tfidf+PRF, the difference between the performance of tfidf-based methods and that of language-model-based methods remains rather significant.

Table 1. The overall performance result is summarized in this table. Regular retrieval runs are listed in the upper-half and expansion runs in the lower-half. Boldfaced values indicate the best-performers. Evaluation results for using the rigid and the relax judgment sets are both listed. Note that improvement (+%) for each expansion run is calculated against the performance of the corresponding regular run.

	Rigid Judgment				Relax Judgment			
Regular	MAP	(+%)	P@5	(+%)	MAP	(+%)	P@5	(+%)
tfidf	0.181		0.264		0.213		0.335	
okapi	0.185		0.278		0.223		0.356	
indri	0.174		0.258		0.216		0.346	
lm	0.170		0.251		0.209		0.322	
Expansion								
tfidf+PRF	0.217	(+19.9%)	0.295	(+11.7%)	0.264	(+23.9%)	0.383	(+14.3%)
okapi+PRF	**0.224**	(+21.1%)	**0.315**	(+13.3%)	**0.270**	(+21.1%)	**0.400**	(+12.4%)
indri+RM	0.180	(+3.4%)	0.271	(+5.3%)	0.222	(+2.8%)	0.342	(-1.2%)
lm+BRM	0.207	(+21.8%)	0.302	(+20.3%)	0.261	(+24.9%)	0.369	(+14.6%)

Table 2. The performance results of all the methods (except the proposed one) using only the top-500,000 bigram representation. Boldfaced values indicate the best performers.

Method	Rigid Judgment		Relax Judgment	
	MAP	P@5	MAP	P@5
tfidf+PRF.500k	0.190	0.288	0.241	0.373
okapi+PRF.500k	0.196	**0.302**	0.247	**0.383**
indri+RM.500k	0.155	0.248	0.197	0.309
(*The above runs were indexed against top-50k bigrams only*)				
lm+BRM	**0.207**	**0.302**	**0.261**	0.369
(*This run was operated on both representations*)				

One thing to note is that readers might argue that the performance improvement of our model was largely contributed by using the terms in the secondary representation as expansion source. Table 2 summarizes the performance results for another round of experiments conducted on the same corpus where only the secondary representation (i.e., top-500,000 bigrams) was available. The result shows that using the secondary representation alone was not enough for achieving high retrieval effectiveness. The performance for all the participating runs except our proposed method decreased due to the choice of the document representation. Note that we do not intend to claim superiority of our method over the other runs, since our model possessed better knowledge about the complete document distribution and making comparison against other approaches in this case would not be appropriate.

3.2   Retrieving Query-Relevant Facets

Faceted search [3,8,7] can be seen as a two-phase extension of the ordinary retrieval task: In the first phase, one populates a set of documents (the *result set*) by querying the underlying retrieval model; then, in the second phase, one exploits the associations between the facet entries and the documents, and returns the facet items back to the users. The collected facets are usually presented in descending order of the corresponding number of occurrences in the result set, which we called the *count-based scheme*. The scheme is mostly preferable because it is fast and easy to implement. However, it treats all the collected facet counts equally important and disregards the differences on the degree of relevance between the retrieved documents. In other words, a facet found in a low-rank document might appear as good as that found in a top-rank one when this simple ranking scheme is employed.

This can also be a problem when the user wants to consult the retrieved facets to guide the subsequent exploratory search. Since the facets are not sorted in terms of relevance, the user might be mislead by top-ranked facets that are not actually relevant to the input query but merely possess more counts in the lower-ranked documents. We argue that a reasonable facet ranking algorithm should always assign higher weights to the facets discovered from the top-ranked documents; therefore, the algorithm itself may need to co-operate with the retrieval model for obtaining better facet ranking. This observation has brought us to a simple solution: We can build in the facets associated with each document as a secondary representation and utilize Equation 2 to rank the facets.

The very nature of this task makes our proposed model feasible. One major difficulty that we faced, however, was the lack of standard benchmark on the facet ranking task. As a result, we went for a custom benchmark based on one text collection in our own applications. The test corpus that we chose was the Tan-Hsin Archive[3], which is currently the most sizable and complete collection of historical documents in Taiwan dating back from 1776 to 1895. We took a subset of 15,314 documents from the collection to form the test set. Each document in the collection is associated with a set of human-annotated facets. By considering topic coverage and ease of evaluation, we tested model performance only on person names as the designated facet set. The number of unique person names in the dataset is 10,918, and the total number of occurrences of these facets is 37,489. Thus, the average number of person names associated with a document is 2.45. All these information were already made available in the metadata of the documents.

To prepare the query topics, we first fetched all the query log entries from the database server. We put together a set of 105 query topics, each of which had obtained more than 50 hits in our database. We randomly chose 28 topics out from the set and used them in the following evaluation. The relevance judgment was made manually. For each query topics, we prepared a list of the top 100 facets returned by the baseline retriever that operated merely based on occurrence counts[4]; the domain expert would then go over the entire list, labeling each facet as relevant or irrelevant accordingly. We considered 3 competing runs in the experiment: (i) `baseline`, with which facets were ranked by the corresponding number of counts in the result set; (ii) `uniform-prior`, with which facets were ranked by the proposed model using uniform prior for β; and (iii) `smoothed-prior`, with which facets were ranked by the proposed model using Dirichlet-smoothed prior for β. Note that the language-model-based approach proposed in [2] was partly involved in this experiment. The method is roughly comparable[5] to a special case of the `uniform-prior` method for $\beta = 0$.

We took the top-1000 documents retrieved by using Dirichlet-smoothed language model with $\mu = 2,500$ as the result set. The hyperparameter was predetermined through experimentation. All the algorithms took the same set of document IDs as input. For our proposed methods, we reused the retrieved scores returned by the document-level retrieval model, as stated in the preceding sections. The output was a sorted list of all the associated facets in descending order of the ranking score. For efficiency, we used only the top-100 facets returned by

---

[3] http://www.lib.ntu.edu.tw/project/en/index.htm

[4] Relevance judgment created this way might greatly favor the baseline method, as noted by the friendly anonymous reviewer. A better way to do this is through pooling. As of writing, we are not able to revise the benchmark; however, the biases result is still able to demonstrate the effectiveness of the proposed method.

[5] The equivalence takes place only when the mixture component λ_{CA} is set to 0.

Table 3. The performance results for all the test runs. The top performers are shown in boldface.

Method		MAP	P@10
baseline		0.2996	0.3857
uniform-prior	$\beta = 0$	0.5775	0.6179
	$\beta = 1$	**0.5899**	**0.6464**
	$\beta = 10$	0.5877	**0.6464**
smoothed-prior	$\mu = 0.01$	0.5781	0.6179
	$\mu = 1$	0.5782	0.6214
	$\mu = 100$	0.4956	0.5429

each run as the final results. The performance was assessed both in terms of mean-average precision and precision-at-10.

The performance of the baseline was quite moderate, with MAP a bit less than 0.3 and P@10 around 0.39. All the other models showed significant improvement over the baseline, ranging from 30% to 100% in terms of MAP. From the result, we find that the performance of our best model (uniform-prior with $\beta = 1$) was slightly better than that of the language-model-based counterpart (uniform-prior with $\beta = 0$), though only to a limited extent, by 2.15% in terms of MAP. Out of curiosity, we also ran a line search for each model by varying the hyperparameter β. We found that model performances were quite stable across different experimental runs. Generally speaking, uniform-prior and smoothed-prior achieved comparable performance. The best one was found in the uniform-prior run with $\beta = 0.2$, achieving 0.591 in MAP. The positive observation in this experiment suggested that a relevance-based model is probably more effective than a count-based model in the facet ranking task.

4   Related Work

Our proposed framework was greatly inspired by the recent advances on language modeling applications in information retrieval, including relevance models [6,5], model-based feedback [10], and Bayesian language model [9]. In this respect, our solution can be seen as a two-stage Bayesian extension of the regular language model over the facet data. Our approach differs from the previous efforts in the formal definition of a secondary document representation and a corresponding generative Bayesian model. Specifically, our work departs from the original relevance model [6] and its cross-lingual counterpart [5] in the way Dirichlet priors are associated with the both representations.

To the best of our knowledge, this work is among the earliest attempt for retrieving relevant facets in the digital library community. Interestingly, we learned that similar attempts were made in the area of expert finding. In [1], Amitay et al. formulated the problem of expert finding as a two-layered retrieval task and proposed a solution based on the *inverse entity-frequency* that achieved moderate performance on the task. Balog et al. [2] followed up in the same direction by proposing a language modeling framework with the similar rationale to extend the use of language model to the underlying co-occurrence statistics by exploiting person-term and person-document links. Our contribution departs from these two previous efforts, not only in the application domain, but in the way document relevance is incorporated into the model and the support for prior belief.

5   Discussion and Concluding Remarks

In this work, we propose a Bayesian framework that enables the use of a secondary document representation in language modeling. The framework extends Lavrenko's relevance model to offer interoperability between two different term domains. Moreover, we show that our method is capable of working with a language-model-based retrieval engine to achieve high efficiency in computation.

Two applications are introduced in this paper to evaluate the performance of the proposed solution. In the first task, we show that the presence of a secondary document layer that is made of a carefully-selected vocabulary could greatly enhance retrieval effectiveness. Even though the proposed query refinement model did not achieve the best performance, the model still beaten the relevance model baseline by 17.6% (rigid) and 22.7% (relax) in term of MAP and gained comparable performance as `tfidf` with pseudo-relevance feedback. The refinement model alone improved the MAP of the regular language modeling run by 21.8% (rigid) and 24.9% (relax). In the second application, where the model was used to rank named entities returned in the query session by the underlying retrieval system, the proposed solution achieved encouraging result on the custom benchmark. Our approach outperformed the baseline and the language-model-based approach by roughly 100% and 2.15%, respectively, in terms of MAP.

Despite the early success in the evaluation results, there is still room for improvements. We see our contributions here as a starting point toward further exploration on several issues that have not yet been covered in this study: the use of different prior families, the formal inference model for the hyperparameters, potential applications on the other datasets, etc. These challenges should be the focus of our future work.

Acknowledgments

We thank Po-Yu Chen and the staff in Special Collection Department, National Taiwan University Library for their support on preparation of the test data. The research efforts described in this paper are supported under the National Taiwan University Digital Archives Project (Project No. NSC-98-2631-H-002-005), which is sponsored by National Science Council, Taiwan.

References

1. Amitay, E., Carmel, D., Golbandi, N., HarEl, N., Ofek-Koifman, S., Yogev, S.: Finding people and documents, using web 2.0 data. In: Proceedings of the SIGIR 2008 Workshop on Future Challenges in Expertise Retrieval (fCHER), pp. 1–6 (2009)

2. Balog, K., Azzopardi, L., de Rijke, M.: A language modeling framework for expert finding. Inf. Process. Manage. 45(1), 1–19 (2009)
3. Hearst, M., Elliott, A., English, J., Sinha, R., Swearingen, K., Yee, K.P.: Finding the flow in web site search. Commun. ACM 45(9), 42–49 (2002)
4. Kishida, K., Chen, K., Lee, S., Kuriyama, K., Kando, N., Chen, H., Myaeng, S., Eguchi, K.: Overview of CLIR task at the fourth NTCIR workshop. In: Proceedings of NTCIR, vol. 4, pp. 1–38 (2004)
5. Lavrenko, V., Choquette, M., Croft, W.B.: Cross-lingual relevance models. In: SIGIR 2002: Proceedings of the 25th Annual International ACM SIGIR Conference on Research and Development in Information Retrieval, pp. 175–182. ACM Press, New York (2002)
6. Lavrenko, V., Croft, W.B.: Relevance based language models. In: SIGIR 2001: Proceedings of the 24th Annual International ACM SIGIR Conference on Research and Development in Information Retrieval, pp. 120–127. ACM Press, New York (2001)
7. Roy, S.B., Wang, H., Das, G., Nambiar, U., Mohania, M.: Minimum-effort driven dynamic faceted search in structured databases. In: CIKM 2008: Proceeding of the 17th ACM Conference on Information and Knowledge Management, pp. 13–22. ACM, New York (2008)
8. Yee, K.P., Swearingen, K., Li, K., Hearst, M.: Faceted metadata for image search and browsing. In: CHI 2003: Proceedings of the SIGCHI Conference on Human Factors in Computing Systems, pp. 401–408. ACM Press, New York (2003)
9. Zaragoza, H., Hiemstra, D., Tipping, M.: Bayesian extension to the language model for ad hoc information retrieval. In: SIGIR 2003: Proceedings of the 26th Annual International ACM SIGIR Conference on Research and Development in Informaion Retrieval, pp. 4–9. ACM Press, New York (2003)
10. Zhai, C., Lafferty, J.: Model-based feedback in the language modeling approach to information retrieval. In: CIKM 2001: Proceedings of the Tenth International Conference on Information and Knowledge Management, pp. 403–410. ACM, New York (2001)
11. Zhai, C., Lafferty, J.: A study of smoothing methods for language models applied to information retrieval. ACM Trans. Inf. Syst. 22(2), 179–214 (2004)

Multi-viewpoint Based Similarity Measure and Optimality Criteria for Document Clustering

Duc Thang Nguyen, Lihui Chen, and Chee Keong Chan

Nanyang Technological University, 50 Nanyang Ave, Singapore 639798
victorthang.ng@pmail.ntu.edu.sg, {elhchen,eckchan}@ntu.edu.sg

Abstract. The aim of this work is to produce fast, easy-to-apply but effective algorithms for clustering large text collections. In this paper, we propose a novel concept of similarity measure among objects and its related clustering algorithms. The similarity between two objects within a cluster is measured from the view of all other objects outside that cluster. As a result, two optimality criteria are formulated as the objective functions for the clustering problem. We analyze and compare the proposed clustering approaches with the popular algorithms for document clustering in the literature. Extensive empirical experiments are carried out on various benchmark datasets and evaluated by different metrics. The results show that our proposed criterion functions consistently outperform the other well-known clustering criteria, and give the best overall performance with the same computational efficiency.

Keywords: Text mining, document clustering, similarity measure.

1 Introduction

The aim of document clustering is to organize a collection of documents into separate clusters, so that documents within one cluster are as similar to each other as possible, while documents in a cluster are as dissimilar as possible from those in the other clusters. Document clustering has many important applications in information retrieval; for example, search result clustering to improve information presentation to user, or cluster-based retrieval for more efficient search. Over the years, there have been countless number of clustering algorithms being proposed. They come from different scientific backgrounds, and employ various techniques and approaches. Some examples of up-to-date development are von Mises-Fisher model-based clustering [1], bipartite graph-based [3], non-negative matrix factorization [16] or co-clustering on manifolds [8]. However, after more than half a century since its introduction, the elementary k-means is still regarded as one of the top 10 algorithms in data mining today [15]. One recent scientific discussion suggests that practitioners in the field prefer to use k-means as their favourite clustering algorithm [9]. Perhaps, despite many of its drawbacks, the reasons for its immense popularity are its simplicity, understandability and scalability.

In general, a formal approach to clustering is to consider it as an optimization problem. An optimal partition is one that optimizes a particular criterion

P.-J. Cheng et al. (Eds.): AIRS 2010, LNCS 6458, pp. 49–60, 2010.

function of similarity or distance among data. Essentially, clustering solutions depend greatly on how this similarity measure is defined, and whether the specified measure suits the intrinsic structure of data. In the original k-means, for example, it is the sum-of-squared-error criterion, which uses Euclidean distance. For very sparse and high-dimensional domains such as document clustering, spherical k-means, which replaces Euclidean distance by cosine similarity, is more suitable than the standard k-means [4]. Banerjee et al. [2] introduced a class of distance measures, called Bregman divergences, which have attracted a lot of attentions. Particularly, KL-divergence, a special case of Bregman divergence, was reported to provide good results on large text datasets. These research findings reveal to us that the nature of similarity measure plays a very important role in the success or failure of a clustering method. More interestingly, non-Euclidean and non-metric measures can be informative for statistical learning of data [12]. There has also been argument that the symmetry and non-negative assumption of similarity measures is a limitation of current approaches to clustering [13].

The above observations are the motivation for our work reported in this paper. Firstly, our main objective is to derive a novel method for measuring similarity between data objects. Our application domain is sparse and high-dimensional data, particularly text documents. Secondly, we formulate clustering criterion functions which lead to high-quality, fast and scalable algorithms.

2 Background and Related Work

In [18], Zhao and Karypis presented their work on hierarchical clustering algorithms for document datasets. Their conclusion was that partitional methods were more effective and efficient than agglomerative ones. These methods were basically developed based on optimizing a set of criterion functions. This set included graph-based edge-cutting functions, intra-cluster similarity measures, inter-cluster dissimilarity measures and combinations of both types of measure. They also compared the performance of these criterion functions in partitional clustering of large document datasets [17]. All of these methods were implemented into a complete software package called CLUTO [10]. CLUTO is well-known because while providing high quality document clustering solutions, it is very efficient computationally. One of its recent applications is, for example, in job information retrieval based on document similarity [14].

In this paper, we review CLUTO's partitional clustering functionality with four of its best criterion functions. These four criteria, summarized in Table 1, were reported in the literature that they produced good clustering results [17], with H_2 being the best overall. In Table 1, d represents a document vector. In document clustering, documents are often represented in vector space model. When a collection S of n documents has a total of m terms, each document is considered as an m-dimensional vector. The vectors are weighted by standard Term Frequency-Inverse Document Frequency (TF-IDF) scheme, and normalized to have unit length, i.e. $\|d\| = 1$. When partitioned into k clusters, the subset of documents in cluster r is denoted by S_r. $D = \sum_{d_i \in S} d_i$ is the composite vector

Table 1. CLUTO's clustering criterion functions

$$\max I_2 = \sum_{r=1}^{k} \sum_{d_i \in S_r} \cos(d_i, C_r) = \sum_{r=1}^{k} \|D_r\|; \quad \min E_1 = \sum_{r=1}^{k} n_r \cos(C_r, C) = \sum_{r=1}^{k} n_r \frac{D_r^t D}{\|D_r\|}$$

$$\max H_1 = \frac{I_1}{E_1} = \frac{\sum_{r=1}^{k} \|D_r\|^2 / n_r}{\sum_{r=1}^{k} n_r D_r^t D / \|D_r\|}; \qquad \max H_2 = \frac{I_2}{E_1} = \frac{\sum_{r=1}^{k} \|D_r\|}{\sum_{r=1}^{k} n_r D_r^t D / \|D_r\|}$$

of all the documents, and $D_r = \sum_{d_i \in S_r} d_i$ is the composite vector of cluster r. $C = D/n$ is the centroid vector of all the documents, while $C_r = D_r/n_r$ is the centroid vector of cluster r, $n_r = |S_r|$.

Among the four criterion functions, I_2 had been popular in text clustering domain, whereas the other three were proposed by Zhao and Karypis. I_2 is actually equivalent to the objective function of Spherical k-means algorithm [4]. Its goal is to maximize the sum of similarities between document vectors and centroid vector of the cluster that they are assigned to. While I_2 is an internal criterion, E_1 is an external one, due to the fact that it aims to minimize the similarity between each cluster's centroid and the centroid of the entire collection. Before summed up, the similarities are weighted by corresponding cluster sizes. H_1 and H_2 are categorized as hybrid criterion functions, since they are formulated by dividing I_1 and I_2 by E_1 respectively. $I_1 = \sum_{r=1}^{k} \|D_r\|^2 / n_r$ is another internal criterion similar to I_2, but because its clustering performance was shown to be pretty poor [17], we choose not to include it in our comparison.

In all the above criterion functions, similarity of two documents, $Sim(d_i, d_j)$, is defined as the cosine of the angle between the corresponding vectors. Since the vectors are of unit length, this is equal to their dot-product:

$$Sim(d_i, d_j) = \cos(d_i, d_j) = d_i^t d_j \tag{1}$$

In the next section, we propose a novel way to evaluate similarity of documents, and consequently formulate new criterion functions for document clustering.

3 Multi-viewpoint Based Clustering

3.1 Our Novel Similarity Measure

The similarity measure in Eq. (1) can be rewritten as follows without affecting its meaning:

$$Sim(d_i, d_j) = \cos(d_i - 0, d_j - 0) = (d_i - 0)^t (d_j - 0) \tag{2}$$

where 0 is vector 0 representing the origin point. According to Eq. (2), we determine the similarity of documents d_i and d_j by the angle between the two points when looking from the origin. Thus, this is based on just one reference point.

To construct a new concept of similarity, our idea is simple: if we look at the two points from a set of different positions, we may have a better judgment of how close or distant they are. This is applicable to everything in real life, too. For example, before giving a decision to any problem, it is always necessary to approach the problem from different perspectives to have a more comprehensive understanding of the problem itself. When looking at an object, for instance a building, we will have a clearer picture of it if we stand to view it from different angles. In the vector-space model, if we stand at not the origin but a third point d_h, the directions and distances from this viewpoint to d_i and d_j will be presented by the difference vectors $(d_i - d_h)$ and $(d_j - d_h)$. By applying this idea, we define a new similarity measure for two documents in a cluster as follows:

$$Sim(d_i, d_j) = \frac{1}{n - n_r} \sum_{d_h \in S \setminus S_r} Sim(d_i - d_h, d_j - d_h) \quad (3)$$
$$\scriptstyle d_i, d_j \in S_r$$

According to this equation, similarity of two documents in the same cluster is defined as the average of similarities measured with respect to all other documents that do not belong to that cluster. Hence, similarity here is defined in close relation to the clustering problem. On the one hand, the two objects of the measure must be in the same cluster. On the other hand, the points from where to establish this measure must be outside the cluster. There is a presumption of cluster memberships prior to the measure. If we further define each relative similarity simply as the dot-product of the difference vectors, we have:

$$Sim(d_i, d_j) = \frac{1}{n - n_r} \sum_{d_h \in S \setminus S_r} (d_i - d_h)^t (d_j - d_h)$$
$$\scriptstyle d_i, d_j \in S_r$$

$$= \frac{1}{n - n_r} \sum_{d_h \in S \setminus S_r} \cos(d_i - d_h, d_j - d_h) \| d_i - d_h \| \| d_j - d_h \| \quad (4)$$

From a viewpoint d_h outside cluster S_r, the similarity between two points d_i and d_j inside this cluster equals to the product of the cosine of the angle looking from d_h and the Euclidean distances from d_h to each of these two points. Hence, through these distances, Eq. (4) also contains a measure of inter-cluster dissimilarity, given that points d_i and d_j belong to cluster S_r, whereas d_h belongs to another cluster.

3.2   The Clustering Criterion Functions

Our first criterion function, called I_R, aims to maximize the cluster size-weighted sum of average pairwise similarities between documents that have the same cluster label. Let us consider function F, which represents this sum:

$$F = \sum_{r=1}^{k} n_r \left[\frac{1}{n_r^2} \sum_{d_i, d_j \in S_r} Sim(d_i, d_j) \right] \quad (5)$$

By applying Eq. (4) for $Sim(d_i, d_j)$ and expanding the sum of vector products, after some derivation steps, we will be able to obtain:

$$\sum_{d_i, d_j \in S_r} Sim(d_i, d_j) = \frac{n + n_r}{n - n_r} \| D_r \|^2 - \frac{2 n_r}{n - n_r} D_r^t D + n_r^2$$

Substituting back into Eq. (5) to give:

$$F = \sum_{r=1}^{k} \frac{1}{n_r} \left[\frac{n+n_r}{n-n_r} \|D_r\|^2 - \left(\frac{n+n_r}{n-n_r} - 1 \right) D_r^t D \right] + n$$

As n is constant, maximizing F above is equivalent to maximizing:

$$\bar{F} = \sum_{r=1}^{k} \frac{1}{n_r} \left[\frac{n+n_r}{n-n_r} \|D_r\|^2 - \left(\frac{n+n_r}{n-n_r} - 1 \right) D_r^t D \right] \tag{6}$$

Comparing $\bar{F}$ to min-max cut graph-based clustering function [5], which is also included in CLUTO as G_1 [17], it is seen that both of them involve the two terms $\|D_r\|^2$ and $D_r^t D$. The former is a measure of intra-cluster similarity, whereas the latter is a form of external measure (similarity between a cluster and the entire document collection). However, while G_1's objective is to minimize the inverse ratio between these two terms, $\bar{F}$ aims to maximize their weighted difference. In $\bar{F}$, this value for each cluster is weighted again by the inverse of cluster's size, before summed up across the clusters. Such a criterion, similarly to some of CLUTO's functions, is expected to be sensitive to cluster size. Following the formulation of COSA, a well-known subspace clustering algorithm [7], it would be better to have a set of weight factors $\{\lambda_r\}_1^k$, which are simple functions of respective cluster sizes $\{n_r\}_1^k$, to regulate the distribution of these cluster sizes in clustering solutions. Consequently, we have $\bar{F}$ become:

$$\bar{F}_\lambda = \sum_{r=1}^{k} \frac{\lambda_r}{n_r} \left[\frac{n+n_r}{n-n_r} \|D_r\|^2 - (\frac{n+n_r}{n-n_r} - 1) D_r^t D \right] \tag{7}$$

And if by letting $\lambda_r = n_r^\alpha$, where α is some constant called regulating factor, $\alpha \in [0,1]$, we arrive at the final criterion function I_R:

$$I_R = \sum_{r=1}^{k} \frac{1}{n_r^{1-\alpha}} \left[\frac{n+n_r}{n-n_r} \|D_r\|^2 - (\frac{n+n_r}{n-n_r} - 1) D_r^t D \right] \tag{8}$$

In our experiments, it has been observed that the criterion function yields relatively good clustering results when $\alpha \in (0,1)$.

The principle for formulation of I_R is related to that of CLUTO's criterion function I_1, in the sense that a cluster quality is measured by the average pairwise similarity between documents within that cluster. An alternative approach is to use similarity between each document vector and its cluster's centroid instead. Based on this ground, our second criterion function, called I_V, is formulated as follows. Considering objective function G:

$$G = \sum_{r=1}^{k} \sum_{d_i \in S_r} \left[\frac{1}{n-n_r} \sum_{d_h \in S \backslash S_r} Sim\left(d_i - d_h, \frac{C_r}{\|C_r\|} - d_h \right) \right]$$

$$G = \sum_{r=1}^{k} \left[\frac{1}{n-n_r} \sum_{d_i \in S_r} \sum_{d_h \in S \backslash S_r} (d_i - d_h)^t \left(\frac{C_r}{\|C_r\|} - d_h \right) \right] \tag{9}$$

By expanding the vector product, after some derivation, we will be able to obtain:

$$\sum_{d_i \in S_r} \sum_{d_h \in S \setminus S_r} (d_i - d_h)^t \left(\frac{C_r}{\|C_r\|} - d_h \right) = (n + \|D_r\|) \|D_r\| - (n_r + \|D_r\|) \frac{D_r^t D}{\|D_r\|}$$
$$+ n_r(n - n_r)$$

Substituting back into Eq. (9), we get:

$$G = \sum_{r=1}^{k} \left[\frac{n + \|D_r\|}{n - n_r} \|D_r\| - \left(\frac{n + \|D_r\|}{n - n_r} - 1 \right) \frac{D_r^t D}{\|D_r\|} \right] + n$$

Since n is constant and does not affect the optimization problem, maximizing the above function is equivalent to maximizing I_V:

$$I_V = \sum_{r=1}^{k} \left[\frac{n + \|D_r\|}{n - n_r} \|D_r\| - \left(\frac{n + \|D_r\|}{n - n_r} - 1 \right) \frac{D_r^t D}{\|D_r\|} \right] \tag{10}$$

Comparing I_V with CLUTO's criterion function H_2, we notice that both of them take in two terms $\|D_r\|$ and $D_r^t D / \|D_r\|$. Though, while H_2 is simply the ratio of two other criterion functions I_2 and E_1, I_V calculates the weighted difference between these two terms for each of the clusters before summing them up. This variation brings about the distinctions in clustering performance between I_V and H_2, since it affects how documents are moved from one cluster to another during the optimization process.

3.3   Optimization Algorithm

Our goal is to perform document clustering by optimizing criterion functions I_R and I_V in Eq. (8) and (10). To achieve this, we utilize the sequential and incremental version of k-means, which is guaranteed to converge to a local optimum [6,17]. This algorithm consists of a number of iterations: initially, k seeds are selected randomly and each document is assigned to cluster of its closest seed based on cosine similarity; in each of the subsequent iterations, the documents are picked in random order and, for each document, a move to a new cluster takes place if such move leads to an increase in the objective function. Particularly, considering that the expression of I_V in Eq. (10) depends only on n_r and D_r, $r = 1, \ldots, k$, let us represent I_V in a general form:

$$I_V = \sum_{r=1}^{k} I_r(n_r, D_r) \tag{11}$$

Assume that, at beginning of some iteration, a document d_i belongs to a cluster S_p that has objective value $I_p(n_p, D_p)$. d_i will be moved to another cluster S_q that has objective value $I_q(n_q, D_q)$ if the following condition is satisfied:

$$\Delta I_V = I_p(n_p - 1, D_p - d_i) + I_q(n_q + 1, D_q + d_i) - I_p(n_p, D_p) - I_q(n_q, D_q) > 0$$
$$\text{st. } q = \arg\max_{r, r \neq p} \{ I_r(n_r + 1, D_r + d_i) - I_r(n_r, D_r) \}$$

Table 2. Document datasets

Data	#Classes	n	m	Data	#Classes	n	m
classic	4	7,089	12,009	fbis	17	2,463	2,000
hitech	6	2,301	13,170	k1a	20	2,340	13,859
k1b	6	2,340	13,859	la12	6	6,279	21,604
new3	44	9,558	36,306	ohscal	10	11,162	11,465
re0	13	1,504	2,886	re1	25	1,657	3,758
reviews	5	4,069	23,220	sports	7	8,580	18,324
tr31	7	927	10,127	tr41	10	878	7,453
wap	20	1,560	8,440	la2	6	3,075	15,211
tr11	9	414	6,424	tr12	8	313	5,799
tr23	6	204	5,831	tr45	10	690	8,260

Hence, document d_i is moved to a new cluster that gives the largest increase in the objective function, if such an increase exists. The composite vectors of corresponding old and new clusters are updated instantly after each move. If a maximum number of iterations is reached or no more move is detected, the procedure is stopped.

A major advantage of our clustering functions under this optimization scheme is that they are very efficient computationally. During the optimization process, the main computational demand is from searching for optimum clusters to move individual documents to, and updating composite vectors as a result of such moves. If τ denotes the number of iterations the algorithm takes, nz the total number of non-zero entries in all document vectors, the computational complexity required for clustering with I_R and I_V is approximately $O(nz \cdot k \cdot \tau)$.

4   Experiments

4.1   Document Datasets

There are twenty benchmark document collections employed in our experiments. Apart from the fifteen datasets used in [17] to demonstrate CLUTO's performance, we used five more collections (*la2, tr11, tr12, tr23, tr45*) to have an even more thorough examination of the clustering methods. All datasets are available with the CLUTO toolkit. These datasets possess diverse characteristics in terms of number of classes, number of documents and number of words. They were already preprocessed by standard procedures, including stop-word removal and stemming. We further removed words that appear in less than two documents or more than 99.5% of the documents. The documents were then weighted by TF-IDF and normalized to unit vectors. Table 2 summarizes these datasets.

4.2   Experimental Setup and Evaluation Metrics

We compare I_R and I_V with the criteria in Table 1 for their performance in document partitional clustering. For I_R, the regulating factor α was set at 0.3

throughout the experiments, after we had observed that this was one of the best values. For CLUTO, there is a C library interface freely available [10]. We used this library to run the tests for I_2, E_1, H_1 and H_2 with direct k-way incremental algorithm. Zhao and Karypis [17] evaluated these four criterion functions based on entropy and purity for $k = 5$, 10, 15 and 20. Hence, we repeated their experiments with those numbers of clusters on each datasets. The same numbers of clusters were also used for I_R and I_V. As a result, there was a total of 480 cases (6 criterion functions, 20 datasets, 4 values of k). Besides, since both entropy and purity are biased towards larger number of clusters, we resorted to an additional evaluation metric: the normalized mutual information (NMI). It was suggested to be a superior measure to entropy and purity [19]. All three metrics have value within [0,1]. For entropy, the smaller value the better; for purity and NMI, greater value indicates better clustering result.

For each of the 480 cases, 10 runs were carried out and the average entropy, purity and NMI were calculated. Besides, to eliminate the effect of random initialization, each run was set to have 10 trials with different initializations, from which the best result (based on objective function) was selected as the final output for that run. This procedure was applied to all the methods in comparison. Due to space limitation, we could not report all individual evaluation values here. We employed the technique used in [17] to present the summarized results over all datasets through *relative entropy*, *relative purity* and *relative NMI*. If $I, J \in \{I_R, I_V, I_2, E_1, H_1, H_2\}$, for each pair of dataset S and cluster number k, the relative evaluation measures corresponding to any criterion function I are:

$$rEntropy_{I,S,k} = \frac{Entropy_{I,S,k}}{\min_{J} Entropy_{J,S,k}}; \qquad rPurity_{I,S,k} = \frac{\max_{J} Purity_{J,S,k}}{Purity_{I,S,k}}$$

where $Entropy_{I,S,k}$ and $Purity_{I,S,k}$ are the entropy and purity resulted from clustering S by I with k. Relative NMI is calculated in similar way to relative purity. Then, according to each relative measure, I is the best performer among all criterion functions if it has a value of 1. Otherwise its value is greater than 1; the larger this value is, the worse it has performed. Since the original evaluation measures on different datasets with different cluster numbers can be very diverse, using the relative metrics enables us to average the results over all the examined datasets. Eventually, the final average measures are calculated over all 4 cluster numbers to yield the overall performance.

4.3   Results

Table 3 summarizes performance of all the clustering criterion functions based on the three evaluation metrics. The average results over all 20 datasets with the different values of cluster number k, as well as the overall average performances, are shown. For each row of the table, the number in bold and underlined is the best value (closest to 1); the one in bold only is the second best. We observe that I_R and I_V consistently outperform the other criterion functions across varied selections of k, under different types of evaluation. In Fig. 1 and Fig. 2, we

Table 3. Three types of average relative metric over 20 datasets

k	I_R	I_V	I_2	E_1	H_1	H_2
Average relative entropy						
5	**1.072**	**1.055**	1.075	1.103	1.115	1.079
10	**1.034**	**1.039**	1.056	1.104	1.059	1.056
15	**1.034**	**1.034**	1.045	1.108	1.050	1.063
20	**1.031**	**1.022**	1.035	1.113	1.039	1.053
Average	**1.043**	**1.037**	1.053	1.107	1.066	1.063
Average relative purity						
5	1.040	**1.029**	1.042	**1.040**	1.066	**1.040**
10	1.014	**1.008**	1.020	1.031	1.020	1.020
15	1.014	**1.009**	1.016	1.027	1.017	1.018
20	1.012	**1.008**	**1.012**	1.027	**1.012**	1.013
Average	1.020	**1.014**	1.022	1.031	1.029	1.023
Average relative NMI						
5	1.041	**1.035**	1.061	1.087	1.083	1.069
10	**1.013**	1.017	1.033	1.066	1.027	1.043
15	**1.011**	1.020	1.028	1.068	1.028	1.050
20	**1.010**	1.015	1.024	1.062	1.025	1.040
Average	**1.019**	1.021	1.037	1.071	1.041	1.051

show the relative NMI performance of the criterion functions, averaged over the numbers of clusters used, on each of the twenty datasets. In the figures, left-to-right in legend corresponds to left-to-right in the plot. It can be noticed that the first and second bars in each subgroup, which represent I_R and I_V respectively, are frequently the shortest and closest to 1. There are only 2 cases, *re0* and *tr12*, where both I_R and I_V are not in the top 2 NMIs. Otherwise, on the rest of the datasets, it appears from the figures' patterns that our two proposed functions consistently provide better clustering results than the others.

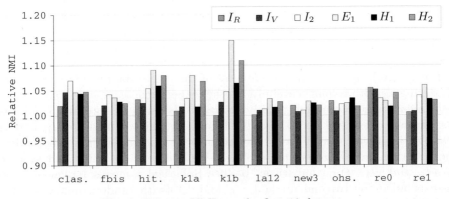

Fig. 1. Relative NMIs on the first 10 datasets

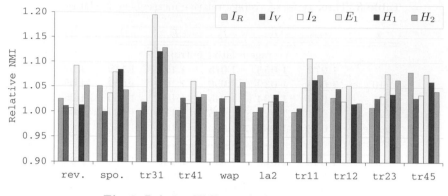

Fig. 2. Relative NMIs on the last 10 datasets

Table 4. Statistical significance of comparisons. "$\gg$" ("$\ll$") means criterion in row is significantly better (worse) than one in column; "$>$" ("$<$") means insignificance.

	I_R	I_V	I_2	E_1	H_1	H_2
			Entropy			
I_R	-	$<$	$>$	$\gg$	$>$	$>$
I_V	$>$	-	$>$	$\gg$	$\gg$	$>$
			Purity			
I_R	-	$\ll$	$>$	$\gg$	$\gg$	$>$
I_V	$\gg$	-	$\gg$	$\gg$	$\gg$	$\gg$
			NMI			
I_R	-	$>$	$\gg$	$\gg$	$\gg$	$\gg$
I_V	$<$	-	$\gg$	$\gg$	$\gg$	$\gg$

To have a statistical justification for our comparisons above, paired t-tests [11] with 5% significance level were conducted. The outcomes in Table 4 show in most cases, performance improvement by I_R and I_V over the others is statistically significant. Additionally, we also examined I_R's performance with different α values from 0 to 1, over all given datasets with $k = 10$. In Fig. 3, top-to-bottom in legend corresponds to left-to-right in the plot. As the figure shows, there is little variation regarding purity and NMI when $0 < \alpha < 1$. In general, relatively good selections of α, applied to all three evaluation metrics, are from 0.2 to 0.8.

Finally, to inspect the appropriateness of the new similarity measure and its clustering algorithms more carefully, another experiment was carried out. Cluster assignment output from Spherical k-means (i.e. I_2), which uses cosine similarity, was further optimized by I_R and I_V. If such refinement made by I_R and I_V leads to improved result, the proposed measure and methods are potentially more suitable for the clustering problem. We denote these refinement schemes as rI_R and rI_V. For comparison, besides Spherical k-means (sp$k$means), we also included the original methods I_R and I_V (with random initializations), CLUTO's graph method with cosine similarity (graphCS) and with extended

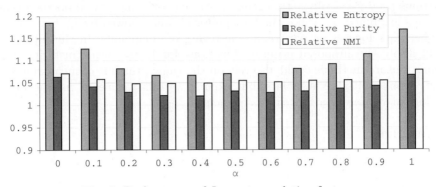

Fig. 3. Performance of I_R w.r.t. regulating factor α

Table 5. Clustering results in NMI with fixed $k=$ number of classes

Data	sp$k$means	rI_R	rI_V	I_R	I_V	graphCS	graphEJ	MMC
fbis	.585	**.604**	.596	**.606**	.595	.527	.524	.556
hitech	.303	**.324**	**.329**	.323	**.329**	.279	.292	.283
k1a	.592	**.612**	.598	**.612**	.594	.537	.571	.588
la12	.567	.579	**.591**	.574	**.584**	.496	.482	.558
re0	.405	**.409**	.408	.399	.402	.367	.342	**.414**
sports	.624	.659	**.684**	.669	**.701**	.578	.581	.591
tr31	.571	.630	**.650**	.613	**.658**	.577	.580	.548
la2	.556	.573	**.589**	.568	**.590**	.496	.478	.566

Jaccard similarity (graphEJ), and the Min-Max Cut algorithm (MMC) [5]. Table 5 presents the NMI clustering results of the clustering approaches on a group of typical datasets, where each k is set to be the actual number of classes. It shows that using I_R or I_V to refine output of sp$k$means does give rise to clustering quality. Such improvement is meaningful, since it demonstrates the suitability and effectiveness of our proposal. Besides, the results also show again the better performance of the original I_R and I_V compared with the other methods.

5   Conclusions and Future Work

In this paper, we propose a multi-viewpoint based similarity measuring method and two novel criterion functions for document clustering. The main principle is that similarity between two objects in the same cluster is assessed from many different viewpoints which are objects outside that cluster. The final estimate is based on a combination, e.g. the average, of all these relative assessments. We deem that this method offers more informative assessment than single origin point based similarity measures. From the proposed similarity measure, we introduce two clustering criterion functions I_R and I_V. They are applied for clustering large document collections. Comparisons with related methods, especially the ones from the well-known software package CLUTO, show that our criterion functions produce significantly better clustering solutions. Based on the twenty datasets examined, I_V yields the best performance, followed by I_R.

This work focuses on partitional clustering of documents. In the future, we could apply the proposed criterion functions for hierarchical clustering algorithms. Future methods could also rely on the same principle of measuring similarity from multiple viewpoints, but explore alternative means instead of dot product of vectors or average of assessments.

References

1. Banerjee, A., Dhillon, I., Ghosh, J., Sra, S.: Clustering on the unit hypersphere using von Mises-Fisher distributions. J. Mach. Learn. Res. 6, 1345–1382 (2005)
2. Banerjee, A., Merugu, S., Dhillon, I., Ghosh, J.: Clustering with Bregman divergences. J. Mach. Learn. Res. 6, 1705–1749 (2005)
3. Dhillon, I.S.: Co-clustering documents and words using bipartite spectral graph partitioning. In: KDD, pp. 269–274 (2001)
4. Dhillon, I., Modha, D.: Concept decompositions for large sparse text data using clustering. Mach. Learn. 42(1-2), 143–175 (2001)
5. Ding, C., He, X., Zha, H., Gu, M., Simon, H.: A min-max cut algorithm for graph partitioning and data clustering. In: IEEE ICDM, pp. 107–114 (2001)
6. Duda, R.O., Hart, P.E., Stork, D.G.: Pattern Classification, 2nd edn. John Wiley & Sons, New York (2001)
7. Friedman, J., Meulman, J.: Clustering objects on subsets of attributes. J. R. Stat. Soc. Series B Stat. Methodol. 66(4), 815–839 (2004)
8. Gu, Q., Zhou, J.: Co-clustering on manifolds. In: KDD, pp. 359–368 (2009)
9. Guyon, I., von Luxburg, U., Williamson, R.C.: Clustering: Science or Art? In: NIPS 2009 Workshop on Clustering Theory (December 2009),
http://clusteringtheory.org/
10. Karypis, G.: CLUTO a clustering toolkit. Tech. rep., Dept. of Computer Science, Uni. of Minnesota (2003), http://glaros.dtc.umn.edu/gkhome/views/cluto
11. Mitchell, T.M.: Machine Learning. McGraw-Hill, New York (1997)
12. Pekalska, E., Harol, A., Duin, R.P.W., Spillmann, B., Bunke, H.: Non-Euclidean or non-metric measures can be informative. In: Yeung, D.-Y., Kwok, J.T., Fred, A., Roli, F., de Ridder, D. (eds.) SSPR 2006 and SPR 2006. LNCS, vol. 4109, pp. 871–880. Springer, Heidelberg (2006)
13. Pelillo, M.: What is a cluster? Perspectives from game theory. In: NIPS 2009 Workshop on Clustering Theory (December 2009), http://clusteringtheory.org/
14. Wang, J., Xia, Y., Zheng, T.F., Wu, X.: Job information retrieval based on document similarity. In: Li, H., Liu, T., Ma, W.-Y., Sakai, T., Wong, K.-F., Zhou, G. (eds.) AIRS 2008. LNCS, vol. 4993, pp. 165–175. Springer, Heidelberg (2008)
15. Wu, X., Kumar, V., Ross Quinlan, J., Ghosh, J., Yang, Q., Motoda, H., McLachlan, G.J., Ng, A., Liu, B., Yu, P.S., Zhou, Z.H., Steinbach, M., Hand, D.J., Steinberg, D.: Top 10 algorithms in data mining. Knowl. Inf. Syst. 14(1), 1–37 (2007)
16. Xu, W., Liu, X., Gong, Y.: Document clustering based on non-negative matrix factorization. In: SIGIR, pp. 267–273 (2003)
17. Zhao, Y., Karypis, G.: Empirical and theoretical comparisons of selected criterion functions for document clustering. Mach. Learn. 55(3), 311–331 (2004)
18. Zhao, Y., Karypis, G.: Hierarchical clustering algorithms for document datasets. Data Min. Knowl. Discov. 10(2), 141–168 (2005)
19. Zhong, S., Ghosh, J.: A unified framework for model-based clustering. J. Mach. Learn. Res. 4(6), 1001–1037 (2004)

A Text Classifier with Domain Adaptation for Sentiment Classification

Wei Chen and Jingyu Zhou

School of Software
MOE-MS Key Laboratory for Intelligent Computing and Intelligent Systems
Shanghai Jiao Tong University
800 Dongchuan Road, Shanghai 200240, P.R. China
sagitchen@sjtu.edu.cn,
zhou-jy@cs.sjtu.edu.cn

Abstract. In sentiment classification, traditional classification algorithms cannot perform well when the number of labeled data is limited. EM-based Naïve Bayes algorithm is often employed to argument the labeled data with the unlabeled ones. However, such an approach assumes the distributions of these two sets of data are identical, which may not hold in practice and often results in inferior performance.

We propose a semi-supervised algorithm, called Ratio-Adjusted EM-based Naïve Bayes (RAEMNB), for sentiment classification, which combines knowledge from a source domain and limited training instances from a target domain. In RAEMNB, the initial Bayes model is trained from labeled instances from both domains. During each EM iteration, we add an extra R-step to adjust the ratio of predicted positive instances to negative ones, which is approximated with labeled instances of target domain. Experimental results show that our RAEMNB approach outperforms the traditional supervised, semi-supervised classifiers.

Keywords: domain adaptation, sentiment classification, Naïve Bayes, EM, semi-supervised.

1 Introduction

Sentiment classification, or polarity classification, is the binary classification task of labeling a document as expressing an overall positive or negative opinion. In recent years, sentiment classification has been widely adopted in many applications, such as analyzing results of political debate [14] and customer reviews [10,16].

Previous research [10,9] has applied various text-categorization algorithms for sentiment classification, which requires a large number of training instances to be effective. For domains that have little or no labeled instances, transfer learning algorithms [1,9,6,12,2] can be applied. Among them, EM-based Naïve Bayes (EMNB) [6] and its extensions have received a lot of attentions. However, the performance of EMNB could degrade during each EM iteration [15].

P.-J. Cheng et al. (Eds.): AIRS 2010, LNCS 6458, pp. 61–72, 2010.
© Springer-Verlag Berlin Heidelberg 2010

An important reason for this phenomenon is that the distributions of source domain and target domain are different, which has an adverse effect on the prediction accuracy for Naïve Bayes classifier.

We propose our Ratio-Adjusted EM-based Naïve Bayes (RAEMNB) algorithm for sentiment classification. RAEMNB is a semi-supervised classifier that utilizes knowledge from a source domain with rich labeled instances and limited training items from the target domain. The limited labeled data from the target domain serves two purposes. First, these data are used as training instances for initial Naïve Bayes model. The second more important usage of these data is for estimating the real distribution of the target domain. Specifically, RAEMNB first trains an initial Naïve Bayes model with labeled data from both source and target domains. Inside each EM iteration step, RAEMNB introduces an extra Ratio-adjustment step (R-step) between E and M step to keep the ratio of the predicted positive and negative instances during EM iteration consistent with the ratio of the target domain. To measure the distance of a predicted document and positive (or negative) labeled instances, we use the Kullback-Leibler divergence [5].

We crawled more than 130,000 online reviews of four categories from Amazon.com to construct 12 domain adaptation tasks for evaluation. In our experiments, we compare our proposed algorithm RAEMNB with traditional supervised, semi-supervised algorithms and ANB [13]. Experimental results show that RAEMNB outperforms all other algorithms with our Amazon online review dataset.

The rest of the paper is organized as follows. Section 2 presents our RAEMNB algorithm. Section 3 evaluates the performance of RAEMNB by comparing with previous supervised, semi-supervised and ANB. Section 4 discusses related work. Finally, Section 5 concludes the paper with future work.

2   Ratio-Adjusted EM-Based Naïve Bayes Algorithm

This section presents our algorithm for sentiment classification. Due to limited labeled instances from the target domain, our approach builds an initial Naïve Bayes classifier from labeled instances of both the source and the target domains. Then EM algorithm is employed to improve the initial classifier. During each EM iteration, we introduce an extra R-step to adjust the ratio for predicted instances during the expectation step, where the ratio is estimated with labeled data in the target domain.

Before describing our algorithm in detail, we define the notations used in this paper in Table 1.

2.1   Train the Initial Naïve Bayes Classifier

Our EM-based Naïve Bayes algorithm first trains the initial Naïve Bayes classifier from labeled instances in both source and target domains. Here we assume the number of labeled instances in the source domain is much larger than the one of the target domain, i.e.,

Table 1. Notations used in the paper

Notations	Description
D_{sl}	Source domain labeled data
D_{tl}	Target domain labeled data
D_{tl}^{+}	Positive instances in D_{tl}
D_{tl}^{-}	Negative instances in D_{tl}
D_{tu}	Target domain unlabeled training data
D_{tu}^{test}	Target domain unlabeled data for testing (different from D_{tu})
D_l	Labeled data from both source and target domain ($=D_{sl} \cup D_{tl}$)
D_t	Target domain data ($=D_{tl} \cup D_{tu} \cup D_{tu}^{test}$)
N_{pos}	numbers of predicted positive instances in D_{tu}
N_{neg}	numbers of predicted negative instances in D_{tu}

Algorithm 1. Ratio-Adjusted EM-based Naïve Bayes

Input: Training set D_{sl}, D_{tl}, and D_{tu}
Output: Naïve Bayes model $\hat{\theta} = \{P_D(C), P_D(W \mid C)\}$

Build initial Naïve Bayes model: $\theta = \{P_{D_l}(C), P_{D_l}(W \mid C)\}$
while the performance improves with estimated $\hat{\theta}$ **do**
    (E Step) Label the document d in the D_{tu} with the model $\hat{\theta}$
    (R Step) Calculate $\gamma = \frac{N_{pos}}{N_{neg}}$
  Let $\hat{\gamma} = \frac{|D_{tl}^{+}|}{|D_{tl}^{-}|}$
  if $\gamma > \hat{\gamma}$ **then**
    for each predicted positive instance d_i **do**
      $LM(d_i) = KL(D_{tl}^{+} \parallel d_i) - KL(D_{tl}^{-} \parallel d_i)$
    end for
    Sort the sequence $LM(d_i)$ $(1 \leq i \leq N_{pos})$ in decreasing order
    Change the label of first $\triangle N_{pos} = \frac{N_{pos} - \hat{\gamma} \cdot N_{neg}}{1 + \hat{\gamma}}$ instances from positive to negative
  else $\{\gamma < \hat{\gamma}\}$
    for each labeled negative instance d_i **do**
      $LM(d_i) = KL(D_{tl}^{-} \parallel d_i) - KL(D_{tl}^{+} \parallel d_i)$
    end for
    Sort the sequence $LM(d_i)$ $(1 \leq i \leq N_{neg})$ in decreasing order
    Change the label of first $\triangle N_{neg} = \frac{\hat{\gamma} \cdot N_{neg} - N_{pos}}{1 + \hat{\gamma}}$ instances from negative to positive
  end if
  (M Step) Re-train the Naïve Bayes classifier to acquire new $\hat{\theta}$
end while

$$\lambda = \frac{|D_{sl}|}{|D_{tl}|} > 1. \tag{1}$$

The initial Naïve Bayes model is calculated with the following formulas:

$$P(c_k) = \frac{\sum_{d_i \in D_l} P(c_k \mid d_i)}{|D_{sl}| + |D_{tl}|}, c_k \in C \tag{2}$$

and

$$P(w_i \mid c_k) = \frac{1 + n(w_i, c_k)}{|W| + n(c_k)}, c_k \in C, w_i \in W \tag{3}$$

where $P(c_k \mid d_i)$ is 1 if d_i is in category c_k, otherwise 0. Here W is the word set and C is the set of categories.

2.2 Ratio-Adjusted EM Steps

Traditional EMNB algorithm often assumes the distributions of labeled and unlabeled data are identical, which leads to classification errors. For instance, assume the actual ratio of the positive instances to negative ones is 1:1 and the Bayes model is trained from data with a distribution ratio of 2:1. Thus, more instances will be predicted as positive during each EM iteration, resulting in low accuracy [15].

Our approach addresses the above problem by introducing an extra R-step between the E and M steps. The extra R-step, i.e., Ratio-adjustment Step, adjusts the labels predicted in the E step so that the distribution ratio is consistent with its real value. We define

$$\hat{\gamma} = \frac{|D_{tl}^+|}{|D_{tl}^-|} \tag{4}$$

$$\gamma = \frac{N_{pos}}{N_{neg}} \tag{5}$$

The predicted distribution γ is adjusted to be close to the actual distribution of D_t. Since the actual distribution for D_t is unknown, our approach is to use the distribution ratio in D_{tl}, i.e., $\hat{\gamma}$, as an approximation. Assuming labeled instances of D_{tl} are randomly sampled from D_t, such an approximation is acceptable and our experiments in Section 3.6 confirm this. Specifically, if $\gamma > \hat{\gamma}$, which indicates that some predicted positive instances are actually negative, then we should adjust some predicted positive instances to be negative. Conversely, if $\gamma < \hat{\gamma}$, we should adjust some predicted negative instances to be positive.

We use Likelihood Measure (LM) to estimate if a document d is more close to positive instances or negative instances:

$$LM(d) = sgn(\gamma - \hat{\gamma}) \cdot (KL(D_{tl}^+ \mid\mid d) - KL(D_{tl}^- \mid\mid d)) \tag{6}$$

Recall that D_{tl}^+ and D_{tl}^- represent positive and negative instances of D_{tl}, respectively. It is natural to estimate the relevance between d and D_{tl}^+ (or D_{tl}^-) with a relevance metric. Kullback-Leibler (KL) divergence [5], is a measure of distance between two probability functions and is used as relevance metric in our algorithm. $KL(\cdot)$ is defined as follows,

$$KL(D_{tl}^+ \| d) = \sum_{w \in d} P(w \mid D_{tl}^+) \cdot \log \frac{P(w \mid D_{tl}^+)}{P(w \mid d)} \qquad (7)$$

$$KL(D_{tl}^- \| d) = \sum_{w \in d} P(w \mid D_{tl}^-) \cdot \log \frac{P(w \mid D_{tl}^-)}{P(w \mid d)} \qquad (8)$$

The complete algorithm is described in Algorithm 1. To determine whether the current model improves, we use the same metric as Nigam et al. [6]:

$$l(\hat{\theta} \mid \hat{D}_l) = \sum_{j=1}^{|C|} \log P(c_j \mid \hat{\theta}) \prod_{k=1}^{|W|} P(w_k \mid c_j; \hat{\theta}) + \sum_{d_i \in \hat{D}_l} \sum_{j=1}^{|C|} z_{ij} \log P(c_j \mid \hat{\theta}) P(d_i \mid c_j; \hat{\theta}) \qquad (9)$$

where $\hat{D}_l$ is labeled positive and predicted positive instances in target domain, $z_{ij} = 1$ if the class label of d_i is c_j, otherwise $z_{ij} = 0$.

3   Evaluation

3.1   Dataset

We crawled more than 130,000 product reviews from Amazon.com within four categories: Books, Grocery, Movie and Sports Instruments. These reviews are scored within the range of 1 to 5 by users, with higher scores representing more positive feedbacks. In the experiments, we assume reviews with scores greater than three are positive and ones whose scores are less than three are negative. Table 2 illustrates the distributions of our crawled data. For domain adaptation tasks, each of the four category can be the source domain and the other three are target domains. Thus, we have a total of 12 domain adaptation problems.

The training and testing sets of each category are generated as follows. We randomly sample 10% instances as labeled data (D_{tl}) and randomly selected another 20% as testing data (D_{tu}^{test}). The rest 70% data is used as unlabeled training data (D_{tu}). Labeled data from source domain is also randomly selected, subjecting to the following limit, i.e., $|D_{sl}| = \min\{\lambda \cdot |D_{tl}|, |D_{sl}|\}$.

We preprocessed the crawled data before applying learning algorithms. Specifically, words are stemmed with the Porter Stemmer [11] and stop words are filtered from texts. Then feature selection method is applied — we employ Document Frequency (DF). As suggested by [18], DF is a simple feature selection method and has a comparable performance with Information Gain and CHI. In the experiments, we keep terms whose DF value is greater than three. In the end, we have 7,248 unigram terms.

Table 2. Positive instance and negative instance distribution of four product types

Product Type	Positive #	Negative #	Ratio of positive to negative
Books	56,377	10,396	5.42
Grocery	13,659	1,818	7.51
Movie	25,463	3,006	8.47
Sports	18,185	2,186	8.32

3.2   Evaluation Metric

The evaluation metric for experiments is accuracy, which is defined as:

$$Accuracy = \frac{TruePositives + TrueNegatives}{TotalNumberOfInstances}. \tag{10}$$

3.3   Overall Performance

This experiment compares the performance of our RAEMNB algorithm with other classifiers. For supervised baseline, we selected Naïve Bayes and SVM. Both classifiers only use D_{tl} as training data. For the SVM algorithm, we employ LibSVM [3] and all parameters are set to the default values. For semi-supervised baseline, EMNB [6] and ANB [13] are chosen for comparison. EMNB use both labeled data D_{tl} and unlabeled data D_{tu} for training. For ANB, the labeled training data is from D_{sl} and D_{tl} while the unlabeled data is from D_{tu}; parameter N_{fce} and δ are 500 and 0.2, respectively, as suggested in [13]. For our RAEMNB, λ is set to 10. All these classifiers are tested with the data from D_{tu}^{test}.

Table 3 shows the results of supervised and semi-supervised baseline algorithms. Table 4 shows the ANB and RAEMNB algorithms results. Naïve Bayes and SVM perform poorly even though both their training and testing data are from the same domain. This is mainly because the number of training data is very limited. The accuracy for Books category of Naïve Bayes is much higher

Table 3. Accuracies of Naïve Bayes, SVM, and EMNB over four product types with limited training instances

Product Type	Naïve Bayes	SVM	EMNB
Books	72.90%	69.55%	67.41%
Grocery	49.35%	68.15%	67.88%
Movie	50.28%	68.53%	67.37%
Sports	50.18%	68.76%	67.58%
Average	55.68%	68.75%	67.56%

Table 4. Accuracies of ANB & RAEMNB over 12 domain adaptation problems

Domain Adaptation Problems	ANB	RAEMNB
Books → Grocery	45.51%	74.13%
Books → Movie	79.70%	84.11%
Books → Sports	36.44%	81.96%
Grocery → Books	76.34%	80.33%
Grocery → Movie	58.43%	82.07%
Grocery → Sports	64.10%	82.31%
Movie → Books	78.10%	79.74%
Movie → Grocery	30.23%	76.23%
Movie → Sports	25.91%	83.36%
Sports → Books	77.70%	79.04%
Sports → Grocery	42.93%	75.55%
Sports → Movie	71.00%	84.49%
Average	57.20%	80.28%

compared with other categories. The reason is that the average length of texts of Books category is much longer than others. As the training data contains more vocabularies than others, Naïve Bayes classifier is trained better for the Books category. Our RAEMNB has an average accuracy of 80.28%, outperforming the semi-supervised EMNB and ANB by about 13% and 23%, respectively. The reason for the inferior performance of the semi-supervised algorithm, EMNB, is that the labeled data is very limited in our experiments so it cannot be fully trained. For ANB, it cannot achieve a high accuracy because the distributions of source domain and target domain are different. While in our RAEMNB, this problem is addressed by the ratio-adjustment step during EM iterations.

3.4   Study on the Effectiveness of R-Step and Sensitivity of λ

This experiment studies the effectiveness of ratio-adjustment step of our RAEMNB algorithm. We compare the performance of RAEMNB initial model, initial model with standard EM iterations, and RAEMNB whose R-step is with LM and Naïve Bayes (NB) ranking (i.e., the probability values predicted by NB). For each scheme, we vary the number of instances in D_{sl} to change λ and the average accuracies of all 12 domain adaptation tasks are illustrated in Figure 1.

We can observe that the RAEMNB scheme performs significantly better than the approach using standard EM iterations, which is in turn better than the RAEMNB initial model. The RAEMNB perform the best because they can adjust the distribution of predicted instances, thus avoiding the drawback of traditional EM algorithm. Additionally, the performance of RAEMNB (with

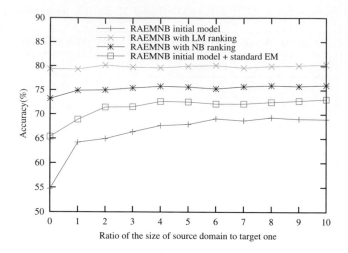

Fig. 1. The accuracies of RAEMNB with LM ranking, RAEMNB with Naïve Bayes ranking, RAEMNB initial model, and initial model with standard EM when λ is changing

either LM or NB ranking) remains stable with varying number of labeled data in the target domain, even when λ is 10. This indicates that our RAEMNB are effective with relatively lower number of labeled instances in the target domain.

This experiment shows that LM ranking outperforms NB ranking with different λ values. The lower performance of NB ranking can be mainly attributed to the imperfect quality of the current Naïve Bayes classifier. In comparison, LM ranking uses relevance between a document and labeled datasets, thus to some extent calibrates the wrong prediction of Naïve Bayes. As a result, our RAEMNB algorithm chooses LM as the ranking method in the R-step.

3.5   Study on the Convergence of RAEMNB

This experiment studies the convergence of our RAEMNB algorithm. Figure 2 illustrates the accuracies of all domain adaptation problems for different iterations. It can observed that our RAEMNB converges in less than five iterations, which indicates the extra R-step does not break the convergence of the traditional EMNB. In particular, we can observe that the first iteration usually has the most significant performance improvement. The reason is that the initial model was established with little target domain training data, thus is not very accurate. On the other hand, this shows that the extra R-step is effective for performance improvement.

3.6   Study on Sensitivity of $\hat{\gamma}$

In RAEMNB, parameter $\hat{\gamma}$ from D_{tl} is estimated as the distribution for the target domain (D_t). Because D_{tl} is only a fraction of target domain data, such

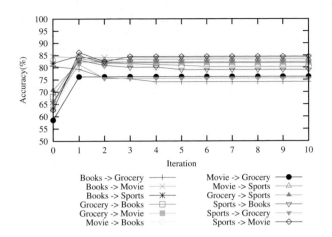

Fig. 2. The accuracies of twelve domain adaptation problems for different iterations ($\lambda = 10$)

an approximation may have some impact on the performance of RAEMNB. Thus, this experiment is designed to study the sensitivity of $\hat{\gamma}$.

To obtain a reasonable range for parameter $\hat{\gamma}$, we perform the following experiment: for a given sampling ratio of target domain data, we random sample D_t 100 times and calculated the $\hat{\gamma}$ value. The results are illustrated in Figure 3. From the figure, we can observe that when sampling ratio is large, the range of $\hat{\gamma}$ becomes smaller. The upper and lower bound for $\hat{\gamma}$ always happens when sampling ratio is smallest (0.02), because samples are more biased.

Then, we use the upper and lower bounds of $\hat{\gamma}$ obtained above, along with the actual distribution value, and study accuracies of RAEMNB for 12 domain adaptation tasks. Table 5 illustrates the average accuracy values with different λ values. For both lower bound and upper bound, the performance is comparable to the one using actual distribution.

In summary, this experiment demonstrates that our RAEMNB is insensitive to parameter $\hat{\gamma}$. In other words, RAEMNB effectively only needs to sample a small amount data from the target domain.

4   Related Work

Previous research [4,10,16] has applied traditional supervised or semi-supervised algorithms for sentiment classification. The domain adaptation problem of has often been studied. ANB [13] is an extension of EMNB [6] for sentiment classification, where co-occurring features from both source and target domains are used to build an initial Naïve Bayes model. Domain adaptation is achieved by increasing of the knowledge from target domain during EM iterations. ANB assumes the distributions of two domains are identical, thus limiting its performance. Structural Correspondence Learning (SCL) [2] employs pivot features to

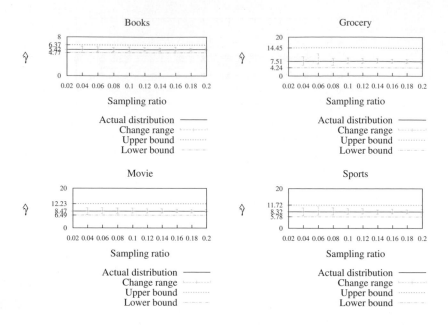

Fig. 3. The range of $\hat{\gamma}$ with respect to different sampling ratios. Each range is obtained by sampling D_{tl} 100 times.

Table 5. The impact of the deviation of $\hat{\gamma}$ to the average accuracy over 12 domain adaptation problems with different λ

λ	Upper bound	Lower bound	Actual distribution
0	79.27%	79.18%	80.86%
1	80.37%	80.01%	79.39%
2	79.95%	79.80%	80.31%
3	79.39%	79.75%	80.96%
4	79.99%	80.09%	80.15%
5	79.85%	80.18%	80.30%
6	80.43%	79.80%	80.42%
7	80.44%	79.39%	80.05%
8	80.92%	79.08%	80.00%
9	79.99%	80.17%	80.45%
10	80.08%	80.20%	80.28%

find the correspondences of features from source and target domains and trains a domain adaptation classifier with pivot and non-pivot features. W-SCL [12] improves SCL by assigning smaller weights to high-frequency domain-specific features and larger weights to the instances whose label is the same as the one of involved pivot features. Spectral Feature Alignment (SFA) [7] employs the domain-independent features as a bridge to align domain-specific features from different domains into the unified cluster. In this way, SFA minimizes the gap between different domains. These approaches perform domain adaptation with consideration of domain-specific and domain-independent features, while our RAEMNB employs a R-step to adjust distributions. Transfer learning [8,17] is another way to solve the domain adaptation problem, which often studies how to classify texts into multiple topics. Our work focuses on sentiment classification, which is often considered to be more challenging [9].

5 Conclusion

In this paper, we have proposed a new semi-supervised classifier, RAEMNB, for sentiment classification with domain adaptation. RAEMNB enhances traditional EMNB [6] algorithm with an additional ratio-adjustment step during each EM iteration so that the distribution of predicted instances does not deviate from real distribution much. We have compared RAEMNB with traditional supervised, semi-supervised classifiers. Our experiments on a dataset of 12 domain adaptation tasks demonstrate that our RAEMNB algorithm performs better than other algorithms. Particularly, even though our estimation of real distribution of target domain data is from a small randomly sampled fraction, experiments show that our algorithm is robust with estimation errors.

Currently, RAEMNB converges over 12 domain adaptation tasks, which indicates the convergence from an empirical perspective. In future work, we plan to study the convergence of RAEMNB from a theoretical perspective. Another direction is to apply ration adjustment for other classifiers and traditional learning applications.

Acknowledgment

We thank anonymous reviews for their comments. This work is supported in part by the National Natural Science Foundation of China (Grant No. 60811130528 and 60725208). Jingyu Zhou is the corresponding author.

References

1. Aue, A., Gamon, M.: Customizing Sentiment Classifiers to New Domains: a Case Study. In: Proceedings of the International Conference on Recent Advances in Natural Language Processing, pp. 207–218 (2005)

2. Blitzer, J., Dredze, M., Pereira, F.: Biographies, Bollywood, Boomboxes and Blenders: Domain Adaptation for Sentiment Classification. In: ACL. pp. 187–205 (2007)
3. Chang, C.C., Lin, J.: LIBSVM: A Library for Support Vector Machines. Software (2001), http://www.csie.ntu.edu.tw/~cjlin/libsvm
4. Kennedy, A., Inkpen, D.: Sentiment Classification of Movie Reviews Using Contextual Valence Shifters. In: Computational Intelligence, vol. 22, pp. 110–125 (2006)
5. Kullback, S., Leibler, R.A.: On Information and Sufficiency. In: The Annals of Mathematical Statistics, vol. 22, pp. 79–86 (1951)
6. Nigam, K., Mccallum, A.K., Thrun, S., Mitchell, T.: Text Classification from Labeled and Unlabeled Documents Using EM. In: Machine Learning, vol. 39, pp. 103–134 (2000)
7. Pan, S.J., Ni, X., Sun, J.T., Yang, Q., Chen, Z.: Cross-domain Sentiment Classification via Spectral Feature Alignment. In: Proceedings of the 19th International Conference on World Wide Web, WWW 2010, pp. 751–760 (2010)
8. Pan, S.J., Yang, Q.: A Survey on Transfer Learning. Technical report. (2009), http://doi.ieeecomputersociety.org/10.1109/TKDE.2009.191 (in press,2009)
9. Pang, B., Lee, L.: Opinion Mining and Sentiment Analysis. In: Foundations and Trends in Information Retrieval, vol. 2, pp. 1–135 (2008)
10. Pang, B., Lee, L., Vaithyanathan, S.: Thumbs up?: Sentiment Classification Using Machine Learning Techniques. In: EMNLP 2002: Proceedings of the ACL-02 Conference on Empirical Methods in Natural Language Processing, pp. 79–86 (2002)
11. Porter, M.F.: An Algorithm for Suffix Stripping. In: Program, vol. 14, pp. 130–137 (1980)
12. Tan, S., Cheng, X.: Improving SCL Model for Sentiment-Transfer Learning. In: Proceedings of Annual Conference of the North American Chapter of the Association for Computational Linguistics, pp. 181–184 (2009)
13. Tan, S., Cheng, X., Wang, Y., Xu, H.: Adapting Naïve Bayes to Domain Adaptation for Sentiment Analysis. In: Boughanem, M., Berrut, C., Mothe, J., Soule-Dupuy, C. (eds.) ECIR 2009. LNCS, vol. 5478, pp. 337–349. Springer, Heidelberg (2009)
14. Thomas, M., Pang, B., Lee, L.: Get out the Vote: Determining Support or Opposition from Congressional Floor-debate Transcripts. In: EMNLP 2006: Proceedings of the ACL 2006 Conference on Empirical Methods in Natural Language Processing,Association for Computational Linguistics. pp. 327–335 (2006)
15. Tsuruoka, Y., Tsujii, J.: Training a Naïve Bayes Classifier via the EM Algorithm with a Class Distribution Constraint. In: Proceedings of the Seventh Conference on Natural language Learning at HLT-NAACL, pp. 127–134 Association for Computational Linguistics. Morristown (2003)
16. Turney, P.D.: Thumbs up or Thumbs down?: Semantic Orientation Applied to Unsupervised Classification of Reviews. In: ACL 2002: Proceedings of the 40th Annual Meeting on Association for Computational Linguistics, Morristown, pp. 417–424 (2002)
17. Xue, G.R., Dai, W., Yang, Q., Yu, Y.: Topic-bridged PLSA for Cross-domain Text Classification. In: Proceedings of the ACM SIGIR Conference on Research and Development in Information Retrieval (SIGIR), pp. 627–634 (2008)
18. Yang, Y., Pedersen, J.O.: A Comparative Study on Feature Selection in Text Categorization. In: Proceedings of ICML 1997, 14th International Conference on Machine Learning, Nashville, US, pp. 412–420. Morgan Kaufmann Publishers, San Francisco (1997)

Effective Time Ratio: A Measure for Web Search Engines with Document Snippets

Jing He[1,2], Baihan Shu[1], Xiaoming Li[1,2], and Hongfei Yan[1]

[1] Department of Computer Science and Technology, Peking University
[2] State Key Laboratory of Software Development Environment, Beihang University
{hj,sbh,lxm,yhf}@net.pku.edu.cn

Abstract. The dominant method for evaluating search engines is the Cranfield paradigm, but the existing metrics do not consider some modern search engines features, such as document snippets. In this paper, we propose a new metric *effective time ratio* for search engine evaluation. *Effective time ratio* measures the ratio between effective time a user spent on getting relevant information and the total search time. For retrieval system without presenting document snippet, its value is identical to *precision*. For search engine with snippet, some theoretical analysis proves that its value can reflect both retrieval system performance and snippet quality. We further deploy a real user study, showing that *effective time ratio* can reflect users' satisfaction better than the existing metrics based on document relevance and/or snippet relevance.

Keywords: Information retrieval, evaluation, metric, snippet.

1 Introduction

Evaluation of information retrieval (IR) systems is critical for improving search techniques. So far, the dominant method for IR evaluation has been the Cranfield evaluation method. It involves creating a test collection with a document collection, a set of topics, and relevance judgments, and then measuring the performance of a retrieval system or comparing the performances of different systems on the test collection. This evaluation methodology has been very useful especially because of the availability of many test collections created in TREC (http://trec.nist.gov).

Although being quite successful and popular, the Cranfield experimental model, has received extensive questioning in the literature, e.g. [1,2]. One major criticism is that the relevance judgment may not represent real users' information need thus the evaluation results may not reflect the real utility of the system. There are some research to investigate the correlation between the Cranfield paradigm experiment and user study. Some early research [3,4] found that the correlation is weak or even negative. However, some recent evaluation work [5,6,7], which employed larger scale of topics and users, reported the positive correlation between the Cranfield evaluation and real user study.

P.-J. Cheng et al. (Eds.): AIRS 2010, LNCS 6458, pp. 73–84, 2010.

In the use of a real search engine, the effectiveness and the satisfaction of a user is also affected by some factors other than retrieval system performance. The document snippet is a very important feature for modern search engine. Good snippets can guide the users to find out the relative documents from the retrieved results, or even contain relative information itself. On the contrary, users may miss relevant documents or waste time clicking and examining irrelevant documents due to bad snippets. However, the traditional metrics used in Cranfield paradigm have not consider the quality of the document snippets.

Turpin et al. [8] investigated the problem of including document snippet quality in search engine evaluation. It extended the existing IR metrics by including snippet quality factor to measure the retrieval performance. Compared to the original metric, the new one changes the absolute retrieval score, topic difficulty and relative system performance. It indicates that it makes change by including snippet quality in search engine evaluation. This work also opens a direction of adding features other than document relevance in search engine evaluation. However, it has not validated that the proposed metric that includes snippet quality can really reflect the user satisfaction. Furthermore, the snippet relevance in the work was simulated from the document relevance, so it may not reflect the real situation.

In this paper, we interpret traditional IR metric *precision* as *effective time ratio* of the real user, i.e, the ratio between the time used in reading relevant information and the total search time. By this interpretation, we can easily extend the *effective time ratio* in the scenario when the search engines provide document snippets. The theoretical analysis proves that this metric can reflect both retrieval performance and snippet quality. We further validate this metric by user study, finding that it has larger correlation with user satisfaction than the existing metrics that consider document relevance only, and the metric proposed by Turpin et al. [8]. Further scenario analysis shows that it can work better on both open-information and close-information questions.

2   Related Work

There are a large body of researches on information retrieval evaluation. Cranfield paradigm is the most commonly used methodology in IR evaluation. It employs a test collection to evaluate retrieval system by some standard performance measures such as MAP and nDCG.

Since there is many known differences between Cranfield paradigm evaluation and evaluation through user studies, it is thus important to understand how they correlate with each other. Some reported negative correlation. For example, [3] asked 24 users for 6 instance-recall tasks, and [4] involved 24 users for 6 question-answer tasks, but there is no significant difference in user task effectiveness found between systems with significantly different metric scores. The limitation of the two studies is that the small number of topics may explain why no correlation was detected.

Some recent and larger scale evaluation work reported positive correlation between batch system evaluation and user evaluation. [5] involved 33 users to search for 45 topics and showed that differences in *bpref* could result in statistically significant differences in user effectiveness of retrieving faceted document passages. Using 7 participants working on 200 Google queries, [6] demonstrated that satisfaction of assessors correlates fairly strongly with relevance among top three documents measured using a version of *DCG*. In [7], 56 users performed a recall-based task on 56 queries on top of "good" and "bad" systems. The authors showed that user effectiveness (time consumed, relevant documents collected, queries input, satisfaction, etc) and system effectiveness ($P@n$, MAP) are correlated.

Turpin et al. [8] suggested that one possible reason for the limited correlation between real users' satisfaction and Cranfield paradigm metric score is that it has not considered snippet quality in calculating the metric score. They proposed one new metric combining document and snippet relevance, finding that it affects the system performance ranking. In this paper, we propose another metric considering snippet relevance, and find that the correlation between user satisfaction and our proposed metric is higher.

3   Effective Time Ratio

Intuitively, for a search engine with snippets, the users' satisfaction is affected by two factors: 1) whether the relevant documents are highly ranked; and 2) whether the snippet can indicate the corresponding document relevance. In this paper, We combine these two factors in one metric *effective time ratio*.

3.1   Precision as Effective Time Ratio

Precision and recall are two most important basic metrics in information retrieval. In the context of Web search engine, it is very difficult to estimate real recall value because it nearly impossible to find out all relevant documents. Some researchers even states that recall is not well founded as a measure of satisfaction [9]. Therefore, precision and its extensions are very important in Web search engine evaluation.

In order to derive the metric that can be used to evaluate search engines with document snippet, we first interpret precision as *effective time ratio* (denoted as *ETR* for short) when using retrieval system without snippet presentation.

Definition 1. *(Effective Time Ratio): Effective Time Ratio is the ratio between effective time used in get relevant information and the total search time.*

A traditional IR system presents to the user a ranked list of documents for a query. We assume the user examines every (top) retrieved document to seek relevant information . We further assume the time spent on examining each document is same (denoted as T). Thus a user needs $T \cdot N$ time to examine top N documents, but the *effective time*, which is used to examine relevant documents, is $T \cdot \sum_{i=1}^{N} R(d_i)$, where d_i is the i-th ranked document in the result list, and R is a binary function, indicating whether a document is relevant or not (1 for relevant and 0 for irrelevant). Thus *effective time ratio* at a cutoff N can be formulated as Equation 1. With very simple derivation, we can find that $ETR@N$ is identical to $P@N$, so we can interpret *precision* as *effective time ratio* when using the retrieval system without providing document snippets.

$$ETR@N = \frac{T \cdot \sum_{i=1}^{N} R(d_i)}{T \cdot N} \tag{1}$$

3.2 Effective Time Ratio for Search Engines with Snippets

The modern search engines usually present the users a list of snippets. The underlying idea is that: 1) the user can judge whether a document is relevant by just examining its snippet; and 2) it costs users less time to examine a snippet than to examine the corresponding document. For a search engine with snippet, the assumption used in section 3.1 that users examine each top retrieved document is not valid. Instead, the users would examine the document snippets before clicking and examining the real documents, and some documents whose snippets seem to be irrelevant would not be examined. The search process can be presented as Figure 1. In the process, a user examines i-th snippet, which is generated from i-th ranked document (i is initially assigned 1). If he finds the snippet is relevant, he would click and examine the corresponding document; otherwise, he would examine the next snippet. After examining a document, the users may quit search or continue to examine $i+1$-th snippet. This process uses examination hypothesis and cascade hypothesis, which are commonly used in modeling user's search behaviors [10,11].

According to the definition of *effective time ratio*, it is easy to include snippet quality. The effective time used in getting really relevant information include the time spent on reading the snippet and the original text of the relevant documents. The total time is composed by two parts: 1) the time spent on reading all snippets of the (top) retrieved documents, and 2) the time spent on reading the text of the clicked documents, whose snippets seem to be relevant. We further assume that the time spent on reading a snippet and a document are two

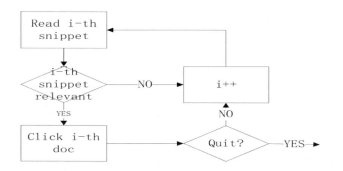

Fig. 1. Using Search Engine with Snippets

static values(T_1 and T_2). In the top N documents, only the relevant documents with relevant snippets can provide relevant information, so the *effective time* is $\sum_{i=1}^{N} R(s_i) \cdot R(d_i) \cdot (T_1 + T_2)$(where d_i the i-th ranked document, s_i is its snippet, and R is a function indicating whether a document or a snippet is relevant or not). Total time spent on reading snippets is $N \cdot T_1$. The user would read all documents with relevant snippet, so the total time spent on reading documents is $\sum_{i=1}^{N} T_2 \cdot R(s_i)$. Thus the *effective time ratio* can be formulated as Equation 2. Though it seems that there are two parameters (T_1 and T_2, we find that their rate affects the *effective time ratio* value. In Equation 3, we rewrite ETR by the reading time rate between reading document time and reading snippet time ($c = T_2/T_1$).

$$ETR@N = \frac{(T_1 + T_2) \cdot \sum_{i=1}^{N} R(d_i)R(s_i)}{T_1 \cdot N + T_2 \cdot \sum_{i=1}^{N} R(s_i)} \tag{2}$$

$$= \frac{(1 + c) \sum_{i}^{N} R(d_i)R(s_i)}{N + c \cdot \sum_{i=1}^{N} R(s_i)} \tag{3}$$

3.3 Theoretical Analysis

To further understand the effect of including snippet quality, we would compare versions of *effective time ratio* implementation with and without snippet quality factor.

Intuitively, high-quality document snippets used in the search engine can guide the users to find relevant information more efficiently, so the *effective time ratio* is supposed to be higher for the search engine with high-quality snippets. The quality of the snippet (or so-called query dependent summarization) is discussed in some early research [12,13]. The objective of these work is to find out query related information from a document. However, in the context of search engine snippet, the objective is to indicate the relevance of the original document accurately. Thus the metrics used in this field can not be directly used here.

A snippet is good if it can indicates the document relevance accurately. Otherwise it may mislead users to miss a relevant document or waste time reading an irrelevant document. Here we define a relevant snippet iff it indicates the corresponding document is relevant. Therefore the quality of snippet can be qualified by possibility two types of errors.

Definition 2. *(First Type Error) Error of generating a relevant snippet for an irrelevant document*

Definition 3. *(Second Type Error) Error of generating an irrelevant snippet for a relevant document*

The first type of errors would lead the users to waste time clicking and examining irrelevant documents, and the users would miss relevant documents because of second type of errors. Given a snippet generation algorithm, we define

$p_1 = Pr(R(s) = 1|R(d) = 0)$ as the possibility of making *first type error* and $p_2 = Pr(R(s) = 0|R(d) = 1)$ as the possibility of making *second type error*. The expected value of effective time and total time of a search engine for a query can be estimated by the *precision* of its underlying retrieval system and possibility of these two types of errors of the snippet generation algorithm. The ratio between expected expected effective time and expected total time (denoted as $EETR$) can be presented as Equation 4 (The derivation is presented in appendix). Because $P@N$ is also an implementation of *effective time ratio* without considering snippet factor, this equation describes the relations of *effective time ratio* with and without including snippet quality.

$$EETR@N = \frac{(1+c)(1-p_2)}{c(1-p_1-p_2) + \dfrac{1+cp_1}{P@N}} \tag{4}$$

We can derive three properties of *expected effective time ratio* from this equation. Proposition 1 shows that a search engine with an error-free snippet generation algorithm has higher *expected effective time ratio* than a retrieval system without snippet. It means that in modern search engine, the high-quality snippet can improve the ratio of effective time that is used in achieving really relevant information.

Proposition 1. $p_1 = 0, p_2 = 0 \Rightarrow EETR@N > P@N$

Proposition 2 validates that the with two different retrieval system and one snippet generation algorithm, the $EETR$ values can reflect the underlying retrieval performance. Similarly, proposition 3 validates that with one retrieval system and two different snippet generation algorithm, the $EETR$ values can reflect the performance of the snippet generation algorithms. These two propositions prove that *effective time ratio* can reflect both retrieval performance and snippet quality.

Proposition 2. $p_1(A) = p_1(B), p_2(A) = p_2(B), P@N(A) > P@N(B) \Rightarrow EETR@N(A) > EETR@N(B)$

Proposition 3. $p_1(A) > p_1(B), p_2(A) > p_2(B), P@N(A) = P@N(B) \Rightarrow EETR@N(A) < EETR@N(B)$

4   Experiment

To validate the *effective time ratio* metric, a user study is designed to resemble the common search engine usage. Some users are employed to collect relevant information for some questions, and they are asked to answer the questions and report the satisfaction in using the search engine. The satisfaction values are compared with scores of various IR metrics including the proposed *effective time ratio*.

4.1   Data Collecting

The user study is designed to resemble the common search engine usage. The study process is quite similar to the user study research deployed by Huffman and Hochster [6]. We recruited 10 college students, and most of them are familiar with using search engines.

The users were asked to answer 50 questions with the help of a search engine. Each question is categorized as either open-information (with many answers) or close-information (with only one answer). Its category is determined by three assessors' voting. Each question is also assigned a difficulty score from 1 to 5. The final difficulty is assigned by three assessor and these three values are averaged. Each question also has a topic category (sports, computers, etc.). The selected 50 questions contain 25 open-information questions and 25 close-information questions. The questions are also uniformly distributed in difficulty and topic. For each question, we designed a query, submitted it to a commercial search engine and collected the top 100 results (including both snippets and documents) from the engine. Some question examples are given in Table 1. In the table, the five columns are the question (information need), its submitted query, topic category, open/close-information type and difficulty.

Table 1. Question Examples

Question	Query	Topic	Type	Diff
The website you can login MSN and chat online	MSN Web	Computer	close	2
When was the movie Avatar online	Avatar online	Entertainment	close	1
How can I reduce the blood pressure without aking medicine	reduce blood pressure	Health	open	2
What are the reviews to Frances Burnett's novel "Secret Garden"	secret garden review	Culture	open	4

In the user study, for each question, a user was presented with the question following top 10 ranked snippets in the result page, and he can jump to other results by clicking "next page", "previous page" or page number link at the bottom of the page. For each question, a user can view totally 100 results from an individual search engine. The user was asked to answer this question with the help of the listed results and he can click the link for browsing the original document. The snippets and documents were crawled and stored on the server, so that all the users are presented with same results. A user can end the search once he thought he was able to answer the current question or he found that the presented results did not contain an appropriate answer. Once ending a question, the user was asked to answer the question and to report his satisfaction, whose values ranging from 1 to 4 (the higher the better).

The manual relevance judgments were also collected. Three assessors were employed to judge relevance of both documents and snippets for the queries. The relevance judgment is binary and the final value is determined by voting.

5   Results and Discussion

With the collected dataset, we can compare the user reported satisfaction with various metric scores.

5.1   Metrics

In this paper, we focus on three groups of metrics. Their scores are used to compare with the user satisfaction score.

The first group of metrics use the document relevance information only, including precision, DCG, RR and cumulated precision. The reason for using cumulated precision instead of average precision is that the total number of relevant documents is unknown.

The second group of metrics have the exactly same forms as those in the first group, but they use both document relevance and snippet relevance. In this group, one document is considered to be relevant if and only if the original document and its snippet are both relevant (see Equation 5). This group of metrics were proposed by Turpin et al. [8].

$$R'(d_i) = \begin{cases} 0, R(d_i) = 0 \text{ or } R(s_i) = 0 \\ 1, R(d_i) > 0 \text{ and } R(s_i) > 0 \end{cases} \tag{5}$$

The third groups of metrics are *effective time ratio* and its extensions. As stated in Section 3.1, precision can be interpreted as *effective time ratio*. As extending precision to cumulated precision, we can also define the *cumulated effective time ratio* as the sum of *effective time ratio* at the cutoffs where both the document and the snippet are relevant. The *cumulated effective time ratio* (denoted as $CETR$) is defined in Equation 6.

$$CETR@N = \sum_{i=1}^{N} R(d_i) \cdot R(s_i) \cdot ETR@i \tag{6}$$

There are two parameters in the metric *effective time ratio*: cutoff N and document/snippet reading time rate $c = T_2/T_1$. For N, we can tune it in the experiment. For c, we can estimate it from the real user query log. We still assume the user search follows the process described in Figure 1. For a query submission and the corresponding clicks, we can get c by six values: the query submission timestamp t_q, the timestamp and the rank of the first click t_{c1} and r_{c1}, the timestamp of the last click t_{c2}, the maximal rank of the clicks r_{c2}, and the total number of clicked documents C.

Before a user's first click c_1, he has examined all snippets above the rank r_{c1}, so the time cost before first click $t_{c1} - t_q$ can be presented as Equation 7.

$$t_{c1} - t_q = r_{c1} \cdot T_1 \tag{7}$$

Similarly, the total time cost before last click is composed by two parts: time spent on reading snippets before maximal rank of the clicks and time spent on reading all clicked documents (not include the last clicked document). So we have:

$$t_{c2} - t_q = r_{c2} \cdot T_1 + (C - 1) \cdot T_2 \qquad (8)$$

From Equation 7 and 8, we can get value of T_1 and T_2 and can further derive c value. To estimate the value, we use two query logs: the log of our user study and a one-month log from a commercial search engine. The estimated c value is 8.25 for the former log and is 10.36 for the later one. We also find that most c values are near 10, so we use 10 as c value in *effective time ratio* metric.

5.2   Basic Results

A good evaluation metric is supposed to reflect the users' satisfaction in using a search engine to find out relevant information for a need. In this paper, we follow Huffman and Hochster's work [6] to use correlation between metric score and user reported satisfaction to validate the metrics. The users' satisfaction of a search engine on a topic is averaged by all users' reported rates. If the correlation is larger, the metric can reflect the users' satisfaction better.

Table 2, 3 and 4 present the correlation results for three groups of metrics respectively. The highest score in each group is in bold. It shows that the *effective time ratio* has overall highest correlation with the users' satisfaction, and RR also has relative high correlation. Surprisingly, though *average precision* is the most commonly used metric in IR, its unnormalized version of *cumulated precision* and *cumulated effective time ratio* work not so well when compared with the real users' satisfaction.

We can also find that the metrics in the second group don't work as well as the correponding metrics in the first group, though they use both document and snippet relevance information. Another finding is that metrics at cutoff 5 can reflect users' satification better than those metrics at other cutoffs. It may be because the user can see about 5 snippets without scrolling the mouse at the search engine result page.

To investigate how good the correlation is, we also calculated the correlation between each invididual user's satisfaction scores and the average users' satisfaction scores of the results. The average correlation is 0.706, so it is higher compared to any metric used. It indicates that the users agree more on the system's performance, so there is still room to improve the metric to reflect users' satisfaction better.

Table 2. Metrics Based on Document Relevance

RR	P@3	P@5	P@10	DCG@3	DCG@5	DCG@10	CP@3	CP@5	CP@10	CP@100
0.497	0.396	0.407	0.286	0.412	0.431	0.366	0.330	0.345	0.286	0.201

Table 3. Metrics Based on Snippet-Document Relevance

RR	P@3	P@5	P@10	DCG@3	DCG@5	DCG@10	CP@3	CP@5	CP@10
0.467	0.344	0.343	0.253	0.366	0.375	0.320	0.283	0.287	0.222

Table 4. Effective Time Ratio and its extension

ETR@3	ETR@5	ETR@10	ETR@20	CETR@3	CETR@5	CETR@10	CETR@20
0.469	**0.537**	0.513	0.383	0.312	0.314	0.239	0.122

5.3 Question Categories

The above experimental results show *effective time ratio* can perform well on average, but they provide limited information on how it performs in multiple scenarios. It would be much more informative to compare these metrics in various scenarios, such as open-information vs. close information query.

In the data collecting, we collect 25 close-information queries (corresponding to the question that can be answered by one document, such as the birthday of Abraham Lincoln) and 25 open-information queries (corresponding to the question that can be answered by multiple document, such as the information about domain IR). We can calculate the correlation between user satisfactions and the metric scores on these two topic categories respectively. Due to the space limit, we just present the 3 metrics with highest correlation from each of three metric groups in Table 5 and 6. *Effcetive time ratio* still has higher correlation with user satisfaction than other metrics. It is obviously that the correlation is higher for the close-information questions. Another finding is that the correlations are larger for metrics with larger cutoffs for open-information questions, because the users are likely to view more documents for such questions.

Table 5. Correlations for Open-information Questions

doc-rel			doc-snippet-rel			ETR		
DCG@10	P@10	P@5	RR	DCG@5	P@5	ETR@10	ETR@20	ETR@100
0.337	0.336	0.355	**0.237**	0.219	0.222	0.368	0.330	**0.379**

Table 6. Correlations for Close-information Questions

doc-rel			doc-snippet-rel			ETR		
RR	DCG@5	DCG@3	RR	DCG@5	DCG@3	ETR@3	ETR@5	ETR@10
0.681	0.580	0.596	**0.682**	0.596	0.617	0.674	**0.734**	0.677

6 Conclusion

Traditional IR metrics can only measure the performance of a pure retrieval system, but the modern search engine includes some other features, such as snippet quality. The users' satisfaction of using a search engine is not only affected by its underlying retrieval system, but is also affected by its snippet generation algorithm. We propose a search engine performance metric *effective time ratio*, in which the snippet quality can be easily embedded. Theoretical analysis proves that it can reflect both retrieval and snippet generation quality. The user study shows that this metric can reflect the real users' satisfaction better than the existing metrics based on document relevance and/or snippet relevance.

Acknowledgments

This work is supported by NSFC grant No.70903008 and 60933004, CNGI grant No.2008-122, 863 Program No.2009AA01Z143, and the Open Fund of the State Key Laboratory of Software Development Environment under Grant No.SKLSDE-2010KF-03, and by 973 Program Grant No.2005CB321901.

References

1. Kagolovsky, Y., Moehr, J.R.: Current status of the evaluation of information retrieval. J. Med. Syst. 27(5), 409–424 (2003)
2. Harter, S., Hert, C.: Evaluation of information retrieval systems: approaches, issues, and methods. In: ARIST, pp. 3–99 (1997)
3. Hersh, W., Turpin, A., Price, S., Chan, B., Kramer, D., Sacherek, L., Olson, D.: Do batch and user evaluations give the same results? In: SIGIR 2000: Proceedings of the 23rd Annual International ACM SIGIR Conference on Research and Development in Information Retrieval, pp. 17–24. ACM, New York (2000)
4. Turpin, A.H., Hersh, W.: Why batch and user evaluations do not give the same results. In: SIGIR '01: Proceedings of the 24th Annual International ACM SIGIR Conference on Research and Development in Information Retrieval, pp. 225–231. ACM, New York (2001)
5. Allan, J., Carterette, B., Lewis, J.: When will information retrieval be "good enough"? In: SIGIR 2005: Proceedings of the 28th Annual Iternational ACM SIGIR Cnference on Research and Dvelopment in information Retrival, pp. 40–433. ACM, New York (2005)
6. Huffman, S.B., Hochster, M.: How well does result relevance predict session satisfaction? In: Proccedings of the 30th Annual International ACM SIGIR Conference on Research and Development in Information Retrieval, pp. 567–574. ACM, New York (2007)
7. Al-Maskari, A., Sanderson, M., Clough, P.: The relationship between ir effectiveness measures and user satisfaction. In: SIGIR 2007: Proceedings of the 30th Annual International ACM SIGIR Conference on Research and Development in Information Retrieval, pp. 773–774. ACM, New York (2007)
8. Turpin, A., Scholer, F., Jarvelin, K., Wu, M., Culpepper, J.S.: Including summaries in system evaluation. In: SIGIR 2009: Proceedings of the 32nd International ACM SIGIR Conference on Research and Development in Information Retrieval, pp. 508–515. ACM, New York (2009)
9. Moffat, A., Zobel, J.: Rank-biased precision for measurement of retrieval effectiveness. ACM Trans. Inf. Syst. 27(1), 1–27 (2008)
10. Chapelle, O., Zhang, Y.: A dynamic bayesian network click model for web search ranking. In: WWW 2009: Proceedings of the 18th International Conference on World Wide Web, pp. 1–10. ACM, New York (2009)
11. Guo, F., Liu, C., Kannan, A., Minka, T., Taylor, M., Wang, Y.M., Faloutsos, C.: Click chain model in web search. In: WWW 2009: Proceedings of the 18th International Conference on World Wide Web, pp. 11–20. ACM, New York (2009)
12. Varadarajan, R., Hristidis, V.: A system for query-specific document summarization. In: CIKM 2006: Proceedings of the 15th ACM International Conference on Information and Knowledge Management, pp. 622–631. ACM, New York (2006)

13. Liang, S., Devlin, S., Tait, J.: Evaluating web search result summaries. In: Lalmas, M., MacFarlane, A., Rüger, S.M., Tombros, A., Tsikrika, T., Yavlinsky, A. (eds.) ECIR 2006. LNCS, vol. 3936, pp. 96–106. Springer, Heidelberg (2006)

Appendix

We derive the Equation 4 from 3 here. From Equation 3, we get:

$$EETR = \frac{(1+c) \cdot \sum_{i=1}^{N} R(d_i)R(s_i)}{N + c \sum_{i=1}^{N} R(s_i)}$$

The *precision* at a cutoff is defined as $P@N = \dfrac{\sum_{i=1}^{N} R(d_i)}{N}$. The snippet is relevant ($R(s_i) = 1$) iff $R(d_i) = 1$ and the second type error does not happen or $R(d_i) = 0$ and the first type error happens. Therefore we have $\sum_{i=1}^{N} R(d_i) = N \cdot P@N$. So the numerator part(denoted as U) of $EETR@N$ can be rewritten as

$$U = (1+c) \sum_{i=1}^{N} R(d_i)(1 - p_2)$$
$$= (1+c)(1 - p_2)N \cdot P@N$$

Similarly, the denominator part(denoted as L) can be written as

$$L = N + c \sum_{i=1}^{N} (R(d_i)(1 - p_2) + (1 - R(d_i))p_1)$$
$$= N + cNp_1 + cN(1 - p_1 - p_2)P@N$$

Therefore, the *expected effective time ratio* can be presented by p_1, p_2 and $P@N$.

$$EETR@N = \frac{U}{L} = \frac{(1+c)(1 - p_2)}{c(1 - p_1 - p_2) + \dfrac{1 + cp_1}{P@N}}$$

Investigating Characteristics of Non-click Behavior Using Query Logs*

Ting Yao, Min Zhang, Yiqun Liu, Shaoping Ma, Yongfeng Zhang, and Liyun Ru

State Key Lab of Intelligent Technology and Systems
Tsinghua National Laboratory for Information Science and Technology
Department of Computer Science and Technology
Tsinghua University, Beijing, 100084, China P.R.
yt596188@gmail.com

Abstract. Users' query and click behavior information has been widely used in relevance feedback techniques to improve search engine performance. However, there is a special kind of user behavior that submitting a query but not clicking any result returned by search engines. Queries ending with non-click make up a large fraction of user search activities, but few studies on them have been done in user behavior analysis. In this paper we investigate non click behavior using large scale search logs from a commercial search engine. We analyze query and non-click behavior characteristics on three levels, i.e., query, session and user level. Query frequency, search engine returned results and category of information need are observed to be relative to non-click behavior. There are significant differences between post-query actions of clicked and non-clicked queries. Users' personal preference can also results in non-click behavior. Our findings have implications for separating queries which are handled well or not by search engines and are useful in user behavior reliability study.

Keywords: Non-click behavior, click-through log, query session analysis.

1 Introduction

User behavior analysis has played an important role in Web information retrieval. A variety of techniques based on user behaviors have been proposed and applied to improve search engine performance. These techniques mainly use query-click data as feedback to gain users' information need and relevance judgments of queries [1].

The optimal situation in Web search is that users submit queries and click a few results to satisfy their need. However, in real Web search process, click behavior doesn't happen certainly. In many cases the user doesn't click any result for the query. Non-click is a kind of special user behavior which may due to complex factors. For example, the results are too irrelevant to worth clicking, or the search engine returns no result so that click is impossible, or the user attains the goal from titles and

* Supported by Natural Science Foundation (60736044, 60903107) and Research Fund for the Doctoral Program of Higher Education of China (20090002120005).

P.-J. Cheng et al. (Eds.): AIRS 2010, LNCS 6458, pp. 85–96, 2010.

abstracts directly so that there is no need to click through. However, Non-click provides valuable information as well as click behavior for search engine optimization.

In this paper we make an empirical study on the characteristics of non-click behavior to investigate the factors affecting users' choice whether to click or not. This study is carried out on three levels based on large scale search logs of a commercial search engine. At first we analyze the features of queries which are without clicks under most of their appearances. Then we make comparative analysis of entire search process (referred as *session*) which originates with a clicked query or non-clicked query. On this session level, post-query actions are taken into account as potential interpretation and consequence of non-click behavior. On user level we focus on some different search customs of users who prefer to click results and rarely click results. From the investigation we find some relationship between non-click behavior and query, resource, user features. We propose to consider these non-click related factors in studies concerning relevance feedback and user reliability.

The rest of the paper is organized as follows. In Section 2 we review related work in user behavior analysis. Section 3 introduces the data we used in our log-based study. Section 4 describes the search features of three levels on which we focus. We present our findings in Section5. Section 6 is about conclusions and future work.

2 Related Work

A variety of research efforts have been made to acquire more knowledge about user behavior. Human-based techniques, such as eye-tracking was used in some studies to look into users' decision process, aiming at finding effectiveness of implicit feedback comparing with manual relevance judgments [2]. The advantage of this method is that we can observe what people are looking at before they click [3], but the disadvantages also exist in its unreal and highly limited experimental environment.

One of the most important methods in user behavior analysis is log-based study [4]. Downey's studies focused on the relationship of queries and destination URLs [5] and the difference between common and rare queries [6]. He also proposed many useful search features. By analyzing interaction style and domain information, two classes of users- navigators and explorers as well as advanced users are separated in [7][8][9]. Users' click and skip information also proves to be effective for query suggestion [10]. All these studies interpreted or modeled general user behaviors including query-click and web browsing, but not analyzed non-click behavior.

Recently user behavior reliability has seized people's attention. Studies about click reliability based on context of click behavior [11] and the reliability of one user [12] give us a wider view of user behavior study except for query-click data. Non-click is an important behavior in user search process, which may provide much information about the interaction between users and search engines, but has hardly been studied in previous work. We make a study of it from query, session and user level through search logs analysis, for a general impression on this special and interesting behavior.

3   Data

We use search logs collected anonymously by a commercial search engine from server-side to perform our study. First of all we deal with the noise in data. Entries of query submission generated by accidentally clicks of hyperlinks are abandoned; we select those log entries originating with user's active submission of a query. Each log entry describes an interactive action between search engines and users. It contains an identifier for the user, a timestamp for the action, some parameters indicating the attributes of the action, the URLs of referred page, current page and destination page.

From the logs we can get all queries and corresponding click or non-click information. We refer to each query submitted by users as a query request. Requests with the same query are put together for analysis of each unique query.

Then we mine sessions. A session refers to an entire search process with a series of interactions to address user's information goal [13]. In our method, we start a session with an user's query submission, and end it if the user makes no action to search engine over 30min or submits an irrelevant query to begin a new search process. We refer to the first query in a session as the *goal query*. When the user is not satisfied with the search engine returned results on the first page, he/she may slide down the list pages to find results or change the query through clicking query suggestion, query correction or re-writing query directly. We refer to all these actions as post-query actions. A session entry records the goal query and post-query actions as a search trail.

Finally we gather all the sessions by individual users through unique identifiers.

Table 1 shows the data on which we make our study of non-click from three levels. In figure 1 we give the long-tailed query frequency distribution of the data set. From the right figure we can see that the top 10% of queries with highest frequency cover 78.2% of all the requests.

Table 1. Users' search and click-through log data information

Request number	Unique query number	Total clicks	Session number	User number
77,820,191	17,236,938	88,987,857	36,618,342	27,107,586

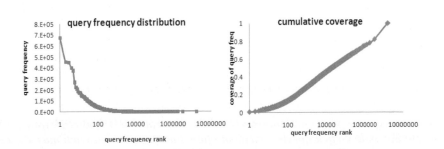

Fig. 1. Query frequency distribution and cumulative coverage. X-axis is query rank.

4 Non-click Analysis on Three Levels

4.1 Query Level Analysis

As there are many query requests with the same query but different click information, on query level, non-click behavior happens with a certain probability for each query. We define a metric namely *click ratio* to approximately describe the probability of a unique query with click. The lower *click ratio* is, the more frequent non-click behavior happens when users search this query.

$$click\ ratio = \frac{\#\text{query request with click}}{\#\text{all the query request}} \tag{1}$$

From Table 2 we can see there are most queries are in two extremes of *click ratio* (i.e. 0 or 1). Only 9.7% of queries are mixed clicked. Figure 2(a) shows more than 80% of these mixed queries are submitted only one or two times, on which click behavior is rather random. This reminds us *click ratio* of rare query is not reliable, so that we just select queries occurring more than three times. There are 1,269,868 unique queries meeting the need, which make up 7.4% of the total unique queries and cover 76.2% of all the query requests. Figure 2 (b) shows their click ratio distribution.

Table 2. Queries with different click ratio

	Number of queries	Query Frequency	Frequency of clicks
All clicked(ratio=0)	8,095,348(**47%**)	10,114,784(**13%**)	22,448,698(**25.2%**)
Never clicked(ratio=1)	7,459,583(**43.3%**)	10,265,055(**13.2%**)	0
Mixed	1,682,007(**9.7%**)	57,440,352(**73.8%**)	66,539,159(**74.8%**)
Total	17,236,938	77,820,191	88,987,857

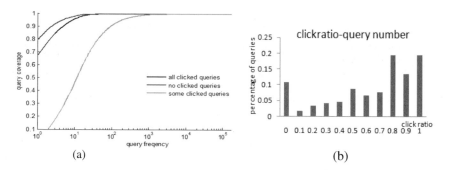

(a)   (b)

Fig. 2. (a) Cumulative coverage along with query frequency. (b) *Click ratio* distribution

We refer queries with *click ratio<=1/3, 1/3<click ratio<2/3*, and *click ratio>=2/3* respectively as *low-click queries, medium-click queries* and *high-click queries*. Features to be compared among the three are listed in Table 3.

We classify these queries into four categories: *navigational, sex/pornography, vanity search* and *the other. Navigational* queries are separated based on the Broder category [14] which assigns queries to be navigational, informational and transactional (the latter two are usually treated as non-navigational). *Sex/pornography* queries are proved to be special in many aspects of user behaviors. *Vanity search* queries are also separated for the reason that they raised more and more attention by commercial search engines. Most of *the other* queries are traditional informational and transactional queries.

Table 3. Query features (per unique query)

Query feature	Description of the feature
QF	Frequency of this query
RN	The latest number of results returned by the search engine
QL	Length of the query
FAT	Average time after query submitting until first action done
QC	Category of the query

4.2 Session Level Analysis

Each session is a search process, in which rare queries are also maintained, since if they are omitted, the session may be incomplete. In order to state our comparative experiments, we define three data sets.

Click Set refers to the sessions whose goal query is with result clicks. That is to say, people begin the search process by submitting a query and clicking some results for this query. *Non-click Set* refers to the sessions whose goal query is without result clicks, while there may be clicks for other queries submitted after the first query. In these sessions there are post-query actions. *Non-action Set* refers to the sessions without any post-query action. That is to say, after submitting the first query, the user doesn't do anything (of course he/she can look at the result list in the first page, but we can't know this action from the logs). The size of each set is shown in Table 4.

Table 4. Click Set, Non-click Set, Non-action Set

	Click Set	Non-click Set	Non-action Set
Number of sessions	21,808,194 (**59.6%**)	6,133,755 (**16.7%**)	8,676,393 (**23.7%**)

A session contains the context of click behavior. We are actually interested in users' activities after they click or do not click results for the goal query. Two features of goal queries and four features of sessions are compared in our experiment as listed in Table 5. The post-query actions include result clicks, page down, query suggestion, query correction and query re-writing after the goal query. As a comparison, actions out of the goal query refer to those activities after the goal query is changed.

Table 5. Features on session level

feature	Description of the feature
G-FAT	Time after the goal query submitting until the first action done
G-QT	Time in the goal query
SQN	The number of queries in the session
AOQ	The number of actions out of the goal query
SPA	The percentage of different post-query actions in sessions

4.3 User Level Analysis

Non-click behavior is relative to user's personality as the same query may be clicked by one user but not clicked by another. We use *user click ratio* to describe the probability of a user performing click action and estimate it with the proportion of sessions in Click Set in all the sessions of the same user. There is also data sparseness problem as with query level that most users only take one or two search process. We omit those users and use remaining 1,399,841 users for experiment. Three kinds of users are defined, i.e., high-click user (*user click ratio* < 1/3), medium-click user (1/3 <= *user click ratio* <= 2/3) and low-click user (*user click ratio* > 2/3) in Table 6.

Table 6. User click ratio partition

	High-click users	Medium-click users	Low-click users
Number of Users	135,033 (**9.6%**)	540,319(**38.6%**)	724,489 (**51.8%**)

We select four features listed in Table 7 to see how a user's preference in query description, effort for finding results, and time spent are related to non-click behavior.

Table 7. Features on user level (per user)

feature	Description of the feature
AQL	Average query length of the user's search process
ASC	Average number of clicks in a session
ASA	Average number of actions in a session
AQT	Average time spent in the goal query

5 Findings

In this section we present our findings of the investigation. We make comments on each feature and give summaries of the characteristics of non-click behavior.

5.1 Query and Non-click Behavior

(I) *QF.* We investigate the relationship of click ratio and query frequency, finding that queries with high frequency are tending to be with a high click ratio. The lower frequency does a query have, the higher probability it has to be with a ratio of 0.5, which is a random click ratio. Table 8 shows the two results.

Table 8. For different query frequency region, the percentage of *click ratio*

ratio\freq	1E+01	1E+02	1E+03	1E+04	1E+05	1E+06
[0,1/3]	22.65%	19.97%	16.96%	27.73%	13.95%	0.00%
(1/3,2/3)	20.87%	22.32%	21.69%	16.22%	19.45%	6.67%
[2/3,1]	56.47%	57.71%	61.35%	56.04%	**66.60%**	**93.33%**
0.5	*10.53%*	*6.23%*	*4.63%*	*3.71%*	*2.95%*	*0.00%*

(II) **RN**. Figure 3(a) shows for high-click queries, the typical RN is from 10^4 to 10^6. As a result, queries with RN in this range are more probable to have higher click ratio in Figure 3(b). By contrast, 8.5% of low-click queries have no resource at all.

In fact resource for the same query varies from time to time in web search environment. We count the resource of all non-click requests. Figure 3(c) indicates that about 15% of non-click requests happen in the condition of no resource.

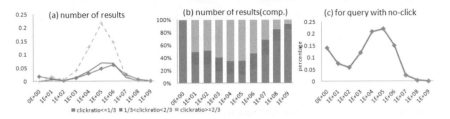

Fig. 3. (a) The distributions of RN feature of three kinds of queries. (b) The composition of click ratio for each RN bin. (c) The percentage of query requests with different RN.

(III) **QL**. Query length is also distinctive in Figure 4(a). We can see that queries containing five to eleven characters (two to four words after segment) are more likely to be with higher click ratio, while the majority of low-click queries contain only three or four characters. Presumably when query is too short to understand the user's information need or too long for the search engine to find resource matching all parts of the query, bad results and non-click behavior may happen.

(IV) **FAT**. We can see from Figure 4(b) the trends of curves are the same while the curve of high-click queries is sharper during 0 to 30s, suggesting a preference to less time to make the first action. For 60% of queries, the average first action time is no more than 10 seconds. That is to say, people will rather quickly make a choice to click a result, change the query, turn to another page or leave the search engine, etc.

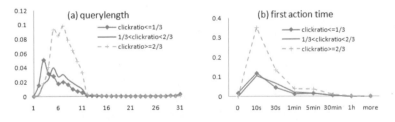

Fig. 4. (a) and (b) are the percentage of queries with different QL and FAT, respectively

(V)**QC**. We find the category of a query has implicit influence on non-click behavior. Percentage of *sex/pornography* category is higher (5.6%) in high-click queries as shown in Figure 5(a). In *navigational* category 83% of queries have higher click ratio as Figure 5(b) shows. This result consists with our knowledge that navigational query is well handled.

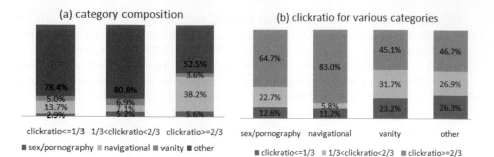

Fig. 5. (a) The percentage of categories in different click ratio region. (b) The percentage of click ratio in different category.

5.2   Non-click and Post-query Actions in Session

(I) *G-FAT.* Consistent to the conclusions stated in *FAT* feature on query level, in over 82% of search process users make the first action in 10s. As Figure 6(a) shows, in Click Set about 80% of the first actions (e.g. clicking) happen in 10s, inflecting that the results are relevant to their information need. In Non-click Set and Non-action Set, there are a large part of goal queries which users make decisions (of course not to click) almost at first sight, so the results should be very bad for users. In Non-click Set there are also 20% of goal queries demanding a little longer time to make the first decision. For example, users scan the list from top to bottom or look at the query suggestions. In this situation the results are not so bad but not relevant enough to the query as users prefer to compare them even though they do not click on any of them.

(II)*G-QT.* Time in goal query can reflect the effort users make to find results without changing the goal query, which has some relationship of the first action time as Figure 6(b). In No-action Set they are the same. In Click Set, except for the region of about 10s, there is an increase in region of 5min to 30min, since users will look into the clicked page and click several times to interact with the search engine. In No-click Set, typical time in goal query is from below 10s to 5min, since users may spend more time to read abstract and think about the results or slide down pages.

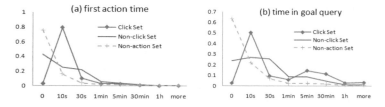

Fig. 6. (a) The G-FAT distribution of each set. (b) The G-QT distribution of each set.

(III) *SQ.* As Figure 7(a) shows, in more than 90% of Non-click sessions the user will resubmit queries, while more than 60% of Click sessions contain only the goal query. That is a significant difference. About 40% of Non-click sessions change the query for one time, as this percentage of Click sessions is 19%.

We did not think users would submit so many queries (e.g. above 5) in a session, especially in Click Set, but the statistic is out of our expectation, indicating that click behavior does not mean satisfaction of users. The clicked result may be not relevant and even if the result is relevant, the user may still change the goal query to make it clearer, or move to another related query for more information. Anyway 90% of sessions contain no more than 9 queries, no matter the goal query is with click or not.

(IV) *AOQ.* Figure 7(b) shows the number of actions after changing the goal query. We can see that in Non-click Set, AOQ is much more than in Click Set. The most sessions will have two actions after changing the goal query, which may be a resubmission and another action on this query. This can also confirm the SQ feature. There are about 10% of all sessions contain more than eight queries, and here the percentage of AOQ>8 is about 30%, which is reconcilable.

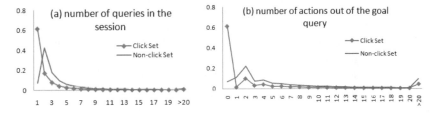

Fig. 7. (a) The percentage of sessions with QN. (b) The percentage of sessions with AOQ.

(V) *SPA.* Figure 8 shows the proportions of five kinds of post-query actions. These actions are not totally mutually-exclusive so that the sum of proportions does not equal 100% for each set. In Click Set nearly 60% of sessions end up with clicks on the goal query, which consists with AOQ feature on the point that 61.4% of sessions in Click Set contain no actions out of the goal query. In Non-click Set this bar is not zero in that users may click some irrelevant things in the result page such as ad-links at the right of pages. In Non-click Set the percentage of query re-writing is 85.5%, meanwhile there is 15.9% of sessions with query suggestion. These can indicate that in Non-click Set users are not satisfied with the goal query performance. Most of users prefer to reorganize the query by themselves and sometimes rely on query suggestions.

When users don't click any result on the first page, they may move down to another page or change the query. We compare SQ and AOQ features between those sessions with and without page down in Non-click Set.

As shown in the Figure 9(a), if users slide page down, about half of them will not resubmit queries any more. The results in Figure 9(b) also support this as 48.7% of sessions with page down have no actions out of the goal query. Compared with Fig. 7 we find that the sessions with page down in Non-click Set are more similar to sessions in Click Set in user behaviors. This may because if people would like to look at next page of result lists, the results hold a little relevance to users' information goal on some degree or users prefer spending more time in looking for proper results. In fact, users are mostly too lazy to look at more than one result page list. Thus the proportion of page change action is no more than 5% and the features of Non-click Set are mainly represented by those sessions without page down.

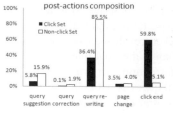

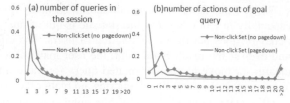

Fig. 8. Comparison on the post-actions (Click vs. Non-click)

Fig. 9. the QN feature, OQA feature in comparison between sessions in Non-click Set with or without page down

From the analysis above, we can derive the impression that Non-action Set on the whole is a little better than Non-click Set on the first action time and time in query (see Fig. 6). This may lie in that non-action behavior sometime can mean very well-done cases such as queries about *the weather of tomorrow, what day is Father's Day* for which the search engine may give answers in the title or abstract of top results. However, if users do not click any result in the goal query but have more actions in the search process, it is probable that the results are not satisfying. In this non-click situation, the features of post-query actions are similar to those with clicks on goal query if users choose to look at other result pages except for the first page (see Fig. 9).

5.3 Non-click and Users' Click Preference

The comparative results of four features on user level are shown in Figure 10.

In Figure 10(a), AQL of medium-click and high-click users is similar. They prefer to use four to seven characters to describe their information goal while low-click users have a certain proportion of using two or three characters. As to AQT in Figure 10(b), the three curves are all double-humped but relative proportions are different. On the whole low-click users spend less time than the other two kinds in a query.

The ASC and ASA features are measured on the whole of users. About 5% of all users never click anything in each session in Figure 10(d). Users would not like to click too many results in a search process in that they want to find answers through the search engine as soon as possible. About 87.3% of users click no more than 6 times in a session on average. The ASA in Figure 10(c) also supports the idea that low-click users do not make much effort in addressing their information need.

Non-click behavior may due to users' habit that they do not like to click more results, or bad cases of returned results which are caused by many factors including their improper organization of queries and other inexperienced interactions. Here we do not make individual analysis of the users so that we can not conclude which users are experts. But we show the three kinds of users are distinguishing in several aspects of user behaviors. These findings convince us we should make a difference of them in user behavior analysis, not only from their retrieval interests and query content, but also from their click behaviors. An easy case supporting this idea can be that there is no need to release ads for users who rarely click results.

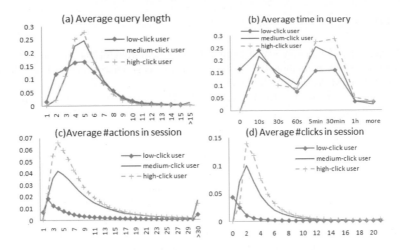

Fig. 10. Comparisons of (a)AQL, (b)AQT, (c)ASA, (d)ASC among different groups of users

6   Conclusions and Future Work

In this paper we present a log-based study on three levels to investigate the influential factors of non-click behavior. We define click ratio of queries and users, and separate sessions by non-click behavior on the goal query. We make a comparative analysis of features concerning various aspects including query, click, action and time. The main conclusions are listed as follows:

(1) Non-click behavior has much relationship with rare queries and resources. Query categories also have potential effect on it as navigational queries usually have a higher click ratio.

(2) Non-click behavior should be treated differently according to the post-query actions. Sessions with post-query actions have different characteristics from those without post-query actions, as the non-action sessions may include extreme satisfying cases. The sessions without clicks on goal query but with page down are more similar to those with clicks.

(3) It is important to distinguish user groups according to their click behavior in user related studies and applications, such as user reliability, browsing models and ads click prediction.

(4) Users will make judgments and do the first action in very short time after getting the search engine returned results. In most situations it is no more than 10s. This is an additional conclusion derived in our study.

The investigation is among the first to give a general insight on non-click behavior. Non-click is a special but frequent behavior in user search process, which implicates valuable information for Web search optimization. In the future, we will make a deep analysis of result relevance and user satisfaction with non-click behavior. Further studies focused on specific aspects we proposed in this paper for techniques of non-click modeling can also be done.

References

1. Joachims, T.: Optimizing Search Engines Using Clickthrough Data. In: Proceedings of 8th ACM SIGKDD International Conference on Knowledge Discovery and Data Mining, pp. 133–142. ACM Press, New York (2002)
2. Joachims, T., Granka, L., Pan, B., Hembrooke, H., Gay, G.: Accurately Interpreting Clickthrough Data as Implicit Feedback. In: Proceedings of the 28th ACM SIGIR Conference on Research and Development in Information Retrieval, pp. 154–161. ACM Press, New York (2005)
3. Visual attention to Online Search Engine Results. A study by Market Research Agency De Vos & Jansen in cooperation with full service Search Engine Media Agency Checkit, http://www.checkit.nl/pdf/eyetracking_research.pdf
4. Silverstein, C., Henzinger, M., Marais, H., Moricz, M.: Analysis of a Very Large Altavista Query Log. Technical Report 1998-014, Digital SRC (1998)
5. Downey, D., Dumais, S., Liebling, D., Horvitz, E.: Understanding the Relationship between Searchers. Queries and Information Goals. In: Proceeding of the 17th ACM CIKM Conference, pp. 449–458. ACM Press, New York (2008)
6. Downey, D., Dumais, S., Horvitz, E.: Heads and Tails: Studies of Web Search with Common and Rare Queries. In: Proceedings of the 30th ACM SIGIR Conference on Research and Development in Information Retrieval, pp. 847–848. ACM Press, New York (2007)
7. White, R.W., Drucker, S.M.: Investigating Behavior Variability in Web Search. In: Proceedings of the 16th International Conference on World Wide Web, pp. 21–30. ACM Press, New York (2007)
8. White, R.W., Dumais, S.T., Teevan, J.: Characterizing the Influence of Domain Expertise on Web Search Behavior. In: Proceedings of the Second ACM International Conference on Web Search and Data Mining, pp. 132–141. ACM Press, New York (2009)
9. White, R.W., Morris, D.: Investigating the Querying and Browsing Behavior of Advanced Search Engine Users. In: Proceedings of the 30th ACM SIGIR Conference on Research and Development in Information Retrieval, pp. 255–262. ACM Press, New York (2007)
10. Song, Y., He, L.W.: Optimal Rare Query Suggestion With Implicit User Feedback. In: Proceedings of the 19th International Conference on World Wide Web, pp. 901–910. ACM Press, New York (2010)
11. Cen, R.W., Liu, Y.Q., Zhang, M., Ru, L.Y., Ma, S.P.: Study on the Click Context of Web Search Users for Reliability Analysis. In: Lee, G.G., Song, D., Lin, C.-Y., Aizawa, A., Kuriyama, K., Yoshioka, M., Sakai, T. (eds.) AIRS 2009. LNCS, vol. 5839, pp. 397–408. Springer, Heidelberg (2009)
12. Xing, Q.L., Liu, Y.Q., Cen, R.W., Zhang, M.: Are Search Engine Users Equally Reliable? In: Proceedings of the 19th International Conference on World Wide Web, pp. 1207–1208. ACM Press, New York (2010)
13. Jansen, B.J., Spink, A.: How are We Searching the World Wide Web? A Comparison of Nine Search Engine Transaction Logs. Information Processing and Management: an International Journal 42, 248–263 (2006)
14. Broder, A.: A Taxonomy of Web Search. ACM SIGIR Forum 36, 3–10 (2002)

Score Estimation, Incomplete Judgments, and Significance Testing in IR Evaluation

Sri Devi Ravana[1,2] and Alistair Moffat[1]

[1] Department of Computer Science and Software Engineering,
The University of Melbourne
[2] University of Malaya, Malaysia

Abstract. Comparative evaluations of information retrieval systems are often carried out using standard test corpora, and the sample topics and pre-computed relevance judgments that are associated with them. To keep experimental costs under control, partial relevance judgments are used rather than exhaustive ones, admitting a degree of uncertainty into the per-topic effectiveness scores being compared. Here we explore the design options that must be considered when planning such an experimental evaluation, with emphasis on how effectiveness scores are inferred from partial information.

Keywords: Retrieval evaluation, effectiveness metric, pooling.

1 Introduction

Two distinct methodologies have emerged for comparing the usefulness of information retrieval systems: subject-based approaches that observe humans as they carry out some information seeking task while aspects of their behavior are monitored; and data-based approaches, in which standard corpora of documents, and the query topics and relevance judgments that accompany them, are used and re-used. The drawback of the first approach is that human experimentation requires great care in experimental design and in data interpretation, and is both difficult to reproduce, and expensive to carry out on a large scale. The drawback of the second approach is that it requires system "usefulness" to be approximated by an effectiveness metric that may or may not adequately represent the facets of performance that can be elicited via a user study [10,19]. Data-driven experiments also require human input while the test sets are being prepared. The preparation of relevance judgments is expensive, and creation of exhaustive relevance judgments for non-trivial topics is beyond the resources of most individuals or organizations, even for relatively modest collection sizes and topic sets.

To identify a subset of the documents for judging, *pooling* is commonly used. Pooling has been the standard approach used in TREC for nearly two decades [20], and selects for judgment documents which are highly ranked by at least one of the contributing systems. The current practice is to pick the top d ranked documents for each system for each topic, identify the set of unique document-topic pairs, and judge them, with the choice of d controlling the cost of the evaluation in a non-linear manner.

This arrangement then gives rise to the question as to how unjudged documents should be handled when they are encountered during the evaluation of whatever effectiveness metric is being used. The conventional and default assumption is to presume

P.-J. Cheng et al. (Eds.): AIRS 2010, LNCS 6458, pp. 97–109, 2010.
© Springer-Verlag Berlin Heidelberg 2010

that unjudged documents are not relevant, arguing that if they were relevant, they should have appeared within the top d for at least one of the systems that gave rise to the pool. This presumption is especially important when effectiveness metrics such as NDCG and AP are being used, since they include a normalization step by R, the total number of relevant documents for that topic. Studies have shown that when d is of the order of 100 to 200, the value of R derived from pooling is a relatively useful estimate [23]. But when a smaller number of judgments are being performed, care is required – it is not at all unusual, for example, for system runs to be generated and evaluated to depth 1,000 even though $d = 100$ is used for the judgments. In this case it is entirely possible for fully 90% of the documents comprising a scored run to be unjudged.

Our work in this paper examines this tension. Specifically, we:

- explore methods for estimating effectiveness scores in the face of missing relevance judgments;
- compare the quality of the system comparisons that result from those estimation techniques; and
- explore the appropriateness of statistical tests when the number of judgments against them is small.

In particular, we demonstrate that the assumption of "not relevant" for unjudged documents, while simplistic, and giving incorrect effectiveness scores, still leads to reliable experimental outcomes.

2   Retrieval Experimentation

The design of a retrieval experiment relies on a number of critical decisions [20]. This section briefly summarizes these different facets.

Collection and topics. The starting point for data-based IR experimentation is a collection of realistic documents, where realistic refers both to content and style, and to scale. In many IR experiments documents are sourced from the public web, but commercial entities may choose to make use of private collections, such as email repositories and the like. A set of realistic topics relative to that data is also required, where a topic is expressed as a query or more detailed information need, and is accompanied by a statement as to the supposed intent of the searcher assumed to have authored that need.

The two systems being compared are then used to create a ranked list of answers, or a *system run* for each of the topics, evaluated in the context of the collection. It is those system runs – containing a thousand or more documents in order, for each of the topics – that are then evaluated in the remaining steps of the experiment.

Effectiveness metrics. A suitable effectiveness metric is then chosen to reflect the assumed model for the anticipated user behavior. For example, if users are presumed to be focussed primarily on quickly identifying a single possible resource in connection with the query, a metric such as "hit at 3" might be appropriate, which assigns "1" to any retrieval run in which one or more of the top-three ranked documents is an answer. The assessment of somewhat more patient user behavior might be modelled by the metric precision at 10 (P@10); and extended searching behaviors might be modelled by a weighted precision metric that reaches further down the ranking, such as that offered by Discounted Cumulative Gain (DCG) [11] evaluated to depth 100 in the rankings.

Formation of relevance judgments. The next step is to form relevance judgments that allow the effectiveness metric to be evaluated. A usual method for building relevance judgments is to *pool* the runs from the systems being compared down to some depth d. This approach yields incomplete judgments, but is necessary because it is beyond most researchers' resources to carry out comprehensive judgments across a non-trivial set of topics for realistic-sized document collections.

Statistical testing. Another important facet of experimental design is the choice of statistical test, and a number of authors have commented in this regard [4,8,13,16,17,18,23]. Parametric statistics such as the t-test are used when assumptions can be made about the distribution underlying the system scores (or more correctly, underlying aggregates of scores), with predictions then possible about future behavior. For the most part, these rely on the scores being normally distributed. Parametric distributions can also be applied to score *differences* when a sufficiently large set is available for analysis, even if the two underlying score distributions are not normal. For typical purposes, most sources agree that "sufficiently large" is attained at around 30–50 independent paired observations. When there is a pre-conceived notion as to which system is being tested for superiority (because, for example, it has the higher mean score across the set of observations) a one-tailed test is appropriate.

Statistical testing also assumes that the observations are independent and drawn randomly from some universe. In the case of an IR experiment, it is hard to provide evidence that the topics are a random subset of all queries; nevertheless, it is an assumption that is made in all statistical testing on IR system scores.

3   Score Estimation

Consider the simple metric *precision at depth* k, computed as the fraction of the top k ranked documents for each system that are relevant. If d, the pool depth, is larger than k, then all of the system-topic scores are fully defined, because every required document has been judged. But when $k > d$, or when a new system that was not a contributor to the pool is being scored, there are three sets of documents, rather than two:

- those that have been judged relevant, r in total;
- those that have been judged irrelevant, n in total; and
- those that have not been judged, $k - (r + n)$ in total.

The effectiveness score for the run can then be expressed as a range $[B, T]$, where $B = r/k$ and $T = 1 - n/k$ are the bottom and top of the range, and $\Delta = T - B = 1 - (r + n)/k$ is the uncertainty, or *residual* associated with the measurement. In the presence of unjudged documents other precision-based effectiveness metrics can also be evaluated to a $[B, T]$ interval rather than a point, including *rank-biased precision* [12], and *discounted cumulative gain* [11]. Moffat and Zobel [12] make explicit reference to the benefits of tracking score uncertainty via a residual, and highlight the lack of fidelity in effectiveness scores that arises when the pool depth d is shallow and significant numbers of unjudged documents are encountered.

In fact, what is desired in order for the system comparison to take place is a *point estimate* that reflects the interval. More precisely, if the interval is taken to be the domain of a probability density function that describes the likelihood of the final score being any value in the interval, then the required point splits the probability density into two parts each of mass 0.5.

When viewed this way, taking B as the representative point is a approach that is open to question, and there are other point estimates that could be considered. In the experiments that are described below, the following four methods are used. In all cases it is assumed that the representative point X is required to lie within $[B, T] \subseteq [0, 1]$.

Simplistic prediction. As already noted, the simplest approach is to take the minimum value of the range, $X_S = B$.

Background prediction. If a global estimate E can be computed for the background probability of a document being relevant, then the unjudged documents can be presumed to be relevant with that probability,

$$X_B = B + \Delta E .$$

In this approach, a fixed fraction of Δ is added to B, regardless of the value of B. The question now is to determine an appropriate value of E; the value $E = 0.01$ is defended below as being a reasonable one.

Interpolated prediction. A third option is to split Δ, based on the ratio of B to $1 - T$, on the assumption that unjudged documents for a particular system are as likely to be relevant as the documents for which judgments are available. This approach yields:

$$X_I = B + \Delta \frac{B}{1 - \Delta} .$$

This method is similar to the RBP projection method discussed by Moffat and Zobel [12]. An obvious drawback is that it cannot be computed when $\Delta = 1$ (that is, when $B = 0$ and $T = 1$), and in this special case $X_I = E$.

Smoothed prediction. The smaller the value of Δ, the greater the confidence in the Interpolated prediction. Conversely, the greater the value of Δ, the more attractive it may be to prefer the background model. This combination leads to point score calculated as:

$$\alpha X_I + (1 - \alpha) X_B ,$$

where α is a parameter that reflects the level of confidence in the Interpolated prediction. If α is chosen to be $1 - \Delta$, this simplifies to

$$X_M = B + \Delta B + \Delta^2 E .$$

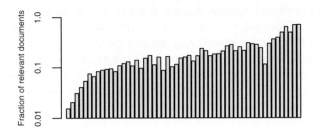

Number of request: 1 through 55

Fig. 1. Fraction of relevant documents, as a function of the number of systems that had that document in their top-d pool for $d = 100$, summed over 50 topics and the 59 systems contributing to the judgment pool in the TREC-9 Web Track

Pessimistic interval comparison. Rather than seek to represent an interval by a point value within the interval, it is also possible to compare corresponding score intervals directly. Suppose two systems are being compared, S_1 and S_2, and their score ranges are $[B_1, T_1]$ and $[B_2, T_2]$ respectively. If $T_1 < B_2$ then S_2 is clearly better (on this topic) than S_1; and vice versa if $T_2 < B_1$. On the other hand, when $B_1 < B_2 < T_1$ or $B_1 < T_2 < T_1$ (or either of two further symmetric cases) the outcome is inconclusive and there is neither evidence in support the hypothesis that S_1 is better than S_2, nor evidence to contradict it.

Estimating the background probability. It was indicated above that $E = 0.01$ would be used in our experimentation. As a justification for this, consider Figure 1, which shows the fraction of the documents in the TREC-9 Web Track that were judged relevant, categorized by the number of the pool-contributing systems that had included that document in their pool with $d = 100$. For example, seven documents were each identified as being in the top $d = 100$ by 55 different systems, of which five were judged relevant, corresponding to the rightmost bar in the graph.

The average fraction across the graph is 0.202, but is biased by the higher values at the right of the distribution. What is of more interest is the trend line, and where that trend line crosses the y-axis. That "zero requests" value can then be interpreted as being the likelihood of relevance for a document that has not been reported into the pool at $d = 100$ by any of the 59 systems. Fitting a cubic polynomial to the data gives a crossing value of 0.043. Over the whole TREC-9 judgment set (the qrels file), the probability of a document being relevant is 0.038.

Based on these values, $E = 0.01$ is not an overestimate. Note that this is not a claim that a randomly selected document in the entire collection has a 1% chance of being relevant for a randomly selected topic, that is clearly excessive. The claim is that, of the documents selected into the top $d = 100$ by a retrieval system of quality comparable to a mid-range TREC one, of the documents that have not already been judged, around 1% can be expected to be relevant.

Metrics. The estimation methods described above can be applied to all weighted-precision metrics. Other members of this family include *rank-biased precision* (RBP) [12], which in principle has no cutoff k because of the geometric weights that are used, but in practice is evaluated over a finite ranking and hence always has a residual; and *discounted cumulative gain* [11], which, like precision, must be evaluated over a finite prefix. In the results below we use both RBP and *scaled discounted cumulative gain*, SDCG, in which the DCG score is divided by the DCG score that would be achieve by an "all relevant" ranking of that depth, so as to obtain scores bounded above by 1.0.

4   Experimental Investigation

Our goal with this investigation was to determine the extent to which the quality of the outcome of an IR experiment is affected by the factors discussed in the previous sections, namely: the volume of judgments performed; the choice of score estimation technique; and the choice of metric. To measure quality, we adopt the approach that has been employed by a number of authors [13,16,23]. Using TREC data, we compare pairs of systems, and count the fraction of them that yield a significant outcome according to the 50-topic comparison. For any chosen metric, if one experimental regime results in a greater fraction of the system pairs being statistically separable in this way than does another, it is more sensitive.

The experimentation is based around the 105 system submissions over 50 topics that comprise the TREC-9 Web Track [9], and the subset of 59 systems that were used to form the pool for the relevance judgments. The qrels file contains ternary judgments rather than binary ones; in our experiment both the "relevant" (category 1) and "highly relevant" (category 2) document were taken to be relevant in a binary sense. The qrels file contains 69,100 judgments, of which 2,614 or 3.8%, are "relevant".

Two sets of system pairs were used in the comparisons. In the first set, each of the 59 runs that contributed to the pooling was compared to each of the other 58, as a set of 1,711 system pairs. In the tables and graphs that follow, this set is called "59-con". The second set, "46-non", was generated by applying the same process to the other 46 systems, to create a set of 1,035 system pairs in which neither of the two systems had contributed to the judgment pool. This latter set represents a typical "judgment reuse" situation, in which two non-contributing runs are to be compared in a post-TREC experiment. To evaluate of the effect of pool depth on metric usefulness, we sorted the qrels file according to the minimum depth at which each document appeared in any of the 59 contributing runs for each topic, with random ordering applied to ties. This arrangement mimics the effect of pooling and allowed, for example, the first 1,000 qrels to be used, simulating a highly resource-limited experiment in which only shallow judgments were undertaken.

Scores and Residuals. Table 1 gives initial results for this experimental framework. Part (a) of the table shows the average base scores B computed for the two sets of systems, using three different effectiveness metrics, and evaluated using shallow, medium, and deep pooled judgments. In all cases the use of the $X_S = B$ approximation leads to non-decreasing score estimates as the number of judgments employed increases, a useful

Table 1. Base effectiveness scores, residuals, and two point estimates within the $[B, T]$ range, in all cases averaged across 50 topics and a set of system runs, for three different effectiveness metrics and three different judgment sets. In each case, two different sets of topic runs are used, the 59-con runs that led to the TREC-9 judgments; and the other 46-non system runs that did not.

Judgments	P@10		SDCG@100		RBP, $p = 0.95$	
	59-con	46-non	59-con	46-non	59-con	46-non
1,000	0.1407	0.1184	0.0509	0.0419	0.0783	0.0647
10,000	0.2362	0.1877	0.1105	0.0900	0.1592	0.1269
69,100	0.2362	0.1923	0.1351	0.1085	0.1748	0.1398
(a) Effectiveness scores, B						
1,000	0.6181	0.6759	0.8356	0.8535	0.7638	0.7921
10,000	0.0000	0.2692	0.4760	0.5670	0.2810	0.4333
69,100	0.0000	0.1631	0.0000	0.2311	0.0019	0.1955
(b) Residuals resulting from unjudged documents, Δ						
1,000	0.3121	0.2718	0.2970	0.2691	0.3148	0.2820
10,000	0.2362	0.2201	0.1987	0.1836	0.2102	0.1980
69,100	0.2362	0.2035	0.1351	0.1257	0.1751	0.1546
(c) Interpolated scores, X_I						
1,000	0.2112	0.1786	0.0992	0.0832	0.1398	0.1169
10,000	0.2362	0.2025	0.1591	0.1318	0.1963	0.1612
69,100	0.2362	0.1981	0.1351	0.1172	0.1751	0.1470
(d) Smoothed scores, X_M						

behavior; and 10,000 judgments is mostly sufficient to get the X_S scores to within around 10% of the values attained at 69,100 judgments.

Table 1(b) lists the average residuals Δ associated with those base scores. Unsurprisingly, the 59-con set of systems has smaller average residuals than the 46-non systems, since the documents to be judged to make the partial relevance judgments were chosen from the 59-con runs. Note also that rank-biased precision has non-zero residuals even when all 69,100 judgments are used. A critical observation in Table 1(b) is that on the 46-non systems the residuals are, for the most part, comparable in magnitude to the scores B that they relate to; that is, $T \geq 2B$. It must be concluded that there is considerable uncertainty associated with the 46-non systems, and that the base scores in Table 1(a) – which are also simplistic point values X_S – may not be at all accurate. The third section of Table 1 shows the average of the X_I point estimates. Now the initial estimates based on shallow and medium judgment pools are uniformly overestimates of the final scores. Taking X_I as the point estimate – and assuming that documents at the tail of a run have the same density of relevance as documents at the start of it – is clearly too generous. Finally, Table 1(d) shows the smoothed scores X_M for the same combinations of metrics and judgments. After 1,000 judgments the point estimates are now all below the at-69,100 values; and at 10,000 judgments they are all somewhat higher than the at-69,100 values, indicating a reasonable compromise between the two options, but also perhaps indicating scope for further refinement.

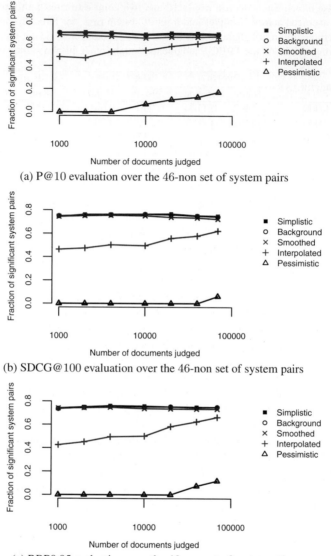

(a) P@10 evaluation over the 46-non set of system pairs

(b) SDCG@100 evaluation over the 46-non set of system pairs

(c) RBP0.95 evaluation over the 46-non set of system pairs

Fig. 2. Separability rates within the 46-non set of systems for three different effectiveness metrics, with pooling across 50 topics and 59 systems, and with the comparison based on use of the t-test at the 0.01 confidence level. Use of the t-test is appropriate for this number of topics.

Significance outcomes. Figure 2 shows system separability as the number of judged documents varies, evaluated over the 46-non set of system pairs. The different curves within each graph correspond to different ways (Section 3) of rendering each of the $[B, T]$ ranges into a single score value. The vertical axis records the fraction of the

Table 2. Percentage of system pairs separable at the $p = 0.01$ level by different experimental approaches, for three sets of judgments, two sets of system pairs, and three effectiveness metrics

Judgments	P@10		SDCG@100		RBP, $p = 0.95$	
	59-con	46-non	59-con	46-non	59-con	46-non
1,000	53.0	68.9	62.0	74.5	61.0	74.1
10,000	55.8	67.3	65.5	76.5	65.2	75.7
69,100	55.8	67.5	61.8	74.9	63.8	74.8

(a) Using X_S, and the t-test

Judgments	P@10		SDCG@100		RBP, $p = 0.95$	
1,000	46.8	47.7	46.3	46.4	44.0	38.6
10,000	55.8	53.3	57.5	49.6	59.6	50.0
69,100	55.8	61.8	61.8	62.1	63.8	61.9

(b) Using X_I, and the t-test

Judgments	P@10		SDCG@100		RBP, $p = 0.95$	
1,000	53.4	66.8	61.4	74.4	60.8	74.0
10,000	55.8	64.1	63.6	75.1	62.1	73.6
69,100	55.8	65.2	61.8	72.3	63.8	73.2

(c) Using X_M, and the t-test

system pairs that were significant at $p = 0.01$. The effectiveness metrics used in the three graphs are P@10, SDCG@100, and RBP (with parameter $p = 0.95$).

Except for the pessimistic interval-overlap method of handling the residuals, even as few as 1,000 judgments is sufficient to obtain relatively high rates of system separability. Perhaps surprisingly, it is the simplistic approach X_S and the background approach X_B that yield the greatest separability, followed by the smoothed approach X_M. Note that the different approaches disagree on outcomes even after the "full" set of 69,100 judgments have been used; the equivalent P@10 graph for the 59-con set of runs shows all lines converging by the time 20,000 judgments are being used, because of the top-centric nature of the P@10 metric. On the 59-con set the SDCG@100 curves also converge, but only after the full set of 69,100 judgments.

Table 2 gives more details of these separability coefficients. The Interpolated score estimation approach gives low separability, and is consistently less useful than the other point estimation methods. This inferior behavior is presumably a consequence of the fact that it badly overestimates the actual scores (Table 1). On the other hand, the simplistic X_S approach provides confident assessments even when startlingly few documents have been judged. There are only 223 relevant documents (including 76 highly relevant documents) in the first 1,000 positions of the TREC-9 qrels file in the ordering that is used in Figure 2 and Table 2, meaning that with 1,000 judgments, 90% of the relevant documents are *not* part of the comparison.

The success of the X_S approach to score estimation is because pooling ensures that it is tantamount to evaluating the same metric, but at a shallower depth – for example, P@10 on the shallow judgment sets is somewhat similar to evaluating P@3 (see the residuals listed in Table 1), and what is being observed in the separability graphs is that P@3 is a reasonably effective mechanism for separating systems across a set of 50 topics. Similar arguments can be made for SDCG@100 – it is sufficiently well correlated

Table 3. Percentage of significant system pairs after one set of judgments that are not identified as being significant once deeper judgments are applied

Starting with	P@10		SDCG@100		RBP, $p = 0.95$	
	10,000	69,100	10,000	69,100	10,000	69,100
1,000 judgments	7.0	8.4	4.2	7.4	4.6	6.7
10,000 judgments	–	2.2	–	3.9	–	3.1
(a) Using X_S, and the t-test						
1,000 judgments	8.0	8.4	5.0	8.5	4.3	6.6
10,000 judgments	–	1.3	–	4.3	–	3.0
(b) Using X_B, and the t-test						
1,000 judgments	9.7	6.1	17.5	11.5	18.4	8.9
10,000 judgments	–	3.3	–	4.9	–	3.3
(c) Using X_I, and the t-test						
1,000 judgments	9.0	8.1	6.0	10.5	7.7	9.1
10,000 judgments	–	0.9	–	5.8	–	2.6
(d) Using X_M, and the t-test						

with SDCG@10 (say), and the pooling approach to judgment discovery sufficiently well focussed on the top of the system runs that the latter is evaluated reasonable accurately.

Convergence. The simplistic X_S point estimate yields high separability rates even when only shallow judgments are being used, despite the actual effectiveness scores generated being under estimates. An important question then becomes the extent to which the significant pairs that are identified after 1,000 judgments remain significant as more judgments are processed. Table 3 evaluates these relationships, using the 46-non system pairs, the three precision-based metrics, and the shallow, medium, and deep judgments. To compute each value in Table 3, the set of system pairs that gave t-test p values less than 0.01 according to the test environment noted in the left-most column were then checked again in the context of the test environment recorded in the heading of the other columns. For example, with 1,000 judgments performed, P@10 resulted in 713 system comparisons (of a total of 1,035 system pairs) being deemed significant at the 0.01 level. Of these, 50 (or 7.0%) were *not* identified as being significant when 10,000 judgments were used; and 60 (that is, 8.4%) system pairs were no longer found to be significant when all 69,100 judgments were employed. What is apparent in these results is that both X_S and X_B appear to be relatively stable in their selections of significant system pairs, with less than 10% "recanting" of previous significance as further judgments are employed. The X_I approach has higher revision rates, even though it is more conservative in awarded significance when using the shallower pool depths. The latter effect is particularly marked for the two effectiveness metrics that carry out deep evaluations and are intended to reflect the behavior of very patient searchers.

Other effectiveness metrics. The use of three weighted precision metrics in the various evaluations presented in this paper is deliberate – with each of these three metrics, discovery of additional relevant documents can only increase the effectiveness score, and so the score that is attained on partial relevance judgments is a lower bound.

But other effectiveness metrics are also amenable to this treatment, with varying degrees of credibility. Average precision (AP), defined as the average of the precision values at the ranks at which relevant documents occur, is particularly challenging. Because it is an average over relevant documents, the discovery of new relevant documents can reduce as well an increase partial scores. A similar observation holds for normalized discounted cumulative gain NDCG [11], in which the scaling factor is the best DCG score attainable given the number of relevant documents available for each topic.

5   Related Work

Other researchers have also considered the issue of partial relevance judgments, and carried out experiments in which TREC (and other) judgments are scaled back and simulated retrieval comparisons carried out. Buckley and Voorhees suggest the use of a modified effectiveness metric denoted as *bpref* in which unjudged documents are by-passed [5]; an approach commented on by Sakai [14] and by Sakai and Kando [15]. The latter work includes discussion and evaluation of a wide range of effectiveness metrics. Aslam and Yilmaz et al. [1,2,22] sample the system runs in order to derive approximate values for average precision and other metrics, and show that the variance of the estimate can be reduced as the number of samples increases. Büttcher et al. [6] consider the related problem of determining and allowing for the bias in favor of pool-contributing systems. Webber and Park [21] have also considered this issue. Bompada et al. [3] consider the similarity of system orderings when compared using incomplete relevance judgments, and demonstrate that partially-evaluated NDCG is more self-consistent than Buckley and Voorhees' bpref metric. Carterette and Smucker [7] quantify the tradeoff between pool depth and pool breadth, and conclude that shallow pooling over many topics is almost certainly more powerful than deep pooling over a restricted set of topics. Our work here, in which shallow judgment pools are demonstrated to still yield significant system comparisons, are a further validation of these various findings.

6   Conclusion

We sought to explore the extent to which the use of incomplete relevance judgments affected retrieval system comparisons. It is clear that the X_S approach of assuming unjudged documents to be irrelevant affects numeric effectiveness scores, and results in values that (for weighted-precision metrics at least) markedly underestimate the true values that would arise from a more costly evaluation. In this sense, it is appropriate to explore other estimation techniques; of the ones considered here, the smoothing approach X_M gives reasonable approximations, but still leaves room for improvement.

When the effectiveness scores are being developed purely as input to a t-test in order to carry out a paired system comparison, the X_S method shed the disadvantage of being inaccurate, and provided consistently reliable outcomes. That is, despite the fact that the scores it produces are a low-fidelity approximation of the eventual scores for that metric, the relativities observed in the system scores can be relied on, and experimental outcomes reasonably determined.

We next plan to undertake similar experiments with AP and NDCG; with different document orderings for the purposes of creating the judgment set; and using other statistical tests, including in situations in which only small numbers of topics are in use.

Acknowledgment. This work was supported by the Australian Research Council, and by the Government of Malaysia.

References

1. Aslam, J., Yilmaz, E.: Inferring document relevance from incomplete information. In: Proc. 2007 ACM CIKM Conf. Lisbon, Portugal, pp. 603–610 (November 2007)
2. Aslam, J.A., Pavlu, V., Yilmaz, E.: A statistical method for system evaluation using incomplete judgments. In: Proc. 29th ACM SIGIR Conf. Seattle, WA, pp. 541–548 (August 2006)
3. Bompada, T., Chang, C.C., Chen, J., Kumar, R., Shenoy, R.: On the robustness of relevance measures with incomplete judgments. In: Proc. 30th ACM SIGIR Conf. Amsterdam, pp. 359–366 (July 2007)
4. Buckley, C., Voorhees, E.M.: Evaluating evaluation measure stability. In: Proc. 23rd ACM SIGIR Conf. Athens, Greece, pp. 33–40 (July 2000)
5. Buckley, C., Voorhees, E.M.: Retrieval evaluation with incomplete information. In: Proc. 27th ACM SIGIR Conf. Sheffield, England, pp. 25–32 (July 2004)
6. Büttcher, S., Clarke, C.L.A., Yeung, P.C.K., Soboroff, I.: Reliable information retrieval evaluation with incomplete and biased judgements. In: Proc. 30th ACM SIGIR Conf. pp. 63–70 (July 2007)
7. Carterette, B., Smucker, M.D.: Hypothesis testing with incomplete relevance judgments. In: Proc. 2007 ACM CIKM Conf, Lisbon, Portugal, pp. 643–652 (November 2007)
8. Cormack, G.V., Lynam, T.R.: Validity and power of t-test for comparing MAP and GMAP. In: Proc. 30th ACM SIGIR Conf. pp. 753–754 (July 2007)
9. Hawking, D.: Overview of the TREC-9 Web Track. In: Proc. 9th Text REtrieval Conf. (TREC-9). Gaithersburg, Maryland (November 2000)
10. Huffman, S.B., Hochster, M.: How well does result relevance predict session satisfaction? In: Proc. 30th ACM SIGIR Conf. Amsterdam, pp. 567–574 (July 2007)
11. Järvelin, K., Kekäläinen, J.: Cumulated gain-based evaluation of IR techniques. ACM Transactions on Information Systems 20(4), 422–446 (2002)
12. Moffat, A., Zobel, J.: Rank-biased precision for measurement of retrieval effectiveness. ACM Transactions on Information Systems 27(1), 1–27 (2008)
13. Sakai, T.: Evaluating evaluation metrics based on the bootstrap. In: Proc. 29th ACM SIGIR Conf. Seattle, WA, pp. 525–534 (August 2006)
14. Sakai, T.: Alternatives to Bpref. In: Proc. 30th ACM SIGIR Conf, Amsterdam, pp. 71–78 (July 2007)
15. Sakai, T., Kando, N.: On information retrieval metrics designed for evaluation with incomplete relevance assessments. Information Retrieval 11(5), 447–470 (2008)
16. Sanderson, M., Zobel, J.: Information retrieval system evaluation: Effort, sensitivity, and reliability. In: Proc. 28th ACM SIGIR Conf. Salvador, Brazil, pp. 162–169 (August 2005)
17. Smucker, M.D., Allan, J., Carterette, B.: A comparison of statistical significance tests for information retrieval. In: Proc. 2007 ACM CIKM Conf, Lisbon, pp. 623–632 (November 2007)

18. Smucker, M.D., Allan, J., Carterette, B.: Agreement among statistical significance tests for information retrieval evaluation at varying sample sizes. In: Proc. 32nd ACM SIGIR Conf. Boston, MA, pp. 630–631 (July 2009)
19. Turpin, A., Scholer, F.: User performance versus precision measures for simple search tasks. In: Proc. 29th ACM SIGIR Conf. pp. 11–18 (August 2006)
20. Voorhees, E.M., Harman, D.K.: TREC: Experiment and Evaluation in Information Retrieval. The MIT Press, Cambridge (2005)
21. Webber, W., Park, L.A.F.: Score adjustment for correction of pooling bias. In: Proc. 32nd ACM SIGIR Conf. Boston, MA, pp. 444–451 (July 2009)
22. Yilmaz, E., Kanoulas, E., Aslam, J.A.: A simple and efficient sampling method for estimating AP and NDCG. In: Proc. 31st ACM SIGIR Conf. Singapore, pp. 603–610 (July 2008)
23. Zobel, J.: How reliable are the results of large-scale information retrieval experiments? In: Proc. 21st ACM SIGIR Conf. Melbourne, Australia, pp. 307–314 (August 1998)

Multi-Search: A Meta-search Engine
Based on Multiple Ontologies

Mohammed Maree[1], Saadat M. Alhashmi[1], Mohammed Belkhatir[2],
Hidayat Hidayat[1], and Bashar Tahayna[1]

[1] Monash University, Sunway Campus, Malaysia
[2] University of Lyon & CNRS-Francesity, France
{mohammed.maree,saadat.m.alhashmi,hhid1,
bashar.tahayna}@infotech.monash.edu.my,
mohammed.belkhatir@iut.univ-lyon1.fr

Abstract. In this paper, we present *Multi-Search* meta-search engine. *Multi-Search* combines three approaches: meta search, ontology-based semantic translation techniques, and statistically-based semantic relatedness measures. *Multi-Search* attempts to employ knowledge represented by multiple ontologies for both query translation and returned results merging. In addition, it utilizes semantic relatedness measures to address the issue of missing background knowledge in the used ontologies. The developed system operates on top of several search engines and can be easily extended. Experimental results indicate that the techniques used to build the meta-search engine are both effective and efficient.

Keywords: meta-search, ontology, query translation, semantic relatedness.

1 Introduction

Current internet search engines have a number of deficiencies. First, these search engines still suffer from low precision/recall ratio [1]. The reason behind this is because these search engines use keyword-based indexing techniques to index Web-Pages. Although this approach assist users in finding information on the Web, many of the returned results are irrelevant to the user's intent. This is due to the "semantic-gap" between the meanings of the keywords that are used to index WebPages and the meanings of the terms used by the user in his query. Second, the web-coverage by a single search engine may be limited. A study conducted by [2] showed that the index intersection between the largest available search engines (Google, Yahoo!, MSN and ASK) is estimated to be 28.8%. Therefore, combing results returned from multiple search engines can be seen as an effective solution to this problem. In this paper, we introduce *Multi-Search,* a meta-search engine for retrieving, merging and ranking results returned by several individual search engines. The proposed system employs knowledge represented by multiple ontologies to derive the semantic aspects of both the user query and returned search results. In addition, statistically-based semantic relatedness measures are utilized to compensate for missing background knowledge in the exploited ontologies. In our approach, we believe that users must be considered as the center of the search process. Therefore, in *Multi-Search,* users can filter and rank

P.-J. Cheng et al. (Eds.): AIRS 2010, LNCS 6458, pp. 110–120, 2010.

the results by giving them weights according to their relevancy to the query intent. To overcome the low coverage problem, the proposed system operates on top of several search engines such as Google (www.google.com), Yahoo! (www.yahoo.com), Bing (www.bing.com), and it can be easily extended by plugging additional search engines. We summarize our contributions as flows:

- Unlike traditional keyword-based indexing approaches, *Multi-Search* employs knowledge represented by multiple ontologies to derive the semantic aspects of both user query and returned search results.
- *Multi-Search* combines semantic and statistical based techniques to compensate for missing background knowledge in the used ontologies.

The rest of the paper is organized as follows. Section 2 presents an overview of the related work. A general overview of the proposed meta-search engine is given in section 3. Section 4 explains in detail the proposed methods. Section 5 discusses experiments carried out to evaluate our meta-search engine. The final section presents the conclusions and outlines the future work.

2 Related Work

2.1 Ontology-Based Semantic Translation (OBST)

Ontologies play a crucial role in deriving the semantic aspects in both text and content-based information retrieval systems. Several OBST systems have been proposed but all of them either use a single ontology or multiple ontologies for a specific domain. Among the first systems that used ontology for this purpose is OntoSeek [3]. This system is designed for content-based information retrieval from online yellow pages and product catalogs. It uses the Sensus ontology which comprises a simple taxonomic structure of approximately 70,000 nodes to represent queries and resource descriptions. The system proposed by [4] uses subject hierarchies provided by online portals such as Yahoo.com and About.com as reference ontology for personalized web search. The authors of [5] propose to use multiple ontologies in specialized domains for information extraction purposes. Their experimental results show that by using multiple ontologies precision can be improved. In *Multi-Search*, we are not interested in a particular domain; therefore, we propose to use general-purpose ontologies that cover knowledge in multiple domains.

2.2 Meta-search Engine Construction

Among the first issues to address in meta-search engine construction is database selection. Most of the approaches rank the databases based on the relevancy of the results. For example, GIOSS [6] uses an approach called metaindex to select databases that are likely to contain the desired information. This approach has been proven not flexible or rather ignorant towards the newly added databases. Therefore, re-training is needed; and it is not very effective as the process of re-training is time consuming [7]. This paper's approach is to select several big search engines, like Google, Bing, Yahoo!, etc. The idea is that these search engines index a big part of the web so the likely hood of users getting their desired information is very high. The second issue in designing a meta-search engine is results merging. Traditionally, a linear combination (LC) of score scheme is used to rank the results from different search engines [8]. Although good results are achieved in specific cases, this technique has not yet been shown to produce reliable improvement [9]. MetaCrawler [10] is a popular meta-search engine that employs LC scheme. [11] introduces a meta-search engine called iXmetafind which uses Mearf instead of the traditional LC scheme. It is stated by the authors of [11] that Mearf outperforms LC scheme because it takes advantage of several observations like: presence of the same documents in the results of different search engines in top ranks, common themes, in addition to personalization and clustering methods.

3 *Multi-search* Architecture

As shown in Figure 1, when a user submits a query, the query analyzer first tokenizes the query into uni-gram, bi-gram and tri-gram tokens. Then, it checks whether each of these tokens is defined in the ontologies or not. For those tokens that are defined in the ontologies, semantic networks that represent the query terms and relations between them are constructed. In this context, an ontology may produce zero, one or more semantic networks. Therefore, a merging mechanism is required to merge the produced semantic networks into a single coherent network. This network represents a cooperative decision made by multiple ontologies on the semantics of the query.

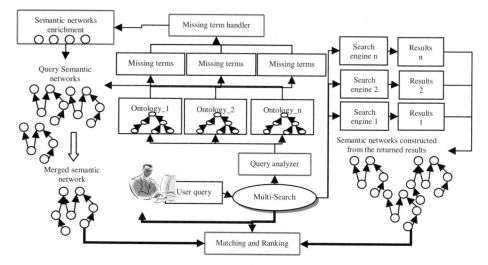

Fig. 1. Architecture of *Multi-Search*

Although using multiple ontologies provides broader domain coverage, we may still have some query terms that are not defined in any of the ontologies. In this case, the missing term handler is utilized to measure the semantic relatedness between the query terms that are missing in the ontologies and those that are defined in them. Based on this technique, a set of additional query terms are suggested to enrich the merged semantic network. On the other hand, *Multi-Search* dispatches the user query into several search engines. At this step, different results may be returned by different search engines. Each returned result is analyzed using the same technique that we used to analyze the user query. As such, semantic networks are constructed from the returned search results. In this context, a returned search result may produce zero, one or more semantic networks. Therefore, *Multi-Search* merges these networks by employing the same technique used to merge the query semantic networks. To filter and rank the results, a scoring function is employed to match the query semantic network and the returned results semantic networks. The higher the similarity, the more it is considered relevant to the query intent. Finally, the user is provided with a decision-oriented mechanism that allows him to contribute in the ranking process.

4 Details of the Proposed Methods in *Multi-Search*

Before we detail the methods of the proposed system, we formalize the use of the terms "Ontology", "Semantic Network", "Semantic Network Merging", "Semantic Network Enrichment", and "Normalized Retrieval Distance (NRD)":

Definition 1: Ontology: An ontology Ω is *quintuple*, $\Omega := \langle C, P, I, V, A \rangle$ where:

- C is the set of concepts of the ontology. The concept hierarchy of Ω is a pair $(C, \leq)$, where $\leq$ is an order relation on C x C. We call $c \in C$ the set of concepts, and $\leq$ the sub-concept relation.
- P is the set of properties.
- I is the set of instances or individuals
- V is the set of property values
- A is the set of axioms (such as constraints)

Definition 2: Semantic Network: A semantic network $\zeta := \langle T, R, A \rangle$ where:

- T is the set of terms in the network. These terms are query terms that are defined in the ontologies.
- R is the set of relations between the query terms. These relations are derived from the ontologies.
- A is the set of axioms defined on the query terms and relations.

Definition 3: Semantic Network Merging: A semantic network merging algorithm takes a given set of semantic networks $S = \{\zeta_1, \zeta_2, \zeta_3, \zeta_n\}$ as input and produces a single merged semantic network ζ_{merged} as output.

Definition 4: Semantic Network Enrichment: A semantic network enrichment algorithm takes a given set of query terms that are not defined in the ontology $W = \{w_1, w_2, w_3, w_n\}$ and the merged semantic network ζ_{merged} as input and produces for each $t \in T$ in ζmerged a set of $S(t) \subseteq W$ as output. where,

- $S(t)$ is the set of suggested enrichment candidates for t. A suggested candidate $w \in W$ is a word or compound word from W.

The set of suggested enrichment candidates $S(t)$ can be obtained using the Normalized Retrieval Distance (NRD) function and based on a threshold value v using equation 1.

$$S(t,v) := \{ w \in W \mid NRD(t,w) \geq v \} \tag{1}$$

Definition 5: Normalized Retrieval Distance (NRD): is a general case of the Normalized Google Distance (NGD) [12] function that measure the semantic relatedness between pairs of terms: Given two terms T_{mis} and T_{in}, the Normalized Retrieval Distance between T_{mis} and T_{in} can be obtained as follows:

$$NRD\ (Tmis\ ,Tin\ ) = \frac{\max\{\log\ \ f\ (Tmis\ ),\log\ f\ (Tin\ )\} - \log\ f\ (Tmis\ ,Tin\ )}{\log\ M\ -\ \min\{\log\ \ f\ (Tmis\ ),\log\ f\ (Tin\ )\}}$$

where,

- T_{mis} is a term that is not defined in the ontology
- T_{in} is a term that exists in the ontology
- $f(T_{mis})$ is the number of hits for the search term T_{mis}
- $f(T_{in})$ is the number of hits for the search term T_{in}
- $f(T_{mis}, T_{in})$ is the number of hits for the search terms T_{mis} and T_{in}
- M is the number of web pages indexed by the search engine

4.1 Query Translation and Returned Search Results Merging

4.1.1 Multiple Ontology-Based Query Translation

First, we apply several Natural Language Processing (NLP) steps on the user query such as stop word removal, n-gram query tokenization, and part-of-speech tagging. After the NLP steps, query tokens are submitted to each of the ontologies to check whether they are defined in them or not. Tokens that are defined in the ontologies are considered as meaningful query terms and thus, semantic networks that represent these terms and relations holding between them are constructed. As a consequence of this step, different number of semantic networks may be produced according to different ontologies. Therefore, we utilize the ontology merging algorithm to merge these networks into a single coherent network. The next example illustrates the NLP steps and the semantic networks construction and merging techniques.

Example1: Query = "Java or jawa the island of Indonesia"

In this example, we use WordNet [13] and OpenCyc [14] ontologies. First, the stop word removal function removes stop words based on a pre-defined list. For example, the words (the, of) are removed from the query. Then, the n-gram tokenization algorithm tokenizes the query into unigram, bigram and trigram tokens. After this step, each token is submitted to each of the ontologies to check whether it is defined in it or not. The algorithm returns that the terms {Java, Island, Indonesia} exist in both WordNet and OpenCyc ontologies. For this set of terms, semantic networks are constructed based on both ontologies as shown in Figure 2.

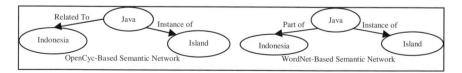

Fig. 2. Query terms represented by semantic networks

As we can see from figure 2, it is not necessarily that the used ontologies produce the same semantic networks. Therefore, due to the semantic heterogeneity between the produced networks, we utilize the merging algorithm described in section 4. In this algorithm, we used the merging techniques proposed in our previous work [15]. The result of merging the semantic networks is shown in figure 3 below.

Fig. 3. Merged Query's Semantic Network

The rest of n-gram tokens such as "jawa" are considered as missing background knowledge from the ontologies. However, we don't ignore such tokens because we believe that they may be related to the query terms and can be further suggested to enrich the merged query semantic network.

4.1.2 Statistically-Based Semantic Relatedness Measures

We utilize statistically-based semantic relatedness measures to compensate for the lack of domain coverage in the used ontologies. For query terms that are not defined in the ontologies, we attempt to find whether they can be suggested as candidates to enrich the merged query semantic network. To do this, first we utilize the NRD function described in section 4. This function measures the semantic relatedness between the query terms in the merged query semantic network and other terms that are not defined in any of the used ontologies. As different semantic relatedness measures are returned according to several search engines, we sum up all NRD values for each candidate term. This summation represents a cooperative decision made by several search engines on the semantic relatedness measurers. Table 1 shows the obtained semantic relatedness measures for the term "jawa".

Table 1. Semantic Relatedness Measures for the Term "jawa"

Term / Term	Java	island	Indonesia
jawa	0.72	0.56	0.69

4.1.3 Semantic Relations Extraction

Obtaining semantic relatedness measures is a prior step towards deriving the actual semantic relation(s) that may hold between semantically related terms. To do this, we defined a list of lexico-syntactic patterns to derive synonymy, hypernymy and hyponymy relations. These types of relations can be automatically obtained by utilizing the Semantic Relation Extractor (SRE) function. For each pair of semantically related terms, the SRE returns the number of their hits by submitting each of the patterns to several search engines. As shown in Algorithm 1 below, for each pattern, the makeQuery function (Line 6) submits exact match queries including both terms. We considered both singular and plural forms of the terms. Patterns that include negation operators such as "No T_*missing* is a(n) T_*in*" are excluded. For instance, to find the relation between the terms "jawa" and "island", we utilize the SRE function by submitting patterns in the form of exact match queries Qi such as, $Q1$= "*jawa is an island*", which outputs 80,700 hits result, $Q2$= "*jawa is a part of island*", which outputs 0 hits result, and $Q3$= "*jawa is same as island*", which outputs 0 hits result.

Algorithm 1. Semantic Relation Extractor Function

Input: Semantically related terms,($T_{\_missing}$, $T_{\_in}$)
Output: suggested relations between terms
1:    String [] suggestedRelations, [] Patterns;
2:    int[] value;
3:        for each t_missing $\in$ $T_{\_missing}$
4:            for each t_in $\in$ $T_{\_in}$
5:                for each pattern $_p$ in Patterns
6:                    value.**add**(**makeQuery**("t_$_{missing}$,$_p$, "t_$_{in}$"));
7:                end for
8:            suggestedRelations.**add**(***max***(value));
9:            end for
10:    end for

Based on the number of hits returned for the queries Qi, relations defined in the patterns are suggested to be used to enrich the semantic network with the term "jawa".

4.2 Returned Results Processing

To process the returned results by individual search engines we utilize the query translation techniques explained in section 4.1. First, each returned result page is processed using the NLP steps. At this step, tokens of the result page are matched to the terms in the merged query semantic network. To do this, we employ the Jaro-Winkler distance function [16] which is a simple technique that measures the similarity between the strings of terms in the returned page results and the merged query semantic network. If the similarity measure is above than a threshold value v=0.92, then both strings are considered as equivalent. For example, if we have the term "Object Oriented Programming" in the query semantic network and the term "Object_Oriented Programming" in one of the result pages, then using the string distance function we find that both terms are equivalent. For other terms in the result pages that didn't match the terms of the merged query semantic network, we utilize the statistical techniques detailed in section 4.1.2. Finally, each returned page result is ranked according to the similarity between the obtained set of its terms and the terms in the query semantic network. Finally, *Multi-Search* provides users with a decision-oriented mechanism that allows them to rank the returned results according to their relevancy to the query intent. In this context, a user can give weights to the returned results and filter out those results that are not semantically related to his query.

5 Experimental Results

This section describes the experiments carried out to evaluate the performance of the proposed meta-search engine. All solutions are implemented in Java and experiments are performed on a PC with dual-core CPU (3000GHz) and 2 GB RAM. The operating system is OpenSuse 11.1. The developed prototype operates on top of big search engines such as (Bing, Google, and Yahoo!). We carried out experiments using WordNet [13], OpenCyc [14], and Yago [17] ontologies. Additional experimentations through a focused study with the help of ten computer science students were carried out to see the significance of the developed system.

5.1 Experiments Using Query Samples

In order to testify our proposal of using multiple ontologies, we selected 45 sample queries (15 per domain) from different domains. We evaluated the precision of the proposed system by comparing human judgments to the automatically returned results when using a single ontology and multiple ontologies. As shown in Table 2, the precision of using multiple ontologies is higher than using a single ontology.

Table 2. Summary of the Obtained Results

Queries per Domain	Precision Using a Single Ontology (WordNet)	Precision Using Multiple Ontologies (WordNet, OpenCyc and Yago)
Countries and Cities	44%	82%
Sports	40%	75%
Programming Languages	42%	71%

5.2 Focused Study Experiments

Phase 1: *Multi-Search* and the search engines that are used in the prototype are disguised so that the users don't not know which one is "*Multi-Search*". Several queries were pre-defined and submitted to these search engines. The interviewees were asked to show which one gives the most relevant results. Among the queries that were given are: "Java Beverage", "Blood Pressure Vital Sign" and "Tree plant".

Phase 2: Given the following scenario, the user has to provide the query:
Let's say you are looking for information about states in the world, you type "state" as your query, but the search engines went off by mixing up your results with "state of mind", "state of health", "state to express", "chemical state", etc. How would you construct a query, so that it will give you, not the list of the states, but specific information about instances of state? The feedbacks from the 10 students were closely considered. Feedbacks were then compiled together to reflect how does the prototype perform. After the interviews, every interviewee had to answer a set of questions:

1. From scale 1 to 5 (1 = Worst, 5 = Best), how would you rate the results relevancy?
2. From scale 1 to 5 (1 = Worst, 5 = Best), how precise it defines the query semantics?
3. From scale 1 to 5 (1 = Worst, 5 = Best), how close it is in defining ambiguous term?
4. How many average links you had to click before you found the desired result?

5.3 Evaluation of the Study

The study results are compiled and shown in Figure 4. For overall performance, the average rate that was given by the users is= 3.7. As it is previously discussed in section

1, among the objectives of *Multi-Search* is to involve users in ranking the returned results. However, some people were confused by the way queries are converted into semantic networks. One argument was that, in most cases, users think of search by submitting keywords instead of actual query semantics.

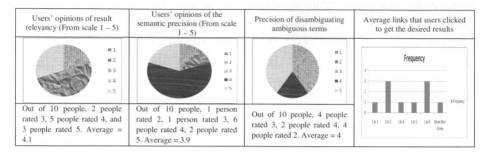

Users' opinions of result relevancy (From scale 1 – 5)	Users' opinions of the semantic precision (From scale 1 – 5)	Precision of disambiguating ambiguous terms	Average links that users clicked to get the desired results
Out of 10 people, 2 people rated 3, 5 people rated 4, and 3 people rated 5. Average = 4.1	Out of 10 people, 1 person rated 2, 1 person rated 3, 6 people rated 4, 2 people rated 5. Average = 3.9	Out of 10 people, 4 people rated 3, 2 people rated 4, 4 people rated 2. Average = 4	

Fig. 4. Evaluation of the Study Results

Table 3. Phase 1 Results

Query \ Search engine	Bing	Yahoo!	Google	Multi-Search
First Query	4	1	2	3
Second Query	3	2	4	2
Third Query	5	0	1	4
Total	12	3	7	9

From the table above, we can see that Bing and *Multi-Search* are favored among the other search engines. Although at this phase of experiments Bing was given high priority, *Multi-Search* is distinguished by the way it involves users in the search process as it provides them with a mechanism for filtering and ranking the results.

Phase 2 Results: To narrow down the results, the interviewee usually added a word before and/or after the term "state". For example: "State Country", "Country State", "State of 'INSTANCE_NAME'" like "State of Malaysia" and "State of Mississippi", etc. For this scenario, the students were not expecting the search engine to understand the meanings of the queries, but they were expecting that keywords of the queries would be exactly matched to their equivalent keywords in Web pages. The reason is because most conventional search engines search the web based on keywords matching. This approach has influenced the way people search for information over the internet. For instance, when searching for something, some people will put all the keywords that they think will appear in a web page. However, as *Multi-Search* combines ontology-based query translation and semantic relatedness measures, it was able to better understand queries by filling the "semantic-gap" between the meanings of keyword used to index WebPages and keywords used by the user. Therefore, in this case, *Multi-Search* was favored among the other search engines.

6 Conclusion and Future Work

In this paper, we proposed *Multi-Search*, a meta-search engine that employs knowledge represented by multiple ontologies and combines semantic and statistical based techniques to derive the semantic aspects of both the user query and the returned search results. Based on these semantic aspects, relevancy rates are given to the user so that he can filter and rank the results. In the developed prototype experimentations were done with the help of 10 computer science students and evaluations were carried out based on the experimental results. Students agree that the prototype has successfully considered semantics of the query instead of matching keywords. Some of the feedbacks that were given stated that the search engine is very useful for people who are new to a certain topic and would like to find legit information about that topic. Among the future works that we plan to do is to exploit additional ontologies to ensure broader domain coverage and more precise query translation. In addition, instead of manually defining the lexico-syntactic patterns, we plan to use automatic pattern acquisition techniques. The benefits of using these techniques are (i) saving the time and effort required to manually define the patterns and (ii) acquiring additional relations other than synonymy and hyponymy.

References

1. Tanaka, K., et al.: Improving Search and Information Creditability Analysis from Interaction between Web1.0 and Web 2.0 Content. Journal of Software 5, 154–159 (2010)
2. Gulli, A., Signorini, A.: The indexable web is more than 11.5 billion pages. In: The 14th International World Wide Web Conference (WWW), pp. 902–903 (2005)
3. Guarino, N., Masolo, C., Vetere, G.: OntoSeek: Content-Based Access to the Web. IEEE Intelligent Systems 14(3), 70–80 (1999)
4. Gauch, S., Chafee, J., Pretschner, A.: Ontology-based personalized search and browsing. In: Web Intelligence and Agent Systems, pp. 219–234 (2003)
5. Wimalasuriya, D., Dou, D.: Using Multiple Ontologies in Information Extraction. In: CIKM 2009, Hong Kong, China, pp. 235–244 (2009)
6. Gravano, L., Garcia-Molina, H.: Generalizing GlOSS to Vector-Space Databases and Broker Hierarchies. In: Proc. of the 21st VLDB Conference, Switzerland, pp. 78–89 (1995)
7. Tseng, J., Hwang, G.J.: A Study of Metaindex Mechanism for Selecting and Ranking Remote Search Engines. Journal of Computer Science and Engineering, 353–369 (2007)
8. Tang, J., Du, Y.J., Wang, K.L.: Design and Implementation of Personalized Meta-Search Engine based on FCA. In: Proceedings of the Sixth International Conference on Machine Learning and Cybernetics, Hong Kong, China, pp. 4026–4031 (2007)
9. Aslam, J., Montague, M.: Models for Metasearch*. In: Proc. of the 24th Annual International ACM SIGIR Conf. on Research and Development in IR, USA, pp. 276–284 (2001)
10. MetaCrawler (2010), http://www.metacrawler.com
11. Han, S., Karypis, G.: Intelligent Metasearch Engine for Knowledge Management. In: Proc. of the CIKM 2003, pp. 492–495 (2003)
12. Cilibrasi, R., Vitanyi, P.: The Google Similarity Distance. IEEE Transactions on knowledge and data engineering 19(3), 370–383 (2007)
13. Miller, G.A.: WordNet: A Lexical Database for English. Communications of the ACM, 409–409 (1995)

14. Matuszek, C., Cabral, J., Witbrock, M., DeOliveira, J.: An Introduction to the Syntax and Content of Cyc. In: AAAI Spring Symposium on Formalizing and Compiling Background Knowledge and Its Applications to Knowledge Representation and Question Answering, Stanford, CA, pp. 44–49 (2006)
15. Maree, M., Belkhatir, M.: A Coupled Statistical/Semantic Framework for Merging Heterogeneous domain-Specific Ontologies. In: Accepted for Publication in the Proceedings of the 22th International Conference on Tools with Artificial Intelligence, France (2010)
16. Winkler, W.E.: The State of Record Linkage and Current Research Problems. Publication R99/04, Statistics of Income Division, Internal Revenue Service (1999),
    `http://www.census.gov/srd/www/byname.html`
17. Fabian, M.S., Gjergji, K., Gerhard, W.: YAGO: A Core of Semantic Knowledge Unifying WordNet and Wikipedia. In: 16th International World Wide Web Conference, pp. 697–706 (2007)

Co-HITS-Ranking Based Query-Focused Multi-document Summarization

Po Hu[1,2], Donghong Ji[1], and Chong Teng[1]

[1] Computer School, Wuhan University,
430072 Wuhan, China
[2] Department of Computer Science, Huazhong Normal University,
430079 Wuhan, China
geminihupo@163.com, donghong_ji2000@yahoo.com.cn,
tchong616@126.com

Abstract. Graph-based ranking methods have been successfully applied to multi-document summarization by adopting various link analysis algorithms such as PageRank and HITS to incorporate diverse relationships into the process of sentence evaluation. Both the homogeneous relationships between sentences and the heterogeneous relationships between sentences and documents have been investigated in the past. However, for query-focused multi-document summarization, the other three kinds of relationships (i.e. the relationships between documents, the relationships between the given query and documents, and the sentence-to-document correlation strength) are seldom considered when computing the sentence's importance. In order to address the limitations, this study proposes a novel Co-HITS-Ranking based approach to query-biased summarization, which can fuse all of the above relationships, either homogeneous or heterogeneous, in a unified two-layer graph model with the assumption that significant sentences and significant documents can be self boosted and mutually boosted. In the model, the manifold-ranking algorithm is employed to assign the initial biased information richness scores for sentences and documents individually only based on the local recommendations between homogeneous objects. Then by adopting the Co-HITS-Ranking algorithm, the initial biased information richness scores of sentences and documents are naturally incorporated in a mutual reinforcement framework to co-rank heterogeneous objects jointly. The final score of each sentence can be obtained through an iteratively updating process. Experimental results on the DUC datasets demonstrate the good effectiveness of the proposed approach.

Keywords: Query-focused multi-document summarization, graph model, Co-HITS ranking.

1 Introduction

The growing availability of text in electronic formats has created an urgent need for the effective technologies that can help users cope with information overload problem. A revival of interest on multi-document summarization is spurred in the circumstances, because it can reduce information overload by synthesizing contents from a

P.-J. Cheng et al. (Eds.): AIRS 2010, LNCS 6458, pp. 121–130, 2010.

large collection of documents to produce a short text that can be read more quickly and digested more conveniently.

Multi-document summarization aims to provide a highly comprehensive overview of a document set. As a particular kind of multi-document summarization, query-focused summarization exhibits high practicability in many demand-driven applications and a great amount of research has been concerned. In [1], a query-biased summary was created by incorporating the content similarity between each sentence and the given query into a generic multi-document summarizer. In [2], a novel query expansion method was presented to improve the sentence ranking result. Wei et al. proposed a cluster-sensitive graph model and the corresponding iterative algorithm for query-focused multi-document summarization [3]. A variety of graph-based sentence ranking approaches have also been proposed recently [4,5,6,7].

However, these methods either make uniform use of inter-sentence recommendation to evaluate the sentence's significance without considering the influence of the document-level information or only divide the links between sentences into intra-document relationship and inter-document relationship without considering the sentence-to-document correlation strength. So in this study, a novel Co-HITS-Ranking based extractive approach is proposed to extend the existing work by naturally fusing three kinds of relationships between sentences and documents, either homogeneous or heterogeneous, in a unified two-layer graph model. Experiments have been performed on the DUC benchmark datasets, and the results demonstrate that the proposed Co-HITS-Ranking based approach can outperform both the lead baseline method and the sentence-based manifold-ranking method on the sentence affinity graph over three ROUGE metrics.

The rest of this paper is organized as follows: the proposed Co-HITS-Ranking based approach is presented in Section 2. The experiments and results are shown in Section 3. Section 4 presents our conclusion.

2   The Proposed Co-HITS-Ranking Based Approach

2.1   Overview

The proposed Co-HITS-Ranking based approach is intuitively based on the following assumptions:

Assumption 1: A sentence should be significant if it is heavily linked with the given query and other significant sentences. A document should be significant if it is heavily linked with the given query and other significant documents.

Assumption 2: A sentence should be significant if it has high correlation strength with the significant documents. A document should be significant if it has high correlation strength with the significant sentences.

Based on the assumptions, we develop a two-layer graph model to fuse three kinds of relationships (i.e. the homogeneous relationships between sentences or documents, and the heterogeneous relationships between sentences and documents), where the significance of a sentence is not only determined by the significances of its related sentences and query, but also the significances of its closely related documents.

2.2 Two-Layer Graph Model

The two layer graph model is denoted as $G=<V_{SD}, E_{SS}, E_{DD}, E_{SD}>$, in which three sub-graphs are involved (i.e. G_{SS}, G_{DD}, and G_{SD}). $G_{SS} = (V_{SS}, E_{SS})$ is the undirected affinity graph of sentences. $V_{SS} =\{S_i \mid 1 \leqslant i \leqslant N\}$ is the set of sentences in a set, while $E_{SS}=\{(S_i, S_j) \mid S_i, S_j \in V_{SS}\}$ includes all possible links between pairs of sentences with the link weight $w(S_i, S_j)$ denoting the pair-wise content similarity between two sentences S_i and S_j. $G_{DD} = (V_{DD}, E_{DD})$ is the undirected affinity graph of documents, where $V_{DD} =\{D_j \mid 1 \leqslant j \leqslant M\}$ is the set of documents, and $E_{DD} =\{(D_i, D_j) \mid D_i, D_j \in V_{DD}\}$ includes all relationships between pairs of documents with the weight $w(D_i, D_j)$ representing the pair-wise similarity between document D_i and D_j. $G_{SD} = (V_{SD}, E_{SD})$ is the bipartite graph denoting the sentence-to-document correlations. $V_{SD} = V_{SS} \cup V_{DD}$. $E_{SD} =\{(S_i, D_j) \mid S_i \in V_{SS}, D_j \in V_{DD}\}$. The element's weight $w(S_i, D_j)$ of E_{SD} represents the correlation strength between the sentence S_i and document D_j. Figure 1 gives an illustration of the two layer graph G and its sub-graphs.

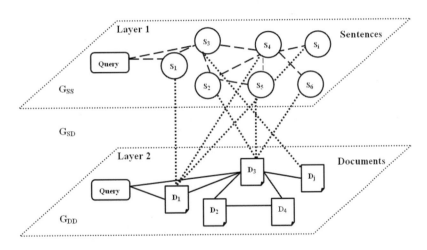

Fig. 1. Illustration of the two layer graph G and its sub-graphs

In Figure 1, the thin dotted lines linking the different kinds of objects from two layers demonstrate the correlation between sentences and documents. The upper layer expresses both the relationships among all the sentences and the relationships between the given query and the sentences. The relationships among all the documents and the relationships between the given query and the documents in the lower layer have been further investigated in this study. The given query q is treated as a pseudo-sentence when building the affinity graph G_{SS} of sentences, which can be processed in the same way as other sentences. Similarly, when building the affinity graph G_{DD} of documents, the same query q is treated as a short pseudo-document, which can then be processed in the same way as other documents.

In the graph model, the link weight $w(S_i, S_j)$ can be computed by adopting the cosine similarity measure between the corresponding term vectors $\overrightarrow{V_{S_i}}$ and $\overrightarrow{V_{S_j}}$ of sentence S_i and S_j, whose element's value can be computed by the $TF_{sk}*ISF_k$ formula, where TF_{sk} is the frequency of term T_k in the corresponding sentence and ISF_k is the inverse sentence frequency of term T_k, i.e.$1+\log(N/N_k)$, where N is the total number of the sentences in a set and N_k is the number of the sentences containing term T_k.

$$w(S_i, S_j) = \frac{\overrightarrow{V_{S_i}} \cdot \overrightarrow{V_{S_j}}}{|\overrightarrow{V_{S_i}}| \times |\overrightarrow{V_{S_j}}|} \qquad (1)$$

Likewise, we can compute the link weight $w(D_i, D_j)$ by adopting the cosine similarity measure between a pair of documents' term vectors $\overrightarrow{V_{D_i}}$ and $\overrightarrow{V_{D_j}}$, whose element's value can be computed by the $TF_{dk}*IDF_k$ formula, where TF_{dk} is the frequency of term T_k in the corresponding document and IDF_k is the inverse document frequency of term T_k.

$$w(D_i, D_j) = \frac{\overrightarrow{V_{D_i}} \cdot \overrightarrow{V_{D_j}}}{|\overrightarrow{V_{D_i}}| \times |\overrightarrow{V_{D_j}}|} \qquad (2)$$

The correlation strength between the corresponding sentence S_i and document D_j can be computed by the cosine similarity measure between the sentence's term vector and the document's term vector.

$$w(S_i, D_j) = \frac{\overrightarrow{V_{S_i}} \cdot \overrightarrow{V_{D_j}}}{|\overrightarrow{V_{S_i}}| \times |\overrightarrow{V_{D_j}}|} \qquad (3)$$

Where $\overrightarrow{V_{S_i}}$ and $\overrightarrow{V_{D_j}}$ are the term vectors of sentence S_i and document D_j.

2.3   Ranking Homogeneous Objects

Manifold-ranking algorithm is a general graph-based ranking method [8], which takes advantage of local recommendations among the neighboring nodes to rank nodes. In this study, when the sentence set S and the document set D are provided, two subgraphs G_{SS} and G_{DD} can be correspondingly constructed on S and D respectively, where S $=V_{SS} \cup \{q\}$, D $=V_{DD} \cup \{q\}$, and q denotes the given query. In the model, the manifold ranking algorithm [7,8] is further used to assign initial ranking scores (i.e. the biased information richness scores) for two kinds of homogeneous objects (i.e. sentences and documents) individually, which is performed as follows:

Table 1. The manifold ranking algorithm for ranking homogeneous objects

---

Input:
G_{SS}: The affinity graph of the sentence set S.
G_{DD}: The affinity graph of the document set D.
N: The number of the total sentences in the document set to be summarized.
M: The number of the total documents in the document set to be summarized.
Output:
The limit value $V_{S_i}^{*}$ of the sentence ranking function $V_S: S \rightarrow \Re$, which can be represented as a vector $V_S = [V_{S_0}, ..., V_{S_N}]^{T}$ with each element V_{S_i} denoting the biased information richness score of the corresponding sentence.

The limit value $V_{D_i}^{*}$ of the document ranking function $V_D: D \rightarrow \Re$, which can be represented as a vector $V_D = [V_{D_0}, ..., V_{D_M}]^{T}$ with each element V_{D_i} denoting the biased information richness score of the corresponding document.

Process:
Step 1: Define a prior sentence vector $Y_S = [Y_{S_0}, ..., Y_{S_N}]^{T}$ and a prior document vector $Y_D = [Y_{D_0}, ..., Y_{D_M}]^{T}$ respectively, in which Y_{S_0} and Y_{D_0} are set to 1 since they both correspond to the given query which can be regarded as the only labeled seed on both of the affinity graphs, and other vector elements in Y_S and Y_D are set to 0.

Step 2: Define the affinity matrix $W_S = \left(w_{S_{i,j}} \right)_{(N+1) \times (N+1)}$ with each element $w_{S_{i,j}}$ denoting the affinity weight $w(S_i, S_j)$ between the sentences S_i and S_j. Define the affinity matrix $W_D = \left(w_{D_{i,j}} \right)_{(M+1) \times (M+1)}$ with each element $w_{D_{i,j}}$ denoting the affinity weight $w(D_i, D_j)$ between the documents D_i and D_j.

Step 3: Normalize W_S and W_D by $N_S = D_S^{-1/2} \cdot W_S \cdot D_S^{-1/2}$ and $N_D = D_D^{-1/2} \cdot W_D \cdot D_D^{-1/2}$ respectively, where D_S is the diagonal matrix whose entry (i, j) equals to the sum of the i-th row of W_S and D_D is the diagonal matrix whose entry (i, j) equals to the sum of the i-th row of W_D.

Step 4: Iterate according to the following equations until convergence.

$V_S (t+1) = \lambda_s N_S V_S (t) + (1 - \lambda_s) Y_S$, $V_D (t+1) = \lambda_D N_D V_D (t) + (1 - \lambda_D) Y_D$

Where the parameter $\lambda_s, \lambda_D \in [0, 1]$ specifies the relative contribution to the ranking scores from the neighborhood homogeneous objects and the initial scores.

Step 5: Let $V_{S_i}^{*}$ and $V_{D_i}^{*}$ denote the limit of the sequence { $V_{S_i}(t)$ } and { $V_{D_i}(t)$ } respectively, each sentence S_i gets its ranking score $V_{S_i}^{*}$ and each document D_i gets its ranking score $V_{D_i}^{*}$.

In the fourth step of the algorithm, all nodes spread their ranking scores to their neighbors via the corresponding affinity graph, and the whole spreading process is repeated until a stable state is achieved.

2.4 Co-ranking Heterogeneous Objects

In Section 2.3, the initial ranking scores are only determined by homogeneous objects. However, the interactions between heterogeneous objects are not considered. To leverage the above information, the Co-HITS-Ranking algorithm is adopted to rank sentences and documents jointly [9], which can be summarized as follows.

Table 2. The Co-HITS-Ranking algorithm for co-ranking heterogeneous objects

---

Input:
G_{SD}: The bipartite graph denoting the sentence-to-document correlations.
N: The number of the total sentences in the document set to be summarized.
M: The number of the total documents in the document set to be summarized.
Output:
The limit value $Z_{S_i}^{*}$ of the sentence ranking function Z_S: $V_{SS} \rightarrow \Re$, which can be represented as a vector $Z_S = [Z_{S_1}, ..., Z_{S_N}]^T$ with each element Z_{S_i} denoting the significance score of the corresponding sentence.

The limit value $Z_{D_i}^{*}$ of the document ranking function Z_D: $V_{DD} \rightarrow \Re$, which can be represented as a vector $Z_D = [Z_{D_1}, ..., Z_{D_M}]^T$ with each element Z_{D_i} denoting the significance score of the corresponding document.

Process:
Step 1: Initialize $Z_S(0)$ and $Z_D(0)$ respectively by set each entry in them to the initial biased information richness score of the corresponding sentence or document.

Step 2: Define the affinity matrix $W_{SD} = \left(w_{SD_{i,j}}\right)_{N \times M}$ of G_{SD} with each element $w_{SD_{i,j}}$ denoting the affinity weight $w(S_i, D_j)$ (i.e the sentence-to-document correlation strength) between sentence S_i and document D_j by the cosine similarity measure. Then normalize $Z_S(0)$, $Z_D(0)$ and W_{SD} respectively.

Step 3: Iterate according to the following equations until convergence.

$$Z_{S_i}(t+1) = (1-\mu_S)Z_{S_i}(t) + \mu_S \sum_{D_j \in V_{DD}} w_{SD_{i,j}} Z_{D_j}(t) \qquad (4)$$

$$Z_{D_j}(t+1) = (1-\mu_D)Z_{D_j}(t) + \mu_D \sum_{S_i \in V_{SS}} w_{SD_{i,j}} Z_{S_i}(t) \qquad (5)$$

Where the parameter $\mu_S, \mu_D \in [0, 1]$ specifies the relative contribution to the ranking scores from the correlated heterogeneous objects and the objects' latest scores.

Step 4: Let $Z_{S_i}^{*}$ and $Z_{D_i}^{*}$ denote the limit of the sequence $\{Z_{S_i}(t)\}$ and $\{Z_{D_i}(t)\}$ respectively, each sentence S_i gets its final significance score $Z_{S_i}^{*}$ and each document D_i gets its final significance score $Z_{D_i}^{*}$.

In the study, the interaction information between sentences and documents is encoded by the bipartite graph G_{SD}, which reflects the sentence-to-document correlations in essence. We believe that the direct links and the corresponding correlation strength between sentences and documents may have significant effect on the sentence ranking, so the Co-HITS-Ranking algorithm is used to incorporate the bipartite graph G_{SD} with the content information from both layers to co-rank sentences and documents more effectively. Here the content information from both layers refers to the initial ranking scores of sentences and documents determined by each layer alone.

The final ranking scores of every sentence and document can be got through the above iteratively updating process, which can take into account the mutual influences between documents and sentences and retain their initial scores to an extent at the same time. Therefore, the significance of a sentence is determined ultimately by both its initial significance and the document's significance that is related with it closely.

After the significance score of each sentence has been obtained, a variant of MMR algorithm is employed to remove redundancy and extract summary sentences.

3   Experimental Evaluation

3.1   Dataset and Evaluation Metrics

DUC is a series of evaluation workshops that have been supported by NIST to further progress in automatic summarization. Query-focused multi-document summarization has become the main task since DUC 2005 with the aim to synthesize from a set of documents a well-organized summary to meet the information need. In this study, we use the DUC 2005 dataset for evaluation. Table 3 gives a brief summary of the dataset.

Table 3. The brief summary of the DUC 2005 dataset

Data Source	TREC collections (Los Angeles Times and Financial Times of London)
Number of Topics	50
Number of Relevant Documents Associated with Each Topic	25-50 documents
Number of Human Model Summaries for Each Topic	either 4 or 9
Summary length	250 words

We use ROUGE toolkit [10] as the evaluation utility, which has provided multiple recall-oriented metrics to evaluate the quality of a candidate summary automatically. In our experiments, documents and queries were firstly segmented into sentences. The stop words in both documents and queries were removed. And the average recall scores of the above ROUGE metrics are demonstrated in the experimental results at a confidence level of 95%.

3.2 Experimental Results

In the experiment, the optimized parameters of our approach are set by empirically. The proposed Co-HITS-Ranking based approach (denoted as "CoHR") was firstly compared with the systems participating in DUC 2005. Table 4 lists the ROUGE scores of our summaries and those of the DUC 2005 runs.

Table 4. The ROUGE scores of our summaries and those of the DUC 2005 runs

	ROUGE-1	ROUGE-2	ROUGE-SU4
CoHR	*0.37011*	*0.07012*	*0.12899*
DUC 2005 Median	0.33612	0.05842	0.11205
DUC 2005 Best	0.37515	0.07251	0.13163
DUC 2005 Worst	0.17935	0.02564	0.05569

From Table 4, we can find that the proposed Co-HITS-Ranking based approach can achieve comparable performance to the state-of-the-art systems on the DUC 2005 dataset. The results also demonstrate the effectiveness of the proposed methods, as compared with many different summarization approaches. In addition, to gain a better insight into the proposed approach, we compared it with two baseline methods. One is the lead baseline method (denoted as "LeadBase"), which simply took the first 250 words of the most recent document for each topic in the final summary. The other is the sentence-based manifold-ranking method (denoted as "SenMR"), which makes use of the sentence-to-sentence relationships and the sentence-to-query relationships in a manifold-ranking process to computes each sentence's information richness score in the documents. Then the same MMR like algorithm with same parameter configuration is applied to reduce redundancy in the ranked sentence list and choose those sentences with highest ranking scores and minimum duplicate information to create the summary according to the length limit.

The "SenMR" method is performed only on the sentence affinity graph G_{SS} without considering the influence of the document-level information that is encoded by G_{DD} and G_{SD}. Specifically, the important information ignored in the "SenMR" includes each document's significance and the sentence-to-document correlation strength. For the purpose of comparison and simplicity, we use the same value of λ_s in the "SenMR" as in the "CoHR". Table 5 shows the comparison results with the above two baseline methods on the DUC 2005 dataset.

Table 5. Comparison results with two baseline methods on DUC 2005 dataset

	ROUGE-1	ROUGE-2	ROUGE-SU4
CoHR	*0.37011*	*0.07012*	*0.12899*
SenMR	0.36102	0.06128	0.12045
LeadBase	0.27523	0.04026	0.08716

The experimental results shown in Table 5 demonstrate that the proposed Co-HITS-Ranking based approach can outperform both the lead baseline method and the sentence-based manifold-ranking method over three ROUGE metrics. The encouraging performance can be attributed to the following major factors.

Factor 1: Evaluating the initial significance of sentences and documents via the local recommendations between homogeneous objects

To collaboratively evaluate single object's importance via the local recommendations within the homogeneous objects, we make use of the manifold-ranking algorithm to integrate the relationships between homogeneous objects as well as the information about the given query in a unified graph-based score propagation process, which has been proved to be effective in the previous research [7].

Factor 2: Updating the significance scores of sentences and documents via the global mutual reinforcement between heterogeneous objects

In the model, by adopting the Co-HITS-Ranking algorithm, the initial biased information richness scores of sentences and documents can be naturally incorporated in a mutual reinforcement framework to co-rank heterogeneous objects jointly and updating their significance scores adaptively. The updating process can be regarded as a bipartite-graph-based score propagation process based on the heterogeneous relationships between sentences and documents, which can be used to co-rank sentences and documents more effectively.

In summary, the proposed Co-HITS-Ranking based approach can benefit from the integration of two single layer's own information as well as the interaction information between both layers into a unified two-layer graph model, which has been investigated in our preliminary experiment and has shown its superiority to the method that only considers the information from one layer.

4 Conclusion

In this paper, we propose a novel approach to query-focused multi-document summarization, which can extend the existing work by incorporating all kinds of relationships between sentences and documents in a unified two-layer graph model. The main feature of the proposed approach is its ability to evaluate sentences comprehensively by making use of local recommendations within homogeneous objects as well as global mutual reinforcement between heterogeneous objects. Preliminary experimental results on the DUC2005 dataset demonstrate the effectiveness of the proposed approach.

Acknowledgments. This work was supported by the Major Research Plan of National Natural Science Foundation of China (90820005, 90920005), National Natural Science Foundation of China (60773011, 60773167) and Wuhan University 985 Project (985yk004).

References

1. Saggion, H., Bontcheva, K., Cunningham, H.: Robust Generic and Query-Based Summarization. In: 10th Conference of the European Chapter of the Association for Computational Linguistics, pp. 235–238 (2003)

2. Zhao, L., Wu, L.D., Huang, X.J.: Using Query Expansion in Graph-Based Approach for Query, Focused Multi, Document Summarization. Information Processing and Management 45, 35–41 (2009)
3. Wei, F.R., Li, W.J., Lu, Q., He, Y.X.: A Cluster-Sensitive Graph Model for Query-Oriented Multi-Document Summarization. In: Macdonald, C., Ounis, I., Plachouras, V., Ruthven, I., White, R.W. (eds.) ECIR 2008. LNCS, vol. 4956, pp. 446–453. Springer, Heidelberg (2008)
4. Erkan, G., Radev, D.R.: LexRank: Graph-Based Centrality as Salience in Text Summarization. Journal of Artificial Intelligence Research 22, 457–479 (2004)
5. Mihalcea, R., Tarau, P.: TextRank–Bringing Order into Text. In: Conference on Empirical Methods in Natural Language Processing, pp. 404–411 (2004)
6. Haveliwala, T.H.: Topic-Sensitive PageRank. In: 11th International Conference on World Wide Web, pp. 517–526. ACM, New York (2002)
7. Wan, X.J., Yang, J.W., Xiao, J.G.: Manifold-Ranking Based Topic-Focused Multi-Document Summarization. In: 20th International Joint Conference on Artificial Intelligence, pp. 2903–2908. Morgan Kaufmann Publishers Inc, San Francisco (2007)
8. Zhou, D., Weston, J., Gretton, A., Bousquet, O., Schölkopf, B.: Ranking on Data Manifolds. In: Advances in Neural Information Processing Systems, vol. 16, pp. 169–176. MIT Press, Cambridge (2004)
9. Deng, H.B., Lyu, M.R., King, I.: A Generalized Co-HITS Algorithm and Its Application to Bipartite Graphs. In: 15th ACM SIGKDD International Conference on Knowledge Discovery and Data Mining, pp. 239–248. ACM, New York (2009)
10. Lin, C.Y., Hovy, E.: Automatic Evaluation of Summaries Using N-Gram Cooccurrence Statistics. In: Conference of the North American Chapter of the Association for Computational Linguistics on Human Language Technology, pp. 71–78 (2003)

Advanced Training Set Construction
for Retrieval in Historic Documents

Andrea Ernst-Gerlach and Norbert Fuhr

University of Duisburg-Essen, Department of Computational and Cognitive Sciences,
Lotharstr. 65, 47048 Duisburg, Germany
ernst@is.inf.uni-due.de,
norbert.fuhr@uni-due.de

Abstract. Retrieval in historic documents with non-standard spelling requires a mapping from search terms onto the historic terms in the document. For describing this mapping, we have developed a rule-based approach. The bottleneck of this method has been the training set construction for the algorithm where an expert has to assign manually current word forms to historic spelling variants. As a better solution, we apply a spell checker on a corpus of historic texts, which gives us a list of candidate terms and associated suggestions. The new method generates possible rules for the suggestions and accepts the most frequent rules. Experimental results with German and English texts from different centuries demonstrate the feasibility of our approach. Thus a training set can be constructed with much less initial effort.

Keywords: Spelling variation, training set construction, historic documents.

1 Introduction

The number of digital historical collections is continually growing. But even though full text search is available, many documents can not be found because they use a non-standard spelling. E. g. the German word *akzeptieren* is the contemporary word of the spelling variant *acceptieren*. The non-standard spelling produces problems when searching in historic parts of digital libraries. Most users will enter search terms in their contemporary language which differs from the historic language used in the documents.

However, even popular digitization initiatives like Google Book Search[1] or the European Digital Library[2] have not integrated a search for spelling variants yet. In order to solve this problem, our project deals with the research and development of a search engine where the user can formulate queries in contemporary language for searching in documents with an old spelling that is possibly unknown to the user (see [5]).

Other approaches use dictionaries for this purpose (e. g. [7]). However, these approaches cover only the words contained in the dictionary. Furthermore, the time and effort for the manual construction of the word entries is rather high. We overcome this

---

[1] http://books.google.com/ access: 13.08.2010.
[2] http://www.europeana.eu/portal/ access: 13.08.2010.

P.-J. Cheng et al. (Eds.): AIRS 2010, LNCS 6458, pp. 131–140, 2010.

disadvantage with a rule-based approach, in order to be able to cover the complete vocabulary (and thus increase recall). For this purpose, we are developing transformation rules for generating historic spellings from a given word.

Due to the dependency of rules on time and region , rule sets have to be generated over a longer period when suitable corpora become available. In order to get a large rule covering at least 1000 training instances are needed. This work manually has to be done by linguists or historians without help from computer scientists. Thus it is necessary to develop a tool for an easy and fast rule development that does not require computer science knowledge.

In the following, we assume that the user has a new collection and wants to enable a full text search for the documents. Let us further assume that there is no rule set available for the time and region of the collection. One first has to collect evidences consisting of contemporary inflected and derived forms of the lemma (in the following denoted by word forms) and their corresponding historic spelling variants. In a second step, the rules can be developed.

Users may have different interests. For example, for a linguist the creation of evidences is already an interesting research task and thus he wants to create each evidence only with semi-automatic support from the tool since he is interested in the development of the language and wants very precise rules. Possibly, he often searches for all occurrences of a word form in his collection, and thus he can only work with a more complete rule set. By contrast, a historian might only be interested in getting relevant documents. Thus he wants to enable a fuzzy full text search as soon as possible. He might prefer an automatic approach even if he misses some documents in the first step, when he has the chance to improve the rule set later on. Depending on his needs the user will concentrate more on the recall or on the precision of the search. The tool should offer the necessary flexibility at this point. Therefore the user will be offered full support but it will be his choice how many of the suggested evidences (and rules) he is accepting.

The remainder of this paper has the following structure: First, we give a brief survey over related work, and then Section 3 briefly introduces the rule generation process. Section 4 describes how the rule generation algorithm can be used to build evidences and rules automatically. Our approach is evaluated in Section 5, and the last section concludes the paper and gives an outlook on future work.

2   Related Work

Gotscharek et. al. [6] developed LeXtractor, a tool for the construction of historical lexica. The lexicon entries can also be regarded as evidences in our approach. On the one hand the user could work on the lexicon construction based on highlighted unknown terms. On the other hand he can work with a ranked list of unknown terms. In order to rapidly increase the percentage of the tokens from the documents that is covered by the lexicon the list is ordered by decreasing frequency. Because they are used for lexicon construction, the results have to be very precise. Thus the expert has to go through the whole collection and look at each reading of an unknown spelling. As support, a list with so called attestations for an unknown word is offered when it is chosen for the construction of a lexicon entry. LeXtractor applies manually collected rules (so called patterns) to find the potential contemporary forms in a modern dictionary.

Pilz and Luther [10] developed a method for supporting evidence collection within their Evidencer tool. The Evidencer uses a Bayesian classifier, assuming that the distribution of the n-grams differs significantly between the standard spellings and the non standard spellings. For the separation of unknown words into spelling variants and correct spellings, the classifier estimates the probability of a word being a spelling variant. After the training phase, a list of unknown words is presented which is ranked by decreasing probability of being a spelling variant. The user can adjust the Bayesian classifier by modifying the corresponding probability threshold for possible spelling variants.

VARD 2 developed by Baron and Rayson [2] also finds contemporary word forms for spelling variants in historic documents. The tool marks all words as potential variants that have not been found in a modern lexicon. For each marked word, a ranked list of candidate modern forms is offered to the user. He can then chose the correct modern form for the possible spelling variant. Additionally, a second mode is offered where the tool can automatically accept suggestions. In this mode, for each potential variant the suggestion with the highest ranking is accepted, if the corresponding score is higher than a user-defined threshold value. For providing the suggestions, Baron and Rayson use a manually created evidence list, a modified version of the SoundEx algorithm and manually created replacement rules. Based on these methods the confidence score for a suggestion is generated. This score is not a fixed value. It is adapted after each process step.

The first approach needs a lot of manual interaction for creating the evidences as well as for the rule development, even with the offered support. The second approach looks more promising regarding the automatic support for the user and the possibility for the user to influence the results by a threshold value, but the Bayesian classifier needs a lot of training data as input. Thus a huge amount of manual work is necessary before the classifier can be used. Additionally, the user can only work document-wise; he can not look at several occurrences of unknown terms in different documents at once. The permanently adapted confidence value for the modern word forms from the third approach is remarkable. The confidence score is comparable to the Bayesian classifier of the Evidencer tool. The disadvantage of VARD 2 are the methods which need a training set and a rule set as input. Both sets are manually created. Additionally, the SoundEx algorithm is a phonetic algorithm which has been developed for contemporary English. Thus the approach is not language-independent.

In summary, none of the presented approaches overcomes the bottleneck. All of them need a lot of manual effort, at least in the beginning, in order to initialise the tools. Thus an approach that can automatically detect evidences for a training set will make the access to historic documents much more comfortable for the user.

3   Generation of Transformation Rules

Now we give a brief overview on the methods for evidence collection and rule-generation methods used in the past (see [4]). In order to generate rules for transforming contemporary query terms onto the historic spelling variants, we first need a training set. By using a spell checker, we are getting a list of candidate words for historic documents in non-standard spelling. We are using Hunspell as spell checker[3], which currently offers dictionaries for 98 different languages. The suggestions for the misspelled word are generated based on n-gram similarity, rules and pronunciation data based on a dictionary. We have to check manually that the words are actually of a non-standard spelling, and have to assign the equivalent words in the contemporary standard spelling. Furthermore, we determine the number of occurrences of each historic word form. Afterwards, we can focus on the second step — the building of new rules.

The automatic rule generation method starts with a training sample of historic texts. Thus, we have sets of triplets containing the contemporary word forms, their historic spelling variant and the collection frequency of the spelling variant.

First, we compare the two words and determine so-called 'rule cores', the necessary transformations, and also identify the corresponding contexts. For example, for the contemporary word form *enclosed* and the historic word form *inclos'd*, we would get the following 2-element set of rule cores: $((e\rightarrow i)nclos)$, $(nclos(e\rightarrow')d)$.

As a second step, we generate rule candidates for each rule core that also takes account of the context information (e. g. consonant (C) or word-ending ($)) of the contemporary word. If we use the example shown above, we find that among others the following candidate rules are generated: $e\rightarrow$ ', $ed\rightarrow$ 'd, $se\rightarrow$ s', $sed\rightarrow$ s'd, $Ce\rightarrow$ C', $ed\$\rightarrow$ 'd\$.

Finally, in the third step, we select the useful rules by pruning the candidate set (where we are taking the collection frequency into account) with a modified version of the PRISM algorithm (see [3]).

4   Automatically Accepting Evidences

The last section showed that up to now, the approach required a substantial manual effort at the beginning. Therefore, a major goal is to reduce the initial work by developing an algorithm for building evidences automatically.

The basis for the rule-based approach is the assumption that the spelling variants have a certain amount of regularity. We take this assumption also as basis for automatically accepting evidences. The correct contemporary form is often among the suggestions from the spell-checker. We assume that these regularities between spelling variants and the contemporary forms are much less frequent between variants and false suggestions. Thus our algorithm concentrates on the problem of finding the correct suggestion for a possible variant. We choose the correct suggestions by taking those with more frequent rule candidates.

An evidence is created from an unknown spelling and each corresponding suggestion (see Table 1). We use these evidences as training set, and generate the possible rule candidates. Since we do not want to apply the rules in this step, we are not interested in the different rule candidates and thus consider the rule cores. In this way we get a more distinct distribution of the rules.

---

[3] http://hunspell.sourceforge.net/ access: 13.08.2010.

Table 1. Example training set and generated rule candidates

suggestion	unknown word	rule candidates
Geschicklichkeit	Geschicklichkeyt	$i \rightarrow y$
Ungeschicklichkeit	Geschicklichkeyt	$un \rightarrow \emptyset, i \rightarrow y$
Gesch**wister**lichkeit	Gesch**ick**lichkeyt	$w \rightarrow \emptyset, ster \rightarrow ck, i \rightarrow y$
jederzeit	jederzeyt	$i \rightarrow y$
jeder**mann**	jeder**zeyt**	$mann \rightarrow zeyt$
derzeitig	jederzeyt	$\emptyset \rightarrow je, i \rightarrow y, ig \rightarrow \emptyset$

Table 2. Example for accepting evidences for the rule core $i \rightarrow y$

suggestion	unknown word	procedure
Geschicklichkeit	Geschicklichkeyt	accept
jederzeit	jederzeyt	accept
obgleich	obgleych	accept
Sonderheit	**In**sonderheyt	mark $i \rightarrow y$ accepted

We are assuming that the more often a rule core appears in different evidences, the higher the probability that it is useful. Accordingly, the precision for evidences based on more frequent rule candidates will also increase. Thus, in each run, the most frequent of the unprocessed rule candidates is accepted. If several rule candidates have the same frequency, substitution rules are preferred, since these rules usually have a higher precision than insertion or deletion ones. E. g., we prefer $i \rightarrow y$ over $s \rightarrow \emptyset, \emptyset \rightarrow h$.

After we have accepted a rule candidate, we look at the corresponding evidences (and thus at the suggestions of the spell checker). If the evidence is based only on the accepted rule candidate, the evidence is directly accepted. If it is based on more than one rule candidate, it is accepted, as long as the other rule candidates also have been accepted. Otherwise it is only marked that the rule candidate has been accepted (see Table 2).

Since we have now accepted a suggestion, we are looking at the other suggestions for the spelling variants of the accepted evidence in the next step. We are assuming that a spelling variant has exactly one corresponding modern spelling. Thus we can delete the other evidences. This is a simplification, since Pilz [9] observed already that e. g. the spelling variant *Hunngern* has the two modern spellings *Ungarn* (Hungary) and *Hungern* (starvation). This simplification is needed in order to enable the process of accepting evidences automatically and thus to reduce the manual effort. However, we use it only for the automatically accepted evidences. If an evidence is missed during the automatic process, we assume that the necessary rule for it is created by another evidence. During the deletion process the evidences are also deleted from their other corresponding rule cores. Afterwards the whole process starts again with the most frequent unprocessed rule candidate. For the remaining unknown words, the user has to manually add different contemporary forms for one spelling variant.

The user can influence this process by setting a minimum word length, a minimal number of rule occurrences and a maximal number of rule applications per word. From these choices the historian might prefer a shorter word length, a smaller number of rule occurrences and a higher maximal application of rule cores, in order to achieve a high recall. Thus he can immediately start his search if he wants to. In contrast to that, a linguist might prefer the opposite settings for improving the precision.

The results of the chosen evidences are offered within the user interface in form of a list where the user can confirm the collected evidences. The overview of the evidence pairs will also offer access to attestations of the spelling variants. Thus the user can also look at to corresponding context.

5   Evaluation

As test collection, we used documents from the Nietzsche reception[4] and other smaller collections. The collection contains around 100 documents. For the evaluation we randomly choose 10 documents for each century from the 16th to 19th century in order to consider the time dependency of the approach. Since we assumed that the number of helpful suggestions from the spell-checker is decreasing, we made different runs for each century. In order to demonstrate the language-independence of our approach, we also applied it to 10 randomly chosen documents from the Shakespeare collection.

For each subcollection, we first applied our approach and then we randomly tooked 200 unknown word types for evaluation. For each subcollection we perform different runs with at most one, two or three rule applications and then we calculated recall and precision values based on the number of the minimum rule occurrences (2, 5 and 10). For all runs we set the minimum word length of the unknown terms to five. The results can be found in Tables 3, 4 and 5. We calculated two different precision values. The first variant is based on the overall number of accepted evidences while the second one only considers those evidences that are really spelling variants. As a baseline for this evaluation, we took the first suggestion from the spell-checker for each unknown word and calculated the corresponding recall and precision values.

5.1   Temporal Evaluation

The spell checker offers on average 5.4 suggestions per unknown word for the 16th century, 4.9 for the 17th and 18th century and 4.6 for the 19th century texts. Thus the number of suggestions is slightly decreasing for the more modern words.

Regarding the precision values for the different centuries, we discover that the precision is increasing over the time, with the exception of the 19th century. The percentage of unknown terms is decreasing over time from 0.33 (16th century) to 0.06 (19th century). Additionally, the number of different types is higher in the 18th century in comparison to the 19th century. Thus there are only half as many unknown types for the 19th century than for the 18th century. The resulting smaller training set leads to the decreasing precision. The recall is also increasing over time, with the exception of three rule applications in the 19th century, and three rule applications with two rules in the 16th century. Therefore, the evaluation shows that the quality of our approach is increasing over time, even though exceptions may occur.

---

[4] http://www2.inf.uni-due.de/Studienprojekte/Nietzsche/pp2001/
die_cd/die_cd.htm

Table 3. Precision based on all unknown terms

Thresholds		German				English
Rule applications	Rule Occurrences	1500-1599	1600-1699	1700-1799	1800-1899	1590-1616
	2	0.50	0.56	0.62	0.60	0.42
1	5	0.51	0.59	0.72	0.63	0.42
	10	0.52	0.61	0.74	0.65	0.46
	2	0.48	0.51	0.65	0.55	0.38
2	5	0.48	0.57	0.71	0.60	0.40
	10	0.52	0.60	0.74	0.64	0.45
	2	0.48	0.48	0.53	0.54	0.38
3	5	0.50	0.53	0.68	0.58	0.39
	10	0.53	0.57	0.71	0.62	0.41
Baseline		0.35	0.32	0.42	0.40	0.44

Table 4. Precision values restricted to spelling variants

Thresholds		German				English
Rule applications	Rule Occurrences	1500-1599	1600-1699	1700-1799	1800-1899	1590-1616
	2	0.58	0.63	0.70	0.71	0.48
1	5	0.59	0.66	0.82	0.75	0.45
	10	0.57	0.66	0.82	0.76	0.50
	2	0.60	0.61	0.75	0.65	0.46
2	5	0.58	0.66	0.78	0.71	0.46
	10	0.62	0.68	0.79	0.74	0.50
	2	0.58	0.57	0.62	0.64	0.46
3	5	0.61	0.61	0.77	0.68	0.45
	10	0.61	0.64	0.77	0.71	0.46
Baseline		0.39	0.36	0.48	0.43	0.58

Table 5. Recall values for the different parameters

Thresholds		German				English
Rule applications	Rule Occurrences	1500-1599	1600-1699	1700-1799	1800-1899	1590-1616
	2	0.56	0.62	0.78	0.79	0.74
1	5	0.52	0.62	0.74	0.77	0.74
	10	0.46	0.61	0.74	0.75	0.74
	2	0.65	0.66	0.80	0.81	0.77
2	5	0.58	0.65	0.77	0.79	0.77
	10	0.53	0.65	0.77	0.79	0.77
	2	0.71	0.66	0.86	0.81	0.77
3	5	0.63	0.65	0.84	0.79	0.77
	10	0.58	0.65	0.84	0.79	0.77
Baseline		0.64	0.56	0.67	0.70	0.66

5.2   Restricted Number of Rule Applications

Precision is decreasing in three of four cases for increasing numbers of rule applications. All recall values are increasing. In spite of the small number of runs it becomes obvious that a restriction on the number of rule applications per word is a useful parameter for controlling the quality of automatic evidence collection. At a closer look the increase in precision is only very small if the number of rule application is more restricted.

5.3   Minimal Number of Rule Occurrences

The minimal number of rule occurrences achieves even better results than the restricted number of rule applications. For the German runs only two cases (both for the 16th century) can be found where the precision is decreasing in between.

The improvements are also higher for more recent texts. A look at the evaluation data showed that the differences for the various number of rule occurrences are only limited. In this case the threshold should be higher in order to get a remarkable effect for the precision values. As expected, the recall is decreasing in all cases for the German runs. Noticeable is the recall for English. There is only a difference when just one rule is applied. The minimal number of rules occurrences has no influence on recall. Since approximately three out of four words are found already it seem that the parameter settings for English are well chosen regarding the recall.

5.4   Different Precision Values

The precision for all unknown terms gives us an indication of the number of generated incorrect evidences. Since we are not missing any rules when we generate rules for evidences that are not spelling variants, it is also interesting to look at the precision that is restricted to the spelling variants.

As expected, the precision values are much higher in this case. The highest precision is 0.82 for the 18th century when only one rule is applied and the rule occurs in at least 5 evidences. None of the restricted precision values is lower than 0.57 for German. Thus more than half of the chosen suggestions are contemporary forms. Even if we regard the lowest precision for all unknown terms (0.48), it turns out that nearly every second evidence is correct.

5.5   Baseline

Regarding the German examples, the precision is always clearly better than the baseline. With an exception for the 16th century, the recall is also better than the baseline. For the 16th century the recall can also be outperformed by those runs with less restrictive parameters.

The results for the runs based on the Shakespeare documents show that the recall is always better than the baseline. Regarding the precision based on all terms, we get mixed results. Looking at the precision restricted to the spelling variants, we detected that the precision for the baseline (0.58), which is much better than the best result for our approach was a precision of 0.50. If we increase the minimum number rule occurrences to 100, we are getting the same precision as the baseline but still achieve a higher recall (0.71 to 0.66). Thus the original parameter setting was unsuitable for the English examples.

5.6   Discussion

The results for the 18th century are remarkable, since the precision is increasing from 0.62 to 0.72 for unknown terms and from 0.70 to 0.82 for the spelling variants in the case when one rule is applied and the threshold for the minimum rule occurrences is increased from two to five. A closer look at the evaluation shows that 5 as minimum number of rule occurrences is a very good threshold in this case, since it cuts out a lot of wrong evidences and thus demonstrates the usefulness of the introduced parameters.

Especially the documents from the 16th and 17th centuries contain a lot of unknown terms in foreign languages, mostly Latin. Some documents even contain complete sentences in Latin. In order to avoid showing these terms as unknown terms, a language identifier could be used. This would also offer the possibility of spell-checking the affected passages in the different language.

For insertion and deletion rules taking minimal context into account might further improve the precision. For example, we could replace the insertion rule $\emptyset \to h$ by rules like $t \to th$.

Based on the evaluation we must correct our assumption: There are also regularities between spelling variants and the false suggestions. Since some rules are the same as those for spelling variant and the correct suggestion (see Table 1), the false suggestions to some extent even confirm the correct suggestions.

6   Conclusion and Future Work

In this paper, we present a method for automatic construction of evidences. The evidences are needed as input for a rule generation process that enables retrieval for texts in non-standard spelling. The presented approach for automatically creating evidences is very flexible, since the user has several parameters in order to control the process according to his needs with respect to recall and precision of evidences and rules.

The evaluation based on the different parameters showed that the approach for accepting evidences automatically can be applied successfully for creating a training set as well as creating a first set of rules directly. The approach is flexible enough to support different types of user needs. Additional experiments for English show the language-independene of the approach.

The remaining unknown terms will be sorted by decreasing irregularity. We will do that by comparing the n-gram relative frequencies of unknown terms with the corresponding relative n-gram frequencies of a modern collection. We are expecting that the more frequent terms have a higher probability for containing historic n-grams and thus are good candidates for possible spelling variants.

A user interface with the described approach has already been developed (see [1]). It is integrated into an interactive tool for collecting evidences and a user driven rule generation process where the user can also modify generated rules and create rules on his own (see [8]). At the moment, the automatic evidences are presented in a list of triples consisting of contemporary word, spelling variant and the corresponding rules. Since the evidences are already ordered depending on their rule frequency, we will rearrange the list and group it by rules in order to increase the usability.

Additionally, we will examine if an integration of the Bayes classifier (see Section 2) can enhance the creation of automatic accepted evidences once we have enough examples to train the classifier. In future work, we will also compare the rules that are generated by the automatic evidences to that of the baseline approach.

References

1. Awakian, A.: Development of a user-interface for an interactive rule development. Master thesis, University of Duisburg-Essen (2010)
2. Baron, A., Rayson, P.: VARD 2: A tool for dealing with spelling variation in historical corpora. In: Proceedings of the Postgraduate Conference in Corpus Linguistics, Aston University, Birmingham (2008)
3. Cendrowska, J.: PRISM: An algorithm for inducing modular rules. International Journal of Man-Machine Studies 27(4), 349–370 (1987)
4. Ernst-Gerlach, A., Fuhr, N.: Generating Search Term Variants for Text Collections with Historic Spellings. In: Lalmas, M., MacFarlane, A., Rüger, S.M., Tombros, A., Tsikrika, T., Yavlinsky, A. (eds.) ECIR 2006. LNCS, vol. 3936, pp. 49–60. Springer, Heidelberg (2006)
5. Ernst-Gerlach, A., Fuhr, N.: Retrieval in text collections with historic spelling using linguistic and spelling variants. In: Proceedings of the 7th ACM/IEEE-CS Joint Conference on Digital Libraries, pp. 333–341. ACM, New York (2007)
6. Gotscharek, A., Neumann, A., Reffle, U., Ringlstetter, C., Schulz, K.U.: Enabling Information Retrieval on Historical Document Collections - the Role of Matching Procedures and Special Lexica. In: Proceedings of the ACM SIGIR 2009 Workshop on Analytics for Noisy Unstructured Text Data (AND 2009), Barcelona, pp. 69–76 (2009)
7. Hauser, A., Heller, M., Leiss, E., Schulz, K.U., Wanzeck, C.: Information Access to Historical Documents from the Early New High German Period. In: Proceedings of the International Joint Conference on Artificial Intelligence (IJCAI 2007) Workshop on Analytics for Noisy Unstructured Text Data, Hyderabad, India, pp. 147–154 (2007)
8. Korbar, D.: Visualisation of rule structures and rule modification possibilities for texts with non-standard spelling. Master thesis, University of Duisburg-Essen (2010)
9. Pilz, T.: Nichtstandardisierte Rechtschreibung - Variationsmodellierung und rechnergestützte Variationsverarbeitung. Doctoral thesis, University of Duisburg-Essen (2009)
10. Pilz, T., Luther, W.: Automated support for evidence retrieval in documents with nonstandard orthography. In: Featherston, S., Winkler, S. (eds.) The Fruits of Empirical Linguistics. Process, vol. 1, pp. 211–228. Mouton de Gruyter, Berlin (2009)

Ontology-Driven Semantic Digital Library

Shahrul Azman Noah, Nor Afni Raziah Alias, Nurul Aida Osman,
Zuraidah Abdullah, Nazlia Omar, Yazrina Yahya, and Maryati Mohd Yusof

Knowledge Technology Research Group, Faculty of Information Science & Technology,
Universiti Kebangsaan Malaysia 43600 UKM Bangi, Selangor, Malaysia
{samn,afni,nurulaida,za,no,yaz,mmy}@ftsm.ukm.my

Abstract. This paper discusses an on-going research project in developing a semantic digital library for academic institution. It provides another view of semantic information retrieval for digital library from the perspective of semantic technology and ontology. We proposed an approach for managing, organizing and populating ontology for document collections in digital library. In this sense the document metadata and content are inserted and populated to a knowledge base which allows sophisticated query and searching. The paper also proposed an ontology based information retrieval model which is based on the classic vector space model which includes document annotation, instance-based weighting and concept-based ranking.

Keywords: digital library, information retrieval, ontology, semantic technology.

1   Introduction

The extensive deployment of digital libraries over the last decades is hardly surprising. They offer remote access to articles, journals and books with many users able to access the same document at the same time. Through the use of search engines, they make it possible to locate specific information more rapidly than ever is possible in physical libraries. Warren et al. [1] describes few challenges of current and future digital libraries, such as interoperability between different libraries or different collection of documents which pose a lot of problems, search and semantic retrieval which need to be enhanced and user interface which need to be improved. Semantic technology seems to offer solutions for the aforementioned challenges in digital library.

Digital libraries contain varieties of documents from newspaper articles to academic journals and even audios and videos collections. These collections of documents are usually described using metadata for easier access, storage and retrieval. Using metadata alone, however, is not enough to describe the semantic of documents and enhanced search is usually not possible. As such ontology is seen potential to support current limitations of digital library. One example of documents is academic thesis which contains numerous knowledge contents. An adaptation of the Dublin core metadata can be used to represent the semantic resources of the theses such as author, title, language etc, but what about the content of the theses, location of which the research presented in the theses were carried out, and how each theses link with the other theses or other resources. Such questions can be potentially answered by an

P.-J. Cheng et al. (Eds.): AIRS 2010, LNCS 6458, pp. 141–150, 2010.

ontology which is considered as a backbone to many semantic applications. A well designed ontology is essential for a successful semantic application. However, the construction of ontology is a complex and tedious process, and further more the management, storing and managing such knowledge resources are often difficult for normal users.

Digital libraries manage various kinds of digital contents and provide services for users to navigate, query, use, produce and disseminate the digital resources [2]. However, in order to provide effective services for users of digital libraries such as conceptual search and semantic navigation, the ontology forms the basis for building such semantic integration functionality. Thus, this paper discusses our on-going research in developing a semantic digital library for academic institution. This paper focuses on the semantic management level of extracting knowledge for the academic theses and populate such knowledge into an ontology in such a way to support the semantic search of digital libraries. We also proposed an ontology-based retrieval model meant for the utilization of complete domain ontologies and knowledge-bases. The search system takes advantage of both detailed instance-level knowledge available in the knowledge base, and topic taxonomies for classification. To manage the large-scale information sources, an adaptation of the classic vector-space model for an ontology-based representation is proposed, upon which a ranking algorithm is defined.

2 Related Research

Enhancing the knowledge access to the Digital Library of the British Telecom is the goal of one of the case studies in the EU IST integrated project Semantically Enabled Knowledge Technologies (SEKT). In current interfaces to Digital Libraries, users pose keyword-based queries to perform document retrieval. However, these keywords do not directly represent the semantics of the information need of the user. Therefore, the implementation uses an approach that allows the user to perform structured natural language queries against the information contained in the Digital Library [1]. The semantics of the information and the user queries is defined by an underlying ontology. The implementation of BT digital library shows how semantic technology is being used to enhance the digital library features through richer metadata, enhanced user-profiling, unlocking the documents, enhanced searching and browsing, and displaying the result.

The work of [3] focuses on the verification and the tracing of information using an information dissemination platform and other Semantic Web-based services. Services on the platform include information dissemination services to support reliable information exchange among researchers and knowledge service to provide unrevealed information. It is difficult to support collaboration among users because additional metadata cannot be inserted into documents or containers.

The work of [4] focus on question answering over heterogeneous knowledge sources that makes use of different ontology management components within the scenario of a digital library application. In particular, ontologies offer a generic solution to the problem of integrating various sources. The documents in the knowledge sources are annotated and classified according to the ontology. The ontology model consists of concepts organized hierarchically in terms of subsumption as well as of (binary) relations together with appropriate domain/range restrictions. The ontological metadata can then be exploited for advanced knowledge access, including navigation, browsing, and semantic search. Advanced semantics-based mining technology can extract fine-grained metadata from articles contained in the digital library. Finally, current reasoning techniques allow to answer structured queries to access full-text content as well as fine-grained metadata from articles from different sources in a uniform way. The knowledge base of the digital library consists of a number of heterogeneous knowledge sources, partially structured in the form of metadata and topic hierarchies, but largely unstructured in the form of full text documents. All these heterogeneous knowledge sources are integrated using a common ontology, name PROTON. The structured information sources are integrated using a mapping of the underlying structures to the ontology. The mapping for the unstructured sources is not as direct and using the help of the ontology learning tool Text2Onto [5].

The work of [6] describe how ontologies can serve as symbolic tools within a community of practice. It combines the central server which is called knowledge server whose main role is to retrieve appropriate learning initiatives from the database from end-user queries. The knowledge server consists of a customized HTTP server which offers a library of high-level Lisp functions to dynamically generate HTML pages, WebOnto Server, an operational knowledge modelling language which provides the underlying representation for the ontologies and knowledge models., a set of knowledge models which includes the observatory ontology used to index the learning initiatives in the good practice database. Connected to the central server is a database containing several hundred summaries of documented examples of life-long learning, Named Entity Recognizer, WebOnto Client and a Semantic Search Service.

The research in [3,4] mainly view the semantic digital library at the upper-level ontology with little or none focusing on domain specific ontology. Such specialized ontology of a particular domain deem important to enhance semantic search from the domain perspectives. Research in [6] although not directly related to digital library, it seems appropriate to be considered in this study. Techniques presented in the research which relates to ontology population can be used in digital library.

Furthermore none of the aforementioned approaches look into the possibility of adapting the available information retrieval model to support semantic. As such most of the approach employ exact matching of documents. Apart from that, as the process of inserting and populating ontology is a complicated process, it is deem appropriate to develop a tool which can assist user in managing knowledge of the theses. We proposed a backend process is to annotate the description of the academic theses using GATE (General architecture for text engineering) [7].

3   The Approach

The focus of this paper is on academic theses under the computing domain. The aim is to build an ontology driven digital library which can support semantic search and retrieval. The prototype assists users in inserting and extracting knowledge from documents and subsequently populated into a knowledge base.

3.1 The Proposed Architecture

Fig. 1 illustrates the general architecture of the proposed digital library. As can be seen, the construction, modelling and querying of documents are all related to the ontology.

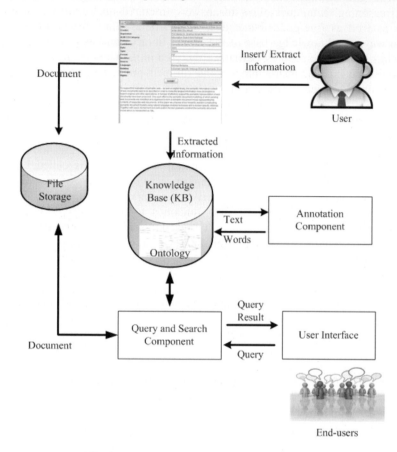

Fig. 1. The general architecture of the prototype

There are two (2) types of ontology, i.e. i) standard ontology; and ii) domain ontology. The standard ontology is an ontology which relates to metadata of the document resources such as creator (author), title, date, and language. We assumed that the standard ontology is consistent for all disciplines or subjects of documents. The standard ontology is mainly derived from the Dublin Core metadata and the PROTON ontology. The domain ontology on the other hand is specific to disciplines or subjects such as computing, health sciences, social sciences and medical. It is basically represented as topic hierarchy (or taxonomy). At the moment, only the computing discipline ontology which is the ACM topic hierarchy is available. The domain ontology is meant to semantically describe the content of documents by annotating terms available in the abstract, the whole documents or only keywords. The domain ontology is also used for automatic semantic indexing.

Logically each document is classified under one subject, however terms available in the documents may be annotated by multiple concepts from different domain ontologies. As such the term 'genetic' might be available in the computing domain or biology domain. Similarly for the term 'social network' which may appear in the computing discipline or the social science discipline. When it comes to annotation, the annotation component allows user to manually annotate or accept suggestions provided by the system. We will discuss annotation in more detail in the next section. Apart from that, the standard ontology is also federated with other domain ontology and even extended with more specialized concepts. For instance in the case of academic theses, the standard ontology is federated with the Geo ontology and extended with further specialized concepts such as research, awards and institutions which relate to the theses. Fig. 2 shows a portion of the ontology used to describe the academic theses.

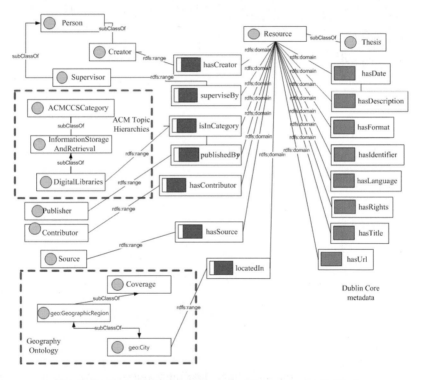

Fig. 2. Portion of domain ontology focusing on academic thesis

Referring again to Fig. 1, a user is responsible to insert the document, data and related information (the extracted information) about the digital contents to the knowledge base. Therefore, the prototype acts as a layer or mediator between users and digital libraries. The prototype provides an interface for user to expand the data/instances of the ontology in the digital libraries. The backend of the system consists of an annotation component and a query and search component, while the front end consists of an interface for end-users to access the digital library. As can be seen in Fig. 1, the process begins with the user insert the extracted information into the prototype. The prototype will populate the information to the ontology based on the information given. Inserted information is the metadata of the thesis which includes the creator, title, year and publisher. These metadata will be populated under the modified Dublin Core ontology represented as OWL. Each inserted thesis will become an instance in the knowledge base.

For example in Fig. 3, the name of the theses' creator will be populated under `Student`, and `Student` is a subclass of `Creator` in the ontology and the title of the theses will be related to the `Creator` with the help of the ontology. This ontology also relate the `Supervisor` of the theses to the `Creator`.

```
  <rdf:Description rdf:about="#hasTitleJournal">
     <rdf:type rdf:resource="http://www.w3.org/2002/07/owl#DatatypeProperty"/>
     <rdfs:label
rdf:datatype="http://www.w3.org/2001/XMLSchema#string"></rdfs:label>
     <rdfs:domain rdf:resource="#Journal"/>
     <rdfs:range rdf:resource="http://www.w3.org/2001/XMLSchema#string"/>
  </rdf:Description>
  <rdf:Description rdf:about="#InformationStorage">
     <rdfs:label rdf:datatype="http://www.w3.org/2001/XMLSchema#string">Information
Storage</rdfs:label>
     <rdfs:subClassOf rdf:resource="#InformationStorageAndRetrieval"/>
     <rdf:type rdf:resource="http://www.w3.org/2002/07/owl#Class"/>
  </rdf:Description>
  <rdf:Description rdf:about="#Paper1">
     <rdf:type rdf:resource="#PublishMaterial"/>
     <rdfs:label rdf:datatype="http://www.w3.org/2001/XMLSchema#string">paper 1
semantic digital library paper</rdfs:label>
  </rdf:Description>
  <rdf:Description rdf:about="#Student1">
     <studentOf rdf:resource="#Academic1"/>
     <studyAt rdf:resource="#Faculty1"/>
     <rdf:type rdf:resource="#Student"/>
     <rdfs:label
rdf:datatype="http://www.w3.org/2001/XMLSchema#string">Afni</rdfs:label>
  </rdf:Description>
  <rdf:Description rdf:about="#ISR_infoSearchAndRetrieval_Clustering">
     <rdfs:label rdf:datatype="http://www.w3.org/2001/XMLSchema#string">information
search and retrieval,clustering</rdfs:label>
     <rdf:type rdf:resource="#InformationSearchAndRetrieval"/>
  </rdf:Description>
  <rdf:Description rdf:about="#Source">
     <rdfs:label
rdf:datatype="http://www.w3.org/2001/XMLSchema#string">Source</rdfs:label>
     <rdf:type rdf:resource="http://www.w3.org/2002/07/owl#Class"/>
  </rdf:Description>
</rdf:RDF>
```

Fig. 3. Example of RDF statements

3.2 Document Annotation

Document annotation is the most important task for representing the semantic meaning of digital collections. Annotation can be considered as the process of populating ontology with instance or literals. It can be done either in a manual or automatic fashion. We proposed a semi automatic approach by employing the GATE (General Architecture for Text Engineering) engine toolkit [8]. The ACM topic hierarchy ontology developed contain all the concepts related to the ACM classification. We decided to represent every topic as instances of a generic class topic. The decision is entirely due to implementation issue which makes it possible to annotate related terms with suitable instances. Each of the topic instances is associated with related terms that represent the topic. These terms were extracted from mining the ACM digital library by extracting keywords defined in articles of the specific category. We assumed that the articles in the ACM digital library were assigned with the correct topic and the associate keywords defined by authors are best to represent the topic. At this point we only annotate the abstract of each thesis. Apart from populating the ACM topic hierarchy, terms extracted from the abstract which are related to other ontologies such as the Geo ontology will also be extracted and populated. Fig. 4 illustrates the proposed approach.

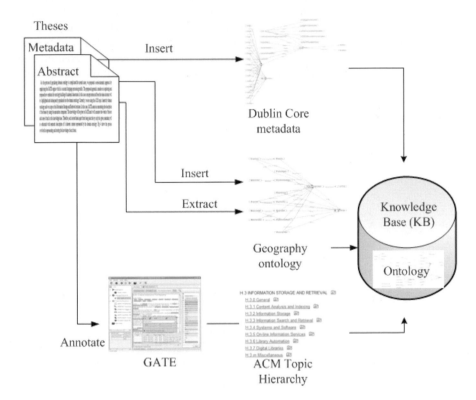

Fig. 4. Document Annotation

The annotation of terms or concepts which relate to the standard ontology is rather a straight forward process whereby if such concepts are found matched with the concepts in the ontology then a new triplet will be added to the knowledge base. However, as users are still favoured keyword search which results a ranked list of documents, few consideration is required. We decided to implement an adaptation of a vector space model to support a so-called ontology-based information retrieval. The model is quite similar to the one that was proposed in [9]. In this case annotation of the terms in the abstract (and may be the whole documents) is not stored as triplets as previously described but instead are represented as a vector space model. This would allow weighting and ranking of retrieved documents. Text in the abstract will undergo the normal indexing process such as tokenisation, frequency calculation and weight assignment.

Terms in the documents are then annotated with concept instances from the existing knowledge base by creating instances of the Annotation Class. Annotation Class is purposely created to facilitate the semantic search. It is a part of the ontology which stored the annotated documents separately in a different database. Annotation Class will link between the knowledge base and the index upon the executed query. Annotation class has two properties which are instance and document, where the concepts and documents are related together. Whenever the label of an instance in the ontology is found, an annotation is created between the instance and the document. It then will be stored in the annotation class under the property of term (instance), concept and document by which are related to each other. Thus, whenever a user sent a search query, the searching will be run upon the ontology first. Whenever the satisfied query found in the domain ontology, it then will be referred to the annotation class and then the documents will be retrieved and presented to the user.

3.3 Semantic Search and Processing

The overall semantic search and processing is as illustrated in Fig. 5.

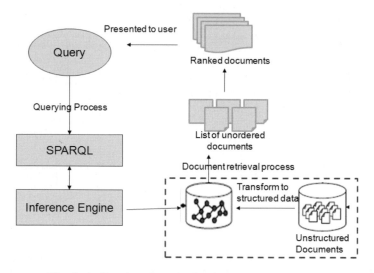

Fig. 5. An Ontology Based Information Retrieval Process

The query process takes an input as a user search request. The search request can be either a list of keywords or a complex natural language query. The search request will be first analysed by a query parser and will be parsed into SPARQL. These queries are then sent to the inference engine which will return a set of RDF (Resource Description Framework) triples containing the related concepts or instances in the knowledge base. For example a query on "digital library technology" will first be transformed into a SPARQL query which will be then submitted to the inference engine. The inference engine will find instances and other "related instances" concerning the submitted terms. The retrieval process will then retrieved all documents which have been annotated with all the instances related to the query terms and subsequently ranked them.

The weighting scheme is based on the modified TFIDF as follows:

$$TFIDF = \frac{freq_{ij}}{max_e freq_{ej}} \times \log \frac{N}{n_i}$$

where $freq_{ij}$ is the total number of instance i in document j; $max_e freq_{ej}$ is the maximum number of any instance e in document j; N is the total number of annotated documents collection and n_i is the total number of documents that contained instance i. The similarity measures is based on the standard cosine measures.

The semantic search facility also allow sophisticated query such as *"Find the supervisor of Arifah Alhadi and the title of her thesis"*. Such a query can be represented as a SPARQL statement as follows:

```
SELECT ?student ?thesis ?academic ?studentname ?svname ?title
WHERE {?student rdf:type :Student.
       ?student rdfs:label ?studentname.
       FILTER(REGEX(?studentname,"Arifah"))
              ?academic rdf:type :Academic.
              ?academic :hasFirstNameAc ?svname.
              ?thesis rdf:type :Thesis.
              ?thesis :supervisedBy ?academic.
              ?thesis :hasTitle ?title}
```

The result for the query will return the following tuples which shows that student001, who is Arifah Alhadi is supervised by supervisor067 who is Shahrul Azman and return the title of the thesis.

student	thesis	academic	svname	title
student001	thesis008	academic067	"Shahrul Azman"	"Semantic Document Modelling"

4   Conclusion

This paper has presented our on-going work in implementing an ontology driven to digital library. Ontology proof to be a powerful tool for supporting complex querying and semantic search of digital library collections. However, to manage a knowledge rich digital collections is difficult for most users. The inherent idea of the proposed approach in this paper is to engaged user in implementing a digital library by inserting, updating and populating the knowledge bases.

A semantic retrieval framework is also proposed in this paper which aims to improve the precision of search results by concentrating on the context of concepts. Document annotation is represented as an extension ontology and stored in a relational database. The triple searching and semantic matching is performed by the inference engine and results are passed to the ranker to sort them according to their relevancy to user's queries. In the current framework we focused on academic theses. Our near future is currently focusing on the aspect of document annotation. Current annotation is purely based on exact match by referring to the labels of each instances stored in the knowledge base. We look into the possibility of doing document annotation by means inexact match or contextual term matching. Other current research work is on evaluating the effectiveness of the proposed instance-based weighting scheme. We are in the process of compiling decent number of test documents in order for the evaluation to be carried out.

Acknowledgments. We would like to thank Universiti Kebangsaan Malaysia for supporting this research project.

References

1. Warren, P., Thurlow, I., Alsmeyer, D.: Applying Semantic Technology in Digital Library: a Case Study. Library Management 26(4/5), 196–205 (2005)
2. Yeh, C.L.: Development of an Ontology-Based Portal for Digital Archive Services. In: Presented in International Conference on Digital Archive Technologies (2002)
3. Jung, H.M., Lee, M., Sung, W.K., Park, D.I.: Semantic Web-Based Services for Supporting Voluntary Collaboration Among Researchers using an Information Dissemination Platform. Data Science Journal 6, S241–S249 (2007)
4. Bloehdorn, S., Cimiano, P., Duke, A., Haase, P., Heizmann, J., Thurlow, I., Völker, J.: Ontology-Based Question Answering for Digital Libraries. In: Kovács, L., Fuhr, N., Meghini, C. (eds.) ECDL 2007. LNCS, vol. 4675, pp. 14–25. Springer, Heidelberg (2007)
5. Cimiano, P., Volker, J.: Text2onto-a framework for ontology learning anda data driven change discovery. In: Montoyo, A., Muñoz, R., Métais, E. (eds.) NLDB 2005. LNCS, vol. 3513, pp. 227–238. Springer, Heidelberg (2005)
6. Domingue, J., Motta, E., Shum, S.B., Vargas-Vera, M., Kalfoglou, Y., Farnes, N.: Supporting Ontology Driven Document Enrichment within Communities of Practice. In: Proceedings of the 1st International Conference on Knowledge Capture, pp. 30–37. ACM Press, New York (2001)
7. Cunningham, H.: GATE, a general architecture for text engineering. Computers and Humanities 36(2), 223–254 (2002)
8. Gaizauskas, R., Cunningham, H., Wilks, Y., Rodgers, P., Humphreys, K.: GATE: An Environment to Support Research and Development in Natural Language Engineering. In: Proceedings of the 8th IEEE International Conference on Tools with Artificial Intelligence, pp. 58–66. IEEE Press, New York (1996)
9. Castells, P., Fernandez, M., Vallet, D.: An Adaptation of the Vector Space Model for Ontology-Based Information Retrieval. IEEE Trans. on Knowledge and Data Engineering 19(2), 261–272 (2007)

Revisiting Rocchio's Relevance Feedback Algorithm for Probabilistic Models

Zheng Ye[1,2], Ben He[2], Xiangji Huang[2], and Hongfei Lin[1]

[1] Department of Computer Science and Engineering, Dalian University of Technology
Dalian, Liaoning, 116023, China
[2] Information Retrieval and Knowledge Managment Lab,
York University, Toronto, Canada
zye@mail.dlut.edu.cn, {benhe,jhuang}@yorku.ca, hflin@dlut.edu.cn

Abstract. Rocchio's relevance feedback method enhances the retrieval performance of the classical vector space model. However, its application to the probabilistic models is not adequately explored. In this paper, we revisit Rocchio's algorithm by proposing to integrate this classical feedback method into the divergence from randomness (DFR) probabilistic framework for pseudo relevance feedback (PRF). Such an integration is denoted by RocDFR in this paper. In addition, we further improve RocDFR's robustness by proposing a quality-biased feedback method, called QRocDFR. Extensive experiments on standard TREC test collections show that our proposed RocDFR and QRocDFR methods significantly outperform the relevance model (RM3), which is a representative feedback model in the language modeling framework. Moreover, the QRocDFR method considerably improves the robustness of RocDFR's retrieval performance with respect to the size of feedback document set.

Keywords: Information Retrieval, Probability Model, Relevance Feedback, DFR, QRocDFR.

1 Introduction

In information retrieval (IR), relevance feedback (RF) can improve query representation by taking feedback information into account. A classical relevance feedback algorithm was proposed by Rocchio in 1971 [14] for the SMART retrieval system [14]. It takes a set of documents as the feedback set. Unique terms in this set are ranked in descending order of TF-IDF weights. A number of top-ranked candidate terms are then added to the original query, and finally, documents are returned for the expanded query. Better performance can always be expected in many IR task.

Many other relevance feedback techniques and algorithms have been developed, mostly derived from Rocchio's algorithm [1,3,12,13]. Feedback documents can be obtained by many possible means. In general, there are explicit evidence, such as the labeled relevant documents from real users, or implicit evidence, such as the click-through data. Obtaining the feedback information involves extra efforts, e.g. real user relevance judgment, and is usually expensive. For every

P.-J. Cheng et al. (Eds.): AIRS 2010, LNCS 6458, pp. 151–161, 2010.

given query, the corresponding feedback information is not necessarily available. An alternate solution is *query expansion* (QE), also called *pseudo-relevance feedback* (PRF), which uses the top-ranked documents in the initial retrieval for the feedback [5]. Its basic idea is to extract expansion terms from the top-ranked documents to formulate a new query for a second round retrieval.

Despite the marked improvement brought by Rocchio's relevance feedback algorithm (RocRF), the overall retrieval performance of RocRF over the vector space model (VSM) [15] is still not satisfying enough as shown in [16]. In particular, with the recent development of feedback methods [7,16], within the language modeling framework [11], such a combination of RocRF with VSM can no longer catch up with the state-of-the-art methods. In [8], Lv *et al.* systematically compare five state-of-the-art approaches for estimating query language models in ad-hoc retrieval, in which an instantiation of the relevance model [7], called *RM3*, not only yields effective retrieval performance in both precision and recall metric, but also performs robustly with different feedback document set sizes.

The aim of this paper is to investigate ways to improve PRF for probabilistic models. Our main contributions are as follows. First, we propose a new PRF paradigm, called RocDFR, by revisiting and adopting the classical Rocchio's relevance feedback framework within a divergence from randomness (DFR) probabilistic framework [1]. Second, we further enhance the robustness of RocDFR by introducing a quality-biased feedback method, called QRocDFR. Finally, extensive experiments also show that the retrieval performance of our proposed RocDFR and QRocDFR significantly outperform the state-of-the-art relevance model within the language modeling framework.

The remainder of this paper is organized as follows. Section 2 surveys previous work on PRF. Section 3 introduces our proposed PRF method adapted for the DFR framework. Section 4 describe our experimental methodology, and Section 5 reports the experimental results and provides the related discussion. Finally, Section 6 concludes on the work and suggested future research directions.

2 Related Work

2.1 Rocchio's Relevance Feedback Method

Rocchio's algorithm [14] is a classic framework for implementing (pseudo) relevance feedback via improving the query representation. It models a way of incorporating (pseudo) relevance feedback information into the vector space model (VSM) in IR. In case of pseudo relevance feedback, Rocchio's method (RocRF) has the following steps:

1. All documents are ranked for the given query using a particular Information Retrieval model, for example the vector space model [15]. This step is called *first-pass retrieval*. The R highest ranked documents are identified as the pseudo relevance set D_R.

2. An expansion weight $w(t, D_R)$ is assigned to each term appearing in the set of the R highest ranked documents. In general, $w(t, D_R)$ is the mean of the weights provided by the IR model, for example the TF-IDF weights [15], computed over the set of the R highest ranked documents.
3. The vector of query terms weight is finally modified by taking a linear combination of the initial query term weights with the expansion weight $w(t, D_R)$ as follows:

$$Q_1 = \alpha * Q_0 + \beta * \sum_{r \in D_R} \frac{r}{R} \tag{1}$$

where Q_0 and Q_1 represent the original and first iteration query vectors, D_R is the set of pseudo relevance documents, r is the expansion term weight vector, and α and β are tuning constants controlling how much we rely on the original query and the feedback information. In practice, we can always fix α at 1, and only study β in order to get better performance.

2.2   The DFR Probabilistic Framework

Divergence from Randomness (DFR) is a componential framework that measures the relevance of documents following the probabilistic paradigm [1]. In the DFR framework, the weight of a document d for a given query term t is given by:

$$w(d, t) = qtw(t) \cdot IG \cdot (-log_2 Prob(tf)) \tag{2}$$

where IG is the information gain, which is given by a conditional probability of success of encountering a further token of a given word in a given document on the basis of the statistics on the retrieved set. *Prob(tf)* is the probability of observing the document d given *tf* occurrences of the query term t. $-log_2 Prob(tf)$ measures the amount of information that term t carries in d. *qtw* is the query term weight component. Similarly to the query model in language modeling [11], *qtw* measures the importance of individual query terms. In the DFR framework, the query term weight is given by:

$$qtw(t) = \frac{qtf(t)}{qtf_{max}} \tag{3}$$

where *qtf(t)* is the query term frequency of t, namely the number of occurrences of t in the query. qtf_{max} is the maximum query term frequency in the query. For example, if all query terms appear only once in the query, which is usually the case for short queries, qtf_{max} is 1 and *qtw(t)* is also 1 for each query term. When PRF is applied, *qtw(t)* is updated according to each query term's importance in the pseudo relevance documents, so that informative query terms can be differentiated from the non-informative ones.

The other two components, namely information gain (IG) and information amount $(-log_2 Prob(tf))$, can be approximated by different statistics such as Poisson distribution and Bose-Einstein statistics, etc. [1]. In this paper, we apply the DPH instantiation of the DFR framework, which is based on the hyper-geometric approximation of the term distribution [2,6]. Using the DPH model, the relevance score of a document d for a query Q can be found in [2]. It is of note that no parameter tuning is required to optimize DPH, and we can rather focus on studying PRF.

The DFR framework provides a componential paradigm to which relevance feedback methods can be easily embedded. In the next section, we describe our method of combining the classical Rocchio's relevance feedback method with the DFR framework.

3   Applying RocRF for DFR Models

In this section, we first demonstrate how to employ the Rocchio's algorithm (RocRF) within the DFR probabilistic framework. The resulting feedback method is denoted by RocDFR. Next, We propose a quality-biased feedback method to enhance the robustness of RocDFR.

3.1   Adopting RocRF for DFR

We propose to integrate Rocchio's relevance feedback (RocRF) method into the divergence from randomness (DFR) probabilistic weighting framework. The proposed method updates the query term weight component of the DFR framework by considering an expansion term's importance in the pseudo relevance set. Our proposed method, called *RocDFR*, has the follows steps:

1. For a given query, performs the first-pass retrieval and considers the R highest ranked documents as the pseudo feedback set D_R. This is the same as step 1 of RocRF described in Section 2.1.
2. Assigns an expansion weight $w(t, D_R)$ to each unique term t in D_R, where $w(t, D_R) = \sum_{d_R \in D_R} w(t, d_R)/R$ is the mean of the expansion weights in each individual feedback document d_R. Unlike step 2 of RocRF in Section 2.1, we apply the document ranking scores from the first-pass retrieval to compute the expansion weight $w(t, d_R)$.
3. Finally, the T most weighted expansion terms are added to the query. In particular, the query term weight vector is updated using Equation 1.

Above we have proposed a standard deployment of the classical RocRF in the DFR probabilistic framework. One of the obstacles that prevents RocRF's from its application to probabilistic models is the robustness problem. The retrieval performance of RocDFR could be highly sensitive to its parameters, in particular the size of the pseudo relevance set. In the next section, we propose a quality-biased feedback method that aims to improve the robustness of RocDFR.

3.2   Quality-Biased PRF

The RocDFR method is simple and computationally efficient, and is usually effective when its parameters are properly optimized, as shown later in our experiments. However, as RocDFR treats each feedback document equally, regardless

of their quality, its retrieval performance is likely to be sensitive to the size of
the pseudo feedback document set. In particular, as shown in our experiments
in Section 5.2, when the feedback document set size is very large, the retrieval
performance is seriously degraded by the low-quality feedback documents on
some test collections. To this end, we propose a quality-biased pseudo relevance
feedback (PRF) method, denoted by QRocDFR, to promote expansion terms in
the high-quality documents, and penalize those in the low-quality documents.

In our proposed QRocDFR method, a quality-biased factor is introduced to
the query term weight updating formula (i.e. Equation 1) as follows:

$$Q_1 = \alpha * Q_0 + \beta * \sum_{r \in R} \frac{r * q(d_r)}{R} \tag{4}$$

where $q(d_r)$ is the quality score of feedback document d_r in the R highest ranked
documents in the first-pass retrieval. The document quality score is given by the
sum of the expansion weight of the original query as $q(d_r) = \sum_{t \in Q} w(t, d_r)$.

In practice, our proposed QRocDFR method is very flexible since the weight
of each feedback document can be determined in different ways. If a uniform
quality score is assigned to all feedback documents, RocDFR can be viewed as
a special case of QRocDFR. In this paper, we choose to infer the document
quality by the expansion weight of the original query terms in the document.
The rationale behind our choice of document quality score is that a high-quality
feedback document is highly related to the query topic, and hence likely to yield
the original query terms. Therefore, our document quality score is given by the
sum of the expansion weight of the original query as $q(d_r) = \sum_{t \in Q} w(t, d_r)$.

4   Experimental Setup

4.1   Test Collections and Evaluation

In this section, we describe three representative test collections used in our experiments: disk4&5 (no CR), WT10G, and GOV2. These three collections are
different in both size and genre. The TREC tasks and topic numbers associated
with each collection are presented in Table 1.

Table 1. The TREC tasks and topic numbers associated with each collection

Collection	Task	Queries	Docs
disk4&5	2004, Robust	301-450	528,155
WT10G	TREC9, 10, Web ad-hoc	451-550	1,692,096
GOV2	TREC04-06, Web ad-hoc	701-850	25,178,548

In all our experiments[1], we only use the *title field* of the TREC queries for
retrieval. In the process of indexing and querying, each term is stemmed using Porter's English stemmer, and standard stopwords are removed. The MAP

---

[1] The experiments are conducted with an in-house integration of Terrier 3.0[10] and
Lucene (http://lucene.apache.org/)

(Mean Average Precision) performance measure for top 1000 documents is used as evaluation metric.

4.2 Baseline Models and Parameter Training

In order to evaluate the performance of our proposed methods, the baseline used is DFR-RF, the DFR relevance feedback method [1] implemented in the Terrier retrieval platform [9]. The DFR-RF method considers the R highest ranked documents as the pseudo feedback document set D_R. Differently from RocDFR, DFR-RF views the R feedback documents as a whole bag of words, and measures the divergence of an expansion term's distribution in D_R from its distribution in the entire document collection. As shown by previous experiments, the DFR-RF method's effectiveness is highly sensitive to the feedback document set size R [6]. Thus, we expect our proposed methods to outperform DFR-RF in terms of both effectiveness and robustness.

In addition, we also compare our proposed methods with relevance model [7], which is a representative and state-of-the-art approach for estimating query language models within language modeling framework[8]. Relevance models do not explicitly model the relevant or pseudo-relevant document. Instead,they model a more generalized notion of relevance R. The formula of RM1 is:

$$p(w|R) \propto \sum_{\theta_D} p(w|\theta_D)p(\theta_D)P(Q|\theta_D) \tag{5}$$

The relevance model $p(w|R)$ is often used to estimate the feedback model θ_F, and then interpolated with the original query model θ_Q in order to improve its estimation. The interpolated version of relevance model is called RM3.

In order to find the optimal parameter setting for fair comparisons, we use the training method in [4] for both the baseline and our proposed approach. In particular, first, for the smoothing parameter μ in LM with Dirichlet prior, we sweep over values from 300 to 1500 with an interval of 50. Second, for the linear combination parameter β of (Q)RocDFR, and the interpolation parameter α of RM3, we sweep over values in the range of $(0.0, 0.1, \ldots, 1.0)$. For the number of expansion terms, we sweep over values in $(10, 20, 30, 40, 50)$. To evaluate the baseline and our proposed approach, we use 2-fold cross-validation, in which the TREC queries are partitioned by the parity of queries number on each collection. Then, the parameters learned on the training set are applied to the test set for evaluation purpose.

5   Experimental Results and Analyses

5.1   Performance of Basic Retrieval Models

Table 2 presents the results of the basic retrieval models. In genereal, LM slightly outperforms DPH on all the test collections. However, there is no signicant difference observed, according to the Wilcoxon matched-pairs signed-ranks test at

Table 2. Performance of basic retrieval models

Basic Models	disk4&5	WT10G	GOV2
DPH	0.2178	0.1961	0.2994
LM	0.2254	0.2077	0.3040

the 0.05 level. It is of note that the results from LM are obtained under optimal parameter, while DPH is a parameter-free model. In this sense, DPH is still a good basic retrieval model. In addition, it is fair to make cross-comparison of different PRF methods in language modeling framework and the DFR framework respectively, since the basic retrieval models are comparable.

5.2   Comparison of the PRF Methods

Tables 3, 4 & 5 present the comparisons of the PRF methods over different numbers of feedback documents. A star and a "+" indicate a statistically significant improvement over the baselines of DFR-RF and RM3 respectively, according to the Wilcoxon matched-pairs signed-ranks test at the 0.05 level.

Generally, as we can see from Tables 3 4 5, QRocDFR is at lease comparable with DFR-RF and RM3 on all the test collections. In some cases, QRocDFR

Table 3. Comparison of different PRF methods On the *disk4&5* collection. The values in the parentheses are the improvements over DFR-RF and RM3.

$|D_f|$	DFR-RF	RM3	RocDFR	QRocDFR
3	0.2486	0.2517	0.2476 (-%0.4, -1.6%)	0.2484 (0%, -1.3%)
5	0.2511	0.2525	0.2511 (0%, -0.5%)	0.2513 (0.1%, 0.46%)
10	0.2552	0.2534	0.2641^{*+} (3.37%, 4.05%)	0.2556 (0.16%, 0.86%)
15	0.2605	0.2522	0.2632^{+} (1.04%, 4.36%)	0.2583 (- 0.84%, 2.42%)
20	0.2506	0.2523	0.2615^{*+} (4.35%, 3.64%)	0.2612^{*+} (4.23%, 3.52%)
30	0.2460	0.2506	0.2531 (2.89%, 1%)	0.2627^{*+} (6.79%, 4.83%)
50	0.2346	0.2495	0.2466^{*} (5.12%, -1.16%)	0.2598^{*+} (10.7%, 4.13%)

Table 4. Comparison of different PRF methods on the WT10G collection. The values in the parentheses are the improvements over DFR-RF and RM3.

$|D_f|$	DFR-RF	RM3	RocDFR	QRocDFR
3	0.2136	0.2215	0.2336^{*+} (9.36%, 5.46%)	0.2348^{*+} (9.83%, 6.00%)
5	0.2085	0.2185	0.2248 (1.53%, 2.88%)	0.2329^{*+} (11.7%, 6.59%)
10	0.2067	0.2169	0.2053 (-0.67%, -5.35%)	0.2337^{*+} (12.67%, 7.38%)
15	0.1959	0.2156	0.2113^{*} (7.86%, -1.99%)	0.2278^{*+} (16.28%, 5.66%)
20	0.1941	0.2153	0.2091^{*} (7.73%, -2.88%)	0.2285^{*+} (17.72%, 6.13%)
30	0.1945	0.2167	0.2015^{*} (8.68%, -7.01%)	0.2260^{*+} (17.46%, 4.29%)
50	0.1922	0.2164	0.1985^{*} (3.28%, -8.27%)	0.2196^{*} (14.25%, 1.15%)

Table 5. Comparison of different PRF methods on the GOV2 collection. The values in the parentheses are the improvements over DFR-RF and RM3.

$|D_f|$	DFR-RF	RM3	RocDFR	QRocDFR
3	0.3426	0.3287	$0.3354(-2.13\%, 2.00\%)$	$0.3494^+(2.80\%, 6.29\%)$
5	0.3454	0.3262	$0.3441(-0.32\%, 5.55\%)$	$0.3496^+(1.21\%, 7.17\%)$
10	0.3327	0.3333	$0.3440^{*+}(3.40\%, 3.21\%)$	$0.3562^{*+}(5.08\%, 4.89\%)$
15	0.3323	0.3330	$0.3463^{*+}(4.21\%, 3.99\%)$	$0.3592^{*+}(8.09\%, 7.87)$
20	0.3264	0.3331	$0.3462^{*+}(6.07\%, 3.93\%)$	$0.3576^{*+}(9.56\%, 7.36\%)$
30	0.3289	0.3328	$0.3405^*(3.53\%, 2.31\%)$	$0.3571^{*+}(8.42\%, 7.15\%)$
50	0.3211	0.3322	$0.3332^*(3.77\%, 0.30\%)$	$0.3432^*(6.88\%, 3.31\%)$

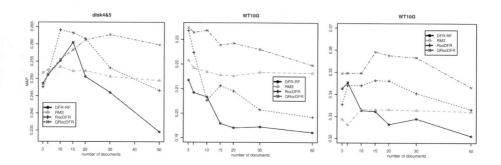

Fig. 1. Robustness of the PRF methods over the number of feedback documents

significantly outperforms both DFR-RF and RM3, especially when a larger number of documents are used for PRF. In addition, QRocDFR and RM3 are more robust with respect to the parameter R, compared with DFR-RF and RocDFR. This is because both QRocDFR and RM3 take into account the quality of the feedback documents in some ways. When low-quality documents are used for PRF, it is likely that noisy terms will be introduced into the query such that the IR performance can be decreased.

A more clear picture of the robustness is depicted in Figure 1. While the performance of RM3 is the most robust on all the three collection, QRocDFR achieves better performance than RM3 does in terms of the MAP measure. It is also of note that when a larger number of documents are used for feedback, QRocDFR still achieves relatively good performance. In addition, on the GOV2 collection, we can see that DFR-RF and RocDFR perform stably over parameter R, although DFR-RF and RocDFR view each document the same. This is probably because most of the top 50 documents are positive for PRF. On WT10G and disk4&5, when R approaches 50, the MAP values of both DFR-RF and RocDFR drop dramatically. In the contrast, QRocDFR and RM3 remain stably to some extent. It indicates that the quality of the feedback documents is importance in the process of PRF.

5.3   Influence of the Control Parameter β

Recall that we incorporate the feedback information to derive a better representation of the query as shown in Equation (4). How much we rely on the feedback information is controlled by the parameter β. In our preliminary experiments, we found that the control parameter β in Equation (4) plays an important role in obtaining good performance. In this section, we empirically study the influence of this parameter on all the test collections. In particular, Figure 2 depicts its influence over different numbers of feedback documents. In this set of experiments, we use 50 terms to expand the original query since QRocDFR archives very good performance under this setting generally. The MAP at $\beta = 0$ is actually the baseline of DPH without query expansion. It is of note that when β takes very large value, it approaches the performance resulting from using only the feedback information.

As we can see from Figure 2, in general, the IR performance can always be boosted when the feedback documents are used to expand the original query. Although the setting of β can affect the retrieval performance significantly, it is always safe to set α to a value around 1 on all our test collections. Similar results can be observed over other numbers of feedback documents, which are not presented as the problem of space limitation.

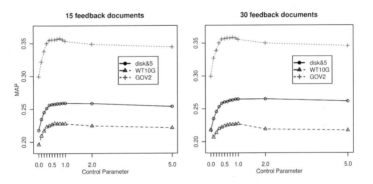

Fig. 2. Influence of the control parameter β

6   Conclusions and Future Work

In this paper, we have revisited the Rocchio's relevance feedback method and integrated it into the divergence from randomness (DFR) probabilistic retrieval models. Moreover, we have proposed a quality-biased feedback method, called QRocDFR, which takes into account the quality of the feedback document. Extensive experiments on three representative TREC test collections show that QRocDFR is not only effective, but also robust with respect to the number of feedback documents. To some extent, we have shown that the classical Rocchio's relevance feedback method can be successfully applied to probabilistic models, and the resulting retrieval performance is at lease as good as those in the existing literature of pseudo relevance feedback methods.

In the future, we plan to study how to automatically determine the control parameter β. Although it is often relatively safe to set β to a value around 1, an automatic way to optimizing β for each individual query sounds more interesting. We also plan to use machine learning techniques to estimate the quality of the feedback documents.

Acknowledgments

This research is jointly supported by NSERC of Canada, the Early Researcher/Premier's Research Excellence Award, the Natural Science Foundation of China (No.60673039 and 60973068) , the National High Tech Research and Development Plan of China (No.2006AA01Z151), National Social Science Foundation of China (No.08BTQ025), the Project Sponsored by the Scientific Research Foundation for the Returned Overseas Chinese Scholars, State Education Ministry and The Research Fund for the Doctoral Program of Higher Education (No.20090041110002).

References

1. Amati, G.: Probabilistic models for information retrieval based on divergence from randomness. Ph.D. thesis, Department of Computing Science, University of Glasgow (2003)
2. Amati, G., Ambrosi, E., Bianchi, M., Gaibisso, C., Gambosi, G.: FUB, IASI-CNR and University of Tor Vergata at TREC 2007 blog track. In: Voorhees, E.M., Buckland, L.P. (eds.) TREC. National Institute of Standards and Technology (NIST), vol. Special Publication 500–274 (2007)
3. Carpineto, C., de Mori, R., Romano, G., Bigi, B.: An information-theoretic approach to automatic query expansion. ACM Trans. Inf. Syst. 19(1), 1–27 (2001)
4. Diaz, F., Metzler, D.: Improving the estimation of relevance models using large external corpora. In: Efthimiadis, E.N., Dumais, S.T., Hawking, D., Järvelin, K. (eds.) SIGIR, pp. 154–161. ACM, New York (2006)
5. He, B.: Query expansion models. In: Encyclopedia of Database Systems, pp. 2257–2260 (2009)
6. He, B., Macdonald, C., Ounis, I., Peng, J., Santos, R.L.T.: University of glasgow at trec 2008: Experiments in blog, enterprise, and relevance feedback tracks with terrier. In: Voorhees, E.M., Buckland, L.P. (eds.) TREC. National Institute of Standards and Technology (NIST), Special Publication 500–277 (2008)
7. Lavrenko, V., Croft, W.B.: Relevance-based language models. In: Croft, W.B., Harper, D.J., Kraft, D.H., Zobel, J. (eds.) SIGIR, pp. 120–127. ACM, New York (2001)
8. Lv, Y., Zhai, C.: A comparative study of methods for estimating query language models with pseudo feedback. In: CIKM, pp. 1895–1898 (2009)
9. Ounis, I., Amati, G., Plachouras, V., He, B., Macdonald, C., Johnson, D.: Terrier information retrieval platform. In: Losada, D.E., Fernández-Luna, J.M. (eds.) ECIR 2005. LNCS, vol. 3408, pp. 517–519. Springer, Heidelberg (2005)

10. Ounis, I., Amati, G., Plachouras, V., He, B., Macdonald, C., Lioma, C.: Terrier: A high performance and scalable information retrieval platform. In: Proceedings of ACM SIGIR 2006 Workshop on Open Source Information Retrieval, OSIR 2006 (2006)
11. Ponte, J.M., Croft, W.B.: A language modeling approach to information retrieval. In: SIGIR, pp. 275–281. ACM, New York (1998)
12. Robertson, S.E.: On term selection for query expansion. Journal of Documentation 46(4), 359–364 (1990)
13. Robertson, S.E., Walker, S., Hancock-Beaulieu, M., Gatford, M., Payne, A.: Okapi at TREC-4. In: TREC, pp. 73–97 (1995)
14. Rocchio, J.: Relevance feedback in information retrieval, pp. 313–323. Prentice-Hall, Englewood Cliffs (1971)
15. Salton, G., Buckley, C.: Improving retrieval performance by relevance feedback. Journal of the American Society for Information Science 41, 288–297 (1990)
16. Zhai, C., Lafferty, J.D.: Model-based feedback in the language modeling approach to information retrieval. In: CIKM, pp. 403–410 (2001)

When Two Is Better Than One: A Study of Ranking Paradigms and Their Integrations for Subtopic Retrieval

Teerapong Leelanupab, Guido Zuccon, and Joemon M. Jose

School of Computing Science, University of Glasgow
Glasgow, G12 8RZ, United Kingdom
{kimm,guido,jj}@dcs.gla.ac.uk

Abstract. In this paper, we consider the problem of document ranking in a non-traditional retrieval task, called *subtopic retrieval*. This task involves promoting relevant documents that cover many subtopics of a query at early ranks, providing thus diversity within the ranking. In the past years, several approaches have been proposed to diversify retrieval results. These approaches can be classified into two main paradigms, depending upon how the ranks of documents are revised for promoting diversity. In the first approach subtopic diversification is achieved implicitly, by choosing documents that are different from each other, while in the second approach this is done explicitly, by estimating the subtopics covered by documents. Within this context, we compare methods belonging to the two paradigms. Furthermore, we investigate possible strategies for integrating the two paradigms with the aim of formulating a new ranking method for subtopic retrieval. We conduct a number of experiments to empirically validate and contrast the state-of-the-art approaches as well as instantiations of our integration approach. The results show that the integration approach outperforms state-of-the-art strategies with respect to a number of measures.

Keywords: Subtopic Retrieval, Subtopic Awareness, Interdependence Document Relevance, Diversity.

1 Introduction

Presenting redundant information in a ranking is undesirable as users have to endure examining the same information repeatedly. A document might be non-relevant if the user has already examined other documents containing similar information [3]. The utility of a document thus depends upon which documents have been ranked in previous positions. In some contexts the user requires a broad view of a search topic, for instance because his information need is unclear or vague. In these situations, a retrieval system should provide a document ranking covering several subtopics that the user might be interested in [16].

Although there is a clear need to account for the influence of previously ranked documents, traditional ranking approaches rely on the assumption that the relevance of a document is independent to other documents, e.g. the probability

P.-J. Cheng et al. (Eds.): AIRS 2010, LNCS 6458, pp. 162–172, 2010.
© Springer-Verlag Berlin Heidelberg 2010

ranking principle (PRP) [13], where documents are ranked exclusively according to their probability of being relevant to a query. In real search scenarios, however, the independent relevance assumption often does not hold and consequently ranking approaches that rely on it, such as the PRP, provide a suboptimal document ranking [7].

Many efforts have been devoted to overcome the limitations of the independent relevance assumption in document ranking. In parallel, several approaches have been devised so as to produce a document ranking that covers many different subtopics of the information need. These approaches can be thought of as two faces of the same coin: generally, diversifying a document ranking implies exploiting document dependencies, and vice versa when accounting for document dependencies (at relevance level) diversification can be achieved. Two different patterns can be recognised from the approaches suggested in the literature in order to achieve ranking diversification:

- **Interdependent document relevance paradigm.** When ranking documents, relationships between documents are considered by promoting documents that differ from each other. These approaches maximise, at each rank position, a function that depends upon both relevance estimates and documents relationships. The intuition underlying this is that novelty and diversity are achieved by ranking relevant documents containing information that has not yet been ranked. A similarity function is usually employed to estimate the novelty of a document (the less a document is similar to the ones already ranked, the more it carries novel information). Examples of heuristic or theoretically driven approaches that implement this paradigm are maximal marginal relevance (MMR) [1], which interpolates document relevance and documents relationships; and portfolio theory (PT) [15], which combines relevance estimates and document correlations.
- **Subtopics aware paradigm.** The need of (subtopic) diversity can be achieved by estimating and modelling subtopics and then selecting documents within them. Regardless of document relevance, relationships between documents are employed to estimate subtopics. Many techniques can be applied to discriminate documents with respect to the possible subtopics they cover: examples are clustering [5], classification [9], latent Dirichlet allocation (LDA) [2], and probabilistic latent semantic analysis (PLSA) [8]. Afterwards, result diversification is achieved by interleaving in a ranking the documents belonging to different estimated subtopics. Several criteria can be applied to select documents after the evidence of the estimated subtopics is obtained.

In this paper, we intend to determine which paradigm, and in turns which approach, performs best in the subtopic retrieval task. Furthermore, we investigate whether a new ranking approach can be devised so that we can integrate the merits of the two ranking paradigms, regardless of the choices of the similarity estimation function, the document dependency function, and the subtopic modelling algorithm. The intuition underlying the integration approach is as follows: if subtopics are estimated in a way that do not corresponds to the user's common perception of subtopics, an interdependent document ranking strategy could assist in correctly ranking documents after the subtopic evidences are given. Possible subtopics are thus explicitly modelled and diversity among ranked documents is promoted. To the best of our knowledge, no empirical study has been performed comparing and integrating the two ranking paradigms in the context of subtopic retrieval.

2   Related Work

2.1   Beyond Independent Relevance

In this paper, we examine just two popular examples of ranking approaches for subtopic retrieval based on the interdependent document relevance paradigm, e.g. MMR [1] and PT [15]. Both approaches have a similar underlying assumption, which combines and maximises the estimated document relevance and diversity during ranking process. For instance, MMR method attempts to maximise marginal similarity between documents and query, and dissimilarity between candidate documents and all documents ranked at previous positions. To rank a document at rank $j + 1$, the MMR strategy is characterised by the following ranking function[1]: $\text{argmax}[\lambda S(x_i, q) + (1 - \lambda) \text{avg} D(x_i, x_j)]$, where x_i is a candidate document that has been retrieved by a traditional ranking method but has not been ranked yet; x_j is a document that has been already ranked; and λ is a tuneable parameter that assigns importance to either similarity or novelty/diversity. The function $S(x_i, q)$ is a normalised similarity function used for document retrieval, whereas $D(x_i, x_j)$ is a normalised diversity metric between documents, such as the cosine similarity. For further details of PT approach, we refer to the paper [15].

2.2   Subtopic Aware Paradigm for Diversity

In the following we revise a number of examples belonging to the subtopics aware paradigm. These approaches have an explicitly indication of which subtopics are covered by each document. The underlying intuition is that once the subtopics have been modelled and the documents that cover these subtopics are identified, a ranking strategy can be devised so that it selects documents that belong to different classes of subtopics. Several techniques can be employed to produce or estimate a hypothetical partition of the retrieved documents according to the subtopics they might cover. For example, in [2] Carterette and Chandar use LDA to estimate the presence of subtopics within documents. Alternative techniques that can be employed to this end are PLSA [8] and clustering (e.g. K-mean clustering). In [5] subtopics are estimated from the retrieved documents using clustering: presenting results that belong to different clusters is meant to guarantee the novelty of subtopics in the document ranking. However, information redundancy and document relevance are ignored in the document selection

---

[1] Note that the ranking formula that we report and use in our work is a modification of the formula originally proposed in [1]. However, the behaviour of the approach and the outcome of the ranking process is equivalent in both versions.

process. Regardless of the specific technique employed to estimate subtopics, a document ranking that exploits such explicit evidence can be formulated in various ways. In the following paragraphs we examine two approaches that follow the subtopic aware paradigm by exploiting evidence drawn from clusters of documents. Common to both approaches is the assumption that each cluster contains documents that address the same subtopic, and thus documents can be divided into classes on the basis of the subtopic (or subtopics) they cover.

Interpolated approach. This approach is directly connected with the cluster hypothesis[2], and it prescribes that the relevance estimation of a document should be interpolated with the information obtained by clusters [10]. Formally, the retrieval score of a candidate document x_i is calculated as: $\hat{p}(x_i, q) = \lambda p(x_i, q) + (1 - \lambda) \sum_{c_j \epsilon C} p(c_j, q) p(x_i, c_j)$, where c_j is a cluster of documents in C, i.e. the set of document clusters modelled by topic modelling approaches; λ[3] is a hyperparameter that controls the balance between the probability of relevance and the probability of the document belonging to a cluster. In the context of our paper, we assume that $p(a, b)$ is a similarity function between the objects[4] a and b. In the following we indicate this approach with **Interp(.)**.

Cluster representative approach. This approach aims to cover the whole set of subtopics at early ranks at least with one representative document. For example, in [6] the document ranking is formed by selecting documents from clusters in a round-robin fashion, i.e. assigning an order to the clusters and selecting a representative document cyclically through all clusters. The same approach might be applied to different algorithms that model subtopics, i.e. K-Mean, EM, and DBSCAN clustering, LDA, PLSA, and relevance models. What differentiates each instantiation of the approach is the function used to select cluster representatives. For example, in [6] cluster representatives are selected according to the order in which documents are added to clusters. An alternative approach is suggested by Deselaers et al. [5] where cluster representatives are selected according to their relevance to the query. In our empirical study we opt to investigate Deselaers's solution, that we denote in the following with **Repre$_{PRP}$(.)**.

3 Integration Approach

In the interdependent document relevance paradigm, subtopic coverage is implicitly achieved by considering both document relevance and a measure of similarity/diversity between documents, where the latter measure indicates the dependency of documents. Nevertheless, since there is no explicit knowledge or model of the subtopics contained in the documents, subtopics coverage is hardly

---

[2] Relevant documents tend to be more similar to each other than non-relevant documents [14].

[3] Note that when $\lambda = 0$, the ranking function returns documents within the cluster with highest similarity to the query, i.e. the cluster with higher $p(c_j, q)$.

[4] These can be queries, documents, or clusters.

addressed although it is a main criterion for assessing ranking quality in the subtopic retrieval task.

In the subtopic aware paradigm, subtopics that a document covers are explicitly identified. However, document relevance is commonly ignored and the novelty of a ranking relies exclusively on the quality of the subtopic estimation techniques employed. Furthermore, these techniques might not be able to precisely model subtopics as they are perceived by users. Therefore there might be, in practice, subtopic redundancy within the ranking formed using this paradigm.

In this section we consider whether the two paradigms we have exposed so far can be integrated in order to form a family of new approaches for subtopic retrieval. Additionally, we hypothesise that the subtopic redundancy can be alleviated by measuring dependencies between documents after imprecisely estimating subtopics. To this end, we suggest to exploit the document dependencies when selecting representatives from subtopic classes (e.g. clusters), obtained employing any of the approaches belonging to the subtopic aware paradigm. We do not focus on the retrieval and relevance estimation, but we assume to have a reliable function that is able to provide an initial set of documents with associated estimations of probability of relevance. Thereafter, the set of retrieved documents is partitioned into classes, for example according to clustering or LDA. The assumption at this stage is that a class corresponds to a subtopic of the information need and thus a class contains all the documents that address a common subtopic. When producing a ranking, we impose that each class has to be represented by a document in the ranking at least once. Specifically, we first rank the subtopic classes according to the average relevance of the documents contained in each class. Given a query q and a class c_k, average class relevance is defined as $S_{avg}(c_k, q) = \frac{1}{|I_k|} \sum_{x_i \in I_k} s(x_i, q)$, where I_k is the set of documents belonging to c_k, $X = \{x_1, ..., x_n\}$ is the initial set of retrieved documents and $s(x, q)$ is the estimated relevance of document x with respect to query q. Average class relevance is employed to arrange the subtopic classes in a decreasing order. Thereafter, a round-robin approach that follows the order suggested by average class relevance is used to select individual documents within the subtopic classes.

To select a specific document within each subtopic class, we employ an intralist dependency-based approach, and thus integrate the two different subtopic retrieval paradigms into a common family of approaches. For example, if at this stage a MMR-like function is used, then the following objective function should be maximised:

$$J_{j+1} = J_j \cup \operatorname*{argmax}_{x_{k,n} \in X_k \setminus J_j} \left[\lambda S(x_{k,n}, q) + (1 - \lambda) \operatorname*{avg}_{x_j \in J_j} D(x_{k,n}, x_j) \right] \tag{1}$$

where $X_k = \{x_{k,1}, x_{k,2}, x_{k,3}, ..., x_{k,n}\}$ is the set of retrieved documents belonging to the subtopic class c_k and J is the set of documents that has been already ranked. Of course, other approaches, such as PT, can be used at this stage.

4   Empirical Study

In the following we present the experimental methodology of the empirical study we perform in this paper. The objectives of our empirical investigation are:

1. to compare different state-of-the-art approaches based on the two ranking paradigms presented in Section 2. Specifically, which paradigm delivers the best document ranking for subtopic retrieval?
2. to investigate and validate the integration approach in a high level regardless of particular techniques of ranking paradigms used. Specifically, we aim to answer the question: does considering at the same time interdependent document relevance and subtopic awareness improve performances in the subtopic retrieval task?

In order to answer these questions, we test state-of-the-art approaches belonging to both paradigms and our integration approach on a number of test collections. In particular, we use the ImageCLEF 2009 Photo Retrieval[5] [12], and the TREC ClueWeb 2009 (limited to part B) [4]. A broader empirical investigation, we refer the interested reader to our extended technical report [11], which includes results based on the TREC 6,7,8 interactive collection [16].

Textual information have been indexed using Lemur[6], which served also as platform for developing the ranking approaches using the C++ API. We removed standard stop-words [14] and applied Porter stemming to both documents and queries. Queries are extracted from the titles of the TREC and CLEF topics.

Okapi BM25 has been used to estimate document relevance given a query; these estimates have been directly employed to produce the PRP run in our experiments. The same weighting schema has been used to produce the relevance estimates and the document term vectors that are employed by some of the re-ranking strategies to compute similarity (e.g. in MMR) or correlation (e.g. in PT). This is consistent with previous works [15]. We experiment with several ranking lengths, i.e. 100, 200, 500, and 1000, but in this paper we report results for ranking up to 100 documents long for space matters.

The MMR approach has been instantiated as discussed in Section 2, where we employed the BM25 score as similarity function between document and query, and the opposite of the cosine similarity between documents as a measure of dissimilarity. Furthermore we varied the value of λ in the range $[0,1]$ with steps of 0.1. When testing PT that requires two setting parameters, we explored values of b in the range[7] $[-9, 9]$; we treat the variance of a document as a parameter that is constant with respect to all the documents, similarly to [15]. We experimented with variance values δ^2 ranging from 10^{-9} to 10^{-1}, and selected the ones that achieve the best performances in combination with the values of b through a grid

---

[5] This collection consists of images with associated text captions. We discard the image features, and just consider the text captions.

[6] http://www.lemurproject.org/

[7] Note that when $b = 0$ the ranking of PT is equivalent to the one of PRP.

search of the parameter space. Correlation between documents is computed by the Pearson's correlation between the term vectors representing documents.

Regarding the runs based on the subtopic aware paradigm, we adopt three techniques to model subtopics: K-mean clustering, PLSA and LDA, although alternative strategies may be suitable. For each query, the number of clusters/classes required by the techniques has been set according to the subtopic relevance judgements for that query. When techniques like LDA and PLSA are used, we obtain an indication of the probability that a subtopic is covered by a document. Because in our study we do not consider overlapping classes of subtopics, we assign to each document only one subtopic: i.e. the subtopic that has been estimated as the most likely for that document. After the classes or clusters are formed, documents are ranked according to the approaches we illustrated in Sections 2.2 and 3, specifically:

- **Interp(.)**: selects documents that maximise the interpolation algorithm for cluster-based retrieval;
- **Repre$_{PRP}$(.)** : selects representative documents in the given classes/subtopics with the highest probability of relevance;
- **Integr$_{MMR}$(.)**: selects documents according to MMR, as an example of strategy based on the interdependent document relevance paradigm.

Interp(.) requires to build a vector representing the cluster/class in order to compute $sim(c, q)$, $sim(c, d)$, and the distance to the centre of the cluster/class. To this aim we create cluster's centroid vector: for a cluster c_k the cluster representative vector is expressed by $(\bar{w}_{1,k}, \bar{w}_{2,k}, ..., \bar{w}_{t,k})$, where $\bar{w}_{t,k}$ is the average of the term weights of all the documents within cluster c_k. Cosine similarity is used to evaluate the similarity of clusters against a query and documents.

Repre$_{PRP}$(.) does not require parameter tuning. On the contrary, when instantiating Interp(.) and Integr$_{MMR}$(.), we varied their hyper-parameter in the range [0,1] and select the value that obtained the best performances. The combinations of the subtopic estimation algorithms and the document selection criteria form in total nine experimental instantiations that we tested in our empirical study, such as Interp(K-Mean), Repre$_{PRP}$(PLSA), Integr$_{MMR}$(LDA) etc.

In addition to the use of subtopic estimation techniques, we investigate the situation where subtopic coverage evidence is drawn from the relevance judgements. We assume that a document can cover only one subtopic: although this assumption is limitative (and not true), it is adequate in the context of our study[8]. Documents that have been judged as belonging to only one subtopic are assigned to a specific cluster that represents the subtopic. These documents are then used to construct clusters' centroid vectors in order to represent the clusters. Afterwards, Euclidean distance is used to assign to a cluster those documents that have been judged to cover two or more subtopics, and the cluster representative is updated. The documents that have not been judged are assigned to clusters using the same procedure. Instantiations of the approaches based on

---

[8] Further work will be directed towards a methodology for generating subtopic clusters/classes where this assumption is relaxed.

this subtopic evidence (denoted by "**Ideal Subtopics**") are an indication of the upper bound performances each approach can achieve.

5   Experimental Results

The results obtained in our empirical investigation are reported in Tables 1, 2 for ImageCLEF 2009 and TREC ClueWeb 2009 collections respectively. Results are evaluated using α-NDCG [3], S-recall and S-MRR [16]; regarding the parametrisation of some approaches, we report here only the best results of each ranking strategy with respect to α-NDCG@10. Parameter values are shown underneath the methods. The results obtained employing *Ideal Subtopics* represent the upper bound each technique can achieve. When statistical significant differences (according to t-test, with $p < 0.05$) against MMR and PT are individuated, we report them with $*$ and $\dagger$ respectively.

The results obtained on the ImageCLEF 2009 collection suggest that instantiations of the subtopic aware paradigm outperform instantiations of the interdependent document relevance paradigm, with respect to α-NDCG@10 and

Table 1. Retrieval performances on the *ImageCLEF 2009 (Photo Retrieval)* collection with % of improvement over PRP. Parametric runs are tuned w.r.t. α-NDCG@10. Statistical significances at 0.05 level against MMR, and PT are indicated by $*$ and $\dagger$ respectively.

		Models	α-*NDCG@10*	S-R@10	S-R@20	S-MRR 25%	S-MRR 50%
		PRP	0.4550	0.5330	0.6235	0.7589	0.5221
		MMR	0.4830	**0.6651**	**0.7315**	0.7297	0.5041
		$(\lambda = 0.7)$	(+6.15%)	(+24.80%)	(+17.33%)	(-3.85%)	(-3.44%)
		PT	0.4450*	0.5648*	0.6636*	0.7307	0.4916
		$(b = 4, \delta^2 = 10^{-1})$	(-2.20%)	(+5.97%)	(+6.44%)	(-3.72%)	(-5.84%)
Subtopic Estimation	KMean	**Interp** $(\lambda = 1.0)$	0.4550 (0.00%)	0.5330* (0.00%)	0.6235* (0.00%)	0.7589 (0.00%)	0.5221 (0.00%)
		Repre$_{PRP}$	0.4660 (+2.42%)	0.5701* (+6.97%)	0.6573* (+5.43%)	0.7503 (-1.13%)	0.5173 (-0.92%)
		Integr$_{MMR}$ $(\lambda = 0.9)$	0.4860† (+6.81%)	0.6256† (+17.39%)	0.6910* (+10.83%)	0.7588 (-0.01%)	0.4985 (-4.53%)
	PLSA	**Interp** $(\lambda = 1.0)$	0.4550 (0.00%)	0.5330* (0.00%)	0.6235* (0.00%)	0.7589 (0.00%)	0.5221 (0.00%)
		Repre$_{PRP}$	0.4730 (+3.96%)	0.5766* (+8.19%)	0.6805* (+9.15%)	0.7608 (+0.25%)	0.5361 (+2.69%)
		Integr$_{MMR}$ $(\lambda = 0.9)$	0.4950† (+8.79%)	0.6520† (+22.33%)	0.7179 (+15.14%)	0.7743 (+2.03%)	0.4865 (-6.81%)
	LDA	**Interp** $(\lambda = 1.0)$	0.4550 (0.00%)	0.5330* (0.00%)	0.6235* (0.00%)	0.7589 (0.00%)	0.5221 (0.00%)
		Repre$_{PRP}$	0.4740 (+4.18%)	0.5683* (+6.62%)	0.6637* (+6.45%)	**0.8104***† (+6.79%)	**0.5406** (+3.55%)
		Integr$_{MMR}$ $(\lambda = 0.9)$	**0.5020**† (+10.33%)	0.6236*† (+17.01%)	0.6842* (+9.74%)	0.7973 (+5.06%)	0.5223 (+0.04%)
Ideal Subtopics		**Interp** $(\lambda = 1.0)$	0.4550 (0.00%)	0.5330* (0.00%)	0.6235* (0.00%)	0.7589 (0.00%)	0.5221 (0.00%)
		Repre$_{PRP}$	0.5700*† (+25.27%)	0.7901*† (+48.24%)	0.8066*† (+29.37%)	0.7440 (-1.97%)	0.5544 (+6.18%)
		Integr$_{MMR}$ $(\lambda = 0.9)$	0.6080*† (+33.63%)	0.8066*† (+51.33%)	0.8066*† (+29.37%)	0.8183*† (+7.83%)	0.6241*† (+19.54%)

Table 2. Retrieval performances on the *TREC ClueWeb 2009* collection with % of improvement over PRP. Parametric runs are tuned w.r.t. α-NDCG@10. Statistical significances at 0.05 level against MMR, and PT are indicated by $*$ and $\dagger$ respectively.

Models	α-NDCG@10	S-R@10	S-R@20	S-MRR 25%	S-MRR 50%
PRP	0.0680	0.1606	0.2719	0.1787	0.0953
MMR ($\lambda = 0.7$)	0.1050 (+54.41%)	0.1664 (+3.65%)	0.2451 (-9.86%)	0.1741 (-2.58%)	0.0786 (-17.53%)
PT ($b = -5, \delta^2 = 10^{-4}$)	0.1510 (+122.06%)	0.2676* (+66.64%)	0.3486* (+28.20%)	0.2179 (+21.90%)	0.1264 (+32.69%)
Subtopic Estimation — KMean Interp ($\lambda = 0.2$)	0.1670* (+145.59%)	0.1682† (+4.77%)	0.2331† (-14.27%)	0.3411* (+90.84%)	0.1367 (+43.44%)
Repre$_{PRP}$	0.1030† (+51.47%)	0.1819† (+13.29%)	0.2466† (-9.32%)	0.2077 (+16.21%)	0.1145 (+20.21%)
Integr$_{MMR}$ ($\lambda = 1.0$)	0.12700 (+86.76%)	0.20191 (+25.74%)	0.26424† (-2.82%)	0.29128 (+62.96%)	0.13653 (+43.31%)
PLSA Interp ($\lambda = 0.3$)	0.1670* (+145.59%)	0.1682† (+4.77%)	0.2331† (-14.27%)	0.3411* (+90.84%)	0.1367 (+43.44%)
Repre$_{PRP}$	0.1160 (+70.59%)	0.1876 (+16.81%)	0.2858 (+5.10%)	0.2265 (+26.73%)	0.1120 (+17.55%)
Integr$_{MMR}$ ($\lambda = 1.0$)	0.1440* (+111.76%)	0.2099 (+30.72%)	0.2926 (+7.62%)	0.3140* (+75.69%)	0.1490* (+56.41%)
LDA Interp ($\lambda = 0.2$)	0.1670* (+145.59%)	0.1682† (+4.77%)	0.2331† (-14.27%)	0.3411* (+90.84%)	0.1367 (+43.44%)
Repre$_{PRP}$	0.1130 (+66.18%)	0.2047 (+27.46%)	0.2902 (+6.74%)	0.2134 (+19.40%)	0.0990 (+3.93%)
Integr$_{MMR}$ ($\lambda = 1.0$)	0.1260 (+85.29%)	0.2149 (+33.84%)	0.2741 (+0.81%)	0.2333 (+30.51%)	0.1211 (+27.15%)
Ideal Subtopics Interp ($\lambda = 0.1$)	0.1670* (+145.59%)	0.1682† (+4.77%)	0.2331† (-14.27%)	0.3411* (+90.84%)	0.1367 (+43.44%)
Repre$_{PRP}$	0.2000* (+194.12%)	0.3332* (+107.53%)	0.3872* (+42.42%)	0.2868* (+60.48%)	0.1780* (+86.85%)
Integr$_{MMR}$ ($\lambda = 0.1$)	0.2330* (+242.65%)	0.3376* (+110.23%)	0.3774* (+38.81%)	0.4041*† (+126.09%)	0.1891* (+98.46%)

when subtopics are estimated using LDA. Other subtopic estimation techniques (PLSA and clustering) obtain comparable results. However, the best results overall (at least when considering[9] α-NDCG@10) are obtained by our integration paradigm using LDA for estimating subtopics. Thus integrating the two retrieval paradigms improves performances in the case of ImageCLEF 2009. The results obtained employing evidences derived from the ideal subtopics configuration indicate how much each subtopic aware strategy would perform if subtopics were correctly identified. In this case, the integration approach performs the best.

In Table 2 we report the results from our investigation on TREC ClueWeb 2009. Approaches based on the subtopic aware paradigm only slightly outperform (with respect to α-NDCG@10) approaches based on the interdependent document relevance. In particular, this is evident when the runs obtained by PT are compared against the runs obtained by Interp(.) and when the MMR runs are compared against the Repre$_{PRP}$(.) runs. However, it can be noticed that the performances of the subtopic aware approaches do not highly vary when considering different subtopic estimation techniques. If the ideal subtopic estimation is considered, then the Repre$_{PRP}$(.) approach is shown to outperform instantiations

---

[9] Note that parameters have been tuned according to this measure.

of the other state-of-the-art approaches. However, in this scenario our integration approach outperforms any other method, and gains up to the 16.5% over the $Repre_{PRP}(.)$. The performance difference between the approaches that use the estimated subtopic evidence and the ones that employ the ideal subtopic evidence suggests that subtopic estimation techniques fail to capture subtopics. This might be because of the more noisy nature of the ClueWeb collection with respect to the ImageCLEF collection.

6   Conclusions

The goal of this paper is to empirically compare state-of-the-art methods and an integration approach we propose for subtopic retrieval. Two test collections has been used to this aim. We find that overall approaches derived from the subtopic aware paradigm perform better (and in many cases significantly better) than approaches based on the interdependent document relevance paradigm. Amongst the techniques for estimating subtopics, LDA and PLSA has been shown to provide better evidences than K-mean clustering. However, all the techniques for estimating subtopics fail to some extent to provide high quality evidences in the case of the TREC ClueWeb 2009 collection. This might be due to the noisy nature of the documents contained in the collections (web pages and newswire articles). The integration approach, that combines implicit and explicit approaches for ranking diversification, has been shown to outperform state-of-the-art approaches, in particular when subtopics are directly derived from the relevance judgements. Thus, the integration approach has the capability to improve subtopic retrieval performances when effective topic estimation is deployed. Further investigation will be directed towards the empirical validation of effective topic estimation techniques.

References

1. Carbonell, J., Goldstein, J.: The use of MMR, diversity-based reranking for reordering documents and producing summaries. In: SIGIR 1998, pp. 335–336 (1998)
2. Carterette, B., Chandar, P.: Probabilistic models of ranking novel documents for faceted topic retrieval. In: CIKM 2009, pp. 1287–1296 (2009)
3. Clarke, C.L.A., Kolla, M., Cormack, G.V., Vechtomova, O., Ashkan, A., Büttcher, S., MacKinnon, I.: Novelty and diversity in information retrieval evaluation. In: SIGIR 2008, pp. 659–666 (2008)
4. Clarke, C.L.A., Craswell, N., Soboroff, I.: Overview of the TREC 2009 Web Track. In: Proc. of TREC 2009 (2009)
5. Deselaers, T., Gass, T., Dreuw, P., Ney, H.: Jointly optimising relevance and diversity in image retrieval. In: CIVR 2009, pp. 1–8 (2009)
6. Ferecatu, M., Sahbi, H.: TELECOM ParisTech at ImageCLEFphoto 2008: Bimodal text and image retrieval with diversity enhancement. In: Working Notes for the CLEF 2008 workshop (2008)
7. Gordon, M.D., Lenk, P.: When is the probability ranking principle suboptimal. JASIS 43, 1–14 (1999)

8. Hofmann, T.: Probabilistic latent semantic indexing. In: SIGIR 1999, pp. 50–57 (1999)
9. Huang, J., Kumar, S.R., Zabih, R.: An automatic hierarchical image classification scheme. In: MM 1998, pp. 219–228 (1998)
10. Kurland, O., Lee, L.: Corpus structure, language models, and ad hoc information retrieval. In: SIGIR 2004, pp. 194–201 (2004)
11. Leelanupab, T., Zuccon, G., Jose, J.M.: Technical report: A study of ranking paradigms and their integrations for subtopic retrieval. Technical report, School of Computing Science, University of Glasgow (2010)
12. Paramita, M.L., Sanderson, M., Clough, P.: Developing a test collection to support diversity analysis. In: Proc. of Redundancy, Diversity, and IDR workshop SIGIR 2009, pp. 39–45 (2009)
13. Robertson, S.E.: The probability ranking principle in IR. J. of Doc. 33, 294–304 (1977)
14. van Rijsbergen, C.J.: Information Retrieval, 2nd edn. Butterworth (1979)
15. Wang, J., Zhu, J.: Portfolio theory of information retrieval. In: SIGIR 2009, pp. 115–122 (2009)
16. Zhai, C.X., Cohen, W.W., Lafferty, J.: Beyond independent relevance: methods and evaluation metrics for subtopic retrieval. In: SIGIR 2003, pp. 10–17 (2003)

Connecting Qualitative and Quantitative Analysis of Web Search Process: Analysis Using Search Units

Hitomi Saito[1], Masao Takaku[2], Yuka Egusa[3],
Hitoshi Terai[4], Makiko Miwa[5], and Noriko Kando[6]

[1] Aichi University of Education, 1 Hirosawa, Igaya, Kariya, Aichi 448-8542, Japan
hsaito@auecc.aichi-edu.ac.jp
[2] National Institute for Materials Science, 1-2-1 Sengen, Tsukuba,
Ibaraki 305-0047, Japan
TAKAKU.Masao@nims.go.jp
[3] National Institute for Educational Policy Research, 3-2-2 Kasumigaseki,
Chiyoda-ku, Tokyo 100-8951, Japan
yuka@nier.go.jp
[4] Nagoya University, Furo-cho, Chikusa-ku, Nagoya, 464-8601, Japan
terai@cog.human.nagoya-u.ac.jp
[5] The Open University of Japan, 2-11 Wakaba, Mihama, Chiba, 261-8586, Japan
miwamaki@ouj.ac.jp
[6] National Institute of Informatics, 2-1-2 Hitotsubashi Chiyoda-ku,
Tokyo 101-8430, Japan
kando@nii.ac.jp

Abstract. Our final goal is to understand exploratory searches as four levels of search processes: search task, intent unit, search unit, and link unit. To complete these objectives, we used qualitative data to categorize participants' information needs for search units and quantitatively analyzed whether differences in the information needs of search units influence users' search processes and how task types and groups affect search units. In the experiment, eleven undergraduates and five graduates conducted information gathering task for writing a report and trip planning. We recorded their verbal protocols during the tasks and post interviews, browser logs, screen captured video, and eye-tracking data. We divided the process of exploratory searches into search units. Then search units were classified into the two types of information needs, navigational and informational, based on qualitative data. We conducted a quantitative analysis to compare between tasks and groups and types of search units. The results showed that there were many differences between the information and navigation search units.

Keywords: Exploratory search, search intent, information seeking behavior.

1 Introduction

Web searches are a part of various daily activities. For instance, people engage in information searches to help them make decisions, learn new things, and conduct

P.-J. Cheng et al. (Eds.): AIRS 2010, LNCS 6458, pp. 173–182, 2010.
© Springer-Verlag Berlin Heidelberg 2010

investigations on many different topics. Bates [1] created the berrypicking model to describe searching behavior in online and information systems and suggested that researchers should focus on the sequence of search behaviors. Marchionini [2] referred to three kinds of search activity: lookup, learning, and investigation and defined an "exploratory search" as one associated with learning and investigation activities. There were a series of studies examining the influence of task types and user attributes on information seeking behaviors in exploratory searches by analyzing various data from client-side search logs, think-aloud protocols, eye-tracking, and post-experiment interviews [3][4][5]. Our approach is to extend them and to establish a situation for exploratory searches in the laboratory where we can observe participants' behaviors.

White and Roth [6] said that people engaged in exploratory searches are generally: (1) unfamiliar with the domain of their goal; (2) unsure about the ways to achieve their goals; and/or even (3) unsure about their goals. The search tasks of our experiments were open-ended (i.e., to collect information for writing a report about world history) and participants had to decide what they would focus on. The aim to correct information for the tasks was shared by the participants, but more their detailed information needs were varied. Participants in our experiments were unfamiliar with their goal or unsure about how to achieve them, and consequently, their searches were exploratory.

Our previous analysis did not examine whether their detailed information needs changed during the search process Moreover, we have analyzed qualitative data and quantitative data separately. Bridging these gaps between qualitative and quantitative is not just problem for us, but for the whole research community investigating information seeking behavior and IR.

In this study, we used qualitative data to categorize participants' detailed information needs during their searches and quantitatively analyzed the categorization results. We used the taxonomy of web searches proposed by Broader [7] to categorize information needs. Our purpose is to reveal how different information needs affected the participants' search processes. Below, we briefly discuss related work and our framework to analyze exploratory search processes.

2   Related Work

Researchers analyzing query logs have often collected transaction logs from search engines. Such studies have used the "session" as a unit of search processes [8]. These studies on query logs in search engines used the interval time from the search engine as criteria to cut a session [9][10].

On the other hand, analyses of client-side logs rely on users' interaction data with Web browsers. These studies have to extract behaviors related to searches. White and Drucker [11] defined a search trail to extract search processes from client-side logs. Search trails start from a directed search and proceed to the following points of termination: return to homepage, check email or logon services, type URL or visit bookmarked pages, page timeout, and close the browser. White and Drucker extracted search trails from client-side logs of two thousand

Table 1. Four Levels of Search Processes

Levels	Definition
Search Task	The overall process to complete the search task. The concept of the search task is similar to the search trail concept of White and Drunker[11]. The range of the search trail is broader than the search task.
Intent Unit	Continuous process while searching for the same target. The concept of the intent unit is similar to that of the search mission by Guo and Agichtein[12].
Search Unit	Continuous process while searching a single query. A search unit ends when users submits new query.
Link Unit	Continuous process while linking non-search results pages. A link unit starts when the user click a link in SERP and ends when he or she returns to SERP.

volunteer users during a six month period and found two types of interaction patterns (navigators and explorers). Guo and Agichtein [12] also used client-side logs to predict changes in search intent. They defined an interaction that leads to results pages as a search and referred to a sequence of consecutive searches as a search mission. A search mission changes when a user submits new query that doesn't overlap with the previous one. They constructed a model to predict whether the user will continue on the same mission or switch to a new one. These studies are strongly associated with our interest. However, our study differs in its methodology from these studies. We used users' own thought in to extract users' information needs.

In accordance with the previous studies, we defined four levels of search processes. Table 1 shows the definition of each level. "Search task" denotes the overall process of searching. "Intent unit" is used to denote changes in the searcher's intent. "Search unit" means a search using a query. "Link unit" starts when users click a link in SERP and ends when users return to SERP.

In this study, we focus on the search unit level and categorize information needs in search units. The research questions are (1) Do differences in the information needs of search units influence users' search processes? and (2) How do task types and groups affect search units?

3   Experiment

The participants were 11 undergraduate students of various (ages: between 19 and 21; male: 5, female: 6) and 5 graduate students (ages: between 23 and 28; male: 4, female: 1). The undergraduate students' academic majors included economics, literature, electronics engineering, Spanish, psychology, chemistry, and civil engineering, and the graduate students' were in library and information science.

The participants conducted two different web searches: the report task and the trip task. In the report task, the students were required to gather information from web pages concerning a topic of world history, a requisite subject for every high school student in Japan. In the trip task, participants were required to gather information from web pages for planning a trip. Participants selected a particular topic for each task based on their own interests, so the experimental searches were exploratory in nature: e.g., aimed at concrete tasks in the Report Task; at destination, trip partner, and traveling season in the Trip Task.

The participants answered a pre-test questionnaire about their information-seeking experiences with web search engines in their daily lives. We set up experimental equipment and calibrated an eye-tracking system. The participants were given a five-minute period to practice a web search and the "think aloud" method, in which they orally described their thought process. The two search tasks were conducted for 15 minutes. The order of the tasks was counterbalanced between participants. After each task, a questionnaire about the degree of difficulty and satisfaction with the search results was completed. Subsequently, we interviewed the participants about their information-seeking process while showing them screen captured video of their PC use with eye-movements to facilitate episodic memory retrieval.

4   Methods of Analysis

In our previous studies based on browser logs and screen capture video, we first used time markers and tags to mark page categories, action categories, and the depth of links from the search engine results, as explained below. Additionally, we divided their search processes into a number of search units according to the following rules.

- Search units changed when users submitted a query or clicked a related search in SERP.
- Search units changed when users moved a SERP that viewed other tab window or added it bookmark in previous searches by clicking a tab or selecting a bookmark.
- Search units did not change when users moved a page except SERP that viewed other tab or added it bookmark in previous searches by clicking a tab or selecting a bookmark.
- In a category search, search units changed when users selected a category first or move from a lower rank category to a higher rank category.
- In a category search, search units did not change when users moved from a higher rank category to a lower rank category.

Next, we categorized the informational needs of search units into navigational or informational based on the participants' verbal protocols during the task and post interview. Navigational needs are those to reach a particular site whereas informational needs are those to acquire information assumed to be present on one or more web pages [7].

In this analysis, we compared users' search processes between tasks, groups, search unit types. We used 5% as the level of statistical significance.

5   Results

5.1   Overview of Results on Search Units

The total number of search units was no significant differences between the two tasks and two groups. Table 2 shows the averages for the number of each type of search unit and the averages for the time of each type of search unit. A two-way ANOVA revealed significant differences between the two search unit types regarding the number of search units and the time. The number of information search units was more than the number of navigation search units . Moreover, the time of navigation search units was longer than the time of information search units .

Table 2 also shows the average number of each type of page and the averaege reading times. The pages participants read while searching were categorized into two types: SERP (Search Engine Results Pages) and nonSERP (non Search Engine Results Pages) based on the URLs.

First, we report the results for the number of pages. We conducted a four-way mixed ANOVA with page type (SERP and nonSERP) as a within participant factor and task type (Report and Trip), participants' group (graduates and undergraduates), and search unit type (information and navigation) as between-participant factors. There were significant interactions between page types and task types , and page types and search unit types . The results of Bonferroni multiple-significance-tests showed that the number of nonSERPs in the trip task was more than the number of nonSERPs in the report task . The results also show that the number of SERPs in information search units was more than the number of SERPs in navigation search units . In contrast, the number of nonSERPs in navigation search units was more than the number of nonSERP in information search units .

Next, we analyze the results of reading time. A three-way mixed ANOVA showed a significant interaction between page types and search unit types . The results of Bonferroni multiple-significance-tests showed that the reading time of SERPs in information search units was longer than the reading time of SERPs in navigation search units . In contrast, the reading time of nonSERPs in navigation search units was longer than the reading time of nonSERPs in information search units .

Table 2. Overview of Results on Search Units

	Undergraduate (n = 11)				Graduate (n = 5)			
	Report		Trip		Report		Trip	
	navi	info	navi	info	navi	info	navi	info
Ave. Num. of SU	1.27	6.27	1.45	5.45	4.00	5.40	2.00	5.80
Ave. Time of SU	187.02	104.94	92.71	98.35	165.63	124.22	175.22	94.10
Ave. Num. of SERP	1.57	2.77	1.13	1.95	1.40	2.41	1.50	2.10
Ave. Num. of nonSERP	7.79	3.71	10.88	8.78	9.80	7.30	14.50	7.52
Ave. Time of SERP	6.96	26.05	9.65	15.84	13.87	34.66	12.15	17.35
Ave. Time of nonSERP	84.78	70.85	164.61	77.25	172.31	69.32	151.26	105.45

Table 3. Average Number of Actions

Action	Undergraduates (n=11)				Graduates (n=5)			
	Report		Trip		Report		Trip	
	navi	info	navi	info	navi	info	navi	info
search	1.00	1.00	0.69	0.97	0.95	0.93	0.90	1.00
link	3.50	2.38	4.63	5.30	3.55	2.70	6.40	3.52
next	0.21	0.03	0.25	0.10	0.10	0.07	0.00	0.03
back	2.86	2.20	3.38	3.18	1.35	0.93	2.20	1.10
jump	0.57	0.22	0.69	0.20	0.30	0.15	0.70	0.31
browse	0.00	0.29	0.00	0.03	0.00	0.15	0.00	0.10
submit	1.00	0.00	1.13	0.25	1.65	0.19	1.70	0.21
bookmark	0.79	0.57	0.81	0.62	1.00	0.74	1.50	0.86
change	0.29	0.33	0.75	0.45	4.15	4.93	4.30	3.41
close	0.07	0.04	0.50	0.30	0.30	0.56	0.50	0.86

5.2   Results of Actions in Each Search Unit

We defined ten categories of action to analyze user behavior on the Web.

- Search: searching with a search engine
- Link: clicking on a page link
- Next: going forward to the next page
- Back: going backward to the previous page
- Jump: going forward or backward to more than one page
- Browse: going to the nth search result in SERP
- Submit: clicking a submit button
- Bookmark: adding bookmarks
- Change: changing from one tab to another
- Close: closing a tab or window

Table 3 lists the average number of actions carried out for each search unit type in each task by the graduate and undergraduate students. In those categories, we did not analyze the "search" action; the number of search actions in most units was 1, because we separated the units on the basis of the search actions. We analyzed each search unit separately, and we conducted a three-way mixed ANOVA with task type, participants' group, and search unit type as between-participant factors. There were significant differences between the two tasks for the Link actions, between the two groups for the Next , Back , and Change actions, and between the two search unit types for the Jump and Submit actions.

The participants were significantly more likely to click links during the trip task than during the report task. The undergraduates forwarded to next pages and clicked back to previous pages more often than the graduates did. The graduates switched more often to different tabs or windows compared with the undergraduates. The participants forwarded or backwarded to more than one page and clicked a submit button more often in the navigation search unit than in the information search unit.

Table 4. SERP Lookzone

Browser control area	SERP contents area
1:Title bar, 2:Menu, 3:Bookmark, 4:Tool bar, 5:URL bar, 6:Search bar, 7:Search bar button, 8:Tab, 12:Scroll bar, 21:Find in a page, 22:Status bar	9:Link for services, 10:Query box, 11:Search button, 13:Number of hits, 14:Sponsor Link, 15:Spell check, 16:Title, 17:Snippet, 18:URL, 19:Related search, 20:Link for next page

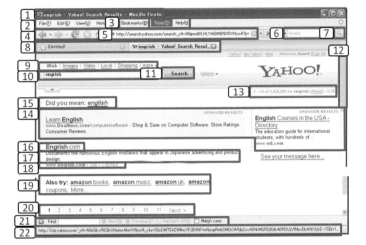

Fig. 1. Location of blocks in Lookzone

5.3   Results of Eye Gaze Points for SERP

We defined 22 Lookzone blocks on the page to classify exactly where participants were looking on the SERP (Table 4 and Figure 1). Next, we captured images from the eye tracking data of the participants at 0.5-second intervals, beginning as soon as the results pages were presented to them. We then manually tagged where the eye gaze points in the extracted images fell within the Lookzone. Table 5 shows the average number of eye gaze points per search unit carried out for each search unit type in each task by the graduate and undergraduate students. We did not analyze 11 underlined Lookzone blocks in table 4 whose average number of eye gaze points was under 0.5. As in the analysis of actions in each search unit, we conducted a three-way mixed ANOVA with task type, participants' group, and search unit type as between-participant factors.

There were significant differences between the two tasks for the Sponsor link , between the two groups for the Search bar , Link for services , and Query box , and between the two search unit types for the Query box and Title lookzone. There were significant interactions between task types and search unit types for the Snippet and URL lookzone.

Regarding the task types, the participants were significantly more likely to gaze at the Sponsor link during the trip task than during the report task. Regarding

Table 5. Average Number of Lookzones

Lookzone		Undergraduates (n=11)				Graduates (n=5)			
		Report		Trip		Report		Trip	
		navi	info	navi	info	navi	info	navi	info
1	Title bar	0.09	0.66	0.13	0.13	0.05	0.04	0.00	0.14
3	Bookmark	0.00	0.76	0.00	0.00	0.00	0.00	0.00	0.03
6	Search bar	0.00	0.00	0.00	0.00	0.85	0.63	0.20	0.66
8	Tab	0.36	1.38	1.67	1.12	0.80	1.63	0.10	1.00
9	Link for services	0.91	2.98	0.13	0.85	0.05	0.41	0.40	0.24
10	Query box	1.27	6.36	1.00	1.88	0.40	0.74	0.30	0.41
14	Sponsor Link	0.09	1.18	1.20	1.81	0.00	0.00	0.60	1.76
16	Title	2.91	10.78	3.80	6.37	1.55	6.56	1.20	6.48
17	Snippet	2.18	15.92	3.47	5.40	2.75	11.81	0.70	4.66
18	URL	0.45	7.36	1.93	2.17	0.45	3.07	0.70	1.90
19	Related search	0.09	0.52	0.20	0.38	0.05	0.19	0.10	0.17

the groups, the undergraduates gazed at the Query box and Link for services more often than the graduates did. In contrast, the graduates gazed at the Search bar more often than the undergraduates did. Regarding the search unit types, the participants gazed at the Query box and Title more often in the information search unit than in the navigation search unit.

Moreover, regarding the interaction between the task types and search unit types, the participants gazed at the Snippet and URL in the information search unit more than in navigation search unit for the report task . The participants also gazed at the Snippet and URL in information search unit for the report task more than for the trip task .

5.4   Results of View Rank and Click Rank

Table 5 shows that there was a clear tendency for students to focus on the titles, URLs, and snippets of the hits displayed on the results pages. We consequently grouped the eye-gaze points on titles, URLs, and snippets and assigned rankings. Then we analyzed which rankings attracted the most views. Figure 2 and Figure 3 show the average number of eye gaze points for each search unit type in each task. Figure 2 shows the results of undergraduates and figure 3 shows the results of graduates. As in the previous analyses, we conducted a three-way mixed ANOVA with task type, participants' group, and search unit type as between-participant factors.

First, we analyzed the view rank. There were significant differences between the two tasks for rank 1 , between the two groups for rank 1 and rank 5 , and between the two search unit types for ranks 1-6, 8, and 10 . There were significant interactions between task types and search unit types for rank 7 .

Regarding the task types, the participants were significantly more likely to gaze at rank 1 during the report task than during the trip task. Regarding the groups, the undergraduates gazed at ranks 1 and 5 more often than the graduates did. Regarding the search unit types, the participants gazed ranks

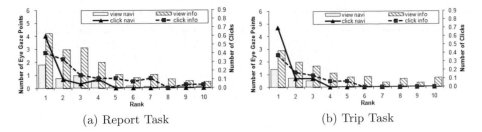

(a) Report Task   (b) Trip Task

Fig. 2. Average number of eye-gaze points and click rank (Undergraduates)

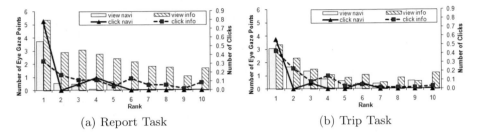

(a) Report Task   (b) Trip Task

Fig. 3. Average number of eye-gaze points and click rank (Graduates)

1-10 more often in the information search unit than in the navigation search unit. Regarding the interaction between the task types and search unit types, the participants gazed at rank 7 in the information search unit more than in the navigation search unit for the report task. The participants also gazed at rank 7 in the information search unit for the report task more than for the trip task.

Next, we analyzed the click rank; there were significant differences between the two search unit types for rank 1 and rank 2. The participants clicked rank 1 more often in the navigation search unit than in the information search unit. In contrast, the participants clicked rank 2 more often in the information search unit than in the navigation search unit.

6   Discussion and Conclusion

In this study, we divided exploratory search processes into search units based on qualitative data and quantitatively analyzed the differences in each type of search unit We also investigated the relationship between the type of task or user group and the type of search unit. This section discusses the results of the analysis.

First, we summarize the characteristics of each type of search unit. The information search units viewed more SERPs as compared with the navigation search units. Moreover, the navigation search units viewed more nonSERPs as compared with the information search units. These results indicate that users thought SERPs were more important in the information search units and thought nonSERPs were more important in the navigation search units.

These differences imply the information needs in each type of search unit. The navigation search unit is to search for a navigation path to a particular site.

In many cases, the target pages in the navigation search units were displayed at a higher rank in SERP. For example, say you wanted to go to Wikipedia; you would submit a query "Wikipedia" and Wikipedia would be ranked first in SERP. Similarly, in the navigation search units, users did not have to look deeply at the SERPs; their target information was beyond it.

On the other hand, the information search unit is to search one or more pages in order to acquire the target information. Therefore, users in the information search units scanned down to the lower ranks of SERP and read snippets to evaluate whether the documents were relevant or not.

This study was our first attempt at bridging the gap between qualitative and quantitative analyses. In the future, we will use these findings to extract search units and predict information needs from client-side logs. Additionally, we will try to extract and categorize the intent unit level in a second attempt to connect qualitative and quantitative data.

References

1. Bates, M.J.: The design of browsing and berrypicking techniques for the online search interface. Online Review 13(5), 407–424 (1989)
2. Marchionini, G.: Exploratory search: from finding to understanding. Commun. ACM 49(4), 41–46 (2006)
3. Terai, H., Saito, H., Egusa, Y., Takaku, M., Miwa, M., Kando, N.: Differences between informational and transactional tasks in information seeking on the web. In: Proceedings of IIiX 2008, pp. 152–159. ACM, New York (2008)
4. Saito, H., Terai, H., Egusa, Y., Takaku, M., Miwa, M., Kando, N.: How task types and user experiences affect information-seeking behavior on the web: Using eye-tracking and client-side search. In: Workshop on Understanding the User (UUIR 2009) (SIGIR 2009 Workshop), pp. 19–22 (2009)
5. Egusa, Y., Saito, H., Takaku, M., Terai, H., Miwa, M., Kando, N.: Link depth: Measuring how far searchers explore web. In: Proceedings of HICSS 2010, pp. 1–8 (2010)
6. White, R.W., Roth, R.A.: Exploratory Search: Beyond the Query-Response Paradigm. Synthesis Lectures on Information Concepts, Retrieval and Services. Morgan & Claypool, San Francisco (2009)
7. Broder, A.: A taxonomy of web search. SIGIR Forum 36(2), 3–10 (2002)
8. Jansen, B., Pooch, U.: A review of Web searching studies and a framework for future research. Journal of the American Society for Information Science and Technology 52(3), 235–246 (2001)
9. Silverstein, C., Henzinger, M., Marais, H., Moricz, M.: Analysis of a very large web search engine query log. SIGIR Forum 33(1), 6–12 (1999)
10. He, D., Göker, A.: Detecting session boundaries from web user logs. In: Proceedings of the BCS-IRSG 22nd Annual Colloquium on Information Retrieval Research, pp. 57–66 (2000)
11. White, R.W., Drucker, S.M.: Investigating behavioral variability in web search. In: Proceedings of WWW 2007, pp. 21–30 (2007)
12. Guo, Q., Agichtein, E.: Beyond session segmentation: predicting changes in search intent with client-side user interactions. In: Proceedings of SIGIR 2009, pp. 636–637 (2009)

Transliteration Retrieval Model
for Cross Lingual Information Retrieval

Ea-Ee Jan[1], Shih-Hsiang Lin[1,2], and Berlin Chen[2]

[1] IBM T.J. Watson Research Center, NY 10598, USA
{ejan,shihhlin}@us.ibm.com
[2] Computer Science and Information Engineering, National Taiwan Normal University,
Taipei, Taiwan
{shlin,berlin}@csie.ntnu.edu.tw

Abstract. The performance of transliteration from a source language to a target language builds the ground work in support of proper name Cross Lingual Information Retrieval (CLIR). Traditionally, this task is accomplished by two separate modules: transliteration and retrieval. Queries are first transliterated to target language using one or multiple hypotheses. The retrieval is then carried out based on translated queries. The transliteration often results in 30-50% errors with top 1 hypothesis, thus leading to significant performance degradation in CLIR. Therefore, we proposed a unified transliteration retrieval model that incorporates the transliteration similarity measurement into the relevance scoring function. In addition, we presented an efficient and robust method in similarity measurement for a given proper name pair using the Hidden Markov Model (HMM) based alignment and a Statistical Machine Translation (SMT) framework. Experimental data showed significant results with the proposed integrated method on the NTCIR7 IR4QA task, which demonstrated a greater flexibility and acceptance in transliteration.

Keywords: cross lingual information retrieval (CLIR), transliteration, retrieval model, statistical machine translation (SMT), NTCIR.

1 Introduction

Proper name transliteration, the pronunciation-based translation of a proper name from a source language to a desired target language, is important to many multilingual natural language processing tasks, including Cross Lingual Information Retrieval (CLIR), multilingual spoken document retrieval and Machine Translation (MT). Traditionally, transliteration is achieved by human translators using hand-crafted translation lexicon and translation rules. However, due to the fast growth of multilingual information, more and more proper names become undefined in the lexicon. These undefined proper names can be referred as Out-Of-Vocabulary (OOV) word, and potentially introduce harm to the system performance, especially in CLIR task. Since proper names usually carry distinctive information, when not carefully handled, the mean average precision (mAP) can reach 50% degradation [1].

P.-J. Cheng et al. (Eds.): AIRS 2010, LNCS 6458, pp. 183–192, 2010.

Transliteration between languages that use irrelevant alphabets and phonemes, e.g. English and Chinese or English and Arabic is especially challenging [1-4]. Due to the pronunciation differences between the source and target languages, particular phonemes in the source language can either have no corresponding phoneme or have a few close phonemes in the target language. These pronunciation differences usually yield "many to one", "one to many" or "one to none" phoneme mappings. Thus, one proper name can be transliterated into multiple foreign names with similar pronunciations. Differential alignment in source language can also lead to different transliteration outcomes in the target language. In addition, because of homophones, a single proper name can be transliterated to multiple foreign names with identical pronunciation. A typical example of multiple transliteration is that "Osama Bin Laden" can be transliterated into "奧薩瑪 賓拉登", "奧薩瑪 本拉丹", "奧薩瑪 本拉登" and so on. These varieties can significantly degrade the CLIR performance when a different set of transliterations was used by the query and its relevant documents. Despite that the state-of-the-art statistical machine translation (SMT) techniques have been developed, the proper name transliteration remains as a challenging task due to its diversity. Hence, alternative methodology that targets multiple transliterations is indispensible.

Proper name CLIR was mostly tackled by two essential steps [1, 4-6]: (1) one or multiple alternative transliterations were generated for each unknown word using transliteration techniques; (2) the expanded alternative transliterations were used for the retrieval module. However, two potential problems remained unaddressed. Firstly, transliteration does not always produce the exact spelling variants used in the document collection. An approximate string matching technique is usually required to alleviate this drawback. Secondly, the retrieval performance will be compromised if inaccurate or confusing transliterations occur in multiple alternative transliterations. To our best knowledge, no unified framework has been used to seamlessly integrate transliteration and retrieval model. Therefore, we proposed a novel transliteration retrieval model that incorporates a transliteration similarity function into the relevance scoring mechanism as a single component. The proposed framework computes the document relevant score of a given query without translation of any words, even the quires and documents are represented in two irrelevant languages. In this framework, we employed an efficient and robust method to measure the similarity of a given proper name pair using a Hidden Markov Model (HMM) based alignment.

2   Background and Related Work

Related work in CLIR can be roughly grouped into two major categories [7]: (1) translating the query into the language used in the document collection and (2) incorporating the statistical translation model into the retrieval model. For the first category, after the queries have been translated into the language used in the document collection, the remaining retrieval procedure can be derived from the standard ad hoc retrieval [3-6]. However, this approach relies on a high quality machine translation method. In the second category, researches have attempted to apply the statistical Language Model (LM) to CLIR [8-10]. The LM aims to capture the regularity in human natural language and to quantify the acceptability of a given word sequence.

The basic idea is that a document is deemed to be relevant to a query if its corresponding document language model is more likely to generate the query. A probabilistic language model is developed explicitly for each individual document in the collection. Therefore, the translation probability $P(t \mid s)$ can be naturally integrated into the retrieval model where s is the source term and t is the target term. However, the diversity of the proper name transliteration makes it difficult to have a translation model that handles all the possible proper name translation.

The proper name transliteration was often modeled by the SMT framework. Virga et al. applied statistical machine translation models to translate English names into Chinese characters for Mandarin spoken document retrieval [4]. Knight and Graehl proposed a generative transliteration model for Japanese and English using finite state transducers [11]. Meng et al. developed an English-Chinese Named Entity (NE) transliteration technique using a pronunciation lexicon and phonetic mapping rules [3]. Most of the above statistical machine translation approaches were based on the IBM noisy source-channel model framework [12]. Instead of using the noisy source-channel model, Gao et al. proposed a direct modeling approach to estimate the posterior probability using phoneme chunks as the contextual features [13]. Li et al. proposed direct orthographic mapping with a joint source-channel model for proper name transliteration [14]. Kumaran and Kellner [15] also implemented a generic transliteration framework using an approach similar to [14]. On the other hand, due to the challenge of machine transliteration, additional data source such as comparable corpora and web were explored to improve the performance [16-17]. All of these approaches had a scoring mechanism to test how likely a given pair of names in source and target languages is the transliteration of each other. This is a key component and is the aspect we focus on in this paper.

One popular approach for proper name CLIR is to translate queries from the source language to the target language. IR module is then applied for document retrieval. By this approach, the CLIR is addressed by two separated tasks. For the LM based IR, a probabilistic language model is developed explicitly for each individual document in the collection. The translation probability $P(t \mid s)$ is needed for retrieval model. However, proper name transliteration is a challenge task. The $P(t \mid s)$ can be less accurate. In this paper, we propose a unified framework which integrates the proper name transliteration similarity measurement into the retrieval model.

3 Our Approach

In this section, we first describe the baseline retrieval model and its extension to the proposed transliteration retrieval model. We then present our approach to calculate proper name transliteration similarity in latter section.

3.1 Retrieval Model

In language model based IR, a probabilistic generative framework is used for ranking each document D in the collection by a given query Q. This concept can be described by $P(D \mid Q)$ [18]. The ranking criterion is usually approximated by the likelihood of Q generated by D, i.e., $P(Q \mid D)$. By this approach, each document is treated as a probabilistic language model for generating the query. If Q is treated as a sequence of words, $Q = w_1 w_2 \cdots w_N$, which is assumed to be independent of each other given D, and the word order is assumed to be irrelevant, (the "*bag-of-words*" assumption), the relevance measure $P(Q \mid D)$ can be decomposed as a product of the probabilities of the query words generated by the document:

$$P(Q \mid D) = \prod_{w \in Q} P(w \mid D)^{c(w,Q)}$$
$$\propto \sum_{w \in Q} c(w, Q) \log P(w \mid D) \quad , \tag{1}$$

where $c(w, Q)$ is the number of times that each distinct word w_i occurs in Q. The document ranking is now simplified by the document model $P(w \mid D)$. The simplest way to construct $P(w \mid D)$ is using the unigram LM, where each document in the collection can respectively offer a unigram distribution for observing a query word.

A similar notion can be applied to CLIR by introducing the translation probability $P(w_e \mid w_f)$ into the formulation where w_e is an English query term and w_f is a Chinese document term[1] [19]. The retrieval model for CLIR given the English query Q_e and the Chinese document D_f can be formulated as:

$$P(Q_e \mid D_f) = \prod_{w_e \in Q_e} P(w_e \mid D_f)^{c(w_e, Q_e)}$$
$$\propto \sum_{w_e \in Q_e} c(w_e, Q_e) \log \left(\sum_{w_f \in D_f} P(w_e \mid w_f) P(w_f \mid D_f) \right) \quad . \tag{2}$$

Due to the OOV and diversity natural of the transliteration, it can be a challenge to estimate the translation probability of $P(w_e \mid w_f)$. We therefore redefine the scoring function as

$$P(Q_e \mid D_f) \propto \sum_{w_e \in Q_e} c(w_e, Q_e) \log \left(\sum_{w_f \in D_f} Transliteration(w_e, w_f) P(w_f \mid D_f) \right) \quad , \tag{3}$$

where $Transliteration(w_e, w_f)$ is an approximated transliteration probability obtained by the following sigmoid operation:

$$Transliteration(w_e, w_f) = \frac{1}{1 + \exp(-\gamma \cdot sim(w_e, w_f) + \beta)} \quad , \tag{4}$$

The weight γ and β describe the steepness and central of the sigmoid function, respectively. The $Sim(w_e, w_f)$ denotes the similarity between the query term w_e and the document term w_f. This sigmoid function is introduced to converts the similarity measure, $Sim(w_e, w_f)$, into a probability measure. The idea underlying the proposed model is that the greater the similarity score implies the greater likelihood of an appropriate transliteration.

---

[1] In the SMT community, e and f are represented as English and foreign language, respectively. In this paper, e denotes English and f is Chinese.

3.2 Transliteration Similarity $Sim(w_e, w_f)$

For a given proper name pair, one from the source language and the other from the target language, our goal here is to explore approaches with reliable similarity scoring mechanism which yields high accuracy with low computational complexity. For ease of illustration, we choose English and Chinese name transliteration for this study.

Intuitively, proper name transliteration "translates" a proper name from the source language to the target language based on pronunciation. Phonetic based edit distance measures should provide a good evaluation method. However, the source and target language can have very different base phone sets. One has to convert these phone sets to a unified phone set for edit distance calculation. Due to pronunciation differences between the source and target languages, the phone set mapping can be "one to many", "many to one" or "one to none". Additionally, pronunciation difference between some phone pairs can be more significant than the other pairs. For example, the transliteration difference caused by /t/ and /d/ should incur less error than the differences cause by /t/ and /e/. Instead of treating all errors with unique cost, we need a similarity measure rather than phonetic based edit distance. Some linguistic background may help hand craft the phone set mapping rules with weights. Instead, we use a phonetic based SMT framework to derive the mapping rules.

We propose a left-to-right discrete HMM based alignment to measure the similarity for a given proper name pair. Prior to alignment, the proper name pairs are converted to phone sequences. In the discrete HMM alignment, we treat each phone to be aligned as a state which is characterized by a multinomial distribution. The emission probability for each state is the conditional probability of phone in target language given by phone in source language $p(f \mid e)$, or by a null probability model. The null probability model is presented by either $p(f \mid \phi)$ or $p(\phi \mid e)$. The phrase-based SMT framework can be utilized to derive the state emission probability $p(f \mid e)$. The valid state transition is from left to right with self looping, and with the maximum jump of two states. A uniform probability is used for all valid state transition. The best path can be calculated by the dynamic time wrapping (DTW). The similarity score is the best alignment score normalized by the total length.

The parallel training corpus for SMT to derive $p(f|e)$ is organized as such that the English phone sequences (in English phone set) are paired with their corresponding Chinese phone sequences (in Chinese phone set). Words with multiple pronunciations are fully enumerated. The SMT models are developed by a commonly used recipe [22]. The phrase table $p(f \mid e)$ is used as the emission probability for the HMM alignment. The phrase table size is set to 2. Thus, one or two phone sequences in the source language can mapped to one or two phone sequences in the target language and vice versa. Please refer to [24] for more details.

4 Experimental Setup

Two consecutive experiments were setup to verify the proposed framework. The first experiment is to assess the performance of proper name transliteration similarity measurement. To this end, a parallel corpus consisting of English and Chinese proper name pairs was extracted from the people section of the multilingual Wikipedia. Approximately 3,000 pairs were used for training and 300 pairs for testing. To evaluate the robustness of the proposed similarity measurement, match and unmatched conditions were both tested. The 300 pairs were used as a matched condition test. A separated 1,000 unmatched test pairs were created randomly from the 300 matched pairs. The English and Chinese pronunciations were obtained by the IBM voice toolkits. Multiple pronunciations for a given word were considered to be uniformly distributed. All possible combinations of pronunciation were created in both training and test set.

The second experiment is document retrieval using the data compiled from the NTCIR-7 Information Retrieval for Question Answering (IR4QA) task [20]. IR4QA evaluates the performance of document retrieval using Average Precision (AP) metrics. This task is embedded in the context of cross language question answering. In this study, we used the EN-CS (English to Simplified Chinese) subtask, which includes 545,162 documents and 97 queries, for the retrieval experiments. Of the original 97 queries, 10 proper name related queries (listed in Table 2) were extracted to verify our proposed method. The retrieval results were presented by AP.

5 Results and Discussion

We first evaluated the performance of the proper name transliteration similarity measurement. The phonetic based transliteration SMT system was developed. The log probability of e2f and f2e from phrase tables were used to calculate the similarity score for both matched and unmatched proper name pair test set. A larger value represents a higher similarity. If the similarity score for a matched pair is lower than a given threshold, this pair is falsely rejected. If the similarity score for an unmatched pair is higher than the threshold, this pair is falsely accepted. The performance metrics can be evaluated by the Equal Error Rate (EER), where the error rate of the false rejection of matched pairs and the false acceptance of unmatched pairs are identical. The EER for our proposed method was 3.47%. This low EER provides a good foundation for proper name CLIR. For comparison, the transliteration employing the commonly used SMT framework was also explored. The translation of a given phone sequence from the source language to the target language was performed. The similarity of the translated phone sequence and true target phone sequence was calculated using BLEU score [23]. While setting the phrase table size equal to 8, the SMT framework yielded the best performance at the EER of 7.1%, which is substantially higher than that of our approach. We also compared the edit distance between spelling of English name and Pinyin of Chinese names. The EER for the orthographic based edit distance is 22%. Table 1 summarizes these results.

Table 1. Equal error rates (EERs) for various similarity measures

Approach	EER(%)
Orthographic Edit distance	22.27%
Phonetic Based SMT	7.10%
Proposed Method	3.43%

Table 2. Baseline retrieval results (in AP) for NTCIR-7 ACLIA EN-CS

Topic	Query	Baseline	NTCIR7(Avg.)
ACLIA-CS-T42	本拉登 (Bin Laden)	0.0585	0.1628
ACLIA-CS-T43	罗讷尔多 (Ronaldo)	0.8664	0.6319
ACLIA-CS-T55	哈塔米 (Khatami)	0.7843	0.5054
ACLIA-CS-T61	克林顿 (Clinton) 莱温斯基 (Lewinsky)	0.6659	0.4514
ACLIA-CS-T338	苏哈托 (Suharto)	0.7747	0.5837
ACLIA-CS-T339	普里马可夫 (Primakov)	0.8304	0.6226
ACLIA-CS-T340	农德孟 (Nong Duc Manh)	0.9485	0.6935
ACLIA-CS-T367	拉纳利 (Ranariddh)	0.7103	0.4774
ACLIA-CS-T376	奥尼尔 (O'Neal)	0.6275	0.3967
ACLIA-CS-T379	郑肯 (Duncan)	0.6442	0.3685
Avg.	-	0.6911	0.4894

For document retrieval, we first evaluated the retrieval model (cf. Eq. (1)) on the monolingual task (CS-CS) using entire 97 queries. The unigram document language model $P(w \mid D)$ is constructed with Dirichlet smoothing where the smoothing parameter μ is determined by maximizing the leave-one-out log likelihood of the entire document collection [21]. The AP of this approach is 0.5764. The best performance for this query set from the NTCIR report is 0.6184 and the average AP from all participated systems is 0.4276. Our monolingual baseline retrieval model is comparable to the best systems of the NCTIR-7 report.

We then performed retrieval experiment using the 10 proper name query topics. Our baseline yielded overall AP of 0.6911, which outperformed the average AP[2] of 0.4894 from all systems (cf. Table 2). However, while examining the AP of each individual query topic, our baseline performed is worse than the average for the query ACLIA-CS-T42. The reason is that the proper name "Bin Laden" has been transliterated as "本拉登", "本拉丹", and so on, in the document collection. This multiple transliterations degrade the performance of our baseline, which uses words as the indexing unit. To address the problem of ACLIA-CS-T42 query topic, it is necessary to extend the baseline to our proposed approach, which integrates the transliteration similarity function into the retrieval model (cf. Eq. (3)). To evaluate the performance of proposed approach, we needed the document collection equipped with controlled multiple transliterations. We created a homogenous name list for those proper names used in the test query topics and uniformly replaced those names into the original document collections. The homogenous names list and associated Pinyin are shown in Table 3. The baseline performance for each original query against the new synthetic document collection was presented at Table 3 (denoted as "**Synthetic**"). When a proper name has n alternatives, the performance degradation will be approximately $(n/n+1)$.

---

[2] The best performance for individual query is not available from NTCIR reports. We can only compare our baseline with the average AP.

Table 3. The homogenous name list and retrieval results (in AP) on the synthetic collection

Original	Alternatives	Synthetic
罗讷尔多 (Ronaldo) /luo na er duo/	罗讷度 罗讷多 罗讷尔度 朗拿度 /luo ne du/ /luo ne duo/ /luo ne er du/ /lang na du/	0.1284
哈塔米 (Khatami) /ha ta mi/	卡塔米 汉塔米 哈他米 肯塔米 /ka ta mi/ /han ta mi/ /ha ta mi/ /ken ta mi/	0.1261
克林顿 (Clinton) /ke lin dun/	柯林顿 科林顿 可林顿 /ke lin dun/ /ke lin dun/ /ke lin dun/	0.2126
莱温斯基 (Lewinsky) /lai wen si ji/	路文斯基 李文斯基 莱文斯基 /lu wen si ji/ /li wen si ji/ /lai wen si ji/	0.2126
苏哈托 (Suharto) /su ha tuo/	撒哈托 苏哈尔托 撒哈尔托 史哈托 /sa ha tuo/ /su ha er tuo/ /sa ha er tuo/ /shi ha tuo/	0.1220
普里马可夫 (Primakov) /pu li ma ke fu/	普林马可夫 普利马可夫 普利马科夫 普利马克夫 /pu li ma ke fu/ /pu lin ma ke fu/ /pu li ma ke fu/ /pu li ma ke fu/	0.1418
农德孟(Nong Duc Manh) /nong de meng/	侬德猛 农德猛 侬得猛 /nong de meng/ /nong de meng/ /nong de meng/	0.2124
拉纳利 (Ranariddh) /la na li/	拉那烈 拉那利 拉纳瑞德 拉那瑞 /la na lie/ /la na li/ /la na rui de/ /la na rui/	0.4564
奥尼尔 (O'Neal) /ao ni er/	欧尼尔 澳尼尔 欧尼而 欧尼耳 /ou ni er/ /ao ni er/ /ou ni er/ /ou ni er/	0.1625
邓肯 (Duncan) /deng ken/	当肯 丹肯 郑肯 /zheng ken/ /dang ken/ /dan ken/	0.1556

We then evaluated the proposed method against the synthetic collection document. We first assumed a perfect similarity function (Eq. (4)): $Sim(W_e, W_f)=1$ if a pair of words is in the homogenous name list; otherwise, $Sim(W_e, W_f)=0$. This ideal function can be the Oracle results of our approach (denoted by "**Oracle**" in Table 4). The Oracle results outperform the baseline results for query topics "ACLIA-CS-T42" and "ACLIA-CS-T367", which suggests that the original document collection may have multiple transliterations for these two query topics. This approach also slightly outperforms the baseline in a few query topics. This performance improvement can stem from the segmentation error. For example, if "科林顿路"is included in the document lexicon, it might be a mis-segmentation of "科林顿", whereas our approach is able to retrieve this document. However, this experiment is impractical since the complete list of transliterations for the document collection is unknown.

Next, we manually tagged 2,000 candidate proper names from the document collection for similarity function evaluation. These 2,000 candidate proper names are related to the homogenous name list. At least one character from the candidate proper name has a similar pronunciation to the homogenous name list. This test data was used to evaluate the robustness of our approach against the false acceptance of OOVs. The similarity scores for these proper names were calculated. The weights of γ and β used in sigmoid operation (cf. Eq. (4)) were optimized based on the experiments shown in Table 1 (with an EER of 4.3%). The corresponding results were shown in Table 4 (denoted by "**Taggers**"). The average of all APs was degraded slightly from 0.7254 to 0.6516, while compared to the Oracle results.

Last, we evaluated the worse scenario by using the vocabulary from the complete set of lexicon with length of 2 to 5, to calculate similarity function. It resembles a scenario when the Named Entities (NE) tagger is not available. This test scenario created the maximum number of false acceptance of OOVs. The average AP for this experiment drops from the Oracle performance of 0.7254 to 0.4040 (denoted by "**Worst**"), but it is still much better than that of 0.1776 obtained by the baseline retrieval approach on synthetic document collection. The results clearly showed that our proposed transliteration retrieval model and the low EER of similarity function can properly handle the multiple proper name transliteration problems. Even without the NE tagger (cf. "**Worst**" in Table 4), the proposed method provides significant improvements over the baseline of the synthetic document collection.

Table 4. Retrieval results (in AP) for the simulated document collection

Topic	Synthetic	Oracle	Tagger	Worst
ACLIA-CS-T42*	0.0585	0.1391	0.0777	0.0522
ACLIA-CS-T43	0.1284	0.8663	0.3870	0.1497
ACLIA-CS-T55	0.1261	0.8014	0.7936	0.2112
ACLIA-CS-T61	0.2126	0.6899	0.6884	0.6977
ACLIA-CS-T338	0.1220	0.7749	0.6642	0.0415
ACLIA-CS-T339	0.1418	0.8304	0.8307	0.8360
ACLIA-CS-T340	0.2124	0.9485	0.9176	0.9117
ACLIA-CS-T367*	0.4564	0.9319	0.8931	0.8784
ACLIA-CS-T376	0.1625	0.6276	0.6293	0.2613
ACLIA-CS-T379	0.1556	0.6442	0.6340	0.0002
Avg.	0.1776	0.7254	0.6516	0.4040

6 Conclusion

Due to the diversity of proper name transliteration, the transliteration accuracy can be impaired, leading to performance degradation in proper name CLIR. We proposed a unified transliteration retrieval framework which integrates the transliteration similarity measurement into the relevance scoring function. Instead of performing proper name transliteration, a transliteration similarity function is used in our framework. The EER of the proposed similarity function can be as low as 3.5%, which reduces the negative impact of proper name CLIR due to the uncertainty of transliteration. The CLIR experiments were conducted using the NTCIR7 IR4QA dataset. The corpus was first corrupted by introducing 4 to 5 different transliterations. These new proper names severely degraded the IR performance. The CLIR performance was recovered by our proposed method.

References

1. Larkey, L., AbdulJaleel, N., Connell, M.: What's in a Name?: Proper Names in Arabic Cross Language Information Retrieval. CIIR Technical Report, IR-278, Univ. of Amherst (2003)
2. Darwish, K., Doermann, D., Jones, R., Oard, D., Rautiainen, M.: TREC-10 Experiments at University of Maryland CLIR and Video. In: 10th TREC, pp. 549–561 (2002)

3. Meng, H., Chen, B., Lo, W.K., Tang, K.: Generating Phonetic Cognates to Handle Named Entities in English-Chinese Cross-Language Spoken Document Retrieval. In: IEEE Workshop on Automatic Speech Recognition and Understanding, pp. 311–314 (2001)
4. Virga, P., Khudanpur, S.: Transliteration of Proper Names in Cross-lingual Information Retrieval. In: ACL Workshop on Multilingual and Mixed-Language Named Entity Recognition, pp. 57–64 (2003)
5. Bellaachia, A., Amor-Tijani, G.: Proper Nouns in English–Arabic Cross Language Information Retrieval. J. American Society for Information Science and Technology 59(12), 1925–1935 (2008)
6. Chen, H.: -S., Huang, S. -J, Ding, Y. -W., Tasi, S. C.: Proper Name Translation in Cross-Language Information Retrieval. In: 17th COLING-ACL 1998, pp. 232–235 (1998)
7. Kishida, K.: Technical Issues of Cross-Language Information Retrieval: A Review. Information Processing & Management 41(3), 433–455 (2005)
8. Xu, J., Weischedel, R., Nguyen, C.: Evaluating a Probabilistic Model for Cross-Lingual Information Retrieval. In: 24th ACM SIGIR, pp. 105–110 (2001)
9. Kraaij, W., Pohlmann, R., Hiemstra, D.: Twenty-one at TREC-8: Using Language Technology for Information Retrieval. In: 8th TREC, pp. 285–300 (2000)
10. Lavrenko, V., Choquette, M., Croft, W.B.: Cross-lingual relevance models. In: 25th ACM SIGIR, pp. 175–182 (2002)
11. Knight, K., Graehl, J.: Machine Transliteration. Computational Linguistics 24(4), 509–612 (1997)
12. Brown, P.E., Pietra, S.A.D., Mercer, R.L.: The Mathematics of Statistical Machine Translation: Parameter Estimation. Computational Linguistics 19(2), 263–311 (1993)
13. Gao, W., Wong, K.F., Lam, W.: Improving Transliteration with Precise Alignment of Phoneme Chunks and Using Context Features. In: Myaeng, S.-H., Zhou, M., Wong, K.-F., Zhang, H.-J. (eds.) AIRS 2004. LNCS, vol. 3411, pp. 106–117. Springer, Heidelberg (2005)
14. Li, H.Z., Zhang, M., Su, J.: A Joint Source-Channel Model for Machine Transliteration. In: 42nd ACL, pp. 159–166 (2004)
15. Kumaran, A., Kellner, T.: A Generic Framework for Machine Transliteration. In: 30th ACM SIGIR, pp. 721–722 (2008)
16. Klementiev, A., Roth, D.: Weakly Supervised Named Entity Transliteration and Discovery from Multi-lingual Comparable Corpora. In: 44th ACL, pp. 817–824 (2006)
17. Jiang, L., Zhou, M., Chien, L.F., Niu, C.: Named Entity Translation with Web Mining and Transliteration. In: 20th ICJAI, pp. 1629–1634 (2007)
18. Ponte, J.M., Croft, W.B.: A Language Modeling Approach to Information Retrieval. In: 10th ACM SIGIR, pp. 275–281 (1998)
19. Berger, A., Lafferty, J.: Information Retrieval as Statistical Translation. In: 22nd ACM SIGIR, pp. 222–229 (1999)
20. Sakai, T., Kando, N., Lin, C.J., Mitamura, T., Shima, H., Ji, D., Chen, K.H., Nyberg, E.: Overview of the NTCIR-7 ACLIA IR4QA Task. In: NTCIR-7 Workshop Meeting, pp. 77–114 (2008)
21. Zhai, C.X., Lafferty, J.: A Study of Smoothing Methods for Language Models Applied to Information retrieval. ACM Trans. on Information Systems 22(2), 179–214 (2004)
22. Och, F., Ney, H.: A Systematic Comparison of Various Statistical Alignment Models. Computational Linguistics 29(1), 19–51 (2003)
23. Papeneni, K.A., Roukos, S., Ward, T., Zhu, W.J.: Bleu: a method for automatic evaluation of machine translation. In: 40th ACL, pp. 311–318 (2001)
24. Jan, E., Ge, N., Lin, S.H., Roukos, S., Sorensen, J.: A Novel Approach to Proper Name Transliteration. Submitted to ISCSLP 2010

The Role of Lexical Ontology in Expanding the Semantic Textual Content of On-Line News Images

Shahrul Azman Noah and Datul Aida Ali

Knowledge Technology Research Group, Faculty of Information Science & Technology,
Universiti Kebangsaan Malaysia, 43600 UKM, Bangi, Selangor, Malaysia
{samn,da41030}@ftsm.ukm.my

Abstract. Using low-level features to support semantic search of images is a difficult task. As a result, textual content is used to provide semantic description or annotation of images. Such textual description of what we may call as 'surrounding text' is a value added features available in most web images particularly on-line news images. Most search engines used them as a feature to provide textual meaning of images. Relying on surrounding text alone, however, unable to provide support for semantic search that go beyond indexed terms. Lexical resources and ontology are potential sources to enhance searching for images. This paper discusses the use of WordNet and ConceptNet to enhance searching for on-line news images. This is further improved with named entity recognition (NER) technique to annotate important entities such as name if a person, location and organization among image searchers. Results show that lexical ontology has the capacity to semantically enhance the meanings of conventional bag of words index.

Keywords: information retrieval, semantic search, image retrieval.

1 Introduction

The important proliferation of digital multimedia content requires tools for extracting useful knowledge from the content to enable intelligent and efficient multimedia organization, filtering and retrieval. Vast amount of images are now available as digital format and many of them are being described either directly or indirectly by some textual information [1]. Such description is useful in many cases particularly for searching. Web images for instance have brought great challenges for search engines. While many search engines mainly focused on keyword spotting for indexing and searching, little have gone beyond the "semantic meaning" of images which are hidden and embedded somewhere in the textual description. Semantically search of images based on its content is highly difficult and little successful stories have been reported. An image in web documents, however, is provided with meaningful description which can be exploited to support keyword searching. Relying on the surrounding text alone however unable to provide meaningful description of the images. The questions of Who? What? When? and Where? are common among image searchers which are not capable of being answered by normal indexing. External sources particularly in the form of ontology and some forms of annotation are required in order to provide such semantic facility.

P.-J. Cheng et al. (Eds.): AIRS 2010, LNCS 6458, pp. 193–202, 2010.

This paper reports our approach in supporting simple semantic search of web images by exploiting lexical ontology. The scope of our work is on on-line newspaper images. Such images are usually provided with short description and elaborated somewhere in the news content. The aim is to extract the 'who', 'what', 'when' and 'where' information from the textual description which represent the images. In a broader sense, the idea is to extract semantic meanings of images based from the free (unstructured) textual description provided by web authors and then subsequently constructs the semantic index. In our approach we employ the Named Entity Recognition (NER) technique and exploit the WordNet [2] and ConceptNet [3] lexical ontologies. NER plays an important role in extracting the information about person, location and time of the textual description. WordNet and ConceptNet on the other hand are used to semantically enhance the index of the stored images. The main purpose is to semantically index images beyond the terms provided in the attached textual description.

This paper is organized into the following five sections. The next section provides some background and related research. Section three discusses our approach and technique to support semantic document retrieval and browsing and followed by section four which provides the evaluation activities. Finally we present the conclusions that may be drawn from our work.

2   Background and Related Research

Search engines used textual information surrounding images as features [4]. In general terms, such information came be loosely considered as annotations containing textual keywords that can be thought of as resembling documents [5]. Such annotations can be semantically enhanced by extending to ontology or any lexical resources. Named Entity Recognition (NER), on the other hand, is one of the techniques in natural language processing (NLP) that can semantically annotate important entities such 'person', 'location' and 'time'. The remaining of this section briefly describes the aforementioned concepts and then proceeds with related works in this area.

Few efforts in semantic retrieval for images are illustrated in the work of [1,6,7]. Benitez and Chang [1] focused on information extraction of semantic or relationship between a collection of images that has been annotated, such as nature images and news images. Among the heuristics considered are: words nearer to the images have semantic relations to the images and, high frequency of words indicates important meanings of images. Three stages involved in extracting such meanings, which are: text preprocessing; extraction of semantic concept and extraction of semantic relationship. Text preprocessing uses syntactic analysis while semantic concept extraction process uses Wordnet and Word Sense Disambiguation (WSD) technique for text clustering. Weights are assigned to chosen concepts using *tf×idf* and *log tf × entropy*. Weights are also given based on synsets (from the WordNet), core meaning and example usage. Semantic relationships extraction of concepts on the other hand is based on the meanings derived from WordNet. Their study shows that the use WordNet gives better for nature images. Furthermore, the use of annotated news images that contain more textual description than those images that only contain keywords also give better result.

The main objective of Gong et al [6] work is to develop indexing scheme of web images using texts that are available in the web. This research emphasizes the principle that every website developer will use images to describe their website and the distance between the word and the image are also important. Therefore, texts that are available in the website will have semantic relations that are linked to the image. Their approach divided the text containing the images into three blocks of semantic segmentation, i.e. (i) TM (Title & Meta); (ii) LT (image location, image name, image hyperlink or ALT); and (iii) BT (body of text). Results from the experiment showed that the texts situated nearest to the image gives recall measure. However, when taking the whole text into account (i.e. by considering the three segments of TM, LT and BT), the recall measure is much better. The work of [6], however, does not consider external resources to provide additional semantic meanings of the indexed terms.

The work of Hua et al [7] combined visual and textual feature for searching images. Semantic information extracted from web pages are text summary, human related information such as name, geographical information such as name of a place and telephone number. Apart from concept extraction as in the previous two approaches, their approach proposed four aspects of semantic information extraction namely: visual weight, total phrases, phrase weight and independent phrases. Result shows that 62% to 90% of web images capable of being semantically described. The proposed approach, however, still could not differentiate between geographical and human name such as McDonald's which should be considered as geographical information and not human's name.

Previous work shows that annotations are important as means to describe the semantics of images. Two obvious forms of annotation exhibited in the related works: structured annotation and unstructured annotation. Structured annotation can be regarded as comments made directly to sources by means of some tools and which are usually seen technically as metadata. This kind of annotation is exhibited by the work of [1]. However, in real life, there are lots of unstructured annotations that can be seen as natural language description attached to either the images, documents or artifacts. We may call this 'unstructured' because it is not represented by means of meta data but usually freely provided by document or web authors. The WordNet has been a popular choice for enhancing semantic meaning of images. However, not all images descriptive terms can be semantically extended by WordNet. Therefore, some common-sense concepts are required. For instance mentioning the word 'bride and groom' or seeing images with similar 'content' will relate to terms such as 'wedding' and 'ring' [8]. Such common-sense concepts can be derived from rich semantically processed resources such as the ConceptNet. This study, therefore, embarks on the possibility of representing semantic and common-sense meanings in images by exploiting the unstructured textual annotations and the surrounding text, and further extended by deriving the semantic and common-sense concepts from the WordNet and ConceptNet respectively.

3   The Approach

Semantic search uses the science of meaning in language—instead of just searching keywords, it checks the context of the words to return more relevant results. Therefore, we view semantic search as searching beyond searchable index. For instance searching for the term "primer minister" will also result in the retrieval of images which contain similar terms such as "head of state" and "Abdullah Badawi" (the prime minister of Malaysia). However, the name "Abdullah" can still be ambiguous as either representing a name of a person, name of a street or even name of a company. Therefore, NER is one of the methods meant to solve such ambiguity. Our approach takes into consideration the aforementioned elements with the use of WordNet and ConceptNet, as well as NER patterns. We scope our work into on-line Malaysian English language newspaper under the nation category. The nation category is related to Malaysian political and local issue news. Our approach is as depicted in Fig. 1 of which containing a number of stages as follows.

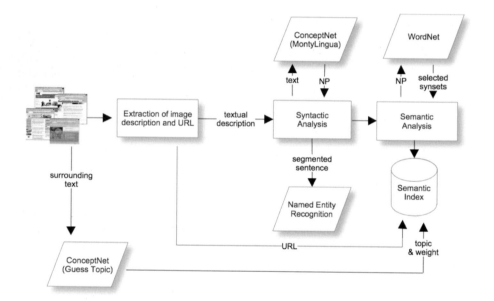

Fig. 1. The process to support semantic search of on-line news images

3.1 Extraction of Image Description, URL and Surrounding Text

As mentioned earlier, textual information surrounding images can be regarded as unstructured annotation of images. Images in on-line newspapers contain such rich and useful annotations. In this stage, tags in HTML documents have to be 'cleaned' with the exception of 'p', 'br', 'div', and 'span' tags. These tags are required as a bookmark for extracting the surrounding text, image description and image location. The HTML documents will then be transformed to ASCII document file type. Image location will be stored directly into the database whereas the associated image's description and surrounding text will be used in the next process. Throughout this paper, image's description refers to textual information right under images as exhibited in many on-line newspaper images. Other textual information is considered as surrounding text.

3.2 Syntactic Analysis

Syntactic analysis is split into two main stages: syntax analysis and NER. The first stage is the syntax analysis that will be processed by the MontyLingua component which is part of the ConceptNet. Every sentence in description image will be tokenized using MontyTokenize classes: 'tokenize' and 'tag_tokenize'. The class tokenize transforms input sentences into sentences without hyphenation, whereas the class tag_tokenize performs the part-of-speech (POS) tagging process according to the Penn TreeBank tagsets. The output of this stage is in the form of " *This/DT is/VB a/DT sentence/NN* ".

After that the sentence will be tagged with a more detail tag in the MontyTagger class and the output sentence will be like this: " *(NX He/PRP NX)(VX is/VB VX) (NX the/DT mailman/NN NX)* ". Only noun phrases will be considered for the next process based on the assumptions that noun phrases are the best lexical category to describe images [9]. Weights for every noun phrases are calculated using the *tf×idf* weighting scheme.

The second stage which is the NER stage contains two sub-processes: the sentence segmentation process and pattern matching process. In sentence segmentation, noun phrases from syntax analysis are used for sentence selection. Fig 2 illustrates an example of a word matching for choosing segmented sentence. In this example, the sentence: *"Friendly visit: Anwar talking to Mohammad Nizar in Ipoh yesterday. With them are (from left) Gopeng MP Dr Lee Boon Chye, Anwar's wife Datin Seri Dr Wan Azizah Wan Ismail and Perak PKR chief Zulkifly Ibrahim"*, will be segmented into "Anwar talking to Mohmmad Nizar", "Mohammad Nizar in Ipoh: and "Gopeng MP Dr Lee Boon Chye" based upon the word matching of the set {"Abdullah', 'Ipoh', 'Anwar' and 'Sungai Dua'}.

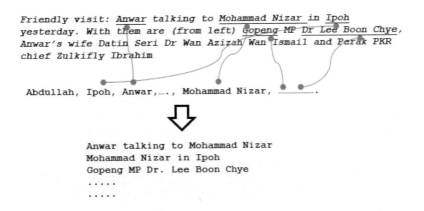

Fig. 2. The process of sentence segmentation

The next process of this second stage is the pattern matching process whereby the segmented sentences are matched with NER patterns developed from the analysis of existing documents. Overall there are 142 patterns meant to extract entities such as 'person', 'location', 'event', 'time', 'title', 'organization' and 'position'. These entities are chosen based on the opinion of Kawata et al. [10] that such entities are the most common information acquired in news. Table 1 lists the example of the patterns used in this study and Fig. 3 illustrates an example of the pattern matching process.

Table 1. Example of the NER pattern

Named entity	Pattern
Person	[person] having, [person] watching her [post] [person]
Location	in [location], [location], [person] at the [location] in [location]
Event	at the [event], the [event] held at
Time	at the [location] on [time], in [location] since the [time]
Title	[post][title][person], [title][person]
Person-post	[post] from the [post], the [person's post] holding up
Organization	at the [organization], [person] from [organization]

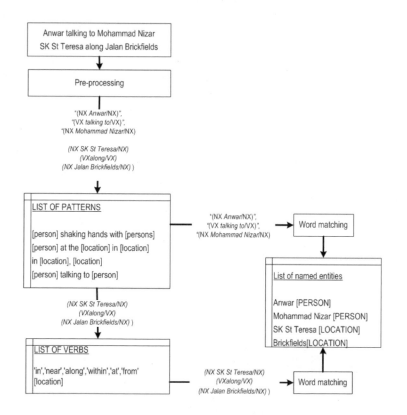

Fig. 3. An example of a pattern matching process

Based on Fig 3, the input for pattern matching are the segmented sentences. The sentences will be parsed to generate the POS tags (text pre-processing). For instance, the sentence *"Anwar talking to Mohammad Nizar"* will be tagged and tokenized as *"(NX Anwar/NX)"*, *"(VX talking to/VX)"*, *"(NX Mohammad Nizar/NX)"*. The tagged sentence is then matched with the appropriate pattern. For this example, it will be matched with the pattern *"[person] talking to [person]"* and subsequently semantically tagged as *"(Anwar [PERSON]) talking to (Mohammad Nizar [PERSON])"*. For those noun phrases in the word list that do not matched with any of the patterns, the process will continue by matching the verbs with the NER patterns. For example the tokenize segmented sentence of *(NX SK St Teresa/NX) (VXalong/VX)(NX Jalan Brickfields/NX))* will resulted in the generation of *"(SK St Teresa[LOCATION]) along (Jalan Brickfields [LOCATION])"*.

3.3 Deriving Semantic Meanings

The main aim of this stage is to add additional semantic information and common sense knowledge of the indexed images using the WordNet and ConceptNet. Noun phrases from the word list are matched with the terms in WordNet. If such matched exists, the hypernyms of the terms will be included as part of the indexed terms. For instance, the phrase *"prime minister"* will generate semantic information such as " *Head of State, Chief of State, Representative, and negotiator.*

As mentioned earlier, ConceptNet is used to derive common-sense knowledge or meanings of sentences. Such meanings can be derived using the topic-jisting module. To achieve this, sentences are first fragmented into verb-subject-object-object (VSOO), of which then used to derive related concepts (or topics) from the Concept-Net. ConceptNet provides weights (saliency weight) based on the relevancy of the topics to the submitted sentences. These weights are based upon lightweight syntactic cues and contextual intersection. It is not realistic, however, to consider all the topics derived from the ConceptNet. Therefore, we consider only top topics, i.e. those top n topics before the weight has converged to specific δ value. The ConceptNet topic jisting module allows terms (or topics) associated with the images (based on the description or surrounding text) to be derived from a large lexical resource. Liu and Lieberman [5] refer these additional terms as common sense knowledge.

4 Evaluation

Initial evaluation was conducted by comparing our proposed approach to semantic search with the conventional bag-of-words vector space model (normal search). As such only 800 images from the Malaysian on-line newspaper (under the nation category) were indexed. On average, each document consists about 85 terms. Ten queries have been articulated, and for each query the relevant images is manually identified and labeled. The constructed queries resembled information related to 'person', 'location', 'event', 'time', 'organization' and 'position'. The query is in the form short natural language sentence such as *"Voter in the 12th general election"*. The popular precision and recall measures [11] were used.

We divided the evaluation into eight groups in order to assess the significant contribution of the WordNet and ConceptNet. The eight groups represent the number of different indexes of which the results are shown in Table 2. The precision-recall graph is shown in Fig. 4. S represents the standard index, S_{CNet} and S_{WNet} represent index expanded from extracting concepts from ConceptNet and WordNet respectively. S_{NER} on the other hand represent index enhanced with NER tags. Therefore $S_{CNet} + S_{WNet}$ represent index semantically expanded from both Concept-Net and WordNet. Cosine similarity is used to measure the similarity between queries and images. During retrieval, two document indexes involved i.e. the standard index and the expanded index. Therefore, the score for each images are combined using a simple equation $S(i) = c_1 S_1(i) + c_2 S_2(i)$ whereby S_1 and S_2 represents the similarity score of image i for the first and second index respectively. c_1 and c_2 are weighted values for first and second index respectively, whereby $c_1 + c_2 = 1$. Table 2 illustrates the average precision for all tests which show that all the semantically enhanced index capable of increasing the average precision of the standard index. In this case $c_1 = 0.2$ and $c_2 = 0.8$. Fig. 5 illustrates the interpolated the precision-recall graph for all the test. The most significant is exhibited by the $S_{NER}+(S_{CNet}+S_{WNet})$ indexes. The results also show that the lexical ontology ConceptNet provides better semantic meaning expansion of the terms associated with each images. Furthermore NER approach was also seen as a useful for improving the precision and recall from its capability for discriminating different named entities found in the extracted terms.

Table 2. Precision at a standard recall level

Recall				Aveage Precision				
	S	$S+$ S_{CNet}	$S+$ S_{WNet}	$S+$ $(S_{CNet}+S_{WNet})$	S_{NER}	$S_{NER}+$ S_{CNet}	$S_{NER}+$ S_{WNet}	$S_{NER}+$ $(S_{CNet}+S_{WNet})$
0.0	0.73	0.84	0.82	0.92	0.82	0.91	0.91	1.00
0.1	0.73	0.84	0.82	0.92	0.82	0.91	0.91	1.00
0.2	0.54	0.74	0.56	0.76	0.73	0.86	0.75	0.88
0.3	0.45	0.61	0.46	0.62	0.65	0.77	0.66	0.78
0.4	0.42	0.57	0.44	0.59	0.58	0.68	0.60	0.69
0.5	0.41	0.56	0.42	0.57	0.56	0.65	0.57	0.66
0.6	0.40	0.56	0.40	0.56	0.52	0.59	0.52	0.60
0.7	0.39	0.53	0.40	0.53	0.50	0.59	0.51	0.59
0.8	0.39	0.51	0.39	0.51	0.48	0.58	0.48	0.58
0.9	0.39	0.50	0.39	0.50	0.48	0.57	0.48	0.57
1.0	0.39	0.49	0.39	0.50	0.48	0.56	0.48	0.57
Avg.	0.48	0.61	0.50	0.63	0.60	0.70	0.62	0.72
Increased %		27.08	4.17	31.25	25.00	45.83	29.16	50.00

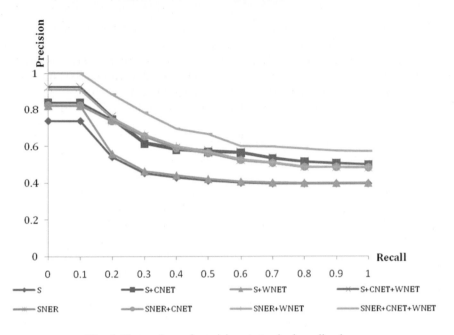

Fig. 4. Comparison of precision at standard recall values

5   Discussion and Conclusion

Semantically searched for images based on the low level features such as color and texture are still difficult to perform and little success development has been reported. The more practical approach is to use annotations or surrounding text for capturing the semantic meanings of images and subsequently extends such meanings to lexical ontology or resources. In this paper, we described an approach for extracting such textual meaning of on-line newspaper images from the description (unstructured annotation) and the surrounding text. The textual meaning is then semantically enhanced by mapping them to WordNet and common-sense concepts (or topics) which are derived from the ConceptNet lexical concepts. A set of NER patterns were designed in order to identify and differentiate important named entities in images. We scope our domain to the 'Nation' category of Malaysian on-line newspaper. Evaluation on the initial 800 images has shown promising result, but further evaluation is definitely required with more queries, larger data sets and on different domains.

WordNet has been the preferred lexical resource among information retrieval researchers for supporting semantic search and query expansion. However, not all terms can be directly associated with WordeNet synsets. While WordNet can provide structured semantic meanings for some terms or concepts, images can go beyond such meanings to common-sense concepts or knowledge. Our approach has shown that how topics or common sense concepts can be derived from the ConceptNet topic_jisting module in order to enhance the semantic search.

References

1. Benitez, A.B., Chang, S.-F.: Semantic Knowledge Construction from Annotated Image Collections, Multimedia and Expo, 2002. In: ICME 2002: Proceedings 2002 IEEE International Conference, vol. 2, pp. 205–208. IEEE Press, New York (2002)
2. Miller, G.A.,, W.: A Lexical Database for English. Communication of the ACM 38(11), 39–41 (1995)
3. Liu, H., Singh, P.: ConceptNet – A Practical Commonsense Reasoning Toolkit. BT Technology Journal 22(4), 211–226 (2002)
4. Noah, S.A., Azilawati, A., Tengku Sembok, T.M., Tengku Siti Meriam, T.W.: Exploiting Surrounding Text for Retrieving Web Images. Journal of Computer Science 4(10), 842–846 (2009)
5. Liu, H., Lieberman, H.: Robust Photo Retrieval Using World Semantics. In: Proceedings of the LREC 2002 Workshop on Creating and Using Semantics for Information Retrieval and Filtering, pp. 15–20 (2002)
6. Gong, Z., Leong, H.U., Cheang, C.W.: Web Image Indexing by Using Associated Data. Knowledge and Information Systems 10(2), 243–264 (2006)
7. Hua, Z., Wang, X.-J., Lui, Q., Lu, H.: Semantic Knowledge Extraction and Annotation for Web Image. In: Proceedings of the 13th Annual ACM International Conference on Multimedia, pp. 467–470. ACM Press, New York (2005)
8. Hsu, M.-H., Chen, H.-H.: Information Retrieval with Commonsense Knowledge. In: Proceedings of the 29th Annual International SIGIR Conference, pp. 651–652. ACM Press, New York (2006)
9. Kuo, C.-H., Chou, T.-C., Tsao, N.-L., Lan, Y.-H.: CANFIND: A Semantic Image Indexing and Retrieval System. In: Proceedings of the 2003 International Symposium on Circuits and Systems, vol. 2, pp. 644–647. IEEE Press, New York (2003)
10. Kawata, K., Sakai, H., Masuyama, S.: QUARK: A Question and Answering System Using Newspaper Corpus as a Knowledge Source. In: Proceeding of the 3rd NTCIR Workshop, National Institute of Informatics, Tokyo (2003)
11. Baeza-Yates, R., Ribeiro-Neto, B.: Modern Information Retrieval, pp. 10–10 6458-0189 18 W. Addison-Wesley, New York (1999)

Order Preserved Cost-Sensitive Listwise Approach in Learning to Rank

Min Lu[1], MaoQiang Xie[2,*], Yang Wang[1], Jie Liu[1], and YaLou Huang[1,2]

[1] College of Information Technology Science, Nankai University, Tianjin, China
[2] College of Software, Nankai University, Tianjin, China
{lumin,wangyang022,jliu}@mail.nankai.edu.cn
{xiemq,huangyl}@nankai.edu.cn

Abstract. The effectiveness of the cost-sensitive listwise approach has been verified in learning to rank. However, the order preservation and generalization of cost-sensitive listwise approach are not studied. The two properties are very important since they can guide to develop a better ranking method. In this paper, we establish a framework for order preserved cost-sensitive listwise ranking approach. The framework yields the conditions of order preservation for the cost-sensitive listwise method. In addition, the generalization of the order preserved cost-sensitive listwise approach is proven. According to the theorem of generalization, a novel loss function for order preserved cost-sensitive listwise approach has been proposed. The loss function not only is order preserved but also penalizes the model complexity by an auxiliary variable. As an example, we propose the order preserved cost-sensitive ListMLE algorithm. Experimental results show the proposed method outperforms the baselines.

1 Introduction

Learning to rank is a popular research area in machine learning and information retrieval(IR). In this paper, we focus on its application to document retrieval in IR. When applied to document retrieval, learning to ranking aims to learn a real-valued ranking function in training. In testing, the ranking function assigns a rank score for each document of a query, and sorts the documents in descending order of rank scores. Several approaches have been proposed, and are summarized into three categories: the pointwise, the pairwise and the listwise approach.

The listwise methods are attracted remarkable attention due to their high performance on the empirical datasets. The representative listwise methods include ListNet[1], RankCosine[2] and ListMLE[3]. In ListNet, the entropy is used to evaluate the similarity between the ranked list and the ground truth list. Nevertheless, the cosine similarity is used in the RankCosine. The ranked list is generated by sorting the documents in descending order of rank scores. The ground truth list is obtained from the descending order of document relevance level. ListMLE maximizes the likelihood probability of the ground truth list.

---

* Corresponding author.

P.-J. Cheng et al. (Eds.): AIRS 2010, LNCS 6458, pp. 203–210, 2010.

Meanwhile, the ranking order on the top of the ranked list is very important in IR, and the correct ranking list of all the documents is usually not needed. For instance, users care much more about the top ranked documents than the whole ranked list in the search engine. As a result, two variants of listwise approach are proposed to emphasize ranking order on the top of the ranked list. They are top-k consistency of ranking approach[4] and cost-sensitive listwise ranking approach [5]. The top-k ListMLE [4] maximizes the likelihood probability of permutation of the top k documents based on plackett-Luce model[6]. The cost-sensitive ListMLE[5] sets large coefficients(*i.e.*, weights) for the documents with higher ranks in the listwise loss function.

The effectiveness of cost-sensitive listwise ranking approach[5] is verified on several benchmark datasets. However, [5] does not study the two important properties: order preservation and generalization. The two properties should be cared about because they can guide to develop a better ranking method. The order preservation in ranking indicates whether the loss function can indeed represent the loss in ranking. Intuitively, suppose there are two ranked lists p_1 and p_2 with respect to the given query. When p_1 is superior to p_2, the value of the loss function on p_2 should be no less than that on p_1. The generalization represents the expected loss for an unseen query.

In this paper, we establish a framework for order preserved cost-sensitive listwise ranking approach. The framework yields the constraints of coefficients for the order preservation of the cost-sensitive listwise methods. It is validated that the cost-sensitive ListMLE[5] violates the constraints. In addition, the generalization of the order preserved cost-sensitive listwise approach is proven. As an example, the cost-sensitive ListMLE is modified into the order preserved cost-sensitive ListMLE, referred to OPCS.ListMLE. Experimental results show OPCS.ListMLE outperforms ListNet[1], Top-k ListMLE[4] and cost-sensitive ListMLE[5].

The rest of the paper is organized as follows. The cost-sensitive listwise approach is shortly introduced in Section 2. Section 3 describes the framework for order preserved cost-sensitive listwise approach. Section 4 presents the experimental results. The last section draws the conclusion.

2   Cost-Sensitive Listwise Approach

The purpose of the cost-sensitive listwise approach[5] was to emphasize the ranking order on the top of the ranked list. To achieve the target, [5] made use of the idea of cost-sensitive learning in the listwise loss function. More precisely, the documents in the listwise loss function were set with coefficients (*i.e.*, weights). The coefficients were computed based on the IR evaluation measure NDCG[7]. NDCG evaluates the performance about ranking order on the top of the ranked list. Moreover, a cost-sensitive ListMLE method was proposed, referred to CS-ListMLE. Its loss function on the query $q = \{(\boldsymbol{x_i}, y_i)\}_{i=1}^{n}$ was defined as:

$$L = Z \sum_{j=1}^{n} \beta_j \log \left(\sum_{t=j}^{n} \alpha_{j,t} \exp \left(\psi \left(f(\boldsymbol{x_t}) \right) - \psi \left(f(\boldsymbol{x_j}) \right) \right) \right) \qquad (1)$$

where x_i denote the feature vector of the document d_i. y_i is the relevance level of the document d_i. f is the ranking function, and $f(x_i)$ is the rank score of the document d_i. ψ denotes an increasing function. For the sake of describing simply, in the paper the documents have been ranked in descending order of document relevance level, i.e., $y_1 \succeq y_2 \ldots \succeq y_n$. The coefficients Z, β_j and $\alpha_{j,t}$ satisfy the following conditions.

$$Z > 0, \quad \beta_1 \geq \beta_2 \geq \ldots \beta_n \geq 0, \quad 0 \leq \alpha_{j,j+1} \leq \ldots, \alpha_{j,n} \leq \alpha_{j,j} = 1 \qquad (2)$$

3   A Framework for Order Preserved Cost-Sensitive Listwise Approach

In the paper, the cost-sensitive listwise approaches are referred to the methods whose loss function are defined in (1). The loss functions of all the cost-sensitive listwise approaches are proved to be bounded by functions being (1) plus a constant. The proof is easily verified for the cost-sensitive variants of ListNet and ListMLE. Regarding the cost-sensitive variant of RankCosine, the proof can be verified with the inequality $-\sqrt{z} < -\log(z)/2$.

3.1   Conditions of Order Preservation for Cost-Sensitive Listwise Approach

The framework first gives the conditions of the order preservation for the cost-sensitive listwise approach on the two ranked lists p_1 and p_2. In the ranked list p_1, the rank scores of the documents are $f(x_1), \ldots, f(x_n)$. The rank list p_2 is obtained by just exchanging the values of $f(x_s)$ and $f(x_t)$ in p_1 only.

Theorem 1. *If $s < t$ and $f(x_s) > f(x_t)$, the value of the cost-sensitive listwise loss function L defined in (1) on p_2 is no less than that on p_1 when the three following constraints are satisfied.*

1. $Z > 0 \quad \forall i, j \quad \beta_i \geq 0 \quad 0 \leq \alpha_{i,j} \leq 1$
2. $j = 1, 2, \ldots, s - 1 \quad \alpha_{j,s} \leq \alpha_{j,t}$
3. $\beta_s > \beta_t \quad \alpha_{s,s} \leq \alpha_{s,t}$

If p_1 is superior to p_2, the theorem 1 demonstrates the constraints of the coefficients for the order preservation on the p_1 and p_2. The proof of the theorem 1 is based on the principle: the value of each item in the loss function L on p_2 is no less than the value of the same item on p_1. The proof is omitted since it is easily verified. However, in theorem 1 the hypothesis is sufficient but not necessary for the conclusion. In other words, there is a case where the conclusion is obtained but the loss function L is not order preserved on the p_1 and p_2. The case is the value of the loss function L being constant. In that case, the value of the loss function on the p_2 is no less than p_1 even though the p_1 is inferior to p_2. Thus, the coefficients should be restricted to prevent the value of the loss function being constant. The sufficient and necessary constraints of the coefficients for order preservation of the cost-sensitive listwise approach are deduced:

1. $Z > 0$
2. $\beta_1 \geq \beta_2 \ldots \geq \beta_n \geq 0$
3. $\forall j \quad 0 \leq \alpha_{j,j} \leq \alpha_{j,j+1} \ldots \leq \alpha_{j,n} \leq 1$
4. $L \neq$ constant

For all j, when let $\alpha_{j,j} = \alpha_{j,j+1} \ldots \alpha_{j,n} = 1$, it is validated the order preservation of ListNet[1], ListMLE[3] and Top-k ListMLE[4]. However, the coefficients in the cost-sensitive ListMLE[5] defined in (2) violate the third constraint. Thus, the cost-sensitive ListMLE can be modified into the order preserved cost-sensitive ListMLE by accommodating the coefficients $\alpha_{j,j}$ for all j.

3.2   Generalization for Order Preserved Cost-Sensitive Listwise Approach

There are many coefficients complying with the constraints for the order preservation of the cost-sensitive listwise approach. Thus, it is necessary to study the effect of the coefficients to the loss on the unseen query. The generalization of the order preserved cost-sensitive listwise approach is proven.

Theorem 2. *Suppose the training set consists of N queries $q_1, q_2, \ldots, q_N$ drawn independently according to an unknown but fixed probability distribution $\mathcal{X} \times \mathcal{Y}$, where $\mathcal{X} \in \mathbb{R}^{n \times d}$ denotes the input space of n documents represented by d dimensional feature vectors, and let $\mathcal{Y}$ be the output space of the permutation of the documents. Each feature vector has norm bound R and model parameters $w \in \mathbb{R}^d$ has norm bound B. Let the loss function L be a lipschitz function with constant l. The expected loss of an unseen query Q is bounded with probability at least $1 - \delta$*

$$\boldsymbol{E}\left[L\left(w, Q\right)\right] \leq \frac{1}{N} \sum_{i=1}^{N} L\left(w, q_i\right) + 3lBR\sqrt{\frac{n}{N}} + \sqrt{\frac{8 \log\left(2/\delta\right)}{N}} \tag{3}$$

where $L(w, q)$ denotes the loss on the query q with model parameters being w. The detail of the proof is referred to [8]. The lipschitz constant l for the order preserved cost-sensitive listwise loss function is

$$l \leq Z \cdot \exp\left(\psi\left(BR\right) - \psi\left(-BR\right)\right) \cdot \sum_{i=1}^{n} \frac{\beta_i}{\sum_{j=i+1}^{n} \alpha_{i,j}} \max\left\{\alpha_{i,i+1}, \ldots, \alpha_{i,n}\right\} \tag{4}$$

The three key points implied in the theorem 2 can guide to develop better order preserved cost-sensitive listwise algorithms. They are listed as follows:

1. The major influence coefficients to the generalization are $Z, \beta_1, \beta_2, \ldots, \beta_n$.
2. The document pair $< d_i, d_j >$ can be emphasized with large value of $\alpha_{i,j}$, which does not affect much in the generalization error.
3. Since the model parameter w has norm bound B, the second term $3lBR\sqrt{\frac{n}{N}}$ in (3) can be interpreted as penalty $||w||_2^2$ in the generalization error.

To obtain good generalization, the empirical risk on the training set and the penalty on the model complexity should be minimized together. Hence, a novel loss function for the order preserved cost-sensitive listwise approach on the query is defined by

$$L = \frac{Z}{\gamma} \sum_{j=1}^{n} \beta_j \log \left\{ \sum_{t=j}^{n} \alpha_{j,t} \exp \left(\gamma \left(\psi \left(f \left(\boldsymbol{x_t} \right) \right) - \psi \left(f \left(\boldsymbol{x_j} \right) \right) \right) \right) \right\} \quad \gamma > 0 \qquad (5)$$

where the coefficients satisfy the conditions of the order preservation for cost-sensitive listwise approach. γ is an auxiliary variable. When the value of γ is large, the L penalizes much for the model parameter w with large value. The above statement can be deduced from the following approximation:

$$0 \leq \frac{1}{\gamma} \log \left(\sum_{i=1}^{n} \exp(\gamma \cdot \lambda z_i) \right) - \lambda \cdot \max \left\{ z_1, z_2, \ldots, z_n \right\} \leq \frac{1}{\gamma} \log n \qquad (6)$$

Compared to the cost-sensitive listwise loss function defined in (1), there are two advantages about the loss function L defined in (5). On the one hand, L has the property of order preservation. The order preservation makes L match the NDCG[7] metric better. On the other hand, L achieves a better generalization error by penalizing the model complexity. Since [5] proved that loss function defined in (1) is the upper bound of NDCG loss, it is deduced that L will achieve less NDCG loss for the unseen query.

3.3   A Case: Order Preserved Cost-Sensitive ListMLE Approach

As case study, the cost-sensitive ListMLE[5] is modified into the order preserved cost-sensitive ListMLE method, called OPCS.ListMLE. The loss function of OPCS.ListMLE on a query is defined in (5). In the experiments, let $\psi(z) = z$. The values of the coefficients in (5) are calculated based on the values of the coefficients in the loss function of CS-ListMLE(*i.e.*, cost-sensitive ListMLE).

With the abuse of notation, z_i, $\beta_{i,j}$ and $\alpha_{i,s,t}$ denote the coefficients Z, β_j and $\alpha_{s,t}$ in the CS-ListMLE loss function on the query q_i. z_i', $\beta_{i,j}'$ and $\alpha_{i,s,t}'$ denote the coefficients Z, β_j and $\alpha_{s,t}$ in the OPCS.ListMLE loss function on the query q_i. The values of the coefficients z_i', $\beta_{i,j}'$ and $\alpha_{i,s,t}'$ is listed in Table 1. The loss function of OPCS.ListMLE is optimized by Stochastic Gradient Descent(SGD) method. Since the loss function is convex, the model parameter converges to a global optimum[9].

Table 1. The Values of the Coefficients in the OPCS.ListMLE Loss Function

Coefficient	z_i'	$\beta_{i,j}'$	$\alpha_{i,s,s}'$
Value	$z_i / \max_j z_j$	$\beta_{i,j} / \max_{k,h} \beta_{k,h}$	$\min_{t=s+1,\ldots,n} \alpha_{i,s,t}$

4 Experiments

The experiments are conducted on the two datasets OHSUMED and TD2003 in Letor2.0[1]. The experiments validate whether OPCS.ListMLE obtains high performance about the ranking order on the top of the ranked list. NDCG@k(N@k) is used as evaluation measures with k taking 1, 3, 5 and 10. The baselines are summarized into three categories: state-of-the-art methods[10,11], representative listwise approaches[1,2,3] and Top-k ranking algorithms[4,5]. The methods Top-k ListMLE[4], CS-ListMLE@k[5] and OPCS.ListMLE@k focus on the ranking order of the top k documents in the ranked list.

4.1 Parameter Setting

Three parameters are manually tuned in the OPCS.ListMLE loss function. Two parameters are the learning rate η and tolerance factor ξ in the gradient descent method. The last parameter is the auxiliary variable γ. If the value of γ is large, the OPCS.ListMLE penalizes more for the model parameter with larger value. In the experiments, η takes 0.01 and 0.001, and ξ takes 1e-05 and 1e-06. The choices of γ are 10, 20, 30, 40 and 50. The combinations of all values of the parameters are tried in the experiments. There are $2 \times 2 \times 5$ experiments conducted for each fold in a dataset. The three parameters are selected on the validation set.

4.2 Experiment Results

The performances of OPCS.ListMLE and CS-ListMLE on the two datasets are reported in Table 2. The OPCS.ListMLE@k(k=5, 10) outperforms the CS-ListMLE@k(k=5, 10) on the dataset OHSUMED at all evaluation measures. The OPCS.ListMLE@1 achieves higher ranking accuracy than all versions of CS-ListMLE on the dataset TD2003. Moreover, OPCS.ListMLE@1 significantly outperforms CS-ListMLE on the two datasets at NDCG@1. We conduct t-test on the improvement of OPCS.ListMLE@1 over CS-ListMLE in terms of NDCG@1. The improvement of NDCG@1 over CS-ListMLE@k(k=3,5,10) on the dataset OHSUMED is statistically significant(p-value<0.05). There is no statistically significant difference on the dataset TD2003.

We take OPCS.ListMLE@1 as an example to compare the ranking accuracy of OPCS.ListMLE with the other baselines. The experimental results are illustrated in Table 3. On the one hand, OPCS.ListMLE@1 obtains the highest NDCG@1 among the methods on the dataset OHSUMED. The t-test on the improvement of OPCS.ListMLE@1 over the baselines in terms of NDCG@1 is conducted. The improvements over Ranking SVM[10], AdaRank[11] and ListNet[1] are statistically significant. On the other hand, OPCS.ListMLE@1 outperforms all the baselines on the dataset TD2003 at all evaluation measures, especially the NDCG@1. The t-test results show that OPCS.ListMLE@1 statistically outperforms Ranking SVM, AdaRank and ListNet. Note that the t-test on the

---

[1] http://research.microsoft.com/en-us/um/beijing/projects/letor/letor-old.aspx

Table 2. Test Results on Datasets OHSUMED and TD2003

	OHSUMED				TD2003			
Methods	N@1	N@3	N@5	N@10	N@1	N@3	N@5	N@10
CS-ListMLE@1	0.555	0.482	0.464	0.446	0.48	0.400	0.362	0.359
CS-ListMLE@3	0.539	0.480	0.458	0.446	0.48	0.400	0.364	0.358
CS-ListMLE@5	0.548	0.468	0.453	0.438	0.48	0.391	0.358	0.355
CS-ListMLE@10	0.536	0.471	0.452	0.439	0.48	0.398	0.362	0.350
OPCS.ListMLE@1	0.573	0.473	0.460	0.444	0.52	0.424	0.390	0.383
OPCS.ListMLE@3	0.567	0.472	0.454	0.441	0.5	0.390	0.367	0.366
OPCS.ListMLE@5	0.555	0.475	0.458	0.443	0.5	0.416	0.378	0.369
OPCS.ListMLE@10	0.539	0.471	0.456	0.443	0.5	0.375	0.359	0.375

Table 3. Ranking Accuracy on Datasets OHSUMED and TD2003

	OHSUMED				TD2003			
Methods	N@1	N@3	N@5	N@10	N@1	N@3	N@5	N@10
RSVM	0.495	0.465	0.458	0.441	0.42	0.379	0.347	0.34
AdaRank	0.514	0.462	0.442	0.437	0.42	0.291	0.242	0.194
RankCosine	0.523	0.475	–	0.437	0.36	0.346	–	0.322
ListNet	0.523	0.478	**0.466**	**0.449**	0.46	0.408	0.382	0.374
ListMLE	0.548	0.473	–	0.446	0.24	0.253	–	0.261
Top-1 ListMLE	0.529	**0.482**	–	0.447	0.4	0.329	–	0.314
Top-3 ListMLE	0.535	0.484	–	0.445	0.44	0.382	–	0.343
Top-10 ListMLE	0.558	0.473	–	0.444	0.5	0.410	–	0.378
OPCS.ListMLE@1	**0.573**	0.473	0.460	0.444	**0.52**	**0.424**	**0.390**	**0.383**

improvement of NDCG@1 over ListMLE, RankCosine and Top-k ListMLE on the two datasets is not conducted. Their performances at each fold on the two datasets are not published.

Experimental results demonstrate that the OPCS.ListMLE achieves higher ranking accuracy on the two dataset. However, the OPCS.ListMLE is a variant of the CS-ListMLE with coefficients normalization. The reason why the OPCS.ListMLE performs better is: the order preservation and generalization are incorporated into the cost-sensitive listwise methods. It demonstrates the effectiveness of the order preserved cost-sensitive listwise approach.

5   Conclusion

To develop better cost-sensitive listwise ranking methods, we study the two important properties: order preservation and generalization. We establish a framework for order preserved cost-sensitive listwise ranking approach. The framework yields the constraints of the coefficients for order preservation of the cost-sensitive listwise approach. In addition, the generalization of the order preserved cost-sensitive listwise approach is proven. We then analyze the effect of the coefficients and model complexity to the generalization error. According to the theorem of generalization, a novel loss function for order preserved cost-sensitive listwise approach has been proposed. The loss function not only is order preserved but also penalize the model complexity by an auxiliary variable. Moreover, the order preserved cost-sensitive ListMLE method is proposed, called OPCS.ListMLE. Experiment results on the benchmark datasets show the effectiveness of the order preserved cost-sensitive listwise methods.

Acknowledgments

Thanks to the anonymous reviewers, especially regarding writing and experiments. This work was supported by the National Natural Science Foundation of China under grant 60673009 and the Fundamental Research Funds for the Central Universities under grant 65010571 at NanKai University.

References

1. Cao, Z., Qin, T., Liu, T.Y., Tsai, M.F., Li, H.: Learning to rank: from pairwise approach to listwise approach. In: Proceedings of the 24th international Conference on Machine Learning, pp. 129–136. ACM, New York (2007)
2. Qin, T., Zhang, X.D., Tsai, M.F., Wang, D.S., Liu, T.Y., Li, H.: Query-level loss functions for information retrieval. Inf. Process. Manage. 44(2), 838–855 (2008)
3. Xia, F., Liu, T.Y., Wang, J., Zhang, W., Li, H.: Listwise approach to learning to rank: theory and algorithm. In: Proceedings of the 25th International Conference on Machine Learning, pp. 1192–1199. ACM, New York (2008)
4. Xia, F., Liu, T.Y., Li, H.: Top-k consistency of learning to rank methods. In: Advances in Neural Information Processing Systems, pp. 2098–2106 (2009)
5. Lu, M., Xie, M., Wang, Y., Liu, J., Huang, Y.: cost-sensitive listwise ranking approach. In: Proceedings of the 14th International Conference on Pacific-Asia Conference on Knowledge Discovery and Data Mining, pp. 358–366 (2010)
6. Marden, J.I.: Analyzing and Modeling Rank Data. Chapman and Hall, Boca Raton (1995)
7. Järvelin, K., Kekäläinen, J.: Cumulated gain-based evaluation of ir techniques. ACM Trans. Inf. Syst. 20(4), 422–446 (2002)
8. Chapelle, O., Wu, M.: Gradient descent optimization of smoothed information retrieval metrics. Information Retrieval
9. Boyd, S., Vandenberghe, L.: Convex Optimization. Cambridge University Press, Cambridge (March 2004)
10. Joachims, T.: Optimizing search engines using clickthrough data. In: Proceedings of the eighth ACM SIGKDD International Conference on Knowledge Discovery and Data Mining, pp. 133–142. ACM, New York (2002)
11. Xu, J., Li, H.: Adarank: a boosting algorithm for information retrieval. In: Proceedings of the 30th Annual International ACM SIGIR Conference on Research and Development in Information Retrieval, pp. 391–398. ACM, New York (2007)

Pseudo-Relevance Feedback Based on mRMR Criteria

Yuanbin Wu, Qi Zhang, Yaqian Zhou, and Xuanjing Huang

School of Computer Science, Fudan University
825 Zhangheng Road
Shanghai, P.R. China, 201203
{ybwu,qz,zhouyaqian,xjhuang}@fudan.edu.cn

Abstract. Pseudo-relevance feedback has shown to be an effective method in many information retrieval tasks. Various criteria have been proposed to rank terms extracted from the top ranked document of the initial retrieval results. However, most existing methods extract terms individually and do not consider the impacts of relationships among terms and their combinations. In this study, we first re-examine this assumption and show that combinations of terms may heavily impact the final results. We then present a novel clustering based method to select expansion terms as a whole set. The main idea is to use first simultaneously cluster terms and documents using non-negative matrix factorization, and then use the Maximum Relevance and Minimum Redundancy criteria to select terms based on their clusters, term distributions, and other features. Experimental results on serval TREC collections show that our proposed method significantly improves performances.

Keywords: Pseudo-relevance Feedback, NMF, mRMR Criteria.

1 Introduction

With the ever-increasing growth of the World-Wide Web, the number of casual search engines users has grown rapidly. However user queries are usually too short to describe the accurate information they need. The analysis [1] shows that the average query length is 1.7 terms for popular queries and 2.2 terms over all queries. In order to address this problem, query expansion has been receiving much attention in a long time [2,3,4,5,6,7,8]. Among all the query expansion methods, pseudo-relevance feedback (PRF) [9,10] is nearly the most attractive one because it does not require any user input. PRF assumes that top ranked documents are relevant. Many approaches have been presented to extract useful terms from those pseudo-relevant documents. Serval criteria have also been proposed to select expansion terms based on term distributions, such as idf, tf, χ^2 statistic, web resource (e.g Wikipedia), linguistic feature, ontology and so on. More recently, supervised learning methods have also been studied[5,11].

However, previous research efforts have mainly focused on extracting terms separately without considering the impacts of relationships among terms and their combinations. Selection of terms is typically performed in a greedy manner using some type of score or rank. As a result, the performances of current models are usually unstable and the improvements are limited. Several experiments in Section 3 show that term combinations can highly impact the final results. This in turn leads to a natural question: how can we select *a set* of expansion terms from pseudo-feedback documents?

P.-J. Cheng et al. (Eds.): AIRS 2010, LNCS 6458, pp. 211–220, 2010.

To address the above question, we propose to seek a set of terms by requiring that: 1) the terms are related to the query and useful for Information Retrieval (IR) according to their distributions, linguistic features, and so on; 2) redundancy of the terms is minimum, in other words, the terms should be maximally dissimilar to each other. In this paper, we use non-negative matrix factorization method to cluster the terms and capture their pairwise correlations. Then a novel expansion term selection algorithm is used to extract a set of terms. We compare the proposed algorithm with the traditional approaches on five TREC test collections. The experimental results show that our proposed term selection method achieves good performance and is able to improve the retrieval effectiveness significantly.

The contributions of our work can be summarized as follows: 1) We thoroughly evaluate impacts of relationships among terms and their combinations for pseudo relevance feedback. 2) We propose a novel maximum relevance and minimum redundancy criteria to select expansion terms. In contrast to existing work, expansion terms are selected as a set, and the relationships among them are considered.

The remaining of the paper is organized as follows: In Section 2, we review a number of related work and the state-of-the-art approaches in query expansion. Section 3 provides experimental examinations of the hypothesis about term combinations and shows that it does hold in practice. In Section 4, we present our expansion criteria. Experimental results on five TREC test collections are shown in Section 5. Finally, Section 6 concludes and suggests some future work.

2   Related Work

The approach presented in this paper is related to previous work on pseudo-relevance feedback and Non-negative Matrix Factorization.

The problem of how to automatically extract useful terms from the top rank initial retrieval set is a long-studied task. Since no user input is required, pseudo-relevance feedback (PRF) has received considerable attentions. Statistical based query expansion is one of the classical methods. Okapi [12] adds the 20 top ranking terms, which is scored by $BM25$ weight, for query expansion. Carpineto et al.[8] introduced an information-theoretic method, including Rocchio's weights, Robertson Selection Value (RSV), CHI-squared, and Kullback-Leibler distance, for query expansion.

Many approaches have been proposed to improve the effectiveness of PRF with external resources, such as Wordnet[13], dependency relations[14], and so on. Xu et al.[2] explored the utilization of wikipedia in PRF. They categorized the TREC topics into three types based on wikipedia and proposed different methods for term selection with wikipedia entity pages. Collins-Thompson and Callan [15] described a Markov chain model that combines multiple sources of knowledge on term associations, and allows chaining of multiple inference steps with different link types to perform "semantic smoothing" on language models, and applied this model to query expansion.

Recently, there has been work focused on selecting better documents for pseudo-relevance feedback. Sakai et al. [16] proposed an approach to skip documents in the initial ranked documents to look for more "novel" pseudo-relevant documents.

They used cluster method to collect novel documents rather than separating relevant documents from non-relevant ones. However, their experiments on NTCIR collections did no show significant improvements. Lee et al.[3] proposed an approach to resample the top-ranked documents using clusters. They assumed that document that appears in multiple highly-ranked clusters would contribute more to the query terms than other documents.

Huang and Croft [17] proposed a framework to expand queries with a small number of opinion words. A number of sentiment expansion approaches were used to find the most appropriate query-independent or query-dependent opinion words. However, the query expansion method they used is query independent. It only forces on the opinion retreval domain.

Supervised learning methods have also been proposed to classify expansion terms. Zhang et al. [11] proposed a method to automatically evaluate the retrieval effectiveness of terms. Then SVM is used to select terms directly based on statistical features. Cao et al. [5] re-examined the assumption of pseudo-relevance feedback and used the similar idea to select expansion terms.

The most similar work to our proposal is the method proposed by Udupa et al. [18]. They claimed that the effect of including a term into an expansion set depended on the rest of the terms in the expansion set. They proposed to use spectral partitioning of term-term interaction matrix to takes into account term interactions. Different from their approach, we propose to use maximum relevance and minimum redundancy criteria to select terms as a whole. The redundancy is captured by term clusters, which is obtained by constrained non-negative matrix factorization method. Term distributions and linguistic features are used to measure the relevance.

3   Motivation

As we mentioned in Section 1, our approach selects expansion terms as a whole set. The general assumption behind it is that the relationships among terms and their combinations can impact the final retrieval result. To evaluate this assumption, we consider all the "good" expansion terms and their combinations.

Suppose $MAP(q)$ represents the mean-average-precision of the original query q and $MAP(q \bigcup t_i)$ represents the MAP of the expanded query(original query with term t_i). Following the formula proposed in [5], the performance change due to t_i is measured by $chg(t_i) = \frac{MAP(q \bigcup t_i) - MAP(q)}{MAP(q)}$. *Good expansion terms* are those whose $chg(t_i)$ is bigger than 0.05[1].

Since the size of vocabulary is too big and the evaluation is a time consuming task, we use the following score function to select top 200 words as candidate terms:

$$Score(t_i, q) = \log \frac{(r_i + 0.5) * (N - n_i - R + r_i + 0.5)}{(R - r_i + 0.5) * (n_i - r_i + 0.5)} \quad (1)$$

where N is the total number of documents, R is the number of relevant documents, the number of documents and relevant documents containing term t_i are respectively

---

[1] Cao et al. [5] set up this threshold to 0.005. Because of the computational limitations, we use a higher threshold to reduce the number of expansion sets.

Table 1. MAP at all test collections with different expansion queries

Collection	BM25	Best	Worst	Top 5
TREC 7	0.1815	0.3792	0.1565	0.3320
TREC 8	0.2385	0.3518	0.2032	0.3194
TREC 10 Web	0.1923	0.4212	0.1636	0.2767
Blog2006	0.3040	0.4560	0.2135	0.3840
Blog2007	0.3744	0.5296	0.2992	0.4687

represented by n_i and r_i[19]. The top 20 documents[2] are regarded as relevant in our experiments. Then, good expansion terms are measured and selected by $chg(t)$ from the candidate terms.

Through the above steps, we can obtain a set of good expansion terms for each topic. In order to evaluate the impact of their combinations, $C_{|G_k|}^5$ expanded queries are generated where $|G_k|$ represents the count of good expansion terms in topic k and $C_{|G_k|}^5$, is the number of 5-combinations from the good expansion terms. In our examination, the maximum size of $|G_k|$ is set to 20. Each expanded query contains both the original query and five additional terms, which are selected by $chg(t_i)$. We use Lemur toolkit[3] to conduct the experiments in this paper.

Five TREC collections are used to examine the assumption and their description can be found in Section 6.1. in TREC 7 (from topic 351 to $C_{|G_k|}^5$ Table 1 shows the summary results in different collections. The fourth column "Top 5" represents the result of combining initial query with five additional terms whose $chg(t_i)$ are the highest among all the candidate terms.

As we can see, pseudo-relevance feedback is effective when good expansion set is selected. In TREC 7, the relative improvement of the best expansion set over the initial result is 108.9%. However, although every single term can improve the retrieval result, their combinations may deteriorate the performance. In all collections, the worst results with query expansions of some topics are even much lower than the result of the initial query without any expansion terms. We also note from the Table 1 that the best expansion set achieves better result than the *Top 5*. In other words, although each single term can only improve the result slightly, their combination can be more effective.

4   Query Expansion Methods

Figure 1 shows the overview of our proposed query expansion methods. First of all the system returns an initial set of retrieval results with the given query. Then the unigram language model is applied to generate term-document matrix. After that non-negative matrix factorization methods are used on term-document matrix. Upon convergence of the matrix factorization algorithm, term-cluster and document-cluster matrices are

---

[2] Both Huang & Croft's results [17] and our experimental results show that the number of pseudo relevance documents from five to twenty are reasonable estimations.

[3] http://www.lemurproject.org/

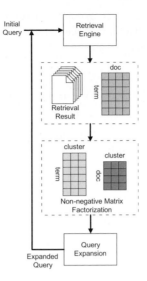

Fig. 1. Overview of our methods

obtained. Given the two matrices, query expansion set can be generated by different query expansion methods, which will be detailedly described in the following parts.

4.1 Coverage Criterion for Query Expansion

From analyzing clustering result of the top-ranked documents, we observe that those documents usually correspond to several different topics. Different clusters usually contain different concepts. Buckley et al.[20] also mentioned the observation. Since the intention of the query cannot be easily detected, including all major topics should be useful for the expansion queries.

In order to improve the coverage of expansion queries, one of the straightforward method is to select terms from each clusters. Since clusters have different size, a balanced way to select terms from the multiple clusters should be considered. We assume that clusters with more documents are more important. Based on this assumption, the number of terms extracted from cluster C_i is set to $\lceil \frac{|C_i|}{N} \rceil$, where N is the total number of documents and $|C_i|$ represents the number of documents in the cluster. In each cluster, terms are ranked by Eq.(1).

4.2 Maximum Relevance and Minimum Redundancy Criterion for Query Expansion (mRMR-QE)

Ding and Peng [21] proposed *minimal-redundancy-maximal-relevance*(mRMR) framework to select promising features. Inspired by their work on feature selection, we redefine the *maximal relevance* constraint and *minimal redundancy* constraint for text retrieval, and combine them as mRMR-QE criterion for query expansion.

The maximal relevance condition is to search a set of terms T satisfying Eq.(2). $Score_{c_i}(t_i, q)$ is similar to that in Eq.(1), except that R is the number of relevant documents in cluster c_i. $\max_{c_i \in C} Score_{c_i}(t_i, q)$ represents the maximum relevance score of the term to a cluster. The relevance between T and q is measured by the sum of individual term t_i and query q.

$$\max Rel(T, q),$$
$$Rel(T, q) = \sum_{t_i \in T} \max_{c_i \in C} Score_{c_i}(t_i, q) \tag{2}$$

However, it is likely that the redundancy among the terms selected according to the maximal relevance criterion could be rich. More over, from the analysis of Section 3, we observe that the including terms which are highly dependent on each other may degrade the result. Therefore, the following minimal redundancy criterion can be used to select mutually exclusive terms.

$$\min Red(T, q),$$
$$Red(T, q) = \frac{1}{|T|^2} \sum_{t_i, t_j \in T} I(t_i, t_j), \tag{3}$$

where $I(x_i, x_j)$ represents the mutual information between term t_i and t_j.

Combing the maximal relevance and minimal redundancy creation, the maximum relevance and minimum redundancy Criterion for query expansion (mRMR-QE) is defined by the Eq.(4).

$$\arg \max_{T \in \mathcal{T}} (Rel(T, q) - Red(T, q)) \tag{4}$$

Following the method proposed in [22], an incremental search method is used in practice. Suppose we already have T_{m-1}, which contains $m - 1$ terms. Then Eq.(5) is used to select the mth term from the remaining set $\{W - T_{m-1}\}$.

$$\arg \max_{t_i \in \{W - T_{m-1}\}} \{Rel(T_{m-1} \cup t_i, q) - Red(T_{m-1} \cup t_i, q)\} \tag{5}$$

5   Experiments

5.1   Collections

We evaluate our methods with three TREC corpus Disk4&5, WT10g and BLOGS06. Five test collections, TREC 7, TREC 8, TREC 10 Web, TREC Blog 2006, and TREC Blog 2007, are used in the experiments. We implement our expansion methods based on Lemur 4.10 [4]. Okapi BM25 ranking function is used as the retrieval model. All test collections and corpus were stemmed using the Porter stemmer provided as part of Lemur. As for performance measures, the mean average precision (MAP) for top 1000 documents is the primary evaluation metric in all the test collections. Other metrics include precision at five documents (P@5), precision at ten documents (P@10), R-precision (R-prec), and binary Preference (bPref). We also conduct τ-test to determine where the improvement on performance statistically significant.

---

[4] http://www.lemurproject.org

Table 2. Ad-hoc retrieval results on all the test collections with Okapi BM25 function and pseudo relevance feedback using coverage criterion. * indicates that the improvement over "BM25+PRF" is statistically significant($p < 0.05$).

Collection	P@10	bPref	R-prec	MAP-P	MAP
TREC 7	0.3920	0.2423	0.2636	0.2303	0.2355
TREC 8	0.4640	0.2574	0.2812	0.2489	0.2555 *
Blog2006	0.6812	0.3615	0.3961	0.3150	0.3095
Blog2007	0.6700	0.4001	0.4111	0.3912	0.3849
TREC10Web	0.3086	0.1809	0.2319	0.2070	0.2086

Table 3. Ad-hoc retrieval results on all the test collections with Okapi BM25 function and pseudo relevance feedback using mRMR-QE criterion. * indicates that the improvement over coverage criterion is statistically significant at level $p < 0.05$.

Collection	P@10	bPref	R-prec	MAP-P	MAP
TREC 7	0.4440	0.2557	0.2775	0.2303	0.2494 *
TREC 8	0.4860	0.2759	0.3046	0.2489	0.2776 *
Blog2006	0.6937	0.3676	0.4106	0.3150	0.3389 *
Blog2007	0.7060	0.4072	0.4227	0.3912	0.4017
TREC10Web	0.3216	0.1862	0.2343	0.2070	0.2109

5.2 Coverage Criterion Evaluation

Table 2 contains the results of experiments in all test collections using Okapi BM25 ranking function and pseudo relevance feedback with coverage criterion. The left column in the table shows the test collections. Each row in the table represents the results of different performance metrics. The column "MAP-P" represents results of the Okapi BM25 ranking function with traditional pseudo relevance feedback. For all four collections, 20 terms are sorted by Eq. 1 and extracted with coverage criterion from 5 top-ranked documents.

From the table we can observe that the coverage criterion achieve better results than the original pseudo relevance feedback method in all four collections. In TREC 8 collection, the criterion achieves significant improvement. The results we obtained in TREC 7 and TREC 8 are the state-of-the-art performance. Compared to "BM25+PRF ", not only the MAP but also most of the other evaluation metrics achieve better results among the collections. Those results can also demonstrate the observation we mentioned in the previous sections.

5.3 mRMR-QE Evaluation

In this experiment, we also use the TREC corpus Disk4&5, WT10g, and BLOGS06 to test the performances. In the same way as previous experiments, five test collections, TREC 7, TREC 8, TREC 10 Web, TREC Blog 2006, and TREC Blog 2007, are evaluated. Table 3 summaries the results of experiments in all test collections using Okapi

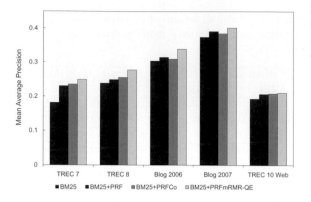

Fig. 2. Performance comparisons of different expansion methods using MAP

BM25 ranking function and pseudo relevance feedback with mRMR-QE criterion. The same parameters are used in this experiment.

From the Table 3, we observe that expansion terms extracted by pseudo relevance feedback with maximum relevance and minimum redundancy criterion can significantly improve the retrieval effectiveness. In all the collections, mRMR-QE criterion achieves better results than coverage criterion in most performance metrics. Figure 2 shows the performance comparisons of different expansion methods. Those results show that mRMR-QE criterion can capture the good expansion terms more effectively than pervious approaches. This is consistent with the observations we studied in the Section 3. We also note from the retrieval result that more than 69.2% of expansion queries give positive impact over the original queries, which is also more robust than coverage criterion.

6   Conclusions

In this paper, we studied the impacts of the relationships among terms and their combinations. Through several empirical experiments, we show that retrieval performance would significantly impacted by the combinations of expansion terms. In all five test collections, the best expansion can significantly improve the retrieval result.

In order to address this problem, we presented a novel clustering based method to select expansion terms as a set. The main idea is to first simultaneously cluster terms and documents, and then use Maximum Relevance and Minimum Redundancy criteria to select terms based on their clusters, term distributions, and other features. We evaluated the results with five different TREC collections. We also discussed the factors in our proposed method, including the number of expansion terms and the number of pseudo relevance documents.

Acknowledgements

The author wishes to thank the anonymous reviewers for their helpful comments. This work was partially funded by 973 Program (2010CB327906), The National High

Technology Research and Development Program of China (2009AA01A346), Shang-hai Leading Academic Discipline Project (B114), Doctoral Fund of Ministry of Education of China (200802460066), National Natural Science Funds for Distinguished Young Scholar of China (61003092), and Shanghai Science and Technology Development Funds (08511500302).

References

1. Beitzel, S.M., Jensen, E.C., Chowdhury, A., Grossman, D., Frieder, O.: Hourly analysis of a very large topically categorized web query log. In: SIGIR 2004: Proceedings of the 27th Annual International ACM SIGIR Conference on Research and Development in Information Retrieval, pp. 321–328. ACM, New York (2004)
2. Xu, Y., Jones, G.J., Wang, B.: Query dependent pseudo-relevance feedback based on wikipedia. In: SIGIR 2009: Proceedings of the 32nd International ACM SIGIR Conference on Research and Development in Information Retrieval, pp. 59–66. ACM, New York (2009)
3. Lee, K.S., Croft, W.B., Allan, J.: A cluster-based resampling method for pseudo-relevance feedback. In: SIGIR 2008: Proceedings of the 31st Annual International ACM SIGIR Conference on Research and Development in Information Retrieval, pp. 235–242. ACM, New York (2008)
4. Collins-Thompson, K., Callan, J.: Estimation and use of uncertainty in pseudo-relevance feedback. In: SIGIR 2007: Proceedings of the 30th Annual International ACM SIGIR Conference on Research and evelopment in Information Retrieval, pp. 303–310. ACM, New York (2007)
5. Cao, G., Nie, J.Y., Gao, J., Robertson, S.: Selecting good expansion terms for pseudo-relevance feedback. In: SIGIR 2008: Proceedings of the 31st Annual International ACM SIGIR Conference on Research and Development in Information Retrieval, pp. 243–250. ACM, New York (2008)
6. Tao, T., Zhai, C.: Regularized estimation of mixture models for robust pseudo-relevance feedback. In: Proceedings of SIGIR 2006, pp. 162–169. ACM, New York (2006)
7. Bhogal, J., Macfarlane, A., Smith, P.: A review of ontology based query expansion. Information Processing & Management 43(4), 866–886 (2007)
8. Carpineto, C., de Mori, R., Romano, G., Bigi, B.: An information-theoretic approach to automatic query expansion. ACM Transactions on Information Systems 19(1), 1–27 (2001)
9. Buckley, C.: Automatic query expansion using SMART: TREC 3. In: Proceedings of The Third Text REtrieval Conference (TREC-3), pp. 69–80 (1994)
10. Yu, S., Cai, D., Wen, J.R., Ma, W.Y.: Improving pseudo-relevance feedback in web information retrieval using web page segmentation. In: Proceedings of WWW 2003, pp. 11–18. ACM, New York (2003)
11. Zhang, Q., Wang, B., Huang, X.H., Wu, L.: FDU at TREC 2007: opinion retrieval of blog track. In: Proceedings of The Sixteen Text REtrieval Conference, TREC-2007 (2007)
12. Robertson, S.E., Walker, S., Hancock-Beaulieu, M.M., Gatford, M., Payne, A.: Okapi at TREC-4. In: Proceedings of The Fourth Text REtrieval Conference, TREC-4 (1996)
13. Moldovan, D.I., Mihalcea, R.: Using wordnet and lexical operators to improve internet searches. IEEE Internet Computing 4(1), 34–43 (2000)
14. Sun, R., Ong, C.H., Chua, T.S.: Mining dependency relations for query expansion in passage retrieval. In: Proceedings of SIGIR 2006, pp. 382–389. ACM, New York (2006)
15. Collins-Thompson, K., Callan, J.: Query expansion using random walk models. In: CIKM 2005: Proceedings of the 14th ACM international conference on Information and knowledge management, pp. 704–711. ACM, New York (2005)

16. Sakai, T., Manabe, T., Koyama, M.: Flexible pseudo-relevance feedback via selective sampling. ACM Transactions on Asian Language Information Processing (TALIP) 4(2), 111–135 (2005)
17. Huang, X., Croft, W.B.: A unified relevance model for opinion retrieval. In: Proceedings of 16th Conference on Information and Knowledge Management (CIKM 2009), Hong Kong, China (2009)
18. Udupa, R., Bhole, A., Bhattacharyya, P.: A term is known by the company it keeps: On selecting a good expansion set in pseudo relevance feedback. In: Azzopardi, L., Kazai, G., Robertson, S., Rüger, S., Shokouhi, M., Song, D., Yilmaz, E. (eds.) ICTIR 2009. LNCS, vol. 5766, pp. 104–115. Springer, Heidelberg (2009)
19. Robertson, S.E.: On term selection for query expansion. Journal of Documentation 46(4), 359–364 (1990)
20. Buckley, C., Mitra, M., Walz, J.A., Cardie, C.: Using clustering and superconcepts within SMART: TREC 6. Inf. Process. Manage. 36(1), 109–131 (2000)
21. Ding, C., Peng, H.: Minimum redundancy feature selection from microarray gene expression data. In: CSB 2003: Proceedings of the IEEE Computer Society Conference on Bioinformatics, Washington, DC, USA, p. 523. IEEE Computer Society Press, Los Alamitos (2003)
22. Peng, H., Long, F., Ding, C.: Feature selection based on mutual information: Criteria of max-dependency, max-relevance, and min-redundancy. IEEE Transactions on Pattern Analysis and Machine Intelligence 27(8), 1226–1238 (2005)

An Integrated Deterministic and Nondeterministic Inference Algorithm for Sequential Labeling

Yu-Chieh Wu[1], Yue-Shi Lee[3], Jie-Chi Yang[2], and Show-Jane Yen[3]

[1] Finance Department and School of Communication, Ming Chuan University,
No. 250 Zhong Shan N. Rd., Sec. 5, Taipei 111, Taiwan
`bcbb@db.csie.ncu.edu.tw`
[2] Graduate Institute of Network Learning Technology, National Central University,
No.300, Jhong-Da Rd., Jhongli City, Taoyuan County 32001, Taiwan, R.O.C.
`yang@cl.ncu.edu.tw`
[3] Department of Computer Science and Information Engineering, Ming Chuan University,
No.5, De-Ming Rd, Gweishan District, Taoyuan 333, Taiwan, R.O.C.
`{leeys,sjyen}@mcu.edu.tw`

Abstract. In this paper, we present a new search algorithm for sequential labeling tasks based on the conditional Markov models (CMMs) frameworks. Unlike conventional beam search, our method traverses all possible incoming arcs and also considers the "local best" so-far of each previous node. Furthermore, we propose two heuristics to fit the efficiency requirement. To demonstrate the effect of our method, six variant and large-scale sequential labeling tasks were conducted in the experiment. In addition, we compare our method to Viterbi and Beam search approaches. The experimental results show that our method yields not only substantial improvement in runtime efficiency, but also slightly better accuracy. In short, our method achieves 94.49 $F_{(\beta)}$ rate in the well-known CoNLL-2000 chunking task.

Keywords: L_2-regularization, part-of-speech tagging, support vector machines, machine learning.

1 Introduction

The sequential chunk labeling aims at finding non-recursive chunk fragments in a sentence. Arbitrary phrase chunking and named entity recognition are the well-known instances. Over the past few years, the structural learning methods, like conditional random fields (CRFs) [8] and maximum-margin Markov models (M^3N) [16] showed great accuracy in many natural language learning tasks. Structured learners also have the advantage of taking the entire structure into consideration instead of a limited history.

On the contrary, the goal of local-classifier-based approaches (e.g. maximum entropy models) is to learn to predict labels with fixed context window features. Those methods need to encode the history to inform the learners explicitly. Although high order features (i.e., large history) maybe useful for prediction, the runtime is often intractable to the case of large-scale and large category tasks. However, the training

P.-J. Cheng et al. (Eds.): AIRS 2010, LNCS 6458, pp. 221–230, 2010.
© Springer-Verlag Berlin Heidelberg 2010

time of local-classifier-based methods is very efficient since the training instances can be treated independently.

Support vector machines (SVMs) which is one of the state-of-the-art supervised learning algorithms have been widely employed as local classifiers to many sequential labeling tasks [7, 5, 19]. In particular, the learning time of linear kernel SVM can now be trained in linear time [4]. Even though local classifier-based approaches have the drawbacks of label-bias problems [8], training linear kernel SVM is not difficult to the case of large-scale and large-category data. By means of so-called one-versus-all or one-versus-one multiclass SVM training, the learning process could be decomposed into a set of independent tasks.

In this paper, we present a hybrid deterministic and nondeterministic inference algorithm based on conditional Markov model (CMMs) framework. The algorithm makes use of the "so-far" local optimal incoming information and traverses all possible incoming arcs to predict current label. Then a modified Viterbi search method could be adopted to find the optimal label sequence with this manner. To utilize the characteristics of sequential chunk labeling tasks, we propose two heuristics to enhance the efficiency and performance. One is to automatically construct the connections between chunk tags, while the other is designed to centralize the computation efforts. To demonstrate our method, we conduct the experiments with six famous chunking tasks. We also compare our method with different inference strategies.

2   Frameworks of Conditional Markov Models

The goal of conditional Markov models (CMMs) is to assign the tag sequence with maximum conditional probability given the observation sequence,

$$P(s_1, s_2, ..., s_n \mid o_1, o_2, ..., o_n)$$

where s_i is the tag of word i. For the first order left-to-right CMMs, the chain rule decomposes the probabilistic function as:

$$P(s_1, s_2, ..., s_n \mid o_1, o_2, ..., o_n) = \prod_{i=1}^{n} P(s_i \mid s_{i-1}, o_i) \tag{1}$$

Based on the above setting, one can employ a local classifier to predict $P(s_i \mid s_{i-1}, o_i)$ and the optimal tag sequence can be searched by using conventional Viterbi search.

Fig. 1 illustrates the graph of employing variant order of the CMMs (0, 1st, 2nd, and the proposed 2nd order CMMs). The chain probability decompositions of the four CMMs types in Fig. 1 can be shown as follows:

$$P(s, o) = \prod_{i=1}^{n} P(s_i \mid o_i) \tag{2}$$

$$P(s, o) = \prod_{i=2}^{n} P(s_i \mid o_i, s_{i-1}) \tag{3}$$

$$P(s, o) = \prod_{i=3}^{n} P(s_i \mid o_i, s_{i-1}, s_{i-2}) \tag{4}$$

$$P(s,o) = \prod_{i=3}^{n} P(s_i \mid o_i, s_{i-1}, \hat{s}_{i-1}) \tag{5}$$

Equation (2), (3), and (4) are merely standard zero, first and second order decompositions, while equation (5) is the proposed hybrid second order CMMs decomposition which will be discussed in next section.

The above decompositions merge the transition and emission probability with single function. McCallum et al. [9] further combined the locally trained maximum entropy with the inferred transition score. However, our conditional support vector Markov models make different chain probability. We replace the original transition probability with transition validity score, i.e.

$$P(s,o) = \prod_{i=2}^{n} \tilde{P}(s_i \mid s_{i-1}) P(s_i \mid o_i) \tag{6}$$

$$P(s,o) = \prod_{i=3}^{n} \hat{P}(s_i \mid s_{i-1}) P(s_i \mid o_i, s_{i-1}, \hat{s}_{i-1}) \tag{7}$$

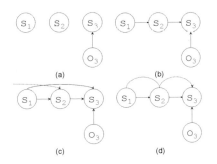

Fig. 1. Variant order of conditional Markov models: (a) the standard 0(zero) order CMMs, (b) first order CMMs, (c) second order CMMs, and (d) the proposed second order CMMs

The transition validity score is merely a Boolean flag which indicates the relationships between two neighbor labels. Equation (6) and (7) are zero-order and *our second order* chain probabilities. We will introduce the proposed inference algorithm and how to obtain the transition validity score automatically without concerning the change of chunk representation.

2.1 Hybrid Deterministic and Nondeterministic Inference Algorithm

In general, incorporating high order information (rich history) could improve the accuracy. However, it is often the case that the inference time of high order CMMs exponentially scales with the number of history, i.e., K. For example, to compute best incoming arc for s_i in the second order CMM, it needs to enumerate all combinations of s_{i-1} and s_{i-2}.

To reduce the curse of high order information, we present an approximate inference algorithm that has the same computational time complexity as first-order Markov models. This method considers all combinations between previous nodes and current node while the history is kept as greedy. More specific, for each previous node s_{i-1}, we traverse the optimal incoming path to incrementally determine s_{i-2}, s_{i-3},...,s_{i-k+1}, instead of enumerating all combinations of the history. This can also be viewed as a variant type of traditional Viterbi algorithm. Fig. 2 illustrates the proposed inference algorithm.

The same as most local classifier-based approaches, in training phase, the history information is known in advanced. In testing, it determines the optimal label sequence by three factors: the accumulated probability, transition validity score, and the output of local classifier. The local classifier (SVMs) should generate different decisions when the given history changes. The algorithm iteratively keeps and stores the optimal incoming arcs in order to trace the local best history. By following this line, the local classifier can concentrate on comparing all possible label pairs (previous and current nodes). Finally, the algorithm traces back the path to determine the output label sequence.

3   Speed-up Heuristics

3.1   Automatic Chunk Relation Construction

In this paper, we argue that the transition probability is not useful to our CMMs framework. Nevertheless, one important property to sequential chunk labeling is that there is only one phrase type in a chunk. For example, if the previous word is tagged as begin of noun phrase (B-NP), the current word must not be end of the other phrase (E-VP, E-PP, etc). Therefore, we only model relationships between chunk tags to generate valid phrase structure. In other words, we eliminate the influence of tag transition probability. Hence the local classifiers play the critical roles in the Markov process.

Wu et al. [19] presented an automatic chunk pair relation construction algorithm which can handle so-called IOB1/IOB2/IOE1/IOE2 [7 17] chunk representation structures with either left-to-right or right-to-left directions. However, the main limitation is that it only works well on IOB or IOE tags rather than more complex phrase structures, for example SBIE. As reported by [20], the use of rich chunk representation such as second begin and third begin of chunk yielded better accuracy in most Chinese word segmentation tasks. It is very useful to represent the Chinese proper name which usually contains more than 5 characters.

To remedy this, we extend the observations from [19] and propose a more general way to automatically build the valid chunk tag relations. The same as previous literature, our method is also applicable to either left-to-right or right-to-left direction. The main concept is to find the valid relationships between leading tags (for example B/I/E/S) and project them to all chunk tags. The summary of this method is listed below.

1.   Enumerate all possible leading tags
2.   Initialize all pairs of leading tags with no relation
3.   Scan the training data and classify the leading tags into the three categories:
     (1)   the same phrase but different leading tag (e.g. B-NP, I-NP)
     (2)   the same phrase and the same leading tag (e.g. I-NP, I-NP)
     (3)   different phrase and different leading tag (e.g. S-NP B-VP)
4.   Construct the chunk pair validity matrix by projecting the leading tag relation

We use the Boolean value to represent the relation score of a pair of chunk tag (0: invalid/ 1: valid). That is, $\tilde{P}(s_i \mid s_{i-1})$ is derived via the above approach.

Initialization:
$$\delta_0(k) := 1$$
$$\psi_0(k) := 0$$
Recursive:
$$\delta_{t+1}(s_j) := \max_{i=1 \sim m} \delta_t(s_i)\tilde{p}(s_j \mid s_i)p(s_j \mid s_i, \hat{s}_{i-1}, o_j)$$
where
$$\hat{s}_{i-1} := \arg\max_{h=1 \sim m} \psi_i(s_h)$$
$$\psi_{t+1}(s_j) := \arg\max_{i=1 \sim m} \psi_t(s_i)\tilde{p}(s_j \mid s_i)p(s_j \mid s_i, \hat{s}_{i-1}, o_j)$$
Termination:
$$\delta_T := \max_{i=1 \sim m} \delta_{T-1}(s_i)$$
Trace back:
$$\psi_t(s_i) := \arg\max_{j=1 \sim m} \psi_{t+1}(s_j)\tilde{p}(s_j \mid s_i)$$

Fig. 2. The proposed hybrid 2-order inference algorithm

3.2 Speed-Up Local Classifiers

As described in Section 2, it is necessary to take all the previous states into account. Directly retrieving the prediction scores from the classifiers might be slow especially when the feature set is large. According to observations, most feature weights can be accessed only once before considering next positions of word. We can use the following techniques to speed up computational efforts in accessing feature weights.

For second order CMMs, the feature set could be decomposed into three parts:

$$F = f_c \cup f_{p1} \cup f_{p2}$$

where f_c is the fixed feature set, f_{p1} and f_{p2} are the state features of previous word and the second words before. The decision function of conventional linear kernel support vector machines has the following form to the input x:

$$g(x; C_i) = \sum_j^F w_{ij} \cdot x_j + b_i$$

w_{ij} is the trained weight of feature j of class i and b_i is the constant of class i. By decomposing the features as above, we can re-write the decision function as:

$$g(x; C_i) = b_i + \sum_j^{f_c} w_{ij} \cdot x_j + \sum_{j \in p1}^{f_{p1}} w_{p1}^i \cdot x_{p1} + \sum_{j \in p2}^{f_{p1}} w_{p2}^i \cdot x_{p2} \tag{8}$$

For each category, the first two terms in Eq. (8) is independent to previous predicted states, while the remaining terms are the sum of weights of the first-order and second-order features. Therefore, we can always keep the values of the first term terms and adding the remaining terms during inference. In this paper, we simply adopt the predicted states of previous 1 and 2 words as features and hence $|f_{p1}|=|f_{p2}|=1$.

This technique is also applicable to maximum entropy models where the category constant b_i is not needed for ME. In addition, the proposed heuristics could also be generalized to different K-order CMMs. Assume the testing time complexity of a full 2-order CMMs is $(C^2*|F|)$ where C is the number of category. By contrast, the testing time complexity is reduced to $(|f_c|+C^2(|f_{p1}|+|f_{p2}|)$ where $|F|=|f_c|+|f_{p1}|+|f_{p2}|$. The time complexity of our hybrid 2-order CMMs is $(|f_c|+|f_{p2}|+C*(|f_{p1}|)$.

4   Experiments

Six well-known sequential labeling tasks are used to evaluate our method, namely, CoNLL-2000 syntactic chunking, base-chunking, CoNLL-2003 English NER, Bio-Text NER, Chinese POS tagging, and Chinese word segmentation. Table 1 shows the statistics of the six datasets.

CoNLL-2000 chunking task is a well-known and widely evaluated in previous work [13 14 7 19 3]. The training data was derived from Treebank WSJ sec. 15-18 while section 20 was used for testing. The goal is to find the non-recursive phrase structures in a sentence, such as noun phrase (NP), verb phrase (VP), etc. There are 11 phrase types in this dataset. We follow the previous best settings for SVMs [7 19]. The IOE2 is used to represent the phrase structure and tagged the data with backward direction.

Second, the base chunking dataset is the extension of CoNLL-2000 phrase recognition in which the goal is to find the base phrase of the full parse tree. The WSJ sec. 2-21 was used for training while sec. 23 was used for testing. We re-trained the Brill tagger with the same training set to label POS tags for both training and testing data.

The training and testing data of the Chinese POS tagging is mainly derived from the Penn Chinese Treebank 5.0. Ninety percent out of the data is used for training while the remaining 10% is used for testing. However, the task of the Chinese POS tagging is very different from classical English POS tagging in that there is no word boundary information in Chinese text. To achieve this, [10] presented a transformation method to encode each Chinese character with IOB-like tags. For example, the tag B-ADJ means the first character of a Chinese word which POS tag is ADJ (adjective). In this task, we simply use the IOB2 to represent the chunk structure. As a result, there are 64 chunk tags.

Similar to the Chinese POS tagging task, the target of Chinese word segmentation (WS) is even simpler. The sequential tagger learns to determine whether the Chinese character is *begin* or *interior* of a word. As discussed in [20], using more complex chunk representation bring better segmentation accuracy in most Chinese word segmentation benchmarks. By following this line, we apply the six tags B, BI, I, IE, E, and S to represent the Chinese word. BI and IE are the *interior after begin* and *interior before end* of a chunk. B/I/E/S tags indicate the begin/interior/end/single of a chunk.

We employed the official provided training/testing data from CoNLL-2003 to run the experiments on the NER task. The BioText NER is a small-scale biomedical named entity recognition task [15]. We randomly split 75% of the data for training while the remaining 25% was used for testing.

For the above six tasks, we do not include any external resources such as gazetteers for NER. This make us clear to see the impact of each search algorithm under full supervised learning frameworks.

Table 1. Statistics of the evaluated sequential labeling tasks

Data Statistics		# of examples	# of sentences	Encoded chunk tags	# of total category	Feature threshold	Learner parameters
CoNLL-	Training	220663	8935	I/E tags	11*2+1=23	f=2	σ=1000;
2000	Testing	49389	2011				C=0.1
Base	Training	950028	39832	I/E tags	20*2+1=41	f=2(SVM);	σ=1000;
Chunking	Testing	56684	2416			f=4(ME)	C=0.1
CoNLL-	Training	204567	14987	B / I tags	4*2+1=9	f=2	σ=1000;
2003	Testing	46666	3684				C=0.1
BioText	Training	20874	773	B / I tags	10*2+1=21	f=2	σ=1000;
	Testing	5250	193				C=0.1
Chinese POS tagging	Training	745215	16909	B / I tags	32*2=64	f=2; f=4(ME)	σ=1000; C=1
	Testing	81674	1878				
Chinese WS	Training	2.64M	57275	S/B/I/E/BI/I E tags	6	f=2; f=10(ME)	σ=1000; C=1
	Testing	357989	7512				

C is the regularized parameter of SVM; σ is the Gaussian prior of the maximum entropy model. f is the feature cutting threshold.

4.1 Settings

Since a couple of the tasks are similar, for example the CoNLL-2000 and base chunking, we adopt three feature types for the six datasets.

We replicated coordinate sub-gradient descent optimization approaches [4] with L_2-SVM as learners. In basic, the SVM was designed for binary classification problems. To port to multiclass problems, we adopted the well-known one-versus-all (OVA) method. One good property of OVA is that parameter estimation process can be trained individually. This is in particularly useful to the tasks which produce very large number of features and categories. To obtain the probability output from SVM, we employ the sigmoid function with fixed parameter A=-2 and B=0 as noted by [11]. On the other hand, the maximum entropy model used in this paper was derived from [6].

As shown in Table1, the parameters of SVM and ME were the same for the six tasks. However, the ME is not scalable to the large-scale and large category tasks, such as base chunking and Chinese WS where more than 80M feature weights needs to be estimated per category. Hence, we incrementally increase the feature threshold until the feature size can be handled in our environment. Though one can increase the hardware performance to cover the shortage, this is not the way to solve problems.

4.2 Overall Results

The first experiment is used to evaluate the benefit of incorporating higher order information and the proposed inference algorithm. We also compared with greedy search and beam search with variant beam width (B=10,50,250) for all tasks. The overall experimental results are summarized in Table 2. Each row indicates the corresponding inference algorithm. The beam search was applied with different width of beams. Term "2⁻ order" is the proposed hybrid deterministic and nondeterministic inference algorithm. Without considering learners, the inference algorithm of MXPOST is beam search-based with combining previous predicted states as features.

Clearly, 2⁻ order inference method seems to be very suitable for SVM. It achieves the best accuracy in four datasets. On the contrary, beam search with ME yields very competitive result as optimal algorithm. In most case, SVM with beam search yields close (but not equal) performance as well as 2⁻ order inference. ME with beam search shows even more close accuracy in most cases. In CoNLL-2003, ME with no history (i.e. 0-order) achieves better performance than the first order and full second order CMMs.

To see the significant difference among these search algorithms, we perform s-test [18] and McNemar-test to examine the statistical test. In most cases, it shows statistical significant difference between our 2⁻ order inference method and Beam search. In BioText and Chinese POS tagging tasks, our method and beam search has the significant difference ($p<0.01$) under 99% confidence.

The proposed 2⁻ order decoding algorithm shows better results than full second order decoders. The main reason is that the history feature is not stable to local classifiers. In the full second order CMMs, all possible triples (s_i,s_{i-1},s_{i-2}) should be taken into consideration, while in the 2⁻ order CMMs, only the first order information is needed. In some cases, enumerating all previous states may misguide the decisions to the local classifier. This also reveals that the local classifier is easily affected by previous predicted decisions, while the 2⁻ order CMMs could reduce the ease of such case.

In addition, we continue the observations and run a trial experiments to CoNLL-2000 with famous structural learning method, namely CRF. Settings of CRF is the same as our ME and we use the same feature set with excepted for history features to train CRF. The overall training and time took 5.62 hours and 4.64 sec. and achieved 94.19 $F(\beta)$ rate. By contrast, the training and testing time of our 2⁻ order CMMs is about 44 sec and 2.82 sec, respectively. Our method achieves better accuracy and runtime efficiency. In base chunking and Chinese word segmentation and POS tagging tasks, CRF showed very limited training scalability. For example, the number of features in Chinese POS tagging task is more 20M per category. By contrast, our 2⁻ order CMMs takes less than 10 minutes to train with the same feature set.

Table 2. Empirical results of the six sequential labeling tasks

Method	CoNLL-2000		Base Chunking		CoNLL-2003		BioText		Chinese POS tagging		Chinese WS	
	SVM	ME	SVM	ME	SVM	ME	SVM	ME	SVM	ME	SVM	ME
0 order	93.83	93.48	92.28	91.73	83.24	81.99	79.22	76.22	90.04	89.58	97.31	94.19
1 order	94.36	94.06	92.48	92.23	84.19	81.62	79.18	76.73	91.47	89.62	97.39	94.19
2⁺ order	94.28	94.06	92.62	92.15	83.7	81.65	80.39	75.11	91.07	90.08	97.18	94.44
2⁻ order	94.49	94.06	92.5	91.84	84.34	82.05	79.79	76.42	91.6	90.71	97.39	94.77
Greedy	94.31	93.99	92.42	92	74.53	81.81	78.34	75.96	91.23	90.36	97.14	94.19
Beam(B=10)	94.46	94.06	92.43	92.17	84.18	82.14	79.26	76.42	91.52	90.71	97.39	94.75
Beam(B=50)	94.46	94.06	92.42	92.17	84.19	82.14	79.32	76.42	91.53	90.71	97.39	94.75
Beam(B=250)	94.46	94.06	92.42	92.17	84.19	82.14	79.32	76.42	91.52	90.72	97.39	94.75

5 Conclusion

In this paper, we present a new search algorithm based on conditional Markov models for sequential labeling tasks. We compare our method to Greedy, Viterbi, and Beam search algorithms. The experiments were conducted on six well-known sequential labeling benchmarks. The experimental results showed that our method scales very well while achieving satisfactory performance in accuracy. In the CoNLL-2000 chunking task, our method outperforms previous best supervised systems. In terms of search algorithms, our method yields more superior accuracy than beam search and runtime efficiency (except for greedy search). The full online demonstration of the proposed conditional support vector Markov models can be found at the web site[1].

References

1. Charniak, E.: A maximum-entropy-inspired parser. In: 6th Applied Natural Language, Processing Conference, pp. 132–139 (2001)
2. Collins, M.: Discriminative training methods for hidden Markov models: theory and experiments with perceptron algorithms. In: Empirical Methods in Natural Language Processing, pp. 1–8 (2002)
3. Daumé, H., Marcu, D.: Learning as search optimization: approximate large margin methods for structured prediction. In: 12th International Conference on Machine Learning, pp. 169–176 (2005)
4. Hsieh, C.J., Chang, K.W., Lin, C.J., Keerthi, S., Sundararajan, S.: A dual coordinate descent method for large-scale linear SVM. In: 15th International Conference on Machine Learning, pp. 408–415 (2008)
5. Giménez, J., Márquez, L.: SVMTool: A general POS tagger generator based on support vector machines. In: 4th International Conference on Language Resources and Evaluation, pp. 43–46 (2004)
6. Kazama, J., Tsujii, J.: Evaluation and extension of maximum entropy models with inequality constraints. In: Empirical methods in natural language processing, pp. 137–144 (2003)
7. Kudo, T., Matsumoto, Y.: Chunking with support vector machines. In: North American Chapter of the Association for Computational Linguistics on Language Technologies, pp. 192–199 (2001)
8. Lafferty, J., McCallum, A., Pereira, F.: Conditional random fields: probabilistic models for segmenting and labeling sequence data. In: 8th International Conference on Machine Learning, pp. 282–289 (2001)
9. McCallum, A., Freitag, D., Pereira, F.: Maximum entropy Markov models for information extraction and segmentation. In: 7th International Conference on Machine Learning, pp. 591–598 (2000)
10. Ng, H.T., Low, J.K.: Chinese part-of-speech tagging. one-at-a-time or all-at-once? word-based or character-based? In: Empirical methods in natural language processing, pp. 277–284 (2004)
11. Platt, J.: Probabilistic outputs for support vector machines and comparisons to regularized likelihood methods. In: Advances in Large Margin Classifiers (1999)
12. Ratnaparkhi, A.: A Maximum Entropy Model for Part-Of-Speech Tagging. In: Empirical Methods in Natural Language Processing, pp. 133–142 (1996)

---

[1] Please refer the website: http://140.115.112.118/bcbb/Chunking.htm

13. Suzuki, J., Fujino, A., Isozaki, H.: Semi-supervised structural output learning based on a hybrid generative and discriminative approach. In: Empirical Methods in Natural Language Processing, pp. 791–800 (2007)
14. Suzuki, J., Isozaki, H.: Semi-supervised sequential labeling and segmentation using giga-word scale unlabeled data. In: 46th Annual Meeting of the Association of Computational Linguistics, pp. 665–673 (2008)
15. Takeuchi, K., Collier, N.: Use of support vector machines in extended named entity recognition. In 6th Conference on Computational Natural Language Learning, pp. 119-125 (2002)
16. Taskar, B., Guestrin, C., Koller, D.: Max-margin Markov networks. In: Advances in Neural Information Processing Systems (NIPS), pp. 25–32 (2003)
17. Tjong Kim Sang, E.F., Buchholz, S.: Introduction to the CoNLL-2000 shared task: chunking. In: 4th Conference on Computational Natural Language Learning, pp. 127–132 (2000)
18. Yang, Y., Liu, X.: A re-examination of text categorization methods. In: 22nd Annual International ACM SIGIR Conference on Research and Development in Information Retrieval, pp. 42–49 (1999)
19. Wu, Y.C., Lee, Y.S., Yang, J.C.: Robust and efficient multiclass SVM models for phrase pattern recognition, Pattern Recognition, vol. Pattern Recognition 41(9), 2874–2889 (2008)
20. Zhang, Y., Clark, S.: Chinese segmentation with a word-based perceptron algorithm. In: 45th Annual Meeting of the Association of Computational Linguistics, pp. 840–847 (2007)
21. Zhao, H., Kit, C.: Incorporating global information into supervised learning for Chinese word segmentation. In: 10th Conference of the Pacific Association for Computational Linguistics, pp. 66–74 (2007)

FolkDiffusion: A Graph-Based Tag Suggestion Method for Folksonomies

Zhiyuan Liu[1,3,4], Chuan Shi[2,3,4], and Maosong Sun[1,3,4]

[1] Department of Computer Science and Technology, Tsinghua University
[2] Department of Electronic Engineering, Tsinghua University
[3] State Key Lab on Intelligent Technology and Systems, Tsinghua University
[4] National Lab for Information Science and Technology, Tsinghua University
lzy.thu@gmail.com, shichuanwuhan@gmail.com, sms@tsinghua.edu.cn

Abstract. Collaborative social tagging is a popular and convenient way to organize web resources. All tags compose into a semantic structure named as folksonomies. Automatic tag suggestions can ease tagging activities of users. Various methods have been proposed for tag suggestions, which are roughly categorized into two approaches: content-based and graph-based. In this paper we present a heat diffusion method, i.e., FolkDiffusion, to rank tags for tag suggestions. Compared to existing graph-based methods, FolkDiffusion can suggest user- and resource-specific tags and prevent from topic drift. Experiments on real online social tagging datasets show the efficiency and effectiveness of FolkDiffusion compared to existing graph-based methods.

Keywords: Folksonomies, tag suggestions, FolkDiffusion, heat diffusion.

1 Introduction

Social tagging is a popular way to organize and share web resources such as documents, bookmarks and photos. Resources, tags and users are three essential parts in a social tagging system, in which users assign tags to resources and share with others. Social tagging systems can be categorized according to the type of resources. For example, Flickr (www.flickr.com) is designed to share photos; CiteULike (www.citeulike.org) and BibSonomy (www.bibsonomy.org) is to share academic references; and del.icio.us (www.delicious.com) is to share bookmarks. A common feature of these tagging systems is they all provide tag suggestions to ease the process of social tagging by recommending tags for a user given a resource.

Many methods have been proposed for tag suggestions. For the resources with rich text contents such as blogs and product reviews, content-based methods are proved to be effective [14]. However, for the resources with less text contents but having rich collaborative information, graph-based methods turn out to be useful. In graph-based methods, users, resources and tags are grouped into a tripartite graph, where there are connections only between users, resources and tags, and there are no connections within users, resources and tags themselves. After that, some ranking algorithms, such as PageRank [12], are performed on the graph. By biasing the ranking values to the given user and resource, we can rank tags specific to the given user and resource. FolkRank is a

P.-J. Cheng et al. (Eds.): AIRS 2010, LNCS 6458, pp. 231–240, 2010.

representative graph-based method based on PageRank on user-resource-tag tripartite graph. FolkRank, proposed as a tag suggestion method in [3], was shown to outperform other content-free methods including collaborative filtering.

FolkRank, however, suffers from the problem of topic drift. Starting from the given user and resource, although FolkRank makes PageRank biased to the given user and resource to a certain extent, it always finally jumps into globally popular tags when reaching stationary state. This is caused by the characteristic of PageRank, which was originally proposed to rank web pages according to their link topology in isolation.

To solve this issue, in this paper we present a new graph-based ranking method, i.e., FolkDiffusion, for tag suggestions. FolkDiffusion is motivated by heat diffusion process. Heat diffusion is a physical phenomenon. The basic theory of heat diffusion is that heat always flows from the position with high temperature to the position with low temperature. Recently, the idea of heat diffusion is introduced in various applications such as dimension reduction [1], classification [6], anti-spam of web pages [17], social network analysis [9] and search query suggestion [8]. In these work, the input data is considered to be a medium and the heat is diffused from a given set of start points to other data points. After iterations of heat diffusion, the heat values of data points indicate their relatedness with the initial start points.

In this paper, we consider tag suggestions as a task of finding most related tags with the given user u and resource r. Firstly, we construct a graph with users, resources and tags, in which edge weights represent the relatedness between them. Based on the idea of heat diffusion, we initially set u and r having the temperature higher than zero. Then we set all tags, users and resources except u and r to be zero temperature. After that, the heat begins to flow from u and r on the graph according to the edges between them. The edge between two vertices can be imagined as the pipe of an air-conditioner for heat flow, and the edge weight indicates the diffusion speed of heat. After several iterations of diffusion, the heat values on tags indicate their relatedness with the original user u and resource r. The most related tags are suggested for u and r.

The important characteristic of FolkDiffusion is that the heat only flows from high temperature to low temperature. We can imagine the process as follows. FolkDiffusion firstly recognizes a group of most related objects. The initially recognized related objects are then endowed with the power to decide which may be further related. This feature prevents FolkDiffusion from topic drift, and guarantees the suggested tags are topically related to the given user and resource. In experiments, we will demonstrate the performance of FolkDiffusion compared with other graph-based methods including FolkRank.

2   Related Work

For resources with rich text contents, many content-based methods have been proposed for tag suggestions. Ohkura et al. [11] proposed a Support Vector Machine-based tag suggestion system. Katakis et al. [5] used a hierarchical multi-label text classifier to find the proper tags for a document. Mishne [10] used a search-based nearest neighbor method to suggest tags, where the tags of a new document were collected from the most relevant documents in the training set. Lipczak et al. [7] extracted keywords from the title of a document, and filtered them with a user's used tags to get final suggestions. Tatu et al. [15] combined tags from similar documents and extracted keywords to provide tag suggestions. We find that most of content-based methods regard tag suggestions as either a text classification problem or a keyword extraction problem. In experiments of this paper, we also demonstrate a simple but effective content-based method, i.e., kNN, as a baseline method for tag suggestions.

Another class of tag suggestion systems is based on the connections between users, tags and resources, which does not take the content of resources into consideration and is thus named as graph-based methods. Xu et al. [16] used collaborative filtering to suggest tags for bookmarks. Jaschke et al. [3] proposed FolkRank, a PageRank-like iterative algorithm to find the most related tags for the given resource and user. PageRank was originally used for ranking web pages according to the topology of web graph. In PageRank we can set preference values to a subset of pages to make the final ranking values biased to these selected pages. In fact, FolkRank computes the relatedness between tags and the specific user and resource by setting the given user and resource to high preference values in PageRank.

3   Graph-Based Tag Suggestions

3.1   Problem Formulation

In social tagging systems, a folksonomy is defined as a tuple $\mathbb{F} = (U, T, R, Y)$, where U is the set of users, T is the set of tags and R is the set of resources. Y is a ternary relation between U, T and R, $Y \subseteq U \times T \times R$. A tuple record $(u, r, t) \in Y$ is called a tag assignment, which means user u assigned tag t to resource r. The goal of tag suggestions is to predict a set of tags $\{t\}$ for a given pair of user and resource (u, r).

The basic idea of graph-based tag suggestions is to construct a graph with users, resources and tags as vertices and build edges according to user tagging behaviors. After building the graph, we can adopt some graph-based ranking algorithms to rank tags for a specific user and resource. Then the top-ranked tags are recommended to users.

To describe the graph-based methods more clearly, we give some mathematical notations. For the folksonomy $\mathbb{F} = (U, T, R, Y)$, we firstly convert it into an undirected tripartite graph $G_{\mathbb{F}} = (V, E)$. In $G_{\mathbb{F}}$, the vertices consist of users, resources and tags, i.e., $V = U \cup R \cup T$. For each tagging behavior of user u assigning tag t to resource r, we will add edges between u, r and t, i.e., $E = \{\{u, r\}, \{u, t\}, \{r, t\} | (u, t, r) \in Y\}$.

In $G_{\mathbb{F}}$, we have the set of vertices $V = \{v_1, v_2, \cdots, v_N\}$ and the set of edges $E = \{(v_i, v_j) \mid$ There is an edge between v_i and $v_j\}$. For a given vertex v_i, let $N(v_i)$ be the neighbor vertices of v_i. We have $w(v_i, v_j)$ as the weight of the edge (v_i, v_j). For an undirected graph, $w(v_i, v_j) = w(v_j, v_i)$. Let $w(v_i)$ be the degree of v_i, and we have

$$w(v_i) = \sum_{v_j \in N(v_i)} w(v_j, v_i) = \sum_{v_j \in N(v_i)} w(v_i, v_j). \tag{1}$$

Based on the graph, we can employ various graph-based ranking methods to recommend tags. In this paper, we first introduce two existing methods, namely *most popular tags* and *FolkRank*. Furthermore, we describe FolkDiffusion for social tag suggestions.

3.2   Most Popular Tags

Here we introduce a simple but effective method for tag suggestions. Some notations are given as below, which is identical with [3]. For a user $u \in U$, we denote all his/her tag assignments as $Y_u = Y \cap (\{u\} \times T \times R)$. Accordingly, we have Y_r and Y_t. Based on the same principle, we can define $Y_{u,t} = Y \cap (\{u\} \times \{t\} \times R)$ for $u \in U$ and $t \in T$. We also have $Y_{t,r}$ accordingly. Furthermore, we denote all tags that user $u \in U$ have assigned as $T_u = \{t \in T | \exists r \in R : (u, t, r) \in Y\}$.

There are variants of *most popular tags* as shown in [4], which are usually restricted in different statistical range. For example, *most popular tags of folksonomy* recommends the most popular tags of the whole set of folksonomy. Therefore, it recommends the same set of tags for any given user and resource pair, which suffers from cold-start problems and has no consideration on personalization.

A reasonable variant of *most popular tags* is recommending the tags that globally are most specific to the resource. The method is named as *most popular tags by resource*

$$T(u, r) = \underset{t \in T}{\operatorname{argmax}^{n}}(|Y_{t,r}|). \tag{2}$$

Since users might have specific preferences for some tags, which should have been used by him/her, thus we can use the *most popular tags by user*. As shown in [4], the performance is poor if we use *most popular tags by user* in isolation. If we mix the *most popular tags by user and resource*, the performance will be much better than each of them in isolation. The simplest way to mix the effect of users and resources on tags is to add the counts and then sort

$$T(u, r) = \underset{t \in T}{\operatorname{argmax}^{n}}(|Y_{t,r}| \times |Y_{u,t}|). \tag{3}$$

3.3   FolkRank

In FolkRank, two random surfer models are employed on the user-resource-tag tripartite graph. The ranking values of vertices are computed with the following formula

$$PR(v_i) = \lambda \sum_{v_j \in N(v_i)} \frac{w(v_j, v_i)}{w(v_j)} PR(v_j) + (1 - \lambda)p(v_i), \tag{4}$$

where $PR(v_i)$ is the PageRank value and p_{v_i} is the preference to v_i. Suppose we have an adjacent matrix $\mathbf{A}$ to represent the graph $G_{\mathbb{F}}$

$$A(i, j) = \begin{cases} 0 & \text{if } (v_i, v_j) \notin E \\ \frac{w(v_i, v_j)}{w(v_j)} & \text{if } (v_i, v_j) \in E \end{cases}$$

With the matrix, we rewrite the Equation 4 as

$$\mathbf{s} = \lambda \mathbf{A} \mathbf{s} + (1 - \lambda)\mathbf{p}, \tag{5}$$

where $\mathbf{s}$ is the vector of PageRank scores of vertices, and $\mathbf{p}$ is the vector of preferences of vertices.

A straightforward idea of graph-based tag suggestions is to set preferences to the user and resource pair to be suggested for, and then compute ranking values using PageRank with Equation (5). However, as pointed out in [4], this will make it difficult for other vertices than those with high edge degrees to become highly ranked, no matter what the preference values are.

Based on the above analysis, we describe FolkRank as follows. To generate tags for user u and resource r, we have to:

1. Let $\mathbf{s}^{(0)}$ be the stable results of Equation (5) with $\mathbf{p} = 1$, i.e., the vector is composed by 1s.
2. Let $\mathbf{s}^{(1)}$ be the stable results of Equation (5) with $\mathbf{p} = 0$, but $p(u) = \frac{|Y_u|}{|Y|}$ and $p(r) = \frac{|Y_r|}{|Y|}$, where $Y_u = Y \cap (\{u\} \times T \times R)$ and $Y_r = Y \cap (U \times T \times \{r\})$.
3. Compute $\mathbf{s} = \mathbf{s}^{(1)} - \mathbf{s}^{(0)}$.

We rank tags according to their final values in $\mathbf{s}$, where the top-ranked tags are suggested to the given user u and resource r.

3.4 FolkDiffusion

For a graph $G = \{V, E\}$, denote $f_i(t)$ is the heat on vertex v_i at time t, we construct FolkDiffusion as follows. Suppose at time t, each vertex v_i receives an amount of heat, $M(v_i, v_j, t, \Delta t)$, from its neighbor v_j during a period Δt. The received heat is proportional to the time period Δt and the heat difference between v_i and v_j, namely $f_j(t) - f_i(t)$. Based on this, we denote $M(v_i, v_j, t, \Delta t)$ as

$$M(v_i, v_j, t, \Delta t) = \gamma(f_j(t) - f_i(t))\Delta t,$$

where γ is heat diffusion factor, i.e. the thermal conductivity. Therefore, the heat difference at vertex v_i between time $t + \Delta t$ and time t is equal to the sum of the heat that it receives from all its neighbors. This is formulated as

$$f_i(t + \Delta t) - f_i(t) = \sum_{v_j \in N(v_i)} \gamma(f_j(t) - f_i(t))\Delta t. \tag{6}$$

The process can also be expressed in a matrix form

$$\frac{\mathbf{f}(t + \Delta t) - \mathbf{f}(t)}{\Delta t} = \gamma \mathbf{H} \mathbf{f}(t). \tag{7}$$

where $\mathbf{f}$ is a vector of heat at vertices at time t, and $\mathbf{H}$ is

$$H(i,j) = \begin{cases} -1 & \text{if } i = j \\ 0 & \text{if } i \neq j \text{ and } (v_i, v_j) \notin E \\ \frac{w(v_i, v_j)}{w(v_j)} & \text{if } i \neq j \text{ and } (v_i, v_j) \in E \end{cases} \tag{8}$$

If the limit $\Delta t \to 0$, the process will turn into

$$\frac{d}{dt}\mathbf{f}(t) = \gamma \mathbf{H} \mathbf{f}(t). \tag{9}$$

Solving this differential equation, we have $\mathbf{f}(t) = e^{\gamma t \mathbf{H}}\mathbf{f}(0)$. Here we could extend the $e^{\gamma t \mathbf{H}}$ as

$$e^{\gamma t \mathbf{H}} = \mathbf{I} + \gamma t \mathbf{H} + \frac{\gamma^2 t^2}{2!}\mathbf{H}^2 + \frac{\gamma^3 t^3}{3!}\mathbf{H}^3 + \cdots . \tag{10}$$

The matrix $e^{\gamma t \mathbf{H}}$ is named as the diffusion kernel in the sense that the heat diffusion process continues infinitely from the initial heat diffusion.

γ is an important factor in the diffusion process. If γ is large, the heat will diffuse quickly. If γ is small, the heat will diffuse slowly. When $\gamma \to +\infty$, heat will diffuse immediately, and FolkDiffusion degrades into PageRank.

Like in PageRank, there are random relations between vertices. To capture these relations, we use a uniform random relation between vertices as in PageRank. Let $1 - \lambda$ denote the probability that random surfer happens and λ is the probability of following the edges. Based on the above discussion, we modify FolkDiffusion into

$$\mathbf{f}(t) = e^{\gamma t \mathbf{R}}\mathbf{f}(0), \quad \mathbf{R} = \lambda \mathbf{H} + (1 - \lambda)\frac{1}{N}\mathbf{1}. \tag{11}$$

In application, a computation of $e^{\gamma t \mathbf{R}}$ is time consuming. We usually approximate it to a discrete form

$$\mathbf{f}(t) = (\mathbf{I} + \frac{\gamma}{M}\mathbf{R})^{Mt}\mathbf{f}(0). \tag{12}$$

Without loss of generality, we use one unit time for heat diffusion between vertices and their neighbors. We have

$$\mathbf{f}(1) = (\mathbf{I} + \frac{\gamma}{M}\mathbf{R})^{M}\mathbf{f}(0). \tag{13}$$

We can thus iteratively calculate $(\mathbf{I} + \frac{\gamma}{M}\mathbf{R})^{M}\mathbf{f}(t)$ by applying the operator $(\mathbf{I} + \frac{\gamma}{M}\mathbf{R})$ to $\mathbf{f}(0)$. Therefore, for each iteration, we could diffuse the heat values $\mathbf{s}$ of vertices using the following formulation

$$\mathbf{s} = (1 - \frac{\gamma}{M})\mathbf{s} + \frac{\gamma}{M}(\lambda \mathbf{A}\mathbf{s} + (1 - \lambda)\frac{1}{N}\mathbf{1}), \tag{14}$$

where M is the number of iterations. As analyzed in [17], for a given threshold ϵ, we can compute to get M such that

$$\|((\mathbf{I} + \frac{\gamma}{M}\mathbf{R})^{M} - e^{\gamma \mathbf{R}})\mathbf{f}(0)\| < \epsilon, \tag{15}$$

for any $\mathbf{f}(0)$ whose sum is 1.0. Similar to [17], in this paper we set $M = 10$ for FolkDiffusion.

Unlike FolkRank, FolkDiffusion sets the initial values $\mathbf{f}(0)$ for vertices to indicate the preferences. To suggest tags to user u for resource r, we set $\mathbf{f}(0) = \mathbf{0}$, but for $\mathbf{f}_u(0) = 1$ and $\mathbf{f}_r(0) = 1$. After running FolkDiffusion on the tripartite graph, we rank tags according to their heat values and the top-ranked tags are suggested to user u for resource r.

3.5   Dynamic Length of Suggested Tag List

For a social tagging system, it is straightforward to suggest dynamic number of tags based on the characteristics of given users and resources instead of fix number of tags. There are several factors that may influence the number of tags for a post:

1. The global factor, which is the global average number of tags for each post, g;
2. The user factor, which is the average number of tags for each post by this user, u;
3. The resource factor, which is the average number of tags for each post for this resource, r.

Motivated by the idea in [13], with the three factors, we estimate the suggested number of tags sn for a given user and resource using formula $sn = \beta_1 g + \beta_2 u + \beta_3 r$, where β_1, β_2 and β_3 are parameters and can be obtained using linear regression using training data. Note that the dynamic length of suggested tag list is independent to tag suggestion methods. The results in the following experiments are all obtained using dynamic length of tag list.

4   Experiments

In experiments, we compare the results of three graph-based methods: most popular tags, FolkRank and FolkDiffusion. Before demonstrating the experiment results, we introduce the dataset and evaluation metric for experiments.

4.1   Dataset and Evaluation Metric

In experiments we use two datasets provided by BibSonomy. BibSonomy is a social bookmark and publication sharing system that supports users to tag and share URLs and bibtexs. After removing all users, tags, and resources which appear in only one post, the datasets contains 253,615 tag assignments, posted by 1,185 users to 14,443 URLs and 7,946 bibtexs using 13,276 unique tags. Since the user behaviors for tagging URLs and bibtexs are quite different, we perform experiments on bookmark posts (41,268) and bibtex posts (22,852) separately. For convenience, we refer to the two parts as *Bookmark* dataset and *Bibtex* dataset respectively.

To ensure the statistical validity of experiment results, we carry out experiments using 5-fold cross validation on datasets Bibtex and Bookmark. The performance of tag suggestions is measured using precision, recall and F_1-measure $= \frac{2 \times \text{precision} \times \text{recall}}{\text{precision} + \text{recall}}$.

4.2   Comparing with Other Methods

In Fig. 1, we show the best performance of various graph-based methods on Bibtex and Bookmark datasets when the maximum of suggested tags are set from 1 to 10. In this figure, we also demonstrate the performance of the content-based method kNN, which finds most k similar resources according to their contents and suggest the tags of the k nearest neighbors to the given resource. kNN achieves the best result when $k = 2$. For the method of most popular tags, we use *mpt+resource* to indicate most popular tags by *resource*, and *mpt+mix* to indicate most popular tags by mixing *resource* and *user*. For

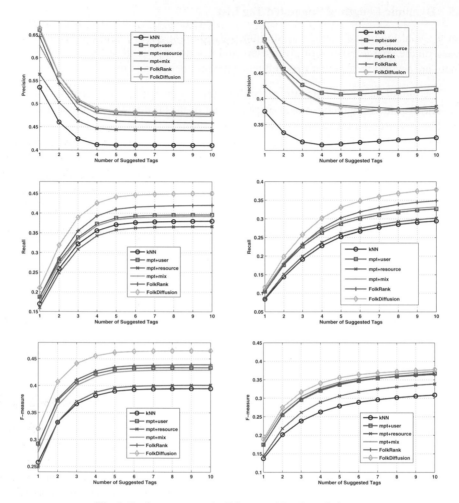

Fig. 1. Performance on the Bibtex and Bookmark datasets

FolkRank, the best result is achieved when damping factor $\lambda = 0.85$ with maximum iterations $max_{it} = 100$. FolkDiffusion obtains the best result when damping factor $\lambda = 0.85$, maximum number of iterations $max_{it} = 10$ and diffusion factor $\gamma = 0.1$.

From the two figures, we have four observations:

1. FolkDiffusion achieves the best F_1-measure on the both datasets. When maximum number of tags is set to 5, FolkDiffusion on Bibtex achieved F_1-measure 0.462 compared to 0.435 of FolkRank. While on Bookmark, FolkDiffusion achieved F_1-measure 0.356 compared to 0.340 of FolkRank and 0.344 of *mpt+mix*.
2. For Bibtex and Bookmark datasets, graph-based methods outperform content-based methods, especially on precision. This is because Bibtex and Bookmark datasets are lack of text information.

3. All graph-based methods perform better on Bibtex than Bookmark. This may because the resources of Bibtex dataset are bibtexs of scientific articles. Users usually
   assign tags to bibtexs mostly based on the themes of the articles, and thus are more
   reasonable and easier for predicting.
4. Since we use dynamic length of suggested tag list, the F_1-measure does not drop
   when the maximum number of suggested tags are growing.

We also explore the performance of FolkDiffusion on training and test dataset
released in Task-2 of *2009 ECML/PKDD Discovery Challenge* (http://www.
kde.cs.uni-kassel.de/ws/dc09) [2]. FolkDiffusion achieves precision $=$
0.327, recall $= 0.321$ and $F_1 -$ measure $= 0.3241$, which ranks the fourth place compared to twelve submission results, which is slightly-lower than the performance of
the second and third places. Note that the evaluation results on the released test set are
much worse than those shown in Fig. 1, which is caused by the different distributions of
resources/users/posts between the training set and test set. In all, the evaluation results
verify the effectiveness of FolkDiffusion.

4.3   Influence of Parameter

We further investigate the influence of dynamic length of suggested tag list. If we do not
use the dynamic length and always suggest 5 tags for each given user and resource, the
F_1-measure of FolkDiffusion will drop to only 0.398 on Bibtex and 0.342 on Bookmark.
The influence is also valid to other graph-based methods.

Besides the above analysis, we also investigate the impacts of FolkDiffusion parameters. In Table 1, we demonstrate the performance of FolkDiffusion on Bibtex and
Bookmark as its parameters change, including the diffusion factor γ and maximum
number of iterations (denoted as *max-it* in tables). Here the damping factor λ is set to
0.85. We find that the performance of FolkDiffusion are not sensitive to its parameters,
which indicates the robustness of FolkDiffusion.

Table 1. Performance of FolkDiffusion on Bibtex (left) and Bookmark (right) dataset. In this
experiment, damping factor λ is set to $\lambda = 0.85$, and the maximum number of suggested tags is
set to 5.

γ	max-it	Precision	Recall	F_1-measure
1.00	10	0.4758	0.4491	0.4621
0.10	10	0.4844	0.4411	0.4618
0.01	10	0.4772	0.4504	0.4634
0.01	100	0.4772	0.4504	0.4634

γ	max-it	Precision	Recall	F_1-measure
1.00	10	0.3834	0.3299	0.3547
0.10	10	0.3878	0.3265	0.3545
0.01	10	0.3844	0.3308	0.3556
0.01	100	0.3844	0.3308	0.3556

5   Conclusion and Future Work

In this paper, we introduce a new graph-based method for tag suggestions, namely
FolkDiffusion, motivated by the idea of heat diffusion. We study the performance of
kNN, most popular tags, FolkRank and FolkDiffusion on real online social tagging
datasets. Experiments show that FolkDiffusion outperforms other graph-based methods

on both Bibtex dataset and Bookmark dataset significantly. This indicates the effectiveness of heat diffusion for modeling user tagging behaviors.

As some recent work indicates, ensembles of various methods will greatly improve the performance of tag suggestions. In future work, we plan to combine FolkDiffusion with other graph-based and content-based methods together to implement a practical social tagging system.

Acknowledgments

This work is supported by the National Natural Science Foundation of China (NSFC) under Grant No. 60873174.

References

1. Belkin, M., Niyogi, P.: Laplacian eigenmaps for dimensionality reduction and data representation. Neural computation 15(6), 1373–1396 (2003)
2. Eisterlehner, F., Hotho, A., Jaschke, R.: ECML PKDD Discovery challenge 2009. In: CEUR-WS. org (2009)
3. Jaschke, R., Marinho, L., Hotho, A., Schmidt-Thieme, L., Stumme, G.: Tag recommendations in folksonomies. In: Kok, J.N., Koronacki, J., Lopez de Mantaras, R., Matwin, S., Mladenič, D., Skowron, A. (eds.) PKDD 2007. LNCS (LNAI), vol. 4702, pp. 506–514. Springer, Heidelberg (2007)
4. Jaschke, R., Marinho, L., Hotho, A., Schmidt-Thieme, L., Stumme, G.: Tag recommendations in social bookmarking systems. AI Communications 21(4), 231–247 (2008)
5. Katakis, I., Tsoumakas, G., Vlahavas, I.: Multilabel text classification for automated tag suggestion. In: ECML/PKDD Discovery Challenge 2008, p. 75 (2008)
6. Lafferty, J., Lebanon, G.: Diffusion kernels on statistical manifolds. The Journal of Machine Learning Research 6, 163 (2005)
7. Lipczak, M.: Tag recommendation for folksonomies oriented towards individual users. In: ECML/PKDD Discovery Challenge 2008, p. 84 (2008)
8. Ma, H., Yang, H., King, I., Lyu, M.R.: Learning latent semantic relations from clickthrough data for query suggestion. In: Proceeding of CIKM, pp. 709–718 (2008)
9. Ma, H., Yang, H., Lyu, M.R., King, I.: Mining social networks using heat diffusion processes for marketing candidates selection. In: Proceeding of CIKM, pp. 233–242 (2008)
10. Mishne, G.: Autotag: a collaborative approach to automated tag assignment for weblog posts. In: Proceedings of WWW, pp. 953–954 (2006)
11. Ohkura, T., Kiyota, Y., Nakagawa, H.: Browsing system for weblog articles based on automated folksonomy. In: Proceedings of WWW (2006)
12. Page, L., Brin, S., Motwani, R., Winograd, T.: The PageRank citation ranking: Bringing order to the web. Tech. rep, Stanford University (1998)
13. Rendle, S., Schmidt-Thieme, L.: Factor models for tag recommendation in bibsonomy. In: ECML/PKDD Discovery Challenge (2009)
14. Sood, S., Owsley, S., Hammond, K., Birnbaum, L.: TagAssist: Automatic tag suggestion for blog posts. In: Proceedings of ICWSM, p. 28 (2007)
15. Tatu, M., Srikanth, M., D'Silva, T.: RSDC 2008: Tag recommendations using bookmark content. In: ECML/PKDD Discovery Challenge 2008(2008)
16. Xu, Z., Fu, Y., Mao, J., Su, D.: Towards the semantic web: Collaborative tag suggestions. In: Collaborative Web Tagging Workshop at WWW 2006 (2006)
17. Yang, H., King, I., Lyu, M.R.: DiffusionRank: a possible penicillin for web spamming. In: Proceedings of SIGIR, pp. 431–438 (2007)

Effectively Leveraging Entropy and Relevance for Summarization

Wenjuan Luo[1,2], Fuzhen Zhuang[1,2], Qing He[1], and Zhongzhi Shi[1]

[1] The Key Laboratory of Intelligent Information Processing, Institute of Computing Technology, Chinese Academy of Sciences, Beijing, 100080, China
[2] Graduate University of Chinese Academy of Sciences, Beijing 100049, China
{luowj,zhuangfz,heq,shizz}@ics.ict.ac.cn

Abstract. Document summarization has attracted a lot of research interest since the 1960s. However, it still remains a challenging task on how to extract effective feature for automatic summarization. In this paper, we extract two features called entropy and relevance to leverage information from different perspectives for summarization. Experiments on unsupervised and supervised methods testify the effectiveness of leveraging the two features.

Keywords: summarization, entropy, relevance, sentence feature extraction.

1 Introduction

With the actual huge and continuously growing of World Wide Web, the amount of information in the public domain grows explosively. As a result, there is a vast demand for new technologies that can effectively process information. Document summarization is an essential technology to overcome this obstacle in technological environments [1].

The main motivation of document summarization is to help users capture the major topics of a document with less effort [2]. Different summarization tasks make the query-oriented summary different from the generic summary [3]. Besides, document summarization can be categorized as abstract-based and extract-based summaries [1]. In this paper, we aim to generate extract-based generic summary, i.e., to select a combination of sentences which are the most important for the overall understanding of the document[4].

Many algorithms, supervised and unsupervised, have been applied for document summarization. Jones [5] gives a review of the research on automatic summarization over the last decade. Based on our study, we argue that a good summary should be compact while cover as many aspects in the document as possible. We propose a feature called entropy to measure the coverage from the inner-sentence level, and another feature called relevance to indicate the compactness from the intra-sentence level:

Entropy–This feature denotes the quantity of information implied by the sentence. As you may notice, long sentences are likely to cover more aspects

P.-J. Cheng et al. (Eds.): AIRS 2010, LNCS 6458, pp. 241–250, 2010.

in the document than short sentences. Note that a long sentence usually has a comparably larger entropy than a short sentence. Hence, a large entropy of sentence possibly implies a large converge.

Relevance–This feature measures the intra-sentence relationships between sentences. On the whole, sentences sharing a considerable number of words with other sentences often have high relevances. Therefore, choosing sentences correlated with each other probably leads to a compact summary.

As you may notice, leveraging the above two features may generate summaries that prefer long sentences which are strongly related to other sentences in the document. We aim to balance the importance within the sentence and between the sentences to generate compact summaries covering as many aspects of the document as possible.

In order to testify the effectiveness of leveraging the two features, or say heuristic rules[6], we firstly score sentences on the strength of these two features and perform a simple sentence selection method for unsupervised summarization. Furthermore, we combine the two features with other features [2,7] extracted from sentences and apply regression methods for supervised summarization.

We evaluate the performance of our methods from DUC01(http://duc.nist.gov) on an open benchmark data set. Experiments show that leveraging the two proposed heuristic rules are contributive to summary generation from both the unsupervised and the supervised perspective.

The rest of the paper is organized as follows: Section 2 introduces the preliminary knowledge and gives the problem definition, Section 3 presents the details of the algorithms, Section 4 gives experimental results and comparisons of our methods with baseline methods, Section 5 describes the related work, and we conclude our paper in Section 6.

2   Preliminary Knowledge

2.1   Feature Extraction

Since sentences could be viewed as a vector of words, in order to analyze the significance within the sentence quantitatively, we adopt entropy as a metric:

$$I(x_i) = - \sum_{j \in x_i} p_{ij} \cdot \log(p_{ij}) \tag{1}$$

where x_i denotes the i-th sentence, $I(x_i)$ denotes the amount of information covered by the i-th sentence, p_{ij} denotes the probability of the j-th word in the i-th sentence. From the above formula, we can see that a longer sentence is more likely to have a larger entropy. Therefore, a sentence of large entropy is very likely to cover more aspects of the document than a sentence of small entropy.

Moreover, we extract another feature called relevance to show the compactness by calculating the relationship of a sentence between other sentences:

$$R(x_i) = \sum_{j \neq i} S(x_j, x_i), \ S(x_j, x_i) = Overlap(x_j, x_i)/length(x_i) \tag{2}$$

where $R(x_i)$ denotes the relevance of the i-th sentence, $S(x_j, x_i)$ is the similarity between the j-th sentence and the i-th sentence based on directed backward graph according to Mihalcea's experiments[8], $Overlap(x_j, x_i)$ denotes the number of words co-occurring in the j-th and the i-th sentence, and $length(x_i)$ is the length of the i-th sentence. Hence, sentences with high relevance probably compose more compact summaries than sentences without.

Besides, for regression methods, we extract entropy and relevance together with other typical features from the document as [2,7] in Table 1.

Table 1. Features for Supervised Summarization

f1	the position of the sentence	f2	the length of the sentence
f3	the likelihood of the sentence	f4	the number of thematic words
f5	the number of low frequency words	f6	the LSA-Score of the sentence
f7	the number of 2-gram keywords	f8	number of words appearing in other sentences
f9	the entropy of the sentence	f10	the relevance of the sentence

2.2 Problem Formulation

Given a document $x = \{x_1, x_2, ..., x_N\} \in \mathcal{X}$, where x is a document, x_i represents the i-th sentence, and $\mathcal{X}$ denotes the space of all the documents.

For a single document, our target is to extract the most representative $y = \{s_1, s_2, ..., s_k\}$ as the final summary, where s_i represents the i-th sentence in the summary.

Unsupervised Summarization. As discussed in Section 2.1, a large $I(s_i)$ of sentence probably suggests a large coverage, and large $R(s_i)$s indicate that sentences are relevant which probably leads to compact summaries. Therefore, in order to generate compact summaries with a large coverage, we aim to maximize the following objective function:

$$\mathbb{S}^* = argmax \sum_{s_i \in \mathbb{S}} \{\alpha \cdot I(s_i) + \beta \cdot R(s_i)\} \tag{3}$$

where $\mathbb{S}^*$ denotes the summary. Take a deep look at Equation (3), substitute the $I(s_i)$ and $R(s_i)$ with Equation (1) and (2), we have:

$$
\begin{aligned}
F(\mathbb{S}) &= \sum_{s_i \in \mathbb{S}} \{\alpha \cdot I(s_i) + \beta \cdot R(s_i)\} \\
&= \sum_{s_i \in \mathbb{S}} \{-\alpha \cdot \sum_{j \in s_i} p_{ij} \cdot \log(p_{ij}) + \beta \cdot \frac{\sum_{x_m \neq s_i} Overlap(s_i, x_m)}{length(s_i)}\} \\
&= \sum_{s_i \in \mathbb{S}} \{-\alpha \cdot \sum_{j \in s_i} p_{ij} \cdot \log(p_{ij}) + \beta \cdot \log(e^{\frac{\sum_{x_m \neq s_i} Overlap(s_i, x_m)}{length(s_i)}})\} \\
&= \sum_{s_i \in \mathbb{S}} \{\log(\prod_{j \in s_i} p_{ij}^{-\alpha p_{ij}} \cdot \prod_{x_m \neq s_i} e^{\frac{\beta Overlap(s_i, x_m)}{length(s_i)}})\}
\end{aligned}
\tag{4}
$$

where x_m is the m-th sentence in the document. After removing stopwords, the number of words in sentences is small, while the effect of $R(s_i)$ grows exponentially as the number of sentences increases. Therefore, if we use relevance in its original form, the $R(s_i)$ will be dominant in the objective function. For a better balance, we adjust our objective function as follows:

$$F(\mathbb{S}) = \sum_{s_i \in \mathbb{S}} \{\alpha \cdot I(s_i) + \beta \cdot \log(R(s_i))\} \tag{5}$$

Supervised Summarization. Given a document $x = \{x_1, x_2, ..., x_N\} \in \mathcal{X}$, for each sentence x_i, there is a corresponding y_i indicating whether the i-th sentence is in the summary. Now assume we have all the training data preprocessed as:

$$\{x_i^{(1)}, x_i^{(2)}, ..., x_i^{(j)}, ..., x_i^{(n)}, y_i | i = 1, 2, ..., n\} \tag{6}$$

where $x_i^{(j)}$ denotes the j-th feature of the i-th sentence, $\{x_i^{(1)}, x_i^{(2)}, ..., x_i^{(j)}, ..., x_i^{(n)}\}$ is the feature vector of x_i, for a classification problem, y_i is either 0 or 1, and for regression problem, y_i denotes the ROUGE-2-P score of the i-th sentence, which will be described in Section 4.2. We aim to construct a discriminant function such that:

$$\mathcal{F}(\mathcal{X}, \mathcal{Y}) : \Psi^T \cdot \mathcal{X} = \mathcal{Y} \tag{7}$$

We attempt to find the Ψ^T with the least generalization error through the training process. The predicted summary y would be extracted according to the following equation:

$$y = argmax\{\Psi^T \cdot x\} \tag{8}$$

The sentences with the highest values of y will constitute the final summary.

3 Proposed Methods

3.1 Entropy-and-Relevance-Based Summarization

As we have given the objective function in Section 2.2, in order to select the most important sentence in the sense of entropy and relevance. As we can see, to maximize the objective function is to find the sentences with highest $I(s_i) + (\beta/\alpha) \cdot \log(R(s_i))$.

Algorithm 1. Entropy and Relevance based Summarization

Input: The term frequency matrix of each document, the number of sentences (k) to be selected as summary, the weight of entropy(α), the weight of relevance(β).
Output: The sequence of sentences selected as final summary.

Step 1: Given the term frequency matrix, construct the backward similarity matrix.
Step 2: For each sentence s_i, calculate its entropy($I(s_i)$) and relevance($R(s_i)$).
Step 3: Calculate the score of $I(s_i) + (\beta/\alpha) \cdot \log(R(s_i))$ for each sentence.
Step 4: Output the top k sentences with highest scores as the final summary.

For a better balance between entropy and relevance, we adopt different α and β to see the effect of leveraging the two features. Specifically, for simplicity, we consider the parameter tuning to be 1 and β/α. Experimental results will be given in Section 4.

3.2 Regression-Based Summarization

From the supervised perspective, we adopt the linear regression [9] and Extreme Learning Machine (ELM) [10] regression to leverage the entropy and relevance. For linear regression, we simply apply the following model:

Given the whole document space $X = \{x_1, x_2, ..., x_N\}$, the feature vector $x_i = (x_i^{(1)}, x_i^{(2)}, ..., x_i^{(n)})$ and its corresponding y_i, for linear regression, we have

$$f(x_i) = \beta_0 + \sum_{j=1}^{n} x_i^{(j)} \beta_j \tag{9}$$

We use the minimum squared errors to estimate β, therefore, we have:

$$RSS(\beta) = \sum_{i=1}^{N} (y_i - f(x_i))^2 = \sum_{i=1}^{N} (y_i - \beta_0 - \sum_{j=1}^{n} x_i^{(j)} \beta_j)^2 \tag{10}$$

In Equation (10), to minimize the RSS with respect to β,

$$\frac{\partial RSS}{\partial \beta} = -2X^T(y - X\beta), \frac{\partial^2 RSS}{\partial \beta \partial \beta^T} = -2X^T X \tag{11}$$

Assume X is full column rank, let $\frac{\partial RSS}{\partial \beta} = 0$, we can obtain a solution of β

$$\beta^* = (X^T X)^{-1} X^T y \tag{12}$$

On the other hand, the ELM regression differs from linear regression in the way how β is obtained. For the single hidden layer feedforward networks (SLFNs) with M hidden neurons, the problem could be modeled as follows:

$$\sum_{i=1}^{N} \|o_i - y_i\| = 0 \text{ , where } o_i = \sum_{j=1}^{M} \beta_j g(w_j x_i^{(j)} + b_j), i = 1, ..., N \tag{13}$$

In Equation (13), the goal of the $g(\cdot)$ function is to approximate all the training data with zero means. Therefore, for all the N training sample, the goal is to minimize the cost function:

$$E = \sum_{i=1}^{N} (\sum_{j=1}^{M} \beta_j g(w_j x_i^{(j)} + b_j) - y_i)^2 \tag{14}$$

Under the ELM model, Huang et al. [10] formularized the problem as:

$$H\beta = Y \text{ where}$$

$$H(w_1, ..., w_M, b_1, ..., b_M, x_1, ..., x_N) = \begin{pmatrix} g(w_1 x_1^{(1)} + b_1), & \cdots, & g(w_M x_1^{(M)} + b_M) \\ \vdots & \cdots, & \vdots \\ g(w_1 x_N^{(1)} + b_1), & \cdots, & g(w_M x_N^{(M)} + b_M) \end{pmatrix}$$

$$\text{and } \beta = [\beta_1^T, \cdots, \beta_M^T]^T, Y = [y_1^T, \cdots, y_N^T]^T \tag{15}$$

According to Equation (15), through the use of the Moore−Penrose generalized inverse, a solution of β is [11]:

$$\beta^* = H^\dagger Y \tag{16}$$

where, $H^\dagger$ is the Moore−Penrose generalized inverse of H. Detail steps of deduction could be found in [10] and [11].

For both kinds of regression, the predictive summary of x could be calculated through:

$$y^* = x\beta^* \tag{17}$$

For each document, we select the sentences with the highest values of y^* into the final summary. As we have mentioned, the goal of using regression methods is to learn how to balance different features through the training procedure. Effectiveness of the leveraging is shown in the next section.

4   Experiments

4.1   Experimental Setting

Experimental Data: The DUC(Document Understanding Conference) 2001 data set is used to evaluate the effectiveness of leveraging the two features. The whole data set includes 147 documents of 6921 sentences together with the corresponding ground-truth summaries.

Baseline Methods: For unsupervised methods, we implement the Luhn's method, RANDOM[7], LSA and HITS to compare with our entropy and relevance based summarization. For supervised methods, the Linear Regression and ELM regression are applied based on different feature sets for evaluation.

Evaluation Metric: The ROUGE evaluation toolkit [12] adopted by DUC for automatic summarization evaluation is highly correlated with human evaluations. In this paper, we employ this toolkit to evaluate the performance of our proposed methods. There are several kinds of ROUGE metrics, here we introduce the most commonly used sub-metrics as follows:

1. ROUGE-N-R is the recall rate of summary from the n−gram point of view. It can be calculated as follows [12]:

$$\text{ROUGE-N-R} = \frac{\sum_{s \in y^*} \sum_{gram_n \in s} Count_{match}(gram_n)}{\sum_{s \in y} \sum_{gram_n \in s} Count(gram_n)}$$

2. ROUGE-N-P is the precision rate summary from the n−gram point of view. It can be calculated as follows :

$$\text{ROUGE-N-P} = \frac{\sum_{s \in y^*} \sum_{gram_n \in s} Count_{match}(gram_n)}{\sum_{s \in y^*} \sum_{gram_n \in s} Count(gram_n)}$$

3. ROUGE-N-F is the F_1 metric of ROUGE-N-R and ROUGE-N-P and could be calculated as follows:

$$\text{ROUGE-N-F} = \frac{2 * \text{ROUGE-N-R} * \text{ROUGE-N-P}}{\text{ROUGE-N-R} + \text{ROUGE-N-P}}$$

In the above equations, N is the length of words in n-gram, s is the sentence in summary, y^* denotes the generated summary and y is the ground−truth summary. $Count_{match}(gram_n)$ is the number of n-gram co-occurring between y^* and y. $Count(gram_n)$ denotes the occurrence number of n-gram words in the corresponding summary.

4.2   Performance Evaluation

Results of Unsupervised Methods: We implement several unsupervised methods for summarization to compare with our ERBS summarization. The results are shown in Table 2.

Table 2. Results of Unsupervised Methods

Name	ROUGE-1-R	ROUGE-1-P	ROUGE-1-F	ROUGE-2-R	ROUGE-2-P	ROUGE-2-F
luhn	0.514	0.510	0.512	0.355	0.353	0.354
RANDOM	0.524	0.552	0.535	0.408	0.428	0.416
lsa	0.506	0.501	0.503	0.351	0.349	0.351
HITS	0.575	0.576	0.575	0.451	0.453	0.452
ERBS	**0.601**	**0.597**	**0.599**	**0.481**	**0.479**	**0.480**

From Table 2, we can find that ERBS achieves the best performance among the unsupervised methods and gains a significant improvement over all baseline methods. This shows the effectiveness of the proposed heuristic rules− entropy and relevance. Moreover, we give the detail results of ERBS with different parameters in Fig. 1.

From the left figure in Fig. 1, we can see that ROUGE-scores changes with different gama, where gama=β/α. From the figure on the right, we can see the best result is obtained when gama=1.2, as is displayed in Table 2. When gama=0, the ERBS just selects sentences with the highest entropy, as gama grows, the ERBS pays more and more attention to relevance. The result of ERBS converges to selecting sentences with the highest relevance when gama grows infinite. As we can see from the figures, leveraging entropy and relevance achieves better performance than emphasizing one single heuristic rule.

Results of Supervised Methods. To further investigate the effect of entropy and relevance, we also listed the compared results of LR, LR+E, LR+R, LR+E+R, ELM, ELM+E, ELM+R and ELM+E+R in Table 3. LR denotes Linear-Regression dealing with features excluding entropy and relevance, while LR+E includes entropy, LR+R includes relevance and LR+E+R includes all the features. The methods based on ELM-regression are named similarly.

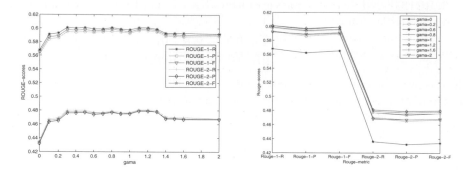

Fig. 1. Rouge-scores of ERBS according to different gama

For a better comparison, we also employ the weighted longest common subsequence (ROUGE-W). And the weight parameter is set to be 1.2 in the experiments. Comparing the LR+E+R with LR, LR+E and LR+R, we can see that LR+E+R performs the best. And it is the same with the ELM. This suggests that leveraging the two features enhances the regression based summarization.

Table 3. Results of Regression Methods

ROUGE-Score	LR	LR+E	LR+R	LR+E+R	ELM	ELM+E	ELM+R	ELM+E+R
ROUGE-1-R	0.54421	0.61309	0.60750	0.61750	0.55229	0.61121	0.60822	**0.62139**
ROUGE-1-P	0.55679	0.60905	0.60333	0.61326	0.55483	0.60670	0.60351	**0.61679**
ROUGE-1-F	0.54926	0.61077	0.60512	0.61510	0.55324	0.60866	0.60556	**0.61879**
ROUGE-2-R	0.42278	0.49969	0.49140	0.50651	0.42557	0.49536	0.49614	**0.51123**
ROUGE-2-P	0.43095	0.49701	0.48867	0.50344	0.42760	0.49234	0.49288	**0.50813**
ROUGE-2-F	0.42615	0.49810	0.48980	0.50473	0.42635	0.49360	0.49427	**0.50943**
ROUGE-W-R	0.22252	0.25208	0.24867	0.25433	0.22445	0.25121	0.25077	**0.25749**
ROUGE-W-P	0.43509	0.48042	0.47382	0.48428	0.43140	0.47752	0.47654	**0.48973**
ROUGE-W-F	0.29333	0.32989	0.32540	0.33274	0.29453	0.32846	0.32786	**0.33673**

5   Related Work

Luhn [13] firstly proposed automatic summarization and addressed the significance of sentences for sentence extraction in the 1960s. Moreover, LSA (Latent Semantic Analysis) was applied to identify semantically important sentences for summarization based on the Singular Vector Decomposition(SVD) of matrix[14] one decade ago. Recently, Lee et al. [1] proposed an unsupervised document summarization method using the Non-negative Matrix Factorization (NMF).

Also, ranking algorithms such as HITS and PageRank could be applied for summarization since documents could be represented as graphs [6]. Mihalcea [8] implemented HITS based on undirected graph, forward directed graph and backward directed graph. Among all the graphs, the method based on the backward directed graph performs best.

Meanwhile, supervised algorithms have also been applied for document summarization. Generally, these methods first extract a set of features from the document, and then train a summarizer to predict whether a sentence should be selected into the summary [6]. Such features include linguistic features and statistical features, such as rhetorical structure [15], the position of the sentence in the document, the sentence length, and so on [2,16]. Some complex features are included in order to improve the performance of supervised algorithms such as, the LSA score of the sentence, the HITS score of the sentence [3], the PageRank score of the sentence [7], and so on.

Learning methods such as Naive Bayes (NB), C4.5 [16], Logistic Regression (LR), and Neural Network (NN) could be applied to train summarizers based on features extracted from sentences [2]. Rijsbergen et al. [17] introduces an SVM-based method aiming at constructing a decision boundary between summary and non-summary sentences. Moreover, HMM(Hidden Markov Models) was proposed by Conroy and O'Leary [3] in 2001 based on three extracted features.

However, HMM could not fully exploit linguistic features of sentences since its independence assumption. Shen et al. [2] proposed Conditional Random Fields(CRF) for summarization, which considers the summarization task as a sequence labeling problem. In order to enhance diversity, coverage and balance for summarization, Li et al. [7] proposed another supervised method through a structure learning framework.

For supervised methods, whether the extracted features indicate the useful information for summarization strongly affects the quality of summaries. Moreover, the capability of the adopted method also influences the quality of summarization.

6 Conclusion

To generate compact summaries with possibly large coverage, we extract entropy and relevance from sentences for summarization. Then we perform unsupervised summarization named ERBS and supervised summarization utilizing Linear Regression and ELM regression in order to validate the effectiveness of leveraging the two features. Experimental results show that the ERBS outperforms other baseline unsupervised methods. Moreover, the results of linear regression and ELM regression based summarization also indicate that leveraging the two features is beneficial for automatic summarization.

Acknowledgements

This work is supported by the National Science Foundation of China (No.60675010, 60933004, 60975039), 863 National High-Tech Program (No.2007AA01Z132), National Basic Research Priorities Programme (No.2007CB311004) and National Science and Technology Support Plan (No.2006BAC08B06).

References

1. Lee, J.-H., Park, S., Ahn, C.-M., Kim, D.: Automatic generic document summarization based on non-negative matrix factorization. Information Processing and Management 45, 20–34 (2009)
2. Shen, D., Sun, J.-T., Li, H., Yang, Q., Chen, Z.: Document summarization using conditional random fields. In: International Joint Conference On Artificial Intelligence, pp. 2862–2867 (2007)
3. Conroy, J.M., O'Leary, D.P.: Text summarization via hidden markov models. In: Proceedings of the 24th Annual International ACM SIGIR Conference on Research and Development in Information Retrieval, pp. 406–407. ACM Press, New York (2001)
4. Aliguliyev, R.M.: A new sentence similarity measure and sentence based extractive technique for automatic text summarization. IExpert Systems with Applications 36, 7764–7772 (2009)
5. Jones, K.S.: Automatic summarizing: The state of the art. Information processing and Management 43, 1449–1481 (2007)
6. Shen, D., Yang, Q., Chen, Z.: Noise reduction through summariation for web-page classification. Information Processing and Management 42, 1735–1747 (2007)
7. Li, L., Zhou, K., Xue, G.-R., Zha, H., Yu, Y.: Enhancing diversity, coverage and balance for summarization through structure learning. In: WWW 2009: Proceedings of the 18th international conference on World wide web, vol. 4825, pp. 71–80. ACM Press, New York (2009)
8. Mihalcea, R.: Language independent extractive summarization. In: Proceedings of the 20th national conference on Artificial intelligence, vol. 4, pp. 1688–1689 (2005)
9. Montgomery, D.C., Peck, E.A., Vinin, G.G.: Introduction to linear regression analysis, 2nd edn. Wiley, Chichester (1992)
10. Huang, G.-B., Zhu, Q.-Y., Siew, C.-K.: Extreme learning machine: A new learning scheme of feedforward neural networks. In: International Joint Conference on Neural Networks 2004, vol. 2, pp. 985–990 (2004)
11. Matrices, D.S.: Theory and Applications, 1st edn. Springer, Heidelberg (2002)
12. Lin, C.Y., Hovy, E.: Automatic evaluation of summaries using n-gram co-occurrence statistics. In: Proceedings of the 2003 Conference of the North American Chapter of the Association for Computational Linguistics on Human Language Technology, vol. 1, pp. 71–78 (2003)
13. Luhn, H.P.: The automatic creation of literature abstracts. IBM Journal of Research and Development 2, 159–165 (1958)
14. Gong, Y., Liu, X.: Generic text summarization using relevance measure and latent semantic analysis. In: Proceedings of the 24th Annual International ACM SIGIR Conference on Research and Development in Information Retrieval, pp. 19–25. ACM Press, New York (2001)
15. MarcuM, D.: From discourse structures to text summaries. In: ACL 1997 Workshop on Intelligent Scalable Text Summarization, pp.82–88 (1997)
16. Neto, J.L., Freitas, A.A., Kaestner, C.A.A.: Automatic text summarization using a machine learning approach. In: Bittencourt, G., Ramalho, G.L. (eds.) SBIA 2002. LNCS (LNAI), vol. 2507, pp. 205–215. Springer, Heidelberg (2002)
17. Rijsbergen, C.V.: Information Retrieval, 2nd edn. Butterworths (1979)

Machine Learning Approaches
for Modeling Spammer Behavior

Md. Saiful Islam[1], Abdullah Al Mahmud[2], and Md. Rafiqul Islam[3]

[1] Institute of Information Technology, University of Dhaka, Dhaka 1000, Bangladesh
[2] Dept. of CSE, Ahsanullah University of Science and Technology, Bangladesh
[3] School of Information Technology, Deakin University, Melbourne, VIC 3216, Australia
saifulit@univdhaka.edu, aamrubel@gmail.com, rislam@deakin.edu.au

Abstract. Spam is commonly known as unsolicited or unwanted email messages in the Internet causing potential threat to Internet Security. Users spend a valuable amount of time deleting spam emails. More importantly, ever increasing spam emails occupy server storage space and consume network bandwidth. Keyword-based spam email filtering strategies will eventually be less successful to model spammer behavior as the spammer constantly changes their tricks to circumvent these filters. The evasive tactics that the spammer uses are patterns and these patterns can be modeled to combat spam. This paper investigates the possibilities of modeling spammer behavioral patterns by well-known classification algorithms such as Naïve Bayesian classifier (Naïve Bayes), Decision Tree Induction (DTI) and Support Vector Machines (SVMs). Preliminary experimental results demonstrate a promising detection rate of around 92%, which is considerably an enhancement of performance compared to similar spammer behavior modeling research.

Keywords: Spam Email, MLA, Naïve Bayes, DTI, SVMs.

1 Introduction

The exponential growth of spam emails in recent years is a fact of life. Internet subscribers world-wide are unwittingly paying an estimated €10 billion a year in connection costs just to receive "junk" emails, according to a study undertaken for the European Commission [1]. Though there is no universal definition of spam, unwanted and unsolicited commercial email is basically known as the junk email or spam to the internet community. Spam's direct effects include the consumption of computer and network resources and the cost in human time and attention of dismissing unwanted messages [2].

Combating spam is a difficult job contrast to the spamming. The simplest and most common approaches are to use filters that screen messages based upon the presence of common words or phrases common to junk e-mail. Other simplistic approaches include *blacklisting* (automatic rejection of messages received from the addresses of known spammers) and *whitelisting* (automatic acceptance of message received from known and trusted correspondents). The major flaw in the first two approaches is that it relies upon complacence by the spammers by assuming that they are not likely to change (or forge) their identities or to alter the style and vocabulary of their sales pitches. Whitelisting risks the possibility that the recipient will miss legitimate e-mail from a known or expected correspondent with a heretofore unknown address, such as correspondence

P.-J. Cheng et al. (Eds.): AIRS 2010, LNCS 6458, pp. 251–260, 2010.

from a long-lost friend, or a purchase confirmation pertaining to a transaction with an online retailer. A detail explanation of these techniques is given in [3].

Machine learning algorithms namely Naïve Bayesian classifier, Decision Tree induction and Support Vector Machines based on keywords or tokens extracted from the email's *Subject*, *Content-Type* Header and Message *Body* have been used successfully in the past [2],[3],[4],[5]. Very soon they fall short to filter out spam emails as the spammer changing themselves in the ways that are very difficult to model by simple keywords or tokens [6]. The tactics the spammer uses follows patterns and these behavioral patterns can be modeled to combat spam. Actually the more they try to hide, the easier it is to see them [6]. This study investigates the possibilities of modeling spammer behavioral patterns instead of vocabulary as features for spam email categorization. The three well-known machine learning algorithms Naïve Bayes, DTI and SVMs are experimented to model common spammer patterns, as these classifiers has already shown great performance in different research in spam classifier [3], [4], [5]. Among the classifiers, Naïve Bayes shows its best suitability.

The paper is organized as follows: section 2 discusses the three machine learning algorithms (MLAs); section 3 presents common spammer patterns, email corpus, feature construction and evaluation measures; section 4 discusses the experimental results; and finally section 5 concludes the paper.

2   Machine Learning Algorithms

The success of machine learning algorithms in text categorization (TC) has led researchers to investigate learning algorithms for filtering spam emails [3], [4], [5]. This paper studies the following three machine learning algorithms to model spammer tricks and techniques.

2.1   Naïve Bayesian Classifier

Bayesian classifiers are based on Bayes' theorem. For a training e-mail E, the classifier calculates for each category, the probability that the e-mail should be classified under c_i, where c_i is the ith category, making use of the law of the conditional probability:

$$P(C_i|E) = \frac{P(C_i)P(E|C_i)}{P(E)}$$

Assuming class conditional independence, that is, the probability of each word in an e-mail is independent of the word's context and its position in the e-mail, $P(E|C_i)$ can be calculated as the product of each individual word w_j's probabilities appearing in the category C_i (w_j being the jth of l words in the e-mail):

$$P(E|C_i) = \prod_{j=1}^{l} P(w_j|C_i)$$

The category maximizing $P(C_i|E)$ is predicted by the classifier [5], [7].

2.2   Decision Tree Induction

A decision tree is a *flow-chart-like* tree structure, where each internal node denotes a test on an attribute, each branch represents an output of the test, and leaf nodes correspond to the classification result [5], [7]. The topmost node in the tree is the root node. An example of a typical decision tree is given below:

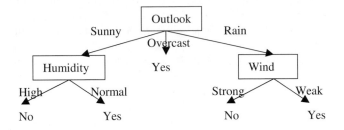

Fig. 1. A decision tree used to determine whether it is suitable to play tennis

To classify an unknown sample the attribute values of the sample are tested against the tree and a path will be traced starting the root to a leaf node that identifies the class prediction for that sample. The commonly used rule learning algorithms J48, ID3 and C4.5 are based on decision trees [5]. The advantage offered by the decision trees is that it can easily be converted to decision rules and comprehended even by a naïve user [7].

2.3 Support Vector Machines

Support vector machines (SVM) are a collection of supervised learning methods that can be applied to classification or regression [4], [7], [8]. Viewing input data as two sets of vectors in a d-dimensional space, an SVM constructs a separating *hyperplane* in that space, one which maximizes the *margin* between the two data sets.

Suppose we are given some training data, a set of points of the form:

$$D = \{(x_i, c_i) \mid x_i \in \Re^d, c_i \in \{-1, \ 1\}\}_{i=1}^n$$

where the c_i is either 1 or -1, indicating the class to which the point belongs. Each x_i is a d-dimensional real vector. We want to find the maximum-margin hyperplane which divides the points having $c_i = 1$ from those having $c_i = -1$. Any hyperplane can be written as the set of points X satisfying

$$W \bullet X - b = 0$$

where $\bullet$ denotes the dot product. The vector W is a normal vector: it is perpendicular to the hyperplane. The parameter $b/\|W\|$ determines the offset of the hyperplane from the origin along the normal vector W.

We want to choose the W and b to maximize the margin, or distance between the parallel hyperplanes that are as far apart as possible while still separating the data. These hyperplanes can be described by the equations:

$$W \bullet X - b = 1 \qquad \text{and} \qquad W \bullet X - b = -1$$

Note that if the training data are linearly separable, we can select the two hyperplanes of the margin in a way that there are no points between them and then try to maximize their instance. By using geometry, we find the distance between these two hyperplanes is $2/\|W\|$, so we want to minimize $\|W\|$.

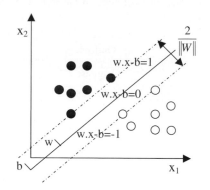

Fig. 2. Maximum-margin hyperplane and margins for a SVM trained with samples from two classes. Samples on the margin are called the support vectors [7], [8].

As we also have to prevent data points falling into the margin, we add the following constraint: for each i either

$$W \bullet x_i - b \geq 1 \text{ for } x_i \text{ of the first class} \qquad \text{or}$$

$$W \bullet x_i - b \leq -1 \text{ for } x_i \text{ of the second.}$$

We can put this together to get the optimization problem:

Minimize (in W, b) $\|W\|$ subject to (for any $i = 1, ..., n$) $c_i(W \bullet x_i - b) \geq 1$

3   Proposed Modeling Approach

People who create spams are called spammers. Electronic mails (emails) are the most common playground of many spammers in the Internet. A tremendous effort has already been invested by the researchers on anti-spamming techniques [4], [5], [12], [13].

3.1   Spammer Behavioral Patterns

The keyword-based statistical analyzers mostly depend on tokenization of the email content and extracting feature from tokenized keywords to model spammer behavior. Tokenization can be misguided in many several ways as today's email supports character sets other than ASCII, non-text attachments and bodies with multiple parts. For example, the following HTML tricks can be used to do this:

GET<!-- banana -->V<!-- 45-->I<!-- wumpus -->A<!-- dskfj -->G <!-- adf -->R<!-- free -->A

Thus above nonsense HTML tags only split the special word "viagra" and disguise the tokenizer though it would be shown as "GET VIAGRA" to email client.

Even a word can be replaced with characters of other languages or like same character. For example, "V1DEO" can be send instead of "VIDEO" and "Fántástïç" instead of "Fantastic". A combination of special characters can used to produce alphabetical characters. For example, char "V" can be represented as the combination of right slash"\" and left slash "/". A list of these kinds of techniques can be found in [9]. A grouping or clustering of these techniques is given Table 1 for quick review.

Table 1. Common spammer tricks

	Java Script	Image	CSS	HTML	MIME/Others
Title Case				Y	
Sticky Finger				Y	
Accent					Y
Readable Spell				Y	
Dot Matrix			Y	Y	
Right-to-Left				Y	
HTML Numbers				Y	
Comments				Y	
Styles			Y		
Invisible Ink			Y	Y	
Matrix			Y	Y	
Encoding of MSG					Y
Encrypted Message Bodies	Y				
Copperfield			Y		
Invisible Image		Y			
Zero Image		Y	Y	Y	
Slice and Dice		Y	Y	Y	
Cross Word			Y	Y	
Honorary Title				Y	
Image Chopping		Y			
Cramp				Y	
Framed				Y	
Big Tag				Y	
Fake Text				Y	
Slick Click				Y	
Phishing				Y	
False Click				Y	
Pump & Dump					Y
I'm Feeling Lucky				Y	

Table 1 has 30 different tricks and one can easily verify that HTML based tactics cover most of them (70%). It can also be shown that 75% of Cascading Style Sheet (CSS) and 50% of Image-based tricks are also covered by HTML-based tactics. It is evident from Table 1 that Java Script and MIME (and/or others) based tricks do not overlap with HTML/CSS based tactics.

In this study, a model has been developed exploiting machine learning algorithms to capture common spammer patterns instead of keyword analysis. The 21 handy crafted features from each e-mail message extracted from subject header, priority & content-type headers and body shown in Table 2 simulate all possible common spammer tricks. These features have also been optimized in their capability of classifying spam emails. The rationale of these features can be verified by their statistics both in spam and non-spam emails. For example, whether a content-type header appeared within the message headers or whether the content type had been set to "text/html" is a common feature of spam, as our investigation revealed. The corpus that has been used in our experimentation, we observed that 98% spam emails include this feature. Similarly, color element (both CSS and HTML format) is also a frequent feature of spam emails. Colorful images those are generally included in the email for X-rated and unwanted internet marketing groups send to catch users' attention. The use of color elements in non-spam mails is very low. We found that that 56% spam emails contain color elements whereas it exists only for 10% non-spam emails. The inclusion of this feature in our classification has improved performance considerably, which shows its practicality. We also added feature 19-21 as in Table 2, which are significant features of recent spams.

Table 2. Features extracted from each e-mail

Feature	Category 1: Features From the Message Subject Header
1	Binary feature indicating 3 or more repeated characters
2	Number of words with all letters in uppercase
3	Number of words with at least 15 characters
4	Number of words with at least two of letters J, K, Q, X, Z
5	Number of words with no vowels
6	Number of words with non-English characters, special characters such as punctuation, or digits at beginning or middle of word
	Category 2: Features From the Priority and Content-Type Headers
7	Binary feature indicating whether the priority had been set to any level besides normal or medium
8	Binary feature indicating whether a content-type header appeared within the message headers or whether the content type had been set to "text/html"
	Category 3: Features From the Message Body
9	Proportion of alphabetic words with no vowels and at least 7 characters
10	Proportion of alphabetic words with at least two of letters J, K, Q, X, Z
11	Proportion of alphabetic words at least 15 characters long
12	Binary feature indicating whether the strings "From:" and "To:" were both present
13	Number of HTML opening comment tags
14	Number of hyperlinks ("href=")
15	Number of clickable images represented in HTML
16	Binary feature indicating whether a text color was set to white
17	Number of URLs in hyperlinks with digits or "&", "%", or "@"
18	Number of color element (both CSS and HTML format)
19	Binary feature indicating whether JavaScript has been used or not
20	Binary feature indicating whether CSS has been used or not
21	Binary feature indicating opening tag of table

3.2 Email Corpus

Classification based spam filtering systems have two major drawbacks. Firstly, building a perfect data set free from noise or imperfection as noise adversely affect the classifier's performance [12]. The nature of spam email is very dynamic and the content of email is textually misleading due to obfuscation as we explained earlier. This remains a continuous challenge for spam filtering techniques. Secondly, most training models of the classifier have limitations on their operations [12]. Classifiers often produce uncorrelated training errors due to the dimension of feature space; a dissimilar output space is generated for changing feature space from small dimension to complex high dimension.

In this work a corpus of 1,000 emails received over a period of several months is used for experimentation. The distribution of both spam and non-spam emails in this collection is equal. The equal distribution is preferred to make the classifier to eliminate the biasness towards a particular category. That is, out of 1,000 emails 500 is spam and 500 is non-spam. The collection of this corpus is selected over a time and latest trend in spamming is kept in mind. Also the author's experience with spam research and statistical selection methodology is applied to the selection, which made this email bank very much representative of current spamming.

3.3 Feature Construction

Each email is parsed as text file to identify each header element to distinguish them from the body of the message. Every substring within the subject header and the message body that was delimited by white space was considered to be a *token*, and an *alphabetic word* was defined as a token delimited by white space that contains only English alphabetic characters (A-Z, a-z)or apostrophes. The tokens were evaluated to create a set of 21 hand-crafted features from each e-mail message (Table 2) of which features 1-17 are proposed in [6]. In addition of these 17 features this study proposes other four features 18-21. The study investigates the suitability of these 21 features in classifying spam emails.

3.4 Evaluation Metrics

Estimating classifier accuracy is important since it allows one to evaluate how accurately a given classifier will classify unknown samples on which the classifier has not been trained. The effectiveness of a classifier is usually measured in terms of accuracy, precision and recall [5], [7]. These measures are calculated using the confusion matrix given below:

Table 3. Confusion matrix

Category C_i	Correct		TP=true positives
Predicted ↓	YES	NO	FP=false positives
YES	TP_i	FP_i	FN=false negatives
NO	FN_i	TN_i	TN=true negatives

Accuracy of a classifier is calculated by dividing the number of correctly classified samples by the total number of test samples and is defined as:

$$Accuracy = \frac{number\ of\ correctly\ classified\ samples}{total\ number\ of\ test\ samples} = \frac{TP + TN}{TP + FP + FN + TN}$$

Precision measures the system's ability to present only relevant items while recall measures system's ability to present all relevant items. These two measures are widely used in TREC evaluation of document retrieval [10]. Precision is calculated by dividing the number of samples that are true positives by the total number of samples classified as positives and is defined as:

$$Precision = \frac{number\ of\ true\ positives}{total\ number\ of\ samples\ classified\ as\ positives} = \frac{TP}{TP + FP}$$

Analogously, recall is calculated by dividing the number of samples that are true positives by the total number of samples that classifier should classified as positives and is defined as:

$$\text{Re}call = \frac{number \quad of \quad true \quad positives}{total \quad number \quad of \quad positive \quad samples} = \frac{TP}{TP+FN}$$

In this study, both precision and recall are kept close to give equal importance on both of them. The block diagram of the proposed model of spam email classification process exploiting spammer behavioral patterns given in Fig 3.

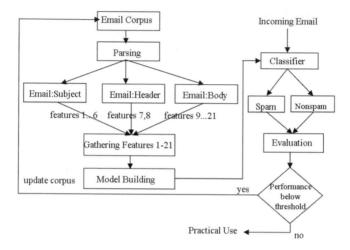

Fig. 3. Block diagram of the proposed model of spam email classification process

4   Experimental Results and Discussion

Table 4 summarizes the comparative results of the three well-known machine learning algorithms namely Naïve Bayesian classifier, decision tree induction and SVM. These algorithms are tested on Weka 3.6.0 suite of machine learning software written in Java, developed at the University of Waikato [11]. It is observed that Naïve Bayesian classifier outperforms than other two machine learning algorithms in all cases. The highest level of accuracy that can be achieved by Naïve Bayesian classifier is 92.2% (shown in yellow color in Table 4) using features from category 2 and 3. The accuracy that can be achieved by any learning algorithms using features from category 1 is negligible. Features from category 2 and 3 contribute mostly in classifying spam emails from non-spam emails for all machine learning algorithm experimented in this study.

Highest number of features is always desirable only if their inclusion increase classifier's accuracy significantly. Growing number of features not only hinders multidimensional indexing but also increases overall execution time. So, this study starves to find an optimal number of features that can be effectively used to lean a classifier without degrading the level of accuracy.

Applying best first forward attribute selection method the study gets only 10 features from category 2 and category 3 useful for classifying the spam and non-spam emails without sacrificing the accuracy as shown in Table 5. The set includes features 8, 9, 10, 12, 13, 14, 15, 16, 17, and 18 of which feature 18 is identified in this study. The Naïve Bayesian classifier again outperforms other two learning algorithms. The optimal feature set obtained by applying best first forward attribute selection method for the features proposed in [6] includes only features 8, 9, 10, 12, 13, 14, 15, 16 and 17, a total of 9 features. In this case decision tree induction outperforms other two machine learning algorithms (shown in light blue in Table 5).

Table 4. Comparison results for Naïve Bayesian Classifier, Decision Tree Induction and SVM

Features	Naïve Bayesian Classifier (Naïve Bayes)			Decision Tree Induction (J48)			SVM (SMO)		
	Acc.	Pre.	Rec.	Acc.	Pre.	Rec.	Acc.	Pre.	Rec.
Cat1 Only	56.5%	55.7%	56.5%	67.8 %	68.9%	67.8%	62.6%	67.8%	62.6%
Cat2 Only	65.2%	75.0%	65.2%	65.2 %	75.0%	65.2%	65.2%	75.0%	65.2%
Cat3 Only	88.7%	88.7%	88.7%	86.9 %	87.4%	87.0%	72.2%	72.5%	72.2%
Cat1+Cat2	66.9%	67.3%	67.0%	73.9%	74.3%	73.9%	68.7	72.6%	68.7%
Cat2+Cat3	92.2%	92.2%	92.2%	86.9 %	87.0%	87.0%	82.6%	83.7%	80.9%
Cat1+Cat3	80.8%	80.9%	80.9%	80.8 %	80.8%	80.9%	76.5%	76.8%	76.5%
Cat1+ Cat2 + Cat3	86.9%	87.0%	87.0%	84.3 %	84.3%	84.3%	74.8%	74.7%	74.8%

The study presented in [6] uses neural network for modeling spammer common patterns and achieved similar performance, but the limitation of neural network is its longer training time and inherent complexity of explaining its derivation, degraded the approach. On the contrary, Bayesian Classifier has the advantage of incremental inclusion of features and beforehand calculation. The decision tree based classification offers the best expressive power and allow better understanding about the classification process and knowledge adoption. Therefore, the proposed modeling approach will have added advantage in this regard.

Table 5. Evaluation of learning algorithms with optimal feature set

Features	Naïve Bayesian Classifier(Naïve Bayes)			Decision Tree Induction (J48)			SVM (SMO)		
	Acc.	Pre.	Rec.	Acc.	Pre.	Rec.	Acc.	Pre.	Rec.
F_1	92.2%	92.2%	92.2%	89.6%	89.9%	89.6%	83.5%	85.5%	83.5%
F_2	86.1%	87.4%	86.1%	91.3%	91.3%	91.3%	83.5%	85.5%	83.5%

F_1: {8, 9, 10, 12, 13, 14, 15, 16, 17, 18} - identified by this study
F_2: {8, 9, 10, 12, 13, 14, 15, 16, 17} - identified in [6]

5   Conclusion and Future Work

This paper studies the modeling of spammer behavior by the well-known machine learning algorithms for spam email classification. Based on examining different features and different learning algorithms, the following conclusions can be drawn from the study presented in this paper: (1) Spammer behavior can be modeled using features extracted from Content-Type header and message Body only, (2) The contribution of features extracted from subject header in spam email detection is negligible or insignificant, (3) Naïve Bayesian classifier best models the spammer behavior than other two machine learning techniques namely Decision Tree Induction and SVMs, and (4) It is possible to get an optimal number of features that can be effectively applied to learning algorithms to classify spam emails without sacrificing accuracy.

The preliminary result presented in this study seems promising in modeling spammer common behavioral patterns compared to similar research. As Naïve Bayes and DTI both offers cost effective framework in classifying spam emails [3], a natural progression will be combining these two ML algorithms in multi-core architecture [13], running both classifier simultaneously in different cores to minimize time and applying voting mechanism to increase positivity, which will give best opportunity to model spammer common patterns. We are also working on developing multi-classifier based spam filters [12] exploiting spammer behavioral patterns with established spam data and benchmarks.

The contribution of this paper is threefold: it shows why keyword based spam email classifier may fail to model spammers' altering tricks, common patterns adopted by spammers and the rationale of using these patterns against them to combat spam; suitability of modeling spammer common patterns using machine learning algorithms and finally, establishment of the four concluding remarks.

References

1. Data protection: Junk E-mail Costs Internet Users 10 Billion a Year Worldwide - Commission Study. In:
   http://europa.eu/rapid/pressReleasesAction.do?reference=IP/01/154 (last accessed on Febuary14th 2009)
2. Aery, M., Chakravarthy, S.: eMailSift: Email Classification Based on Structure and Content. In: Proc. of 5th IEEE Intl. Conf. on Data Mining, pp. 1–8 (2005)
3. Islam, M.R., Chowdhury, M.U.: Spam Filtering using ML Algorithms. In: Proc. of IADIS International Conf. on WWW/Internet, pp. 419–426 (2005)
4. Drucker, H., Wu, D., Vapnik, V.N.: Support Vector Machines for Spam Categorization. IEEE Transactions on Neural Networks 10(5), 1048–1054 (1999)
5. Eichler, K.: Automatic Classification of Swedish Email Messages. B.A Thesis, Eberhard-Karls-Universitat Tubingen (2005)
6. Stuart, J.I., Cha, S., Tappert, C.: A Neural Network Classifier for Junk E-mail. In: Marinai, S., Dengel, A.R. (eds.) DAS 2004. LNCS, vol. 3163, pp. 442–450. Springer, Heidelberg (2004)
7. Han, J., Kamber, M.: Data Mining Concepts and Techniques. Academic Press, London (2001) ISBN 81-7867-023-2
8. Islam, M.S., Amin, M.I.: An Architecture of Active Learning SVMs with Relevance Feedback for Classifying E-mail. Journal of Computer Science 1(1), 15–18 (2007)
9. Common Spammer Techniques,
   http://www.process.com/precisemail/spamtricks.pdf
10. Makhoul, J., Kubala, F., Schwartz, R., Weischedel, R.: Performance Measures for Information Extraction. In: Proc. of DARPA Broadcast News Workshop, pp. 249–252 (1999)
11. Holmes, G., Donkin, A., Witten, I.H.: Weka: A machine Learning Workbench. In: Proc. 2nd Australia and New Zealand Conference on Intelligent Information Systems, Brisbane, Australia, pp. 357–361 (1995)
12. Islam, M.R., Zhou, W., Xiang, Y., Gao, M.: An Innovative Analyser for Multi-Classifier Email Classification Based on Grey List Analysis. The Journal of Network and Computer Applications 32(2), 357–366 (2009)
13. Islam, M.R., Zhou, W., Xiang, Y., Gao, M., Mahmood, A.N.: Spam Filtering for Network Traffic Security on a Multi-Core Environment. Concurrency and Computation: Practice and Experience 21(10), 1307–1320 (2009)

Research of Sentiment Block Identification for Customer Reviews Based on Conditional Random Fields

Lei Jiang, Yuanchao Liu, Bingquan Liu, Chengjie Sun, and Xiaolong Wang

School of Computer Science and Technology, Harbin Institute of Technology,
150001, Harbin, China
{ljiang,lyc,liubq,cjsun,wangxl}@insun.hit.edu.cn

Abstract. Many customer reviews are expressed freely and informally, thus it will bring obstacle for sentiment analysis. In this paper, we aim at finding a method to identify sentiment block from the consumer reviews. The main idea of this paper is to treat this task as a word sequence labeling problem and solved with conditional random fields model (CRF) by introducing template feature. Experimental results show that our approach can identify most sentiment blocks from customer reviews and correspondingly find the sentiment polarity of the blocks correctly.

Keywords: Customer review mining, sentiment block identification, conditional random fields, template feature.

1 Introduction

The customer reviews for products provided by many websites are very helpful for potential buyers. In this paper, we aim at identifying sentiment block from the consumer reviews. The main idea is to treat sentiment block identification task as a word sequence labeling problem, thus it can be solved with conditional random fields model (CRF) by introducing template feature. In this paper, Sentiment blocks mean the phrases with sentiment polarity. For many user reviews in forums, the expressions are usually arbitrary, such as: "要是屏幕再大点就好了。"("If only the screen is bigger"), "这款手机的电池不到两天就没电了"("The energy of the battery is exhausted in less than two days"), here "不到两天" is sentiment blocks. Obviously the traditional methods can not identify such blocks very well and are not sensitive to such valuable information; correspondingly the overall system performance will be adversely affected.

2 Related Work

Early sentiment analyses focus on coarse-grained sentiment analysis [1-6], and word-level sentiment analysis [3-5]. As a coarse-grained analysis, document-level and sentence-level sentiment analysis has some limitations, an article may contain positive parts and negative parts, document-level sentiment analysis is obviously too rough. Word-level sentiment analysis is the basis of all other granularity of the sentiment analysis, but often a word can not represent the emotion of the entire sentence.

P.-J. Cheng et al. (Eds.): AIRS 2010, LNCS 6458, pp. 261–269, 2010.

Phrase-level sentiment analysis mainly has the following difficulties: 1. From a certain perspective, it is an information extraction task, 2. To judge the emotional phrases, we often have to consider its context. In recent years, the phrase-level sentiment analysis is also increasing. Jeonghee Yi includes noun phrase with emotional word, and emotional words into the sentiment blocks [7], Turney [3], considers noun phrase containing adjectives or adverbs as the sentiment blocks, some other studies take into account the context of sentiment blocks (phrase). Wilson [8,9] considers the part of speech of words near the current word, the location of the current word in the syntactic tree, and the relationship between current word and other words. Tianfang Yao [10] and others make in-depth study in fine-grained sentiment analysis, and their focus is to find the relationship between themes and sentiment-descriptive term. However the sentiment-descriptive term, i.e. the sentiment blocks mentioned above, can only be extracted around the emotional word.

3   Our Approach

In this paper, we adopt a flexible mining method using CRF model and introducing the template feature to identifies the sentiment blocks from the user reviews. Given a sequence of words, $X = x_1 x_2 ... x_n$, we generate a sequence of labels $Y = y_1 y_2 ... y_n$, $y_i \in \{O, UB, UE, UBE, DB, DE, DBE\}$,where 'UB' is the first word of positive sentiment block, 'UE' is the non-initial word of positive sentiment block, 'UBE' is positive sentiment block with only one word, 'DB','DE','DBE' is label corresponding to negative sentiment block, 'O' is a word which is not part of any sentiment block. For example: "有时候/O 爱/DB 死机/DE ， /O 外屏(F6)/O 有/DB 问题 /DE， /O 很/DB 烦/DE 。/O". The detailed description of CRF can be found in [11].

We introduce some sequence features, such as word sequence feature, POS (Part-of Speech) sequence feature, emotional words feature, modifier feature, and bug feature. In addition, we also introduce the template feature.

We try to extract templates from training data which may be helpful to sentiment block identification. For example, sentiment block such as "非常漂亮"("very beautiful"),"很不错"("very good"), the corresponding template is "modifier + emotional word", while sentiment block such as "不到两天就没电了"("(battery) is exhausted in less than two days"),"不到三个月就坏了"("(The mobile phone) is broken in less than three months"), the corresponding template is "'不到'+numeral+ quantifier+'就'".

After the Chinese word segmentation and part of speech tagging on the training data, we determine the attribute set of each word with the help of emotional words dictionary, modifier dictionary and mobile phone bug dictionary. The attribute set of each word includes POS tagging *pos*, bug label *bug* , emotional word label *pol*, modifier label *mod*, where $bug \in \{BUG, O\}$, $pol \in \{UP, DOWN, O\}$, $mod \in \{UP, DOWN, O\}$. We say w_1 matches with w_2 (also w_2 matches with w_1), if and only if one of the following conditions are met: (1) $w_1 = w_2$; (2) $bug_1 = bug_2 = BUG$; (3) $pol_1 = pol_2 = UP$ or $pol_1 = pol_2 = DOWN$; (4) $mod_1 = mod_2 = UP$ or $mod_1 = mod_2 = DOWN$; (5) $pos_1 = pos_2$.

Input: Sentiment blocks set in training data $S = \{b_1, b_2, ...b_n\}$

Output: Template set $T = \{t_1, t_2, ...t_m\}$

Initialization: $i = 1$, $T = \varnothing$

Begin:

(a) if $i > n$, stop; otherwise, goto (b);

(b) Consider LCS between b_i and other blocks in S, then calculate the average matching degree of this LCS and current two blocks;

$$MatchDegree(b_i, b_j) = \frac{1}{2}(\frac{len(LSC(b_i, b_j))}{len(b_i)} + \frac{len(LSC(b_i, b_j))}{len(b_j)})$$

Where $len(LSC(b_i, b_j))$ is the length of LCS of b_i, b_j, $len(b_i)$ is the length of b_i, and $len(b_j)$ is the length of b_j.

(c) If the maximum of average matching degrees is greater than the threshold value λ, and the corresponding template hasn't been in T, add the template to T;

(d) $S = S - b_i$, $i = i + 1$, goto (a)

End

Fig. 1. Template extraction algorithm

From (1) to (5) the priority is decreasing. After the two words match with each other, we give them a common marker, which is the so-called match-marker. The decreasing priority from (1) to (5) means that when the two matching words meet two or more condition, we consider the highest-priority matching condition as their final match conditions, and offer them the corresponding tag. For example, two sentiment block: "非常漂亮"("very beautiful") and "很不错"("very good"), they meet two matching condition: $pol_1 = pol_2 = UP$ and $pos_1 = pos_2$, but as we choose the highest-priority condition, that is $pol_1 = pol_2 = UP$, and offer them corresponding tag: UP_P. Next, we will consider the LCS (Longest Common String) between two blocks, and follow the matching method describe above. Template extraction algorithm is shown in Fig. 1.

The features we choose include: (1) word sequence feature, (2) part of speech sequence feature, (3) emotional words feature, (4) modifier feature, (5) mobile phone bug feature (6) template feature.

(1) Word sequence. For the word sequence feature, we mainly select the current word and words in [-2,2] window, that is, the current term, the word before current word, the word after current word, the second word before current word, the second word after current word .

(2) POS sequence. For the POS sequence feature, we select POS of current word and POS of words in its [-2,2] window, that is, POS of the current word, POS of word before the current word, POS of word after the current word, POS of second word before the current word, POS of second word after the current word .

(3) Emotional words. Considering sentiment block such as "非常漂亮", emotional words often appear in the 1-2 position behind the modifiers, so we introduce the emotional word feature. We set the window [0,2] starting from current word, that is, the current word, first word after current word, second word after current word, we consider whether they are emotional words. Word with positive polarity is marked as UP, word with negative polarity is marked as DOWN, non-emotional word is marked as O.

(4) Modifiers features. Similar to (3), modifiers often appear in the 1-2 position before the emotional words, so we introduce the modifiers feature. We set the window [-2,0] starting from current word, that is the current word, first word before current word, second word before current word. We consider whether they are modifiers. Positive modifiers are marked as UP, negative modifiers are marked as DOWN, non-modifiers are marked as O.

(5) Mobile phone bug features. Considering bug-words often express strong feeling of people, so the introduction of mobile phone bug feature is necessary. We consider whether a word is a bug-word, bug-word is marked as BUG, otherwise marked as O.

(6) Template features. For the current term, if it matches a template, we mark the word with corresponding template label, such as D_1, where D represents the polarity of the template, 1 represents the template label. If it does not match any template, it is marked as O.

4 Experiments

In order to evaluate the performance of our approach, we conducted our experiments using the customer reviews downloaded from the mobile phone website it168 (http://pinglun.it168.com), we manually annotated 1000 user reviews (including 3941 compound sentences) as our experimental data.

4.1 Baseline

In our experiments, the Baseline method is as follows: first find the emotional word, and then find modifiers around the emotional word, and we consider the emotional words and their corresponding modifiers together as one sentiment block. We use the emotional words as the center, and set a [-5,5] window. The border isn't beyond current sentence borders. For example, for the sentence "铃声效果不错，屏幕比较清晰！"（"The ringtone is pleasant, and the screen is clear"）,the phrase "不错" and "比较清晰" are sentiment blocks, which is underlined.

4.2 Tagging with CRF model

According to different feature combination, we design three experiments. The feature combination of each experiment is shown in Table 1, in which T1 represents words

Table 1. Feature combination

Experiment Methods	Feature combination
CRF_1	T1
CRF_2	T1+T2
CRF_3	T1+T2+T3

sequence feature and POS sequence feature, T2 represents modifier feature and emotional words feature, T3 represents the template feature.

4.3 Experimental Strategy and Results

In the experiment, we adopted human-tagged sentiment block as the standard to test the performance of our approach. For a standard sentiment block $s_1 = (w_{11}, w_{12}, ... w_{1n})$ and the sentiment block identified $s_2 = (w_{21}, w_{22}, ... w_{2m})$ (see Fig.2). We say s_2 matches with s_1 (also s_1 matches with s_2) if and only if $MD(s_1, s_2) > \eta$, by experience we set $\eta = 0.6$, we use $MD(s_1, s_2)$ to measure how well s_1 and s_2 match with each other. $MD(s_1, s_2) = \frac{1}{2}(\frac{len(Com(s_1, s_2))}{len(s_1)} + \frac{len(Com(s_1, s_2))}{len(s_2)})$. Where $len(Com(s_1, s_2))$ is the

length of common part of s_1, s_2 (Common part here refer to parts completely overlapped in position, which is different from the one mentioned in formula (1).).

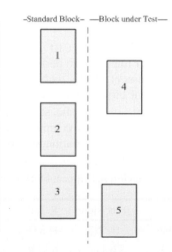

Fig. 2. Corresponding Blocks Illustration（Block 1 corresponds with block 4, block 3 corresponds with block 5）

Experiment 1: Threshold Selection. The purpose of experiment 1 is to determine the optimal threshold λ in template extraction step. The result is shown in Fig. 3. It can be seen that when λ is 0.7, the performance is optimal.

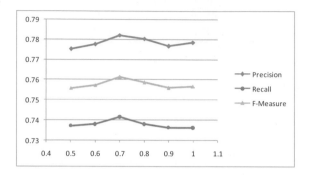

Fig. 3. Result for different λ

Experiment 2: Comparison of precision, recall and F-measure for four different methods. The comparison of precision, recall, F-measure for four methods is given in Table 2. The result shows that:

1. The word sequence labeling method based on the CRF model is better than the Baseline method. This shows that the Baseline method has obvious limitations. Whereas by using CRF model, the context of sentiment blocks can be taken into account to a certain extent, and the modes of sentiment blocks identified are more flexible.
2. According to the results of CRF_2 and CRF_1, we can see the introduction of modifiers feature and emotional words feature can improve the performance, especially the recall value.
3. According to the results of CRF_3 and CRF_2, we can see the introduction of the template feature can further improve the performance. This is because for CRF_1 and CRF_2, only the sentiment blocks with continuous word sequences can be identified, for the sentiment blocks with discontinuous word sequences, CRF_1 and CRF_2 perform worse, such as the sentiment block"要是…就好了"("If only…"), while the CRF_3 includes the template features, so it can do better in identifying sentiment blocks with discontinuous word sequence.

Table 2. Result for sentiment block identification

	Precision	Recall	F1
Baseline	41.55%	44.33%	42.90%
CRF_1	76.41%	68.71%	72.35%
CRF_2	76.48%	72.12%	74.24%
CRF_3	78.22%	74.14%	76.13%

Experiment 3: Comparison of average matching degree. The method of calculating matching degree is shown in formula (2), the experimental result are shown in Fig.4. It suggests that: For methods based on CRF model, the average matching degree can achieve more than 60%. CRF_3 is still the best method, whose average matching degree can achieve almost 70%.

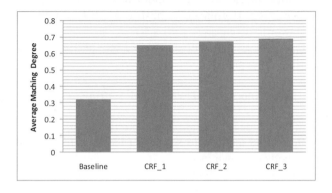

Fig. 4. Comparison of average matching degree

Experiment 4: We design 2 sub-experiments, in each experiment we divide the sentiment blocks into different group according to certain strategies, and then we compare performance of the four methods.

1. Positive sentiment blocks & Negative sentiment blocks

In this experiment, we divide sentiment blocks into positive blocks and negative blocks, and then we compare performance of the four methods. The experimental result is shown in Table 3, it suggests that: 1) Overall, the performance of positive sentiment block identification is superior to that of negative sentiment block identification. Because compared to positive sentiment block, negative sentiment block contains relatively more colloquial expression, like "气死我了", "老死机" and etc. Colloquial expression makes the sentiment block identification more difficult; 2). CRF_3's performance is the best. especially the most obvious increase of the recall value for negative sentiment block identification has been achieved. Template feature can help CRF model perform better in such colloquial expression.

Table 3. Comparison for Positive sentiment blocks and Negative sentiment blocks

	Precision (Positive)	Recall (Positive)	F1 (Positive)	Precision (Negative)	Recall (Negative)	F1 (Negative)
Baseline	38.90%	62.09%	47.83%	46.60%	30.17%	36.63%
CRF_1	77.74%	71.97%	74.75%	75.32%	66.18%	70.45%
CRF_2	78.61%	74.74%	76.62%	74.85%	69.87%	72.27%
CRF_3	80.33%	75.97%	78.09%	76.45%	72.84%	74.61%

In this experiment, we divide sentiment blocks into sentiment blocks with emotional words and that without emotional words, and then we compare performance of the four methods. The experimental result is shown in Table 4, it suggests that: 1) generally the performance of sentiment blocks identification with emotional words is superior to that of sentiment blocks identification without emotional words. The reason is that sentiment blocks without emotional words are mostly very colloquial expression; 2) CRF_3's performance is best, especially for the sentiment blocks without emotional words. Compared with CRF_2, the recall value of CRF_3 has increased about 5 percentages, it is because the template feature can help model do better in such colloquial expression.

2.Two-word sentiment blocks & Three-word sentiment blocks & Multi-word sentiment blocks

In this experiment, we divide sentiment blocks into two-word sentiment blocks, three-word sentiment blocks and multi-word sentiment blocks. The experimental comparison of the four methods is shown in Fig. 5. It reveals similar phenomenon as above from a different perspective: 1) generally, the performance of two-word sentiment blocks identification is better than that of three-word and multi-word sentiment blocks identification. It is because there is a lot of colloquial expression in three-word and multi-word sentiment blocks; 2) CRF_3's performance is best, and for the multi-word sentiment blocks, the performance gets the most obvious increase because template feature can help model do better in such kind of sentiment blocks.

Table 4. The performance comparison on sentiment blocks with emotional words and that without emotional words

	Sentiment blocks with emotional words			Sentiment blocks without emotional words		
	Precision	Recall	F1	Precision	Recall	F1
Baseline	41.70%	67.29%	51.50%	—	—	—
CRF_1	83.11%	71.97%	77.14%	65.04%	62.47%	63.73%
CRF_2	81.48%	77.60%	79.50%	66.93%	61.67%	64.19%
CRF_3	83.32%	78.86%	81.03%	68.43%	65.32%	66.84%

5　Conclusions

In this paper, we have proposed a sentiment block identification method which is based on CRF model. Some different feature combinations have been tried, and found that the introduction of template feature can enhance the performance of the CRF model. Our approach has two advantages: 1). to some extent, it takes into account the context of sentiment blocks, thus it can determine the polarity of sentiment block effectively; 2). Such method performs better in the colloquial expression, especially multi-word blocks or blocks with discontinuous word sequence.

Acknowledgments. This research was supported by "the Fundamental Research Funds for the Central Universities" （Grant No.HIT.NSRIF.2009065） and Key Laboratory Opening Funding of China MOE－MS Key Laboratory of Natural Language Processing and Speech (HIT.KLOF.2009022), the project of The National High Technology Research and Development Program (863 program) of PR China under a research Grant No.2007AA01Z172, Special Fund Projects for Harbin Science and Technology Innovation Talents (2010RFXXG003).

References

1. Tony, M., Nigel, C.: Sentiment Analysis using Support Vector Machines with Diverse Information Sources. In: Proceedings of EMNLP 2004, Barcelona, pp. 412–418 (2004)
2. Pang, B., Lee, L., Vaithyanathan, S.: Thumbs Up? Sentiment Classification Using Machine Learning Techniques. In: Proceedings of the Conference on Empirical Methods in Natural Language Processing (EMNLP), Philadelphia, pp. 79–86 (2002)
3. Turney, P.: Thumbs Up or Thumbs Down? Semantic Orientation Applied to Unsupervised Classification of Reviews. In: Proceedings of ACL 2002, 40th Annual Meeting of the Association for Computational Linguistics, Philadelphia, pp. 417–424 (2002)
4. Minqing, H., Bing, L.: Mining and summarizing customer reviews. In: Proceedings of the 2004 ACM SIGKDD international conference on Knowledge discovery and data mining, Seattle, Washington, pp. 168–177 (2004)
5. Turney, P., Littman, M.: Measuring praise and criticism: Inference of semantic orientation from association. ACM T. Inform. Syst. 21, 315–346 (2003)
6. Chaovalit, P., Zhou, L.: Movie review mining: A comparison between supervised and unsupervised classification approaches. In: Proceedings of the 38th Hawaii international conference on system sciences, Hawaii, pp. 1–9 (2005)
7. Yi, J., Nasukawa, T.: Sentiment analyzer: Extracting sentiments about a given topic using natural language processing techniques. In: 3rd IEEE Conf. on Data Mining (ICDM 2003), Melbourne, Florida, pp. 423–434 (2003)
8. Wilson, T., Wiebe, J.: Recognizing Contextual Polarity in Phrase-Level Sentiment Analysis. In: Proceedings of Human Language Technologies Conference on Empirical Methods in Natural Language Processing, Vancouver, Canada, pp. 347–354 (2005)
9. Theresa, W., Janyce, W., Paul, H.: Recognizing Contextual Polarity: An Exploration of Features for Phrase-Level Sentiment Analysis. Comput. Linguist. 35, 399–433 (2009)
10. Yao, T.: Research on Semantic Orientation Analysis for Topics in Chinese Sentences. Journal of Chinese Information Processing 23, 73–79 (2007)
11. John, L., Andrew, M.: Conditional Random Fields: Probabilistic Models for Segmenting and Labeling Sequence Data. In: Proceedings of 18th International Conf. on Machine Learning, pp. 282–289. Morgan Kaufmann, San Francisco (2001)

Semantic Relation Extraction
Based on Semi-supervised Learning

Haibo Li, Yutaka Matsuo, and Mitsuru Ishizuka

University of Tokyo
7-3-1 Hongo, Bunkyo-ku, Tokyo, Japan
lihaibo@mi.ci.i.u-tokyo.ac.jp,
matsuo@biz-model.t.u-tokyo.ac.jp,
ishizuka@i.u-tokyo.ac.jp

Abstract. Many tasks of information extraction or natural language processing have a property that the data naturally consist of several views—disjoint subsets of features. Specifically, a semantic relationship can be represented with some entity pairs or contexts surrounding the entity pairs. For example, the *Person-Birthplace* relation can be recognized from the *entity pair* view, such as (*Albert Einstein, Ulm*), (*Pablo Picasso, Malaga*) and so on. On the other side, this relation can be identified with some contexts, such as "*A was born in B*", "*B, the birth place of A*" and so on.

To leverage the unlabeled data in the training stage, semi-supervised learning has been applied to relation extraction task. In this paper, we propose a multi-view semi-supervised learning algorithm, Co-Label Propagation, to combine the 'information' from both the *entity pair* view and the *context* view. In propagation process, the label scores of classes are spread not only in the *entity pair* view and the *context* view, but also between the two views. The proposed algorithm is evaluated using semantic relation classification tasks. The experiment results validate its effectiveness.

Keywords: semi-supervised learning, multi-view learning, relation extraction.

1 Introduction

Relationship extraction is a task of recognizing a particular relationship between two or more entities in documents. However, a large amount of manually labeled data is demanded when the supervised learning methods are used to address this problem. But annotating training data is a very tedious and time consuming work [1]. Meanwhile, semi-supervised learning addresses this problem by combining a large amount of unlabeled data with a small set of labeled data to train a classifier, such as co-training, label propagation and so on.

Recently, label propagation, a graph-based semi-supervised learning method, has increasingly attracted research attention [1,2,3]. The label propagation algorithm constructs a graph with both labeled and unlabeled data. The seed nodes in the graph propagate their labels to neighbors according to their similarity. In label propagation process, the label distribution of initial labeled seeds are clamped in each iteration to replenish

P.-J. Cheng et al. (Eds.): AIRS 2010, LNCS 6458, pp. 270–279, 2010.

the label sources from these labeled data. With this spreading from labeled examples, the class boundaries are spread through edges with large weights and settle in gaps along edges with low weights.

Generally, many tasks of information extraction or natural language processing have a property that the data naturally consist of several views—disjoint subsets of features. For instance, web pages can be described by their contents or hyperlinks pointing to these pages [4]. A popular paradigm of multi-view learning is the co-training algorithm, which splits all features into two subsets and trains two classifiers by the labeled seeds in each view. Each classifier classifies the unlabeled data in the unlabeled data pool and provides the other classifier with the few unlabeled examples as training seeds that receive the highest confidence from the first classifier.

In relation classification task, a semantic relationship can be represented with two different kinds of "information": the entity pair itself and the context surrounding it. Given an instance of data for relation classification as follows:

$$s = (C_{pre}, e_1, C_{mid}, e_2, C_{post})$$

where e_1 and e_2 are nouns or noun phrases and C_{pre}, C_{mid}, and C_{post} are the contexts before, between, and after the nominal pairs. We split s into two parts: entity pair (e_1, e_2) and contexts $(C_{pre}, C_{mid}, C_{post})$. Many features can be extracted from the two parts respectively and applied to learning.

In this paper, we propose a label propagation based multi-view learning algorithm, Co-Label Propagation (Co-LP), which combines the information of the *entity pair* view and the *context* view. Let $S = \{s_i | i = 1, \cdots, u\}$ be a set of sentence tuples. A instance $s_i = (a_j, b_k)$ is composed of two parts: entity pair a_j and context b_k. Let $A = \{a_j | j = 1, \cdots, n\}$ and $B = \{b_k | k = 1, \cdots, m\}$ be sets of entity pairs and contexts respectively. A entity pair a_j occurs in S at least once with one or more context(s). A context b_k signify at least one or more entity pair(s). The proposed Co-LP algorithm constructs three graphs: $G_A = < A, E_A >$, $G_B = < B, E_B >$ and $G_{AB} = < A \cup B, E_{AB} >$. A and B represent the data point set of *entity pair* view and *context* view respectively, and E_A, E_B are edges that connect intra-view data points. Graphs G_A and G_B represent the similarities among data points in each view respectively. The inter-view graph G_{AB} is a bipartite graph which describes the correlation between data points of two different views. The graph G_{AB} uses the correlation of the entity pair a_j and context b_k to combine the label score of data points in the two views.

The remainder of this paper is organized as follows: In section 2, we outline related works of relation extraction and semi-supervised learning. In section 3, we present our Co-Label Propagation algorithm in detail. Section 4 presents some experiments and discussion of the results. Finally, in section 5, we discuss our conclusions.

2   Related Work

To leverage the unlabeled data in the training stage, semi-supervised learning has been applied to relation extraction task. As mentioned in previous section, Chen et al. explored a graph based semi-supervised learning for relation extraction, which makes use of unlabeled data [5]. Niu et al. investigated label propagation for a word-sense disambiguation task [6].

Co-Training is a semi-supervised, multi-view algorithm that uses the initial seeds to learn a classifier in each view [4]. Then each classifier is applied to classify all unlabeled data. The examples on which each classifier makes the most confident predictions are selected and added to the training set. Based on the new training set, a new classifier is learned in each view, and the whole process is repeated for several iterations.

The proposed Co-LP is based on label propagation which models an entire dataset as a weighted graph and propagates labels through the graph along its high-density areas [3]. Zhou et al. proposed another graph-based algorithm, the local and global consistency algorithm, in which the function at each node receives contribution from its neighbors in each step [2].

3   Co-label Propagation

3.1   Preliminaries

We presume that each data point s has two views—$s =< a, b >$—where a and b denote data points constructed respectively from *entity pair* view and *context* view. Let u be the number of data points in the feature space built with all features. Similarly, n and m respectively signify the quantities of data points in the feature space generated with *entity pair* view and *context* view. More formally, the dataset $S \subseteq A \times B$, $|S| = u$, $|A| = n$, $|B| = m$, where $u \geq n, m$, each example $s \in S$ is given as (a, b). Actually, $L = \{l_1, l_2, \cdots, l_c\}$ is the set of labels and $|L| = c$.

Let $T^A = (T^A_{ij}, \quad i, j = 1, 2, \cdots, n)$ be an $n \times n$ similarity matrix constructed from A in which T^A_{ij} represents the similarity between a_i and a_j calculated from *entity pair* view. Let T^B be defined similarly, as shown above from B.

Let $W^{AB} = (W^{AB}_{ij}, \quad i = 1, 2, \cdots, n; j = 1, 2, \cdots, m)$ be an $n \times m$ matrix defined as the correlation matrix between *entity pair* view and *context* view. In addition, $T^{AB} = (T^{AB}_{ij}, \quad i = 1, 2, \cdots, n; j = 1, 2, \cdots, m)$ is the row-normalized W^{AB}, as Eq. 1 shows, where T^{AB}_{ij} denotes the normalized correlation between a_i and b_j. In addition, $T^{BA} = (T^{BA}_{ij}, \quad i = 1, 2, \cdots, m; j = 1, 2, \cdots, n)$ is the transposed matrix of column-normalized W^{AB} as presented in Eq. 2.

$$[T^{AB}]_{ij} = \frac{[W^{AB}]_{ij}}{\sum_{k=0}^{m} [W^{AB}]_{ik}}. \tag{1}$$

$$[T^{BA}]_{ij} = \frac{[W^{BA}]_{ji}}{\sum_{k=0}^{n} [W^{BA}]_{ki}}. \tag{2}$$

Let Y^A_t be a $n \times c$ labeling matrix, where $[Y^A_t]_{ij}$ denotes the probability of a_i labeled as l_j in t-*th* round propagation. Let Y^A_0 be initialized by the labeled data as

$$[Y^A_0]_{ij} = \begin{cases} 1 & \text{if } a_i \text{ is labeled as } l_j \\ 0 & \text{otherwise} \end{cases}.$$

Similarly, Y_t^B is an $m \times c$ labeling matrix, whose i-th row represents the label probability distribution of data point b_i and Y_0^B is initialized similarly as Y_0^A. Let Y be an $u \times c$ labeling matrix, where $[Y]_{ij}$ denotes the label probability distribution of data point $s_i \in S$.

Table 1. Co-Label Propagation algorithm

Given:
- Intra-view similarity matrices T^A, T^B
- Inter-view correlation matrices T^{AB}, T^{BA}
- Initial label matrices of each view Y_0^A, Y_0^B

1. Propagate in each view

$$[Y_{t+1}^A]' \leftarrow T^A Y_t^A$$
$$[Y_{t+1}^B]' \leftarrow T^B Y_t^B$$

2. Propagate between different views

$$[Y_{t+1}^A]'' \leftarrow T^{AB} Y_t^B$$

$$[Y_{t+1}^B]'' \leftarrow T^{BA} Y_t^A$$

3. Combine the label score

$$Y_{t+1}^A \leftarrow [Y_{t+1}^A]' + [Y_{t+1}^A]''$$

$$Y_{t+1}^B \leftarrow [Y_{t+1}^B]' + [Y_{t+1}^B]''$$

4. Row-normalize Y_{t+1}^A and Y_{t+1}^B to maintain the class propagation interpretation.

$$[Y_t^A]_{ij} = [Y_t^A]_{ij} / \sum_{k=0}^{c} [Y_t^A]_{ik}$$

$$[Y_t^B]_{ij} = [Y_t^B]_{ij} / \sum_{k=0}^{c} [Y_t^B]_{ik}$$

5. Clump the labeled data: replace the rows of labeled data in Y_t^A and Y_t^B with the corresponding rows of Y_0^A and Y_0^B respectively:

6. Repeat from step 2 for f times:

7. Combine the two matrices: Y_t^A and Y_t^B. For each node $s_i = <a_j, b_k>$, construct an $u \times c$ matrix Y with the labeling matrix of both views.

$$[Y]_{il} = [Y_t^A]_{jl} [Y_t^B]_{kl}$$

3.2   Intra-view and Inter-view Label Propagation

In the proposed algorithm, we construct two intra-view graphs: $G_A = < A, E_A >$, $G_B = < B, E_B >$; one inter-view graph $G_{AB} = < A \cup B, E_{AB} >$. A, B represents the data point in *entity pair* view and where *context* view. G_{AB} represent similarities between data points in different views. Following [1], we use both labeled and unlabeled nodes to create a fully connected intra-view graph in each view. The edge between node i, j is weighted as

$$T_{ij} = \exp\left(-\frac{sim_{ij}^2}{\alpha^2}\right). \tag{3}$$

where sim_{ij} signifies the similarity of x_i and x_j calculated using some similarity measure, and α is used to control the weight. As described in this paper, we set α as the average similarity between labeled examples from different classes.

In the first step of propagation, every node in each view receives a contribution from the linked nodes in the same view. The second step is to spread label scores among different views. We build an inter-view graph $G_{AB} = < A \cup B, E_{AB} >$ between *entity pair* view and *context* view, which is used to amend the class distributions of each node. The weight of edge in E_{AB} is given as W^{AB}. In addition, T^{AB} is row-normalized by Eq. 1 and T^{BA} is line-normalized by Eq. 2. Table 1 presents the proposed algorithm concretely.

3.3   Rebalance the Label Distribution Using Label Bidding

After the matrix Y is learned, the label bidding process is executed to rebalance the label distribution. When data classes are very close or when labeled data are very few, rebalancing the label distribution can improve the final classification performance. Initially, the number of each type of labels can be estimated from labeled data. In the label bidding process, the learned label score of each node in Y is regarded as a bid for the labels. For example, if Y_{il} is the highest bid currently and class l has labels remained, then data point i is labeled as l. Then the data point i exits from bidding and the label number of class l subtracts 1. The second highest bid is processed if class l has no labels. This process will be repeated until all the labels are 'sold'.

4   Experiments

4.1   Evaluation of the Semantic Relation Classification Performance

In this section, we present our empirical study using SemEval-2007 Task 04: Classification of Semantic Relations between Nominals [7]. This dataset consists of seven semantic relations and every semantic relation is a separate binary classification task. Table 2 presents the number of positive and negative examples of each relation.

In our experiment, we first put the training set and test set of SemEval-07 Task 04 together; then we randomly select different percentages of data point as labeled seeds and others as unlabeled data. All data are projected into context and nominal pair views. To test the efficiency of inter-view label propagation algorithm, we also use the other algorithm named UnIVLP. This algorithm uses the same feature splitting and only propagates label scores in each view. In other words, UnIVLP merely skip over steps 2 and 3 portrayed in Table 1.

Table 2. SemEval-07 Task 04 Dataset Statistics

Relation Type	Training Data (positive)	Test Data (positive)
Cause-Effect	140 (65)	80 (41)
Instrument-User	140 (65)	78 (38)
Product-Producer	140 (65)	93 (62)
Origin-Entity	140 (65)	81 (36)
Theme-Tool	140 (65)	71 (29)
Part-Whole	140 (65)	72 (26)
Content-Container	140 (65)	74 (38)

Intra-View Similarity. To weight the similarity graph of each view, we use a frequently used measure, the cosine similarity measure (as Eq. 4), to calculate the similarity between any two data nodes in each view.

$$\cos(x, y) = \frac{\sum_{i=1}^{n} x_i \cdot y_i}{\sqrt{\sum_{i=1}^{n} x_i^2} \sqrt{\sum_{i=1}^{n} y_i^2}}. \tag{4}$$

Matrices T^A and T^B, are constructed and normalized as previous mentioned.

Inter-View Similarity. Mutual information is an efficient measure of the relation between two random variables. Therefore, we use mutual information (as Eq. 5) between a_j and b_k to measure the relevance between data points of different views. Actually, $P(a_j)$, $P(b_k)$ respectively represent the probabilities of node a_j and b_k in V. Furthermore, $P(a_j, b_k)$ is the joint probability distribution of the node pair.

$$[W^{AB}]_{jk} = \log_2 \frac{P(a_j, b_k)}{P(a_j) \cdot P(b_k)}. \tag{5}$$

Features and View Splitting. In this experiment, as Table 3 shows, we use 13 features extracted from the SemEvald-07 Task 04 dataset. Because of the property of this problem, the features are divisible into two subsets: Context and Nominal pair. We put the first four features in Table 3 into the Nominal pair feature set; all other features are distributed to the Context feature set. It is different general semantic relation classification tasks, we only used the surface token of nominals and contexts. Because we specifically examine testing the classification performance of the algorithm, the syntactic features of words are unimportant.

Experiment Results. For semantic relations of all types, the proposed method is compared with the algorithms: 1) using label propagation, treating all features as one view (LP-ALL); 2) using label propagation in each view without inter-view propagation (UnIVLP);

Figure 1 presents the average accuracy of seven relation types. It is apparent from Figure 1 that inter-view propagation can reduce the classification error in most cases.

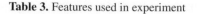

Table 3. Features used in experiment

Feature	Description
Nom1	Surface tokens of the first nominal
Nom2	Surface tokens of the second nominal
N1_ NET	WordNet senses of the first nominal
N2_ NET	WordNet senses of the second nominal
WBNUL	Whether a word exists in between
WBO1	The only word in between when only one is word in between
WBF	The first word in between when at least two words are in between
WBL	The last word in between when at least two words are in between
WBO	Other words in between except the first and last words when at least three words are in between
BN1F	The first word before the first nominal
BN1L	The second word before the first nominal
AN2F	The first word after the second nominal
AN2L	The second word after the second nominal

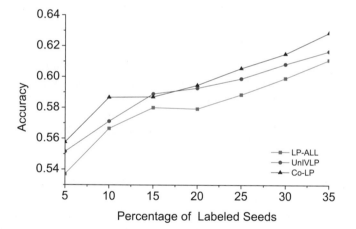

Fig. 1. Average Accuracy of seven relation types in the in SemEval-07 dataset

However, when the labeled seed percentage is 15%, Co-LP cannot beat UnIVLP, indicating that inter-view exchanging the label score cannot improve the performance of the classifier in these cases. Comparing UnIVLP with LP-ALL, it is apparent that UnIVLP works better than single view label propagation, although UnIVLP linearly combines results from separate views. Comparing Co-LP, UnIVLP with LP-ALL, the practice of regarding all features as two views always outperforms their treatment as a single view: Co-LP achieves the best accuracy. Therefore, a classifier trained on one view cannot provide useful information to another classifier. One possible explanation of Co-LP outperforming LP-ALL is that the feature space is provided with a considerable amount of redundancy. This redundancy, in effect, improved the classification accuracy.

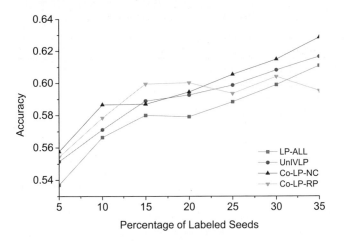

Fig. 2. Average classification accuracy of Co-LP with the Random Projected feature

Comparing Co-LP with UnIVLP, Co-LP employs the relation of different views; such information might improve the classification accuracy.

4.2   Different Feature Splitting

In this experiment, we specifically examine the sensitivity of Co-LP to feature splitting. This will elucidate the dependence of the proposed algorithm for feature splitting. To this end, we split the feature randomly into two disjoint subsets and repeat the above semantic relation classification experiment on the same dataset. We compare the new feature splitting to the (nominal pair, context) feature splitting (Co-LP-NC) in the experiment presented above. We can observe from Figure 2 that, although we randomly split the feature (Co-LP-RP), Co-LP-RP still outperforms label propagation (LP-ALL) in most cases. With labeled data of 15 and 20 percent, Co-LP-RP even outperforms Co-LP-NC, but after 25 percent, Co-LP-NC works better than either of the other two algorithms. When we randomly label 35 percentages of data as seeds, the proposed algorithm with random projected features (Co-LP-RP) cannot beat the LP-ALL algorithm.

4.3   Robustness with Respect to the Inter-view Correlation Measure

For studying the robustness of the proposed method to the correlation measures between different views, we use two similarity measures that are often used in the Natural Language Processing community: the matching coefficient and dice coefficient. The Eq. 6 and Eq. 7 respectively show the Matching coefficient and Dice coefficient. We use the same sampled data to test the sensitivity of Co-LP algorithm to the correlation measure.

– Matching coefficient:

$$[W^{AB}]_{jk} = P(a_j, b_k). \tag{6}$$

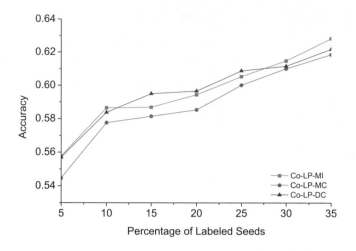

Fig. 3. Average classification accuracy of Co-LP with different correlation measures

– Dice coefficient:

$$[W^{AB}]_{jk} = \frac{2 \cdot P(a_j, b_k)}{P(a_j) + P(b_k)}. \tag{7}$$

Figure 3 portrays the average accuracies of different correlation measures: the mutual information measure (MI), matching coefficient (MC), and Dice coefficient (DC). We observe that the accuracy using DC closely resembles that using MI. Furthermore, we can find that the accuracies of MI and DC are each better than that used MC.

5   Conclusion

In this paper, we propose the Co-Label Propagation algorithm, which is based on the generalized cluster assumption. The experiment results show that our proposed algorithm can improve the performance of the label propagation algorithm, a well-known graph-based algorithm, on the SemEval-07 task 04 dataset. We also show that Co-LP works well with different splitting of feature set and choice of the inter-view correlation measure.

References

1. Zhu, X., Ghahramani, Z., Lafferty, L.: Semi-Supervised Learning Using Gaussian Fields and Harmonic Functions. In: Proceedings of the 20th International Conference on Machine Learning, pp. 912–919 (2003)
2. Zhou, D., Bousquet, O., Lal, T.N., Weston, J., Scholkopf, B.: Learning with local and global consistency. In: Advances in Neural Information Processing Systems, vol. 16, pp. 321–328. MIT Press, Cambridge (2004)

3. Zhu, X., Ghahramani, Z.: Learning from Labeled and Unlabeled Data with Label Propagation. Technical Report CMU-CALD-02-107 (2002)
4. Blum, A., Mitchell, T.: Combining Labeled and Unlabeled Data with Co-Training. In: Proceedings of the Eleventh Annual Conference on Computational learning theory, pp. 92–100 (1998)
5. Chen, J., Ji, D., Tan, C., Niu, Z.: Relation Extraction Using Label Propagation Based Semi-Supervised Learning. In: Proceedings of the 21st International Conference on Computational Linguistics and 44th Annual Meeting of the Association for Computational Linguistics, pp. 129–136 (2006)
6. Niu, Z., Ji, D., Tan, C.: Word sense disambiguation using label propagation based semi-supervised learning. In: Proceedings of the 43rd Annual Meeting of the Association for Computational Linguistics, pp. 395–402 (2005)
7. Girju, R., Nakov, P., Nastase, V., Szpakowicz, S., Turney, P., Yuret, D.: SemEval-2007 Task 04: Classification of Semantic Relations between Nominals. In: Proceedings of the Workshop SemEval-2007, the 45rd Annual Meeting of the Association for Computational Linguistics, pp. 13–18 (2007)
8. Li, H., Matsuo, Y., Ishizuka, M.: Graph Based Multi-View Learning for CDL Relation Classification. In: Proceedings of the 3rd IEEE International Conference on Semantic Computing, pp. 129–136 (2006)

Corpus-Based Arabic Stemming Using N-Grams

Abdelaziz Zitouni, Asma Damankesh, Foroogh Barakati, Maha Atari,
Mohamed Watfa, and Farhad Oroumchian

University of Wollongong in Dubai, POBox 20183, Dubai, UAE
az688@uow.edu.au, adamankesh@acm.org, shamim_66_87@yahoo.com,
maoa704@uow.edu.au, {MohamedWatfa,FarhadOroumchian}@uowdubai.ac.ae

Abstract. In languages with high word inflation such as Arabic, stemming improves text retrieval performance by reducing words variants. We propose a change in the corpus-based stemming approach proposed by Xu and Croft for English and Spanish languages in order to stem Arabic words. We generate the conflation classes by clustering 3-gram representations of the words found in only 10% of the data in the first stage. In the second stage, these clusters are refined using different similarity measures and thresholds. We conducted retrieval experiments using row data, Light-10 stemmer and 8 different variations of the similarity measures and thresholds and compared the results. The experiments show that 3-gram stemming using the dice distance for clustering and the EM similarity measure for refinement performs better than using no stemming; but slightly worse than Light-10 stemmer. Our method potentially could outperform Light-10 stemmer if more text is sampled in the first stage.

Keywords: Arabic Stemmer, Information Retrieval, N-Gram, Corpus-based Stemmer.

1 Introduction

The rapid growth of the internet has increased the number of documents available online. The latest statistics show that Arabic is the 7th most popular language used over the net by the end of the year 2009 [10]. Arabic Information retrieval faces many challenges due to the complex and rich nature of the Arabic language. Stemming is one of the techniques used to improve the Arabic information retrieval by reducing the words' variants into the base words like stems or roots.

Stemming improves the information retrieval by reducing the word mismatch between the query and the document. This will result in returning more relevant documents to the query. Stemming has a great effect on the retrieval when the language is highly inflected for example Arabic language [4]. There has been several attempts to solve the Arabic text stemming including constructing manual dictionary [2], affix removal which is also called light stemming [5,4,11,13], morphological stemming [2,6] and statistical stemming [3,12].

P.-J. Cheng et al. (Eds.): AIRS 2010, LNCS 6458, pp. 280–289, 2010.
© Springer-Verlag Berlin Heidelberg 2010

In this paper, we have used a technique called Corpus-based Stemming that generates lists of words from the same root [19]. Then we have used these lists in Arabic information retrieval experiments and compared the results with a more complex and linguistic-based stemming approach known as Light-10 stemmer.

The remaining of this paper is structured as follows. In the next section, we describe the complexity of the Arabic language. Section 3 describes and compares similar stemming approaches to our proposed approach. Section 4 explains our approach to Arabic stemming for information retrieval. The results of experiments are described in section 5. Section 6 concludes this paper and suggests some potential improvements and future work.

2   The Arabic Language

The Arabic language is complex and has a rich grammar; it consists of 28 letters and a set of short vowels *(harakat)*, long vowels and nunation (تنوين , tanwin).

Arabic text is written from right to left where some letters are "vocalized" and embrace diacritics. Interestingly enough the meaning of a word might change based on its diacritics (i.e. the word كَتَبَ [kataba: he wrote] is different from the

word كُتُب [kotob: books] although they both written with the same three letters (k,t,b)).

Moreover, the Arabic language has a very complex morphology. Most of the words are created from a root of 3 letters. Other words have 4, 5 or 6 letters roots. Some of the words are constructed by attaching a prefix at the beginning or a suffix at the end of the root word. But, most of the adjectives, nouns and verbs are generated by infixing the root. The most challenging morphological problem in the Arabic language is that plural and singular forms of nouns are mostly irregular which makes it difficult to conflate them. Consequently, Arabic morphological analysis is a very complicated task and so far no single stemming technique has been able to resolve all the issues for all the cases.

These complexities in the Arabic language make it a highly inflated language where many similar words have variant morphological forms. This increases the likelihood of word mismatch in information retrieval systems. Therefore, stemming is a very important process in information retrieval where word conflation can be found and word matching between existing documents and queries can be improved to return more relevant documents. In the next section, we describe a number of stemming techniques focusing on the statistical stemming approach.

3   Related Research

Xu and Croft [19] have used a two stage approach in their pioneering work on corpus-based stemming. In the first stage, they experimented with both aggressive stemmers such as Porter and K-stem and also a trigram matching approach.

They created equivalence classes that contained all the words with the same root. In the aggressive stemming method, they grouped all the words that generated the same root with the stemmer in an equivalence class. In the trigram approach, they put all the words that started with the same three letters in the same equivalence class. In the second stage, they refined these equivalence classes by using a variation of the Expected Mutual Information Measure (EMIM) called EM to calculate the closeness of each pair of words in the same equivalence classes. The EM unlike $EMIM$ does not favor words with high frequency. For two terms a and b, the EM is calculated as below:

$$EM(a,b) = \max(\frac{n_{ab} - En(a,b)}{n_a + n_b}, 0) \tag{1}$$

Where n_{ab} is the number of times a and b co-occur within a window in the corpus, n_a and n_b are number of times a and b appear in the corpus. $En(a,b)$ is the expected number of co-occurrences assuming a and b are statically independent and it is calculated as $k_{n_a n_b}$ where k is a constant calculated based upon the window size.

The Connected Component and Optimal Partition algorithms were used to cluster the words within the same equivalence classes into more refined groups of similar words based on their EM similarity values. Their experiments showed that using their approach, aggressive stemmers like Porter for English can be improved. They also showed that a crude method like trigram can be employed in the first stage of that process with little loss of performance. They have also applied their trigram approach to other languages such as Spanish [20]. The main assumption in this approach is that words that belong to the same equivalence class (i.e. have the same root) will co-occur in the same document or text window.

The N-gram is a language-independent approach in which each word is broken down into substrings of length N. This approach has been applied to information retrieval in many languages such as English [9], Turkish [8], Malay [16] and Farsi [1] with varying degrees of success. In [13], Larkey et al. have used the bigram and trigram string similarity approach for Arabic text retrieval. In their experiment, bigrams have performed better than the trigrams; however the N-gram approach did not perform well in general. Authors have traced back the problem to the peculiarities imposed by the Arabic infix structure that increases the N-gram mismatches. However, they did not use stemming in their approach. In [19], the N-gram is used with and without stemming and it was shown that stemming resulted in minor improvements in the search results.

Light-10 [13] is a stemming tool based on Arabic morphological analysis that uses a rule-based affix-removal technique for light stemming. The prefix and suffix of words are removed if certain conditions were satisfied. For example the letter ' ' can be removed from the beginning of the word if the remaining of the word has three or more characters. Light-10 was claimed to perform better than the other affix-removal approach proposed by Khoja and Garside [11], and Backwater Morphological Analyzer [3] . In Backwater Morphological Analyzer approach each word is segmented into a prefix, a stem and a suffix using three dictionaries and three compatibility tables. It then produces a list of all the possible analysis of each word. In [14], Larkey et al. have applied the approach proposed by Xu and Croft [19] on the Khoja stemmer [11] and Light-10 stemmer [13] and concluded that co-occurrence analysis has not improved the performance of the retrieval compared to the base stemmers. However, they reported that the corpus-based approach breaks down the equivalence classes into precise conflation groups with average size of five words. The reason for the low performance of their stemming strategy is claimed to be the complexity and the nature of the Arabic language. In the next section, our approach to the Arabic word conflation is explained in details.

4   N-Gram Conflation and Co-occurrence Analysis for Language-Independent and Corpus-Based Stemming

Our approach is based on the corpus-based approach developed by Xu and Croft [19] with some subtle differences. In their approach, they have used a trigram prefix matching for forming crude equivalence classes. That approach is not useful for Arabic because many nouns in Arabic have irregular plural forms.

Table 1. A few examples of conflation in Arabic words

Word	Letters	Pronunciation	Meaning	New word	PoS	Letters
كتاب	KTAB	k e t A b	book	كتب	plural	KTB
قوم	QVM	q o m	nation	اقوام	plural	AQVAM
رسول	RSVL	r a s u l	prophet	رسل	plural	RSL

As it is depicted in Table 1 the plural forms of the nouns have different trigrams than the original words. That is why, we have used an N-gram approach instead of relying on only 3-letter prefixes in forming equivalence classes.

An N-gram is a string of consecutive N characters. Generally an N-gram approach involves representing a word with a vector of strings of length N formed from the consecutive letters of the word. The N-gram approach has mixed performances in information retrieval. In some languages like English, it results in a poor performance however in languages like Farsi, it has an acceptable performance [1]. As mentioned earlier, most Arabic words are made up of roots with three letters which led us to use trigrams for word segmentation. The general process undertaken is as follow:

1. The corpus is normalized by removing all the stopwords, numbers and diacritics, and then the set of unique words in the corpus is generated.
2. Words are passed to the N-gram algorithm and a set of overlapping trigram substrings is generated for each unique word. For example the 3-grams for

the word كتاب are: كتا – تاب

3. A distance matrix is constructed and the Dice Distance is measured for each pair of words and recorded in this matrix. For two words a and b, the Dice measure (S_{ab}) is

$$S_{ab} = \frac{2C_{ab}}{C_a + C_b} \qquad (2)$$

where S_{ab} is the similarity between a and b, C_{ab} is the number of trigrams shared by a and b, and C_a and C_b are number of trigrams in each word a and b.

4. The words have been clustered into large equivalence classes based on their pair wise Dice similarity measure and the Complete Linkage clustering Algorithm (CLA). We have assumed that if the similarity of the two words is less than a threshold then those words are not similar. This decision is made to increase the similarity of the words that are assigned to the same equivalence class. In total, we have experimented with three different thresholds ($t = 0.5$, $t = 0.6$ and $t = 0.7$).

5. The EM measure described in the previous section is used to calculate the significance of the co-occurrence of each pair of words in the same equivalence class. In this experiment, the window size for calculating the co-occurrence is set to two paragraphs (approximately 50-100 words). The k value for this size of window is 2.75×10^{-6} as reported in [19].

6. The Optimal Partition Algorithm (OPA) is used for clustering within the equivalence classes with the EM score. In order to measure the drawbacks of keeping a and b in the same class, Xu and Croft have proposed using a constant $\delta = 0.0075$ where the net benefit of keeping a and b is $EM(a, b) - \delta$. In this way, OPA improves the *recall* measure while preserving the *precision* measure. The OPA algorithm refines each cluster by partitioning and keeping only very related words in the same partition.

7. We have also experimented with combining the EM(a,b) and the Dice similarity measures. So, in some experiments we calculated a new matrix using the mean of *Dice* and *EM* measures.

$$SEM = \frac{S_{ab} + EM(a, b)}{2} \qquad (3)$$

For those experiments two new sets of equivalence classes are constructed using $t = 0.5$ and $t = 0.6$ thresholds.

Table. 2 Conflations for the word معلومات based on different measures

N-grams: معل , طو , لوم , وما , مات		
DiceDistance	*EM*	*SEM*
ومعلومات , معلوماتنا , معلومات, للمعلومات , لمعلومات , المعلوماتی, المعلوماتيه, معلوما , معلومه, بمعلومات , لمعلوماتها , بالمعلومات, معلوماتك, معلوماته, معلوماتی معلوماتها , والمعلومات , المعلومات	معلوماتنا , معلومات ومعلومات, للمعلومات , المعلوماتی, المعلوماتيه, معلوما , بمعلومات , لمعلوماتها , بالمعلومات, معلوماتك معلوماته , والمعلومات , المعلومات	معلوماتنا , معلومات ومعلومات, المعلوماتی, لمعلومات , للمعلومات, المعلوماتیه معلومه, معلوما بالمعلومات, لمعلوماتها , بمعلومات معلوماته , معلوماتك, معلوماتی معلوماتها , والمعلومات , المعلومات

Table 2 illustrates the conflations generated for the word معلومات using Dice distance, EM and SEM average with $t = 0.5$.

5   Experiments

We have used a portion of INFILE 2009 Arabic text collection for running our experiments. This collection contains $100,000$ Arabic newswires from Agence France Presse (AFP) for the years 2004, 2005 and 2006. There are also 50 queries (30 general queries about sport, international affair, politics, etc and 20 scientific and technology related queries). All the documents and queries are in xml format consisting of headline, keyword and description tags. This corpus is used because of the diversity in the documents and queries. In these experiments, due to limited computational power and memory issues, only 10% of the corpus is used for generating the equivalence classes but the information retrieval experiments are conducted on the whole collection. We used python for processing the XML files and working with matrix using Numpy and Scipy plug-ins. The Java Lucene is used as the default search engine for all runs. The TREC Eval tool [18] is used for evaluating the search results and calculating the *recall* and *precision*.

Table 3 reports the characteristics of the eight different sets of the conflation classes that have been generated for these experiments. Although it has been stated in [13] that large number of Arabic words in any corpus is unique, a large number of these words can be conflated with at least one other word using the Dice distance or the average of the *Dice* and EM measures. However, when using the EM measure, more precise classes are generated which might sometimes lead to having only one word in most of the clusters. The first three runs in Table 3 (*Dice*0.5, *Dice*0.6 and *Dice*0.7) are single stage runs. In these runs, the Dice distance and Complete Linkage clustering algorithm with different thresholds (0.5, 0.6 and 0.7) were used to create the equivalence classes which were later used in stemming the entire corpus. All of the queries were used for retrieval and the precision, recall and precision at document cut-off measures were calculated for each run.

Table 3. Description of the eight different equivalence classes

Experiment (trigram is used for all)	t	#of Words	#of Clusters with more than 1 word	#of words in the largest cluster	Average #of words in clusters
*Dice*0.5	0.5	59,251	12,069	59 (1 *cluster*)	2.68
*Dice*0.6	0.6	69,265	14,440	51 (1 *cluster*)	2.44
*Dice*0.7	0.7	69,265	15,002	43 (1 *cluster*)	1.79
*EM*0.5	0.5	59,251	3,259	23 (2 *clusters*)	1.13
*EM*0.6	0.6	59,251	3,116	23 (1 *cluster*)	1.19
*EM*0.7	0.7	59,251	2,781	17 (1 *cluster*)	1.44
*SEM*0.5	0.5	59,251	12,069	59 (1 *cluster*)	4.9
*SEM*0.6	0.6	55,413	14,439	51 (1 *cluster*)	3.8

Table 4. The precision of 8 experiments at different document cutoffs

Cut-off	Dice0.5	Dice0.6	Dice0.7	EM0.5	EM0.6	EM0.7	SEM0.5	SEM0.7
5	0.32	0.312	0.328	0.328	0.336	0.316	0.32	0.316
10	0.282	0.286	0.294	0.29	0.294	0.298	0.282	0.288
15	0.26	0.258	0.264	0.28	0.265	0.266	0.26	0.261
20	0.242	0.244	0.245	0.264	0.257	0.243	0.242	0.246
30	0.213	0.222	0.218	0.246	0.232	0.226	0.213	0.222
100	0.118	0.119	0.120	0.123	0.120	0.118	0.118	0.119
200	0.069	0.070	0.071	0.071	0.070	0.067	0.069	0.070
500	0.033	0.033	0.032	0.032	0.031	0.031	0.033	0.033
1000	0.017	0.017	0.017	0.017	0.017	0.017	0.017	0.017

The other runs are two stage runs as described in *Section4*. The next three runs ($EM0.5$, $EM0.6$ and $EM0.7$) applied the Optimal Partition Clustering algorithm and EM measure on the equivalence classes generated from the first stage with different thresholds. The last two runs ($SEM0.5$, $SEM0.6$) applied the average *Dice* and EM measures along with the OPA clustering algorithm. In order to get a better understanding of the performance of the proposed methods, we created two extra runs. One run used the Light-10 stemmer [14] for stemming the Arabic words and another run applied no stemming at all. Table 5 shows a comparison of these two runs with $EM0.6$ run which is the best run in Table 4. By analyzing these results one can conclude that using any sort of stemming technique improves the precision by at least 50%. It can also be inferred that the precisions obtained using EM based clustering are very close to those obtained using the Light-10 stemmer. This implies that although the numbers of conflation classes with more than one word are not many, they still had a positive impact. These results also show that mere statistical analysis produced results comparable to stemming with linguistic knowledge. Figure 1 depicts the *precision recall* graph for the top3 runs along with Light-10 and no-stemming runs. As shown in Tables 4 and 5 and Figure 1, the Light-10 stemmer which uses linguistic knowledge is the best run. Most runs are similar to each other.

Table 5. Comparison of EM0.6 run with Light-10 stemming and no stemming runs

Cut-off	no stem	Light-10	EM0.6
5	0.061	0.34	0.336
10	0.063	0.336	0.294
15	0.057	0.302	0.265
20	0.055	0.279	0.257
30	0.053	0.254	0.232
100	0.034	0.143	0.120
200	0.022	0.083	0.070
500	0.011	0.037	0.031
1000	0.00	0.020	0.017

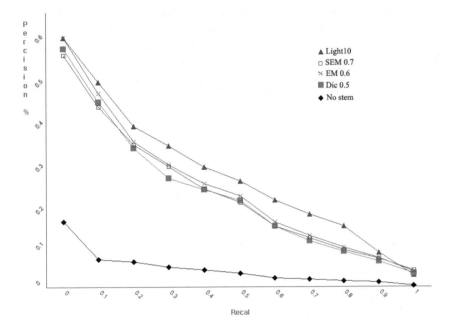

Fig. 1. Precision-Recall graph comparing our top 3 experiments with Light-10 and no-stemming

However, the results from $EM0.6$ run are very close to those of the Light-10 stemmer. It is safe to say that the EM measure in the second stage is necessary for eliminating erroneous conflations. It is also clear that using the Dice measure alone produces clusters that have disimilar conflated words. Since only 10% of the documents are used in generating the equivalence classes, it seems reasonable to believe that the result of $EM0.6$ will reach or exceed Light-10 if a higher percentage of the text is used.

6   Conclusion and Future Work

In this paper, we have successfully modified the corpus-based stemming proposed by XU and Croft to be used for Arabic text. We generated many different variations of our approach and compared them to the Light-10 stemming which used linguistic knowledge and no stemming approaches. Our comparison was based on precision, recall and precision at document cut-off values of retrieving 50 standard queries on a large text collection. The experiments show that using stemming without any linguistic knowledge can perform less than but comparable to well known approaches based on the morphological analysis. In our approach, we used one stage and two stage models and our findings indicate that the second stage co-occurrence analysis is necessary to improve the conflation classes and weed out incorrect groupings of the first stage. It was also noticed that using trigram reduces the chance of word conflation and results in the construction of many single word clusters. Therefore, it is possible that bi-grams will perform better by conflating more words and reducing the number of clusters with only one word. As part of the future work, we will use bigrams and hexagrams on the same corpus in order to investigate the effects of the length of roots in the Arabic language. Another future goal of ours is to improve our best performer ($EM0.6$) method with some linguistic knowledge. In this new approach, we will use a few clues to even further refine the equivalence classes produced. This refinement will be in the form of post processing and will include removing some words from equivalence classes or combining some the classes into larger units. We also intend to use only minimum morphological analysis in this new approach. We can also look into the implications behind other distance and similarity measures and different threshold values.

References

1. AleAhmad, A., Hakimian, P., Oroumchian, F.: N-Gram And Local Context Analysis For Persian Text Retrieval. In: International Symposium on Signal Processing and its Applications (ISSPA 2007), Sharjah, United Arab Emirates, pp. 12–15 (February 2007)
2. Al-Kharashi, I., Evens, M.W.: Comparing words, stems, and roots as index terms in an Arabic information retrieval system. JASIS 45(8), 548–560 (1994)
3. Buckwalter, T.Q.: Arabic lexicography, http://www.qamus.org/
4. Chen, A., Gey, F.: Building an Arabic stemmer for information retrieval. In: Proceedings of TREC 2002, pp. 631–639. NIST, Gaithersburg (2002)
5. Darwish, K., Oard, D.W.: CLIR Experiments at Maryland for TREC-2002: Evidence combination for Arabic-English retrieval. In: Proceedings of TREC 2002, pp. 703–710. NIST, Gaithersburg (2002)
6. De Roeck, A.N., Al-Fares, W.: A morphologically sensitive clustering algorithm for identifying Arabic roots. In: Proceedings of the 38th Annual Meeting on Association for Computational Linguistics, ACL 2000, Hong Kong, pp. 199–206 (2000)
7. Diab, M., Hacioglu, K., Jurafsky, D.: Automatic tagging of Arabic text: From raw test to base phrase chunks. In: Proceedings of the Human Language Technology Conference of the North American Chapter of the Association for Computational Linguistics: HLT-NAACL (2004)
8. Ekmekcioglu, F.C., Lynch, M.F., Willett, P.: Stemming and N-gram matching for term conflation in Turkish texts. Information Research News 7(1), 2–6 (1996)
9. Frakes, W.B.: Stemming algorithms. In: Baeza-Yates, W.B.F.a.R. (ed.) Information retrieval: Data structures and algorithms. ch. 8, Prentice Hall, Englewood Cliffs (1992)
10. Internet Word Stats (2010), http://www.internetworldstats.com/stats7.htm
11. Khoja, S., Garside, R.: Stemming Arabic text, http://zeus.cs.pacificu.edu/shereen/research.htm
12. Khreisat, L.: Arabic Text Classification Using N-Gram Frequency Statistics A Comparative Study. In: Proceedings of the 2006 International Conference on Data Mining, Las Vegas, USA, pp. 78–82 (2006)
13. Larkey, L.S., Connell, M.E.: Arabic information retrieval at UMass. In: Proceedings of TREC 2001, NIST, Gaithersburg (2001)

14. Larkey, L.S., Ballesteros, L., Connell, M.E.: Improving stemming for Arabic information retrieval: Light Stemming and co-occurrence analysis. In: Proceedings of SIGIR 2002, Tampere, Finland, pp. 275–282 (2002)
15. Mustafa, H.S., Al-Radaideh, Q.: Using N-Grams for Arabic Text Searching. Journal of the American Conference on Data Mining, Society for Information Science and Technology 55(11), 1002–1007 (2004)
16. Oard, D.W., Levow, G.A., Cabezas, C.I.: CLEF experiments at Maryland: Statistical stemming and backoff translation. In: Peters, C. (ed.) CLEF 2000. LNCS, vol. 2069, pp. 176–187. Springer, Heidelberg (2001)
17. Oroumchian, F., Garamaleki, F.M.: An Evaluation of Retrieval Performance Using Farsi Text, In: Workshop On Knowledge Foraging for Dynamic Networking of Communities and Economies. First Eurasia Conference on Advances in Information and Communication Technology, Shiraz, Iran (2002)
18. Trec eval Tool (2010), `http://trec.nist.gov/trec_eval/`
19. Xu, J., Croft, W.B.: Corpus-based stemming using co-occurrence of word variants. ACM Transactions on Information Systems 16(1), 61–81 (1998)
20. Xu, J., Fraser, A., Weischedel, R.: Empirical Studies in Strategies for Arabic Retrieval. In: SIGIR 2002, Tampere, Finland, pp. 269–274 (2002)

Analysis and Algorithms for Stemming Inversion

Ingo Feinerer

Vienna University of Technology, Austria
ingo.feinerer@tuwien.ac.at

Abstract. Stemming is a fundamental technique for processing large amounts of data in information retrieval and text mining. However, after processing the reversal of this process is often desirable, e.g., for human interpretation, or methods which operate on sequences of characters. We present a formal analysis of the stemming inversion problem, and show that the underlying optimization problem capturing conceptual groups as known from under- and overstemming, is of high computational complexity. We present efficient heuristic algorithms for practical application in information retrieval and test our approach on real data.

Keywords: Stemming, inversion.

1 Introduction

Stemming has been widely used as a fundamental technique in information retrieval, especially in the context of web search engines [19], in text mining [20] and sentiment analysis [1] as a preprocessing technique, and for databases when building large indices on documents [18]. The main reasons are reduced memory and computing demands which are necessary to handle large amounts of data, however once stemmed it is hard for humans to work with the underlying material for manual inspection. Further, methods which directly operate on character sequences, like string kernels [10], or computer-assisted approaches for content analysis of textual data which involve exact word matching, like the General Inquirer [17], may return unexpected results. One can address this problem in multiple ways. First, we could avoid the "design error" of deleting information we need later on, e.g., store both the original and stemmed representation. However, this introduces significant space overhead for large corpora, and ignores the fact that many text mining routines only return stems due to their internal representation. Second, one can use the context, i.e. the order of the stems appearing in the original texts, to better reconstruct the original words. Computational morphology also provides techniques for implementing reversible methods, nevertheless, the stemming process cannot be directly reverted. A far more conservative assumption, which will ground our further considerations, is that the original words to stems can only be restored from a dictionary. This is especially relevant for large amounts of (very) short texts (like blogs or Twitter) as context is hardly preserved due to abbreviations or stemming. Based on a dictionary the main challenge is now to find completions for individual stems along compatible semantic groups.

P.-J. Cheng et al. (Eds.): AIRS 2010, LNCS 6458, pp. 290–299, 2010.

2 Stemming

Stemming denotes the process of conflating words to their stems, e.g. by deleting word suffixes. Formally stemming can be seen as a surjective function $s: \Sigma^* \to \Sigma^*$ mapping words from an alphabet Σ to words from the same alphabet. Stemming functions can be evaluated e.g. by under- and overstemming errors [14], by checking whether words of the same conceptual group are actually conflated to the same stem.

Example 1. Table 1 shows words (completions) and their word stems (c_i and s_i are shortcuts for completions and stems, respectively), and the effect of over- vs. understemming. All words starting with `exp` are conflated to the same stem `experi` ($= s_1$) although the first two belong to another conceptual group (*overstemming*) as the rest, whereas `adhe` words have different stems (s_2 and s_3) although describing a similar semantic concept (*understemming*).

Table 1. Completions and stems

C Completion	Word Stem	S
c_1 experimental		
c_2 experiment	experi	s_1
c_3 experience		
c_4 experiences		
c_5 adhere	adher	s_2
c_6 adhesion	adhes	s_3

Prominent stemmer implementations are the Porter [15], Lovins [11], Paice [13], Dawson [2] and Krovetz [7] stemming algorithms.

3 The Stemming Inversion Problem

Given two sets of terms—word stems and possible completions—we want to find an assignment of stems to completions in such a way that as many of the original, i.e. before initial stemming, words (or at least its semantics) are restored. Conceptually, the best solution to this optimization problem is exactly the inversion of the implemented stemming procedure. However, since stemming is surjective a one-to-one inversion is in general not always possible, and we need a notion of optimality in terms of choosing completions for given stems. We formalize this as follows:

Definition 1 (Stemming Inversion Problem). *Let S be a set of stems, and C be a set of completions. Note that both sets are not necessarily disjoint, i.e. $S \cap C \neq \emptyset$. Let $\mathcal{G}_C$ be a collection of sets (groups) of completions of related semantic interpretation, and there may exist sets of stems $\mathcal{G}_S$ which group stems of related meaning (e.g., when stems are considered as equivalent which is useful for combining stemming and lemmatization tasks). The sets in $\mathcal{G}_C$ can be used to* *indicate that a single completion of the same group suffices to participate in the matching. Finally, let $\mathcal{L}$ contain all links between stems and valid corresponding possible completions. Note that not all stems need to have a link to a completion (e.g., if there is a completion missing due to an incomplete dictionary).*

The stemming inversion problem *is to choose the minimal number of links $l \in \mathcal{L}$ and groups in $\mathcal{G}_C$, $\mathcal{G}_S$, such that all stems $s \in \mathcal{S}$ and completions $c \in \mathcal{C}$ which are present in at least one link or group in $\mathcal{G}_C$, $\mathcal{G}_S$ in the input, are covered. An element is covered if it is present in at least one link or group in the solution.*

Note that this definition allows isolated stems or completions (and e.g. $\mathcal{C}$ to be a dictionary) which are simply ignored. Also note that it is allowed to choose multiple completions for a given stem. We present completion strategies for choosing a single element out of multiple completions at the end of this section.

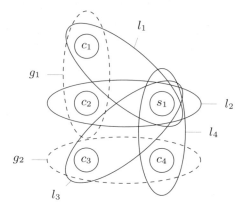

Fig. 1. A subset of the inversion problem instance of Ex. 2 for the `experi*` cluster

Example 2. A corresponding instance to the stemming inversion problem for Ex. 1 is defined by $\mathcal{S} = \{s_1, s_2, s_3\}$, $\mathcal{C} = \{c_1, c_2, c_3, c_4, c_5, c_6\}$, $\mathcal{G}_C = \{g_1 = \{c_1, c_2\}, g_2 = \{c_3, c_4\}, g_3 = \{c_5, c_6\}\}$, $\mathcal{G}_S = \emptyset$, and $\mathcal{L} = \{l_1 = \{c_1, s_1\}, l_2 = \{c_2, s_1\}, l_3 = \{c_3, s_1\}, l_4 = \{c_4, s_1\}, l_5 = \{c_5, s_2\}, l_6 = \{c_6, s_3\}\}$, where the c_i and s_i correspond to the shortcuts defined in Tab. 1. Figure 1 depicts the situation for the subset induced by the terms starting with `experi`. The assignment of stems, completions, and links (solid lines) between stems and possible completions follows directly by definition. The assignment of groups (dashed lines) is given by the observation that c_1 and c_2 have a similar semantics as a completion, whereas c_3 and c_4 are different and thus are in another group. Similarly, we define c_5 and c_6 to be in the same semantic group. A solution to this instance is given by choosing the links l_3, l_5, l_6, and the groups g_1 and g_2, as this covers all stems and completions. Note that the groups allow us to choose one out of several choices, but only if the links allow us this.

This formalism allows us to model important notions for stemming inversion. However this comes at a computationally high price as we show the problem to be NP-hard via a polynomial-time reduction from the set cover problem.

Definition 2 (Set cover problem). *Let U be a universe of elements, and S be a family of subsets of U. The* set cover optimization problem *is now to find the minimal number of subsets T_i of S such that $\bigcup T_i = U$.*

This problem is NP-hard [6,4]. For the reduction we need to encode every possible instance of the set cover problem to our stemming inversion problem:

Proof. For a given set cover problem with the universe U we define $\mathcal{C} = U$, i.e., all elements of the set cover problem are assumed to be completions, and we set $\mathcal{G}_\mathcal{C} = S$, i.e., the groups of the completions directly correspond to the subsets of the set cover problem.   □

Note that we do not even need links between completions and stems since already the problem of choosing a minimal number of semantically equivalent groups is expensive. However we argue that the inversion problem in its full generality cannot be simplified as we observe that stemming functions can be arbitrary surjective functions, and as such can have one or multiple completions, and that groups of completions and stems depend on semantic notions and language properties, and as such can overlap and intersect each other.   ·

Nevertheless, in many languages, the underlying problem is not that complex since there is normally no deep nesting or overlapping between groups. That means that naive brute-force algorithms will work reasonably well in practical applications since the search space that needs to be explored is separated in local components (e.g. see the two clusters in Ex. 1).

So far we were only concerned about finding optimal assignments between stems and completions respecting the semantics of related conceptual groups. In addition we need a local criterion which tells us which element should be chosen out of multiple completions. E.g., in Ex. 2 we could prefer to choose c_3 or c_4 out of group g_2 as completion for stem s_1, depending on our notions of optimality. A description of possible completion heuristics follows:

Prevalent. Choose the completion c with the maximal number of occurrences in a corpus, i.e. such that $\max_{i=1,\dots,n} |c_i| = c$, where n denotes the total number of completions for a single stem.

First. Choose the completion c which is first found in a dictionary, i.e., $c_1 = c$.

Shortest. Choose the completion c with the minimal number of characters of all suitable completions, i.e., $\min_{i=1,\dots,n} |\text{char}(c_i)| = c$, where n denotes the total number of completions for a given term.

Longest. Symmetric to the previous case, i.e., the completion with the maximal number of characters: $\max_{i=1,\dots,n} |\text{char}(c_i)| = c$.

Random. Choose a random item c out of the possible completions, i.e., $c_i = c$ with $i \in \{1, \dots, n\}$.

The actual implementation of the strategies is slightly more complicated due to some intricacies of prominent stemming algorithms. In detail it does not suffice just to search for completions only but also consider insertion or deletion of characters. E.g., the Porter stemming algorithms produces `berri` out of `berry`. A solution is to use completions with minimal Levenshtein distance [8] regarding insertion/deletion for such special cases.

4   Experiment

To evaluate our presented approaches we implement a benchmark consisting of three test suites working on real data in an information retrieval setting.

Reconstruction. Given a text corpus we build a dictionary consisting of the terms. Successively, we draw samples of the terms in the corpus, and apply the Porter [15] stemming algorithm. The stems are now completed with the different inversion heuristics presented in the previous section. The results from the completion are compared to the original samples, and a matching statistics is computed. This gives us information on how much information from the original corpus can directly be reconstructed.

Text clustering. Our second test suite measures the performance of our approximation heuristics if applied to text clustering. We cluster the original, the stemmed, and each corpus obtained by applying every completion heuristic on top of the stemmed version. In detail we use the classical k-means algorithm [5,12] which minimizes the objective function $\sum_{j=1}^{k} \sum_{x_i \in \pi_j} \|x_i - m_j\|^2$, where π_j are clusters and $m_j = \frac{1}{\|\pi_j\|} \sum_{x_i \in \pi_j} x_i$ is the mean of cluster π_j.

Sentiment Analysis. Our final procedure tests for the effect of inversion in a slightly more involved scenario. We implement a sentiment analysis using word lists as found in the General Inquirer [17], both on the stemmed and the completed words in our data set, and compare the results. Sentiment analysis can be seen as text mining for opinions, and is typically implemented by counting words of specific categories (e.g., the General Inquirer word list for the *Positive* category includes "good", "extraordinary", or "outstanding"), and computing scores (e.g., the sum) for each category $\mathcal{C}_j$: $\text{score}(\mathcal{C}_j, \tau) = \sum_{w_i \in \mathcal{C}_j} \Phi(w_i, \tau)$, where $\Phi(w, t)$ counts the frequency of a word w in a text t, and τ denotes the underlying corpus.

4.1   Data

We use the Reuters-21578 data set [9] as the basis for our experiments. It contains stories covering a broad range of topics, like mergers and acquisitions, finance, or politics, and was collected by the Reuters news agency. The data set is publicly available[1] and has been widely used in text mining and information retrieval within the last decades. It contains 21578 short to medium length documents.

4.2   Procedure

The experiment is carried out using the R [16] statistical computing and graphics environment since it provides a text mining infrastructure [3] which makes it easy to implement a prototype and apply user-defined algorithms, in our case the five presented completion heuristics, provides a broad spectrum of clustering and classification tools, and has support to access the General Inquirer word lists

---

[1] http://www.daviddlewis.com/resources/testcollections/reuters21578/

and score documents accordingly. For the first part (*Reconstruction*) we built a dictionary out of the corpus, resulting in—after some preprocessing like removal of punctuation marks, numbers, and common stopwords—about 45000 unique terms. Next, we drew samples consisting of 100 randomly chosen terms out of this dictionary. The terms were stemmed and heuristically completed with the five presented procedures. We independently repeated the sample, stemming, and completion steps up to 100 times, resulting in up to 100 different runs. The results of the individual runs are analyzed such that for a given sample we compare the completions of each individual completion heuristics with the original unstemmed terms, and compute the percentage of matching terms. This corresponds to the relative amount of terms where a perfect inversion (reconstruction) was possible. In the second experiment (*Text clustering*) we extracted all documents of the Reuters-21578 corpus with topics *acq* (acquisitions; 2125 documents) or *crude* (crude oil; 355 documents). These documents are the input for a k-means clustering procedure (averaging over 100 runs to compensate for local minima due to unfortunate (randomized) initial start assignments) with two desired clusters ($k = 2$, modeling the two chosen topics). Since we have the true class/topic ids from the annotations in the corpus, we compute cross-agreements using maximal co-classification rate (i.e., the maximal rate of objects with the same class ids in both clusterings). The third part (*Sentiment analysis*) implements a sentiment analysis by scoring individual documents according to occurrences of matching terms from word lists as provided by the General Inquirer. These word lists are carefully chosen for specific categories (we use *Positive, Negative, Strong, Weak, Active, Passive, Rise* and *Fall*) by the creators of the General Inquirer, and are as such highly sensitive to individual word forms. I.e., it might happen that a word matches, but its stem does not, but also vice versa. We then compute word scores for documents consisting of stemmed words and compare their scores when using our presented inversion heuristics.

5   Results

For the first part of our experiment, Fig. 2 depicts the percentage of matching terms for the five completion strategies `prevalent`, `first`, `shortest`, `longest`, and `random` for 15 independent runs. Note that although the runs are independent we connect points of the same method to visualize their relative positions among each other throughout the experiment. Also be aware that we only visualize 15 runs instead of 100 to see more details but the results hold for the full experiment in the same way. For comparison we also have a `none` entry which corresponds to the stemmed terms. I.e., if there is a match for `none` this means the stem and the completion is identical, which is the case for about 43% of the terms in average in Fig. 2. We see that `prevalent`, `first`, and `shortest` are comparable in performance with about 67% which corresponds to a relative increase of about 55%. Interestingly, even `random` outperforms `longest` which has the lowest matching rate of all strategies.

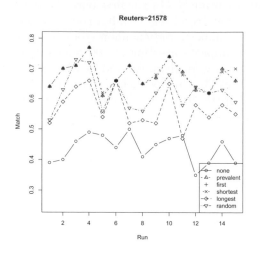

Fig. 2. Match results of the five stemming inversion heuristics for 15 independent runs

Table 2. Percentage of matches between original terms and stemmed terms with applied completion heuristic (*Reconstruction*), and percentage between cross-agreements using maximal co-classification rate for k-means ($k = 2$) clustering for stemmed and completed terms in the Reuters-21578 corpus (*Clustering*)

	Reconstruction	Clustering
none	43.95	0.00
prevalent	67.09	**15.99**
first	67.09	6.42
shortest	**67.46**	3.14
longest	56.60	-0.04
random	61.24	6.39

Table 2 gives exact numbers for this observed behavior. The column "Reconstruction" lists the percentage of matches between the original terms and the stemmed terms with completion for all 100 runs.

Column "Clustering" is relevant for our text clustering experiment and shows the relative performance of k-means clustering for the two ($k = 2$) clusters of known topics *acq* and *crude* both for the stemmed corpus and the corpora obtained by first applying our completion heuristics. Relative performance measures the cross-agreements (between cluster labels obtained from the k-means clustering procedure and the true class ids available as annotations from the corpora) using maximal co-classification rates. The zero entry for *none* forms the base line as no relative improvement can be achieved (obviously, since no heuristics is applied). Interestingly, *longest* has a negative impact on the clustering results. I.e., it is better to use no heuristics than this one on the Reuters-21578 data set. Strategies *shortest* and *first* perform about 3% and 6% better than

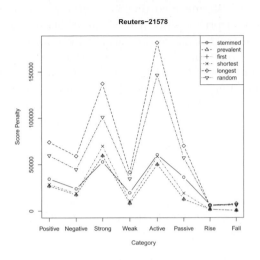

Fig. 3. Score penalties for the inversion heuristics for the categories *Positive*, *Negative*, *Strong*, *Weak*, *Active*, *Passive*, *Rise* and *Fall*

Table 3. Score penalties for the inversion heuristics for the categories *Positive*, *Negative*, *Strong*, *Weak*, *Active*, *Passive*, *Rise* and *Fall*

	prevalent	first	shortest	longest	random
Positive	**26,966**	**26,966**	28,513	73,971	59,567
Negative	**17,469**	**17,469**	19,017	59,020	44,716
Strong	**59,343**	**59,343**	69,626	137,152	100,899
Weak	**8,269**	**8,269**	10,888	41,577	34,617
Active	**49,995**	**49,995**	58,579	181,767	146,397
Passive	**12,658**	**12,658**	19,078	69,942	57,072
Rise	1,686	1,686	**1,629**	5,335	5,785
Fall	**505**	**505**	**505**	7,897	6,206

none. Heuristic *prevalent* outperforms all others with a relative performance increase of almost 16%.

For the third part, the application of our methods in the context of sentiment analysis, Fig. 3 depicts summarized score penalties for the whole Reuters-21578 corpus for individual categories from the General Inquirer word lists. Summarized score penalties $|\text{score}(\mathcal{C}_i, \tau_O) - \text{score}(\mathcal{C}_i, \tau_S)|$ for a category $\mathcal{C}_i$ correspond to the sum of word frequencies which are different from the original corpus τ_O considering that the stemmed corpus τ_S has negative impact on the individual scores. A penalty of 0 means that an inversion method produces exactly the same score as the original document, i.e., the smaller the penalty, the better. Table 3 shows corresponding numbers for Fig. 3.

By combining the results from the different conducted experiments we observe that the method `prevalent` performs best and yields a notable improvement compared to just using a stemmed corpus, i.e., without any completion strategy. This result is in so far surprising since it holds in *all* of our experiments; it could be expected for reconstruction since the terms which occur most often are also likely to be the correct ones for completion. However, this is not necessarily true for text clustering, and especially not for text mining on sentiments. Clusterings are selective to large numbers of identical observations; a strategy in favor of prevalent terms can merge different stems to a single one occurring quite often. Similarly, joining different stems to a common word might trigger different semantics related to sentiments in text mining. Nevertheless, our experiments show that a prevalent strategy works in these two settings satisfactorily. For special settings `shortest` is a viable alternative, especially for runtime sensitive applications. Given a sorted dictionary finding the shortest completion is easy compared to determining the most prevalent terms in a corpus which involves counting word frequencies. We note that both the `random` (as expected) but also the `longest` completion strategy are unsatisfactory, and should not be used in general.

6   Conclusion

We presented the stemming inversion problem which is motivated by the fact that stemming is a central technique in information retrieval but the reversal of this process is often desirable, either for human consumption, or for word sensitive methods. Although being a natural and important research question, to the best of our knowledge this problem has not been addressed in the literature in a systematic way we do. We proved that the problem in its full generality is NP-hard. We introduced efficient approximation algorithms which solve the inversion problem based on a set of heuristics. Experiments on real data show the applicability of the presented heuristics for word reconstruction, text clustering, and text mining. We obtain strong results for a strategy based on prevalent term completions, yielding observable better results than just the stemmed words without completion heuristics, in all categories of our benchmarks. It remains open to investigate to which extent alternative strategies depend on the corpus language. This is highly relevant in an international context, e.g. for Internet search engines [19] due to user provided queries. Another remaining issue is the extension of our implementation into a stand-alone library. This would allow easy integration of the proposed inversion strategies into existing information retrieval frameworks. Finally there are plans to incorporate context-aware techniques in our setting.

Acknowledgments. This work is supported by the Vienna Science and Technology Fund (WWTF), project ICT08-032.

References

1. Annett, M., Kondrak, G.: A comparison of sentiment analysis techniques: Polarizing movie blogs. In: Bergler, S. (ed.) Canadian AI. LNCS (LNAI), vol. 5032, pp. 25–35. Springer, Heidelberg (2008)

2. Dawson, J.L.: Suffix removal for word conflation. Bulletin of the Association for Literary and Linguistic Computing 2(3), 33–46 (1974)
3. Feinerer, I., Hornik, K., Meyer, D.: Text mining infrastructure in R. Journal of Statistical Software 25(5), 1–54 (2008), http://www.jstatsoft.org/v25/i05
4. Garey, M.R., Johnson, D.S.: Computers and Intractability: A Guide to the Theory of NP-Completeness. W.H. Freeman, New York (1979)
5. Hartigan, J.A., Wong, M.A.: Algorithm AS 136: A K-means clustering algorithm (AS R39: 81V30 p355-356). Applied Statistics 28, 100–108 (1979)
6. Karp, R.M.: Reducibility among combinatorial problems. In: Miller, R.E., Thatcher, J.W. (eds.) Complexity of Computer Computations, pp. 85–103 (1972)
7. Krovetz, R.: Viewing morphology as an inference process. Artificial Intelligence 118(1–2), 277–294 (2000)
8. Levenshtein, V.: Binary codes capable of correcting deletions, insertions and reversals. Soviet Physics Doklady 10(8), 707–710 (1966)
9. Lewis, D.: Reuters-21578 text categorization test collection (1997), http://www.daviddlewis.com/resources/testcollections/reuters21578/
10. Lodhi, H., Saunders, C., Shawe-Taylor, J., Cristianini, N., Watkins, C.: Text classification using string kernels. J. of Machine Learning Research 2, 419–444 (2002)
11. Lovins, J.B.: Development of a stemming algorithm. Mechanical Translation and Computational Linguistics 11, 22–31 (1968)
12. MacQueen, J.: Some methods for classification and analysis of multivariate observations. In: Proceedings of the Fifth Berkeley Symposium on Mathematical Statistics and Probability, vol. 1, pp. 281–297. University of California Press, Berkeley (1967)
13. Paice, C.D.: Another stemmer. SIGIR Forum 24(3), 56–61 (1990)
14. Paice, C.D.: Method for evaluation of stemming algorithms based on error counting. Journal of the American Society for Information Science 47(8), 632–649 (1996)
15. Porter, M.: An algorithm for suffix stripping. Program 3, 130–137 (1980)
16. R Development Core Team: R: A Language and Environment for Statistical Computing. R Foundation for Statistical Computing, Vienna, Austria (2010), http://www.R-project.org ISBN 3-900051-07-0
17. Stone, P.J.: Thematic text analysis: new agendas for analyzing text content. In: Text Analysis for the Social Sciences. ch. 2, Lawrence Erlbaum Associates, Mahwah (1997)
18. Strzalkowski, T., Vauthey, B.: Information retrieval using robust natural language processing. In: Proc. of the 30th annual meeting on ACL, Association for Computational Linguistics, Morristown, NJ, USA, pp. 104–111 (1992)
19. Uyar, A.: Google stemming mechanisms. J. of Inf. Sci. 35(5), 499–514 (2009)
20. Weiss, S., Indurkhya, N., Zhang, T., Damerau, F.: Text Mining: Predictive Methods for Analyzing Unstructured Information. Springer, Heidelberg (2004)

Top-Down and Bottom-Up:
A Combined Approach to Slot Filling

Zheng Chen, Suzanne Tamang, Adam Lee, Xiang Li, Marissa Passantino, and Heng Ji

Computer Science Department, Queens College and Graduate Center
City University of New York, New York, NY 13367, USA
hengji@cs.qc.cuny.edu

Abstract. The Slot Filling task requires a system to automatically distill information from a large document collection and return answers for a query entity with specified attributes ('slots'), and use them to expand the Wikipedia infoboxes. We describe two bottom-up Information Extraction style pipelines and a top-down Question Answering style pipeline to address this task. We propose several novel approaches to enhance these pipelines, including statistical answer re-ranking and Markov Logic Networks based cross-slot reasoning. We demonstrate that our system achieves state-of-the-art performance, with 3.1% higher precision and 2.6% higher recall compared with the best system in the KBP2009 evaluation.

Keywords: Slot Filling, Information Extraction, Question Answering.

1 Introduction

The increasing number of open evaluations and shared resources has made it possible for many natural language processing tasks to benefit from system combination. Fortunately, the Slot Filling track of the recently launched Knowledge Base Population (KBP) task[1] at the Text Analysis Conference (TAC) provides a platform to attempt system combination for information extraction.

The KBP Slot Filling task involves learning a pre-defined set of attributes for person and organization entities based on a source collection of documents. A query contains a name-string, docid, entity-type, node-id (entry ID) in Wikipedia, an optional list of slots to ignore. For example, *[Andy Warhol, ABC-20080611-9372, PER, SF7, per:date_of_birth]* is a query for the painter "*Andy Warhol*", for which a system should return all slot types except *per:date_of_birth*. KBP 2010 defined 26 slot types for persons and 16 slot types for organizations. This task has attracted many participants from Information Extraction (IE) and Question Answering (QA) communities. In addition, a large amount of system or human annotated data are shared as a community effort.

In this paper we present a state-of-the-art Slot Filling system that includes two bottom-up IE style pipelines and a QA style pipeline, with several novel enhancements including statistical answer re-ranking and Markov Logic Networks (MLN) based

---

[1] http://nlp.cs.qc.cuny.edu/kbp/2010/

P.-J. Cheng et al. (Eds.): AIRS 2010, LNCS 6458, pp. 300–309, 2010.

cross-slot reasoning. We evaluate performance across our pipelines, with the systems from KBP2009 and human annotators.

2 System Overview

Figure 1 depicts the general procedure of our approach. All three pipelines begin with an initial query processing stage where query expansion techniques are used to improve recall. The next step of the system is pipeline dependent, representing three alternative approaches to the KBP task: IE, pattern matching and QA. After generation of the best answer candidate sets form the individual systems, they are combined to re-rank confidence on the system-wide answer set and for cross-slot reasoning.

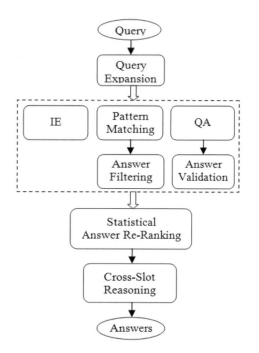

Fig. 1. Slot Filling System Pipelines

3 Bottom-Up and Top-Down Pipelines

These pipelines are organized in two forms: bottom-up IE based approaches that extract all possible attributes for a given query and then fill in the slots by mapping and inference (Section 3.1 and 3.2); and top-down QA based approach that search for answers constructed from target entities and slot types (Section 3.3).

3.1 Pattern Matching

In pattern matching approach, we first automatically obtain the ranked patterns by learning from *query-answer (q-a)* pairs, and then apply these patterns to find answers to unseen queries. For example, given the pair *(Michael Jackson, 50)* for slot *per:age*, we can extract sentences in which Michael Jackson and 50 co-occur:

(1) Michael Jackson died at the age of 50 ; (2) Michael Jackson (50) …

Pattern can be constructed as

(1) *<Q>* died at the age of *<A>* ; (2) *<Q> (<A>)*

This approach consists of the following steps:

(1) Selection of query-answer pairs
We extract *q-a* pairs from the facts listed in Wikipedia infobox[2] by some mappings from infobox fields to KBP slots. *q-a* pairs are split into two sets: half for pattern extraction, and the other half for pattern assessment.

(2) Pattern extraction
For each *q-a* pair from the training set, we use a search engine[3] to retrieve the top 1000 documents in the source collection, and pick out sentences in which the query and answer co-occur. In addition to populating static patterns for different *q-a* pairs, we also apply entity type replacement and regular expressions to make patterns as general as possible.

(3) Pattern assessment
For each *q-a* pair from a stand-alone development set, we search the top 1000 documents and pick out the sentences in which the query occurs. We apply patterns for each sentence and if it can be matched, extract the entity at the exact place as the answer. We sort the patterns in the descending order of precision (matching rate), and filter those with precision below a threshold.

(4) Pattern matching
To obtain candidate answers for slot filling, we locate the sentences where *q* occurs, apply the patterns generated by step (3) and extract the answer when there is a pattern match. We then rank the answers according to the sum of precisions of all patterns that produce the answer.

(5) Filtering answers
We set a low threshold to include more candidate answers, and then apply several filtering steps to distill the best answers. Filtering steps include removing answers with inappropriate entity types, erroneous answers that are not in dictionary resources (e.g., the country dictionary for slot *per:country_of_birth*) or inappropriate answers whose dependency parsing paths to the query do not satisfy certain constraints (e.g., for slot o*rg:subsidiaries, org:parents*, the query and the answer should not have a conjunction relation).

3.2 Supervised IE

We apply a cross-document English IE system (Ji et al., 2009) to extract relations and events defined in NIST Automatic Content Extraction Program (ACE 2005)[4].

---

[2] http://en.wikipedia.org/wiki/Help:Infobox
[3] http://lucene.apache.org/
[4] http://www.nist.gov/speech/tests/ace/

Relation extraction and event extraction are based on maximum entropy models, incorporating diverse lexical, syntactic, semantic and ontological knowledge. ACE2005 defines 6 main relation types and 18 subtypes; 8 event types and 33 subtypes. We apply the following mapping between ACE relation/event and KBP.

Given a 3-tuple $<em_i, em_j, r>$ from relation extraction which indicates that the entity mentions em_i and em_j holds a relation r, and if r matches a slot type r' and em_i matches the query entity q in slot filling, then the answer a in the uncompleted 3-tuple $< q, a, r'>$ for slot filling is em_j.

Given a 3-tuple $<t, arg, e>$ and arg = $\{em_i, em_j, ...\}$ from event extraction which indicates that the trigger word t indicates an event type e and the involving arguments in arg include em_i, em_j, and so on. If the event type e matches a slot type e', em_i matches the query entity q in slot filling and em_j satisfies the role constraint, then the answer a is em_j. For example, if a *MARRY* event matches *per:spouse* slot, and one person entity em_i matches the query, and the other involved entity em_j satisfies the role constraint *of PERSON*, then we return em_j as the answer.

3.3 Question Answering

We also apply the web module of an open domain QA system, OpenEphyra (Schlaefer et al., 2007) to retrieve candidate answers for the KBP slot filling task. Since candidate answers must be entailed in the KB and a corresponding document id identified, additional answer processing is necessary to determine the candidate answer's relevance and retrieve the corresponding docid(s) for the document collection.

To estimate the relevance, R, of a q-a pair, we use the joint probability of observing both the query and answer by means of the answer pattern probability:

$$P (q, a) = P (q\ NEAR\ a)$$

where *NEAR* is defined as within the same sentence boundary. At the sentence level, we calculate the frequency of q-a pair occurrence in the reference corpus and modify the related Corrected Conditional Probability (CCP) formula to assess R for query pattern q and answer pattern a:

$$R(q,a) = \frac{frequency(qNEARa)}{frequency(q)*frequency(a)} *\#totalsentences$$

After the relevance scores are calculated, the values for each KBP slot are rescaled from 0-1 in order to facilitate the comparison of relevance values among different slot.

4 More Queries and Fewer Answers

We enhance the above three pipelines based on the following extensions. We hypothesize that cleverly designed query expansion techniques (Section 4.1) will improve recall of candidate answers to the query. By obtaining more potential correct answers in the ranked list, we can exploit effective learning-to-rank technique to select the best answer (Section 4.2). Furthermore, most slot filling methods often produce logically incoherent answers. We design a novel cross-slot reasoning approach based on Markov Logic Networks (MLN) to further refine the quality of answers and predict new answers (Section 4.3).

4.1 Query Expansion

In order to generate informative natural language questions from each pair of <query name, slot type>, we develop the following expansion methods.

(1) Template expansion

We generated 59 question templates for the 16 organization slots and 62 question templates for the 26 person slots. For example, the following semantically equivalent questions are generated for the "person: age" slot type:

- What is <per>'s age?
- How old is <per>?
- When was <per> born?

During candidate answer generation, the tag <per> is replaced by the target. On average, each target value produced an initial set of 112 candidates per slot. After filtering by stop words, and sufficient co-occurrence with the query and answer pattern in the reference corpus, queries averages 4.9 answers each in the baseline results, which suggests a very high rate of spurious results from the web module. For this reason, query expansion is a necessary step in the QA pipeline and a rough estimate using a small set of queries without enhanced expansion suggests the impact of this step on recall leads to approximately a four-fold improvement.

(2) Name expansion

The query name may be mentioned in its alternative names in the corpus, thus, name expansion can help improve the recall of slot filling. Wikipedia uses redirect links to indicate navigations among pages that mention the same entity. For example, the entity name "Seyed Ali Khamenei" is redirected to "Ali Khamenei". We mine redirect links from Wikipedia database (dump up to Mar., 2010) and use them as dictionary resources to form extra query names.

4.2 Statistical Re-ranking

We develop a Maximum Entropy (MaxEnt) based supervised re-ranking model to re-rank candidate answers for the same slot. We train our model from 452 labeled *q-a* pairs to predict the confidence of each candidate answer's correctness. We incorporate the following semantics and global statistics based features into the re-ranker:

- **Web Module Rank.** We use the answer confidence assigned by the OpenEphyra system as a re-ranking feature. For a query, this feature can provide information on the confidence of the answer based on web results.
- **Answer Validation Score.** We calculate the answer relevance $R(q, a)$ for each query pair in the answer validation procedure. This feature provides confidence information based on co-occurrence in the document collection.
- **Answer Name Type.** We incorporate the name type of the candidate answer (persons, geo-political, organizations, etc.) as an additional feature for re-ranking. Names are tagged using dictionary files compiled by the Ephyra project.
- **Slot Type.** Using the KBP slot type as a feature allows us to re-rank slot types so that our QA system is more likely to get correct answers for a slot type with a higher confidence.

4.3 MLN Based Cross-Slot Reasoning

In the slot filling task, each slot is often dependent on other slots, but systems built for the slot filling task often ignore these dependencies and process each slot individually. In particular, the family slots include such dependency relationships (e.g. X is *per:children* of Y ➜ Y is *per:parents* of X; X is *per:spouse* of Y ➜ Y is not likely to be *per:siblings* of X). Therefore we develop a reasoning component to approach a real world acceptable answer in which all slot dependencies are satisfied. On the other hand, we can design propagation rules to enhance recall, for example, X was born on date Y ➜ X's age is approximately (the current year – Y).

We noticed that heuristic inferences are highly dependent on the order of applying rules, and the performance may have been limited by the thresholds which may over-fit a small development corpus. We use Markov Logic Networks (Richardson and Domingos, 2006), a statistical relational learning language, to model these inference rules more declaratively. Markov Logic extends first order logic in that it adds a weight to each first order logic formula, allowing for violation of those formulas with some penalty. We use the Alchemy toolkit (Kok et al., 2007) to encode inference rules such as:

$$SpouseOf(a,b) \rightarrow (\sim\!ChildOf(a,b) \wedge \sim\!ParentOf(a,b) \wedge \sim\!OtherFamilyOf(a,b) \wedge \sim\!SiblingOf(a,b))$$

Then our remaining uncertainty with regard to this formula will be captured by a weight associated with it. Markov Logic will make it possible to compactly specify probability distributions over these complex relational inferences, and easily capture non-deterministic (soft) rules that tend to hold among slots but do not have to. We incorporate hard rules such as name/date/number/title format constraints for slots including *per:title*, *per:country_of_death* and *org:number_of_em ployees/members*, as well as soft rules such as *per:birth_of_date* to *per:age* propagation.

5 Experimental Results

In this section we present the overall performance of our three pipelines by comparing to the best system at KBP2009 evaluation and human annotation, and break down the performance to demonstrate the impact of key techniques.

5.1 Data and Scoring Metric

We randomly select 21 queries (11 persons and 10 organizations) and the entire source collection (1,289,649 documents in total) from KBP 2009 evaluation corpora o evaluate our methods[5]. For each query, we combine the human annotation from LDC based on exhaustive search (110 instances) and the correct answers from KBP 2009 human assessment (195 instances) to form our initial answer keys (K) including 263 unique instances.

---

[5] In order to compare with KBP2009 participants, we mapped some fine-grained KBP 2010 slot types back to KBP2009 slot types (e.g. maped "country_of_birth", "stateor-province_of_birth" and "city_of_birth" back to "place_of_birth").

Despite of the requirement conducting search as exhaustive as possible, a single human annotator can only achieve lower than 50% recall, we follow the human assessment procedure as in KBP 2009 evaluation. We ask another human annotator to manually check all those instances generated by the system but not in human annotation, and if an instance is correct, it will be added to form the expanded answer key set (K'). Since this human assessment procedure is time consuming, we only apply it to the final best pipeline for comparison, while use relative scores for the detailed break down analysis experiments.

We follow the KBP 2010 scoring metric[6] to evaluate each pipeline. This is a uniform scoring metric based on standard Precision, Recall and F-measure. Since only non-NIL answers are informative in applications, we focus on scoring non-NIL answers. A unique answer instance <query, slot type, answer> is considered as correct if it matches any instance in the answer key. We added additional answer normalizations to the scorer in order to get more reliable scores and speed up human assessment (normalized 6% instances in the test set). The normalizations are based on a list of 362 country name variants (e.g. "the United States = USA") and a list of 423 person fullname-nickname pairs. If a system returns an answer set S, we compute the following scores:

- Relative Precision = $\# (K \cap S) / \# S$ Relative Recall = $\# (K \cap S) / \# K$
- Precision = $\# (K' \cap S) / \# S$ Recall = $\# (K' \cap S) / \# K'$

5.2   System/Human Comparison

Table 1 presents the relative scores for three single pipelines. Although these scores were evaluated against an incomplete answer key set, it indicates that pattern matching can achieve the best result. Supervised IE method performs the worst because not all of the slot types have corresponding relation and event types. QA method obtained comparable precision but much lower recall because the candidate answers are restricted by query template design and the annotations (e.g. name tagging) used for answer validation.

Table 1. Pipeline Relative Performance against Incomplete Answer Keys (%)

Pipeline	Relative Precision	Relative Recall	Relative F-measure
Supervised IE	13.09	12.82	12.95
Pattern Matching	18.95	18.46	18.70
QA	18.97	11.11	14.02

One advantage of QA is that answer candidates can still receive a high confidence despite the context sentence structure. For example, the QA system is the only approach that returned a correct answer for the slot *org:headquarters*, producing the query answer pair <*Convocation of Anglicans in North America, Nigeria*> and returning the context sentence "*In May, Global South spokeman and Nigerian Archbishop Peter Akinola consecrated Martyn Minns of Virginia as Bishop of the*

---

[6] http://nlp.cs.qc.cuny.edu/kbp/2010/scoring.html

Church of Nigeria for an outreach programme called Convocation of Anglicans in North America."

The most common mistakes of the QA pipeline are directly related to the use of co-occurrence statistics. Although semantic evidence indicates an answer is invalid, it is still returned.   For example, the QA pipeline identified context sentence, *"Masked fighters parade beneath yellow flags beside the faces of Nasrallah and Abbas Moussawi , Nasrallah's predecessor who was assassinated, along with his wife and son, in an attack by an Israeli helicopter pilot"*, but since only co-occurrence were used, the following inaccurate answer pair was generated for the slot *per:title <abbas moussawi, assassinated>* and should have been returned for *per:cause_of_death.*

In addition, we compared our absolute scores with the LDC human annotator and the top slot filling system in KBP2009 evaluation which achieved the best score for non-NIL slots. The results are shown in Table 2.

Table 2. Performance Comparison with State-of-the-art System and Human Annotator (%)

System/Human	Precision	Recall	F-Measure
Pattern Matching	**35.26**	**34.36**	**34.81**
09 Best System	32.12	31.79	31.96
Single LDC Human Annotator	100	41.83	58.99

From Table 2 we can see that our pattern matching approach achieved significantly better results than the top site at KBP2009 evaluation, on both precision and recall. We can also conclude that Slot Filling is a very challenging task even for human because the human annotator can only find 41.83% answers.

5.3   Impact of Statistical Re-ranking

We then evaluate the impact of combination methods and will demonstrate they are also essential steps to achieve good slot filling results. We will describe the results for statistical re-ranker in this subsection and cross-slot reasoning in 5.4 respectively.

We evaluate the impact of re-ranking on the QA pipeline. The relative scores are presented in Table 3. We can see that statistical re-ranking significantly improved (about 5%) both precision and recall of the QA pipeline.

Table 3. Statistical Re-ranking on QA (%)

QA Pipeline	Relative Precision	Relative Recall	Relative F-measure
Before Re-ranking	16.41	6.54	9.36
After Re-ranking	18.97	11.11	14.02

Supervised Re-ranking helps to mitigate the impact of errors produced by scoring based on co-occurrence. For example, when applied to our answer set, the answer *"Clinton"* for the query *"Dee Dee Myers"*, had a system relevance score for the attribute *per:children* due to frequent co-occurrence that was reduced and consequently removed by re-ranking. Alternatively, the query *"Moro National Liberation Front"* and answer *"1976"*did not have a high co-occurrence in the text collection, but was bumped up by the re-ranker based on the slot type feature *org:founded* .

5.4 Impact of Cross-Slot Reasoning

Experimental results demonstrate the cross-slot reasoning approach described in Section 4.3 can enhance the quality of slot filling in two aspects: (1) It can generate new results for the slots which the pipelines failed altogether; (2) It can filter out or correct logically incoherent answers. For the test set, this method significantly improved the precision of slot filling without any loss in recall. Table 4 presents the number of spurious errors removed by this approach when it is applied to various pipelines.

Table 4. Impact of Cross-slot Reasoning

Applied Pipeline		#Removed Errors
QA	Baseline	30
	+Validation	23
	+Re-ranking	16
Supervised IE		7
Pattern Matching		3

6 Related Work

The task of extracting slots for persons and organizations has attracted researchers from various fields, e.g., relation extraction, question answering, web people search, etc. Most KBP systems follow one of the three pipelines we described, such as IE-based approaches (Bikel et al., 2009) and QA based methods (Li et al., 2009). Some previous work (e.g. Schiffman et al., 2007) demonstrated that IE results can be used to significantly enhance QA performance.

Answer validation and re-ranking has been crucial to enhance QA performance (e.g. Magnini et al., 2002; Peñas et al., 2007). Recent work (Ravichandran et al., 2003) has showed that high performance for QA systems can be achieved using as few as four features in re-ranking. Our results on the QA pipeline support this finding. The same related work (Huang et al., 2009) reports that systems viewed as a re-ranker work clearly outperforms classifier based approaches, suggesting a re-ranking was a better implementation choice.

(Bikel et al., 2009) designed inference rules to improve the performance of slot filling. We followed their idea but incorporated inference rules into Markov Logic Networks (MLN).

7 Conclusion

We developed three effective pipelines for the KBP slot filling task. We advance state-of-the-art performance using several novel approaches including statistical answer re-ranking and cross-slot reasoning based on Markov Logic Networks (MLN). Experimental results demonstrated that the pattern matching pipeline outperforms the top system in KBP2009 evaluation.

Acknowledgement

This work was supported by the U.S. Army Research Laboratory under Cooperative Agreement Number W911NF-09-2-0053, the U.S. NSF CAREER Award under Grant IIS-0953149, Google, Inc., DARPA GALE Program, CUNY Research Enhancement Program, PSC-CUNY Research Program, Faculty Publication Program and GRTI Program. The views and conclusions contained in this document are those of the authors and should not be interpreted as representing the official policies, either expressed or implied, of the Army Research Laboratory or the U.S. Government. The U.S. Government is authorized to reproduce and distribute reprints for Government purposes notwithstanding any copyright notation here on.

References

1. Bikel, D., Castelli, V., Florian, R., Han, D.: Entity Linking and Slot Filling through Statistical Processing and Inference Rules. In: Proc. TAC 2009 Workshop (2009)
2. Huang, Z., Thint, M., Celikyilmaz, A.: Investigation of question classifier in question answering. In: Proc. EMNLP 2009, pp. 543–550 (2009)
3. Ji, H., Grishman, R., Chen, Z., Gupta, P.: Cross-document Event Extraction, Ranking and Tracking. In: Proc. RANLP 2009, pp. 166–172 (2009)
4. Kok, S., Sumner, M., Richardson, M., Singla, P., Poon, H., Lowd, D., Domingos, P.: The Alchemy system for statistical relational AI. Technical report, Department of Computer Science and Engineering, University of Washington (2007)
5. Li, F., Zheng, Z., Bu, F., Tang, Y., Zhu, X., Huang, M.: THU QUANTA at TAC 2009 KBP and RTE Track. In: Proc. TAC 2009 Workshop (2009)
6. Magnini, B., Negri, M., Prevete, R., Tanev, H.: Mining Knowledge from Repeated Co-occurrences: DIOGENE at TREC 2002. In: Proc. TREC (2002)
7. Peñas, A., Rodrigo, A., Verdejo, F.: Overview of the Answer Validation Exercise 2007. In: Peters, C., Jijkoun, V., Mandl, T., Müller, H., Oard, D.W., Peñas, A., Petras, V., Santos, D. (eds.) CLEF 2007. LNCS, vol. 5152, pp. 237–248. Springer, Heidelberg (2008)
8. Ravichandran, D., Hovy, E., Och, F.J.: Statistical QA -classifier vs. reranker: what's the difference? In: Proc. ACL 2003 Workshop on Multilingual Summarization and Question Answering (2003)
9. Richardson, M., Domingos, P.: Markov Logic Networks. Machine Learning 62, 107–136 (2006)
10. Schlaefer, N., Ko, J., Betteridge, J., Sautter, G., Pathak, M., Nyberg, E.: Semantic Extensions of the Ephyra QA System for TREC 2007. In: Proc. TREC 2007 (2007)
11. Schiffman, B., McKeown, K., Grishman, R., Allan, J.: Question Answering Using Integrated Information Retrieval and Information Extraction. In: Proc. NAACL 2007, pp. 532–539 (2007)

Relation Extraction between Related Concepts by Combining Wikipedia and Web Information for Japanese Language

Masumi Shirakawa[1], Kotaro Nakayama[2], Eiji Aramaki[2],
Takahiro Hara[1], and Shojiro Nishio[1]

[1] Department of Multimedia Engineering, Graduate School of Information Science
and Technology, Osaka University
1-5 Yamadaoka, Suita, Osaka 565-0871, Japan
{shirakawa.masumi,hara,nishio}@ist.osaka-u.ac.jp
[2] The Center for Knowledge Structuring, The University of Tokyo
7-3-1 Hongo, Bunkyo-ku, Tokyo 113-8656, Japan
nakayama@cks.u-tokyo.ac.jp, eiji.aramaki@gmail.com

Abstract. Construction of a huge scale ontology covering many named entities, domain-specific terms and relations among these concepts is one of the essential technologies in the next generation Web based on semantics. Recently, a number of studies have proposed automated ontology construction methods using the wide coverage of concepts in Wikipedia. However, since they tried to extract formal relations such as is-a and a-part-of relations, generated ontologies have only a narrow coverage of the relations among concepts. In this work, we aim at automated ontology construction with a wide coverage of both concepts and these relations by combining information on the Web with Wikipedia. We propose a relation extraction method which receives pairs of co-related concepts from an association thesaurus extracted from Wikipedia and extracts their relations from the Web.

Keywords: ontology, natural language processing, thesaurus.

1 Introduction

In these years, a considerable number of studies have been made on the Semantic Web. Especially, construction of a huge scale ontology covering many named entities, domain-specific terms and relations among these concepts is demanded as an essential technology for various applications such as information retrieval. Most researches on ontology construction are divided into two categories; researches on constructing a task (or domain)-specific ontology, and researches on constructing an upper ontology. The former is primarily the development of tools which help users to build ontologies by hand according to the requirements of tasks. The latter is on constructing multi purpose (general) ontologies whose scope is the entire world. Most of the common upper ontologies, for example

P.-J. Cheng et al. (Eds.): AIRS 2010, LNCS 6458, pp. 310–319, 2010.

OpenCyc[1] and WordNet [8], define only general cencepts and formal relations such as is-a and a-part-of relationships. However, in order to fulfill the requirements of various applications such as information retrieval, a large-scale ontology which defines named entities, domain-specific terms, and various relationships among these concepts is needed. Recently, Wikipedia, a large-scale Web-based encyclopedia, is used in a notable number of studies which automatically build ontologies covering named entities and domain-specific terms. This is because Wikipedia has a wide coverage of concepts and its potency has been demonstrated in those conventional studies. However, although these studies have insisted the coverage of concepts in Wikipedia, they have rarely payed attention to the variety of relationships among concepts.

In this work, we aim at automatically constructing a large scale ontology by combining information from Wikipedia and the Web. In the construction of the ontology, we focus on the following two points.

- the coverage of named entities and domain-specific terms
- the variety of relations among concepts

To achieve these points, we use Wikipedia Thesaurus [10], an association thesaurus which defines relatedness among concepts, to cover numerous named entities and domain-specific terms. This has advantages not only to cover large numbers of named entities and domain-specific terms, but also to refine concept pairs between which relationship should be defined. After finding strongly related concept pairs from Wikipedia Thesaurus, we use a Web search engine to extract a variety of relations. In this phase, how we create Web search queries is important to filter Web pages which are suitable for relation extraction. Hence we add *case particles* (one of postpositions in Japanese, which have similar function to prepositions in English) to related concept pairs for generating Web search queries. Then we analyze the responses to extract relations among concepts.

2   Related Work

In the past, a considerable number of studies have been made for automatically constructing a large scale ontology. Recently, many researchers have payed attention on Wikipedia mining, a research area that is similar to Web mining but highly specialized for Wikipedia, to automatically construct a large scale ontology. Since Wikipedia is based on Wiki, anyone can edit and refine the articles by using a Web browser, that makes Wikipedia high quality and huge scale. As for the quality, according to the statistics of Nature [3], Wikipedia is almost as accurate in covering scientific topics as the Encyclopedia Britannica. As for the scale, Wikipedia contains not only general concepts but also a large number of named entities and domain-specific terms which belong to various kinds of categories such as culture, history, mathematics, science, society, and technology. As of May 2010, the English version of Wikipedia contains more than

---

[1] http://www.opencyc.org/

3.3 million articles, and the Japanese version contains more than 670 thousands articles. Moreover, Wikipedia has various advantages such as dense and multiple link structure, high-quality anchor texts, and concept identification by URL [11]. Because of these advantages, Wikipedia have become one of the most major corpora over the past several years.

DBpedia [1] and YAGO [13] are typical instances of constructing a large scale ontology by analyzing Wikipedia. DBpedia focuses on the infobox, a template to describe attributes on articles in Wikipedia, and simply translates it into RDF (Resource Description Framework) to construct a large scale multilingual ontology. YAGO also constructed a large scale ontology by using NLP (Natural Language Processing) techniques specialized for English grammar for mapping classes in WordNet [8] to categories in Wikipedia. Although these researches have insisted the coverage of concepts, they have rarely payed attention to the variety of relationships among concepts.

The case frame dictionary [5] is one of the dictionaries defining a variety of relations among terms. A case frame consists of nouns, *case particles* and a verb, e.g. "{employee} *ga* {car, truck, airplane} *ni* {package, commodity} *wo tsumu* (load)". *Case particle* is one of postpositions in Japanese language and it has similar function to prepositions in English. Case frames are created by analyzing a large amount of documents and conducting clustering from co-occurrence data of nouns, case particles and verbs. Since the case frame dictionary defines relations among nouns by verbs and case particles, it can be regarded as a kind of ontology. However, the case frame dictionary covers few named entities and domain-specific terms because they occur not as often as general terms.

Though the purpose is different from constructing an ontology, Suhara et al. [14] proposed a relation extraction method which can extract a variety of relations among named entities. This method extracts verb relations among related named entities by analyzing snippets in results of Web search in blogsphere and connecting the named entities centering on verb and case particle pairs. In addition, Suhara et al. mentioned that their method sometimes received many irrelevant Web pages not suitable for extracting relations such as itemizations and lists. On the other hand, Ohshima et al. [12] proposed a method that efficiently makes a short list of Web pages suitable for relation extraction by adding a parallel particle (one of postpositions in Japanese language) to Web search queries.

From these conventional studies, we can see that Wikipedia mining and Web mining are usable for relation extraction. However, few studies have paid attention to both Wikipedia and the Web for relation extraction. In 2009, Yan et al. [15] used information on both Wikipedia and the Web to extract relations. Though they did not intend to construct an ontology, their method outperformed a relation extraction method using only the Web information.

3   Method

In this work, we propose a relation extraction method combining Wikipedia and the Web information.

3.1   Extraction of Related Concept Pairs

Our method first extracts strongly related concept pairs by utilizing Wikipedia Thesaurus. Wikipedia Thesaurus is a dictionary which defines relatedness among concepts in Wikipedia that we developed in our former research [10]. For example, the relatedness between "iPhone" and "iPod Touch" is 0.016 (means high-relative pairs), and the one between "iPhone" and "BlackBerry" is 0.0053 (means medium-relative pairs). Though we can gain strongly related concept pairs by using Wikipedia Thesaurus, we cannot acquire their relations. However, strongly related concept pairs are likely to have some relations. Additionally, it defines relatedness among named entities and domain-specific terms such as "Harry Potter" and "J. K. Rowling," "Dijkstra's algorithm" and "Edsger Dijkstra." For these reasons, we reached an assumption that Wikipedia Thesaurus can be used to extract relations among specialistic concept pairs which are not defined in existing ontologies.

3.2   Relation Extraction between Concepts by Web Search

Our method uses Web search to find concrete relations after extracting related concept pairs. In this phase, a concept pair is given as an input, and relations between concepts with the ranking according to the importances are the output. An extracted relation consists of a verb and case particles. As described in section 2, case particles are postpositions in Japanese language, e.g. *ga* means nominative, *ni* means accusative, *wo* means dative and so on. The importance is calculated based on the frequency on the Web and the reliability as a synonym. For example, if a concept pair "Masayoshi Son" and "SoftBank" is given as input, the output may be as "Masayoshi Son *ga* SoftBank *wo sougyousuru*" (Masayoshi Son establishs SoftBank) and "Masayoshi Son *ga* SoftBank *wo keieisuru*" (Masayoshi Son manages SoftBank) ordered by their importances. Our method adds case particles to concept pairs to generate Web search queries. Then it extracts sentences from top responses in the Web search results, and applies morphological analysis and dependency parsing to them to extract verbs as their relations. We describe the detail on each process in the following clauses.

Acquisition of Synonyms and Reliability of Concepts. In NLP-based relation extraction, the problem of identifying concepts in texts is inevitable. For instance, the concept of a company "Apple Inc." has many representations (synonyms) like *Apple Inc.*, *Apple Computer*, and just *Apple*. We should figure out these synonyms in order to extract relations with high coverage from texts. Whereat, we utilize anchor texts linked to concepts in Wikipedia as their synonyms [9]. In Wikipedia, since the text part of a link (anchor text) is a summary of the linked page in most cases, we can extract synonym candidates by analyzing the anchor texts of a Web page.

Given a list of anchor texts L_c linked to the concept (page) c, the number of occurrences $M_c(l_i)$ of the anchor text $l_i \in L_c$, reliability $R_c(l_i)$ is defined by the following equation.

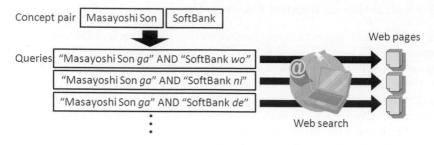

Fig. 1. An example of query generation with case particles

$$R_c(l_i) = \frac{\ln(M_c(l_i))}{\ln(\max(M_c(l_k)))}, \quad l_k \in L_c \tag{1}$$

Reliability $R_c(l_i)$ indicates how suitable an anchor text l_i is as a synonym of the concept c. If the max number of occurrences $\max(M_c(l_k))$ is 0 or 1, we just use the name of the URL assigned to the concept page as a sole synonym. Reliability $R_c(l_i)$ is used for calculating importance I, as described later. Additionally, we adopt the synonym with the highest reliability among R_c as the label of the concept. This label is used for generating Web search queries as described in the next clause.

Generation of Web Search Queries with Case Particles. Our method generates Web search queries from related concept pairs extracted from Wikipedia Thesaurus. Moreover, it adds case particles after each concept in queries. A query with case particles filters search results which are suitable for extracting relations. Suhara et al. [14] does not add case particle to queries, which makes search results noisy. For example, for the concept pair "Masayoshi Son" and "SoftBank", case particles *ga* and *wo* are added after each concept to generate a query "Masayoshi Son *ga*" "SoftBank *wo*". As the result, the search engine returns a set of Web pages definitely including "Masayoshi Son *ga*" and "SoftBank *wo*". These pages tend to include not itemizations or lists but normal texts. Consequently, these pages include more verbs than that gained by a simple query "Masayoshi Son" "SoftBank".

In particular, as shown in Fig. 1, Web search queries are generated for each combination of case particles. Then, sets of responses are gained by these queries. We acquire top N Web pages and the number of all hit counts H for each query. The number of all hit counts H is used for calculating importance I, as described later.

Relation Extraction by Analyzing Responses. After acquiring top N Web pages for each query, our method divides them into each sentence according to delimiters such as period and line feed. Then it extracts sentences which include the concept pair with case particles. To identify whether the concept is included in a sentence or not, we use synonyms described above.

It applies dependency parsing by CaboCha [6] and morphological analysis by MeCab [7] to the sentences which include the concept pair with case particles (Fig. 2). As a result, it can gain verbs that has a modification relation with the concept pair.

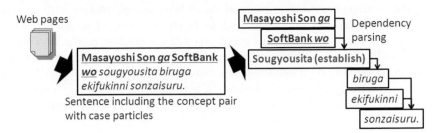

Fig. 2. An example of relation extraction by analyzing responses

For given variables including an extracted verb v, a concept pair (c_1, c_2), case particles following each concept (p_1, p_2), it calculates the number of occurrences $F(c_1, p_1, c_2, p_2, v)$ for each relation as follows.

$$F(c_1, p_1, c_2, p_2, v) = \sum_{l_1 \in L_{c_1}} \sum_{l_2 \in L_{c_2}} \frac{R_{c_1}(l_1) + R_{c_2}(l_2)}{2} \cdot S(l_1, p_1, l_2, p_2, v) \qquad (2)$$

Here, L_{c_1} and L_{c_2} respectively denotes all the synonyms for concepts c_1 and c_2. $S(l_1, p_1, l_2, p_2, v)$ denotes the number of occurrences for a sentence including synonyms l_1 and l_2, case particles p_1 and p_2, and verb v. It calculates a weighted number of occurrences by reliability R determined for each synonym as mentioned above. After analyzing all sentences, it calculates the importance $I(c_1, p_1, c_2, p_2, v)$ for each relation from the number of occurrences $F(c_1, p_1, c_2, p_2, v)$.

$$I(c_1, p_1, c_2, p_2, v) = \max \left(\frac{H(c_1, p_1, c_2, p_2)}{N}, 1 \right) \cdot F(c_1, p_1, c_2, p_2, v) \qquad (3)$$

$H(c_1, p_1, c_2, p_2)$ denotes the all hit count in Web search by a query consisting of a concept pair (c_1, c_2) followed respectively by case particles p_1 and p_2. N denotes the max number of Web pages which should be analyzed. When the hit count $H(c_1, p_1, c_2, p_2)$ is larger than N, the equation (3) speculates how many the relation exists on the Web. Importance I is used for ranking extracted relations.

4   Evaluation

We conducted an experiment to evaluate our proposed relation extraction method. To verify the effectiveness of adding case particles to Web search queries, we compared our method with a method without case particles. In addition, we looked into the extracted relations whether they are unlikely to be defined in existing ontologies.

4.1   Experimental Environment

We evaluated the relations among related concepts extracted by each method by hand. In particular, we randomly selected 306 named entity pairs from Wikipedia

Thesaurus and generated 20 combinations of Web search queries with *case particles* (postpositions) *ha, ga, wo, ni,* and *de*. In this evaluation, we gained 50 Web pages for only top 5 combinations of case partices according to the hit count H. Then we judged top 5 relations according to the importance I into three groups: the correct group X, the partially correct group Y and the wrong group Z. The criteria of the judgment were as follows; if a relation is apparently understandable then it is *correct*, if a relation is understandable with some supplementary information or it is sometimes correct and sometimes wrong then it is *partialy correct*, and the others are *wrong*. Moreover, we judged uncertain rumors into the correct relation group.

We adopted the following three metrics used in the study [14] to evaluate how extracted relations were appropriate.

1. Accuracy of the highest rank
   This is the precision of the highest ranked relations.
2. Mean Reciprocal Rank (MRR)
   The average of reciprocals of the highest ranked correct relations. If there is no correct relation for a concept pair, the score is set as 0.
3. Discounted Cumulative Gain (DCG)
   This metric was proposed by Jarvelin et al. [4]. In the research area of Information Retrieval (IR), DCG is often used for evaluating multiple-rank precision, which is defined as below.

$$dcg(i) = \begin{cases} g(1) & \text{if } i = 1 \\ dcg(i-1) + \dfrac{g(i)}{log_c(i)} & \text{otherwise} \end{cases}, \quad g(i) = \begin{cases} x \text{ if } r(i) \in X \\ y \text{ if } r(i) \in Y \\ z \text{ if } r(i) \in Z \end{cases} \quad (4)$$

Here, $r(i)$ denotes a relation ranked as i-th, $g(i)$ denotes the accuracy level of $r(i)$, and $dcg(i)$ denotes the discounted sum of $g(i)$ from 1st to i-th. The parameters were set to $(x, y, z) = (3, 2, 0)$ and $c = 2$ following these works [14,2].

We distinguished the case regarding partially correct relations as correct and the case regarding them as wrong. For DCG, we calculated the score for two cases: from 1st to 5th and from 1st to 3rd.

4.2   Experimental Results

Table 1 shows the experimental results. First of all, the proposed method extracted relations for 101 pairs while the compared method extracted relations only for 49 pairs. This simply means that the proposed method could extract relations twice larger than by the compared method. In addition, while the compared method extracted 1.60 relations per concept pair, the proposed method extracted 2.60 relations per concept pair. That is, the proposed method (which added case particles to Web search queries) could extract not only relations for more concept pairs but also more relations per concept pair than the compared method (which did not add case particles to Web search queries).

Table 1. Results

Metrics	Compared method (without case particles)	Proposed method (with case particles)
Number of concept pairs between which the relation could be extracted	49	101
Accuracy of the highest rank (including partialy correct)	0.878	0.782
Accuracy of the highest rank (excluding partialy correct)	0.510	0.485
MRR (including partialy correct)	0.908	0.825
MRR (excluding partialy correct)	0.541	0.549
DCG (from 1st to 5th)	3.419	3.861
DCG (from 1st to 3rd)	3.241	3.443

As for the accuracy of the highest rank and MRR, the proposed method shows slightly lower score than the compared method. However, if the partially correct relations are not regarded as correct, the proposed method shows as almost same score as the compared method. Moreover, in terms of DCG, the proposed method shows higher scores than the compared method. This is because DCG is affected by all extracted relations and based on a point-addition scoring system. Briefly, a method which can extract more correct relations achieves higher DCG. Thus we see the proposed method could extract more correct relations than the compared method with almost same precision.

4.3   Extracted Relations

Table 2 shows an example of extracted relations by the proposed method. This represents the first-ranked relations for each concept pair. Looking at Table 2, a variety of relations which are unlikely to be defined in existing ontologies are extracted; relations of consciousness such as "Schubert *ha* Beethoven *wo sonkei* (respect)", and relations between an actor and the role such as "Hiroshi Fujioka *ga* Kamen Rider *ni henshin* (disguise)". Moreover, in relations such as "Pro Wrestling Noah *wo* Mitsuharu Misawa *ga hataage* (launch on an enterprise)" and "Kyoto Sangyo University *ni* Kyoto Seian High School *wo ikan* (place under the control of another department)", the most appropriate verb is extracted among various similar verbs. What's interesting is that the fact that Shingo Katori was absent from the idol group SMAP due to the flu at the beginning of January 2010 could be extracted as a relation at the end of January 2010. Relations about new topics and news tend to be extracted more prior than steady relations. These relations are beneficial because existing ontologies do not possess these information. The relation "NEWS *wo* Tomohisa Yamashita *ga dattai* (drop out)" is not a fact but just a rumor on January 2010. Considering applications on the Web, these relations can be also beneficial.

Table 2. An example of extracted relations

Concept A	Concept B	Extracted relations
Expo 2005	Nagakute	A *ga* B *de kaisai* (be held at)
Berryz Kobo	Miyabi Natsuyaki	A *ni* B *ga kanyu* (join)
NEWS	Tomohisa Yamashita	A *wo* B *ga dattai* (drop out)
ZARD	Izumi Sakai	A *ha* B *ga utau* (sing)
Southern All Stars	Keisuke Kuwata	A *wo* B *ga daihyou* (stand for)
Salzburg	Mozart	A *de* B *ga sakkyoku* (compose music at)
Northwest Airlines	Delta Air Lines	A *ga* B *ni kyushu* (be absorbed)
Fiat	Lancia	A *ga* B *wo seisan* (put out)
Schubert	Beethoven	A *ha* B *wo sonkei* (respect)
Pro Wrestling Noah	Mitsuharu Misawa	A *wo* B *ga hataage* (launch on an enterprise)
Ichinoseki	Higashiyama	A *ni* B *ha gappei* (be merged)
Kyoto Sangyo University	Kyoto Seian High School	A *ni* B *wo ikan* (place under the control of another department)
Atsuya Furuta	Tokyo Yakult Swallows	A *ga* B *ni nyudan* (join a team)
Hiroshi Fujioka	Kamen Rider	A *ga* B *ni henshin* (disguise)
Shingo Katori	SMAP	A *ga* B *wo yasumu* (be absent from)

5 Conclusion

In this paper, we proposed a relation extraction method to construct a large scale ontology which has a wide coverage of concepts as well as a variety of relationships by combining information on both Wikipedia and the Web. In particular, our method utilizes Wikipedia Thesaurus [10] for discovering strongly related concept pairs and generates Web search queries with case particles. Then it analyzes texts in the Web search results to extract relations between the related concept pairs.

From the result of the evaluation, we confirmed the effectiveness of adding case particles to Web search queries. It could extract correct relations twice larger than the compared method, which did not add case particles, with almost same precision. In addition, our method could extract a variety of relations which were not defined in existing ontologies. That is, our method is efficient to construct a large scale ontology which has a variety of relations.

In our future work, we plan to construct a large scale ontology by our method. Constructing and releasing a large scale ontology is important for the advancement of many research areas that use ontologies. For example, researchers who are engaged in ontology construction may construct a more superior ontology based on it. Engineers who are engaged in research and development of applications based on ontologies may develop useful services by using it.

Acknowledgment

This research was supported in part by Grant-in-Aid for Scientific Research (B)(21300032), Grant-in-Aid for Scientific Research (C)(20500093), Grant-in-Aid for the Global COE Program (J101413001) and the Microsoft Research IJARC Core Project.

References

1. Auer, S., Bizer, C., Kobilarov, G., Lehmann, J., Cyganiak, R., Ives, Z.G.: DB-pedia: A Nucleus for a Web of Open Data. In: Aberer, K., Choi, K.-S., Noy, N., Allemang, D., Lee, K.-I., Nixon, L.J.B., Golbeck, J., Mika, P., Maynard, D., Mizoguchi, R., Schreiber, G., Cudré-Mauroux, P. (eds.) ASWC 2007 and ISWC 2007. LNCS, vol. 4825, pp. 722–735. Springer, Heidelberg (2007)
2. Eguchi, K.: Overview of the Topical Classification Task at NTCIR-4 WEB. Working Notes of the 4th NTCIR Meeting, Supplement 1, 48–55 (2004)
3. Giles, J.: Internet encyclopedias go head to head. Nature 438(7070), 900–901 (2005)
4. Järvelin, K., Kekäläinen, J.: IR Evaluation Methods for Retrieving Highly Relevant Documents. In: Proc. of International ACM SIGIR Conference on Research and Development in Information Retrieval (SIGIR), pp. 41–48 (2000)
5. Kawahara, D., Kurohashi, S.: Case Frame Compilation from the Web using High-Performance Computing. In: Proc. of International Conference on Language Resources and Evaluation, (LREC) (2006)
6. Kudo, T., Matsumoto, Y.: Fast Methods for Kernel-Based Text Analysis. In: Proc. of Annual Meeting on Association for Computational Linguistics (ACL), pp. 24–31 (2003)
7. Kudo, T., Yamamoto, K., Matsumoto, Y.: Applying Conditional Random Fields to Japanese Morphological Analysis. In: Proc. of Conference on Empirical Methods in Natural Language Processing (EMNLP), pp. 230–237 (2004)
8. Miller, G.A.: WordNet: A Lexical Database for English. Communications of the ACM (CACM) 38(11), 39–41 (1995)
9. Nakayama, K., Hara, T., Nishio, S.: A Thesaurus Construction Method from Large Scale Web Dictionaries. In: Proc. of IEEE International Conference on Advanced Information Networking and Applications (AINA), pp. 932–939 (2007)
10. Nakayama, K., Hara, T., Nishio, S.: Wikipedia Mining for An Association Web Thesaurus Construction. In: Benatallah, B., Casati, F., Georgakopoulos, D., Bartolini, C., Sadiq, W., Godart, C. (eds.) WISE 2007. LNCS, vol. 4831, pp. 322–334. Springer, Heidelberg (2007)
11. Nakayama, K., Pei, M., Erdmann, M., Ito, M., Shirakawa, M., Hara, T.: Shojiro: Wikipedia Mining - Wikipedia as a Corpus for Knowledge Extraction -. In: Proc. of Wikimedia International Conference, (Wikimania) (2008)
12. Ohshima, H., Tanaka, K.: High-speed Detection of Ontological Knowledge and Bi-directional Lexico-Syntactic Patterns from the Web. Journal of Software 5(2), 195–205 (2010)
13. Suchanek, F.M., Kasneci, G., Weikum, G.: YAGO: A Large Ontology from Wikipedia and WordNet. Journal of Web Semantics 6(3), 203–217 (2008)
14. Suhara, Y., Toda, H., Sakurai, A.: Extracting Related Named Entities from Blogosphere for Event Mining. In: Proc. of International Conference on Ubiquitous Information Management and Communication (ICUIMC), pp. 242–246 (2008)
15. Yan, Y., Okazaki, N., Matsuo, Y., Yang, Z., Ishizuka, M.: Unsupervised Relation Extraction by Mining Wikipedia Texts using Information from the Web. In: Proc. of Annual Meeting on Association for Computational Linguistics, International Joint Conference on Natural Language Processing of the Asian Federation of Natural Language Processing (ACL-IJCNLP), pp. 1021–1029 (2009)

A Chinese Sentence Compression Method for Opinion Mining

Shi Feng[1], Daling Wang[1], Ge Yu[1], Binyang Li[2], and Kam-Fai Wong[2]

[1] Northeastern University, Shenyang, China
{fengshi,wangdaling,yuge}@ise.neu.edu.cn
[2] The Chinese University of Hong Kong, Shatin, N.T., Hong Kong, China
{byli,kfwong}@se.cuhk.edu.hk

Abstract. The Chinese sentences in news articles are usually very long, which set up obstacles for further opinion mining steps. Sentence compression is the task of producing a brief summary at the sentence level. Conventional compression methods do not distinguish the opinionated information from factual information in each sentence. In this paper, we propose a weakly supervised Chinese sentence compression method which aiming at eliminating the negligible factual parts and preserving the core opinionated parts of the sentence. No parallel corpus is needed during the compression. Experiments that involve both automatic evaluations and human subjective evaluations validate that the proposed method is effective in finding the desired parts from the long Chinese sentences.

Keywords: Sentence Compression, Opinion Mining.

1 Introduction

"What other people think" has always been an important piece of information for most of us during the decision-making process [15]. The goal of opinion mining is to extract and summarize opinionated contents from news, blogs, comments and reviews. It has recently attracted much attention because of its wide range of applications, such as marketing intelligence, government policy making and so on.

Opinion holder and target extraction are fundamental task of opinion mining, and a lot of literatures have been published in this area [1,2,10]. However, the accuracy of this task for Chinese news articles is far from acceptable [17]. This is partially because Chinese sentences are usually very long and often connects two or more self-complete sentences together without any indicating word or punctuation. Therefore, the parsing approach will bring in more errors and noisy for the extraction models and methods.

Sentence compression is a recent framework that aims to select the shortest subsequence of words that yields an informative and grammatical sentence [12]. Most previous studies focus on preserving the critical information of the sentence. However they do not differentiate the opinionate part of the sentence from the factual ones. Table 1 shows a compressed sentence addressing the conventional content-oriented compression task (CS) and an example of opinion-oriented compressed sentence (OOCS).

P.-J. Cheng et al. (Eds.): AIRS 2010, LNCS 6458, pp. 320–329, 2010.

Table 1. The example of conventional and opinion-oriented compressed sentences

Original Sentence (OC)	700多名群众聚集在西南部胡齐斯坦省首府阿瓦士的一家神学院门前，强烈抗议美英对伊拉克发动军事打击。 More than 700 people gathered in front of a theological school in the southwestern Khuzestan province, capital of Ahvaz, and strongly protested against the United States and Britain launching a military strike against Iraq.
Compressed Sentence (CS)	群众聚集在神学院门前，抗议美英对伊拉克发动军事打击。 People gathered in front of theological school, and protested against the United States and Britain launching a military strike against Iraq.
Opinion-Oriented Compressed Sentence (OOCS)	群众强烈抗议美英对伊拉克发动军事打击。 People strongly protested against the United States and Britain launching a military strike against Iraq.

From Table 1 we can see that the conventional compression task can get the core information of each sub-sentence. Different from that, the goal of opinion-oriented sentence compression (OOSC) is to eliminate non-opinionated sub-sentence and retain the opinionate part of the sentence. The "gathered" part of the sentence is deleted because it does not express any opinion information. Therefore, the result words in OOCS yield a shortest opinionated and grammatical sentence, which paves the way for the further opinion mining steps.

The traditional sentence compression method could not meet the goal of opinion-oriented sentence compression, because it may retain unnecessary factual part of the sentence. Moreover, it sometimes ignores the opinion words which are very important for OOSC task. On the other hand, an ideal opinion-oriented compressed sentence should not only preserve the opinion holder, target information of the sentence, but also eliminate non-opinionate part of the sentence. It provides a brief summary of the opinion expressed in the sentence, and the shorten sentence brings in a higher parsing accuracy, which will facilitate opinion extraction task in the next mining steps.

Until recently, many papers have been published for sentence compression using both supervised and unsupervised method. However, there are still important challenges to be tackled for opinion-oriented sentence compression:

(1) The Chinese sentences in news articles are usually very long, which brings in errors for parsing based compression methods;

(2) The opinion-oriented sentence compression is lack of parallel corpus;

(3) The compression approach should not only consider the term information importance and grammatical consistency, but also the opinion-related weights of each word.

In this paper, we propose a scoring based opinion-oriented compression method for Chinese news sentences. To best of our knowledge, this is the first paper that seeks to compress Chinese sentences for opinion mining task. The rest of the paper is organized as follows. Section 2 introduces the related work on opinion mining and sentence compression. Section 3 presents the proposed dynamic programming approach for opinion-oriented Chinese sentence compression. Section 4 provides experimental results on Chinese news datasets, including automatic evaluations and human subjective evaluations. Finally we present concluding remarks and future work in Section 5.

2   Related Work

Recently, opinion mining has become a hot topic in research area. For sentiment classification task, documents are classified into positive and negative according to the overall sentiment expressed in them. Turney et al. [18] measured the strength of sentiment by the difference of the Pointwise Mutual Information (PMI) between the given phrase and the seed words. In [14], Pang et al. employed three machine learning approaches (Naive Bayes, Maximum Entropy, and Support Vector Machine) to label the polarity of IMDB movie reviews.

Extracting opinion holders, targets and expressions from documents have attracted many researchers' attentions [3,4,10]. Choi et al. presented an integer linear programming approach for the joint extraction of entities and relations in the sentence. Performance of the system could be further improved when a semantic role labeling algorithm is incorporated [2]. Wu et al. proposed a novel phrase dependency parsing approach for mining opinions from product reviews, where it converted opinion mining task to identify product features, expressions of opinions and relations between them [20]. Although these methods have achieved relatively high extraction accuracy, they are still sensitive to the parsing errors, which set up obstacles for extracting opinions from long Chinese news sentences.

Sentence compression could be usefully employed in wide range of applications. For example, it can be used to automatically generate headline of an article [6]; Other applications include compressing text to be displayed on small screens [5] such as mobile phones or PDAs, and producing audio scanning devices for the blind [7]. However, there is no study on how sentence compression can improve the performance of opinion mining in the previous work.

Most existing studies relied on a parallel corpus to learn the correspondences between original and compressed sentences. Typically sentences are represented by features derived from parsing results, and used to learn the transformation rules or estimate the parameters in the score function of a possible compression. A variety of models have been developed, including but not limited to the noisy-channel model [11], support vector machines [13] and large-margin learning [4]. However, for opinion-oriented Chinese sentence compression, no existing parallel corpus can be directly used to training these models.

An algorithm making limited use of training data was proposed by Clarke and Lapata [3] for English text. Their model searched for the compression with highest score according to the significance of each word, the existence of Subject-Verb-Object structures and the language model probability of the resulting word combination. The weight factors to balance the three measurements were experimentally optimized by a parallel corpus or estimated by experience.

3   Proposed Approach

3.1   Problem Definition

Sentence compression is defined as follows: given a sequence of words $W=w_1w_2...w_N$ (of N words) that constitute a sentence, find a subsequence $V=v_1v_2...v_M$ (of M words, $M<N$), that is a compressed version of W. To take the sentences in Table 1 as an example, we have the following explanations in Figure 1.

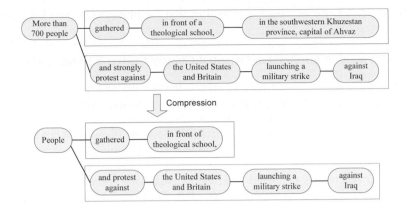

Fig. 1. The traditional sentence compression result for the origin sentence

We can see from Figure 1 that the original sentence can be divided into two self-completed sub-sentence. The conventional compression method can eliminate some modifier words and location words which are less important information for the original sentence. However, since the Chinese sentence are usually very long, not all parts of the sentence contain the opinion-related information that the readers concern. For example, the upper rectangle part of the sentence in Figure 1 describes the fact that "People gathered in front of theological school", which does not include any opinion of "People". For opinion-oriented sentence compression, we intend to get the reduced sentence as shown in Figure 2.

Fig. 2. The opinion-oriented sentence compression result for the origin sentence

In Figure 2, the factual part of the sentence is eliminated, and the opinionated part is retained. We can see that the opinion-oriented compression also preserves the modifier "强烈"(strongly), which is eliminated in the conventional compression method. From the compressed version of the sentence, the opinion is expressed more concise and it will be easier for people to get the opinion holder, target and other related information from the compressed sentence.

Here we give the formal definition of opinion-oriented sentence compression:

Definition 1. (Opinion-Oriented Sentence Compression). Given a sequence of words $W=w_1w_2...w_N$ (of N words) that constitute a sentence, find a subsequence $V=v_1v_2...v_M$ (of M words, $M<N$), that is a compressed version of W. W not only is a informative and grammatical sentence but also eliminates the factual part and preserves the opinionated part as much as possible.

In the Section 3.2, we introduce a score function for opinion-oriented Chinese sentence compression.

3.2 Score Function for Opinion-Oriented Chinese Sentence Compression

Notice that there is no existing parallel corpus for opinion-oriented Chinese sentence compression. To alleviate this problem, we employ a weakly supervised word deletion algorithm based on score function to compress a sentence.

Inspired by the work of Clark and Lapata [3], the score function in our approach is defined as a measure indicating the appropriateness of a compressed sentence. Based on the definition of opinion-oriented sentence compression, a set of words maximizing the score function is extracted from the original sentence using a dynamic programming technique. The score function is defined as the sum of word significance score I, the linguistic score L of the word string in the compressed sentence and the opinion score O of each word in the original sentence.

The score function of the sentence is given by:

$$S(V) = \sum_{i=1}^{M} \{\lambda_I I(v_i) + \lambda_L L(v_i) + \lambda_o O(v_i)\} \tag{1}$$

where $I(v_i)$, $L(v_i)$, $O(v_i)$ is the significance score, linguistic score and opinion score of the word v_i. λ_I, λ_L, λ_O are the weighting factors to balance the dynamic ranges of I, L, O, where the value can be set manually or optimized using a small amount of training data.

Word Significance Score. The word significance score I measures the relative importance of a word in the original sentence. Given a word w_i in the original sentence, the function I is defined as:

$$I(w_i) = f_i \log \frac{F_A}{F_i} \tag{2}$$

where f_i is the frequency of w_i in the document, F_i is the number of occurrences of w_i in all the documents and F_A is the sum of F_i in all the documents ($\sum_i F_i$).

In Clark and Lapata's work, the authors only focused on nouns and verbs as potential significant words. However, adjectives and adverbs are also good indicators for people's opinions. Therefore, in our study, we treat nouns, verbs, adjectives and adverbs equally for calculating the word significance score.

Linguistic Score. Using linguistic score L we can select some function words, thus ensuring that the compression results remain grammatical. We apply n-gram probability estimate the linguistic score of each word in the sentence.

$$L(w_i) = \log P(w_i \mid w_{i-2} w_{i-1}) \tag{3}$$

Opinion Score. Based on the assumption that the opinion words should have more opportunity to be preserved during the compression approach, we assign an opinion score to each word which belongs to a predefined dictionary.

$$O(w_i) = \begin{cases} \log f_i & \text{if } w_i \text{ belongs to opinion dictionary} \\ O_{const} & \text{otherwise} \end{cases} \tag{4}$$

where f_i is the document frequency of the word w_i, O_{const} is a balance weight given to all other words.

3.3 Compression Generation and Selection

Based on the score function, we employ a dynamic programming algorithm to find the best composition of M words in the sentence with N words. Given an original sentence, the dynamic programming algorithm searches different M value to maximize the score function, which generates a list of candidate compressed sentence with different length. Then the final selection of the best candidate compression is a trade-off between sentence and the value of score function. An information density score $D(V_M)$ is used to measure the quality of the candidate compression:

$$D(V_M) = \frac{S(V_M)}{M} \tag{5}$$

The best compression V is selected with the highest density score:

$$V = \arg\max_{V_M} D(V_M) \quad (\alpha N \le M \le \beta N) \tag{6}$$

where α and β are the minimum and maximum compressed ratio of the original sentence, which restrict the final length of the compressed sentence.

4 Experiments

4.1 Experiment Setup

Our intent is to check if the proposed method is effective for opinion-oriented sentence compression. Since there is no existing parallel corpus available, we build a new evaluation dataset for opinion-oriented Chinese sentence compression. The original data come from NTCIR Multilingual Opinion Mining Task, which consist of about 30,000 documents and totally 3,120,000 sentences. From these documents, we randomly pick up 100 opinionate sentences on the topic of "*Iraq War*" for the compression task. One annotator majoring in opinion mining was asked to manually delete the words of sentence, and several rules must be followed during the annotation: (a) the preserved words should not only contain the most important information, but also contain the opinionate content of the original sentence as much as possible; (b) the compressed sentence should remain grammatical. Finally, this annotation result is set to be the gold standard for the opinion-oriented Chinese sentence compression.

Recall that the score function for sentence compression has three components: the significance score, linguistic score and opinion score. The significance score was trained using the NTCIR MOAT corpus which total contain 30,000 documents. The linguistic score was calculated using a trigram language model. In this paper, we use

Google search results to estimate the linguistic score of the give words. Given the word w_i, w_{i-1}, w_{i-2}, the linguistic score is defined as $\log P(w_i|w_{i-1}w_{i-2})$. So we have:

$$L(w_i) = \log P(w_i \mid w_{i-2}w_{i-1}) = \frac{C_{Google}(w_{i-2}w_{i-1}w_i)}{C_{Google}(w_{i-2}w_{i-1})} \tag{7}$$

where $C_{Google}(w_{i-2}w_{i-1})$ and $C_{Google}(w_{i-2}w_{i-1}w_i)$ is the number of search results when launch the query words "$w_{i-2}w_{i-1}$" and "$w_{i-2}w_{i-1}w_i$" to Google search engine. Zhu et al have validated that the web search results can effectively estimate the given trigram language model [21].

The sentiment lexicon is the fundamental tools for estimating the opinion score of each word in the sentence. Our sentiment lexicon is built based on following resources: (a) The Lexicon of Chinese Positive Words and the Lexicon of Chinese Negative Words; (b) The opinion word lexicon provided by National Taiwan University (NTU); (c) Sentiment word lexicon and comment word lexicon from HowNet [9]. The lexicon is manually verified. Totally, 14,201 positive words, 17,372 negative words and 478 neutral words are obtained.

4.2 Evaluation Methods

Both automatic evaluation and human subjective evaluation are employed to measure the correctness of the compressed sentences generated by the proposed approach. The parsing based automatic evaluation methods are not appropriate for the long Chinese sentence, because errors may be brought in during the parsing approach for the original and compressed sentence.

For automatic evaluation, we measure each sentence compression method using BLEU scores [16]. BLEU scores are firstly proposed for evaluating machine translation quality and recently it has been used for measuring the quality of compressed sentences [8,19]. A BLEU score is defined as the weighted geometric average of n-gram precisions with length penalties. 4-gram precision and uniform weights are used for the BLEU scores in this paper.

For human subjective evaluation, one native Chinese speakers majoring in opinion mining was asked to rate the grammatically of compressed sentence using the 1 to 5 scale. Notice that the student has placed more emphasis on whether the opinion information is preserved in the final compressed result. At the same time, the semantic and grammatical correctness is also considered during the evaluation.

4.3 Experiment Results

Our goal of the experiments is to answer this question: whether the proposed algorithm can meet the need of the opinion-oriented sentence compression task.

We check the compression rate of the proposed method and the gold standard, as shown in Table 2. In Table 2, gold standard means the human generated compressed sentence; OOSC denotes the opinion-oriented sentence compression method; TSC denotes the conventional sentence compression method. In this paper, for conventional method, we use significance and linguistic score together and do not consider opinion score. The compression rate is the ratio of the number of Chinese characters in a compressed sentence to that in its original sentence. For OOSC method, there is no compression rate limitation parameter except α and β, which restrict the length of the compressed sentence. In this paper, we set $\alpha=0.2$ and $\beta=0.5$ for the proposed algorithm. In this way, we can limit the range of the compressed sentence range from 20% to 50% of the original sentence. From Table 2, we can see that the human generated results are about 60% size of the original sentences. The compression rate of proposed method OOSC is under fifty percent of the original sentence.

Table 2. Average compression rate

Method	Compression Rate
Gold Standard	63%
OOSC	46%
TSC	47%

To check the effectiveness of the proposed algorithm in compressing Chinese sentence, we evaluate our method using BLUE scores, as shown in Table 3. And the human subjective evaluation results in shown in Table 4. Here we set $\lambda_I=1$, $\lambda_L=5$, $\lambda_O=2$. $O_{const}=0.01$. We can see from Table 3 and Table 4 that the proposed OOSC method outperforms the TSC method which does not consider the opinion information.

Table 3. Automatic evaluation for the compressed results of Chinese sentence

Method	BLEU score
OOSC	0.281
TSC	0.210

Table 4. Human evaluation for the compressed results of Chinese sentence

Method	Score
OOSC	3.2
TSC	2.6

5   Conclusion and Future Work

Compared to Web comments and reviews, the Chinese news articles usually have very long sentences, which bring in new challenge for opinion mining in this area. Conventional sentence compression methods can compress a sentence without changing its meaning. However, these methods do not distinguished opinionated information from factual information. In this paper, an opinion-oriented Chinese sentence compression method is proposed. The weight of each word in original sentence is measured by its information significance, linguistic consistence and opinion score. A dynamic programming algorithm is employed to find the best combination of the words in the original sentence. Automatic evaluations and human subjective evaluations demonstrate that the proposed method is effective in finding the desired parts from the long Chinese sentences.

Future work will consider more linguistic features and constraints to improve the grammatical consistence of the compressed sentence. We also intend to further evaluate the compressed results by applying opinion holder and target extraction algorithms.

Acknowledgments. This work is partially supported by National Natural Science Foundation of China (No.60973019, 60973021), National 863 High Technology Development Program of China (2009AA01Z131, 2009AA01Z150) and HKSAR ITF (No. GHP/036/09SZ). The authors would like to thank Donghao Fang for developing parts of algorithms in this paper.

References

1. Choi, Y., Breck, E., Cardie, C.: Joint Extraction of Entities and Relations for Opinion Recognition. In: Proceedings of the Conference on Empirical Methods in Natural Language Processing (EMNLP), pp. 431–439 (2006)
2. Choi, Y., Cardie, C., Riloff, E., Patwardhan, S.: Identifying Sources of Opinions with Conditional Random Fields and Extraction Patterns. In: Proceedings of Human Language Technology Conference and Conference on Empirical Methods in Natural Language Processing, pp. 355–362 (2005)
3. Clarke, J., Lapata, M.: Models for Sentence Compression: A Comparison across Domains, Training Requirements and Evaluation Measures. In: Proceedings of the 21st International Conference on Computational Linguistics and 44th Annual Meeting of the Association for Computational Linguistics, pp. 377–384 (2006)
4. Cohn, T., Lapata, M.: Large Margin Synchronous Generation and its Application to Sentence Compression. In: Proceedings of the Conference on Empirical Methods in Natural Language Processing and on Computational Natural Language Learning, pp. 73–82 (2007)
5. Corston-Oliver, S.: Text Compaction for Display on Very Small Screens. In: Proceedings of the NAACL Workshop on Automatic Summarization, pp. 89–98 (2001)
6. Dorr, B., Zajic, D., Schwartz, R.: Hedge trimmer: A Parse-and-Trim Approach to Headline Generation. In: Proceedings of HLT-NAACL Text Summarization Workshop and DUC, pp. 1–8 (2003)
7. Grefenstette, G.: Producing Intelligent Telegraphic Text Reduction to Provide an Audio Scanning Service for the Blind. In: Proceedings of the AAAI Symposium on Intelligent Text Summarization, pp. 111–117 (1998)
8. Hirao, T., Suzuki, J., Isozaki, H.: A Syntax-Free Approach to Japanese Sentence Compression. In: Proceedings of Joint Conference of the 47th Annual Meeting of the Association for Computational Linguistics and the 4th International Joint Conference on Natural Language Processing of the Asian Federation of Natural Language Processing, pp. 826–833 (2009)
9. HowNet, http://www.keenage.com
10. Kim, S., Hovy, E.: Extracting Opinions, Opinion Holders, and Topics Expressed in Online News Media Text. In: Proceedings of the ACL Workshop on Sentiment and Subjectivity in Text, pp. 1–8 (2006)
11. Knight, K., Daniel, M.: Summarization Beyond Sentence Extraction: A Probabilistic Approach to Sentence Compression. Artificial Intelligence 139(1), 91–107 (2002)
12. Martins, T., Smith, A.: Summarization with A Joint Model for Sentence Extraction and Compression. In: Proceedings of NAACL-HLT Workshop on Integer Linear Programming for NLP, pp. 1–9 (2009)

13. Nguyen, M., Akira, S., Susumu, H., Tu, B., Masaru, F.: Probabilistic Sentence Reduction Using Support Vector Machines. In: Proceedings of the 20th International Conference on Computational Linguistics, pp. 743–749 (2004)
14. Pang, B., Lee, L., Vaithyanathan, S.: Thumbs up? Sentiment Classification Using Machine Learning Techniques. In: Proceedings of the Conference on Empirical Methods in Natural Language Processing, pp. 79–86 (2002)
15. Pang, B., Lee, L.: Opinion Mining and Sentiment Analysis. Foundations and Trends in IR 2(1-2), 131–135 (2008)
16. Papineni, K., Roukos, S., Ward, T., Zhu, W.: BLEU: A Method for Automatic Evaluation of Machine Translation. In: Proceedings of the 40th Annual Meeting of the Association for Computational Linguistic, pp. 311–318 (2002)
17. Seki, Y., Evans, D., Ku, L., Sun, L., Chen, H., Kando, N.: Overview of Multilingual Opinion Analysis Task at NTCIR-7. In: Proceedings of the Seventh NTCIR Workshop Meeting on Evaluation of Information Access Technologies: Information Retrieval, Question Answering, and Cross-Lingual Information Access (2008)
18. Turney, P.: Thumbs Up or Thumbs Down? Semantic Orientation Applied to Unsupervised Classification of Reviews. In: 40th Annual Meeting of the Association for Computational Linguistics, pp. 417–424 (2002)
19. Unno, Y., Ninomiya, T., Miyao, Y., Tsujii, J.: Trimming CFG Parse Trees for Sentence Compression Using Machine Learning Approach. In: Proceedings of the Joint Conference of the International Committee on Computational Linguistics and the Association for Computational Linguistics, pp. 850–857 (2006)
20. Wu, Y., Zhang, Q., Huang, X., Wu, L.: Phrase Dependency Parsing for Opinion Mining. In: Proceedings of Joint Conference of the 47th Annual Meeting of the Association for Computational Linguistics and the 4th International Joint Conference on Natural Language Processing of the Asian Federation of Natural Language Processing, pp. 1533–1541 (2009)
21. Zhu, X., Rosenfeld, R.: Improving Trigram Language Modeling with the World Wide Web. In: Proceedings of the International Conference on Acoustics Speech and Signal Processing, pp. 533–536 (2001)

Relation Extraction in Vietnamese Text Using Conditional Random Fields

Rathany Chan Sam, Huong Thanh Le, Thuy Thanh Nguyen, and The Minh Trinh

Hanoi University of Technology, 1 DaiCoViet street, Hanoi, Vietnam
rathany_cam@yahoo.com, {huonglt,thuynt}@it-hut.edu.vn,
minhthe87@gmail.com

Abstract. Relation extraction is the task of finding semantic relations between entities from text. This paper presents our approach to relation extraction for Vietnamese text using Conditional Random Field. The features used in the system are words, part-of-speech tag, entity type, type of other entities in the sentence, entity's index and contextual information. In order to evaluate the effect of the contextual information to the system performance, different window sizes have been tested in our experiments. It shown that the system performance is affected by the window size, but it is not directly proportional to the F-score of the system. Our future work includes: (i) testing the system with a larger corpus in order to get a more accurate evaluation of the system; (ii) investigating other features used in the CRF algorithm to increase the system performance; and (iii) researching methods to extract relations outside the sentence's scope.

Keywords: information extraction, relation extraction, CRF.

1 Introduction

Relation extraction (RE) is a subtask of information extraction. Its purpose is to recognize relationships between entities in text. For example, the text fragment "Mr. Kien lives in Hanoi" contains a Person – Location relation between the Person entity "Kien" and the Location entity "Hanoi".

There are several research on relation extraction for English text. However, in Vietnam, this is still a new research area. Our paper is a contribution to this domain. We present a relation extraction system for Vietnamese text. The input is a set of documents that have been tagged for name entities including Person, Position, Organization, and Location. The output is relations between these entities including Per_Loc (i.e., Live_in relation), Per_Pos (i.e., Position relation), and Per_Org (i.e., Work_for relation). Our system firstly finds pairs of entities in each sentence, then it predicts entities' relations based on features related to these pairs using the Conditional Random Field (CRF) method.

The rest of this paper is organized as follows. Section 2 presents recent studies on relation extraction and works that inspire our research. Section 3 briefly introduces the CRF, the training and inference in CRF. Section 4 discusses the RE problem for Vietnamese text and our solution to this problem. Section 5 analyzes our experimental results. Finally, our conclusions and future work are given in Section 6.

P.-J. Cheng et al. (Eds.): AIRS 2010, LNCS 6458, pp. 330–339, 2010.
© Springer-Verlag Berlin Heidelberg 2010

2 Related Work

Recent studies on relation extraction often use statistical machine learning such as Hidden Markov Models, Conditional Random Fields [1, 2], Maximum Entropy Models [5], Support Vector Machines [3, 4, 12, 13].

Giuliano et al. [4] extracted relations Location - Location, Person - Organization, Organization - Location, Person - Location, and Person - Person in documents based on a kernel method, using shallow language processing such as tokenization, sentence splitting, part-of-speech (POS) tag, and lemmatization. This approach uses the sentence that contains entities as the global context for extracting process. The features using in this approach are: the context between the two entities (before, between, and after the two entities), lexicon, POS tag, bag-of-word, entity, chunk types, and WordNet synsets.

Culotta et al. [2] used the CRF for relation extraction. The purpose is to predict relations between entities and the page topic from a set of given relations. The list of features includes relation pattern, context words (such as the token identity within a 6-word window of the target token), lexicons (such as whether a token appears in a list of cities, people, or companies), regular expressions (such as whether the token is capitalized or contains digits or punctuation), part-of-speech, word prefix/suffix, and offset conjunctions (combinations of adjacent features within a window of size six).

Banko and Etzioni [1] created a O-CRF (Open CRF) system for large-scale extraction of relations without any relation-specific user input. The system is self-supervised by applying relation-independent knowledge to Penn Treebank and collect samples which were labeled as relational tuples. Eight lexico-syntactic patterns that captured relations for binary relationships are produced in this work. For example, the sentence "*<Einstein>received<the Nobel Prize> in 1921*" matches the lexico-syntactic pattern E1-verb-E2, thus there is a relation between *<Einstein>* and *<the Nobel Prize>*. The features used in O-CRF are POS tag, context words, and a connection of features between 6 words on the left and 6 words on the right of the current word. O-CRF uses only context words that belong to closed class (e.g., preposition and determiner), not Noun or Verb.

Skounakis et al. [10] used Hierarchical Hidden Markov Models (HHMM) to extract subcellular-localization relations from text using shallow parsing, POS tag, and context words. Kambhatla [5] employed Maximum Entropy models for relation extraction with features derived from word, entity type, mention level, overlap, dependency tree and parse tree.

There are several research on information extraction in Vietnamese. However, most of them focus on entity extraction. As far as we know, there is only one work related to relation extraction [11]. The purpose of relation extraction in [11] is to identify relation between entities in question of a question answering system. Based on a set of basic examples (called seeds) for each relation, the system in [11] repeatedly carries out the learning process to produce patterns and a larger set of seeds for the relation. Rough patterns are created from occurrences. After the rough patterns being clustered, the centroids of clusters, which are called refined patterns, are determined. To generate new seeds, the system creates queries from these refined patterns and uses Google search engine to get snippets that contain new seeds. To identify relation that question asks about, the system chooses the best match pattern to the question. The relation that the pattern belongs to is the relation that question asks about.

Our approach inherits the ideas of Banko and Etzioni [1] by using the string between two entities as a signal to detect relations and by considering the RE problem as the problem of sequential labeling using the CRF. The first-order Markov model is used as assumption about state dependency. The CRF will be introduced next.

3   Conditional Random Field

Before introducing the CRF, we first look at how to formulate the RE task as a sequential labeling problem. Given a tokenization of an observation sequence and three relations named Per_Loc, Per_Pos, Per_Org for any particular relation type R_X, relation label could be one of the forms B_R_X (Begin of the relation R_X), I_R_X (Inside of the relation R_X), or O (not of the relation). RE can be reduced to the problem of assigning one label in 5*2+1 =11 labels to each token. For example, the sentence "Anh/*he,brother* Nguyễn văn Nam/*Nguyen van Nam* đang/*is* sống/*living* ở/*in* Hà Nội/*Hanoi*" has a Per_Loc relation, then this sentence can be labeled as "O O O O O B_R_Per_Loc I_R_Per_Loc O O".

3.1   Definition of Conditional Random Field

Conditional random fields are undirected graphical models trained to maximize a conditional probability [8].

A linear-chain CRF with parameters $\Delta = \{ \lambda, ... \}$ defines a conditional probability for a state (or label) sequence $y = y_1 ... y_T$ given an input sequence $x = x_1 ... x_T$ (where T is the length of sequence) to be

$$P_\lambda(y \mid x) = \frac{1}{Z_x} \exp\left(\sum_{t=1}^{T} \sum_k \lambda_k f_k(y_{t-1}, y_t, x, t) \right)$$ where Z_x is the normalization constant

that makes the probability of all state sequences sum to one, $f_{k(y_{t-1}, y_t, x, t)}$ is a feature function which is often binary-valued, but can be real-valued, and λ_k is a learned weight associated with feature f_k. Large positive values for λ_k indicate a preference for such an event, while large negative values make the event unlikely. There are two types of features: node feature and edge feature.

The node feature $f_k^{node}(y_t, x, t) = \delta[y_t, l] g_m(x, t)$ takes care of label y_t at time t, where $\delta[y_t, l]$ returns 1 if $y_t = l$ and 0 otherwise, $g_m(x, t)$ takes care of the raw data and returns a (real or binary) value.

For example, $f_1^{node}(y_{10}, x, 10) = g_{100}(x, 10)$ if y_{10} = B_R_Per_Loc; =0 otherwise. And $g_{100}(x, 10) = 1$ if x = "sống/*live*"; =0 otherwise.

The edge feature $f_k^{edge}(y_t, y_{t+1}, x, t) = \delta[y_t, l] \delta[y_{t+1}, l']$ realizes the relationship between the two nearly labels y_t and y_{t+1}. For example, $f_2^{edge}(y_{10}, y_{11}, x, 10) = 1$ if y_{10} = B_R_Per_Loc and y_{11} = I_R_Per_Loc; $f_2^{edge}(y_{10}, y_{11}, x, 10) = 0$ otherwise.

3.2 Training CRF

The weights of a CRF, $\Delta = \{\lambda, \ldots\}$, are a set to maximize the conditional log-likelihood of labeled sequences in some training set, $D = \{(x,1)^{(1)}, (x,1)^{(2)}, \ldots, (x,1)^{(N)}\}$:

$$L_{\Delta} = \sum_{j=1}^{N} \log(P_{\Delta}(l^{(j)} \mid x^{(j)})) - \sum_{k} \frac{\lambda_k^2}{2\delta^2}$$

where the second sum is a Gaussian prior over parameters (with variance δ) that provides smoothing to help cope with sparsity in the training data.

When the training labels make the state sequence unambiguous (as they often do in practice), the likelihood function in exponential models such as CRF is convex, so there are no local maxima, and thus finding the global optimum is guaranteed. It has recently been shown that quasi-Newton methods, such as L-BFGS, are significantly more efficient than traditional iterative scaling and even conjugate gradient [8, 9].

3.3 Inference in CRF

Inference in CRF is to find the most probably state sequence y* corresponding to the given observation sequence x.

$$y^* = \arg\max_{y^*} p(y \mid x)$$

In order to find y*, one can apply the dynamic programming technique with a slightly modified version of the original Viterbi algorithm for HMMs.

4 Relation Extraction in Vietnamese Text

Our relation extractor takes as input a set of Vietnamese documents that have been annotated for name entities including Person, Position, Organization, Location. It derives relations between these entities including Per_Loc, Per_Pos, Per_Org. In the scope of this research, only relations within a sentence are considered. Let us look at the nature of these relations expressed in Vietnamese sentences first.

4.1 Relations in Vietnamese

Entity relations in Vietnamese sentences can be expressed in several ways. In most of cases, there are characters, words, or phrases that can signal such relations. These cases are shown below.

Case 1: The main verb phrase in a sentence signals a relation.
Simplified pattern: E1 <verb phrase> E2

Example 1:
Ông Nguyễn Tất Đắc (E1) đang làm việc tại **Trường Đại học Bách khoa Hà Nội** (E2).
   Mr. Nguyen Tat Dac (E1) is working at Hanoi University of Technology (E2)

The verb "làm việc/*work*" in the above sentence denotes a **Per_Org** relation between two entities, "Ông Nguyễn Tất Đắc/*Mr. Nguyen Tat Dac*" and "Trường Đại học Bách khoa Hà Nội/*Hanoi University of Technology*".

Example 2:

Ông Nguyễn Cảnh Lương (E1) hiện giữ chức vụ **phó hiệu trưởng** (E2) Trường Đại học Bách khoa Hà Nội.

*Mr.Nguyen Canh Luong (E1) currently keeps the position of **vice-president** (E2) of Hanoi University of Technology.*

The verb phrase "giữ chức vụ/ *keeps the position*" indicates a Per_Pos relation between two entities "Ông Nguyễn Cảnh Lương/*Mr. Nguyen Canh Luong*" and "phó hiệu trưởng /*vice-president*".

Case 2: Two entities are separated by comma, colon, or hyphen.
Simplified pattern: E1 < , | : | - > E2 E3 <remaining text>

Example 3:

Ông Lê Minh Đạt (E1), **trưởng** (E2) **Trạm Thú y huyện Gia Lâm** (E3) cho biết, xã Kim Sơn là nơi dịch lây lan nhanh nhất.

*Mr. Le Minh Dat (E1), **chief** (E2) of **the veterinary station of Gia Lam district** (E3), said Kim Son commune is the place where the epidemic is spreading fastest.*

The comma in Example 3 separates the Person entity "Ông Lê Minh Đạt /*Mr. Le Minh Dat*" and the Position entity "trưởng/*chief*". A Per_Pos relation is held between these two entities. The above example also has another relation: a Per_Org relation between the Organization entity "Trạm Thú y huyện Gia Lâm/*the veterinary station of Gia Lam district*" and the Person entity "Ông Lê Minh Đạt /*Mr. Le Minh Dat*". By this example, we also would like to illustrate a fact that an Organization entity always stands right after a Position entity in Vietnamese text.

Case 3: Two entities are adjacent.
Simplified pattern: E1 E2 <remaining text>

Example 4:

Thủ tướng (E1) **Nguyễn Tấn Dũng** (E2) cùng nguyên Tổng bí thư Lê Khả Phiêu đã đến thăm hỏi và trao huân chương lao động hạng nhì cho cán bộ nhân viên ban quản lý cụm phà.

*Prime Minister (E1) **Nguyen Tan Dung** (E2) and the former General Secretary Le Kha Phieu visited and awarded the second-class labor medal for management staffs of the ferry clusters.*

The Position entity "Thủ tướng/*Prime Minister*" and the Person entity "Nguyễn Tấn Dũng/*Nguyen Tan Dung*" are adjacent in Example 4. These two entities are related by a Per_Pos relation.

Example 3 above is also an example for Case 3, in which the Position entity is adjacent to the Organization entity.

Case 4: Two entities are separated by another entity.
Simplified pattern: E1 E2 E3 <remaining text>

Example 5:

Bộ trưởng (E1) **Bộ Giáo dục và Đào tạo** (E2) **Nguyễn Thiện Nhân** (E3) đến thăm trường Đại học Quốc gia Hà Nội.

The Minister (E1) of the Ministry of Education and Training (E2) Nguyen Thien Nhan (E3) visited the Hanoi National University.

There is a Per_Pos relation between the Position entity "Bộ trưởng/*The Minister*" and the Person entity "Nguyễn Thiện Nhân/*Nguyen Thien Nhan*". These entities are separated by a third entity – the Organization entity "Bộ Giáo dục và Đào tạo/*the Ministry of Education and Training*".

The following conclusions are withdrawn from the about cases:

- Words and phrases near the two entities, especially the words/phrases between them, are important factors in finding the relation between two entities.
- In recognizing a relation between two entities in a sentence, information about other entities in the sentence is also an important signal.

From this point of view, the features used in our system to recognize relations between entities are shown in Table 1.

Table 1. Features used in our system to recognize relations

Feature	Meaning	Example
word	words within a sentence	làm việc/*work*, sống ở/*live in*
POS tag	Part of Speech	N, V, Adj, Adv
Entity type	The type of the entity that belongs to the considered relation	Organization (*công ty phát triển nông thôn/rural development company*), Location (*Hà Nội/ Ha noi*).
OutR_Entity	The type of the entity that is in the same sentence with the considered relation and does not belong to the relation	Person (*Ông Thanh Minh/Mr.Thanh Minh*), Organization (*công ty phát triển nông thôn/ rural development company*), Location (*Hà Nội/ Ha noi*).
Entity's index	The index of an entity in a sentence	Ông Thanh Minh/*Mr.Thanh Minh* (E1) giám đốc/*director* (E2) công ty phát triển nông thôn/*rural development company* (E3).

4.2 Relation Extraction

4.2.1 Training

The input of this process is training documents whose entities and theirs relations have been annotated. An example of the training documents is shown below:

Example 6:

Ông <Per:1>Nguyễn Việt Hùng</Per:1> hiện tại đang sống ở <Loc:2>Hà Nội</Loc:2> và <r-per-org:1-3>làm việc tại</r-per-org:1-3><Org:3>Trường Đại học Bách khoa Hà Nội</Org:3>.

Mr. <Per:1>Nguyen Viet Hung</Per:1> is living in <Loc:2>Hanoi<Loc:2> and <r-per-org:1-3>is working at<r-per-org:1-3><Org:3>Hanoi University of Technology</Org:3>.

The numbers inside a tag are indexes of entities in the sentence. For example, <r-per-org:1-3> means there is a Per_Org relation between the first entity "Nguyễn Việt Hùng/*Nguyen Viet Hung*" and the third entity "Trường Đại học Bách khoa Hà Nội/*Hanoi University of Technology*".

Actually, there are two relations in this sentence: Per-Loc and Per-Org. We only consided the Per-Org relation by tagging the phrase signalling for this relation: <r-per-org:1-3>làm việc tại</r-per-org:1-3>. This tag means the phrase "làm việc tại/is working at" signals a Per-Org relation between the first entity and the third entity.

The training documents is first parsed by a POS tagger to separate documents into words and to get the syntactic role of words in the sentences. Then different features that are used in the CRF algorithm are calculated. To evaluate the effect of window sizes of the contextual information to the system performance, different window sizes are used in the learning process. The window size is considered as n words on the left, the word itself, and n words on the right of the current word. In our experiment, n is chosen to be equal of 2, 4, 6, and 8.

4.2.2 Inference

The input for the inference process are documents whose entities have been annotated. Sentences with more than one entity are considered for the relation extracting process. These sentences are first analyzed by a POS tagger. Then they are parsed by the CRF inference module using features mentioned in Table 1.

5 Experiments and Discussion

Our experiments used a data set of 720 Vietnamese sentences taken from VnExpress (http://www.vnexpress.net) and DanTri (http://dantri.com.vn/) newspapers that were annotated manually. Each of these sentences has at least two entities and one relation. Per_Loc, Per_Pos, and Per_Org relations are used in the data set, in which the number of examples for each relation are 240, 260, and 220, respectively. When learning one relation, positive examples of other relations are considered as negative examples for the relation being learned (see Example 6).

The data set of each relation was randomly partitioned into six subsets of equal size (in number of sentences). Five subsets were used for training and the remaining subset was used for testing. Only relations within a sentence are considered. The experiments were repeated five times. The performances (Precision P, Recall R, and F-score F) reported in this paper are the average results over these experiments.

The window sizes of n words on the left and n words on the right of the current word are used in the experiments. The values of n used in our experiments are 2, 4, 6, and 8.

In order to evaluate the effect of the OutR_Entity feature to the system performance, experiments have been carried out in both cases: with this feature and without this feature.

Table 2 shows the highest F-score of the relation Per_Org when using information about the Position entity is received at the window size of 5 (n=2) and the lowest one at the window size of 13 (n=6). The average F-score when using information about the Position entity (82.10%) is higher than when this information is not used (69.26%). It proves that information about the Position entity increases the accuracy of recognizing the Per_Org relation.

Table 2. Performance of the Per_Org relation

Window size (n words on the left, n words on the right)	Using information about the **Position** entity			Without using the **OutR_Entity** feature		
	P (%)	R (%)	F (%)	P (%)	R (%)	F (%)
2-2	94	76.66	84.44	64	54.66	58.96
4-4	91	76.66	83.22	86.66	61.16	71.71
6-6	94.66	68.66	79.60	87.14	63.66	73.57
8-8	90.33	73.66	81.15	85	63.66	72.80
Average	92.50	73.91	82.10	80.7	60.79	69.26

Table 3. Performance of the Per_Pos relation

Window size (n-n)	Using information about the **Organization** entity			Without using the **OutR_Entity** feature		
	P (%)	R (%)	F (%)	P (%)	R (%)	F (%)
2-2	93	86	89.36	95	73	82.56
4-4	95	81	87.44	95	73	82.56
6-6	95	72	81.92	90	73	80.61
8-8	92	86	88.90	94	63	75.44
Average	93.75	81.25	86.91	93.5	70.5	80.29

Table 3 also proves that information about the Organization entity increases the accuracy of recognizing the Per_Pos relation.

Table 4. Performance of the Per_Loc relation

Window size (n-n)	Using information about the **Position** entity and the **Organization** entity			Without using the **OutR_Entity** feature		
	P (%)	R (%)	F (%)	P (%)	R (%)	F (%)
2-2	90.06	87.5	88.76	90.14	82.5	86.15
4-4	92	90	90.99	93.55	92.5	93.02
6-6	93.55	85	89.07	95.14	87.5	91.16
8-8	90.5	75	82.02	90.14	82.5	86.15
Average	91.53	84.38	87.71	92.24	86.25	89.12

Table 4 shows the average F-score of the Per_Loc relation when using information about OutR_Entity (the Organization entity and the Position entity) is lower than when such information is not used. This is because information about the Organization entity and the Position entity does not involve in the Per_Loc relation. Therefore, using such information only adds noise to the system.

There are two important conclusions withdrawing from our experiments. First, it is not true that the higher window size, the higher the F-score of the entity relation. Previous works on relation extractions for English using CRF often used the window size of thirteen (n = 6). However, this window size is not the optimal value in our system.

Second, some entity types can be used as signals to detect relations between other entities. The application of the OutR_Entity feature increases the system perfomance in such cases. In other cases, it will reduce the system performance.

The closest research to this paper is [1] and [11]. The differences between Banko and Etzioni's research [1] and ours are: (i) Banko and Etzioni's work do not need any relation-specific input; (ii) context words in Banko and Etzioni belong to closed class (preposition, determiner) , whereas our context words can also be verbs or nouns; and (iii) the entity that do not belong to the relation is also considered in determine the relation name in our research.

Since Banko and Etzioni [1] do not use the same corpus as ours, we cannot compare directly the performance of the two systems. Banko and Etzioni [1] received the average precision of 75% for four entities: Acquisition, Birthplace, InventorOf, and WonAward. However, the average recall of this system is quite low (18.4%).

In [11], 100 questions for 10 relations are used for the testing experiment in the travelling domain. Each relation presents a relationship between two entity classes, one of which is the travelling point, another is the corresponding place (e.g., the relation "Festival – Place"). The system achieved 89.7% precision and 91.4% ability to give the answer. Since relations used in [11] are different than ours, we cannot compare the two systems.

6 Conclusions

This paper represented a relation extraction system for Vietnamese text using Conditional Random Fields. The features used in the system are word, POS tag, entity type, entity's index and contextual information. In order to evaluate the effect of the contextual information to the system performance, different window sizes have been tested in our experiments. It shown that the window size is an important factor to the system accuracy. The experiments also indicated that the window size is not directly proportional to the F-score of the system.

We also investigated the effect of information about other entities (OutR_Entity) in recognizing the relation between two entities in the same sentence. It shown that the system performance increases in case OutR_Entity can signal the relation.

The limitation of this research is that only relations between entities within a sentence are considered, as some other English research did. Our future work concentrates on finding methods to extract relations between entities in different sentences. We also investigate other features to increase the system performance. In addition, we also would like to test the system with a larger corpus in order to get a more accurate evaluation of the system.

Acknowledgments. The research leading to this paper was supported by the National Project DTDL2009G/42 "Study, design and develop smart robots to exploit multimedia information", under grant 42/2009G/HD-DTDL. We would like to thank the project and people involved in this project.

References

1. Banko, M., Etzioni, O.: The tradeoffs between open and traditional relation extraction. In: Proceedings of the 46th Annual Meeting of the Association for Computational Linguistics, pp. 28–36 (2008)
2. Culotta, A., McCallum, A., Betz, J.: Integrating probabilistic extraction models and data mining to discover relations and patterns in text. In: Proceedings of HLT-NAACL 2006, pp. 296–303 (2006)
3. Giuliano, C., Lavelli, A., Romano, L.: Exploiting Shallow Linguistic Information for Relation Extraction from Biomedical Literature. In: Proceedings of EACL (2006)
4. Giuliano, C., Lavelli, A., Romano, L.: Relation extraction and the influence of automatic named-entity recognition. ACM Transactions on Speech and Language Processing (TSLP) 5(1) (2007)
5. Kambhatla, N.: Combining Lexical, Syntactic, and Semantic Features with Maximum Entropy Models for Extracting Relations. In: Proceedings of the 42nd Annual Meeting of the Association for Computational Linguistics (2004)
6. Lafferty, J., McCallum, A., Pereira, F.: Conditional random fields: probabilistic models for segmenting and labeling sequence data. In: Proceedings of ICML, pp. 282–290 (2001)
7. McCallum, A.: Efficiently Inducing Features of Conditional Random Fields. In: Nineteenth Conference on Uncertainty in Artificial Intelligence (2003)
8. Malouf, R.: A comparison of algorithms for maximum entropy parameter estimation. In: Sixth Workshop on Computational Language Learning (2002)
9. Sha, F., Pereira, F.: Shallow Parsing with Conditional Random Fields. In: Proceeding of Human Language Technology NAACL (2003)
10. Skounakis, M., Craven, M., Ray, S.: Hierarchical hidden Markov models for information extraction. In: Proceedings of the 18th International Joint Conference on Artificial Intelligence, Mexico, Acapulco (2003)
11. Tran, M.V., Nguyen, V.V., Pham, T.U., Tran, T.O., Ha, Q.T.: An Experimental Study of Vietnamese Question Answering System. In: Proceedings of the International Conference on Asian Language Processing, pp. 152–155 (2009)
12. Zhao, S., Grishman, R.: Extracting relations with integrated information using kernel methods. In: Proceedings of the 43rd Annual Meeting of the Association for Computational Linguistics, pp. 419–426 (2005)
13. Zhou, G., Su, J., Zhang, J., Zhang, M.: Exploring various knowledge in relation extraction. In: Proceedings of the 43rd Annual Meeting of the Association for Computational Linguistics, pp. 427–434 (2005)

A Sparse L_2-Regularized Support Vector Machines for Large-Scale Natural Language Learning

Yu-Chieh Wu[1], Yue-Shi Lee[3], Jie-Chi Yang[2], and Show-Jane Yen[3]

[1] Finance Department and School of Communication, Ming Chuan University,
No. 250 Zhong Shan N. Rd., Sec. 5, Taipei 111, Taiwan
bcbb@db.csie.ncu.edu.tw
[2] Graduate Institute of Network Learning Technology, National Central University,
No.300, Jhong-Da Rd., Jhongli City, Taoyuan County 32001, Taiwan, R.O.C.
yang@cl.ncu.edu.tw
[3] Department of Computer Science and Information Engineering, Ming Chuan University,
No.5, De-Ming Rd, Gweishan District, Taoyuan 333, Taiwan, R.O.C.
{leeys,sjyen}@mcu.edu.tw

Abstract. Linear support vector machines (SVMs) have become one of the most prominent classification algorithms for many natural language learning problems such as sequential labeling tasks. Even though the L_2-regularized SVMs yields slightly more superior accuracy than L_1-SVM, it produces too much near but non zero feature weights. In this paper, we present a cutting-weight algorithm to guide the optimization process of L_2-SVM into sparse solution. To verify the proposed method, we conduct the experiments with three well-known sequential labeling tasks and one dependency parsing task. The result shows that our method achieved at least 400% feature parameter reduction rates in comparison to the original L_2-SVM, with almost no change in accuracy and training times. In terms of run time efficiency, our method is faster than the original L_2-regularized SVMs at least 20% in all tasks.

Keywords: L_2-regularization, part-of-speech tagging, support vector machines, machine learning.

1 Introduction

Mining large-scale unlabeled data has received a great attention in recent years. Such methods bring important impacts on not only the system accuracy but also the scalability problems. Though one could train the learners with cloud computing servers, this is not the true way of handling large-scale natural language learning problems.

Kernel machines, such as support vector machines (SVMs) had been wildly used as learners in many natural language learning tasks [8]. Nevertheless, the training time of linear kernel SVM (with either L_1-norm [5] or L_2-norm [4, 7]) is now can be obtained in linear time. It is usually the case that the L_2-regularized SVMs achieves slightly better accuracy than the L_1-regularized SVMs. Unfortunately, L_2-SVM often generates dense models where most feature weights are small but non-zero. The situation is even more salient when training large-scale natural language learning tasks,

P.-J. Cheng et al. (Eds.): AIRS 2010, LNCS 6458, pp. 340–349, 2010.
© Springer-Verlag Berlin Heidelberg 2010

like Chinese word segmentations. Maintaining such high-dense feature weights is not easy for common processors. In addition, the denser the model, the slower the testing it achieves.

In this paper, we present a cutting-weight algorithm for L_2-SVM for sequential labeling tasks. Our method iteratively guides the L_2-SVM optimization process toward sparse by disregarding a set of weak features. The classic feature selection approaches can also provide downstream input to the cutting-weight algorithm. To validate the effectiveness, we compare our method on three well-known benchmark corpora, namely, CoNLL-2000 syntactic chunking [14], SIGHAN Chinese word segmentation [13, 17, 18], and Chinese word dependency parsing [15]. The experimental result shows that our method is not only faster than the original L_2-SVM but also with no change in accuracy.

2 L_2-Regularized SVMs

Assume a binary classification problem with n labeled examples, $(x_1, y_1), (x_2, y_2),...,(x_n, y_n)$ where $x_i \in \Re^d$ and $y_i \in \{+1,-1\}$. To obtain the linear classifier W (hypothesis) $y = W \cdot x + b$ the modified finite Newton L_2-SVM solves:

$$\min\{\frac{\lambda}{2}W^T W + \frac{1}{2}\sum_{i=1}^{n}\xi_i^2\} \text{ s.t. } \forall i, y_i(W \cdot x_i + b) \geq 1 - \xi_i \tag{1}$$

For simplicity, bias b can be easily modeled by adding an additional of routine constant to each x_i [11]. $\lambda(=1/C)$ is the regularization parameter that controls the trade-off between margin size and training error.

Following [7], the function of L_2-SVM is a strictly convex, quadratic, and first order differentiable function and has a unique solution. The solution of L_2-SVM objective function is to minimize for:

$$\frac{\partial(2)}{\partial W} = \lambda \times W + X^T(X^T W - Y) \text{ and } (\lambda \times I + X^T X)W = X^T Y \tag{2}$$

where X is the training data matrix (i.e. $X \in \Re^{n \times d}$) and Y is the column vector which contains the label of training examples. I is the identity matrix. Keerthi and DeCoste further introduce the modified finite Newton method to solve (2) with Conjugate Gradient (CG) [2] scheme refer to as CGLS.

3   Sparse L_2-Regularized SVMs Optimization

One good property of the L_2-SVM is that its objective function is strictly convex, first order derivable, and can be directly optimized in primal form. By following this line, we propose a cutting-weight algorithm to guide the *dense* weight vector into *sparse*. First, we decompose the weight vector into two different parts, weight vector W_1 (representative) and vector W_2 (non-representative), and $W = W_1 + W_2$. Thus the original objective function of (1) can be re-written as:

$$\min\{\frac{\lambda}{2}(W_1 + W_2)^T(W_1 + W_2) + \sum_{i=1}^{n}\xi_i^2\} \quad \text{s.t. } \forall i, \; y_i(W_1 \cdot x_i + W_2 \cdot x_i + b) \geq 1 - \xi_i \tag{3}$$

The optimization problem is similar to solve:

$$(\lambda \times I + X^T X)(W_1 + W_2) = X^T Y \quad \text{and} \quad (W_1 + W_2) = (\lambda \times I + X^T X)^{-1} X^T Y \tag{4}$$

Clearly if W_1 (derived from W) is close enough to abstract W, say $W_1 \cong W$, then solving (1) is almost the same as solving (3). In this way, by assuming that W_2 is far *limited* to a zero weight vector and can be further disregarded from the objective function, then the objective function becomes:

$$\min\{\frac{\lambda}{2}W_1^T W_1 + \sum_{i=1}^{n}\xi_i^2\} \text{ s.t. } \forall i, \; y_i(W_1 \cdot x_i + b) \geq 1 - \xi_i \tag{5}$$

In other words, (5) is the exact solution of (1) iff $W_1 = W$, otherwise it is the approximate solution of (3). This implies that the feature weights in W_2 directly affect the degree of approximation.

One important property of L_2-norm regularization is that it pushes a value less and less as it moves toward zero [3]. To find sparse model for L_2-SVM, we start to find W_2 which can be searched from 0. We present a cutting-weight method to construct W_2 in which W_1 can be easily obtained by $W_1 = W - W_2$. That is for each feature weight w_i in W_2, it satisfies:

$$\forall w_i \in W_2 \quad -\varepsilon \leq w_i \leq \varepsilon$$

Similarly for each feature weight w_i in W_1, it satisfies:

$$\forall w_i' \in W_1 \quad w_i' > \varepsilon \text{ and } w_i' < -\varepsilon$$

ε is the cutting-weight parameter which controls the model sparsity and approximation of (5). It can also be interpreted as a threshold for distinguishing relevant (representative) or irrelevant (non-representative) feature values.

Obviously the parameter ε determines the trade-off between the model sparsity and how approximate W_1 reaches. By setting up this technique, we modified the original training algorithm. Fig. 1 outlines the presented sparse L_2-SVM optimization algorithm. The general optimization technique is the same as the modified finite Newton method for L_2-SVM [7]. The difference is that our method refines the weight vector by preserving the relevant features before checking the L_2-SVM optimality. Such technique could also be applied to the other gradient descent-based linear SVM optimization methods. For example, line 6-8 in Fig. 1 can be replaced by introducing the dual-coordinate descent algorithms [4]. Line 12 can be replaced by verifying the difference between maximum and minimum projected gradient (Property 3 of Theorem 2 in [4]).

1. Initialize W^0 ;
2. $iter := 0$;
3. While (! converged) {
4. **Set up (3) using**
5. $SV^k := \{i \mid y_i(W^k \cdot x_i) < 1\}$ //**Get the support vectors**
6. **Solve (3) with CG methods and obtain** $\hat{W}^k$;
7. Let $S^k := \hat{W}^k - W^k$, do a line search to find:
8. $\alpha^k := \arg\min_{\alpha \geq 0} f(W^k + \alpha \times S^k)$;
9. Update weight vector
10. $W^{k+1} := W^k + \alpha^k \times S^k$;
11. s.t. $\forall w_i \in W^{k+1}$ $w_i > \varepsilon$ and $w_i < -\varepsilon$ otherwise $w_i := 0$;
12. if ($\nabla f(W^k) == 0$)
13. stop;
14. $iter := iter + 1$;
15. }

Fig. 1. Sparse L_2-SVM optimization algorithm

3.1 Speed-Up Local Classifiers

For an m class multiclass problem, it needs to manage at least m weight vectors. Usually the larger the m and dimension are, the slower testing time is obtained. Usually the weight vectors are stored in an $m \times d$ matrix. However, it is not a good idea to represent the sparse model since most of the feature weight is zero. When m and d become large, the matrix will be unmanageable in practice.

To solve it, we further introduce the indexing idea from the Information Retrieval (IR) community to represent the sparse weight vectors. The basic concept is to *retrieve* the testing vector in the index file. Fig. 2 illustrates an example of the index file. For each dimension, we store the set of non-zero feature weight with as postings (linked list structures). The posting directly indicates the corresponding class id and its feature weight. Therefore, for each feature weight f_i in testing vector, by walking at the index file, we can easily retrieve a set of relevant categories that contains the same feature.

We do not discuss how to construct the index file and its complexity here since it can be done with existing IR approaches [12]. Therefore, the computational time complexity of multiclass SVM is $O(m \times f_{avg})$ where f_{avg} is the average length of testing example. On the contrary, the testing time complexity of the sparse multiclass representation depends on the number of *relevant* items, i.e. $O(m_{avg} \times f_{avg})$ where m_{avg} is the average number of relevant items per feature and $m_{avg} \leq m$.

The use of indexing file to SVM is not new. For example, [9] introduced a similar idea to manage large number of support vectors generated from the polynomial kernel SVM.

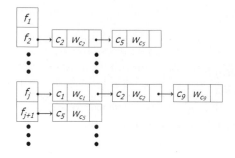

Fig. 2. An example of index file representation

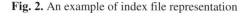

1.	F_{base} : the basic feature set;
2.	F_{cand} : a set of feature candidates;
3.	γ: a threshold parameter that is used to control the goodness of a newly added feature;
4.	δ: a threshold parameter that is used to control the goodness of one iteration;
5.	*Inner_acc* : the accuracy of the F_{base};
6.	While (! converged) {
7.	*Best_Acc* := *Inner_acc*;
8.	for (i :=1~| F_{cand} |) {
9.	Derive one feature F_i from F_{cand};
10.	F := F_{base} + F_i;
11.	Train SVM model by the feature set F;
12.	Evaluate the accuracy Acc_i with the trained model;
13.	if (Acc_i > *Inner_acc*+γ) {
14.	F := F_{base} + F_i;
15.	*Inner_acc* := Acc_i;
16.	}
17.	}
18.	if ((*Inner_acc* - *Best_acc*) < δ)
19.	converged := true;
20.	}

Fig. 3. An algorithm for bottom-up feature search

3.2 Search the Optimal Feature Set

To further enhance the accuracy, we also design a simple feature selection algorithm which makes use of bottom-up search. Fig. 3 gives the designed feature search algorithm.

Before start search, a set of basic feature set is pre-defined and the set of candidates are stored in F_{cand}. The algorithm runs iteratively add one feature from F_{cand} and check whether the new feature leads to better accuracy or not. Line 13 of Fig. 3, we set a parameter γ which is used to control the quality of a new feature. If the resulted performance is greater than the threshold, the feature is added while the resulted accuracy will be kept. The algorithm will stop when the resulted accuracy no significant change. That means the for-loop (Line 8 to Line 17) should produce better results over the threshold δ.

4 Experiments

To evaluate our method, we ran experiments on three tasks: CoNLL-2000 syntactic chunking, three Chinese word segmentation tasks that derived from SIGHAN-3, and the Chinese Dependency parsing [16]. Table 1 shows the statistics of those datasets.

By following most literatures, we adopted the IOB2 with forward direction chunking scheme for CoNLL-2000 chunking task. As encouraged by [18], incorporating global information (AV feature) and extending the boundary information can improve the accuracy. In this paper, we include the AV features and make use of 6-tags[1] rather than I and B two tags for Chinese word segmentation task. The feature set and the settings of the Chinese dependency parsing were set the same as previous work [16].

To validate the proposed idea, we re-implemented SVM-MFN (L_2-norm with modified finite Newton method) [7] and LibLinear-L_2 [4]. To handle multiclass problems, we adopted the well-known one-versus-all (OVA) method. For the remaining experiments, we simply set the feature cut as 2 for all linear SVMs and $\varepsilon = 10^{-4}$ for our method. For a fair comparison, these methods received the same input training data, the same regularization parameter[2], and the same feature set. Table 2 lists the used feature set. All of the experiments were performed under the E6300 OC 3.2 GHz with 4GB RAM under the Server 2003 32bit environment.

Table 1. Dataset used in our experiments

Statistics		# of examples	# of sentences	# of categories
CoNLL-2000	Training	220K	8,935	11*2+1=23
	Testing	48K	2,011	
SIGHAN-3 UPUC	Training	500K	18,804	6
	Testing	154K	5,117	
SIGHAN-3 MSRA	Training	2.16M	46,364	6
	Testing	63K	4,365	
SIGHAN-3 CityU	Training	1.6M	57,274	6
	Testing	220K	7,511	
Chinese word dependency parsing	Training	740K	16,909	12*2+2=26
	Testing	82K	1,878	

4.1 Results

Table 3 lists overall experimental results of the selected three tasks. The table contains accuracy ($F_{(\beta)}$ rate), training time (sec.) and testing time (sec.), the difference between objective goals, and the number of iterations the learner takes. The model size implies the memory requirement in run-time. The larger number the model is, the larger memory usage requires. As shown in Table 3, our method produced much smaller model size without changing in accuracy. In terms of training, our method truncates near-zero features and makes tight model. Intuitively, the calculation cost of the objective function (eq. (3)) is reduced.

---

[1] Similar to IOB2 tagging scheme, the 6-tags: S/B/BI/I/IE/E indicate the Single/Begin/ SecondBegin/Interior/BeforeEnd/ End of a chunk.
[2] $C=0.1/1$ for the CoNLL-2000 chunking task and SIGHAN-3 datasets.

Table 2. Feature templates used in our experiments

Feature type	CoNLL-2000	SIGHAN-3 Chinese word segmentation
Unigram	$w_{-2} \sim w_{+2}$	$w_{-2} \sim w_{+2}$
Bigram	$(w_{-2},w_{-1}),(w_{-1},w_0),(w_0,w_{+1}),$ $(w_{+1},w_{+2}),(w_{+1},w_{-1})$	$(w_{-1},w_0),(w_0,w_{+1}),$ (w_{+1},w_{-1})
POS	$p_{-2} \sim p_{+2}$	
POS bigram	$(p_{-2},p_{-1}),(p_{-1},p_0),(p_0,p_{+1}),$ $(p_{+1},p_{+2}),(p_{+1},p_{-1})$	
POS trigram	$(p_{-2},p_{-1},p_0),(p_{-1},p_0,p_{+1}),$ $(p_{-3},p_{-2},p_{-1}),(p_0,p_{+1},p_{+2}),\ (p_{+1},p_{+2},p_{+3})$	
Word+POS bigram	$(w_{-1},p_0),(w_{-2},p_{-1})\ (w_0,p_{+1}),\ (w_{+1},p_{+2})$	
Other features	2~4 suffix letters 2~4 prefix letters Orthographic feature	AV feature [17] of 2~6 grams
History	$Prev.chunk_{-1}, Prev.chunk_{-2}$	

We also run another experiment to compare with the "final cutting" method. This method simply eliminates the weights after the conventional SVM training with the same ε. Table 4 lists the comparison result of the final-cut. In this experiment, we scale down the epsilon to 0.05 since there will be no accuracy difference when epsilon is larger than 0.005. As shown in Table 4, clearly, our method yields more superior results than f-cut in terms of model size and accuracy. In this experiment, we fail to train SVM-MFN with (ε=0.05) in short time. It takes more than 20 hours to train while resulting slightly worse result than f-cut (93.96 v.s. 93.90).

Note that we should carefully select suitable value for parameter ε. The input feature value is either 0 or 1 in many natural language learning tasks. There is no need to use large epsilon. Observing by the above experiments, we found that $\varepsilon=10^{-3} \sim 10^{-15}$ usually yield much smaller model size, better training/testing time cost.

Table 3. The overall performance results of the selected tasks

Tasks			# of Iterations	Model Size (non-zero entries)	Sum of the objective goals	Training Time (sec.)	Testing Time (sec.)	Accuracy $(F_{(\beta)})$
CoNLL-2000	SVM-MFN	ε=0	290	4.20M	-2945.39	576.16	8.42	94.11
		ε=0.0001	305	0.36M	-2945.37	555.98	3.30	94.11
	LibLinear	ε=0	1134	0.40M	-2945.33	76.58	3.54	94.11
		ε=0.0001	1130	0.36M	-2945.33	77.34	3.29	94.11
SIGHAN3-CityU	SVM-MFN	ε=0	103	9.52M	-119927.00	13947.08	4.91	97.41
		ε=0.0001	103	2.21M	-119927.00	10713.27	3.70	97.41
	LibLinear	ε=0	424	2.32M	-119924.00	595.59	3.73	97.41
		ε=0.0001	424	2.22M	-119924.00	585.48	3.69	97.41
Chinese word dependency parsing	SVM-MFN	ε=0	332	51.36M	-6785.00	9455.59	7.95	81.71
		ε=0.0001	333	4.78M	-6810.19	9233.88	6.30	81.73
	LibLinear	ε=0	470	49.51M	-6810.06	591.33	7.23	81.71
		ε=0.0001	491	4.79M	-6810.06	591.50	6.31	81.71

Table 4. Performance comparison between simple "final-cut" and our approach

CoNLL-2000		Model size (non-zero weights)	Acc.
LibLinear	Our method	68,027	94.03
(ε=**0.05**)	F-cut	156,386	93.94
LibLinear	Our method	286,892	94.10
(ε=0.005)	F-cut	313,762	94.10
SVM-MFN	Our method	305,597	**94.14**
(ε=0.005)	F-cut	313,706	94.10

Table 5 lists the detail comparisons among the selected SVM optimization techniques in the CoNLL-2000 and SIGHAN-3 datasets. In this experiment, we still set (ε=0.0001) as default parameter value for our method.

In summary, our cutting-weight algorithm shows better training and testing time performance for most dataset with excepted for Liblinear(Multi). In terms of accuracy, the L_2-regularized groups such as SVM-MFN and Liblinear(L_2) yield more superior $F_{(\beta)}$ rate than the others. In terms of training time cost, the SVM-light performs significantly worse than the others and the Liblinear (multi) won the best training time efficiency. Even Liblinear (multi) shows great training time performance, it does not as accurate as the L_2-regularized groups. Also, its testing time is not fast.

By applying the proposed cutting-weight algorithm to SVM-MFN and Liblinear (L_2), both learners obtains better training and testing time costs than the original while resulting almost no change in accuracy. As compared to SVM-MFN, our cutting-weight optimization technique usually produces better training and much reduced testing time costs while keeping the same accuracy.

In this paper, we do not successfully conduct all experiments for SVM-light since the training time is not human-tolerable. For example, it costs more than one week to train one class with the MSRA and CityU dataset. That means it takes at least 6 weeks to train one Chinese word segmentor.

Table 5. Experimental results of different SVM optimization techniques

Tasks		**This paper**		SVM-MFN	Liblinear (L_2)	Liblinear (L_1)	SVM-perf	SVM-light	Liblinear (Mutli)
		SVM-MFN	Liblinear (L_2)						
CoNLL-2000	Tr.Time	556	77	576	77	73	336	2881	40
	Te.Time	3.30	3.29	8.42	3.54	3.30	4.52	3.97	3.42
	$F_{(\beta)}$	94.11	94.11	94.11	94.11	93.96	93.98	93.85	92.26
Chinese word dependency parsing	Tr.Time	6229	245	6859	246	312	4941	97538	312
	Te.Time	6.28	6.33	6.56	6.34	6.75	7.67	6.66	6.66
	$F_{(\beta)}$	81.72	81.71	81.72	81.71	81.66	80.42	79.90	81.83
SIGHAN-3 UPUC	Tr.Time	1247	138	1246	140	150	816	64657	93
	Te.Time	2.36	2.37	3.45	2.72	2.36	2.41	2.42	2.39
	$F_{(\beta)}$	93.95	93.95	93.95	93.95	93.99	93.94	93.91	93.89
SIGHAN-3 MSRA	Tr.Time	7398	481	8440	465	591	4323	Out-of-time-bound*	440
	Te.Time	1.63	1.63	2.66	1.95	2.06	2.05		2.08
	$F_{(\beta)}$	95.93	95.93	95.93	95.93	95.95	95.81		95.43
SIGHAN-3 CityU	Tr.Time	10713	585	13947	596	608	5119		408
	Te.Time	3.70	3.69	4.91	3.73	3.70	3.70		3.69
	$F_{(\beta)}$	97.41	97.41	97.41	97.41	97.30	97.33		97.34

* In our experiments, the overall training time of SVM-light is more than 1 week to train one category.

5 Conclusion

We presented a cutting-weight algorithm for L_2-SVM (online demo can be found here[3]) to save the model space for handling large-scale data. The experimental results show that our method achieves better accuracy on three well-known datasets, namely, CoNLL-2000 syntactic chunking, SIGHAN-3 Chinese word segmentation, and Chinese word dependency parsing. In addition, the results also show that there is no change in accuracy between our method and the original L_2-SVM, while it greatly reduced the model size and also reaches slightly faster training time and at least 20% improvement in runtime efficiency.

References

1. Collins, M.: Discriminative training methods for hidden Markov models: theory and experiments with perceptron algorithms. In: Empirical Methods in Natural Language Processing, pp. 1–8 (2002)
2. Frommer, A., Maaß, P.: Fast CG-based methods for Tikhonov-Phillips regularization. Journal of Scientific Computing 20(5), 1831–1850 (1999)
3. Gao, J., Andrew, G., Johnson, M., Toutanova, K.: A comparative study of parameter estimation methods for statistical natural language processing. In: 45th Annual Meeting of the Association of Computational Linguistics, pp. 824–831 (2007)
4. Hsieh, C.J., Chang, K.W., Lin, C.J., Keerthi, S., Sundararajan, S.: A dual coordinate descent method for large-scale linear SVM. In: 15th International Conference on Machine Learning, pp. 408–415 (2008)
5. Joachims, T.: Training linear SVMs in linear time. In: ACM Conference on Knowledge Discovery and Data Mining, pp. 217–226 (2006)
6. Keerthi, S., Sundararajan, S., Chang, K.W., Hsieh, C.J., Lin, C.J.: A sequential dual method for large scale multi-class linear SVMs. In: ACM Conference on Knowledge Discovery and Data Mining, pp. 408–416 (2008)
7. Keerthi, S., DeCoste, D.: A modified finite Newton method for fast solution of large scale linear SVMs. Journal of Machine Learning Research 6, 341–361 (2005)
8. Kudo, T. and Matsumoto, Y.: Chunking with support vector machines. In: North American Chapter of the Association for Computational Linguistics on Language Technologies, pp. 192-199 (2001)
9. Kudo, T., Matsumoto, Y.: Fast methods for kernel-based text analysis. In: The 41st Annual Meeting of the Association of Computational Linguistics, pp. 24–31 (2003)
10. Lafferty, J., McCallum, A., Pereira, F.: Conditional random fields: probabilistic models for segmenting and labeling sequence data. In: 8th International Conference on Machine Learning, pp. 282–289 (2001)
11. Mangasarian, O.L., Musicant, D.: Lagrangian support vector machines. Journal of Machine Learning Research 1, 161–177 (2001)
12. Manning, C., Raghavan, P., Schutze, H.: Introduction to Information Retrieval. Cambridge University Press, Cambridge (2008)
13. Ng, H.T., Low, J.K.: Chinese part-of-speech tagging: one-at-a-time or all-at-once? Word-based or character-based? In: Empirical Methods in Natural Language Processing, pp. 277–284 (2004)

---

[3] http://140.115.112.118/bcbb/CMM-CoNLL/sparseSVM.htm

14. Tjong Kim Sang, E.F., Buchholz, S.: Introduction to the CoNLL 2000 shared task: chunking. In: 4th Conference on Computational Natural Language Learning, pp. 127–132 (2000)
15. Wu, Y.C., Yang, J.C., Lee, Y.S.: An approximate approach for training polynomial kernel SVMs in linear time. In: The 45th Annual Meeting of the ACL on Interactive Poster and Demonstration Sessions, pp. 65–68 (2007)
16. Wu, Y.C., Lee, Y.S., Yang, J.C.: Robust and efficient Chinese word dependency analysis with linear kernel support vector machines. In: proceedings of 22nd International Conference on Computational Linguistics Poster, pp. 135–138 (2008)
17. Zhang, Y., Clark, S.: Chinese segmentation with a word-based perceptron algorithm. In: 45th Annual Meeting of the Association of Computational Linguistics, pp. 840–847 (2007)
18. Zhao, H., Kit, C.: Incorporating global information into supervised learning for Chinese word segmentation. In: 10th Conference of the Pacific Association for Computational Linguistics, pp. 66–74 (2007)

An Empirical Comparative Study
of Manual Rule-Based and Statistical Question Classifiers
on Heterogeneous Unseen Data

Cheng-Wei Lee, Min-Yuh Day, and Wen-Lian Hsu

Institute of Information Science, Academia Sinica, Taiwan, R.O.C.
{aska,myday,hsu}@iis.sinica.edu.tw

Abstract. Question Classification (QC) is critical in many natural language applications, especially factoid question answering (QA). Although a substantial number of studies have addressed QC, most of them have focused on statistical QC. The consensus in the literature is that rule-based QC is high cost and unportable, however, the fact is that rule-based QC is still the primary method in most top-performing factoid QA systems.

Just as statistical QC needs proper feature engineering, we argue that rule-based QC should be based on proper knowledge engineering guidelines, an aspect that has been overlooked in QC works thus far. To address this gap in the literature, we conducted a statistical case study of rule-based and statistical QC. We performed paired t-tests of the classifiers on several heterogeneous unseen datasets, which showed that rule-based QC significantly outperformed statistical QC in terms of fine-grained accuracy.

Keywords: Question Answering, Question Classification.

1 Introduction

Question Classification (QC) plays an important role in various natural language applications, especially in question answering (QA) domains, such as Factoid Question Answering [1-3] and Community Question Answering [4]. According to [5], 36.4% of the Factoid QA errors were derived from question classifiers, which influenced the overall performance a great deal.

The goal of question classification is to accurately classify a question into a question type, which is then used to reduce the search space for candidate answers. For example, given a question "Where is the original site of the Olympics?", if we can accurately classify the question as "LOCATION" type, only answers labeled as "LOCATION" need to be evaluated. Thus, the accuracy of the system as well as the computation cost could be improved.

Because of the importance of QC, a substantial number of works have addressed the issue in recent years. QC approaches can be classified into two broad categories, namely, rule-based approaches and statistical approaches. In rule-based approaches, usually domain experts produce a number of rules, which could be regular expressions, grammar rules, or just a set of phrases. By contrast, in statistical approaches, a

P.-J. Cheng et al. (Eds.): AIRS 2010, LNCS 6458, pp. 350–359, 2010.

sufficiently large collection of labeled questions is used instead of expert knowledge and a model is trained in hopes that useful patterns for classification can be captured automatically. Most existing works are based on closed homogeneous data. To the best of our knowledge, there is currently no empirical comparison of rule-based and statistical approaches on heterogeneous unseen data as we did in this work.

Many successful QA systems [6-8] rely on rule-based question classifiers, which seems to contradict the fact that nearly all recent QC works have focused on statistical approaches and regarded rule-based approaches as impractical or high cost, unportable solutions. To understand the reason for the contradiction, we compared the performance of a manually created rule-based question classifier and a statistical question classifier. We believe the comparison was empirical and unique because of the following characteristics.

First, the experiments were conducted on unseen datasets collected after the question classifiers had been created. This eliminated the possibility that the question classifiers could have been influenced by the test data. Second, to test the strength of the question classifiers on heterogeneous data, we collected data from various sources, such as QA task organizers, QA task participants, and real QA system users. Finally, the approaches we adopted for the question classifiers in comparison have achieved high performance accuracy and have been used successfully in a state-of-the-art Chinese QA system [6].

The remainder of the paper is organized as follows. We review related work in Section 2, and introduce the compared question classifiers in Section 3. The development data and the heterogeneous unseen datasets are presented in Section 4. We describe the experiments and report the results in Section 5. In Section 6, we discuss the experiment results; and in Section 7, we summarize our conclusions.

2   Related Work

Originally, most QA systems [9-11] used rule-based question classifiers with manually created rules or templates (rule and template are interchangeable words in this paper) for all or some question types. However, as rule-based question classifiers were regarded as unportable, the research focus shifted to statistical (or machine learning) approaches.

Extensive works on statistical question classification using various models and features have been reported in the literature. Studies have shown that classifying questions semantically yields better factoid question-answering results than employing conceptual categories [12]. For example, using the Sparse Network of Windows (SNoW), Li and Roth [12] achieved over 90% accuracy. Meanwhile, many works have adopted Support Vector Machine (SVMs) as the machine learning method. Zhang and Lee [13] used SVM with only surface text features (bag-of-words and bag-of-ngrams) to derive coarse-grained categories with 0.86 accuracy and fine-grained categories with approximately 0.80 accuracy. By adding syntactic information, including sub-trees of the parse tree that has at least one terminal symbol or one production rule, Zhang and Lee achieved an accuracy rate of 0.90 for coarse-grained classes. Suzuki et al. [14] used a hierarchical SVM to experiment on four feature sets: (1) words only; (2) words and named entities; (3) words and semantic information; and

(4) words and NEs with semantic information. They measured on a question type hierarchy at different depths and achieved accuracy rates ranging from 0.95 at depth 1 to 0.75 at depth 4.

Although statistical question classifiers have dominated research in recent years, most state-of-the-art QA systems in evaluation forums, such as CLEF, NTCIR, and TREC, still used rule-based question classifiers as their main QC approaches. For example, it seems that Language Computer Corporation's question answering system [8], which has been a top-performing English QA system at TREC conferences for many years, still uses a rule-based question classifier to classify questions and extract related semantic information.

To the best of our knowledge, there have been very few comparative studies between rule-based question classifiers and statistical question classifiers. Radev et al. [15] compared a rule-based question classifier and a Ripper-based question classifier, both of which were created automatically; however, neither question classifier is comparable to state-of-the-art question classifiers. Similar to this study, Day et al. [16] compared a rule-based question classifier and an SVM-based question classifier; however, they only experimented on a closed development set, not on heterogeneous unseen data as we used in this work.

3   The Compared Chinese Question Classifiers

Comparison of manual and statistical question classifiers needs to be handled carefully because the development processes and resources (or features) are substantially different. By definition, creating a manual question classifier involves a great deal of manual effort, while the cost of a statistical question classifier mainly involves choosing proper features and machine learning models. On one hand, the features used for a manual question classifier are almost unlimited in that any features can be referenced for a set of rules or for a special case. However, such classifiers are usually developed in an ad hoc manner, so the quality of the classifier is less predictable. (We introduce a test-assisted approach in Section 3.1 to improve the ad hoc process.) On the other hand, statistical classifier features are usually constrained by the adopted machine leaning model and the amount of training data. Moreover, the same set of features is applied to all the data without exception. The development process of a statistical question classifier is thus almost standardized and easy to follow.

Because of the above differences, we believe that to make an effective comparison of the two types of classifiers, the features and accuracy as well as the development process must be considered. This because the development process plays a key role especially for manual question classifiers. We view our comparison in this work more like a case study than an experiment because only a few independent variables were controlled.

The compared question classifiers were created during the development of a state-of-the-art Chinese QA system. The development times of the question classifiers were almost the same (approximately six months). For the rule-based question classifier, there were two rule creators and one developer. Most of the time was devoted to developing rules. For the statistical question classifier, there was one developer, who used the training data labeled by the above two rule creators. In this case, most of the time was expended on feature engineering, which involved choosing an optimum set of features. All the question classifiers can classify a question into any of 6 coarse-grained classes or 62 fine grained-classes.

3.1 Test-Assisted Rule-Based Question Classifier

In contrast to other rule-based question classifier approaches, we regard the creation of a rule-based question classifier as a knowledge engineering[1] process, which needs guidelines and tools to minimize the rule maintenance costs and maximize the coverage and accuracy.

We used a knowledge representation framework called InfoMap with a test-assisted rule creation process. InfoMap consists of a knowledge editor and a matching engine that can extract important concepts from a natural language text [17, 18]. The framework is designed to represent and match complex templates, which are syntactic rules with semantic labels. A template is comprised of several parts, such as a string, a semantic label, or a reference to other templates. By referencing a part of a template to another template, the number of distinct templates can be reduced. To enable human experts to maintain rules safely and quickly, we adopted a test-assisted approach that was inspired by the test-driven development (TDD)[2] [19] concept in agile software development. Each rule can be associated with a set of questions or phrases as its "tests." With this approach, it is safer to share rules between experts so that no expert will become a bottleneck that slows down the rule development process.

All the templates and rules are maintained by InfoMap knowledge editor, which provides a hierarchical editing interface that allows several domain experts to edit rules from the same server simultaneously. We also have a continuous integration[3] server that periodically checks whether any templates or tests have been modified. Whenever templates or tests are modified, a test process is triggered automatically and uses the matching engine to compare the rules with the "tests" to determine if any test cases have been broken. The server then provides feedback to the human experts. The feedback includes information about how many questions have been tested as well as details of failed tests. The integration process runs on a separate machine so that the human experts do not have to wait for the results and can continue with rule development.

Human experts were asked to increase the question coverage (i.e., the number of training questions that could be categorized by the rules) while maintaining high accuracy. Some questions will not be covered if they cannot be confidently categorized by rules or the cost of creating rules for them is too high.

Fig. 1 shows an example of QC knowledge representation in InfoMap. The two-layer question taxonomy is created in a hierarchical way. For example, the fine-grained category "LOCATION_CITY" is a sub node of the coarse-grained category "LOCATION." Each coarse-grained and fine-grained question type node has two function nodes, "HAS-PART" and "Rule". The rules for a question type are stored

---

[1] http://en.wikipedia.org/wiki/Knowledge_engineering
[2] TDD (http://en.wikipedia.org/wiki/Test-driven_development) is used to facilitate the creation and design of high quality software programs.
[3] Continuous integration: http://en.wikipedia.org/wiki/Continuous_integration

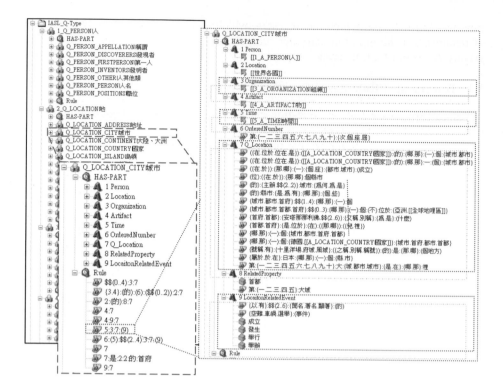

Fig. 1. An example of QC rules in InfoMap

under the "Rule" node. To reduce the number of redundant rules, sub-phrases or sub-rules shared by more than one rule are described by rules stored under the "HAS-PART" node. For example, the rule or template for the LOCATION_CITY question "2004年奧運在哪一個城市舉行? (In which city were the Olympics held in 2004?)" in InfoMap can be formulated as: [Time]:[Organization]:[Q_Location]: ([LocationRelatedEvent]) under the "Rule" node of LOCATION_CITY. This rule has four elements (referenced from the nodes under "HAS-PART"), i.e., "Time", "Organization", "Q_LOCATION", and "LocationRelatedEvent." They are stored by rules under the "HAS-PART" node to match "2004年(Year 2004)", "奧運(the Olympics)", "在哪一個城市(in which city)", and "舉行(is held)" respectively.

3.2 The SVM-Based Question Classifier

We adopted SVM as the statistical (machine learning) approach as it has been the most popular technique used in question classification [13, 20, 21]. We used SVMlight [22] to train the question classifier with the following syntactic features and semantic features reported in [16] for Chinese questions.

Syntactic features: Our SVM model incorporates two syntactic features: bag-of-words (ngrams) and part-of-speech (POS). (a) Bag-of-Words: Character-based bigram and word-based bigram features were used. (b) Part-of-Speech (POS): We used AutoTag[23], a Chinese segmentation tool developed by CKIP, Academia Sinica, to obtain the POS of given Chinese questions, and then adopted the POS features for QC.

Semantic Features: We used "HowNet"[4] to derive the semantic features of given Chinese questions. Our SVM model uses two semantic features: HowNet Main Definition and HowNet Definition.

We tuned the SVM-based question classifier on the development data with 10-fold cross-validation and then trained the final SVM models on all the development data.

Table 1. Datasets Used in the Chinese Question Classification Experiments

Develop. Dataset	# of Qs	Source	Target Corpus
Q-NTCIR5D	1312	300 from NTCIR5 CJ development set	
		200 from NTCIR5 CC development set	CIRB40
		812 from an NTCIR5 participant	CIRB40
Test Datasets	**# of Qs**	**Source**	**Target Corpus**
Q-TREC	384	translated from TREC QA questions	
Q-CIRB20	221	from an NTCIR6 participant	CIRB20
Q-NTCIR5T	200	from NTCIR5 test Set	CIRB40
Q-CTS	205	from an NTCIR6 participant	CTS (a TV news site: http://www.cts.com.tw)
Q-CorpusDemo	186	from an online QA system demo site	CIRB40+CIRB20
Q-WebDemo	167	from an online QA system demo site	Web
Q-NTCIR6T	150	from NTCIR6 test Set	CIRB40+CIRB20

4 The Datasets

We collected question classification datasets from various sources, as shown in Table 1. In contrast to most existing QC experiments, the test datasets used in our experiments were created, collected or translated after the question classifiers had been developed. A QC dataset consists of pairs of questions and standard question types. The standard question types were designated by the human experts and used to judge the correctness of the results yielded by the question classifiers in our experiments.

The dataset used to develop the three question classifiers were collected in 2005, which contains distinct questions created by the NTCIR-5 CLQA organizers (300 questions for the C-J subtask and 200 questions for the C-C subtask) and 850 questions created by a task participant.

The test data comprised seven datasets: Q-TREC, Q-CIRB20, Q-NTCIR5T, Q-NTCIR6T, Q-CTS, Q-CorpusDemo and Q-WebDemo. The Q-TREC dataset was translated from some TREC QA track English questions. The Q-CIRB20, Q-NTCIR5T, and Q-NTCIR6T datasets were created from Chinese newspapers. Since most QA experiments are conducted on newspaper data, we created a new dataset

---

[4] HowNet: http://www.keenage.com/

from a different medium, i.e., the Q-CTS dataset of TV news reports. In addition to these artificially created questions, we collected real user questions posted on an online Chinese QA demo site (http://asqa.iis.sinica.edu.tw/) since 2005. The site targeted two types of answer corpora: a news corpus and a web corpus. We compiled the Q-CorpusDemo and Q-WebDemo datasets according to the answer corpus that the question was posted on.

Table 2. Accuracy scores of the InfoMap-based and SVM-based question classifier

	Q numbers		InfoMap accuracy		SVM accuracy	
	total	fine	coarse	fine	coarse	fine
Dev. Dataset						
Q-NTCIR5D	1312	722	0.992	0.983	0.997	0.983
Test Datasets						
Q-CTS	205	64	0.902	0.828	0.863	0.625
Q-NTCIR5T	200	80	0.925	0.875	0.765	0.563
Q-CIRB20	221	90	0.824	0.656	0.810	0.611
Q-TREC	384	162	0.740	0.543	0.867	0.685
Q-CorpusDemo	186	65	0.823	0.662	0.785	0.492
Q-WebDemo	167	48	0.820	0.583	0.844	0.458
Q-NTCIR6T	150	51	0.900	0.725	0.853	0.627
Mean accuracy			0.848	0.696	0.827	0.580

5   Experiments

We applied the heterogeneous unseen data mentioned in section 4 to the InfoMap-based and the SVM-based question classifiers. To the best of our knowledge, this is the first empirical study of the issue. To date, most research has focused on homogeneous data with statistical question classifiers. In some studies, the development and test datasets were even chosen at random from the same question pool; hence, we think the experiments were not empirical enough to test a question classifier's robustness and portability. A question classification system is evaluated in terms of its accuracy. Since the accuracy depends on the granularity of the question types, we defined two kinds of accuracy to assess a question classifier's performance: the coarse-grained accuracy and the fine-grained accuracy, which focus on the question classifier's ability to classify questions as either coarse-grained and fine-grained types respectively.

As shown in Table 2, both question classifiers fit the development data well with very high accuracy, but the accuracy declines on the unseen test datasets. Overall speaking, the InfoMap-based question classifier outperformed the SVM-based question classifier in terms of the mean accuracy. According to t-test, only the comparison of fine-grained accuracy were significant (p-value < 0.037).

6   Discussion

As shown by the experiment results, surprisingly, the InfoMap-based question classifier performed better than the SVM-based question classifier on most of the heterogeneous unseen data. This seems to contradict the claims made in most question classification papers, such as [21], that rule-based question classifiers lack robustness and portability. We found that when a given question contained unpredicted words, the InfoMap-based question classifier was more likely to get the right question type. Unpredicted words are words that do not exist in the training data; or they appear in the training data, but in a different context to that of the input question.

To deal with unpredicted words, a statistical question classifier could incorporate semantic features, such as the HowNet features we used in the SVM-based question classifier. The objective is to enable the statistical model to learn useful semantic categories for each question type from the training data. However, since the quality and granularity of the used semantic categories varies, some semantic categories may not be suitable features for the question domain; and if the model learns such semantic categories, its performance on unseen data could be impacted.

The semantic categories used in the SVM-based question classifier could also be referenced in the rules created by the human experts. But unlike the SVM-based question classifier, experts could review and judge the content of the referenced semantic categories, remove noisy content, and merge or split categories into the appropriate granularity, thereby alleviating some of the unsuitable semantic category problem.

In addition, we observed that, under the test-assisted approach (which associates rules with tests to verify the rules during development) and the guidelines given to human experts (to only create high accuracy and high confidence rules), the cost of creating the InfoMap-based question classifier was reduced and the experts had more time to improve the quality and coverage of the rules. "Rule bugs" could be detected quickly by running the "tests" after the introduction of new rules or improper modifications. If "bugs" are not detected early, it could be much more expensive if the rules have to be fixed at a later stage, since some new rules could be based on the buggy rules.

With the test-assisted approach, rules are well-protected by the tests and the continuous integration process, it is easier to maintain collective ownership so that everyone is responsible for all the rules and any expert can fix broken rules caused by someone else; thus, the incidence of bottlenecks and risks can be reduced. (The risk in this context is similar to the Bus Factor[5] concept in software development.)

Although the rules of the InfoMap-based question classifier were created carefully with the tools and guidelines, some questions could not be categorized correctly, especially on the Q-TREC dataset. Our analysis of the results revealed three problems: 1) The rules of some question types handled by InfoMap (such as DEFINITION) but not included in our experiments were not carefully handled, which resulted in false positive cases. This showed that, similar to software programs, every piece of rules involved in the computation should be well-maintained or separated. 2) The Q-TREC dataset was translated from English questions. Some of the translations were not appropriate, so the rules output the wrong question type. Since the SVM-based question classifier did not use complex features, it was not seriously affected by the problem. 3) A number of unseen questions could not be matched with any rules. Some of them were deliberately ignored because the cost of creating rules for them

---

[5] Bus Factor: http://en.wikipedia.org/wiki/Bus_factor

would have been too high; and some were just not discovered by the human experts during the development phase.

7 Conclusion

This is a preliminary work designed to investigate the real-world performance of rule-based and statistical question classifiers. The results demonstrated the potential of rule-based QC approaches. Because manually created classifiers are influenced by various factors introduced by the engineering work conducted by humans, method-ologies commonly used to compare machine-learning or statistical methods are not suitable for our work. Therefore, we used post-hoc empirical experiments with het-erogeneous datasets sampled from various sources.

The statistical hypothesis tests showed that, even when dealing with heterogeneous unseen datasets, the InfoMap-based question classifier (a manually created rule-based classifier) performed significantly better than the SVM-based question classifier in terms of fine-grained accuracy. This finding suggests that with proper design, a rule-based method can handle real-world cases with a high degree of confidence. The InfoMap-based question classifier did not encounter any serious robustness and port-ability issues reported in many QC works. We attribute the success of the rule-based question classifier to the test-assisted development process and the guideline whereby question coverage is traded in favor of high accuracy rules.

Acknowledgements

This research was supported in part by the National Science Council of Taiwan under Grants NSC 96-2752-E-001-001-PAE and 95-2416-H-002-047, and the Thematic Program of Academia Sinica under Grant AS95ASIA02.

References

1. Forner, P., Peñas, A., Agirre, E., Alegria, I., Forăscu, C., Moreau, N., Osenova, P., Pro-kopidis, P., Rocha, P., Sacaleanu, B., Sutcliffe, R., Sang, E.T.K.: Overview Of The CLEF 2008 Multilingual Question Answering Track. In: Cross-Language Evaluation Forum (CLEF) Workshop (2008)
2. Dang, H.T., Kelly, D., Lin, J.: Overview of the TREC 2007 Question Answering Track. In: Proceedings of The Sixteenth Text REtrieval Conference, TREC (2007)
3. Mitamura, T., Nyberg, E., Shima, H., Kato, T., Mori, T., Lin, C.-Y., Song, R., Lin, C.-J., Sakai, T., Ji, D., Kando, N.: Overview of the NTCIR-7 ACLIA Tasks: Advanced Cross-Lingual Information Access. In: The 7th NTCIR Workshop (2008)
4. Li, B., Liu, Y., Ram, A., Garcia, E.V., Agichtein, E.: Exploring Question Subjectivity Pre-diction in Community QA. In: Proceedings of 31st Annual International ACM SIGIR Con-ference, pp. 735–736 (2008)
5. Moldovan, D., Paşca, M., Harabagiu, S., Surdeanu, M.: Performance Issues and Error Analysis in an Open-Domain Question Answering System. ACM Transactions on Infor-mation Systems 21, 133–154 (2003)

6. Lee, C.-W., Day, M.-Y., Sung, C.-L., Lee, Y.-H., Jiang, T.-J., Wu, C.-W., Shih, C.-W., Chen, Y.-R., Hsu, W.-L.: Chinese-Chinese and English-Chinese Question Answering with ASQA at NTCIR-6 CLQA. In: Proceedings of NTCIR-6 Workshop, Tokyo, Japan, pp. 175–181 (2007)
7. Laurent, D., Séguéla, P., Nègre, S.: Cross Lingual Question Answering using QRISTAL for CLEF 2006. In: CLEF (2006)
8. Moldovan, D., Clark, C., Bowden, M.: Lymba's PowerAnswer 4 in TREC 2007. In: The Sixteenth Text REtrieval Conference, TREC 2007 (2007)
9. Prager, J., Brown, E., Coden, A., Radev, D.: Question-Answering by Predictive Annotation. In: Proceedings of the 23rd Annual International ACM SIGIR Conference, pp. 184–191 (2000)
10. Pasca, M.A., Harabagiu, S.M.: High Performance Question/Answering. In: Proceedings of the 24th Annual International ACM SIGIR Conference, pp. 366–374 (2001)
11. Hull, D.A.: Xerox TREC-8 Question Answering Track Report. In: Proceedings of the 8th Text Retrieval Conference (TREC-8), vol. 8, pp. 743–752 (1999)
12. Li, X., Roth, D.: Learning Question Classifiers. In: International Conference on Computational Linguistics, Taipei, Taiwan, pp. 1–7 (2002)
13. Zhang, D., Lee, W.S.: Question Classification Using Support Vector Machines. In: Proceedings of the 26th Annual International ACM SIGIR Conference, pp. 26–32 (2003)
14. Suzuki, J., Taira, H., Sasaki, Y., Maeda, E.: Question Classification Using HDAG Kernel. In: Proceedings of the ACL 2003 Workshop on Multilingual Summarization and Question Answering, pp. 61–68 (2003)
15. Radev, D., Fan, W., Qi, H., Wu, H., Grewal, A.: Probabilistic Question Answering on the Web. In: Proceedings of the 11th International Conference on World Wide Web, pp. 408–419 (2002)
16. Day, M.-Y., Lee, C.-W., Wu, S.-H., Ong, C.-S., Hsu, W.-L.: An Integrated Knowledge-based and Machine Learning Approach for Chinese Question Classification. In: IEEE International Conference on Natural Language Processing and Knowledge Engineering, pp. 620–625 (2005)
17. Hsu, W.-L., Wu, S.-H., Chen, Y.-S.: Event identification based on the information map-INFOMAP. In: IEEE International Conference on Systems, Man, and Cybernetics, Tucson, AZ, USA, vol. 3, pp. 1661–1666 (2001)
18. Wu, S.-H., Day, M.-Y., Hsu, W.-L.: FAQ-centered Qrganizational Memory. In: Knowledge Management and Organizational Momery Workshop on the Seventeenth International Joint Conference on Artificial Intelligence, pp. 112–120 (2001)
19. Beck, K.: Test-Driven Development by Example. Addison-Wesley Professional, Reading (2002)
20. Moschitti, A., Quarteroni, S., Basili, R., Manandhar, S.: Exploiting Syntactic and Shallow Semantic Kernels for Question Answer Classification. In: ACL, pp. 776–783 (2007)
21. Metzler, D., Croft, W.B.: Analysis of Statistical Question Classification for Fact-Based Questions. Information Retrieval 8, 481–504 (2005)
22. Joachims, T.: Text Categorization with Support Vector Machines: Learning with Many Relevant Features. In: Proceedings of the European Conference on Machine Learning, pp. 137–142 (1998)
23. CKIP: Autotag. Academia Sinica (1999)

Constructing Blog Entry Classifiers Using Blog-Level Topic Labels

Ken Hagiwara[1], Hiroya Takamura[2], and Manabu Okumura[2]

[1] Department of Computer Science,
Tokyo Institute of Technology,
4259 Nagatsuta Midori-ku Yokohama, Japan, 226-8503
hagiwara@lr.pi.titech.ac.jp
[2] Precision and Intelligence Laboratory, Tokyo Institute of Technology,
4259 Nagatsuta Midori-ku Yokohama, Japan, 226-8503
{takamura,oku}@pi.titech.ac.jp

Abstract. Identification of a blogger's interest is usually solved as a classification problem of a sequence of his/her blog entries. In constructing a blog entry classifier, we need as training data a rather large set of blog entries that are manually labeled with a class label. In contrast, we can easily obtain a set of blog sites with class labels. In this paper, we present a method for constructing a blog entry classifier using only a set of blog sites with class labels. Our method is based on the Naive Bayes classifier coupled with the EM algorithm.

Keywords: text classification, Naive Bayes classifier, EM algorithm.

1 Introduction

Weblogs (blogs) are now considered as an attractive information source. It is generally understood that they are personal web pages authored by a single individual and made up of a sequence of dated entries of the author's thoughts, a sort of short-term journal, that are arranged chronologically. Blogs tend to be frequently updated and include links to others' blogs. The content and purposes of blogs varies greatly from links and commentary about other web sites, to news about a company/person, to diaries, photos, and so on[1]. It is said that blogs date back to 1996, but they exploded in popularity during 1999 with the emergence of blogger(http://www.blogger.com) and other easy-to-use publishing tools[5].

Recently, the study on analyzing the space of weblogs has become a hot topic, as the blogspace has started to exhibit explosive growthenlarge of its size [5]. Identifying the bloggers' characteristics, such as age, gender[4], interest[8,11], emotion, etc., has attracted much attention in blog analysis recently. Identifying the bloggers' interest provides many applications, such as to investigate the distribution of bloggers' interest, and monitor their change over time; and to link bloggers by their interest and form a community.

---

[1] http://new.blogger.com/

P.-J. Cheng et al. (Eds.): AIRS 2010, LNCS 6458, pp. 360–369, 2010.

Identification of a blogger's interest is usually solved as a classification problem of a sequence of his/her blog entries. Classifying blog entries into class labels, we can guess the blogger's interest by investigating a sequence of class labels on entries. This is based on the fact that people usually write some things in which they are interested. Consider a blogger with high interest in computers. He/She will tend to write entries on computers to represent his/her interest.

Text classifiers are usually built with supervised learning where inputting manually constructed, rather large training data to a machine learning framework can produce a text classifier. Therefore, in constructing a blog entry classifier, we need as training data a rather large set of blog entries that are manually labeled with a class label. However, manual labeling is quite a time consuming and costly task. In contrast, we can easily obtain a set of blog sites with class labels. Web directories contain a manually classified set of web sites, including a set of blog sites. Furthermore, there exist web directories that contain only blog sites, such as `http://www.blogmura.com/`.

In this paper, we present a method of constructing a blog entry classifier by using only a set of blog sites with class labels. Our method is based on the Naive Bayes classifier coupled with the EM algorithm. The remainder of this paper is organized as follows. Section 2 describes related work. Section 3 describes the proposed method. Section 4 reports the results of experiments on blog data.

2 Related Work

Automatic identification of bloggers' interests has been addressed as a text classification task [11,8]. Teng and Chen [11] presented a method of the detection of bloggers' interest with three kinds of features in blogs: textual, temporal, and interactive features. Ni et al. [8] used a technique of combining heterogeneous classifiers and a technique of hierarchical classification. Their methods are both based on the traditional supervised approach for text classification.

Automatically tagging blog entries with social tags is a similar task to blog entry classification, though the tags are not well organized class labels. In automatic tagging of blog entries, unsupervised and supervised machine learning framework have been used [1,7,10], since a rather large set of training data (tagged blog entries) is readily available.

In the area of machine learning for text classification, using labeled and unlabeled examples together has often been found effective [9]. Nigam et al. showed that semi-supervised learning, with adding a huge amount of unlabeled examples to a small set of labeled examples, improves the performance of text classification, in cases of difficult availability of a large set of labeled examples.

In this paper we adopted the combination of the EM algorithm and the Naive Bayes classifier, because Nigam et al. [9] already showed that the combination shows better performance in the text classification. Their method is not applicable to the situation we are interested in, that is, when only blog-level topic labels are available. We are going to modify their idea so that we can construct entry classifiers from blog-level topic labels.

3   Classification of Blog Entries

Usually, each training instance is given a training label in classification tasks. However, we suppose that labels are not given to each instance, but to each blog consisting of multiple entries. More precisely, each blog in the training data has one or more labels, and the label of each entry in the blog is often one of those labels, but not always. We construct our entry classifier by imposing the relaxed version of the assumption that the label of each entry of a blog is one of the labels of the blogs.

3.1   Introduction of the Model and Q-Function

In order to construct a classifier from the blog-level class labels, we use the Expectation-Maximization (EM) algorithm [2], which is used to estimate the parameters when some variables are unobserved in the training data.

Nigam et al.,[9] used the EM algorithm to incorporate unlabeled documents into the training of a text classifier. The current situation is different from Nigam et al.'s. Our training instances (entries) are not unlabeled, but incompletely labeled; only blog-level labels are given. By assuming that each label of the entry is selected from the blog-level labels, we can use the EM algorithm to construct a classifier for entries.

Let B denote a set of blogs and their topic labels. We estimate parameters θ by means of maximum a posteriori estimation, i.e., by maximizing

$$\log P(\theta) + \log P(B \mid \theta). \tag{1}$$

The likelihood $\log P(B \mid \theta)$ can be decomposed as (for simplicity, we do not write θ explicitly on the right hand side)

$$
\begin{aligned}
\log P(B \mid \theta) &= \log \prod_{(b_i, T_i) \in B} P(T_i) P(b_i \mid T_i) \\
&= \sum_{(b_i, T_i) \in B} \log P(T_i) P(b_i \mid T_i) \\
&= \sum_{(b_i, T_i) \in B} \log P(T_i) \prod_{e_{ij} \in b_i} P(e_{ij} \mid T_i) \\
&= \sum_{(b_i, T_i) \in B} \left(\log P(T_i) + \sum_{e_{ij} \in b_i} \log P(e_{ij} \mid T_i) \right)
\end{aligned}
$$

where b_i is a blog consisting of entries, T_i is the set of topic labels given to b_i, and e_{ij} is an entry in blog b_i.

We then use the above assumption that each label of the entry is selected from the blog-level labels. That is, if we know the selected label t_n, $P(e_{ij} \mid T_i)$ would be decomposed as $P(e_{ij} \mid T_i) = P(t_n \mid T_i) P(e_{ij} \mid t_n)$. However, since we do not know t_n, we regard the selected label as latent variable, and apply the

EM algorithm with the following Q-function (the expected value of Equation (1) over the latent variable):

$$\log P(\theta) + \sum_{(b_i,T_i)\in B}\left(\log P(T_i) + \sum_{e_{ij}\in b_i}\sum_{t_n} P(t_n|e_{ij},T_i)\log P(t_n \mid T_i)P(e_{ij} \mid t_n)\right).$$

We also assume that $P(T_i)$ is constant and redefine Q-function:

$$Q(\theta) = \log P(\theta) + \sum_{(b_i,T_i)\in B}\sum_{e_{ij}\in b_i}\sum_{t_n} P(t_n|e_{ij},T_i)\log P(t_n \mid T_i)P(e_{ij} \mid t_n).$$

We use the multinomial model of Naive Bayes classifiers [6] for the generative probability of an entry given the label :

$$P(e_{ij} \mid t_n) = P(|e_{ij}|)\frac{|e_{ij}|!}{\prod_w n_{ij}(w)!}\prod_w P(w \mid t_n)^{n_{ij}(w)},$$

where w is a word type, $n_{ij}(w)$ is the frequency of w in entry e_{ij}, and $|e_{ij}|$ is the number of word tokens in e_{ij}. Therefore, we obtain $P(e_{ij} \mid t_n) \propto \prod_w P(w \mid t_n)^{n_{ij}(w)}$. We use the Dirichlet prior for $P(\theta) \propto \prod_{t_n}\left(P(t_n)^{\alpha-1}\prod_w P(w \mid t_n)^{\alpha-1}\right)$, where α is a hyper-parameter. Hence, the Q-function is expressed as follows :

$$Q(\theta) = \sum_{t_n}\left((\alpha-1)\log P(t_n) + \sum_w(\alpha-1)P(w \mid t_n)\right)$$
$$+ \sum_{(b_i,T_i)\in B}\sum_{e_{ij}\in b_i}\sum_{t_n}\bar{P}(t_n \mid e_{ij},T_i)\log P(t_n|T_i)$$
$$+ \sum_{(b_i,T_i)\in B}\sum_{e_{ij}\in b_i}\sum_{t_n}\sum_w n_{ij}(w)\bar{P}(t_n \mid e_{ij},T_i)\log P(w \mid t_n)$$
$$+ (constant). \tag{2}$$

3.2   The EM Algorithm

The EM algorithm consists of two steps: E-step and M-step. These two steps will be performed iteratively in turn until it converges.

E-step
At E-step, the posterior probability of the unobserved variable $\bar{P}(t_n \mid e_{ij},T_i)$ is calculated:

$$\bar{P}(t_n \mid e_{ij},T_i) = \frac{P(t_n,e_{ij},T_i)}{\sum_t P(t,e_{ij},T_i)}$$
$$= \frac{P(T_i)P(t_n|T_i)P(e_{ij}|t_n,T_i)}{\sum_t P(T_i)P(t|T_i)P(e_{ij}|t,T_i)} \tag{3}$$
$$= \frac{P(t_n|T_i)P(e_{ij}|t_n,T_i)}{\sum_t P(t|T_i)P(e_{ij}|t,T_i)}. \tag{4}$$

We assume that, when t is given, e_{ij} is independent of T_i, resulting in $P(e_{ij}|t, T_i) = P(e_{ij}|t)$. We also assume that $P(t_n|T_i)$ is represented as follows :

$$P(t_n|T_i) = \frac{\delta(t_n \in T_i)P(t_n)}{\sum_t \delta(t \in T_i)P(t)}, \tag{5}$$

where

$$\delta(t \in T_i) = \begin{cases} 1 \ (t \in T_i) \\ 0 \ (t \notin T_i) \end{cases} \tag{6}$$

Then, we obtain

$$\bar{P}(t_n \mid e_{ij}, T_i) = \frac{P(t_n|T_i)P(e_{ij}|t_n)}{\sum_t P(t|T_i)P(e_{ij}|t)} \tag{7}$$

$$= \frac{\delta(t \in T_i)P(t_n)P(e_{ij}|t_n)}{\sum_t \delta(t \in T_i)P(t)P(e_{ij}|t)} \tag{8}$$

$$= \frac{\delta(t \in T_i)P(t_n) \prod_w P(w|t_n)^{n_{ij}(w)}}{\sum_t \delta(t \in T_i)P(t) \prod_w P(w|t)^{n_{ij}(w)}}. \tag{9}$$

M-step

At M-step, we obtain the parameters θ (i.e., $P(w \mid t_n)$ and $P(t_n)$) that maximize Q-function. The formula for M-step can be derived through the standard Lagrangian method. We are going to maximize the Q-function (Equation (2)) under the constraints : $\sum_w P(w \mid t_n) = 1$, $\sum_{t_n} P(t_n) = 1$. The Lagrangian $L(\theta)$ is defined to be

$$L(\theta) = Q(\theta) + \sum_{t_n} \beta_{t_n} \left(\sum_w P(w \mid t_n) - 1 \right) + \gamma \left(\sum_{t_n} P(t_n) - 1 \right),$$

where β_{t_n} and γ are Lagrange multipliers. By differentiating $L(\theta)$ with each parameter and setting the derivative to be 0, we obtain the following equations :

$$\frac{\partial}{\partial P(w \mid t_n)} L(\theta) = \frac{\alpha - 1}{P(w \mid t_n)} + \sum_{b_i \in B} \sum_{e_{ij} \in b_i} \frac{n_{ij}(w)}{P(w \mid t_n)} \bar{P}(t_n \mid e_{ij}, T_i) + \beta_{t_n}$$

$$= 0 \tag{10}$$

$$\frac{\partial}{\partial \beta_{t_n}} L(\theta) = \sum_w P(w \mid t_n) - 1 = 0 \tag{11}$$

$$\frac{\partial}{\partial P(t_n)} L(\theta) = \frac{\alpha - 1}{P(t_n)} + \sum_{b_i \in B} \sum_{e_{ij} \in b_i} \frac{1}{P(t_n)} \bar{P}(t_n \mid e_{ij}, T_i) + \gamma$$

$$= 0 \tag{12}$$

$$\frac{\partial}{\partial \gamma} L(\theta) = \sum_{t_n} P(t_n) - 1 = 0. \tag{13}$$

From these equations, we obtain the following update formula in M-step :

$$P(w \mid t_n) = \frac{\sum_{(b_i, T_i) \in B} \sum_{e_{ij} \in b_{ij}} n_{ij}(w) \bar{P}(t_n \mid e_{ij}, T_i) + \alpha - 1}{\sum_{(b_i, T_i) \in B} \sum_{e_{ij} \in b_i} \sum_w n_{ij}(w) \bar{P}(t_n \mid e_{ij}, T_i) + (\alpha - 1)|e_{ij}|}, \quad (14)$$

$$P(t_n) = \frac{\sum_{(b_i, T_i) \in B} \sum_{e_{ij} \in b_i} \bar{P}(t_n \mid e_{ij}, T_i) + \alpha - 1}{\sum_{(b_i, T_i) \in B} \sum_{e_{ij} \in b_i} \sum_{t_n} \bar{P}(t_n \mid e_{ij}, T_i) + (\alpha - 1)|C|}, \quad (15)$$

where $|C|$ is the number of categories.
   We set the initial value of the posteriors to be :

$$P(t_n \mid e_{ij}, T_i) = \left\{ \begin{array}{l} \frac{1}{|T_i|} \ (t_n \in T_i) \\ 0 \ \ (t_n \notin T_i) \end{array} \right. .$$

3.3   The Tempered EM

A number of variants to the EM algorithm have been proposed. Among them, the tempered EM[3] has a good property that it can control the smoothness of the posterior probability $P(t_n|e_{ij}, T_i)$ used during the training. The tempered EM is implemented by slightly modifying the E-step :

$$\bar{P}(t_n \mid e_{ij}, T_i) = \frac{\{\delta(t_n \in T_i) P(t_n) \prod_w P(w \mid t_n)^{n_{ij}(w)}\}^\beta}{\sum_{t_n} \{\delta(t_n \in T_i) P(t_n) \prod_w P(w \mid t_n)^{n_{ij}(w)}\}^\beta}, \quad (16)$$

where β is a user-given hyper-parameter.

4   Experiments

4.1   Experimental Setting

The dataset we used in experiments is written in Japanese and was originally collected by blogWatcher corporation[2]. It consists of 634 blogs (75,161 entries). 532 blogs (64,463 entries) out of the 634 blogs above were used as training data. There are 33 topic labels such as computers, life, outdoor, art, sports, travel. 2,415 entries that were randomly chosen from the remaining entries were manually labeled with one of those 33 topics by one of the authors and used as test data. Blog-level labels were given by users of the blog site. Note that 396 blogs out of the 532 training blogs have only one topic label. The other 136 blogs have multiple topic labels. In the model construction in Section 3.1, we assumed that each label of the entry is selected from the blog-level labels. However, this assumption was only used for model construction and we should be aware that the actual dataset does not follow this assumption in both the training and the test datasets. As a result of the morphological analysis with

---

[2] http://www.blogwatcher.co.jp

MeCab,[3] 61,149 word types were found in the training data and used in training and classification. As evaluation measure, we use accuracy, which is defined to be the number of correctly classified entries divided by the number of all the entries in the test data.

We set two baseline methods.

- **NB0:** the Naive Bayes classifier constructed with only the blogs with a single topic label; blogs with multiple topic labels are simply discarded.
- **NB-init:** the Naive Bayes classifier at the initial condition of the proposed method, i.e., no EM training was applied. The blogs with multiple topic labels allocate its probability equally to the member entries.

As a reference, we also add the result of the Naive Bayes classifier constructed with labeled entries. This result was obtained through 10-fold cross-validation on the test data.

4.2   Results

Experiment 1

We are going to examine the classification ability of the proposed method in the general situation where blog-level topics are not available. The topic labels t_n are predicted by means of the following formula :

$$\arg\max_{t_n} P(t_n \mid e_{ij}) = \arg\max_{t_n} \frac{P(t_n) \prod_w P(w \mid t_n)^{n_{ij}(w)}}{\sum_{t_n} P(t_n) \prod_w P(w \mid t_n)^{n_{ij}(w)}}.$$

The result is shown in Table 1. The table shows that the baseline2 (NB-init) outperforms the baseline1 (NB0), which is unable to use multiple-label blogs. It also shows that NB+EM yields a better accuracy than two baselines (NB0 and NB-init). Since the only difference between NB+EM and NB-init is that the EM algorithm is applied on NB+EM, the result suggests that the proposed method, NB+EM, succeeded in making good use of blog-level topic labels. The difference in accuracy between NB-init and NB+EM was statistically significant in the sign test with 5% significance level.

Figure 1 shows how the accuracy of NB+EM changes during the iterations. The accuracy becomes stable after 15 iterations. The best number of iterations is around 5. An appropriate early stopping would still increase the final accuracy.

As mentioned above, the actual dataset does not follow the assumption that each label of the entry is selected from the blog-level labels. Our model stipulates that this assumption should be true. We come up with a natural question of what would happen if we relax this assumption. We therefore tested a slightly modified method in which the value of the delta function in Equation (6) for $(t \notin T_i)$ is changed from 0 to 0.1, 0.5 or 1.0. With this setting, we executed NB+EM and obtained Table 2. In the table, the accuracy is highest when δ for $t_n \notin T_i$ is 0.0. It suggests that, in our experimental setting, the strict use of the above-mentioned assumption is effective, though the assumption is not completely true.

---

[3] `http://mecab.sourceforge.net`

Table 1. Accuracy of each method

method	accuracy(%)
baseline 1 (NB0)	42.3
baseline 2 (NB-init)	44.0
NB+EM	45.2
NB+tempered EM	45.4
supervised	64.3

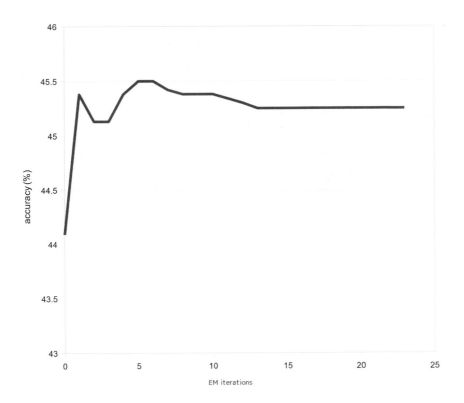

Fig. 1. Accuracy of NB+EM at each iteration

Experiment 2

In Experiment 1, we evaluated the proposed method in a general situation where blog-level topic labels are not given. In Experiment 2, we evaluate the proposed method in a situation where blog-level topic labels are available. In this setting, the model predicts the topic label of an entry e_{ij} as

$$\arg\max_{t_n} P(t_n \mid e_{ij}) = \arg\max_{t_n} \frac{\delta(t_n \in T_i)P(t_n)\prod_w P(w \mid t_n)^{n_{ij}(w)}}{\sum_{t_n} \delta(t_n \in T_i)P(t_n)\prod_w P(w \mid t_n)^{n_{ij}(w)}}.$$

Table 2. Accuracy NB+EM with modified δ

method	δ for $t_n \notin T_i$	accuracy(%)
NB+EM	0.0	**45.2**
NB+EM	0.1	36.9
NB+EM	0.5	25.2
NB+EM	1.0	24.5

Table 3. Accuracy when blog-level topic labels are available

method	accuracy(%)
random	63.7
baseline 2 (NB-init)	67.1
NB+EM	67.4

Thus we can choose a topic label from the set of topic labels assigned to the blog that e_{ij} belongs to. In this setting, we compare the proposed method with the above-mentioned baseline 2 (NB-init) and also with the random classification which randomly selects a topic label from the blog-level topic labels. The accuracy of the random classification was averaged over 5 trials. The result was shown in Table 3. This table shows that, although NB+EM significantly outperforms the random classification, it shows only a slight (non-significant) improvement over the baseline 2 (NB-init).

5   Conclusion

We proposed a method for constructing an entry classifier using blog-level topic labels. We used the Naive Bayes classifier enhanced with the EM algorithm for this purpose. The proposed method outperformed the Naive Bayes classifier without the EM algorithm in a general situation where blog-level topic labels are not available. In future work, we will investigate the proposed method in more details, especially in a situation where there are more blogs that have multiple topic labels. We also plan to incorporate the reliability of blog-level topic labels into the model, because some blogs are assigned with unreliable topic labels, which probably would degrade the classification performance.

References

1. Brooks, C.H., Montanez, N.: Improved annotation of the blogosphere via autotagging and hierarchical clustering. In: Proc. of the 15th International World Wide Web Conference, pp. 625–632 (2006)
2. Dempster, A.P., Laird, N.M., Rubin, D.B.: Maximum likelihood from incomplete data via the EM algorithm. Journal of the Royal Statistical Society Series B 39(1), 1–38 (1977)

3. Hofmann, T., Puzicha, J.: Statistical models for co-occurrence data. Technical Report AIM-1625, Artifical Intelligence Laboratory, Massachusetts Institute of Technology (1998), `citeseer.nj.nec.com/hofmann98statistical.html`

4. Ikeda, D., Takamura, H., Okumura, M.: Semi-supervised learning for blog classification. In: Proc. of the Twenty-Third AAAI Conference on Artificial Intelligence (AAAI 2008), pp. 1156–1161 (2008)

5. Kumar, R., Novak, J., Raghavan, P., Tomkins, A.: On the bursty evolution of blogspace. In: Proc. of the 12th International World Wide Web Conference, pp. 568–576 (2003)

6. McCallum, A., Nigam, K.: A comparison of event models for naive bayes text classification. In: Proceedings of AAAI 1998 Workshop on Learning for Text Categorization, pp. 41–48 (1998)

7. Mishne, G.: Autotag: A collaborative approach to automated tag assignment for weblog posts. In: Proc. of the 15th International World Wide Web Conference, pp. 953–954 (2006)

8. Ni, X., Wu, X., Yu, Y.: Automated identification of chinese weblogger's interests based on text classification. In: Proc. of the 2006 IEEE/WIC/ACM International Conference on Web Intelligence (WI 2006), pp. 247–253 (2006)

9. Nigam, K., McCallum, A., Thrun, S., Mitchell, T.: Text classification from labeled and unlabeled documents using EM. Machine Learning 39(2/3), 103–134 (2000)

10. Ohkura, T., Kiyota, Y., Nakagawa, H.: Browsing system for weblog articles based on automated folksonomy. In: Proc. of the WWW 2006 Workshop on the Weblogging Ecosystem: Aggregation, Analysis and Dynamics (2006)

11. Teng, C.Y., Chen, H.H.: Detection of bloggers' interests: Using textual, temporal, and interactive features. In: Proc. of the 2006 IEEE/WIC/ACM International Conference on Web Intelligence (WI 2006), pp. 366–369 (2006)

Finding Hard Questions by Knowledge Gap Analysis in Question Answer Communities

Ying-Liang Chen and Hung-Yu Kao[*]

Department of Computer Science and Information Engineering,
National Cheng Kung University, Tainan, Taiwan, R.O.C.
hykao@mail.ncku.edu.tw

Abstract. The Community Question Answer (CQA) service is a typical forum of Web2.0 in sharing knowledge among people. There are thousands of questions have been posted and solved every day. Because of the above reasons and the variant users in CQA service, the question search and ranking are the most important researches in the CQA portal. In this paper, we address the problem of detecting the question being easy or hard by means of a probability model. In addition, we observed the phenomenon called knowledge gap that is related to the habit of users and use knowledge gap diagram to illustrate how much knowledge gap in different categories. In this task, we propose an approach called knowledge-gap-based difficulty rank (KG-DRank) algorithm that combines the user-user network and the architecture of the CQA service to solve this problem. The experimental results show our approach leads to a better performance than other baseline approaches and increases the F-measure by a factor ranging from 15% to 20%.

Keywords: CQA portal, difficulty, knowledge gap, link analysis, expert finding.

1 Introduction

Recently, the forum system of Web 2.0 is more and more popular and interesting. People can share or seek any information from any place in the world. One of the most popular and useful forum system is Community-based Question-Answering (CQA) portals. For example, the typical CQA portals such as Yahoo! Answers[1] in English, Naver[2] in Korean, and Baidu Knows[3] in Chinese, can be regarded as variations of online forums. In this paper, We choose Yahoo!Answers where approximately over one hundred million resolved questions in English for our research .

On account of the increasing progressively increasing questions and answers, user may not find the questions they want to know or discuss efficiently. Thus, most of

---

[*] Corresponding author.
[1] http://answers.yahoo.com
[2] http://www.naver.com
[3] http://zhidao.baidu.com

P.-J. Cheng et al. (Eds.): AIRS 2010, LNCS 6458, pp. 370–378, 2010.

works in CQA service are to improve their functionalities like question ranking, question search, and question recommendation. However, the output of the prior work do not consider the expertise (or authority) of users, i.e., for question ranking, the user may be an amateur in this area and the outputs of the search engine are so hard to understand for them. Moreover, an expert may wants to search the harder questions but the top results are too easy to contain rich information for them. Thus, in this paper, *we concerned with how to rank questions by their difficulty levels*.

Moreover, the work of expert finding is highly associated with our task. The expert can be considered a user who is familiar with the particular topic or category, and the expert can solve most of questions in the particular category. In short, the difference between an easy question and a hard question is the ratio of non-experts and experts participating in this question respectively, and we can separate the task as the two parts: expert finding and question ranking. In this paper, the "expert" we want to find is different from the prior works, comparatively, we want to find the *answer-hard-question-frequently expert*. That is to say, we want to find the user that not only is an expert but also focuses on answering hard questions more than other users.

However, the fact in the real world is that the experts not only answer hard questions but also easy questions and it bring about the difficulty of determining a question is easy or hard. We observe a phenomenon called the *knowledge gap* existing in the CQA service. The knowledge gap is a phenomenon which associates with the expertise of users. There are two main principles on the knowledge gap. First, *the non-experts have no ability to answer the question that over their knowledge*. Second, *the experts have less interesting in the question that under the certain the degree of difficulty*. In this paper, we investigate the knowledge gap how to effect a CQA service and we propose a knowledge-gap-based difficulty rank (KG-DRank) algorithm calculating in probability to tackle the task that determine the question is easy or hard.

The rest of this paper is structured as follows. In Section 2, we briefly discuss related work. In Section 3, we define our task by the probability model and we present our approach called KG-DRank algorithm to solve this task. Next, experimental results are reported in Section 4. Section 5 concludes this work and our future work.

2   Related Work

There are several researches focusing on how to find expert by modeling and computing user-user graph such as [6,11,14]. McCallum [11] et al. utilize the user-user graph to find the experts for particular topics and then Zhang et al. [14] use the network-based ranking algorithms HITS [9] and PageRank [2] to identify users with high expertise. Their results show high correlation between link-based metrics and the answer quality. Next, Liu et al [10] use the features such as author's activity, number of clicks for finding the best answers for a given question. Then [6,7] use HITS algorithm to find the authority of users in question/answering network that an asker is linked to an answerer if the answerer replies the question that asker has been asked. The experiments show that the obtained authority score is better than simply counting the number of answers an answerer has given. Although the results demonstrate that HITS algorithm is a good approach to find expert, but there are some potential factor like the habit of asking questions and replying answers may reduce the performance. Unlike [6] and [14], Zhou et al. [15] utilize the structural relations among users in the forum system and use content-based probability model to find the experts for the particular question.

Question ranking is to rank the results for purpose of browsing-time decreasing, the typical approach is using the information of Q&A content such as best ratings such as [3].Jeon et al. [8] addressed the answer quality problem in a community QA portal and tried to estimate it, they used a set of non-textual features such as answer length, number of points received, etc. for determining answer quality. Agichtein et al. [1] expands on [8] by exploring a larger range of features including both structural, textual, and community features. Su et al. [13] analyzed the quality of each answers varies significantly. Bian et al. [3] proposed to solve collaborative QA by considering both answer quality and relevance and also used content-based quality answers without considering user expertise. Because of the answer quality problem on [3,8,13], Suryanoto et al. [12] propose a quality-aware framework that considers both answer relevance and answer quality derived from answer features and expertise of answerers.

3 Problem Definition and Our Approach

3.1 Problem Definition

We state the problem of the degree of difficulty on questions q is by means of a probability model. Given a question q, the probability of the question q being hard is estimated as follows:

$$p(h|q) = \frac{p(q|h)p(h)}{p(q)} \tag{1}$$

where $p(h)$ is the probability of a question being hard in the particular category and $p(q)$ is the probability of a question generated by users, and the two variables are the same for all questions. Thus, our task is therefore to capture how much hard on the question q by $p(q|h)$.

3.2 The KG-DRank Algorithm

The progress of our system only has iterations of the two steps: the expert finding and the difficulty degree detecting. The expert finding concludes the expertise model and reinforcement model, while the difficulty degree detecting concludes the difficulty degree model and question ranking model.

3.2.1 Expertise Model
We cite the prior work [6] as our expertise model.

3.2.2 Difficulty Degree Model
The question can be divided to the two parts: the asking and answering. Thus, the probability of a question q given the degree of difficulty being hard is obtained by taking the summation across the users of the two parts on the question:

$$p(q|h) = \alpha * p\left(c_q^a|h\right) + (1 - \alpha) * p\left(c_q^r|h\right) \tag{2}$$

Where $p\left(c_q^a|h\right)$ represents how much hard in asking, and while $p\left(c_q^r|h\right)$ represents how much hard in answering. In asking, we capture an estimate of $p\left(c_q^a|h\right)$ by means of three types of architecture of CQA service, and it means how much expertise asker has in asking. It can be expressed as:

$$p(c_q^a|h) = p(c_q^a|q) * p(q|a) * p_{ask}(a|\theta h) \tag{3}$$

Where $p(c_q^a|q)$ is the probability of the content that asker a asks on the question q and $p(q|a)$ is how much knowledge that the asker a contribute to the question q and $p_{ask}(a|\theta h)$ is the probability of an asker-expert of the asker a given the difficulty degree model θh. The value of $p_{ask}(a|\theta h)$ is initialized to the hub value that section 3.2.1 referred and we will discuss the change of the next value later in this section.

To compute an estimation of $p(c_q^a|q)$, we use the length of the content and normalize it by the square root such as the following:

$$p(c_q^u|q) = \frac{\sqrt{l_q^u}}{\sqrt{(\Sigma_{i \epsilon q} l_q^i)}} \tag{4}$$

Where c_q^u is the content that user u has posted on the question q and l_q^u is the length of c_q^u and $\Sigma_{i \epsilon q} l_q^i$ is the summation of the length of all the posts on the question q. According to above estimation, the estimation of $p(q|a)$ is defined by:

$$p(q|u) = \frac{\sqrt{l_q^u}}{\max_{q' \epsilon u} \sqrt{l_q^u}} \tag{5}$$

Where $\max_{q' \epsilon u} \sqrt{l_q^u}$ is the maximum of the length that user u had asked before. The estimation of $p(q|u)$ is similar to $p(c_q^u|q)$, but we use maximum instead of summation to compute $p(q|u)$. It is reasonable that the hard questions must be using more words to ask and the easy questions instead. For the same asker, the question which the asker uses more words to describe has stronger probability of being hard question than the other questions the same asker asked.

In answering, we also divided it into two parts: the best answerer and the other repliers, so how much difficulty given by the answerers can be obtained as follows:

$$p(c_q^r|h) = \beta * p(c_q^b|h) + (1 - \beta) * p(c_q^{r'}|h) \tag{6}$$

3.2.3 Reinforcement Model

The main idea of reinforcement model is that the more hard questions user participates in, the more expertise user obtains and the expertise can be divided into the asking and the answering. In this model, we define two types of association between difficulty and users. One of them is defined as :

$$p_{ask}(h|u) = \frac{|A_u \cap H|}{|A_u|} \quad , \quad p_{ans}(h|u) = \frac{|R_u \cap H|}{|R_u|} \tag{7}$$

Where $|A_u|$ is the number of questions that user has asked, while $|R_u|$ is the number of questions that user has replied. And $|A_u \cap H|$ represents the number of hard questions that user has asked, while $|R_u \cap H|$ represents the number of hard questions that user has replied, furthermore, we use equation 9 to represent the notation *local difficulty probability model*. The other association between difficulty degree and user is that how much ratio of hard questions user participates in his/her all participating questions, and it can be expressed as:

$$p_{ask}(u|h) = \frac{|A_u \cap H|}{|H|} \quad , \quad p_{ans}(u|h) = \frac{|R_u \cap H|}{|H|} \qquad (8)$$

Where $|H|$ is the total number of hard questions in category C, and we called this equation as *global difficulty* probability module. Therefore, the global KG-DRank (**GKG-DRank**) of $p_{ask}(u|\theta h)$ and $p_{ans}(u|\theta h)$ is represented as:

$$p_{ask}(u|\theta h)^{k+1} = \lambda * p_{ask}(u|h) + (1 - \lambda) * p_{ask}(u|\theta h)^k \qquad (9)$$

$$p_{ans}(u|\theta h)^{k+1} = \lambda * p_{ans}(u|h) + (1 - \lambda) * p_{ans}(u|\theta h)^k \qquad (10)$$

Where $p_{ask}(u|\theta h)^k$ and $p_{ans}(u|\theta h)^k$ are the kth-iteration-number score of $p_{ask}(u|\theta h)$ and $p_{ans}(u|\theta h)$ which $p_{ask}(u|\theta h)^0$ and $p_{ans}(u|\theta h)^0$ are hub and authority that base HITS algorithm computes in the prior section, and $\lambda \epsilon [0,1]$. The other way is local KG-DRank (**LKG-DRank**) is represented as :

$$p_{ask}(u|\theta h)^{k+1} \propto \lambda * p_{ask}(h|u) + (1 - \lambda) * p_{ask}(u|\theta h)^k \qquad (11)$$

$$p_{ans}(u|\theta h)^{k+1} \propto \lambda * p_{ans}(h|u) + (1 - \lambda) * p_{ans}(u|\theta h)^k \qquad (12)$$

4   Experiments

We crawled 40,000 resolved questions from Yahoo! Answers service in English for our experiments, and these questions from five categories respectively such as *Martial arts, Cycling, Health, Pets,* and *Software,* and there are 8,000 questions among each category. For each category, ten colleague students volunteer to be our assessors and each assessor also has interesting and basic knowledge at one or more categories. In general, we let assessors choose questions from each category randomly and label the question as 'hard' if they think that the question is hard to answer, otherwise, they label the question as 'easy' if they think the question is easy to answer. In this step, although people consider the question as easy or hard is subjective, we do our best to label it and omit the ambiguous questions, and Table 1 is our answer set for each category.

Table 1. The answer set for each categories

	Martial arts	Cycling	Health	Pets	Software
# Hard Q	93	75	70	70	70
# Easy Q	93	75	70	70	70

4.1   Baseline

We utilized five baseline methods in order to demonstrate the effectiveness of our approach:

1. Eigenrumour [4] algorithm: the linked based algorithm for ranking blogs, and the relationship between users and blogs in Eigenrumour is similar to the relationship between users and questions in our approach.
2. Base probability: the score that only do a half of KGB-DR, i.e., the iteration number is 1 in KGB-DR
3. Base Hits: there are two steps in this approach. First, calculate the auth score and hub score of users by [6]. Second, compute the score of the question by the sum of the hub score of asker and auth score of answerers.
4. #Words: the number of words in the question included answers
5. #Answerers: the number of answerers in the question

4.2 Evaluation Metrics

In order to evaluate the performance of our system, we use the four evaluation metrics such as the precision, the recall, the F-measure. In general, we set a variable "N" as a threshold, i.e., if the rank of the question is more than N, the question is regarded as a hard question, and while the question is regarded as an easy question instead. Furthermore, as same as the prior work [1], we utilize the above evaluation metrics for "hard question" and "easy question" separately, and both are measured when the experiment threshold N is set to maximize the F-measure. We will use these evaluating strategies to show how the performance of our methodology.

4.3 Comparison to Baseline

The final tuning of parameters for our two models is reported in Table 2 and the comparison of methods for each category is represented later.

Table 2. The parameters for the two models

	i	α	β	λ	t
LKG-DRank	15	0.3	0.7	0.001	15%
GKG-DRank	10	0.4	0.6	0.4	15%

4.3.1 F-measure of Easy Question and Hard Question

The performance of the methods for all test data sets with the F-measure of hard question is summarized in Table 3. The results presented in the table show that our approach with the LKG-DRank exhibits the best performance among all the other methods in detecting the hard question. The performance of the method we presented with the GKG-DRank is similar to the Base probability and the two methods show the second to the best performance. The #Answerers showed the worst performance and it shows that the more the answerers in the question, the easier the question becomes. Although EigenRumor also utilize the relationship between users and questions, the method shows poor performance due to the phenomenon of the experts can answer easy questions.

Table 3. The F-measure of hard question for each method and each category

	Martial arts	Cycling	Health	Pets	Software
LKG-DRank	**0.77**	**0.71**	**0.79**	**0.81**	0.50
GKG-DRank	0.67	0.70	0.66	0.68	0.55
Base probability	0.68	0.70	0.64	0.68	**0.59**
Base Hits	0.66	0.64	0.60	0.69	0.53
EigenRumor	0.50	0.54	0.61	0.64	0.41
#Words	0.67	0.60	0.55	0.53	0.38
#Answerers	0.48	0.41	0.50	0.46	0.31

Table 4 represents the performance of the methods for all test data sets with the F-measure of hard question. Compare with Table 3, the performance with all methods are increasing, but our approach with LKG-DRank also exhibits the best performance for all categories. It is reasonable that the part of the expert computed in KGS is higher than the part of the non-expert among all categories. In Table 4, the method that the performance is most increasing compared to Table 3 is #Answerers. It represents that the easy question is identified easier than the hard question via #Answerers.

Table 4. The F-measure of easy question for each method and each category

	Martial arts	Cycling	Health	Pets	Software
LKG-DRank	**0.78**	**0.73**	**0.81**	**0.83**	**0.69**
GKG-DRank	0.73	**0.73**	0.75	0.76	**0.69**
Base probability	0.75	**0.73**	0.75	0.76	**0.69**
Base Hits	0.70	0.72	0.71	0.71	0.68
EigenRumor	0.67	0.67	0.67	0.69	0.64
#Words	0.72	0.66	0.73	0.66	0.63
#Answerers	0.68	0.59	0.61	0.62	0.59

4.3.2 The Examples of the Outputs Compared with the Basic Approaches
In order to compare the effectiveness of our approach, we give the particular query for searching questions in the particular category with cosine similarity. For example, we give the query "karate" in the category Martial arts and there are 358 questions in the output. For the purpose of more showing the effectiveness of our approach, we list the other questions and rank the questions with different methods and the outputs is shown in Table 5. The numbers in the brackets in Table 5 represent the corresponding methods. For example, the number 2,768 in No1 question represents there are 2,768 words in the question including asking and answering and the number 161 represents the order of the question is 161 of 358 by ranking with #words. The top three questions in Table 5

are detected as hard questions by our approach and the order of the rank is 36, 39, and 56 respectively. The score of the top three questions computed by our approach is higher and we can tell the three questions as hard by the question title, however, the order of the same questions is last by the other two methods due to the less words and number of answers in the questions. On the contrary, the last two questions in Table 5 are detected as easy question by our approach and it is easy to tell by the title of the questions. But the two easy questions attract some non-experts to answer it and it bring about the high order in the methods with number of words and answers. In addition, the question of No2 and the question of No4 are similar in the particular viewpoint, however; the different type of asking may make question be easy or hard. The question of No4 is the popular question of the amateur, but the question of No2 repeats asking the same thing by the different viewpoints and it would make this question hard. The two examples can prove the two similar questions may not be same degree of difficulty.

Table 5. The example of questions with query "karate" by our approach (358 total questions)

No.	Question title	Rank with our method	Rank with #words	#Answers	Degree of difficulty
1	would shotokan karate help for a mma career?	36	161(2768)	5	Hard
2	what age would you consider being to old to start karate?	39	255(1393)	8	Hard
3	Any karatekas who train with partial or minimal meniscus?	56	162(2757)	2	Hard
4	Starting karate at 16?	317	45(6133)	22	Easy

5 Conclusion

In this paper we defined the problem of detecting the question is easy or hard in YA and addressed it as a probability model and then utilize the phenomenon called knowledge gap in CQA service to solve this task. The contributions of this paper include:

1. We observe the unreasonable relationship between users from knowledge gap diagram, i.e., the expert can also answers the easy question in YA and it is not a good situation for the expert-finding via link analysis.
2. We present the approach called KG-DRank algorithm combining the relationship between users and the architecture in YA or CQA service, and the experiments shows the performance of our approach with LKG-DRank is the best among all baseline.
3. We demonstrate that the phenomenon of knowledge gap in our experiments and the performance reflect to the strength of the knowledge gap in the particular category.

References

1. Agichtein, E., Castillo, C., Donato, D., Gionis, A., Mishne, G.: Finding high-quality content in social media. In: Proceedings of the International Conference on Web Search and Web Data Mining, pp. 183–194. ACM, Palo Alto (2008)
2. Brin, S., Page, L.: The anatomy of a large-scale hypertextual Web search engine. In: Proceedings of the Seventh International Conference on World Wide Web 7, pp. 107–117. Elsevier Science Publishers B. V., Brisbane (1998)
3. Bian, J., Liu, Y., Agichtein, E., Zha, H.: Finding the right facts in the crowd: factoid question answering over social media. In: Proceeding of the 17th International Conference on World Wide Web, pp. 467–476. ACM, Beijing (2008)
4. Fujimura, K., Inoue, T., Sugisaki, M.: The EigenRumor Algorithm for Ranking Blogs. In: WWW 2005 Workshop on the Weblogging Ecosystem 2005 (2005)
5. Fang, H., Zhai, C.: Probabilistic models for expert finding. In: Amati, G., Carpineto, C., Romano, G. (eds.) ECIR 2007. LNCS, vol. 4425, pp. 418–430. Springer, Heidelberg (2007)
6. Jurczyk, P., Agichtein, E.: Discovering authorities in question answer communities by using link analysis. In: Proceedings of the Sixteenth ACM Conference on Conference on Information and Knowledge Management, pp. 919–922. ACM, Lisbon (2007)
7. Jurczyk, P., Agichtein, E.: Hits on question answer portals: exploration of link analysis for author ranking. In: Proceedings of the 30th Annual International ACM SIGIR Conference on Research and Development in Information Retrieval, pp. 845–846. ACM, Amsterdam (2007)
8. Jeon, J., Croft, W.B., Lee, J.H., Park, S.: A framework to predict the quality of answers with non-textual features. In: Proceedings of the 29th Annual International ACM SIGIR Conference on Research and Development in Information Retrieval, pp. 228–235. ACM, Seattle (2006)
9. Kleinberg, J.M.: Authoritative sources in a hyperlinked environment. J. ACM 46, 604–632 (1999)
10. Liu, X., Croft, W.B., Koll, M.: Finding experts in community-based question-answering services. In: Proceedings of the 14th ACM International Conference on Information and Knowledge Management, pp. 315–316. ACM, Bremen (2005)
11. McCallum, A., Corrada Emmanuel, A., Wang, X.: Topic and role discovery in social networks. In: Proceedings of the 19th International Joint Conference on Artificial Intelligence, pp. 786–791. Morgan Kaufmann Publishers Inc., Edinburgh (2005)
12. Suryanto, M.A., Lim, E.P., Sun, A., Chiang, R.H.L.: Quality-aware collaborative question answering: methods and evaluation. In: Proceedings of the Second ACM International Conference on Web Search and Data Mining, Spain, pp. 142–151. ACM, Barcelona (2009)
13. Su, Q., Pavlov, D., Chow, J.-H., Baker, W.C.: Internet-scale collection of human-reviewed data. In: Proceedings of the 16th International Conference on World Wide Web, pp. 231–240. ACM, Banff (2007)
14. Zhang, J., Ackerman, M.S., Adamic, L.: Expertise networks in online communities: structure and algorithms. In: Proceedings of the 16th International Conference on World Wide Web, pp. 221–230. ACM, Banff (2007)
15. Zhou, Y., Cong, G., Cui, B., Jensen, C.S., Yao, J.: Routing Questions to the Right Users in Online Communities. In: Proceedings of the 2009 IEEE International Conference on Data Engineering, pp. 700–711. IEEE Computer Society, Los Alamitos (2009)

Exploring the Visual Annotatability of Query Concepts for Interactive Cross-Language Information Retrieval

Yoshihiko Hayashi[1], Masaaki Nagata[2], and Bora Savas[1]

[1] Graduate School of Language and Culture, Osaka University
Toyonaka 560-0043, Japan
[2] NTT Communication Science Laboratories
Kyoto 619-0237, Japan
hayashi@lang.osaka-u.ac.jp, nagata.masaaki@lab.ntt.co.jp,
bsavas@gs.lang.osaka-u.ac.jp

Abstract. In interactive CLIR (Cross-Language Information Retrieval), it is crucial to provide users with useful clues for signifying the word senses that a translated query term can have. Among the possible means, visual clues can be effectively employed, as they are intuitive and language-neutral to some extent. This paper therefore examined the possibility of Web images as an intuitive and effective clue for the purpose of signifying word senses. We designed an experiment to collect human assessments of the relevance of Web images. Through statistical analyses applied to the assessment data, this paper shows: (1) the semantic class of a word sense together with familiarity is a good indicator for predicting the applicability of Web images as a word sense clue; (2) Web biases should be considered when gathering Web images, particularly for terms used as entity names.

Keywords: cross-language information retrieval, interactive interface, query translation, word sense, visual annotation.

1 Introduction

Among the considerable problems in query-translation-based CLIR, the most crucial one is the proper selection of translation candidates. Given a conceivable situation in which a user is not familiar with the target languages, the CLIR system should be able to automatically and accurately translate user queries. To this end, several approaches have been pursued [9], including the incorporation of (pseudo-)relevance-feedback, application of statistical language models, utilization of off-the-shelf MT systems, and combinations of these.

On another extreme, a different scenario can be drawn, if an *interactive* search setting is possible: the user is able to select appropriate translations by consulting the clues provided by the system [10]. Here, the clues should not be dependent on the target language; they should be language independent and preferably intuitive. Along the lines of this interactive scenario, The authors proposed to

P.-J. Cheng et al. (Eds.): AIRS 2010, LNCS 6458, pp. 379–388, 2010.

present images gathered from the Web (hereafter, Web images) as a clue for the word senses of a translated query term, and experimentally showed that an interactive CLIR interface using such Web images could help users select relevant query translations correctly and efficiently [6].

Although the results are substantially informative, it has not been very clear *what kind of query concepts (word senses) can be effectively illustrated by Web images.* Therefore this paper further explores the visual annotatability of word senses based on a human assessment experiment on the relevance of Web images. The results acquired through statistical analyses from the viewpoints of semantic class and word sense familiarity will provide insights that should be considered in the design of an interactive CLIR system, as well as a principled way to construct a test query set.

2   An Interactive CLIR Interface

Figure 1 shows the system organization of the experimental interactive CLIR interface that we have proposed in [6]. The system accepts queries in a source language and searches for relevant information in user-designated target languages by invoking a target Web search engine that is external to the system.

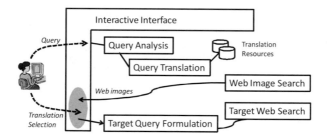

Fig. 1. Organization of an interactive CLIR system

The system first analyzes the input query and assigns translation candidates for each term extracted from the query. A set of translation resources such as bilingual dictionaries is utilized to retrieve translation candidates in the target languages.

The system then invokes an external image search engine on the Web in order to collect Web images for each of the translation candidates. To do this, each translation candidate is employed as a query term submitted to the image search engine, resulting in multiple invocations of the external image search.

The resulted Web images, each accompanied by a check-box, as shown in Figure 2, are then presented to the user so that he or she can generate a query formula to be submitted to the target Web search engine. The point is that the Web images should be presented in an intelligible yet concise manner. Thumbnails provided by Web image search engines fulfill this requirement nicely.

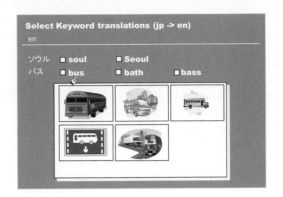

Fig. 2. Displaying Web Images with check-boxes

3   Experiment to Collect Human Assessments

Figure 3 illustrates the general flow of the experiment to collect human assessments of the relevance of Web images, in which we envision Japanese-to-English retrieval. Each of the steps is described as follows.

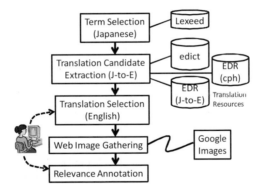

Fig. 3. Flow of the experiment to collect human assessments of Web image relevance

1. **Japanese term selection:** To conduct the experiment, we first need to construct a reasonable set of Japanese target terms. We selected these terms from the Japanese lexical resource Lexeed [11], first by applying the following conditions.

   – the term is a noun
   – it has at least two and at most five word senses after filtering out unfamiliar word senses with the word sense familiarity score threshold 2.0.

   The first condition is not essential, but we limited ourselves to nominal concepts to initiate the presented line of research. The second, on the other hand, is crucial: a monosemous term is of less interest, but one with too many senses may be highly abstract and thus difficult to handle. Fortunately, every entry in Lexeed is sufficiently annotated with grammatical information (POS), semantic information (word senses distinction and the corresponding semantic categories in the semantic hierarchy system given in [8]), and *word sense familiarity scores.* A word sense familiarity score that shows how a word sense is familiar to native speakers is assigned to every word sense of every word entry in Lexeed. These scores were determined by averaging ratings (on 7-point scale) acquired through carefully designed psychological experiments [2] involving around 50 Japanese participants. Lexeed is also valuable in the sense that it gathers a set of 28,113 basic words (45,691 word senses total) that were identified through the experiments as the most essential vocabulary of Japanese language.

2. **Translation candidate extraction:** English translation candidates for the selected Japanese terms were extracted by looking up bilingual translation resources: edict[1] and the EDR Electronic Dictionary[2]. Translation candidates that were recognized as Multi-Word Expressions (MWEs)[3] were discarded, because it was expected that appropriate Web images are hardly assigned to the *complex concept* denoted by an MWE. Moreover, Japanese terms with unique translation candidates in English, even polysemous in Lexeed, were excluded. After applying these filters, a set of 2,380 Japanese target terms (5,540 word senses total) were obtained by setting the word sense familiarity score threshold to 4.3.

3. **Translation selection:** Based on the translation candidates obtained through the above mentioned process, alignments between Japanese target word senses and the English translations were determined by human assessors. Only 37 word senses were left unaligned with appropriate translations after allowing the assessors to make minor revisions to the translation candidates.

4. **Web image gathering:** A set of Web images was gathered for each word-sense/English-translation pair by using `Google Images`[4]. Here we simply supplied `Google Images` with the English translation as a query term without performing any query expansions or refinements. We retained only the images acquired from the first screen returned by `Google Images`.

5. **Relevance annotation:** Finally, the participants were asked to annotate relevance of the Web image set obtained for each Japanese word-sense/English translation pair. The relevance score was given according to the following four point scale.

   - **3:** A number of relevant images are presented in higher ranks.
   - **2:** Around four or five relevant images are presented in the set.

---

[1] http://www.csse.monash.edu.au/~jwb/edict.html
[2] http://www2.nict.go.jp/r/r312/EDR/index.html
[3] English translations consisting of five or more words were naively marked as MWEs this time.
[4] http://images.google.com/

- **1:** At least one relevant image is found in the set.
- **0:** There are no relevant images found in the set.

Three participants in all took part in the annotation work. Of these, one lead person was responsible for determining the final relevance scores.

4 Results and Analyses

4.1 Overall Result

Table 1 summarizes the distribution of the relevance scores of the target Japanese word senses. As shown, almost two-thirds of the word senses were successfully annotated by the associated Web image set. We hereafter classify the Japanese word senses into two groups: *pos* for those whose relevance score is greater than zero, and *neg* for those whose relevance score is zero.

Table 1. Distribution of the relevance scores (total # of word senses: 5,540)

Relevance score	# of Word senses (%)	Relevance group (%)
3	1,803 (32.5)	
2	1,114 (20.1)	*pos* (67.0)
1	794 (14.3)	
0	1,829 (33.0)	*neg* (33.0)

4.2 Semantic Class and Relevance

To examine the results in terms of noun semantics, we made a two-by-two contingency table (Table 2), that shows the relationships between binary semantic classes (`abstract`, `concrete`) and the relevance groups (*neg*, *pos*).

Table 2. Contingency table: binary semantic classes versus relevance groups

Semantic class	*neg*	*pos*
abstract	1,517	2,116
concrete	312	1,575

A chi-square test of independence was performed on the contingency table. The result was statistically significant ($\chi^2 = 364.69$) with p-level ($p < .001$), indicating that word senses that represent a concrete object are better annotated with the Web images[5] compared to those that represent an abstract object.

Note here that we can obtain corresponding semantic classes in Goi-Taikei[8] for each word sense in Lexeed thanks to the semantic links between these two

---

[5] ImageNet [3] actually assigns photographs available on the Web only to the `physical entity` WordNet synsets.

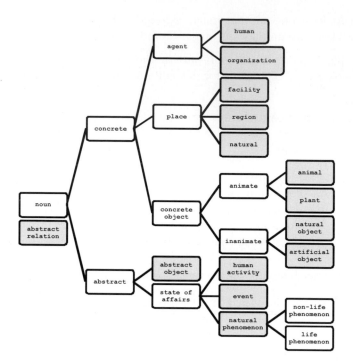

Fig. 4. Upper part of the noun semantic hierarchy in Goi-Taikei [8]

lexical resources. Figure 4 illustrates the upper part of the noun semantic hierarchy in Goi-Taikei, in which all Japanese nouns are first classified into `concrete`
or `abstract`, then further classified into more specific classes[6].

This result may agree with our intuition: objects that have a shape/figure
can be visualized. However to further explore the relationships, we broke down
the binary semantic classes into 14 more specific semantic classes, which are
represented by shaded nodes in Fig. 4. We again conducted a chi-square test
of independence and also performed Haberman's adjusted residual analysis in
order to see which semantic classes exhibit a remarkable tendency.

The result detailed in Table 3 was again statistically significant ($\chi^2 = 491.48$)
with p-level ($p < .001$), indicating that word senses that belong to particular
semantic classes are significantly better or worse being annotated with Web
images. In Table 3, each cell shows the observed frequency and expected frequencies; the expected frequency is marked by either * or ** if it is statistically
significant with p-level ($p < .005$ or $p < .001$).

Table 3 reveals the following anomalies.

– `organization` ($\subset$ `concrete`): Although the observed *pos* number exceeds
  the expected number, it is not statistically significant even with p-level ($p <$

---

[6] Although the entire structure of the system is not shown in Fig. 4, it has almost
2,700 nodes arranged in a tree with a maximum depth 12.

.0.05). This is because the semantic class includes nouns that exhibit so-called *systematic polysemy*, such as "head office" or "mecca" (the attractive place sense), which are hard to visualize.

- `activity` (⊂ `abstract`): Although the observed *neg* number exceeds the expected number, it is not statistically significant with p-value 0.096. This is conceivable, because the semantic class includes many human activities that can be photographed or illustrated. Examples include physical activities such as "jump" and "fishing" and mental activities such as "surprise" and "forgiveness." The formers can be photographed while the latters are tend to be illustrated.

- `natural phenomenon` (⊂ `abstract`): This class exhibits the most prominent anomaly. In spite of belonging to `abstract` class, the observed *pos* number significantly exceeds the expected number, meaning more word senses were annotated with Web images than expected. We can accept this apparent anomaly, if we look further into the semantic system. The semantic class `natural phenomenon` is sub-categorized into `non-life phenomenon` or `life phenomenon`. The former semantic class, for example, includes `meteorological phenomenon`, and the latter includes `physiological phenomenon`; many items in these two classes are photographable or can be illustrated.

4.3   Familiarity and Relevance

Given that the target Japanese word senses are annotated with the word sense familiarity scores, we also examined the relationship between the familiarity level and the relevance of the Web images. Here the familiarity level was derived for each word sense by discretizing the assigned familiarity score f. We once again constructed a contingency table (Table 4) and applied statistical tests. As the both variables are deemed as ordered categorical variables, we applied the asymptotic linear-by-linear association test (lbl_test in [7]) as well as a standard chi-square test.

Statistical significance was once again confirmed with p-level ($p < .005$) by the lbl_test ($\chi^2 = 127.61$) as well as by the standard chi-squre test ($\chi^2 = 152.58$), thus showing that familiarity levels can affect the relevance of the associated Web images. We again added stars in the table to the expected numbers, that show statistical significance through the residual analysis.

The results shown in the table are quite impressive, because they clearly indicate that:

- the highest relevance (r3) was achieved largely by highly familiar word senses (c6 and c7),
- whereas the lowest relevance (r0) was brought about by less familiar word senses (c5, c4, and c3);
- middle-level relevance (r1, r2) was almost independent of the familiarity levels.

Table 3. Contingency table: 14 semantic classes versus relevance groups

Semantic class	neg	pos
human	135	388
	172.67**	350.33**
organization	14	46
	19.81	40.19
facility	12	88
	33.01**	66.99**
region	25	107
	43.58**	88.42**
nature	10	59
	22.78**	46.22**
animal	10	123
	43.91**	89.09**
plant	1	45
	15.19**	30.81**
natural	13	50
	20.80*	42.20*
artificial	92	689
	257.84**	523.16**
abstract	270	373
	212.28**	430.72**
activity	322	588
	300.43	609.57
event	94	143
	78.24	158.76*
natural phenomenon	55	183
	78.57**	159.43**
abstract relation	776	829
	529.88**	1075.12**

Table 4. Contingency table: familiarity levels versus relevance scores (rs)

Familiarity level	rs=0	rs=1	rs=2	rs=3	# of Word senses
c3	55	17	20	21	113
($f \leq 3.0$)	37.31**	16.20	22.72	36.78**	
c4	255	97	123	169	644
($3.0 < f \leq 4.0$)	212.61**	92.30	129.50	209.59**	
c5	781	305	422	567	2,075
($4.0 < f \leq 5.0$)	685.05**	297.39	417.25	675.31**	
c6	662	329	486	854	2,331
($5.0 < f \leq 6.0$)	769.57**	334.08	468.72	758.63**	
ch	76	46	63	192	377
($f > 6.0$)	124.46**	54.03	75.81	122.70**	
# of rs class instances	1829	794	1114	1803	

Further, it can be said that a nearly 70% of word senses located at the highest familiarity levels (c6 or c7) are well annotated ($rs \geq 2$). Although this result might not be incompatible with our intuition, it should be further investigated. One of the possibilities is hidden dependency between semantic class and the word sense familiarity score. For example, many words in `concrete` semantic class could have higher familiarity scores; hence they are likely to be well visualized. The results from a chi-square test of dependence, however, were not statistically significant, suggesting that some words in some `abstract` classes still can have higher familiarity scores. At the same time, the results show that some `concrete` classes, such as `animal`, are tend to have higher average familiarity scores. Therefore it could be said that familiar word senses, in general, can be well visualized.

5   Discussion

As Table 1 shows, around one-third of the word senses were not adequately annotated with the set of Web images gathered by the described simple image gathering method. This difficulty can be mainly attributed to the following two reasons. In either case, any member of the presented set of Web images had nothing to do with the intended word sense.

1. Some word senses might be intrinsically un-visualizable: As discussed in this paper, some of the word senses of this type can be predicted by using the semantic class and the familiarity score. In an actual interactive CLIR system, a translated query term with this kind of word sense can be flagged for the user.
2. Relevant images may exist on the Web, but not included in the presented set of images: This can happen when the translated query term is polysemous, and the intended word sense is *minor* in a sense on the Web. It is quite natural that the frequency distribution of a word's senses is not balanced, rather biased [5] reflecting some characteristics of the Web. Although it has not been as serious as expected in our experiment, we should note a prominent problematic pattern here by citing an example: when we conducted `Google Images` with the query "weaver", intending it in the sense of "a craftsman who weaves cloth" (WordNet gloss), the search returned only a set of pictures of *Sigourney Weaver*, a famous actress. This problem can be partly addressed if a term is recognized as one of the frequently used names on the Web. The system then can let the user know the term of this kind, or even suggest a disambiguation strategy. For instance, the query "weaver -sigourney" (with the term exclusion prefix '-') can greatly improve the Web image set to annotate the intended sense.

6   Conclusive Remarks

This paper examined the possibility of Web images as an intuitive and effective clue for for representing the word senses of a translated query term in CLIR. We designed an experiment to collect human assessments of the relevance of Web images. Statistical analyses applied to the assessment data provided insights that should be considered in the design of an interactive CLIR system. These insights include: (1) the semantic class of a word sense together with familiarity is a good indicator for predicting the applicability of the Web images as a word sense clue; (2) Web biases should be considered when gathering Web images, particularly for terms used as the name of an entity.

Although the presented research has been conducted in relation to an interactive CLIR interface, it obviously pertains to research efforts on image sense disambiguation [1] and lexical resource enrichment [4]. In particular, the results from the latter research should be appreciated: by using lexical semantic relations encoded in monolingual lexical resources, they perform a kind of query expansion to overcome the Web bias issue in gathering appropriate images even for minor word senses. By doing similarly, a translated query term whose Web images are predicted to be less applicable can be annotated with a better set of Web images.

References

1. Alm, C., Loeff, N., Forsyth, D.A.: Challenges for Annotating Images for Sense Disambiguation. In: Workshop on Frontiers in Linguistically Annotated Corpora, pp. 1–4 (2006)
2. Amano, S., Kondo, T.: Estimation of Mental Lexicon Size with Word Familiarity Database. In: International Conference on Spoken Language Processing, vol. 5, pp. 2119–2122 (1998)
3. Deng, J., Dong, W., Socher, R. Li, L.-J., Li. K., Fei-Fei, L.: ImageNet: A Large-Scale Hierarchical Image Database. In: CVPR 2009, pp.248–255 (2009)
4. Fujita, S., Nagata, M.: Enriching Dictionaries with Images from the Internet. - Targeting Wikipedia and a Japanese Semantic Lexicon: Lexeed. In: COLING 2010, pp. 331–339 (2010)
5. Gonzalo, J., Verdejo, F.: Automatic Acquisition of Lexical Information and Examples. In: Agirre, E., Edmonds, P. (eds.) Word Sense Disambiguation, pp. 253–274. Springer, Heidelberg (2006)
6. Hayashi, Y., Bora, S.A., Nagata, M.: Utilizing Images for Assisting Cross-Language Information Retrieval on the Web. In: The 2009 IEEE/WIC/ACM International Joint Conference on Web Intelligence and Intelligent Agent Technology, vol. 3, pp. 100–103 (2009)
7. Hothorn, T., Hornik, K., Wiel, M., Zeileis, A.: coin: A Computational Framework for Conditional Inference,
   http://cran.r-project.org/web/packages/coin/vignettes/coin.pdf
8. Ikehara, S., Miyazaki, M., Shirai, S., Yokoo, A., Nakaiwa, H., Ogura, K., Ooyama, Y., Hayashi, Y.: Goi-Taikei. - A Japanese Lexicon. Iwanami Shoten (1997)
9. Nie, J.: Cross-language Information Retrieval. Morgan & Claypool, San Francisco (2010)
10. Oard, D.W., He, D., Wang, J.: User-Assisted Query Translation for Interactive Cross-Language Information Retrieval. Information Processing and Management 44(1), 181–211 (2008)
11. Kasahara, K., Sato, H., Bond, F., Tanaka, T., Fujita, S., Kanasugi, T., Amano, S.: Construction of a Japanese Semantic Lexicon: Lexeed. In: IEICE Technical Report: 2004-NLC-159, pp. 75–82 (2004) (in Japanese)

A Diary Study-Based Evaluation Framework for Mobile Information Retrieval

Ourdia Bouidghaghen, Lynda Tamine, and Mohand Boughanem

IRIT-University Paul Sabatier, 118 Route de Narbonne, 31062, Toulouse, cedex 09
{bouidgha,tamine,bougha}@irit.fr

Abstract. In this poster, we propose an evaluation framework that investigates the integration of the user context (interests, location and time) into the evaluation process of mobile IR. Our approach is based on a diary study where users are asked to log their queries annotated by their location and time. Users' interests are explicitly acquired or implicitly learned based on users' relevance judgments for the retrieved documents answering their queries. We propose two evaluation protocols namely training/test in chronological order and k-fold cross validation. We exploit this framework in order to evaluate the performance of our context-based personalized mobile search approach. Experimental results show the stability performance of our approach according to the proposed evaluation protocols and demonstrate the viability of the diary approach as a means to capture context in evaluation.

Keywords: Experimental evaluation, evaluation framework in mobile context, diary study, location, time, user's interests.

1 Introduction

Within the emerging mobile IR environment, the focus is over context models including user's interests and environmental data (time, location, near persons, activity, device and networks) [1]. Contextual IR evaluation in this environment aims at measuring the system performance by integrating the user context in the evaluation process [2]. We can classify evaluation methodologies within mobile contextual IR, to two main types: evaluation by context simulations and evaluation by user studies.

The first kind of evaluation simulates users and interactions by means of well defined retrieval scenarios (hypothesis). Contextual simulation frameworks allow systems to be evaluated, according to a formative view, with less regard for constraints that arise from using sensor technologies, and several social and personal differences of users in interaction with the system. The contextual simulation framework proposed in [3] is based on hypothetic user search context and queries. User context is represented by a set of possible locations and users' interests are integrated in the evaluation strategy according to a simulation algorithm that generates them using hypothetic user interactions for each query.

P.-J. Cheng et al. (Eds.): AIRS 2010, LNCS 6458, pp. 389–398, 2010.

In [4], authors propose a contextual simulation framework based on a set of simulated context descriptors that include location, time and user activities. User's queries are automatically formulated from the context descriptors using different techniques. Context simulation based evaluation method is worthwhile since it is less time consuming and costly than experiments with real users. However, the method has still areas of uncertainty, for example the choice of assumptions underlying the major scenarios is open to criticism for its lack of realism.

The evaluation by user studies is carried out with real users, called participants, to test the system performance through real user's interactions with the system. To evaluate the performance of contextualized search, each participant is required to issue a certain number of test queries and determine whether each result is relevant in its context. There are two types of user studies adopted in the domain. The first one [5] is based on the evaluation framework proposed in [6] which makes use of "simulated work task situations" and where users are assigned a set of predefined tasks to perform in predefined situations. This kind of user studies is criticized because it still rely on artificial information needs and may be confounded by inter-subject and order effects. The second kind of contextual evaluation by user studies [7] is carried out in realistic use settings. In these latter, users are free to use the system as they would wish to use it and for only as long as they want, submitting their own queries arising from their natural information needs within real and natural situations, rather than asking them to perform some predefined series of tasks. The advantage of user studies based evaluation is that they are conducted with real users and thus the relevance can be explicitly specified by them. The main limitation is that experiments are not repeatable, the extra cost they induce and they may be of little use if the system is not fully developed.

In the absence of a standard evaluation benchmark for a mobile contextual IR task, we propose in this poster an evaluation framework based on a diary study. Our evaluation framework keeps up the benefits of user study based evaluation by allowing evaluation with real users and real contexts and alleviates its requirement that the system be fully developed by allowing the evaluation of an early stage development system; moreover we estimate our framework to be easily extensible to include any other contextual aspects from the mobile environment (eg. near persons, activity, . . .). Our approach is based on a diary study where mobile users are asked to log their queries annotated by their search context, here location and time. User's interests are explicitly acquired or implicitly learned based on their expressed relevance judgments for the retrieved documents for their queries. Two evaluation protocols training/test in chronological order and cross validation are experienced within this framework.

This poster is organized as follows: we first present our evaluation framework and introduce our experimental design in Section 2. We then present our approach for mobile search personalization, and its performance evaluation using the proposed evaluation framework in Section 3. Finally, we conclude and give perspectives for future work.

2   Proposition of an Evaluation Framework Based on a Diary Study

In our previous work [3] we have proposed an evaluation framework based on context simulation. The contribution of this poster is twofold: first we proposed a new evaluation framework based on a diary study as a tool that enables evaluation with real users in real contexts, second we compared evaluation results obtained using the two evaluation protocols.

Diary study is a method that has its roots in both psychological and anthropological research. In its simplest form, it consists of a representative sample of subjects recording information about their daily lives in situ for a given period. The data captured can then be analyzed in a variety of ways depending upon the nature of the data. Diary studies are presented in an early work by Rieman [8] as a workplace-oriented tool to guide laboratory efforts in the HCI field, they are exploited in [9] to analyze mobile information needs. In our work, we propose to undertake a diary study as a basis for collecting mobile information queries together with their external context namely time and location in situ. The diary entries are used as building blocks that compose the evaluation framework datasets.

2.1   Methodology

The focus of our framework is the evaluation of the effectiveness of a context-aware personalization technique for mobile search, in an early stage development. Such techniques involve the consideration of mobile search user's contexts namely interests, location and time in the development and the evaluation processes. The general process we adopted to build our framework is shown in Figure 1.

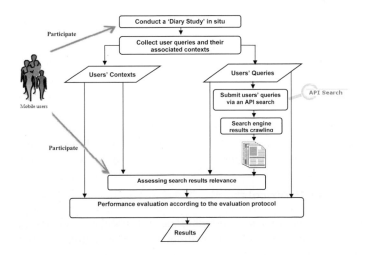

Fig. 1. Our diary study based evaluation framework

First, a diary study is conducted in situ, were real users are asked to log their queries together with their context whenever and wherever it occurs. The entire resulting diary entries are processed to extract user queries and contexts. Then, users queries are submitted to a standard search engine via an API. After, the resulting top N search engine documents are crawled, users are asked to judge these documents according to their queries and contexts. Finally, user's queries and contexts are integrated in the evaluation protocols. The general guidelines for conducting the diary study are: (1) Set the number of participants and the time of the diary study. (2) Assure that all the participants already have experience with using search engines on the web, using a PC or a mobile phone. (3) Set a description of the recording activities your are asking for, namely: recording the date, the time, the location, and the query the user have while he is mobile. (4) To avoid participants forgetting to record entries, send periodic reminders in order to keep participants on track. In what follows, we describe our datasets and evaluation protocols.

2.2   Datasets

Contextual Query Set. The diary study entries constitute a set of contextual queries. While many contextual information can be recorded, in this paper we only focused on the spatio-temporal context and users's interests. A contextual query can then be represented by: $Q_i^u =< q_i^u, l_i^u, t_i^u, g_i^u >$, where q_i^u (resp. l_i^u, t_i^u, and g_i^u) represents the ith query (resp. time, location and interests) of the diary entries of a user u. Each contextual query is annotated with a description of its associated information needs and a narrative about what would be a relevant document belonging to it. Location (l_i^u) and time (t_i^u) information can be expressed as low level data or using semantic concepts depending on the application needs. The user interests (g_i^u) can be manually specified by participants themselves or automatically learned from the user manual judgments of returned documents for their past queries.

Ground Truth in Context. The document collection is to be built by collecting the top N results retrieved from a publicly available Web search API for each query blind of context. The relevance assessments for the documents are to be collected through an assessment tool (available on line). To do, each user who submitted a query (in the diary study), is asked to judge whether a document from the set of top N retrieved results as response to his query was relevant or not according to his query and its context. Relevance judgments are to be made using a three level relevance scale: relevant, partially relevant, or not relevant.

2.3   Evaluation Protocols

In order to evaluate contextualized techniques for mobile search, the set of queries is to be divided into two sets: a training set for learning the parameters of the underlying contextualization technique, and a testing set to evaluate the effectiveness of this technique. Having a set of K contextual queries by user, that contains time information, two evaluation protocols are possible: training/test in chronological order and K-fold cross validation, to be applied on each users' set of queries. The only recommendation to be observed is to respect a *minimum* of 25 testings queries [10] in order to make the evaluation process outcomes significant. These two evaluation strategies are described as follows:

1. **Training/Test in Chronological Order:** this strategy keeps queries in their temporal order of emission, uses $Q_1^u \cdot \cdot Q_{i-1}^u$ past queries as the training set for the learning step, and tests with the following queries $Q_i^u \cdot \cdot Q_K^u$. This strategy is the simplest and more natural one, however effectiveness evaluation may depend heavily on which data points end up in the training set and which end up in the test set.

2. **K-fold Cross Validation:** this strategy divides the query set into k equally sized subsets, then uses *k-1* training subsets for learning and the remaining subset as a test set. The holdout method is repeated k times, each time, one of the k subsets is used as the test set and the other *k-1* subsets are put together to form a training set. The advantage of this method over the first protocol, is that all the queries are used for both training and testing and avoid consequently the bias on the choice of the training set.

We expect that the two protocols are applicable, and despite the difference between the two protocol strategies and the number of queries they allow to test, the evaluation results are expected to be consistent between them.

3   Evaluation Framework Application and Results

We have deployed our proposed evaluation framework and exploited it to validate the performance of our spatio-temporal personalization approach for mobile users [11]. The main objectives of the experimental evaluation are 1) showing the feasibility of our evaluation framework within a real testing scenario, 2) measuring the consistency of results using the two evaluation protocols. In what follows we first give an overview of our personalization approach, describe the framework evaluation in a real diary study and then present a comparative evaluation of the two protocols.

3.1   Our Approach for Personalizing Mobile Search Using a Spatio-Temporal User Profile

Here we give an overview of our approach for personalizing mobile search developed in our previous work [11]. It will serve as a testing scenario for our evaluation framework. Our personalization technique aims to adapt search results according to user's interests in a certain situation. A user U is represented by a set of situations with their corresponding user profiles (interests), denoted: $U = \{(S^i, G^i)\}$, where S^i is a situation and G^i its corresponding conceptual graph user profile. A situation S^i refers to the geographical and temporal context of the user when submitting a query to the search engine. Each situation can be represented by an aggregation of four dimensions:

- Location type: refers to a class name (such as beach, school, ...) extracted from a classification category of location types (like ADL feature type thesaurus[1]),
- Season: refers to one of the year's seasons,
- Day of the week: refers either to workday, weekend or holiday,
- Time of the day: refers to time zone of the day: morning, midday, afternoon, evening and night.

User profiles are built over each identified situation by combining graph-based query profiles. A query profile G_q^s is built by exploiting clicked documents D_r^s by the user and returned with respect to the query q^s submitted at time s. First a keyword query context K^s is calculated as the centroid of documents in D_r^s:

$$K^s(t) = \frac{1}{|D_r^s|} \sum_{d \in D_r^s} w_{td} . \tag{1}$$

K^s is matched with each concept c_j of the ODP[2] ontology represented by single term vector $\vec{c_j}$ using the cosine similarity measure. The scores of the obtained concepts are propagated over the semantic links as explained in [12]. The user profile G_i, within each identified situation S^i, is initialized by the profile of the first query submitted by the user at the situation S^i. It is updated by combining it with the query profile G^* of a new query for the same situation as follows:

$$sw_{c^i}(c_j) = \begin{cases} \eta * sw_{c^i}(c_j) + (1 - \eta) * sw_{c^*}(c_j) \\ \quad if \ c_j \in G^i \\ \\ \eta * sw_{c^*}(c_j) \ \ otherwise \end{cases} \tag{2}$$

where $sw_{c^i}(c_j)$ is the weight of concept c_j in the profile G^i and $sw_{c^*}(c_j)$ is the weight of concept c_j in the profile G^*. A case-based reasoning approach is adopted for selecting the most similar profile G^{opt} to use for personalization according to a new situation by exploiting a similarity measure between situations as explained in [11]. Personalization is achieved by re-ranking the search results of queries related to the same search situation. The search results are re-ranked by combining for each retrieved document d_k, the original score returned by the system $score_o(q^*, d_k)$ and a personalized score $score_c(d_k, G^{opt})$ obtaining a final $score_f(d_k)$ as follows:

$$score_f(d_k) = (1 - \gamma) * score_o(q, d_k) + \gamma * score_c(d_k, G^{opt}) \tag{3}$$

---

[1] http://www.alexandria.ucsb.edu/gazetteer/FeatureTypes/ver100301/
[2] The Open Directory Project (ODP): http://www.dmoz.org

Where γ ranges from 0 to 1. The personalized score $score_c(d_k, G^{opt})$ is computed using the cosine similarity measure between the result d_k and the top ranked concepts of the user profile C^{opt} as follows:

$$score_c\left(d_k, G^{opt}\right) = \sum_{c_j \in C^{opt}} sw\left(c_j\right) * \cos\left(\vec{d_k}, \vec{c_j}\right) \qquad (4)$$

Where $sw\left(c_j\right)$ is the similarity weight of the concept c_j in the user profile G^{opt}.

3.2   Evaluation Framework Application

We conducted a diary study, where users were asked to record the date, the time, the location, and the query they have while they are mobile (out of desk and home). Seven volunteers participated to our study (3 female and 4 male), ages ranged from 21 to 36. The diary study lasted for 4 weeks and it generated 79 diary entries, with an average of 11.28 entries per person. Table 1 shows an example of such diary entries, each diary entry represents a userid, date, time, place and the user query. From the diary study entries, we obtained a total of 79 queries expressed principally in the French language. Query length varies between 1 and 5, with an average of 2,99. The user intent behind these queries is mostly informational *"velo hauteur selle"* or transactional *"paris hotel cardinal"*. From the diary study entries, we extract location and time information associated with each query. While the location information is already expressed in semantic concepts, the time entries are not. Thus, according to our personalization approach, we transformed each date time on a semantic period of the day or the week. We totally obtained 36 different situations, with an average of 5 different situations by user (min=2, max=12) and an average of 3 (min=1, max=8) queries within a same situation. We submit the total queries to Yahoo boss search API[3], and crawled the top 50 obtained results for each query. These documents are presented for relevance judgment to our diary study participants via an assessment tool available on line and developed in our lab[4]. The user interests are integrated in the evaluation protocol according to an automatic algorithm that generates them based on the users manual judgments of the documents like described in section 3.1.

Table 1. An example of some diary entries

User	Date	Hour	Place	Query
1	20-fvr	14h30	place de la concorde	"histoire obélisque"
2	27-fvr	11h10	périphérique	"parking relais bordeaux"
6	16-fvr	16h30	musée	"exposition beaubourg artistes"
7	02-mars	19h40	station bus	"tisseo horaire bus 2"

---

[3] http://developer.yahoo.com/search/boss/
[4] https://osirim.irit.fr developed at IRIT lab.

This first diary study allows us to verify the feasibility of our evaluation framework and its ability to provide as with the desired functionality. In what follows we present our experiment to test results consistency over the two evaluation protocols.

3.3   Measuring Results Consistency over the Two Evaluation Protocols

The goal here is to measure results consistency over the two proposed evaluation protocols. For this aim, we applied these latter for evaluating the effectiveness of our personalized approach. We mention here that the two protocols satisfy the minimum of 25 testing queries, and as it can be expected, the k-fold cross validation allows us to test more queries (68 against 29 for the training/test in chronological order protocol). We first study the effect of combining the original document's rank of Yahoo boss (corresponding to the original document score in formula 3) and the personalized document rank obtained according to our approach, on the retrieval effectiveness. Figure 2 (resp. Figure 3) shows the improvement of our personalized search in terms of P@10,P@20, nDCG@10 and nDCG@20 obtained when using the training/test in chronological order protocol (resp. when using the cross validation protocol) with varying the combination parameter γ in the interval $[0\ 1]$. Results show that the best performance is

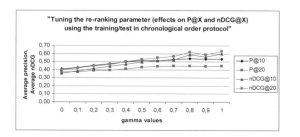

Fig. 2. Effect of the parameter gamma on Precision and nDCG in the combined ranks using the training/test in chronological order protocol

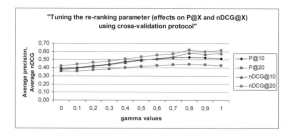

Fig. 3. Effect of the parameter gamma on Precision and nDCG in the combined ranks using the k-fold cross validation protocol

obtained when γ is between 0.8 and 1 for the two protocols. This is likely due to the fact that all the results on the top 50 match the query well and thus the distinguishing feature is how well they match the user profile.

In a second time, we compare our personalized retrieval effectiveness to the baseline search using the best γ value for each protocol. Table 2 shows the improvement of our personalized search in terms of P@10, P@20, nDCG@10 and nDCG@20 over the two protocols. Significant improvement are noted by * in table 2 according to a statistical t-test assuming the significance level fixed at $\alpha = 5\%$. Results prove that personalized search achieves higher retrieval precision of almost the queries. Moreover, our approach enhances the initial nDCG@10 and nDCG@20 obtained by the standard search and improve thus the quality of the top search results lists.

Table 2. Average Top-n precision and nDCG comparison between our personalized search and Yahoo boss over the two evaluation protocols

Evaluation protocol	System/ improvement	Average precision		Average nDCG	
		P@10	P@20	nDCG@10	nDCG@20
training/test	Yahoo boss	0,41	0,37	0,35	0,40
in chronological	Our approach	0,53	0,45	0,59	0,63
order	Improvement	31,14%*	20,72%*	67,65%*	58,80%*
k-fold	Yahoo boss	0,39	0,36	0,37	0,42
cross	Our approach	0,52	0,43	0,58	0,61
validation	Improvement	32,14%*	19,58%*	55,84%*	44,48%*

When comparing the two protocols results, we can observe that there is some difference in improvement of our approach over the two protocols. To determine whether or not an evaluation protocol might be better than another, we conducted a t-test. More precisely, we stated the null hypothesis (denoted H0) specifying that both evaluation protocols achieved similar performance levels, here evaluated between the means obtained on P@10, P@20, nDCG@10 and nDCG@20 over the common queries. This hypothesis would be rejected at the significance level fixed at $\alpha = 5\%$. We obtained a p-value of 0.434 for P@10, 0.478 for P@20, 0.387 for nDCG@10 and 0.365 for nDCG@20, wich are all greater than 0.05. We can then accept the null hypothesis and conclude that there is no significant difference between the two protocols.

4   Conclusion

In this poster we have presented a new evaluation framework for evaluating context-aware personalization techniques for mobile search. It is based on a diary study approach. More precisely, we exploit diary study entries to collect mobile queries, an API web search service and real user judgments to construct our ground truth, in context. We have deployed our proposed framework and exploit it for evaluating the search effectiveness of our personalized approach comparatively to a standard search. We compared the two evaluation protocols training/test in chronological order and K-fold cross validation and showed the consistency of the obtained results. Our example application illustrates the feasibility and usefulness of our proposed evaluation framework. In future, we plan scaling our diary study to include more users and for more long time in order to collect more contextual search situations.

Acknowledgments

The authors acknowledge the support of the project QUAERO, directed by OSEO agency, France, and thank all persons who participated in the experiment.

References

1. Brown, P.J., Jones, G.J.F.: Context-aware retrieval: Exploring a new environment for information retrieval and information filtering. Personal Ubiquitous Computing 5(4), 253–263 (2001)
2. Tamine-Lechani, L., Boughanem, M., Daoud, M.: Evaluation of contextual information retrieval effectiveness: Overview of issues and research. KIS 24(1), 1–34 (2009)
3. Bouidghaghen, O., Tamine, L., Daoud, M., Laffaire, C.: Contextual evaluation of mobile search. In: Doan, B.-L., Jose, J., Melucci, M., Tamine, L. (eds.) Workshop on Contextual Information Access, Seeking and Retrieval Evaluation, Milton Keynes, CEUR Workshop Proceedings, vol. 569 (2010)
4. Mizzaro, S., Nazzi, E., Vassena, L.: Retrieval of context-aware applications on mobile devices: How to evaluate? In: Proceedings of IIix, pp. 65–71. ACM, NY (2008)
5. Göker, A., Myrhaug, H.: Evaluation of a mobile information system in context. Information Processing and Management 44(1), 39–65 (2008)
6. Borlund, P., Ingwersen, P.: Measures of relative relevance and ranked half-life. In: 21st annual international ACM SIGIR conference on Research and development in information retrieval, pp. 324–331. ACM, NY (1998)
7. Mountain, D., MacFarlane, A.: Geographic information retrieval in a mobile environment: evaluating the needs of mobile individual. JIS 33(5), 515–530 (2007)
8. Rieman, J.: The diary study: a workplace-oriented research tool to guide laboratory efforts. In: INTERACT 1993 and CHI 1993 conference on Human factors in computing systems, pp. 321–326. ACM, NY (1993)
9. Sohn, T., Li, K.A., Griswold, W.G., Hollan, J.D.: A diary study of mobile information needs. In: CHI, pp. 433–442. ACM, New York (2008)
10. Voorhees, E.M.: The Philosophy of Information Retrieval Evaluation. In: Peters, C., Braschler, M., Gonzalo, J., Kluck, M. (eds.) CLEF 2001. LNCS, vol. 2406, pp. 355–370. Springer, Heidelberg (2002)
11. Bouidghaghen, O., Tamine-Lechani, L., Boughanem, M.: Dynamically personalizing search results for mobile users. In: Andreasen, T., Bulskov, H. (eds.) FQAS 2009. LNCS, vol. 5822, pp. 99–110. Springer, Heidelberg (2009)
12. Daoud, M., Tamine, L., Boughanem, M.: Towards a graph based user profile modeling for a session-based personalized search. KIS 21(3), 365–398 (2009)

Dynamics of Genre and Domain Intents

Shanu Sushmita, Benjamin Piwowarski, and Mounia Lalmas

School of Computing Science,University of Glasgow,
Scotland, G12 8QQ, United Kingdon
{shanu,bpiwowar,mounia}@dcs.gla.ac.uk

Abstract. As the type of content available on the web is becoming increasingly diverse, a particular challenge is to properly determine the types of documents sought by a user, that is the domain intent (e.g. image, video) and/or the genre intent (e.g. blog, wikipedia). In this paper, we analysed the Microsoft 2006 RFP click dataset to obtain an understanding of domain and genre intents and their dynamics i.e. how intents evolve within search sessions and their effect on query reformulation.

1 Introduction

The diversity of the content available on the web has dramatically increased in recent years. Multimedia content such as images, videos, maps, has been published more often than before. Document genres have also been diversified, for instance, news, blogs, FAQs, wikipedia. Such growth in the diversity of information on the web raises two main questions. First, do users actually access various categories of documents to satisfy their information need? Second, are there particular patterns in how users access these various categories of documents?

Understanding the information need behind a user query, i.e. the *query intent*, is an important goal in web search. There are different ways to classify query intents. A query intent may refer to the type of interaction, e.g. navigational, transactional or informational. It may also relate to some predefined general topics, e.g. travel, sport, shopping. Finally, it may refer to the category of information being sought, e.g. image, video, blog. In this paper, we are concerned with the latter, more precisely, in *domain* (e.g., image, video) and *genre* (e.g., blog, wikipedia) intents.

In this paper, we analysed the Microsoft 2006 RFP click dataset to understand query intents in terms of domain and genre. We looked at three domains, namely, image, video, and map, and three genres, namely, news, blog and wikipedia. All other categories of intent were viewed as standard "web", i.e. the typical web search result. These six "non-web"[1] categories of intent were chosen on the basis of a survey [4], which shows that images, news, and videos were the three most frequently accessed "non-web" results. Map and wikipedia were chosen

---

[1] We use the term "non-web" to distinguish these documents to the standard web documents. In current search engine terminology, these "non-web" documents could be retrieved directly from verticals.

P.-J. Cheng et al. (Eds.): AIRS 2010, LNCS 6458, pp. 399–409, 2010.
© Springer-Verlag Berlin Heidelberg 2010

because results of these categories are now frequently included within the top ten result list by major search engines. This paper has two parts. We first propose a methodology to identify domain and genre intents, allowing us to learn whether users actually access documents of various categories to satisfy their information need. We then study the dynamics of these intents to uncover patterns in how users access documents of various categories.

2   Data Set

We used the Microsoft 2006 RFP Dataset, containing 13,279,076 log entries [6] corresponding to a subset of web search logs from US users spanning over a month. Each log entry corresponds to a click and contains the following information:

1. The **timestamp** (time and date), used to order the clicks within a session.
2. A unique **session id** representing a search session. A session is the entire series of queries, one to several, submitted to the search engine by a user over some given time.
3. A unique **query id** given to each distinct query submitted during a search session.
4. The **query terms** used by the search engine to display results.
5. The **URL** of the clicked result.

We used three sources of evidence: (1) the query itself, more precisely the use of *intent-specific terms* such as "video", "map", etc; (2) the clicked URLs; and (3) the titles of the corresponding web documents. Previous work, e.g. [3], has shown that result snippets (title, URL and excerpt) of the clicked web documents could be used to determine query intents. For instance, a log entry in our dataset corresponds to a document with title "images and diagrams of human muscular system" after having entered the query "muscular system". The term image in the document title, and the fact that the user has accessed that document, may be a good indication that the user is looking for images.

Table 1. Statistics about the click dataset used in our study

Total number of entries	6,637,590
Total number of sessions	3,960,541
No of sessions with 1 click	2,654,794
No of sessions with 2 clicks	721,223
No of sessions with 3 clicks	282,980
No of sessions with 4 clicks	132,834
No of sessions with 5 clicks	68,403
No of sessions with > 5 clicks	100,307
Average duration of a session	00:03:44

Table 2. Percentage of sessions with one, two, ... , six and seven different intents

Number of distinct intents	Original	Random
Seven	0.000	0.000
Six	0.000	0.000
Five	0.000	0.002
Four	0.005	0.034
Three	0.121	0.470
Two	3.385	6.354
One	96.489	93.140

We did not use document excerpts as we did not have access to them. As the data set did not contain the titles of the clicked documents, we had to retrieve these. We therefore downloaded the clicked documents. Given the time lag between when the dataset was created and our download of the clicked documents (approximately 3 years), we were able to obtain the titles for only 50% of the clicked documents. We then used those sessions for which we could download the titles for all clicked documents. The statistics reported in Table 1 correspond to these log entries.

3   Determining Domain and Genre Intents

The first stage of our work is to determine the intended domains and genres for given queries. We first used a rule-based classifier, whose output was used to build the features used by a machine learning classifier.

Table 3. Left: Percentages of classified clicks into the different intents with the rule-based "Rule", the machine learning "SVM" methods, and combined together "Both". **Right:** Percentage of correctly classified/ mis-classified intents. **N** is number of training examples (values above 0.05 in bold).

Intent	Rule	SVM	Both	N	image	video	blog	map	wiki	news	web
image	1.10	0.32	1.42	98	**0.30**	**0.18**	0.01	0.00	0.00	0.01	**0.49**
video	0.64	0.86	1.50	131	0.02	**0.46**	0.02	0.00	0.00	0.03	**0.47**
news	0.71	1.43	2.14	62	**0.08**	**0.12**	**0.27**	0.00	0.01	0.03	**0.49**
map	1.50	0.03	1.54	25	0.00	0.00	0.00	**0.63**	0.00	0.00	**0.37**
blog	0.03	0.15	0.17	66	0.04	0.02	0.04	0.00	**0.74**	0.00	**0.17**
wiki	0.07	0.89	0.96	75	**0.08**	0.04	0.02	0.02	0.01	**0.32**	**0.52**
web	NA	92.27	92.27	3354	0.04	0.04	0.02	0.01	0.00	0.02	**0.87**

3.1   Rule-Based Classifier

Our aim here is to classify as accurately as possible some of the log entries. This was important as these classifications were to be used as inputs to calculate the features for the machine learning approach. To build a high precision classifier, we used the most reliable source of evidence, namely the query terms. For example, if the user has explicitly typed *photo* in the query, we deduced that the user is looking for image, i.e. has an image intent. Here *photo* is referred to as an "intent-specific" term. We use the following intent-specific terms to classify the clicks into domains/genres:

Image: *image, images, photo, photos, picture, pictures.*
Video: *video, videos, movie, movies.*
News: *news.*
Map: *map, maps.*
Blog: *blog, blogs.*
Wikipedia: *wiki, wikipedia.*

Although not exhaustive, these intent-specific terms are a good approximation of how users would search, in terms of the queries they would submit to a search engine, for documents of particular domains or genres. With this approach, 268,491 log entries (i.e. clicked URLs), that is 4% of the total log entries, were identified to be of one of the six intents.

3.2   Machine Learning Classifier

To identify additional non-web intents, we make use of machine learning techniques. This requires (1) a manually labelled set of log entries; (2) designing features correlated with the possible intents that can be computed for every log entry; (3) training a classifier to predict the intent given (1) and (2). Finally, we predict the intent of the non-manually classified log entries using the classifier given their features.

For (1), we randomly sampled 3800 log entries and manually classified them into one of the following six *category* intents – image, video, blog, map, wikipedia, and news. A click was classified as having a web intent (our unclassified category) when it could not be classified into any of the above six categories. A web intent corresponds mostly to the typical web search result, and we expect it to be the predominant intent. We used the query terms, the URL and the document title for this purpose. The outcomes of the manual classification is shown in Table 3, the **N** column. As expected, web corresponds to the predominant query intent.

Step (2) aims at defining a set of features associated with each log entry, where each feature should be a good predictor for identifying a subset of intents (ideally one). In our case, the set of features were based on the language models computed from the dataset (classified intents) obtained through the rule-based approach. We build a language model for each source of evidence and each category. We also build a background language model for the source of evidence itself, which estimates the probability of a term to appear in the given source regardless of the intent. We chose to model separately the three sources of evidence since they are of very different nature.

Our hypothesis is that each category uses a vocabulary often associated with explicit intent-specific terms. For instance, in a query, if "Aniston" is often associated with "photo", the term "Aniston" will be associated to a large number of log entries classified as an image intent by the rule-based classifier. As a result, the query language model for the intent "image" will give a higher probability to "Aniston" than the background language model, and thus comparing both probabilities gives the classifier an indication of how likely a term (or a set of terms) is generated by an intent-specific language model rather than by the background one. We estimated the parameters of each language model[2], one for each source of evidence s and intent i (21 in total, i.e. one for each of the 3 sources and for

---

[2] For the URLs, we considered that terms were any maximal sequence of alphanumeric characters. For example, `http://www.abc.com/video` has four terms, www, abc, com and video.

each of the 6 intents plus the background model). We estimated the probability that a term t occurs using the standard maximum likelihood estimate, and smoothed it using the background language model for a given source of evidence.

$$P(t/\mathbf{i}, \mathbf{s}) = \lambda P_{ML}(t/\mathbf{i}, \mathbf{s}) + (1 - \lambda) P_{ML}(t/\mathbf{s}) \tag{1}$$

$$= \lambda \frac{c_{\mathbf{i},\mathbf{s}}(t)}{\sum_{t'} c_{\mathbf{i},\mathbf{s}}(t')} + (1 - \lambda) \frac{c_{\mathbf{s}}(t)}{\sum_{t'} c_{\mathbf{s}}(t')} \tag{2}$$

The probability P_{ML} is the maximum likelihood estimate of the probability of a term occurring in a given source of evidence $\mathbf{s}$, and if given, for the intent $\mathbf{i}$ (otherwise, it is the background language model). Here, $c_{\mathbf{i},\mathbf{s}}(t)$ denotes the number of times the term t appeared for source $\mathbf{s}$ with the intent $\mathbf{i}$, and $c_{\mathbf{s}}(t)$ is the number of times term t appeared for source $\mathbf{s}$. These were computed from the set of automatically classified clicks using the rule-based classifier. The smoothing parameter λ was heuristically set to 0.95, to emphasize the importance of the intent. We then compute the probability that a sequence of terms T is generated by any of the language models by

$$P(T/\mathbf{s}, \mathbf{i}) = \prod_{t \in T} P(t/\mathbf{s}, \mathbf{i}) \tag{3}$$

We then use the logarithmic ratio of the probability (for a given source) of observing T given the intent to the probability of observing T:

$$R_{\mathbf{i},\mathbf{s}}(T) = \log \frac{P(T/\mathbf{s}, \mathbf{i})}{P(T/\mathbf{s})} \tag{4}$$

whose value is above 0 if it is more likely that the text was generated given the intent than in general, and below 0 in the opposite case. This gives rise to a set of 18 features (one for each of the 6 categories and 3 sources) that are used as an input to build a multi-class classifier.

We use an SVM classifier[3] [1] because it performed the best when evaluated with a 10-fold cross-validation, described further below (using nine tenth of the manually classified data to learn, and one tenth to compute the performance, and repeating this operation 10 times). During the selection process, we preferred models that predicted either the correct or the web intents, over those with better performance that predicted an incorrect non-web intent.

The SVM classifier was then trained using a 3-fold cross validation and a Gaussian radial basis function. With respect to the manually labelled data, to give less importance to the web intent, we down-sampled the number of corresponding examples and only chose 20% of those, which gives a total of 817 manually labelled examples. In addition, we added an equal number of automatically labelled log entries (randomly sampled among the 224,241 classified log entries), using the same rules as in Section 3.1 but using the title and URL as sources of evidence. We experimentally found that using this set of data for training did improve the performance of the classifier.

---

[3] We used the implementation of [2].

Table 3 (Right) shows the confusion matrix with our final settings. The correct classification rate is low (between 0.27 and 0.87), but most of the time, when a click is misclassified its predicted intent is web. The only exceptions are for image (18% are classified as video) and blog (20% are classified as either image or video). Nonetheless, given that web is our unclassified category, the results show that we have improved recall without hurting precision too much.

Table 3 (Left) shows the statistics about the intent classification (rule-based, using SVM as our machine learning approach, and merged together) of all the log entries. It is this *merged* labelled log that was used in the remaining analysis of this paper. We see that approximately 8% of the total log entries were identified to have a domain or genre intent other than web. This is not negligible considering the large size of the log data analyzed, and is compatible (although not directly comparable) to the results reported in [5].

4   Research Questions and Methodology

To study the domain and genre intents, and their dynamics, we posit the following three research questions, each investigated in separate sections next: (**R1**) What are the frequent combinations of domain and genre intents within a search session? (**R2**) Do domain and genre intents evolve according to some patterns? and (**R3**) Is there a relation between query reformulation and a change of intent?

From Table 2, column "Original", around 96.48% of the sessions have only one underlying intent. However, most sessions are composed of one or two clicks (85%, computed from Table 1), and web is the most likely intent (92.28% in Table 3 Left). We can expect that a high percentage of sessions will be one- or two-click sessions with a web intent, and hence will be single-intent sessions. It is therefore not possible to know whether our statistics of 96.48% is due to the fact that users do not combine intents, or that the click and intent distributions are highly skewed. To overcome this, we compare statistics with those obtained from a *random log*. This random log is exactly similar to the real log, but instead of using a classifier to assign an intent to each log entry we have to select one by random, in accordance with the intent distributions presented in Table 1. The random log is a log where the intent would be independent of what the user is searching for, and of his or her search history. To compute statistics for this random log, we average over all the possible random intent assignments.

We thus report statistics computed for both the real and the random logs. Going back to the example of the 96.48% of single-intent sessions in Table 2, we can see (Table 2, column "Random") that we would expect 93.14% of the sessions to be single-intent in the random log. This sets the following limit: if the real number was below this limit (even with a percentage as high as 90%), then we could say that users tend to combine more than one intent within a session; instead, we observe that our statistic is higher (96.48%) which means that sessions are indeed generally single-intent.

5   Combination of Query Intents

We investigate the existence of frequent combinations of query intents in search sessions (**R1**). We compute how often query intents, as classified with the approach described in Section 3, co-occur within the same search session. Table 2 shows the percentage of sessions that contain two or more different intents. We observe that there are very few sessions with more than two different query intents. This is in accordance with the study reported in [5].

Table 4. Percentage of sessions with corresponding pair of intents, where L stands for original log, and R for random log, n= News, m= Map, i= Image, v=Video, w= Wikipedia, b=Blog and W= Web. Column % 1/2 (respectively % 2/1) reports the percentage of sessions with the first intent of the pair (respectively second) that also had the second (respectively first) intent.

Comb	% L	% R	% 2/1 L	% 2/1 R	% 1/2 L	% 1/2 R
bm	0.00	0.02	0.5	4.6	0.1	0.5
nb	0.01	0.03	0.3	0.5	2.6	6.2
vm	0.01	0.2	0.3	4.5	0.4	4.4
bw	0.02	0.01	4	2.8	0.7	0.5
ib	0.02	0.02	0.8	0.5	4.1	4.3
im	0.02	0.19	0.9	4.5	1.1	4.1
in	0.04	0.26	1.5	6.2	1.1	4.2
nm	0.04	0.28	1	4.5	1.8	6.2
nw	0.04	0.18	1.1	2.8	1.6	6.2
vb	0.04	0.02	1.4	0.5	7.8	4.5
wm	0.04	0.13	1.5	4.5	1.9	2.8
vn	0.05	0.27	1.7	6.2	1.3	4.4
iw	0.09	0.12	3.3	2.8	3.4	4.1
iv	0.10	0.18	3.6	4.4	3.5	4.2
vw	0.06	0.12	2.1	2.8	2.2	4.4

Comb	% L	% R	% 2/1 L	% 2/1 R	% 1/2 L	% 1/2 R
bb	0.09	0.00	18.9	0.2	18.9	0.2
ww	0.50	0.04	18.6	1.5	18.6	1.5
mm	1.11	0.1	51.8	2.3	51.8	2.3
vv	1.17	0.1	43.1	2.2	43.1	2.2
nn	1.33	0.2	35.5	3.2	35.5	3.2
ii	1.40	0.09	52.5	2.1	52.5	2.1
bW	0.43	0.51	88.6	97.1	0.4	0.5
mW	1.35	4.42	62.7	97.3	1.4	4.4
iW	1.85	4.09	69.2	97.3	1.9	4.1
vW	1.99	4.31	73.1	97.3	2.1	4.3
wW	2.48	2.77	92.9	97.2	2.6	2.8
nW	2.87	6.1	76.5	97.4	3	6.1
WW	91.77	91.41	94.9	91.7	94.9	91.7

The ratio between the original and the random log statistics show that the fact that a session is associated with a low number of intents is not due to chance. Moreover, the ratio increases as the number of intents increase, which shows that when users have diverse intents, it is generally restricted to at most two. Therefore, we computed the percentage of sessions where at least two intents appeared among sessions with two intents or more (Table 4). For instance, the value 0.01% for "nb" means that there are very few sessions with a blog and a news intents. We also computed for each pair of intents the % that given one intent the second was observed within the same session, and vice versa (3rd and 4th group of columns). For instance, for "vw", the value 2.1% means that 2.1% of the sessions that had a video intent also had a wikipedia intent.

We can observe that most users do not mix intents. Indeed, rows "bm" to "vw" and rows "bW" to "nW" show that users are less likely to combine two different intents in the same session than what would be expected by random (around 3 times less likely in average). Looking at the rows "bb" to "ii", it is on average around ten times more likely that users repeat a click on the same intent than what would be expected by random. In sessions made of two or more clicks, when one intent is map, video, image or news, then there is above 35% of chance to observe a second click with the same intent (third and fourth group of columns). For blog and wikipedia, the probability is lower although still high (around 19%). This could be because users might consider wikipedia and blog result pages as web pages and hence do not differentiate them as belonging to different categories. We however observe some potential exceptions for the pairs blog/wikipedia ("bw"), image/blog ("ib"), and video/blog ("vb"). These three pairs occur more often together that would be expected by random. However, the difference in percentages (≈ 0.01) are so low that this is likely due to noise from the classification.

A last observation is that when there are two intents, these are often a web intent and any non-web intent, as shown in the last series of rows in the table. This is not surprising, and means that search results should continue to contain mostly web results, and when appropriate, images, videos, blogs, etc in addition. This is nowadays the approach followed by all major search engines.

6   Patterns of Query Intents

We investigate how domain and genre intents evolve within search sessions (**R2**). We restrict ourselves to sessions with two query intents. We consider the five most frequent co-occurrences of two query intents (other co-occurrences were too low): image+web, wiki+web, video+web, news+web, map+web. For each such pair intent+web, we looked at all possible sequences of changes of query intents. The four most frequent ones, for all five pairs, were of the form, web $\rightarrow$ intent, intent $\rightarrow$ web, intent $\rightarrow$ web $\rightarrow$ intent, and web $\rightarrow$ intent $\rightarrow$ web. In Table 5, we report for each pair the percentage of sessions containing each of the identified four sequences. All the others come under "Other". In our calculation, we excluded sessions with less than three clicks, to avoid results biased towards the large number of two-click sessions.

First, for the wikipedia intent, users do not follow any particular pattern. Indeed, the sequences obtained are close to what would be expected by random. This confirms the findings of the previous section, where we made the hypothesis that users do not differentiate between wikipedia and web documents. Second, when the intent is news, video and map, users switch from one intent to another, but do not tend to switch back to the first intent. By random we would expect more users to move back and forth between intents. This can be seen in the difference between the random and real logs for the four sequences. Third, in the case of image intents, we observe that users are less likely to move back and forth between intents. However, different from news, video and map intents, users are more likely to begin with a web intent before looking at images, rather than start with an image intent and then switching to a web intent.

Table 5. Sequence of intents in search sessions, for each pair web+non-web. Where, Orig = original log and Rand = random log. Percentage numbers for the most frequent sequences are in bold.

Sequence	Orig	Rand
wiki → web	25	26
web → wiki	30	26
web → wiki → web	**41**	**46**
wiki → web → wiki	1	0
Other	3	1
image → web	27	26
web → image	**37**	26
web → image → web	31	**46**
image → web → image	1	0
Other	4	1

Sequence	Orig	Rand
video → web	32	26
web → video	**34**	26
web → video → web	31	**46**
video → web → video	1	0
Other	2	1
map → web	**36**	26
web → map	34	26
web → map → web	28	**46**
map → web → map	1	0
Other	1	1
news → web	**34**	26
web → news	31	26
web → news → web	32	**45**
news → web → news	1	1
Other	2	1

There is a common sequence in the intents for all except for wikipedia. Users have a tendency to go from one intent to the other, and then to end the session, rather than switching several times between intents within the same session.

7 Query Intents and Query Re-formulation

We study both quantitatively (how many) and qualitatively (how) the effect of a change of intent on a user query (**R3**). We thus compare pairs of consecutive queries with two different intents, within the same session. For each such pair, we computed the numbers of queries that were exactly the same, modified or completely different. Results are shown in Table 6.

For blog and wikipedia, over 50% of the users did not usually change their query (going from a blog or wikipedia intent to web intent or vice versa). It is likely that this happens because both types of results are present in the top ranked documents for the same query. Users do not have to change their queries to obtain results from blog/wikipedia and then web sources (and vice versa). The situation is reversed for news, image, video, and map. Most of the time, users did change their query (over 65%). We also observed that there was a slight difference between news/map/video and image intents. For the former, users issued different queries, whereas for the latter, in half of the cases, users modified their queries by adding or removing terms. We found that, for news/map/video, often users often changed their search topic (e.g. "sovereign bank center trenton" to "art of 1769") and hence modified the query completely, whereas for image users seem to have looked at the results and then added intent-specific terms (e.g., "photo").

Table 6. Percentage of sessions where a query was not modified, was modified (i.e. by adding or removing terms (Mod)), and was different (no terms in common)

Sequence	Exact	Mod	Different
web → blog	**56**	24	19
blog → web	**52**	23	25
web → wiki	**59**	18	23
wiki → web	**54**	20	26
web → news	21	21	**58**
news → web	18	19	**63**

Sequence	Exact	Mod	Different
web → video	35	25	**40**
video → web	33	24	**43**
web → image	30	**40**	29
image → web	30	34	**37**
web → map	4	24	**73**
map → web	3	21	**76**

When a query was modified, we also looked at which terms were added or removed. We easily identified terms linked with an intent, i.e. intent-specific terms; e.g. "wikipedia", "what", "how" for wikipedia; "blog", "how", for blogs;' 'news", "newspaper", and "press" for a news intent; etc. Some of these terms were present in the rule-based classifier described in Section 3.1.

8   Conclusion

We analysed a click dataset to obtain an understanding of domain (image, video, and map) and genre (news, blog and wikipedia) intents, and their dynamics. The first step was to identify the domain and genre intents behind a query. Using a rule-based and an SVM classifier, we classified approximately 8% of the total click dataset to have one of the six domain or genre intents. We looked at how intents co-occur within a session. We observed that users do not often mix intents, and if they do, they mostly use two intents. Furthermore, these were often a web intent and any of the non-web one. Second, we investigated if these intent combinations evolve according to some patterns. Our results show that, except with wikipedia, users in general tend to follow the same intent for a while and then switch to another intent. In other words, users do not switch back and forth between intents. Third, we were interested to see if there were relations between query re-formulation and change of intent. We observed that for video, news and map intents, often completely different queries were submitted, whereas, for blog and wikipedia intents, the same query was used. Further, intent-specific terms were often used when the query was modified.

Acknowledgements. This work was carried out in the context of research partly funded by a Yahoo! Research Alliance Gift.

References

1. Crammerand, K., Singer, Y.: On the Learnability and Design of Output Codes for Multiclass Problems. Computational Learning Theory, pp. 35–46 (2000)
2. Karatzoglou, A., Meyer, D., Hornik, K.: Support Vector Machines in R. Journal of Statistical Software 15(9), 1–28 (2006)

3. He, K-Y., Chang, Y-S., Lu, W-H.: Improving Identification of Latent User Goals through Search-Result Snippet Classification. WI, pp 683–686 (2007)
4. (2008),
   http://www.iprospect.com/about/researchstudy__blendedsearchresults.htm
5. Arguello, J., Diaz, F., Callan, J., Crespo, J.: Sources of Evidence for Vertical Selection. In: ACM SIGIR, pp. 315–322 (2009)
6. Craswell, N., Jones, R., Dupret, G.,Viegas, E. (eds).: Proceedings of the 2009 workshop on web Search Click Data (2009)

Query Recommendation Considering Search Performance of Related Queries[*]

Yufei Xue, Yiqun Liu, Tong Zhu, Min Zhang, Shaoping Ma, and Liyun Ru

State Key Laboratory of Intelligent Technology and Systems,
Tsinghua National Laboratory for Information Science and Technology,
Department of Computer Science and Technology, Tsinghua University,
Beijing, 100084, China
yufei.xue@gmail.com

Abstract. In this paper, we propose a new query recommendation method. This method is designed to generate recommended queries which are not only related to input query, but also provide high quality search results to users. Existing query recommendation methods are mostly focused on users' intention or the relationship between input query andrecommended queries.Because the limitation of Web resource and search engine's index, not all recommended queries lead to good search results. Such recommendation will not help users to find the information they need. In our work, we use machine learning methods to re-rank a pre-generated recommendation candidate list. We select some user behavior features to filter out the queries which have poor search performance. The experiment results show that our method can recommend queries which are related and provide useful results to users.

Keywords: Query Recommendation, User Experience, User Behavior.

1 Introduction

Popular commercial search engines usually provide related search queries to users in search result page. Since users prefer using short queries [1,2] which may not express their information needs exactly, the recommended queries can help them to submit more precise query to search engine and search engine can satisfy users' information needs more easily. Also, when some users do not know how to describe what they exactly desire, query recommendation can guide them to refine their queries in precise terms. We have analyzed large amounts of user query logs(same as the data which weintroduce in Section 5.4)and find that users click recommended related queries in about 15% query sessions.So recommending adequate related queries to users is very important for enhancing the user experience.

Considering a typical search session with query recommendation clicks,a user inputs a query with ambiguous information needs. Unfortunately, the search results do not satisfy his needs, and he turns to query recommendation. The user may find that

---

[*] Supported by Natural Science Foundation (60736044, 60903107) and Research Fund for the Doctoral Program of Higher Education of China (20090002120005).

P.-J. Cheng et al. (Eds.): AIRS 2010, LNCS 6458, pp. 410–419, 2010.

some recommended query exactly describes what he wants, and he clicks it. After reviewing the new results list, he may get what he wants, or go on changing his query for more information, or even end his attempt.

In such a session, any step may affect user experience. No matter how many times a user has changed his query, only when the search engine provides useful results, the user may get satisfied.Most research on query recommendation are focused on how to recommend queries which can describe users' needs, despite whether the search engine can return high-quality results for recommended queries. In this case, a user may find some attractive queries by recommendation, but he will not get useful information after he clicked on it and get another result page. It can be conceivable that this kind of related queries has nothing to do with user experience.

To improve user experience, we would like to progress the recommendation method to avoid providingthe queries which do not give users useful search results. The key to this problem is developing an automatic method which can judge whether the search results of a query will satisfy the users.

Many reasons cause a query doesnot have good results: no related resource on Internet, no related resource indexed by search engine, or useful web pages not shown in top results. Although we can analyze the reason of bad search results, it is still unfeasible to evaluate the results by the possible reasons.In recent years, some works on user browsing information provide us new perspective for search result evaluation. In our work, we use some features based on user browsing information to help us evaluate search results.

2 Related Work

The work [3] of Baeza-Yates etc. uses click-through data in user query log clustering similar queries for query recommendation. In [3], term-wcight vectors of the clicked URL's for queries are used for aggregating the queries. Query-click bipartite graph is presented in [4] for query recommendation. Wen [5], Zaiane [6] and Cucerzan [7] also use information of clicked URLs in user query log to find similar queries. [8] introduces user's query refinement information in logs for evaluating the similarity of different queries and the most similar queries are used for recommendation. Liu's work [9] considers the relationship between two queries more complicated. In [9], the recommendation method is asymmetrical which means two related queries may have different strength to recommend each other.

In these works, different methods are tried to recommend related queries. Most efforts of these works are trying to evaluate the semantic similarity and recommend the queries may interest users. No related work has considered the search performance of recommended queries, which has great impact on user experience.

There are some works trying to evaluate search performance of a query from user's perspective. The work [10] investigated the strong relationship between result relevance and user satisfaction, but they had not proposed an automatic prediction process. Fox et al. [11] attempted to predict user-annotated levels of satisfaction using a variety of implicit features based on search behavior. Hassan et al. [12] proposed an evaluation method which predicts user search goal success by modeling user behavior. They use sequences of search actions to represent users' search process and estimate the probability of being successful with a continuous time Markov model.

In our work, we consider the search performance of related queries from the users' point of view while recommending related queries. We propose some search perform- ance features base on behavior features and combine them with other typical features of query recommendation. With these features, we develop a new recommendation method which ensures the recommended queries to show useful results and provide better user experience to users. To the best of our knowledge, our method is the first one which take the factor of user satisfaction into consideration.

3 Recommendation Candidates Generation

In our query recommendation method, we need a list of recommendation candidates first. The list could be raw, but it has to contain high-quality related queries as many as possible. A lot of methods, such as the ones we mentioned in Section 2, can be used for generating the candidates. In our work, we present a method different from related works in recommendation candidates generation.

We collect query log data from a commercial search engine during a time period of 60 daysand extract all queries from these logs. We build an inverted index for the queries so that all the queries can be retrieved by some input query. While indexing, stop words are removed. Some thesaurus and different names of same entity are merged in inverted index.

For any input query, we can segment it into terms and retrieve them from the in- verted index. Thus a lot of similar queries will be returned in a ranked list as recom- mendation candidates.

4 Query Recommendation Re-ranking

In the candidates generation step, we extract a collection of queries from user query log. While we generate the candidates, we mainly focus on the similarity of queries. This section presents the query recommendation re-ranking method with considering user experience. Thesection is organized with four parts. Section 4.1 gives some as- sumptions of high quality query recommendation. Section 4.2and 4.3 introduce the user behavior features and some other features we used for recommendation candi- dates re-ranking, and Section 4.4 shows how we use SVM to re-rank the candidates with the features we selected.

4.1 Query Recommendation with Good User Experience

Before we discuss recommendation re-ranking, we should firstlydefine what an effec- tive query recommendation is. In other words, we should give a definition of a high- quality query recommendation which leads to good user experience.

With analysis into user behavior information recorded in query log data, we pro- pose 3 criteria to judge whether a query recommendation is effective or not. For a certain query Q proposed by a user U, a query recommendation R is effective if:

1. R is relevant with Q, and
2. R is better atdescribing U's potential information needs, and
3. Search results of$R$ can meet U's potential information needs.

The basic demands of the query recommendation we want is described above. In a search session with query recommendation clicks, these criteria are all important for user experience. When a user U inputs a query Q, U should be interested in something about Q. So it is unhelpful to recommend an irrelevant query R. If R is relevant to Q, but does not satisfy Criterion 2, it is still unhelpful. For Example, when the input query is "Windows Live Messenger download", a query recommendation "MSN Messenger download" may not be a high-quality one. Although it is relevant to input query, but the old version "MSN Messenger" may not satisfy the user. Criterion 3 is also necessary since a query recommendation with poor-performance search results leads to bad user experience, too. In the following work, the feature selection, training annotation, and recommendation evaluation are all based on these.

4.2 User Behavior Features

As we present 3 basic criteriain the section before, the features for re-ranking should be indicative of some demands. While extracting candidates from user log as the described ofSection 3, the method prefers to select the queries which related in literal. Now we would like to choose more user behavior features which help us to evaluate whether a query may satisfy users. Note that all the features are for "input query Q_i – recommendation candidate Q_r," pair, although some are only related to Q_r.

Table 1. User Behavior Features

Feature Name	Description
FirstClickRank	Average ranking of the result which users firstly click for Q_r
LastClickRank	Average ranking of the result which users finally click for Q_r
HintClick	% of sessions of Q_r in which users click the "related queries" (or called hint queries) provided by search engines
NextPage	% of sessions of Q_r in which users view other result pages besides the first page
AllClickNum	Average number of actions (all kinds of clicks) in sessions of Q_r
AllLogRec	Average number of log records in sessions of Q_r
AdvancedSearch	% of sessions of Q_r in which users adopted advanced search function

After a user submits a query (either by input or by clicking related search) to search engine, he gets a result list page returned by search engine. While reviewing the result page, he may havesome interaction with the elements on the page, such as clicking some result items or clicking "Next Page" for more results. These behaviors may contain information of user satisfaction on query Q_r. The user behavior features are listed in Table 1. Introduction and analysis of some user behavior features is given after the table.

FirstClickRank&LastClickRank. The two features are about users' clicks on search results. If a query performsvery well, the users may tend to click only top 2 or 3 results. For such well-performance query, values of the two features will be relatively small. Conversely, if a query performs badly, a user may find the result he desires has a low rank, or the user could not find any useful result after clicking a few results. However, the values of these features will be larger.

For experimental analysis, we select a set of queries, and ask 3 annotators to search the queries as ordinary users do. The annotators review the search results and judge whether a query performs well. Then we can get the distribution of the two features for well-performance queries and poor-performance queries. The distributions are shown in Fig. 1. It provides us the effectiveness of the features.

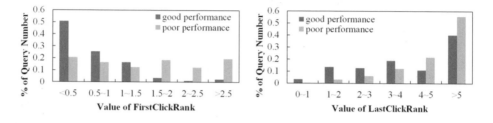

Fig. 1. Feature effectiveness of FirstClickRank&LastClickRank

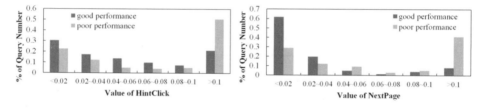

Fig. 2. Feature effectiveness of HintClick&NextPage

HintClick&NextPage. These two features are about users' interaction with search engine's functional hyperlink. Similar to previous analysis, if a query performs well, the user should be able to find what he desires in top results. So the user does not need to click any related queries or review the results in following pages. In this case, the values of the two features should be smaller than the feature values of poor-performance queries.With the same annotated query set, we can also see the effectiveness of these features in Fig. 2by the distribution.The feature AdvancedSearch is similar to the two features. We will not go into analysis of it.

AllClickNum. This feature is about users' actions in a whole search session. Its value is the average number of users' clicks in the session of a specific search query. When the query performs well, the session may end with few actions. But, if the query performs badly, a user may spend quite a lot of actions in finding satisfactory results.

The effectiveness of AllClickNum is shown in Fig. 3. The figure presents that more than 82% of the well-performance search queries' AllClickNum values are less than 3. In contrast, more than 50% of poor-performance search queries' AllClickNum values are greater than 2.The feature AllLogRec is similar to AllClickNum.

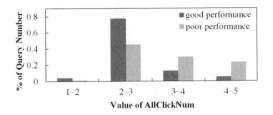

Fig. 3. Feature effectiveness ofAllClickNum

4.3   Other Features

Some other features are also used in our method. They can be easily obtained from search engine, query log or the Q_i-Q_r pair. They are shown in Table 2.

Table 2. Other Features

Feature Name	*Description*
EditDistance	Edit distance between $Q_i$and Q_r.
NormNumOfResults	Number of results of Q_r / Number of results of Q_i
NormQueryFreq	Search frequency of Q_r / Search frequency of Q_i

It is obvious that EditDistance shows the literal similarity of $Q_i$and Q_r. NormNumOfResults presents the quantity of the resources related to Q_r in search engine's index, which may seriously affect the search results of Q_r. NormQueryFreq presents comparatively popularity of Q_r, which is also important to a query recommendation.

4.4   Re-ranking via SVM

With the selected features, we can re-rank the candidates and get the query recommendation by algorithms based on machine learning. For the recommendation in a web search engine, we always need top N best related queries, so the algorithm should evaluate each candidate query with a continuous function and re-rank them by the evaluation result.SVM algorithm can give each sample a decision function value besides a classification result, and it usually performs well in solving this kind of problem. With the decision function values, we can sort the candidates and get top queries forrecommendation.

5   Experiments

5.1   Training Data Annotation

In order to re-rank the candidates, we have to construct a sample set of annotated "input query – recommendation candidate query" pairs. The sample set should contain both high-quality "input query – recommendation candidate query" pairs and bad case pairs.

For constructing the set, we extract top 2,000 hot queries from a commercial search engine's query log. For each query, we extract at most 100 recommendation candidates by the method in Section 3, and get about 200,000 "input query – recommendation candidate query" pairs. Among these pairs, we choose some obvious high-quality recommendation pairs as positive cases, and choose the pairs not related or not unable to provide useful search results as negative cases. The pairs hard to evaluate should not be annotated.

Two annotators have worked for the annotation. Only when two annotators have agreement on a recommendation pair, the annotation of the pair can be used. After annotation, we get 1,065 positive pairs and 681 negative pairs, which come from 123 input queries. These annotated pairs form a training set for re-ranking algorithm.

5.2 Recommendation Experiment

With annotated data, we use SVM algorithm to build a recommendation candidates re-ranking model. We filtered out pornography queries from top 2,000 hot queries and get 1,499 input queries for the following experiment.

We use the trained model to re-rank the recommendation candidates of 1,499 input queries, and get top 10 candidate queries of each input query for recommendation. Altogether, 14,413 recommended queries are generated for 1,499 input queries.

5.3 Evaluation of Recommendation's Relevance and Search Performance

5.3.1 Evaluation Framework and Indicator

In Section 4.1, we propose 3 criteria to judge whether a query recommendation is effective. With the criteria, we can evaluate a query recommendation's effectiveness. The experiment in Section 5.3 shows a framework which we propose for evaluating an "input query – recommended query" pair with Criterion 1 and 3.

For evaluating an "input query – recommended query" pair (A, B), we use three factors C_B, $R_{A, B}$, and E_B. Table 3 shows the meaning and the range of the factors.

C_B is a basic requirement for an effective recommended query. $R_{A,B}$ is corresponding to Criterion 1. The value of E_B indicates how much B's search results satisfy users' information needs, and it is an indicator of Criterion 3.

Table 3. Factors of Evaluation

Factor	Meaning and Range
C_B	Whether B is a correct and regular query. In details, B should be spelled correctly, understandable, not porn, not a URL or hostname.(0forfalse; 1fortrue)
$R_{A,B}$	The relevance of A and B. (0 for irrelevant; 1 forweakly relevant; 2forstrongly relevant)
E_B	The evaluation value of B's search result. In our experiment, we use DCG_5 of B.

For evaluation, we select 29 input queries with different search frequency of the 1,499 input queries. For each input query, we have 10 related queries recommend by our method and 10 queries recommend by the commercial search engine we mentioned before. So we need to annotate C_B and $R_{A, B}$ for at most 580 "input –recommended" pairs (since there are overlaps between our recommendation and the search engine's). For each recommend queries B, we have to annotate the relevance between query B and each of its top 5 search results, and then we can getDCG$_5$ of B.

After the annotation, we can calculate the overall score $S_{A, B}$ for an "input query – recommended query" pair (A, B) by the following equation.

$$S_{A, B} = C_B \cdot R_{A, B} \cdot E_B$$

5.3.2 Evaluation Results

We calculate the recommendation score $S_{A, B}$ for 280 related queries recommend by our method and 280 queries recommended by the search engine. The average score of our recommendation is 10.49 while the average score of the search engine's recommendation is 9.51. Fig.4 shows the distribution of $S_{A, B}$ values of different recommendation. In Fig.4, we can find that the queries recommended by the search engine has a lot more ones with $S_{A, B}$=0. Since every factor with a value of 0 may cause $S_{A, B}$=0, we look into the values of the factors and find that for any factor the recommended queries of the search engine have more value of 0 than the ones recommended by us.

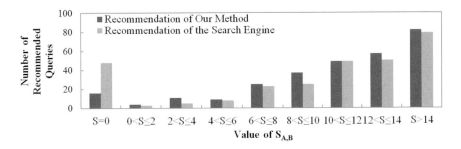

Fig. 4. Distribution of $S_{A, B}$ Values of Different Recommendation

For an input query A, our method gives a group of recommended queries B_1, B_2, …, B_{10} and the search engine give another group with B'_1, B'_2 …, B'_{10}. So we can calculate the average score of each group and have a comparison. Of 29 input queries we annotated, 22 groups of our method's recommendation have higher scores than the search engine's recommendation.

5.4 Popularity of Recommended Queries

As the assumptions of a high-quality query recommendation in Section 4.1, a good recommended query should describe users' needs and attract users to click. This characteristic of recommended queries can be evaluated by analyzing the recommended queries' click frequency in search engine log. The following work would evaluate the popularity of the query recommendation generated by our method.

We collect 30-days click-through log of a popular commercial search engine in China from Nov 2009 to Dec 2009. We extract 30,057 different clicked recommended queries of 1,499 input queries. Of the 30,057 recommended queries, there are 6,967 also recommended by our method, which is called subset *A*. The collection of the other queries which we do not recommend is called subset *B*.

We count the click frequency for all 30,057 extracted recommended queries, and compare the click frequency of the queries recommended by our method(subset *A*) and the ones we do not recommend(subset *B*). The average click frequency of subset *A* is 253.97, while subset *B*'s average click frequency is 230.22.

For a more detailed analysis, we put the queries in different buckets by their click frequency. Then we can compare the distribution in different buckets of subset *A*'s queries to subset *B*'s. The division of buckets and the ratio of different buckets for each subset are shown in Fig. 5.

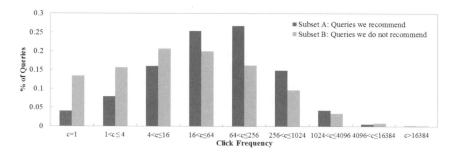

Fig. 5. Queries' Distribution in Buckets Divided by Click Frequency *c*

Fig. 5shows that queries in subset *A* are more concentrated in high-frequency buckets than the ones in subset *B*. But we can also find that in the two buckets with highest frequency queries, subset *A* does not have a higher ratio than subset *B* while subset *A* performs much better than *B* in the buckets with frequency from 64 to 1,024. We look into the recommended queries with top click frequencies in subset *B*and find that there are a lot of porn queries which do not provide users any useful search results. But it doesnot happen in subset *A*. The contrast shows our method can filter out the queries with poor search performance.

In summary, theexperiment results show us that the recommendation of our method is more popular than the recommendation of the commercial search engine in average while popular queries with bad search results are not recommended by us.

6   Conclusion and Future Work

We have presented a new point of view on good query recommendation. We gave some assumptions of high quality query recommendation, and proposed a new query recommendation method which can recommend relevant, popular queries with high performance search results. Then we evaluated the query recommendation generated by our method. It is shown that our recommendations perform better than a commercial search engine in different aspects.

Future study will focus on the performance of our methodon long queries and low search frequency queries. Traditional query recommendation method can also be introduced into our framework.

References

1. Silverstein, C., Henzinger, M., Marais, H., et al.: Analysis of a very large Web search engine query log. In: SIGIR Forum, vol. 33(1), pp. 6–12. ACM, New York (1999)
2. Jansen, M., Spink, A., Bateman, J., Saracevic, T.: Real life information retrieval: a study of user queries on the Web. In: SIGIR Forum, vol. 32(1), pp. 5–17. ACM, New York (1998)
3. Baeza-Yates, R., Hurtado, C., Mendoza, M.: Query recommendation using query logs in search engines. In: Lindner, W., Mesiti, M., Türker, C., Tzitzikas, Y., Vakali, A.I. (eds.) EDBT 2004. LNCS, vol. 3268, pp. 395–397. Springer, Heidelberg (2004)
4. Baeza-Yates, R., Tiberi, A.: Extracting semantic relations from query logs. In: KDD 2007, pp. 76–85. ACM, New York (2007)
5. Wen, J., Nie, J., Zhang, H.: Clustering user queries of a search engine. In: 10th WWW, pp. 162–168. ACM, New York (2001)
6. Zaiane, R., Strilets, A.: Finding similar queries to satisfy searches based on query traces. In: Bruel, J.-M., Bellahsène, Z. (eds.) OOIS 2002. LNCS, vol. 2426, pp. 207–359. Springer, Heidelberg (2002)
7. Cucerzan, S., White, R.W.: Query suggestion based on user landing pages. In: 30th SIGIR, pp. 875–876. ACM, New York (2007)
8. Zhang, Z., Nasraoui, O.: Mining search engine query logs for query recommendation. In: 15th WWW, pp. 1039–1040. ACM, New York (2006)
9. Liu, Z., Sun, M.: Asymmetrical query recommendation method based on bipartite network resource allocation. In: 17th WWW, pp. 1049–1050. ACM, New York (2008)
10. Huffman, S.B., Hochster, M.: How well does result relevance predict session satisfaction? In: 30th SIGIR, pp. 567–574. ACM, New York (2007)
11. Fox, S., Karnawat, K., Mydland, M., Dumais, S., White, T.: Evaluating implicit measures to improve web search. ACM Trans. Inf. Syst. 23(2), 147–168 (2005)
12. Hassan, A., Jones, R., Klinkner, K.: Beyond DCG: user behavior as a predictor of a successful search. In: WSDM 2010, pp. 221–230. ACM, New York (2010)

A Local Generative Model
for Chinese Word Segmentation

Kaixu Zhang[1], Maosong Sun[1], and Ping Xue[2]

[1] State Key Lab of Intelligent Technology and Systems
Tsinghua National Laboratory for Information Science and Technology
Department of Computer Science and Technology
Tsinghua University, Beijing, 100084, China P.R.
`zhangkx03@mails.thu.edu.cn`, `sms@thu.edu.cn`
[2] The Boeing Company
`ping.xue@boeing.com`

Abstract. This paper presents a local generative model for Chinese word segmentation, which has faster learning process than discriminative models and can do unsupervised learning. It has the ability to make use of larger resources. In this model, four successive characters are used to determine whether a character interval should be a word boundary or not. The Gibbs sampling algorithm, as well as three additional rules, is applied for the unsupervised learning. Besides words, the word candidates that are generated by our model can improve the performance of Chinese information retrieval. The experiments show that in supervised learning our method outperforms a language model based method. And the performance on one corpus is better than the best one reported in SIGHAN bakeoff 05. In unsupervised learning, our method achieves the comparable performance compared to the state-of-the-art method.

Keywords: probability model, natural language processing, Chinese word segmentation.

1 Introduction

Being different from English, there are no delimiters in Chinese text to indicate words. The words are potentially existent, in a certain sense, and important for further NLP tasks or information retrieval (IR). The fundamental task to segment characters in Chinese text into words is named as Chinese word segmentation (CWS).

Xue [1] presented a maximum entropy (ME) based model for CWS as character tagging using local context as evidence. To avoid the weakness of these local models, conditional random field (CRF) models [2], perceptrons [3] and other global discriminative models [4] were introduced. Global models, namely sentence models, deal with each sentence or paragraph as a whole. Indirectly, long-distance relations can be taken into account. These models get good performance in the literature. However, the learning process of these models are time-consuming.

P.-J. Cheng et al. (Eds.): AIRS 2010, LNCS 6458, pp. 420–431, 2010.

Language models, which estimate the generating probability of each sentence, are used for CWS. As generative models, language models can learn from corpora much faster than discriminative models, and can be easily adapted for unsupervised learning [5], [6].

In this paper, we present a local generative model, which has not been explored before. The relationship between our model and existent models is shown in Table 1.

Table 1. The relationship between our model and other models for CWS

	local model	global model
generative	our model	language models
discriminative	ME based	CRF based

Following the notation of [7] and [8], the *interval* between two successive characters in Chinese can be classified into two types, namely *separated* and *combined*. A separated interval indicates that those two characters belong to two separated words, while a combined interval indicates that those two characters belong to the same words. The separated intervals are therefore recognized as word boundaries.

Our local generative model estimates the probability of four successive characters, called the *context*, given the type of the interval in the middle of these characters. And the model predicts the interval type separately and only based on the corresponding context.

We also provide a method to generate *word candidates* based on our model. The word candidates are the words that an input sentence could contain at some segmentation granularity. Comparing to using words, using word candidates can improve the performance of IR.

Notice that the traditional output of CWS may not fit the purpose of Chinese IR. Due to the lack of explicit word boundaries in Chinese text, there is no commonly accepted definition of words among Chinese speakers and even linguists. The difference is mainly about the segmentation granularity in some situations. That causes the granularity of the words in queries may differ from the ones in the CWS. Indexing only segmented Chinese words can not get a good performance for Chinese IR.

A binary tree based segmentation representation for Chinese IR was introduced by [9]. The result shows that indexing all word candidates at different granularity improves the performance of IR. However, the method proposed by [9] needs a specific annotated corpus and a ranking-based model.

Using the output of our model, we can get all word candidates without any specific annotation on the training corpus. All the word candidates of a sentence correspond to all the nodes in the binary tree of the corresponding sentence. So indexing word candidates benefits Chinese IR as well as the binary tree based method does.

The experiments are on SIGHAN bakeoff 05 [10] corpora in both supervised and unsupervised CWS.

The contributions of this paper are two-fold. (1) We introduce a local generative model. This simple model has a competitive performance in both supervised and unsupervised CWS, while it enjoys a faster learning process and has the ability to make use of larger resources. (2) We find a general way to generate all the possible segmented word at any segmentation granularity, which may benefit IR and other applications.

2   The Local Generative Model

2.1   The Model

We denote the type of interval I by y, which can be either a separated interval s or a combined interval c, and denote the corresponding context consisting of four successive characters $l_2 l_1 r_1 r_2$ by x. Each pair of interval type and its context is treated as a sample (x, y). Examples can be found in Table 2.

Table 2. Part of samples from the sentence '材料利用率低' (The utility rate of the material is low) segmented as '材料 | 利用率 | 低' (material | utility rate | low). The '(-1)' and the '(-2)' are two additional pseudo characters

x (context)	y (type of the interval)
(-2)(-1)材料	s (separated)
材料利用	s
料利用率	c (combined)

The aim of our model is to estimate the generative probability of the samples $p(x, y) = p(y)p(x|y)$. For x is only based on local information and the probability we use is of the generative form, we call our model local and generative.

The priori $p(y)$ is easy to be estimated appropriately by the maximum likelihood estimation. And there could be various way to estimate the likelihood $p(x|y)$, which is the more complicated part. The choice needs to show the relationship between the interval type and the context, and to be dependent on the size of the corpus.

In supervised learning, the estimations we used for both separated interval and combined interval are in the same form

$$\begin{cases} p(x|s) = p_{s1}(l_1, r_1)p_{s2}(l_2|l_1, r_1)p_{s3}(r_2|l_1, r_1) \\ p(x|c) = p_{c1}(l_1, r_1)p_{c2}(l_2|l_1, r_1)p_{c3}(r_2|l_1, r_1) \end{cases} \qquad (1)$$

The probabilistic graphical model representation of this model is shown in Figure 1. These two characters, l_1 and r_1, in the middle are first generated together according to the interval type, for they are strongly dependent on the interval type. Then two distinct trigram models are used to generate the outer two characters l_2 and r_2 respectively.

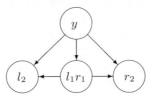

Fig. 1. The probabilistic graphical model representation of the local generative model

Unlike the n-gram language models, these probabilities in the right side of Equation 1 are distinct and estimated individually.

2.2 Predicting

In the learning phrase, the probabilities of the model, $p(y)$, $p(x|s)$, and $p(x|c)$, are estimated. In the predicting phrase, which can be roughly regarded as a binary classification task, for each new context x^* in the training data, a predicted interval y^* can be obtained by the following approach based on Bayesian decision theory. This approach is for both supervised and unsupervised learning.

We define a discriminate function $g(x^*)$ as:

$$g(x^*) = \log \frac{p(s|x^*)}{p(c|x^*)} = \log \frac{p(x^*|s)}{p(x^*|c)} \frac{p(s)}{p(c)} \tag{2}$$

The interval y^* to be predicted can be got by:

$$y^* = \begin{cases} s \text{ , if } g(x^*) > 0 \\ c \text{ , if } g(x^*) < 0 \end{cases} \tag{3}$$

2.3 Unsupervised Learning and the Rules

Following Mochihashi et al. ([6]), we use Gibbs sampling method in the unsupervised learning to learn the model from the raw text.

With slight changes, the local generative model is suitable for the unsupervised Chinese word segmentation, which is usually not feasible for most discriminative models. We also slightly modify the Gibbs sampling method. Details are in the next section.

Three additional rules used in the sampling are introduced below. Wherever these rules are applied, the type of intervals can be determined without any other processes.

The first rule is that any interval is the separated interval, if one of the two immediate characters of this interval is a Chinese character, and the other is a punctuation mark. This idea is from [11], where punctuation marks in raw Chinese text were used as the implicit annotations for unsupervised CWS. So we can say that the punctuation marks make unsupervised CWS semi-supervised. For example, the interval in ', 按' is a separated interval.

Besides, we create the second rule based on Arabic numerals, that any interval is the combined interval, if two immediate characters of this interval are both Arabic numerals. For example, the interval in '1 0' of '又要忙活 1 0 多亩责任田' is a combined interval.

Finally, The third rule is that any intervals at the beginning or at the end of the sequences are all separated intervals.

Table 3 gives us an overview of how the rules work on the raw Chinese text. We found that nearly 1/5 intervals in the raw Chinese text can be determined by the three simple rules in the first three corpora.

Table 3. The statistical information of the SIGHAN bakeoff 05 corpora about the intervals that rules can be applied on

	MSR	CTU	PKU	AS
total intervals	4,325,733	2,525,555	2,020,181	9,289,116
rules can be applied	850,870	492,357	394,889	2,411,779
rate	19.7%	19.5%	19.5%	26.0%

3   Algorithm Detail

3.1   Interpolated Kneser-Ney Smoothing

Unlike the n-gram language model, where we estimate different probabilities for the characters in different positions in the context x, similar smoothing technique is needed in the probability estimation process since the size of corpus is limited. The final performance of this model is sensitive with the smoothing technique.

Here we only discuss the smoothing method for supervised learning. The smoothing method for unsupervised learning is similar. There are two kinds of smoothing needed for the probabilities for supervised learning. One is for the probability of the bigram $p(l_1, r_1)$ in the middle, the other is for the probabilities of the unigram given a bigram, $p(l_2|r_1 l_1)$ and $p(r_2|l_1 r_1)$. We employ an n-gram language model smoothing method called interpolated Kneser-Ney smoothing to smoothen the probabilities. The notation is mainly based on the technical report by [12].

The probability of x with the interpolated Kneser-Ney smoothing is

$$p(x) = P_{\text{bi}}^{\text{IKN}}(l_1, r_1) P_{r_1, l_1}^{\text{IKN}}(l_2) P_{l_1, r_1}^{\text{IKN}}(r_2) \tag{4}$$

This probability is for both separated and combined intervals, only with different contexts to be estimated.

First, we introduce the smoothed probabilities of the unigram given a bigram, $P_{r_1, l_1}^{\text{IKN}}(l_2)$ and $P_{l_1, r_1}^{\text{IKN}}(r_2)$.

The probability of character unigram c given the context n-gram $\mathbf{u}$ is

$$P_{\mathbf{u}}^{\text{IKN}}(c) = \frac{\max(0, C_{\mathbf{u}c} - d_{|\mathbf{u}|})}{C_{\mathbf{u} \cdot}} + \frac{d_{|\mathbf{u}|} t_{\mathbf{u} \cdot}}{C_{\mathbf{u} \cdot}} P_{\pi(\mathbf{u})}^{\text{IKN}}(c) \tag{5}$$

where $C_{\mathbf{u'}}$ is the count of certain sequence $\mathbf{u'}$ appearing in the training data, $t_{\mathbf{u}\cdot} = |\{c'|c_{\mathbf{u}c'} > 0\}|$ is the number of different characters following the context $\mathbf{u}$, d_i is the discount, $\pi(\mathbf{u})$ is the postfix of the context $\mathbf{u}$ which has length of $|\mathbf{u}| - 1$, and $P_{\pi(\mathbf{u})}^{\mathrm{IKN}}(c)$ is the back-off probability.

For the back-off probabilities, modified counts are used and defined as follows:

$$t_{c'\mathbf{u}c} = \begin{cases} 1 & \mathrm{if} c_{c'\mathbf{u}c} > 0 \\ 0 & \mathrm{if} c_{c'\mathbf{u}c} = 0 \end{cases} \tag{6}$$

$$C_{\mathbf{u'}c} = t_{\cdot\mathbf{u'}c} = \sum_{c'} t_{c'\mathbf{u}c} \tag{7}$$

The back-off probabilities can be defined recursively until the context $\mathbf{u}$ is $\emptyset$. When the context $\mathbf{u}$ is $\emptyset$, we use a maximum entropy estimation as the final back-off probability:

$$P_{\emptyset}^{\mathrm{IKN}}(c) = \frac{\max(0, C_c - d_0)}{C_.} + \frac{d_0 t_.}{C_.} P_{\mathrm{ME}}^{\mathrm{IKN}}(c) \tag{8}$$

The maximum entropy probability is

$$P_{\mathrm{ME}}^{\mathrm{IKN}}(c) = \frac{1}{N} \tag{9}$$

where N is the size of the set of all possible characters.

Then we introduce the smoothed probability of the bigram, $P_{\mathrm{bi}}^{\mathrm{IKN}}(l_1, r_1)$.

When apply the interpolated Kneser-Ney smoothing method to estimate the probability of bigram (l_1, r_1) in the middle, an adapted version is used as:

$$\begin{aligned} P_{\mathrm{bi}}^{\mathrm{IKN}}(l_1, r_1) &= \frac{\max(0, c_{l_1, r_1} - d_2)}{c_.} \\ &+ \frac{d_2}{t_{l_1, r_1}} c_{l_1, r_1} P_{\emptyset}^{\mathrm{IKN}}(l_1) P_{\emptyset}^{\mathrm{IKN}}(r_1) \end{aligned} \tag{10}$$

where the back-off probability, which is a product of $P_{\emptyset}^{\mathrm{IKN}}(l_1)$ and $P_{\emptyset}^{\mathrm{IKN}}(r_1)$, assumes that l_1 and r_1 are generated individually. This is quite different from the ordinary n-gram language model back-off method.

The discount d_i can be optimized by holding out a development set or be assigned empirically. The whole learning process for the generative model is to process the samples of contexts and intervals once, without any iteration to optimize any coefficients of the model as the maximum entropy models, CRFs or perceptron methods do. This makes the learning process of our model much faster than those of the discriminative models.

3.2   Adapted Gibbs Sampling

In unsupervised learning, we modify our model and the Gibbs sampling method to learn a model from the raw corpus.

First of all, we slightly change the generative model when we apply this model to unsupervised learning for CWS, for the convergence will be slow and difficult if we use the original model.

The probabilities of the model we use for unsupervised CWS are

$$\begin{cases} p(x|s) = p_s(l_2, l_1)p_s(r_2, r_1) \\ p(x|c) = p_c(l_1, r_1)p_c(l_2|l_1, r_1)p_c(r_2|l_1, r_1) \end{cases} \tag{11}$$

where the probability of the combined intervals is the same as the one for the supervised learning, but the probability of the separated intervals ignores the relationship between these two characters from different words, for this relationship is hard to learn from the raw corpus.

The adapted algorithm of Gibbs sampling [13] is described in Figure 2. There are two changes from the original Gibbs sampling algorithm. The function add() remove() and sample() are the operations for the estimation of the $p(x, y)$ in Gibbs sampling.

Adapted Gibbs sampling algorithm

input x_i, λ
$k := 1000$
$n := 0$
$n_s := 0$
for $t := 1 \dots T$
    for $i := 1 \dots I$
        remove(x_i, y_i^{t-1})
        if rule-can-be-applied(x_i) **then**
            $y_i^t :=$ rule(x_i)
        else
            $y_i^t :=$ sample$(p(x_i|s)e^{k(n_s - n\lambda)}, p(x_i|c))$
        add(x_i, y_i^t)
        $n := n + 1$
        if $y_i^t = s$ **then** $n_s := n_s + 1$
output $p(y)$, $p(x|y)$

Fig. 2. The adapted Gibbs sampling algorithm

First, three rules introduced in Section 2 are used in this algorithm. The interval types of the samples that those three rules can be applied is not sampled but assigned directly according to those rules.

Another change is for the priori $p(y)$ when we apply the sampling. The Gibbs sampling may cause the priori probability we learn from the data set to be quite different from the real value that we can get from the gold standard segmented corpus, even if we set a priori to the $p(y)$. Thus, we adapt the Gibbs sampling in order to fix the $p(y)$ that the Gibbs sampling could converge to. The total number of intervals n and the number of sampled separated intervals n_s are recorded. And this algorithm uses a term $e^{k(n_s - n\lambda)}$, which can restrict the priori $p(s)$ strongly close to a given value λ, instead of $p(y)$ as the priori in sampling. The strength is controlled by k.

3.3   Word Candidates at Different Granularity

Using the output of our model, we can get all word candidates, at different granularity without any specific annotation on the corpus. The aim of using word candidates is to improve the performance of IR.

For an input sentence $c_1c_2\ldots c_n$, we can calculate the degree of confidence $q(c_i)$ that there is a word boundary after c_i:

$$q(c_i) = g(c_{i-1}, c_i, c_{i+1}, c_{i+2}) \qquad (12)$$

A substring $c_a \ldots c_b$ of the sentence is a word candidate if and only if:

$$\min\left(q(c_{a-1}), q(c_b)\right) > \max\left(q(c_a), q(c_{a+1}), \ldots, q(c_{b-1})\right) \qquad (13)$$

That is, if two intervals right before and after a substring are more likely to be the word boundary than any inner intervals in the substring, this substring can be identified as a word at some granularity.

We can define the word as a substring $c_a \ldots c_b$ such that

$$\min\left(q(c_{a-1}), q(c_b)\right) > 0 > \max\left(q(c_a), q(c_{a+1}), \ldots, q(c_{b-1})\right) \qquad (14)$$

The only difference is that there is a zero in the middle of the inequations. This means that words are only generated at a certain granularity which the training corpus has. Interestingly, we can say that the definition of word candidates is the generalization of the definition of words.

For example, given a input sequence '年轻人有学问' (The youngsters have a lot of knowledge) , we have $q(年) = -2.517$, $q(轻) = -2.194$, $q(人) = 2.027$, $q(有) = 1.791$ and $q(学) = -1.644$. For this sequence, all the word candidates are '年', '轻', '人', '有', '学', '问', '年轻', '学问', '年轻人', '有学问' and '年轻人有学问'.

Generally, all the word candidates of a sentence correspond to all the nodes in the binary tree [9] of the same sentence. So indexing word candidates benefits Chinese IR as well as the binary tree based method does.

4   Experiments

4.1   Experiment Setup

All our experiments of supervised and unsupervised learning are on four corpora in SIGHAN bakeoff 05. Two corpora provided by Academia Sinica (AS) and City University of Hong Kong (CTU) are in traditional Chinese, while the other two corpora provided by Peking University (PKU) and Microsoft Research (MSR) are in simplified Chinese. The overview of these corpora are in Table 4. The OOV (out of vocabulary) rate is the rate of the words in the test set that do not appear in the training set.

The discounts in the interpolated Kneser-Ney smoothing need to be assigned. Empirically, the discounts d_0, d_1 and d_2 are assigned to 0.25 0.85 and 0.95

Table 4. Overview of the four corpora in SIGHAN bakeoff 05

	MSR	CTU	PKU	AS
Training set size (words)	2,368,391	1,455,630	1,109,947	5,449,581
test set size (words)	106,873	40,936	104,372	122,610
OOV rate	0.026	0.074	0.058	0.043

respectively for the smoothing of the probabilities for unigram given bigram, and d_0 and d_1 are assigned to 0.4 and 0.75 respectively for the smoothing of the probabilities for bigram. Those values are for all corpora and both supervised and unsupervised learning. Notice that the discounts could also be optimized by holding out a development set.

The f1 measure based on the precision and recall [10] is the commonly used measurement for the evaluation for CWS. We use the f1 measure for our evaluation and comparison.

4.2 Supervised Learning

The learning process for generative models is much faster than the one for discriminative models. The whole learning and predicting process for each corpus terminated in minutes.

Results are shown in Table 5. Here we only concern about the f1 measure for each corpus. It shows that the performances of our model are competitive with the best performances reported by SIGHAN [10], all except one of which are based on discriminative models. Especially on CTU corpus, our performance is better than the best one reported by SIGHAN. And the performances of our model are better than those of the language model [6], which is also a generative model.

There is an interesting observation on the types of segmentation errors. We can adjust the output by replacing some words with corresponding word candidates at finer or coarser granularity according to the gold standard result. The performance could be significantly improved, which is shown in the parentheses of Table 5.

Table 5. Results of supervised learning on SIGHAN bakeoff 05 corpora. The values in the parentheses are the f1 measures that we adjust the result by replacing some words with corresponding word candidates according to the gold standard result to maximize the recall. Results of the language model are from the paper by [6]

method	MSR	CTU	PKU	AS
our model	0.961 (0.995)	0.947 (0.986)	0.945 (0.991)	0.946 (0.990)
language model	0.945	0.941	-	-
SIGHAN reported best	0.964	0.943	0.950	0.952

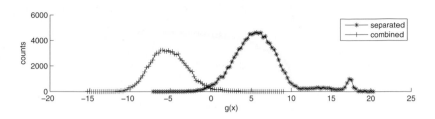

Fig. 3. Distributions of $g(x)$ of the separated and combined intervals on the MSR corpus in supervised learning

Fig. 3 shows the distributions of $g(x)$ for the separated and combined intervals on the MSR corpus in supervised learning. This figure indicates that the $g(x)$ of misclassified samples centers near 0. For the predicting approach is based on the Bayesian decision theory, the value $g(x)$ can be recognized as the degree of confidence. A majority of the types of the intervals could be predicted with high confidence.

4.3   Unsupervised Learning

For unsupervised learning, we directly assign λ in the adapted Gibbs sampling to the value calculated based on the training corpus. In fact, empirical experiments show that this value is not the best estimation for λ.

Table 6 shows the results of experiments on unsupervised learning. The models are learned in two ways, one is to normally use training data, the other is to use test data only for the Gibbs sampling. Figure 4 shows two learning curves of both ways on MSR corpus. The performances of our model are comparable with the state-of-the-art unsupervised method reported by [6].

Similar phenomena occur in the unsupervised learning if we adjust the output using word candidates. The f1 can significantly increase if the result is at a good granularity.

Table 6. Result of unsupervised learning on SIGHAN bakeoff 05 corpora. The values in the parentheses are the f1 measures that we adjust the result by replacing some words with corresponding word candidates according to the gold standard result to maximize the recall. Results of the language model are from the paper by [6].

method	MSR	CTU	PKU	AS
test set only	0.801 (0.941)	0.723 (0.908)	0.774 (0.935)	0.761 (0.937)
training set only	0.819 (0.957)	0.778 (0.951)	0.800 (0.950)	0.796 (0.961)
language model	0.807	0.824	-	-

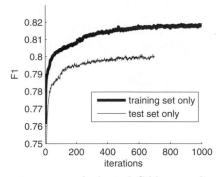

Fig. 4. The learning curve of adapted Gibbs sampling on MSR corpus

5   Discussion and Conclusion

The experiments on SIGHAN bakeoff 05 data show that our model are better than the language model in the supervised learning, and with much faster learning process comparing to discriminative models like CRFs and perceptron. The f1 measure in one of four corpora is better than the best one reported in SIGHAN bakeoff 05. The performance of unsupervised learning of this model is comparable with the state-of-the-art.

In our model, comparing to existent linear discriminative models, information of character trigrams are used, when we calculate the probabilities of l_2 and r_2. And the smoothing technique makes our formulas nonlinear, although there's no coefficients optimization. This may be the reason for why our model can get better performance than the common expectation for the generative models. In addition, four successive characters as the context are proved to be enough for determine a interval type in most of the cases.

For the sake of IR, we define the word candidates for CWS. A previous study already showed that it benefits the performance of IR. The word candidates can be got by our model naturally and directly. Notice that they can also be got by global models such as CRFs, if we redefine the degree of confidence $q(c_i)$ as some marginal probability.

Another interesting result indicated by our experiment is that the errors of CWS are mainly caused by the segmentation granularity difference, without which the performance will increase significantly.

We believe that larger training data or even larger raw data will be helpful to improve the performance. Our model with the advantage shown in this paper is suitable for learning from larger resources. We will work on these issues.

Acknowledgments. This research is supported by the Boeing-Tsinghua Joint Research Project "Robust Chinese Word Segmentation and High Performance English-Chinese Bilingual Text Alignment".

References

1. Xue, N.: Chinese word segmentation as character tagging. Computational Linguistics and Chinese Language Processing 8, 29–48 (2003)
2. Peng, F., Feng, F., McCallum, A.: Chinese segmentation and new word detection using conditional random fields. In: COLING 2004, vol. 1, pp. 562–568 (2004)
3. Gao, J., Li, M., Wu, A., Huang, C.: Chinese word segmentation and named entity recognition: A pragmatic approach. Computational Linguistics 31, 531–574 (2005)
4. Kruengkrai, C., Uchimoto, K., Kazama, J., Wang, Y., Torisawa, K., Isahara, H.: An Error-Driven Word-Character Hybrid Model for Joint Chinese Word Segmentation and POS Tagging. In: 47th Annual Meeting of the ACL, vol. 1, pp. 513–521 (2009)
5. Goldwater, S., Griffiths, T., Johnson, M.: Contextual Dependencies in Unsupervised Word Segmentation. In: 21th Annual Meeting of the ACL, vol. 1, pp. 673–680 (2006)
6. Mochihashi, D., Yamada, T., Ueda, N.: Bayesian unsupervised word segmentation with nested Pitman-Yor language modeling. In: 47th Annual Meeting of the ACL, vol. 1, pp. 100–108 (2009)
7. Sun, M., Shen, D., Tsou, B.: Chinese word segmentation without using lexicon and hand-crafted training data. In: Proceedings of the 17th International Conference on Computational Linguistics, vol. 2, pp. 1265–1271 (1998)
8. Huang, C., Šimon, P., Hsieh, S., Prévot, L.: Rethinking Chinese word segmentation: tokenization, character classification, or wordbreak identification. In: 45th Annual Meeting of the ACL on Interactive Poster and Demonstration Sessions, vol. 1, pp. 69–72 (2007)
9. Liu, Y., Wang, B., Ding, F., Xu, S.: Information retrieval oriented word segmentation based on character associative strength ranking. In: The Conference on EMNLP, vol. 1, pp. 1061–1069 (2008)
10. Emerson, T.: The second international chinese word segmentation bakeoff. In: The Fourth SIGHAN Workshop on Chinese Language Processing, vol. 1, pp. 123–133 (2005)
11. Li, Z., Sun, M.: Punctuation as implicit annotations for Chinese word segmentation. Computational Linguistics 35, 505–512 (2009)
12. Teh, Y.: A Bayesian interpretation of interpolated Kneser-Ney. Technical Report (2006)
13. Bishop, C.: Pattern recognition and machine learning. Springer, Heidelberg (2006)

Re-ranking Summaries Based on Cross-Document Information Extraction

Heng Ji[1], Juan Liu[1], Benoit Favre[2], Dan Gillick[3], and Dilek Hakkani-Tur[3]

[1] Computer Science Department, Queens College and Graduate Center,
City Univeristy of New York,
New York, NY 11367, USA
[2] LIUM, Université du Maine,
Avenue Laënnec, 72085 Le Mans Cedex 9, France
[3] Computer Science Department and International Computer Science Institute,
University of California, Berkeley,
Berkeley, CA 94704, USA
hengji@cs.qc.cuny.edu

Abstract. This paper describes a novel approach of improving multi-document summarization based on cross-document information extraction (IE). We describe a method to automatically incorporate IE results into sentence ranking. Experiments have shown our integration methods can significantly improve a high-performing multi-document summarization system, according to the ROUGE-2 and ROUGE-SU4 metrics (7.38% relative improvement on ROUGE-2 recall), and the generated summaries are preferred by human subjects (0.78 higher TAC Content score and 0.11 higher Readability/Fluency score).

Keywords: Multi-document Summarization, Information Extraction.

1 Introduction

Since about one decade ago Information Extraction (IE) and Automated Text Summarization have been recognized as two tasks sharing the same goal [1] – extract accurate information from unstructured texts according to a user's specific desire, and present the information to the user in a compact form. These two tasks have been studied separately and quite intensively over the past decade. Various corpora have been annotated for each task, a wide range of models and machine learning methods have been applied, and separate official evaluations have been organized. There has clearly been a great deal of progress on the performance of both tasks.

Because a significant percentage of queries in the summarization task involve facts (entities, relations and events), it is beneficial to exploit results extracted by IE techniques in automatic summarization. Some earlier work (e.g. [2], [3]) used Message Understanding Conference (MUC) [4] IE to generate or improve summaries. The IE task has progressed from MUC-style single template extraction to the more comprehensive Automatic Content Extraction (ACE) that targets at more fine-grained types of facts. The IE methods have also been advanced from single-document IE to cross-document dynamic event chain extraction (e.g. [5]) and static attribute extraction

P.-J. Cheng et al. (Eds.): AIRS 2010, LNCS 6458, pp. 432–442, 2010.

[9]. In addition, a lot of current IE systems couple supervised learning techniques with traditional pattern matching approaches, which enable them to produce reliable confidence values (e.g. [5]). Therefore a summarization process can have more flexibility to choose using IE results or the original sentences [6]. Based on the above reasons we feel the time is now ripe to explore some novel methods to marry these two tasks again and raise summarization to a higher level of performance.

From a collection of documents for a specific query, we extract facts in both queries and the documents. We use a high-performing multi-document extractive summarizer as our baseline, and tightly integrate IE results into its sentence ranking and compression. Experiment results show this integration method can achieve significant improvement on both standard summarization metrics and human judgement.

2   Task and Baseline System

2.1   TAC Summarization Task

The summarization task we are addressing is that of the NIST Text Analysis Conference (TAC) multi-document summarization evaluation [7]. This task involves generating fixed-length summaries from 10 newswire documents, each on a given query including a specific topic. For example, given a query "Judge Joan Lefkow's Family Murdered/Describe the murders of Judge Joan Lefkow's husband and mother, and the subsequent investigation. Include details about any evidence, witnesses, suspects and motives." and 10 documents, a summarization system is required to generate a summary about specific entities ("Judge Joan Lefkow"), relations ("family") and events ("murder" and "investigation").

2.2   Baseline Summarization System

We apply a top-performing TAC summarization system [8] as our baseline. In this model, a summary is the set of sentences that best covers the relevant concepts in the document set, where concepts are simply word bigrams valued by their document frequency. The concepts with low-frequency or stop-words are filtered. The value of a sentence is the sum of the concept values it contains. The goal of summarization is modeled in a way to find the collection with maximum value, subject to a length constraint. This problem is solved efficiently with an integer linear programming (ILP) solver. A sentence compression component is used to post-process candidate sentences. The compression step consists of dependency tree trimming using high-confidence semantic role labeling decisions. Non-mandatory temporal and manner arguments are removed and indirect discourse is reformulated in direct form.

3   Cross-Document IE Annotation

We apply a state-of-the-art English cross-document IE system ([6], [9]) to extract facts from the input documents. This system was developed for the NIST Automatic Content Extraction Program (ACE 2005)[1] and TAC KBP 2010 Program[2].

---

[1] http://www.nist.gov/speech/tests/ace/
[2] http://nlp.cs.qc.cuny.edu/kbp/2010/

ACE2005 defined 7 types of entities, 18 types of relations and 33 distinct types of relatively 'dynamic' events. KBP2010 defined 42 types of relatively 'static' slots (e.g. "*Ruth D. Masters is the wife of Hyman G. Rickover*" indicates that the "*per:spouse*" slot for person "*Hyman G. Rickover*" is "*Ruth D. Masters* ").

The IE pipeline includes name tagging, nominal mention tagging, coreference resolution, time expression extraction and normalization, relation extraction and event extraction. Names are identified and classified using an HMM-based name tagger. Nominals are identified using a maximum entropy-based chunker and then semantically classified using statistics from the ACE training corpora. Relation extraction and event extraction are also based on maximum entropy models, incorporating diverse lexical, syntactic, semantic and ontological knowledge. At the end an event coreference resolution component is applied to link coreferential events, based on a pairwise maximum entropy model with linguistic attributes and a graph-cut clustering model. Then an event tracking component is applied to identify important entities which are frequently involved in events as 'centroid entities'; link and order the events centered around each centroid entity on a time line.

Our slot filling system includes a bottom-up pattern matching pipeline and a top-down question answering pipeline, with several novel enhancements including statistical answer re-ranking and Markov Logic Networks (MLN) based cross-slot reasoning. From both extraction systems confidence values are produced on various levels: name identification and classification, relation and event labeling and corresponding argument identification and classification.

Based on the assumption that the documents for a given query are topically related, we apply the extraction methods to the each 'super-document' that includes the query and the related documents. As a result we can obtain a knowledge base including entities, relations, events, event chains and coreference links between the query and documents.

This method can be considered as a combination of query expansion and fact retrieval. We not only obtain a 'profile' (potential fact categories) for the query so that we can design corresponding templates for abstractive summarization, but also assign weights to sentences including these specific categories of facts.

4   Motivation of Using IE for Summarization

Using the combination of fact types in ACE and KBP, we can cover rich information in news articles. For example, among the 92 TAC queries, 28 queries include explicit ACE events and their corresponding input documents include 2739 event instances. Some queries include specific events such as "*Provide details of the **attacks** on Egypt's Sinai Penninsula resorts targeting Israeli tourists.*", while others only inquire about a general series of events: "*Describe the views and **activities** of John C. Yoo.*"

Previous work has extensively focused on using entity extraction to improve summarization, so we only present some concrete examples of using relations and events to improve summarization quality as follows.

4.1 Relations/Events Can Push Up Relevant Sentences

Traditional sentence ranking methods in summarization used key word matching, and the knowledge acquisition bottleneck still remains due to sparse data. In other words, the training data for similarity matching may not be available for each test instance.

In order to learn a more robust sentence ranker, the method of matching query and sentences should go beyond lexical and syntactic level in order to capture semantic structures. A lot of current extractive summarizers use semantic relations in WordNet [10]. This approach has two main limitations: (1) It cannot address broader semantic relatedness; (2). It cannot address the semantic relations between two words with different part-of-speech tags. Semantic relation and event classification can provide a more flexible matching framework. Our basic intuition is that a sentence should receive a high rank if it involves many relations and events specified in the query, regardless of the different word forms to indicate such relations and events. For example, for the following query and sentences with high ranks:

[**Query**]
London Subway Bombing/Describe the July 7, 2005 **bombings** *in* **London, England** *and the events, casualties and investigation resulting from the attack.*

[**High-Rank Sentence 1**]
The **attacks***, the deadliest ever carried out on* **London** *in peacetime, coincided with a summit of the Group of Eight in Gleneagles, Scotland.*

[**High-Rank Sentence 2**]
A group called Secret al-Qaida Jihad Organization in Europe claimed responsibility, saying the **attacks** *were undertaken to avenge* **British** *involvement in the wars in Afghanistan and Iraq.*

[**High-Rank Sentence 3**]
The **bomb exploded** *in the lead car moments after the train pulled out of the* **King's Cross station***, blowing apart the car and making it impossible to reach the dead and injured from the rear.*

In sentences 1 and 2, the baseline summarizer is not able to detect "*attacks*" as the same events as "*bombings*" because they have different lexical forms. The event extraction component, however, predicts "*conflict-attack*" events and labels "*London/British*" as "*place*" arguments in both sentences. This provides us much stronger confidence in increasing the ranks of sentence 1 and 2.

Furthermore, even if the event triggers in sentence 3 "*bomb*" can be matched with "*bombings*" in the query, the baseline summarizer assigns a low weight to sentence 3 because it cannot detect the "located-in" relation between "*King's Cross station*" and "*London*". But the relation extraction component can successfully identify this "*PHYS/Located*" relation from another sentence in the same document set: "*The* *subway tunnel between **King's Cross** and Russell Square is one of several "deep tubes" bored through **London**'s bedrock and clay more than a century ago".*

4.2 Relations/Events Can Push Down Irrelevant Sentences

On the other hand, relations and events can filter some irrelevant sentences by deep semantic structure analysis. For example,

> **[Query]**
> *Judge Joan Lefkow's Family Murdered / Describe the **murders** of **Judge Joan Lefkow**'s **husband and mother**, and the subsequent investigation. Include details about any evidence, witnesses, suspects and motives.*

> **[*Low-Rank Sentence 4*]**
> *They remembered that he would sometimes show up at the federal courthouse to take his **wife**, U. S. District Judge **Joan Humphrey Lefkow**, to lunch and brought her flowers.*

The baseline summarizer mistakenly assigns a high rank to sentence 4 because it involves a name *"Joan Humphrey Lefkow"* specified in the query, and *"wife"* can be recognized to match *"husband"* by semantic clusters. However, event extraction can be used to successfully push down this sentence because it does not include any "Conflict-attack (murder)" events.

4.3 Event Coreference Can Remove Redundancy

What we have presented in section 4.1 and 4.2 is advancing summaries in terms of their *Content* quality. Another central track of summarization research is the issue of *readability* – especially how to remove redundancy existing in summaries from multiple documents.

In this paper we propose an approach of using event coreference resolution to reach this goal. Compared to similarity computation methods based on lexical features, our method can detect similar pairs of sentences even if they use completely different expressions. For example, we can fuse the following sentences because they include coreferential *"Conflict-attack"* event instances = Both include indicative words *"blasts/bombings"* and involve "London" as their place arguments:

> **[*Sentence 5*]**
> *It was the deadliest of the four bomb **blasts** in **London** last week.*

> **[*Sentence 6*]**
> *The bus explosion was one of four co-ordinated **bombings**, the others on **London** Underground subway trains.*

It is challenging for the baseline summarizer to detect this sentence pair because most words don't overlap.

5   IE-Integrated Summarization

IE provides an effective way of modeling the central information described in the source documents. This model consists of entities, relations and events involving these entities. Even if this model described perfectly such information, it does not tell us what subset of this model should appear in a summary.

The first question we have to tackle is "What is most relevant in IE output?" A baseline estimation method would be to look at the frequency of IE elements in the input and ensure that frequently described events appear in the summary. Another approach would be to build a graph of IE elements, and perform a random walk of this graph to weigh the most relevant nodes. However, both approaches do not account for three factors: relevance prior, coverage and confidence of the extraction.

Another question is "How can we incorporate IE-derived model in a summarization system?" Only considering extractive summarization, approaches vary from scoring sentences directly with supervised or unsupervised relevance assessments, to scoring sub-sentence units and finding best covering sentences. Under those models, IE can be integrated as an extra set of features to characterize either sentences or sub-sentence units. For the purpose of this work, we focus on a simple linear model to blend sentence-level IE scores and a baseline summarizer.

5.1   Approach Overview

Figure 1 depicts the general procedure of our approach to integrate IE results into our baseline summarizer.

5.2   IE-Based Re-ranking and Redundancy Removal

Because the human summaries are not necessarily created from the original sentences of the input documents, we cannot adopt a supervised learning based re-ranking approach. For each sentence we adjust its rank produced from the baseline summarizer based on IE confidence values.

Each IE component includes a statistical classifier and thus can generate reliable confidence values. For example, for each event mention in D, the baseline Maximum Entropy based classifiers produce three types of confidence values:

- *Conf(trigger,etype)*: The probability of a string *trigger* indicating an event mention with type *etype*; if the event mention is produced by pattern matching then assign confidence 1.
- *Conf(arg, etype)*: The probability that a mention *arg* is an argument of some particular event type *etype*.
- *Conf(arg, etype, role)*: If *arg* is an argument with event type *etype*, the probability of *arg* having some particular *role*.

For a given query Q and a collection of 10 documents D that includes N sentences, we generate a summary based on an integrated approach as follows. For any sentence s in D, we extract various confidence values in Table 1 and combine them to form the final IE confidence for s:

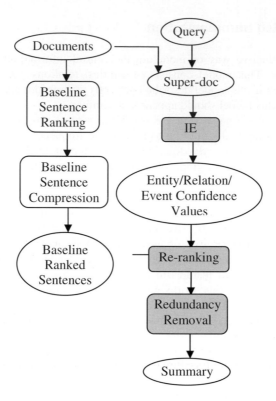

Fig. 1. Pipeline of Integrating IE into Summarization

$$c_{ie}(s) = \alpha_1 \times \sum_j c_1(s,e_j) + \alpha_2 \times \sum_k c_2(s,r_k) + \alpha_3 \times \sum_l c_3(s,e_l) + \alpha_4 \times \sum_m c_4(s,e_m)$$

Table 1. IE Confidence Values

Confidence	Description
$c_1(s,e_j)$	confidence of s including an entity e_j relevant to Q (coreferential)
$c_2(s,r_k)$	confidence of s including a relation r_k relevant to Q (relation type and relation arguments match)
$c_3(s,ev_l)$	confidence of s including an event mention ev_k relevant to Q (event type and event arguments match)
$c_4(s,evcoref_m)$	confidence of s including a link $evcoref_m$ between two coreferential event mentions which are relevant to Q

Assuming the ranking confidence from the baseline summarizer is $c_{baseline}(s)$, then we can get the combined weight for s:

$$w_{summary}(s) = \lambda_1 \times (c_{baseline}(s) / \sum_{i=1}^{N} c_{baseline}(s_i)) + \lambda_2 \times (c_{ie}(s) / \sum_{i=1}^{N} c_{ie}(s_i))$$

We believe that incorporating these confidence values into a unified re-ranking model can provide a comprehensive representation of the concepts in the source collection of documents. Based on the combined weights, we select top sentences to form a summary according the number of words specified in the task. The parameters α and λ are optimized from a development set. In order to achieve better readability (non-redundancy), we conduct a greedy search through the high-ranked sentences for redundancy removal. If all facts in a sentence pair $<s_i, s_j>$ are determined to be coreferential by our entity and event coreference resolvers, we remove the shorter one.

6   Experimental Results

In this section we present the results of applying IE to improve TAC summarization.

6.1   Data and Evaluation Metrics

We randomly selected 30 topics from TAC 2008 and TAC 2009 summarization task as our development set to optimize parameters and another separate set of 31 topics as our blind test set. The summaries are evaluated automatically with ROUGE-2 and ROUGE-SU4 metrics [13]. In order to focus more on evaluating the ordering of sentences and coherence across sentences, we extend the length restriction in TAC setting from 100 words to 20 sentences. We also asked 16 human subjects to manually evaluate summaries based on the TAC Responsiveness metric [7] consisting of Content and Readability/Fluency measures. In order to compare different methods extensively, we ask the annotators to give a real-value score between [1, 5] (1-Very Poor, 2-Poor, 3-Barely Acceptable, 4-Good, 5-Very Good).

6.2   ROUGE Scores

The parameters α and λ are optimized from a separate development set. We use the following optimized α values: $\alpha_1=1$, $\alpha_2=2$, $\alpha_3=3$, $\alpha_4=1$. Figure 2 presents the effect on ROUGE-2/ROUGE-SU4 scores of varying the IE weight λ, from 0 (baseline summarizer) to 1 (using IE only).

We can see that our method achieved significant improvement on Recall. When we use $\lambda = 0.7$, which is also the best weight optimized from the development set, our methods achieved 7.38% relative ROUGE-2 gain. In order to check how robust our approach is, we conducted the Wilcoxon Matched-Pairs Signed-Ranks Test on ROUGE scores for these 31 topics. The results show that we can reject the hypothesis that the improvements were random at a 95.7% confidence level. From these curves we can also conclude that using IE results only ($\lambda=1$) for sentence ranking produced worse ROUGE scores than the baselines.

6.3   TAC Responsiveness Scores

Table 2 presents the average scores across all topics based on manual evaluation using TAC Responsiveness metrics.

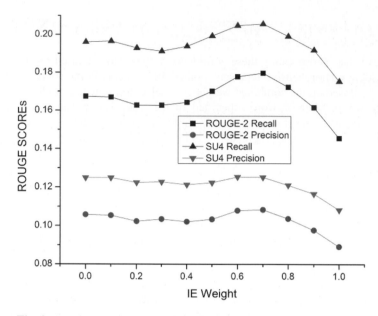

Fig. 2. Applying IE to Re-rank the Baseline with Sentence Compression

Table 2. TAC Responsiveness Comparison

Method	Content	Readability	Responsiveness
Baseline	3.11	3.56	3.39
IE-integrated	3.89	3.67	3.61

Table 2 shows that our IE-integrated method received much better Content scores based on human assessment. For example, for the query "Provide details of the kidnapping of journalist Jill Carroll in Baghdad and the efforts to secure her release", the baseline summarizer received a score '2' because of mis-match between 'kidnapping' in the query and the 'arrest' events involving other person and place arguments in the source documents. In contrast, our method received a score '4', because of the effective integration of 'kidnap' event detection results to re-rank sentences. Furthermore, according to the user feedback, our method produced fewer redundant sentences for most topics.

6.4 Discussion

Error analysis shows that for 3 topics IE had negative impact because of incorrect event categorization for the queries, and missing/spurious extraction errors. For example, for the query *"BTK/Track the efforts to identify the serial killer BTK and bring him to justice."*, IE mistakenly recognized 'Justice' as the main event type while missed a more important event type 'Investigation' which was not defined in the 33 event types. In these and other cases, we could apply salience detection to assign weights to different facts types in the query. Nevertheless, as the above results indicate, the rewards of using the IE information outweigh the risks.

7   Related Work

Our work is a re-visit on the idea of exploiting IE results to improve multi-document summarization proposed by Radev et al. [2] and White et al. [3]. In [2], IE results such as entities and MUC events are combined with natural language generation techniques in summarization. White et al. [3] improved Radev et al.'s method by summarizing larger input documents based on relevant content selection and sentence extraction. They also formally evaluated the performance of this idea. More recently, Filatova and Hatzivassiloglou [14] considered the contexts involving any pair of names as general 'events' and used them to improve extractive summarization. Vanderwende et al. [15] explored an event-centric approach and generated summaries based on extracting and merging portions of logical forms. Biadsy et al. [16] exploited entity and time facts extracted from IE to improve sentence extraction for biographical summaries. Hachey [11] used generic relations to improve extractive summarization and remove redundancy. Compared to these previous methods, we extend the usage of IE from single template to much more complete relation/event types. To the best of our knowledge our approach is the first work to use the information extracted from KBP project in summarization and apply event coreference resolution to remove summary redundancy.

In addition, our work is related to the summarization research that incorporates semantic role labeling (SRL) results (e.g. [12, 17]). SRL has a higher coverage on event categories than IE, while IE can provide additional annotations such as entity resolution and event resolution which are beneficial to summarization.

Our approach of selecting informative facts is also similar to defining Summarization Content Units (SCUs) in the Pyramid Approach [18] because both methods aim to maximize the coverage of logical 'concepts' in summaries..

8   Conclusion

We investigated the once-popular IE-driven summarization approaches in a wider IE paradigm. We demonstrated that a simple re-ranking approach can achieve improvement over a high-performing extractive summarizer. We expect that as IE is further developed to achieve higher performance in wider domains, the summarization task can benefit more from extended semantic frames.

Acknowledgement

This work was supported by the U.S. Army Research Laboratory under Cooperative Agreement Number W911NF-09-2-0053, the U.S. NSF CAREER Award under Grant IIS-0953149, Google, Inc., DARPA GALE Program, CUNY Research Enhancement Program, PSC-CUNY Research Program, Faculty Publication Program and GRTI Program. The views and conclusions contained in this document are those of the authors and should not be interpreted as representing the official policies, either expressed or implied, of the Army Research Laboratory or the U.S. Government. The U.S. Government is authorized to reproduce and distribute reprints for Government purposes notwithstanding any copyright notation here on.

References

1. Grishman, R., Hobbs, J., Hovy, E., Sanfilippo, A., Wilks, Y.: Cross-lingual Information Extraction and Automated Text Summarization. Linguistica Computazionale, XIV–XV (1997)
2. Radev, D.R., McKeown, K.R.: Generating natural language summaries from multiple online sources. Computational Linguistics 24(3), 469–500 (1998)
3. White, M., Korelsky, T., Cardie, C., Ng, V., Pierce, D., Wagstaff, K.: Multidocument Summarization via Information Extraction. In: Proc. HLT 2001, pp. 263–269 (2001)
4. Grishman, R., Sundheim, B.: Message Understanding Conference - 6: A Brief History. In: Proc. COLING 1996, pp. 466–471 (1996)
5. Ji, H., Grishman, R., Chen, Z., Gupta, P.: Cross-document Event Extraction, Ranking and Tracking. In: Proc. RANLP 2009, pp. 166–172 (2009)
6. Ji, H., Chen, Z., Feldman, J., Gonzalez, A., Grishman, R., Upadhyay, V.: Utility Evaluation of Cross-document Information Extraction. In: Proc. NAACL/HLT 2010, pp. 285–288 (2010)
7. Dang, H.T., Owczarzak, K.: Overview of the TAC 2009 Summarization Track. In: Proc. TAC 2009 (2009)
8. Gillick, D., Favre, B., Hakkani-Tur, D., Bohnet, B., Liu, Y., Xie, S.: The ICSI/UTD Summarization System at TAC 2009. In: Proc. TAC 2009 (2009)
9. Chen, Z., Tamang, S., Lee, A., Li, X., Passantino, M., Ji, H.: Top-down and Bottom-up: A Combined Approach to Slot Filling. In: P.-J. Cheng et al. (eds.) AIRS 2010. LNCS, vol. 6458, pp. 300–309. Springer, Heidelberg (2010)
10. Fellbaum, C. (ed.): WordNet: An Electronic Lexical Database. The MIT Press, Cambridge (1998)
11. Hachey, B.: Multi-Document Summarisation Using Generic Relation Extraction. In: Proc. EMNLP 2009, pp. 420–429 (2009)
12. Melli, G., Wang, Y., Liu, Y., Kashani, M.M., Shi, Z., Gu, B., Sarkar, A., Popowich, F.: Description of SQUASH, the SFU Question Answering Summary Handler for the DUC-2005 Summarization Task. In: Proc. DUC workshop 2005 (2005)
13. Lin, C., Hovy, E.: Automatic Evaluation of Summaries Using N-gram Co-occurrence Statistics. In: Proc. HLT-NAACL 2003, pp. 150–156 (2003)
14. Filatova, E., Hatzivassiloglou, V.: A Formal Model for Information Selection in Multi-Sentence Text Extraction. In: Proc. COLING 2004 (2004)
15. Vanderwende, L., Banko, M., Menezes, A.: Event-Centric Summary Generation. In: Proc. DUC 2004 (2004)
16. Biadsy, F., Hirschberg, J., Filatova, E.: An Unsupervised Approach to Biography Production using Wikipedia. In: Proc. ACL 2008, pp. 807–815 (2008)
17. Melli, G., Shi, Z., Wang, Y., Liu, Y., Sarkar, A., Popowich, F.: Description of SQUASH, the SFU Question Answering Summary Handler for the DUC 2006 Summarization Task. In: Proc. DUC 2006 (2006)
18. Nenkova, A., Passonneau, R.: Evaluating Content Selection in Summarization: The Pyramid Method. In: Proc. NAACL 2004 (2004)
19. Filatova, E., Hatsivassiloglou, V.: Event-based extractive summarization. In: Proc. ACL Workshop on Summarization (2004)

A Two-Stage Algorithm for Domain Adaptation with Application to Sentiment Transfer Problems

Qiong Wu[1,2], Songbo Tan[1], Miyi Duan[1], and Xueqi Cheng[1]

[1] Institute of Computing Technology, Chinese Academy of Sciences, China
[2] Graduate University of Chinese Academy of Sciences, China
{wuqiong,tansongbo,duanmiyi}@software.ict.ac.cn, cxq@ict.ac.cn

Abstract. Classification systems are typically domain-specific, and the performance decreases sharply when transferred from one domain to another domain. Building these systems involves annotating a large amount of data for every domain, which needs much human labor. So, a reasonable way is to utilize labeled data in one existing (or called source) domain for classification in target domain. To address this problem, we propose a two-stage algorithm for domain adaptation. At the first transition stage, we share the information between the source domain and the target domain to get some most confidently labeled documents in the target domain, and at the second transmission stage, we exploit them to label the target-domain data via following the intrinsic structure revealed by the target domain. The experimental results on sentiment data indicate that the proposed approach could improve the performance of domain adaptation dramatically.

Keywords: Domain Adaptation, Sentiment Classification, Information Retrieval.

1 Introduction

Text classification [7, 16] is a critical technique in the Natural Language Processing (NLP) community. Many research tasks rely on accurate classification. For example, sentiment classification [4][10] is essentially a text classification problem, and it classifies documents into positive or negative category.

In most cases, a variety of supervised classification methods can perform well. But when training data and test data are from different domains, the supervised classification methods often cannot perform well [8,11,12]. The reason is that training data do not have the same distribution as test data, so test data could not share the information from training data. Therefore, the labeled data in the same domain with test data is considered as the most valuable resources for classification. However, such resources in different domains are very imbalanced. In some traditional domains or domains of concern, many labeled data are freely available on the web, but in other domains, labeled data are scarce and it involves much human labor to manually label reliable data. So, the challenge is how to utilize labeled data in one domain (that is, source domain) for classification in another domain (that is, target domain). This raises a fundamental and important task, domain adaptation.

Realizing the challenges posed by domain adaptation, some researchers have explored a number of techniques to improve the performance of domain adaptation.

P.-J. Cheng et al. (Eds.): AIRS 2010, LNCS 6458, pp. 443–453, 2010.

However, the difficulties for domain adaptation are as follows: the first one is that the distribution of the target domain is not same with that of the source domain, and hence we need to share the information got from the source domain; the second one is the intrinsic structure of the target domain is static, so we need to utilize the intrinsic structure collectively revealed by target domain. In brief, a good method for domain adaptation is expected to utilize the information contained in the source domain as much as possible, and moreover, follow the intrinsic structure revealed by target domain as much as possible.

In light of the difficulties for domain adaptation, we propose a novel system algorithm which is composed of two stages. The first stage is called transition stage, where we firstly share information between the source and target domains by applying the adapted Prototype algorithm to label the target-domain documents initially, and then choose some high-quality seeds from the target domain which are most confidently labeled. The second stage is called transmission stage, where we utilize the intrinsic structure of the target domain by employing the manifold-ranking process to compute the manifold-ranking score for every document that denotes the degree of belonging to a category. So we can label the target-domain data based on these scores.

Our contribution is as follows. First, while existing domain-adaptation approaches typically rely on a generative model, our approach associates two domains to get some high-quality seeds from the target domain, and then follows the structure embodied by the seeds to improve the performance of domain adaptation. Second, while existing manifold-ranking-based approaches typically start with manually labeled seeds, our approach relies only on seeds that are automatically extracted and labeled from the target domain.

For evaluation, we use the proposed algorithm for sentiment classification problem, and evaluate it on three domain-specific sentiment data sets. The experiment results show that our approach can dramatically improve the accuracy when transferred to another target domain.

2   A Two-Stage Algorithm for Domain Adaptation

2.1   The Transition Stage

2.1.1   Overview

At this stage, we take into account these two objectives: we aim to (1) get the labels of the target-domain documents while utilizing the information of the source domain, and then (2) identify the high-quality documents which are most confidently labeled.

As we know, the features of source domain can be divided into two categories: domain-specific and nondomain-specific, and only nondomain-specific features can be used as a bridge between the source domain and the target domain. That is, we can use nondomain-specific features to train a classifier for target domain. For the sake of convenience, we call nondomain-specific features as "generalization features". As mentioned in Section 1, traditional Prototype classifier requires both source domain and target domain have the same distribution, which couldn't be satisfied in domain-adaptation problems. So we use an adapted Prototype classifier to solve this problem. An intuitive description is as follows: We pick up generalization features utilizing Frequently Co-occurring Entropy (FCE) [11], and then we only use these features in both source domain and target domain. After that, we assign a score for every unlabeled document to denote its extent to each category, and then the score is calculated by making use of a Prototype classifier trained by the accurate labels of source-domain data. The final score for classification is achieved when the algorithm ends, so the target-domain data can be labeled based on these scores.

2.1.2 Frequently Co-occurring Entropy

In order to pick out generalization features, we use Frequently Co-occurring Entropy (for simplicity, we call it as "f-score" in this work) proposed in [11]. The criteria behind FCE are: (1) occur frequently in both domains; (2) has similar occurring probability. The formula that satisfies these criteria is as follows:

$$f_w = \log(\frac{P_S(w) \cdot P_T(w)}{|P_S(w) - P_T(w)|})$$

(1)

where $P_S(w)$ and $P_T(w)$ denote the probability of word w in the source domain and the target domain respectively:

$$P_S(w) = \frac{(N_w^S + \alpha)}{(|D^S| + 2 \cdot \alpha)}$$

(2)

$$P_T(w) = \frac{(N_w^T + \alpha)}{(|D^T| + 2 \cdot \alpha)}$$

(3)

where N_w^S and N_w^T is the number of examples with word w in the source domain and the target domain respectively; $|D^S|$ and $|D^T|$ is the number of examples in the source domain and the target domain respectively. And according to [11], α is set to 0.00001.

After computing the f-score of every word, we rank the words in descending order according to their f-scores. Then, we choose the first $K_{FEATURE}$ documents as generalization features.

In formula (1), "$P_S(w) \ P_T(w)$" embodies the first criterion, and "$|P_S(w)-P_T(w)|$" embodies the second criterion. For the sake of being easy to adjust the weight of the two factors, a trade-off parameter π is introduced in the formula. Meanwhile, in case of $P_S(w)$ $=P_T(w)$, a parameter β is introduced. Therefore, the formula is modified as follows:

$$f_w = \log(\frac{(P_S(w) \cdot P_T(w))^\pi}{(|P_S(w) - P_T(w)| + \beta)^{(1-\pi)}})$$

(4)

where β is set as 0.0001 according to [11].

2.1.3 Prototype Classifier

Since we have got generalization features, we process both source-domain and target-domain data so that they only contain generalization features. After that, we assign every unlabeled document a score to represent its degree of belonging to a category, and the score is a real number between -1 and 1. Here, we assume that we classify the documents into two categories: category 1, and category 2. Therefore, when the score is between 0 and -1, the document should be classified as "category 1". The closer its score is near -1, the higher the "category 1" degree is, when the score is between 0 and 1, the document should be classified as "category 2". The closer its score is near 1, the higher the "category 2" degree is. We use S^{Target} to denote the score set of target domain.

In order to compute the score vector S^{Target}, we need to use a traditional classifier. There are many kinds of classifiers. For simplicity, we take prototype classification algorithm [7] as an example here. And its process in our context can be described as follows:

1. Compute the center vector C_1 and C_2 for document set belonging to category 1 (D_1^{SOURCE}) and document set belonging to category 2 (D_2^{SOURCE}) of source domain as follows:

$$C_l = \sum_{i \in D_l^L} d_i \Big/ \left| D_l^{SOURCE} \right|, \quad l \in \{1, 2\}$$

(5)

where |.| is the cardinality of a set.

2. Calculate the similarity between $d_i \in$ target domain ($i = 1,...n$) and each center vector with the cosine measure as follows:

$$Sim_l = \frac{d_i \cdot C_l}{\|d_i\| \times \|C_l\|}, \quad l \in \{1, 2\}$$

(6)

3. Assign $d_i \in$ target domain ($i= 1,...n$) a class label corresponding to the more similar center vector.

4. Give the opposite number of similarity value with C_1 to s_i if d_i's label is "category 1", e.g. if d_i's label is "category 1", and its similarity value with C_1 is 0.5, then set s_i to -0.5. Give the similarity value with C_2 to s_i if d_i's label is "category 2", e.g. if d_i's label is "category 2", and its similarity value with C_2 is 0.5, then set s_i to 0.5.

2.1.4 Identify the High-Quality Documents

Next, we find the high-quality documents from the target domain. To do this, we make use of the score which denotes its corresponding document's extent to "category 1" or "category 2". Firstly, we rank the target-domain documents in descending order according to their scores. So the more forward the document is ranked, the more likely it belongs to category 2; the more backward the document is ranked, the more likely it belongs to category 1. Then, we choose the first K documents and last K documents as the high-quality documents. In the rest of the paper, we will refer to these high-quality documents as seeds.

2.2 The Transmission Stage

The adapted Prototype classifier allows us to share information between the source domain and the target domain, but we haven't utilized the distribution of the target domain. In fact, being able to follow the intrinsic structure of the target domain is important for domain adaptation, as discussed before. Now that we have a small, high-quality seed set which embodies the intrinsic structure of the target domain, we can make better use of the seeds by utilizing the manifold-ranking method and having it improve the performance of domain adaptation.

The manifold-ranking method [13] is a universal ranking algorithm and it is initially used to rank data points along their underlying manifold structure. The prior assumption of manifold-ranking is: (1) nearby points are likely to have the same ranking scores; (2) points on the same structure (typically referred to as a cluster or a manifold) are likely to have the same ranking scores. An intuitive description of manifold-ranking is as follows: a weighted network is formed on the data, and a positive rank score is assigned to each known relevant point and zero to the remaining points which are to be ranked. All points then spread their ranking score to their nearby neighbors via the weighted network. The spread process is repeated until a global stable state is achieved, and all points obtain their final ranking scores.

Given that we now have a high-quality seed set, we build the weighted network whose points denote documents in target domain. Also, we integrate the scores of the seeds into the manifold-ranking process. So the manifold-ranking process used for domain adaptation can be formalized as follows:

Given a point set $\chi = \{x_1,\ldots,x_K,x_{K+1},\ldots,x_{2K},\ x_{2K+1},\ldots,x_n\} \subset R^m$, the first K points x_i $(1 \leq i \leq K)$ are the seeds which are labeled "category 2", the second K points x_j $(K+1 \leq j \leq 2K)$ are the seeds which are labeled "category 1", and the remaining points x_u $(2K+1 \leq u \leq n)$ are unlabeled. Let $F : \chi \rightarrow R^2$ denote a ranking function which assigns to each point x_i $(1 \leq i \leq n)$ a ranking value vector F_i. We can view F as a matrix $F = [F_1^T,\ldots,F_n^T]^T$. We also define a $n \times 2$ matrix $Y = [Y_1,Y_2]$, where $Y_1 = [Y_{11},\ldots,Y_{K1},Y_{K+1,1},\ldots,Y_{n1}]^T$ and $Y_2 = [Y_{12},\ldots,Y_{K2},Y_{K+1,2},\ldots,Y_{n2}]^T$ with $Y_{i1}=1$ if x_i is labeled as "category 2" and $Y_{i2}=1$ is x_i is labeled "category 1". The manifold ranking algorithm used for domain adaptation goes as follows:

1. Compute the pair-wise similarity values between points using the cosine measure. The weight associated with term t is calculated with the tf_t*idf_t formula, where tf_t is the frequency of term t in the document and idf_t is the inverse document frequency of term t, i.e. $1+\log(N/n_t)$, where N is the total number of documents and n_t is the number of the documents containing term t. Given two points x_i and x_j, the cosine similarity is denoted as $sim(x_i,x_j)$, computed as the normalized inner product of the corresponding term vectors.

2. Connect any two points with an edge if their similarity isn't 0. We form the affinity matrix W defined by $W_{ij}=sim(x_i,x_j)$ if $i \neq j$, and we let $W_{ii}=0$ to avoid loops in the graph built in the next step.

3. Construct the matrix $S=D^{-1/2}WD^{-1/2}$ in which D is a diagonal matrix with its (i, i)-element equal to the sum of the i-th row of W.

4. Iterate $F(t+1)=\alpha SF(t)+(1-\alpha)Y$ until convergence, where α is a parameter in $(0,1)$.

5. Let F^* denote the limit of the sequence $\{F(t)\}$. Then every document x_j $(K+1 \leq j \leq n)$ gets its ranking score vector F_j^*.

In the manifold-ranking algorithm, the weight matrix W is normalized symmetrically in the third step, which is necessary to prove the algorithm's convergence. During the fourth step, every point receives the information from its neighbors (first term), and also retains its initial information (second term). The parameter of manifold-ranking weight α specifies the relative contributions to the ranking scores from its neighbors and its initial ranking scores. According to [13], in our experiment, we set α to 0.6. It is worth mentioning that self-reinforcement is avoided since the diagonal elements of the affinity matrix are set to zero in the second step. Moreover, the information is spread symmetrically since S is a symmetric matrix.

Zhou et al. [13] proves that the sequence $\{F(t)\}$ converges to

$$F^* = \beta(I - \alpha S)^{-1} Y \tag{7}$$

In the above formula, $\beta = 1 - \alpha$. Note that although F^* can be expressed in a closed form, for large scale problems, the iteration algorithm is preferable due to computational efficiency. Usually the convergence of the iteration algorithm is achieved when the difference between the scores computed at two successive iterations for any point falls below a given threshold (0.00001 in this study).

Finally, we label the documents in target domain according to their ranking score vector. For each document x_i ($1 \leq i \leq n$), if $Y_{i1} > Y_{i2}$, assign the document the label "category 2"; if $Y_{i1} < Y_{i2}$, assign the document the label "category 1".

3   Evaluation

We evaluate our two-stage algorithm in the field of sentiment classification. In order to highlight the domain-specific nature of sentiment expression, we use reviews not only from different web sites, but also from domains with less similarity. Aimed at Chinese applications, we conduct the experiments based on the characteristics of the Chinese, and verify the performance on Chinese web reviews. However, the main proposed approach in this paper is language independent in essence.

3.1   Experimental Setup

For evaluation, we use three Chinese domain-specific data sets from on-line reviews, which are: Book Reviews[1] (B, from http://www.dangdang.com/), Hotel Reviews[2] (H, from http://www.ctrip.com/) and Notebook Reviews[3] (N, from http://www.360buy.com/). Each dataset has 4000 labeled reviews (2000 positives and 2000 negatives). We choose one of the three data sets as source-domain data, and another data set as target-domain data.

3.2   Baseline Systems

In this paper we compare our approach with the following baseline methods:

Proto: This method applies a traditional supervised classifier, Prototype classifier [7], for the sentiment transfer. And it only uses source domain documents as training data. Results of this baseline are shown in column 1 of Table 1. As we can see, accuracy ranges from 61.25% to 73.5%.

---

[1] http://www.searchforum.org.cn/tansongbo/corpus/Dangdang_Book_4000.rar
[2] http://www.searchforum.org.cn/tansongbo/corpus/Ctrip_htl_4000.rar
[3] http://www.searchforum.org.cn/tansongbo/corpus/Jingdong_NB_4000.rar

TSVM: This method applies transductive SVM for the sentiment transfer which is a widely used method for improving the classification accuracy. In our experiment, we use Joachims's SVM-light package (http://svmlight.joachims.org/) for TSVM. We use a linear kernel and set all parameters as default. This method uses both source domain data and target domain data, obtaining the results in column 2 of Table 1. As we can see, accuracy ranges from 61.42% to 77.17%, which are better than Proto.

EM: We implement the EM algorithm [6] based on Prototype classifier. Specifically, we train the Prototype classifier on the data labeled so far, use it to get the sentiment scores of unlabeled documents in the target domain, and augment the labeled data with K_E most confidently labeled documents. We test values for K_E from 10 to 300, an increase of 20 each, and reported in column 4 of Table 1 the best results. As we can see, since EM is based on Prototype, its accuracy ranges from 65.7% to 76.5% which are better than other baselines except Manifold.

Manifold: Our last baseline implements the manifold-ranking procedure [13] adaptable for sentiment transfer. Specifically, we begin by training a prototype classifier on the training data. Then we use the similarity scores between the documents and the positive central vector and the similarity scores between the documents and the negative central vector to separately initialize the ranking score vectors of the test data. Finally, we choose K_M documents that are most likely to be positive and K_M documents that are most likely to be negative as seeds for manifold-ranking. We test values for K_M from 10 to 300, an increase of 20 each, and reported in column 5 of Table 1 the best results. As we can see, accuracy ranges from 66.5% to 78.4% which are better than all other baselines.

Table 1. Accuracy comparison of different methods

Domain	Proto	TSVM	Adapted Proto	EM based on Proto	Manifold based on Proto	Our Approach
B->H	0.735	0.749	0.751	0.765	0.761	**0.766**
B->N	0.651	0.769	0.678	0.667	0.745	**0.748**
H -> B	0.645	0.614	0.670	**0.723**	0.677	0.695
H ->N	0.729	0.726	0.744	0.657	**0.784**	0.775
N-> B	0.612	0.622	0.653	**0.763**	0.665	0.702
N-> H	0.724	0.772	0.783	0.765	0.779	**0.806**
Aver	0.683	0.709	0.713	0.723	0.735	**0.748**

3.3 Our Approach

In this section, we compare the adapted Prototype classifier (Adapted Proto in Table 1) and the two-stage approach (Our Approach in Table 1) with three baseline methods. There is a parameter, K, in our two-stage approach. We set K to 290 to show we choose $2K$ seeds for manifold-ranking algorithm.

Results of the adapted Prototype classifier are shown in column 3 of Table 1. As we can observe, the adapted Prototype classifier produces much better performance than Proto. The greatest average increase of accuracy is achieved by about 3% compared to

Proto. The great improvement indicates that the adapted Prototype classifier is more effective to share information between source domain and target domain.

Results of our approach are shown in column 6 of Table 1. As we can observe, our approach produces much better performance than all the baselines. The greatest average increase of accuracy is achieved by about 6.5% compared to Proto. The great improvement compared with the baselines indicates that our approach performs very effectively and robustly.

Table 1 shows the average accuracies of Adapted Proto and TSVM are higher than Proto: the average accuracy of Adapted Proto is about 3% higher than Proto, and the average accuracy of TSVM is about 2.6% higher than Proto. As we know, Adapted Proto and TSVM utilize information of both source domain and target domain while Proto not, so this proves that utilizing the information of two domains is better than utilizing the information of only one domain for improving the accuracy of sentiment transfer.

Seen from Table 1, the average accuracies of the last three columns are higher than the first three columns. As we know, the last three approaches are all two-stage approaches while the first three approaches are not, so this indicates that two-stage transfer approach is more effective for sentiment transfer.

Meanwhile, the average accuracy of Manifold based on Adapted Proto showed in column 6 is higher than Manifold based on Proto showed in column 5: the average increase of accuracy of Manifold based on Adapted Proto is achieved by about 1.3% compared to Manifold based on Proto, which proves that Adapted Proto can choose higher quality seeds that embody the intrinsic structure of the domain for next stage.

Table 1 shows the Manifold based on Proto approach outperforms EM: the average accuracy of Manifold based on Proto is about 1.3% higher than EM based on Proto, and the greatest increase of accuracy is achieved by about 13% on the task "H->N" compared to EM based on Proto. This is caused by two reasons. First, EM is not dedicated for sentiment-transfer learning. Second, the manifold approach can follow the intrinsic structure of the target domain better.

4   Related Work

4.1   Classification

Classification is a traditional and widely-used problem, which includes two steps. The first step is to establish a classifier which describes the predefined training data. This is called training stage. The second step is using the classifier to classify test data. This is called test stage. It generally includes supervised classification and semi-supervised classification. Supervised classification is used when there are a lot of labeled data. Effective methods include Naïve Bayes classifiers [17]、 KNN [18]、 decision tree [19] 、 neural network [20] and support vector machines [21] et al. Semi-supervised classification (e.g. [22]~[24]) is used when labeled data are not sufficient to build a classifier. It uses both a small amount of labeled data and a large amount of unlabeled data to build a classifier. Nigam [22] used EM algorithm [6] to get pseudo labels of unlabeled data, and then incorporate them into Naïve Bayes classifier. Lanquillon [23] put forward a framework to utilize unlabeled data using an Expectation-Maximization-like scheme. Joachims [24] exploited the unlabeled date to modify SVM.

Typical classification requires the labeled and unlabeled data should be under the same distribution. So the classifier built by the labeled data could be well applied to the unlabeled data. But in our domain adaptation problem, the labeled and unlabeled data are from different domains, and often have different distributions. This is inconsistent with the basic requirement of typical classification, and the effect methods cannot be directly used in our problem.

4.2 Domain Adaptation

Domain adaptation aims to utilize labeled data from other domains or time periods to help current learning task, and the underlying distributions are often different from each other.

In the past years, many researchers have been working on this field and have proposed many approaches, including classifier adaptation [5], two-stage approach [8], consensus regularization framework [9] and so on. DaumeIII and Marcu [14] studied the domain-transfer field in statistical natural language processing using a specific Gaussian model. Then they presented an instantiation of this framework to Maximum Entropy classifiers and their linear chain counterparts. Xing et al. [15] proposed a novel algorithm, namely bridged refinement. They took the mixture distribution of the training and test data as a bridge to better transfer from the training data to the test data. Jiang and Zhai [8] presented a two-stage approach for transfer learning. At the first generalization stage, they got a set of features generalizable across domains, and at the second adaptation stage, they picked up useful features specific to the target domain. Then they also proposed a number of heuristics to approximately achieve the goal of generalization and adaptation.

Recently, some researchers attempted to address sentiment domain adaptation [3][12].

Some studies rely on only the labeled documents to improve the performance of sentiment transfer (e.g. [2]; [11]). Aue and Gamon [2] used four different approaches to customize a sentiment classification system to a new target domain using a small amount of labeled training data. Tan et al. [11] proposed Frequently Co-occurring Entropy to pick out generalizable features that occurred similarly in both domains, and then proposed Adapted Naïve Bayes to train a classifier suitable for the target-domain data.

Moreover, some studies rely on only the sentiment words to improve the performance of sentiment transfer (e.g. [1]). Andreevskaia and Bergler [1] presented a sentiment annotation system that integrated a corpus-based classifier trained on a small set of annotated in-domain data and a lexicon-based classifier trained on WordNet.

However, most of the existing studies rely on only utilizing the information from the source domain to address the task of domain adaptation, while ignoring the intrinsic structure of the target domain.

In this paper, we design an algorithm for domain adaptation by taking into account the relationship between source domain and target domain as well as the intrinsic structure of the target domain.

5   Conclusions

We propose a two-stage algorithm for domain adaptation. Our key idea is to share information between the source domain and the target domain, and follow the intrinsic structure of the target domain to improve the performance of domain adaptation. Specifically, the algorithm consists of a transition stage and a transmission stage. At the transition stage, we (1) share the information between the source domain and the target domain with the help of an adapted Prototype classifier to get the scores of the target-domain documents, (2) utilize the scores to identify a small number of most confidently labeled documents as high-quality seeds. At the transmission stage, we (3) employ the manifold-ranking algorithm to spread the seeds' ranking scores to their nearby neighbors to compute the ranking score for every unlabeled document, (4) label the target-domain data based on these scores.

Experimental results on three domain-specific sentiment data sets demonstrate that our approach can dramatically improve the accuracy, and can be employed as a high-performance domain adaptation system.

In future work, we plan to evaluate our algorithm to many more tasks. Also, we plan to try more algorithms for each stage of our algorithm.

Acknowledgments

This work was mainly supported by two funds, i.e., 60933005 & 60803085, and two other projects, i.e., 2007CB311100 & 2007AA01Z441.

References

1. Andreevskaia, A., Bergler, S.: When Specialists and Generalists Work Together: Overcoming Domain Dependence in Sentiment Tagging. In: ACL 2008, pp. 290–298 (2008)
2. Aue, A., Gamon, M.: Customizing sentiment classifiers to new domains: a case study. In: RANLP 2005 (2005)
3. Tan, S., Wang, Y., Wu, G., Cheng, X.: A novel scheme for domain-transfer problem in the context of sentiment analysis. In: CIKM 2007, pp. 979–982 (2007)
4. Cui, H., Mittal, V., Datar, M.: Comparative experiments on sentiment classification for online product reviews. In: AAAI 2006, pp. 1265–1270 (2006)
5. Dai, W., Xue, G., Yang, Q., Yu, Y.: Transferring Naive Bayes Classifiers for Text Classification. In: AAAI 2007, pp. 540–545 (2007)
6. Dempster, A.P., Laird, N.M., Rubin, D.B.: Maximum Likelihood from Incomplete Data via the EM algorithm. Journal of the Royal Statistical Society 39(B), 1–38 (1977)
7. Tan, S., Cheng, X., Ghanem, M., Wang, B., Xu, H.: A Novel Refinement Approach for Text Categorization. In: CIKM 2005, pp. 469–476 (2005)
8. Jiang, J., Zhai, C.X.: A Two-Stage Approach to Domain Adaptation for Statistical Classifiers. In: CIKM 2007, pp. 401–410 (2007)
9. Luo, P., Zhuang, F., Xiong, H., Xiong, Y., He, Q.: Transfer learning from multiple source domains via consensus regularization. In: CIKM 2008, pp. 103–112 (2008)
10. Pang, B., Lee, L., Vaithyanathan, S.: Thumbs up? Sentiment classification using machine learning techniques. In: EMNLP 2002, pp. 79–86 (2002)
11. Tan, S., Cheng, X., Wang, Y., Xu, H.: Adapting Naïve Bayes to Domain Adaptation for Sentiment Analysis. In: ECIR 2009, pp. 337–349 (2009)
12. Wu, Q., Tan, S., Cheng, X.: Graph Ranking for Sentiment Transfer. In: ACL 2009, pp. 317–320 (2009)

13. Zhou, D., Weston, J., Gretton, A., Bousquet, O., Schölkopf, B.: Ranking on data manifolds. In: NIPS 2003, pp. 169–176 (2003)
14. DaumeIII, H., Marcu, D.: Domain adaptation for statistical classifiers. Journal of Artificial Intelligence Research 26, 101–126 (2006)
15. Xing, D., Dai, W., Xue, G.-R., Yu, Y.: Bridged refinement for transfer learning. In: Kok, J.N., Koronacki, J., Lopez de Mantaras, R., Matwin, S., Mladenič, D., Skowron, A. (eds.) PKDD 2007. LNCS (LNAI), vol. 4702, pp. 324–335. Springer, Heidelberg (2007)
16. Tan, S.: An Effective Refinement Strategy for KNN Text Classifier. Expert Systems With Applications 30(2), 290–298 (2006)
17. Lewis, D.: Representation and Learning in Information Retrieval. PhD thesis, Amherst, MA, USA (1992)
18. Cover, T.M., Hart, P.E.: Nearest neighbor pattern classification. IEEE Transactions on Information Theory 13, 21–27 (1967)
19. Quinlan, J.R.: Induction of decision trees. Machine Learning 1, 81–106 (1986)
20. Carrol, S.M., Dickinson, W.: Construction of Neural Nets Using Radom Transform. In: Proc. IJCNN 1989, vol. (1), pp. 607–611 (1989)
21. Joachims, T.: Text Categorization with Support Vector Machines: Learning with Many Relevant Features. In: ICML 1998, pp. 137–142 (1998)
22. Nigam, K., McCallum, A.K., Thrun, S., Mitchell, T.: Text Classification from Labeled and Unlabeled Documents using EM. Machine Learning 39(2-3), 103–134 (2000)
23. Lanquillon, C.: Learning from Labeled and Unlabeled Documents: A Comparative Study on Semi-Supervised Text Classification. In: Zighed, D.A., Komorowski, J., Żytkow, J.M. (eds.) PKDD 2000. LNCS (LNAI), vol. 1910, pp. 167–194. Springer, Heidelberg (2000)
24. Joachims, T.: Transductive inference for text classification using support vector machines. In: ICML 1999, pp. 200–209 (1999)

Domain-Specific Term Rankings Using Topic Models

Zhiyuan Liu and Maosong Sun

Department of Computer Science and Technology
State Key Lab on Intelligent Technology and Systems
National Lab for Information Science and Technology
Tsinghua University, Beijing 100084, China
lzy.thu@gmail.com, sms@tsinghua.edu.cn

Abstract. A widely used approach for keyword extraction and content-based tag recommendation is ranking terms according to some statistical criteria. In many cases documents such as news articles and product reviews are in some specific domains. Domain knowledge may be important information for term rankings. In this paper, we present to model domain knowledge using latent topic models, referred to as Domain-Topic Model (DTM). Using DTM we perform domain-specific term rankings according to the relatedness between terms and domains. Experimental results on both keyword extraction and tag recommendation show advantages of DTM for domain-specific term rankings.

Keywords: Domain-Topic Model, term ranking, keyword extraction, social tag recommendation.

1 Introduction

Keyword extraction for documents such as research papers and news articles is widely used in digital library and information retrieval. Content-based tag recommendation for web resources such as blogs and product reviews is an important application in Web 2.0, which can ease the process of social tagging for users. Since both keyword extraction and content-based tag recommendation seek to identify most representative terms from document contents, ranking terms thus plays a crucial role in the both applications.

Previous methods simply rank terms by frequency measures such as $tfidf$ or χ^2 statistics, which are found to lead to poor results. In recent years, there is a surge of studies on graph-based methods for term rankings. These methods apply graph-based ranking algorithms, such as PageRank [4] and HITS [15], to rank terms in given document and select those with the highest ranking values as keywords or tags [20].

Domain knowledge is the knowledge of some specialized disciplines. In practice, there is usually domain information in addition to documents, which indicates the domain knowledge shared by the document and other documents in the same domain. The domain of a document can be either large or small. Here are two examples of domain information of documents. For news websites such as CNN.com, news articles are classified into different categories such as *sports*, *science*, *business* and *politics*. These category-like domains are large. Meanwhile, these news articles are also organized according to various popular themes, such as *financial crisis*, *air pollution* and *world cup*

P.-J. Cheng et al. (Eds.): AIRS 2010, LNCS 6458, pp. 454–465, 2010.

football match. These theme-like domains are small. Similar to news articles, for online bookstores such as `Amazon.com`, book reviews are divided into categories such as *arts*, *literature*, *philosophy* and *history*. The reviews under the same category share a large category-like domain knowledge. Meanwhile, according to some popular themes, various books on the same themes are collected together and their reviews share a small theme-like domain.

Generally, for a document under a specific domain, we are usually more interested in the part that is related to the domain. Domain knowledge of a document may thus play an important role in keyword extraction and tag recommendation, which can help focus on the important part of documents and filter out noise. In order to apply domain knowledge, we have to find a method to represent both terms and domains, and then rank terms by measuring their relatedness with given domains. In this paper, we use latent topic models to represent terms and domains, and then perform domain-specific term rankings.

The key idea of latent topic models is to represent terms and document as a mixture over latent topics. In a pioneer work [6], a topic model, i.e., probabilistic latent semantic analysis (pLSA), is proposed to rank documents in a corpus. Latent Dirichlet allocation (LDA) [3] was further proposed by adding Dirichlet priors on pLSA to avoid over-fitting problem. The success of latent topic models for modeling documents motivates us to propose a new latent topic model, referred to as Domain-Topic Model (DTM), for modeling domain knowledge of documents. Given a set of documents where each document has one or more domain labels, either category-like or theme-like, DTM learns topic distributions of words as well as topic distributions of domains. Using a learned DTM, we can rank term w in domain c by comparing their topic distributions. In this paper we investigate various measures of computing relatedness between domains and terms using their topic distributions.

2   Related Work

Existing methods for keyword extraction can be categorized into supervised classification-based approach and unsupervised ranking-based approach. For the former approach, some researchers adopted supervised learning methods to build two-class (is a keyword or not) classifiers to identify keywords, which is first proposed by [27] and the following supervise-based methods mostly considered more linguistic features of terms for developing classification system [12]. Since the supervised approach needs manually annotated training set, it is sometimes not practical under web circumstance. Starting from TextRank [20], graph-based ranking methods are becoming the most widely used ranking approach for keyword extraction. In recent years, many extensions of TextRank have been proposed for keyword extraction [17,29,28,18]. Besides, clustering methods on word graphs are also proposed for keyword extraction [19,10]. Unsupervised ranking terms is a practical approach for keyword extraction.

Some researchers have noticed the importance of domain knowledge [8,13]. In these work, however, human annotations are required to reflect domain knowledge in keyword extraction, either by building separate training set of different domains for classifiers [8] or using human-defined domain specific thesaurus as external knowledge [13].

The method in this paper, in contrast, can extract domain knowledge in an unsupervised manner.

Social tagging, as known as folksonomy, is a popular approach to organize online resources like documents, bookmarks and photos. Tag recommendation systems are usually designed to ease the process of social tagging, which can suggest tags to a new object based on previous tagged objects, user preferences or keyword extraction from the text content of the object. Most tag recommendation methods focus on analyzing the relations between object, tags and users. For some special online resources such as blogs and product reviews, it is may be practical to recommend tags based on contents. Many supervised methods have been proposed for content-based tag recommendation [21,14,26]. None of these methods, however, have taken domain knowledge into account for content-based tag recommendation. Since we focus on investigating the usefulness of domain knowledge for term rankings, our method is thus only compared with TextRank, without considering the supervised methods mentioned above.

3   Domain-Specific Term Rankings Using Domain-Topic Model

3.1   Domain-Topic Model

DTM models documents composed of words and domain labels. Each document d consists of N_d words $\boldsymbol{w}_d = \{w_{d,1}, \ldots, w_{d,N_d}\}$ and L_d domain labels $\boldsymbol{y}_d = \{y_{d,1}, \ldots, y_{d,L_d}\}$. The words are selected from a vocabulary of V unique words, and the domain labels are selected from a set of C unique labels.

Under the assumption that most words in a document describe the domain information of the document, we define DTM as a generative process as follows:

1. For each domain $c \in \{1, \ldots, C\}$, choose $\theta^{(c)} \sim Dir(\alpha)$.
2. For each topic $k \in \{1, \ldots, T\}$, choose $\phi^{(k)} \sim Dir(\beta)$.
3. For each document $d \in \{1, \ldots, D\}$, given the domain labels $\boldsymbol{y}_d$ For each word w_i, out of the N_d words:
   (a) Choose a domain label $u_i \sim Uni(\boldsymbol{y}^d)$
   (b) Choose a topic $z_i \sim Mul(\theta^{(u_i)})$
   (c) Choose a word $w_i \sim Mul(\phi^{(z_i)})$

where $Dir(*)$, $Uni(*)$ and $Mul(*)$ indicate the Dirichlet distribution, Uniform distribution and Multinomial distribution, respectively. In the generative process, θ_c is the topic distributions of domain c, drawn from a symmetric Dirichlet prior α; ϕ_k is the word distributions of topic k, drawn from a symmetric Dirichlet prior β. α and β are predefined as prior knowledge. Empirically we set $\alpha = 50/T$ and $\beta = 0.01$ where T is the topic number [9].

Figure 1 shows the graphical representation of DTM in comparison with LDA. DTM is identical with Author-Topic Model (ATM) [25] in form, while ATM was proposed for modeling documents with authors.

Let $\boldsymbol{w}$, $\boldsymbol{z}$ and $\boldsymbol{u}$ be the vectors of all words and their topic and domain label assignments of the whole document collection D. Given observed words and domain labels of a set of documents, the problem is inferring the hidden topics $\boldsymbol{z}$. Since estimating posterior is intractable, various approximate methods could be used to estimate DTM.

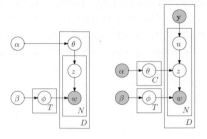

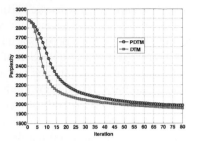

Fig. 1. Graphical model representations of LDA and DTM

Fig. 2. Comparison between PDTM ($P = 10$) and DTM on perplexity versus Gibbs Sampling iterations

In this paper, we use Gibbs Sampling [9] to learn DTM by sampling u_i and z_i for each word w_i. The topic assignment for a particular word depends on the current topic assignments of all the other words. That is, the domain and topic of a particular word w_i in document d with domain labels $\boldsymbol{y}_d$ is sampled from the following distribution:

$$P(u_i = c, z_i = k \mid \boldsymbol{w}, \boldsymbol{z}_{-i}, \boldsymbol{u}_{-i}, \boldsymbol{y}_d, \alpha, \beta) = \frac{n_{-i,k}^{(w_i)} + \beta}{\sum_{w'} n_{-i,k}^{(w')} + V\beta} \frac{n_{-i,k}^{(c)} + \alpha}{\sum_{k'} n_{-i,k'}^{(c)} + T\alpha} \quad (1)$$

where $\boldsymbol{w}_{-i}$, $\boldsymbol{z}_{-i}$ and $\boldsymbol{u}_{-i}$ are all other words in $\boldsymbol{w}$ except current word w_i and their corresponding topic and domain label assignments, $n_{-i,k}^{(w_i)}$ is the number of times that topic k is assigned to word w_i, and $n_{-i,k}^{(c)}$ is the number of times that topic k is assigned to domain c. The $-i$ indicates the counts are taken by not including the value of w_i.

When finishing Gibbs Sampling, we obtain the model consisting of both topic distributions of each word w, i.e., $\phi^{(w)}$, and topic distributions of each domain c, i.e., $\theta^{(c)}$. The probabilities of word w and domain c given topic k are computed as follows:

$$P(w|k) = \phi_k^{(w)} = \frac{n_k^{(w)} + \beta}{\sum_{w'} n_k^{(w')} + V\beta}, \quad P(c|k) = \theta_k^{(c)} = \frac{n_k^{(c)} + \alpha}{\sum_{k'} n_{k'}^{(c)} + T\alpha} \quad (2)$$

where $n_k^{(w)}$ is the total number of times that topic k is assigned to word w, and $n_k^{(c)}$ is the total number of times that topic k is assigned to domain c. Correspondingly, we can also obtain the probabilities of topic k given word w, i.e., $P(k|w)$ and given domain c, i.e., $P(k|c)$ using $n_k^{(w)}$ and $n_k^{(c)}$ for all words, topics and domains. These will be used for domain-specific term rankings, which is introduced in the following section.

3.2 Distributed Gibbs Sampling of DTM

To handle large-scale learning tasks, in this paper we implement a parallel version of DTM using the MapReduce parallel programming model [7], namely PDTM, where training documents are distributed over distinct processors for distributed Gibbs Sampling. The basic idea of PDTM is motivated by [22]. Here is an overview of PDTM algorithm. Given P processors, we partition documents and corresponding assignments into P disjoint subsets. Then simultaneous Gibbs Sampling is performed independently on each processor, as each processor thinks it is the only processor and updates it own copy of DTM. After each Gibbs Sampling iteration, each processor outputs its update to the model. Then an operation is performed to collect and merge the outputs from all processors, and broadcast the new model to all processors.

Our experiments consistently showed that the convergence rate for the distributed algorithms is as rapid as for the single processor case. As an example, Figure 2 shows test perplexity versus iteration number of Gibbs Sampling (NIPS data, $T = 50$ and $P = 10$). Despite having no guaranteed formal convergence, PDTM works very well empirically.

3.3   Ranking Terms Using DTM

To investigate the performance of DTM for domain-specific term ranking, we focus two important applications, keyword extraction and content-based tag recommendation.

A term for rankings usually contains more than one words. For a given term t, we compute

$$P(t|k) = \prod_{w \in t} P(w|k) \tag{3}$$

and

$$P(k|t) = \frac{P(t|k)\,P(k)}{P(t)} = \frac{n_k}{n_t} \prod_{w \in t} P(w|k) \tag{4}$$

where the fraction $\frac{P(k)}{P(t)}$ is approximated by the number of times that topic k occurs in training corpus, i.e., n_k, divided by the number of words in term t, i.e., n_t.

After obtaining $P(t|k)$ and $P(k|t)$, using DTM we can rank term t given domain c by *characteristics* measure [6]:

$$\text{char}(t; c) = P(t|c)\,P(c|t) = \left[\sum_{k=1}^{T} P(t|k)\,P(k|c)\right]\left[\sum_{k=1}^{T} P(c|k)\,P(k|t)\right] \tag{5}$$

This measure can identify what terms are *characteristic* of a domain c. A rarely-used term that is mainly used in domain c is not characteristic of c; neither is a term with high frequency in domain c, if it is also heavily-used by all other domains. The idea is similar to the measure of $tfidf$. That is, the former factor is controlled by $P(t|c)$ and the latter is by $P(c|t)$.

Given a domain, we can also rank terms by KL-divergence between the topic distributions of terms and the domain. KL-divergence is a asymmetric measure of the difference between two probability distributions by computing the expected extra information of one distribution compared to another distribution. By representing both terms and domains using topic distributions, we can use KL-divergence to measure the semantic diversity between terms and domains:

$$D_{\text{KL}}(t||c) = \sum_{k=1}^{T} P(k|t) log \frac{P(k|t)}{P(k|c)} \tag{6}$$

The third method to rank terms is predictive likelihood [11]:

$$P(t|c) = \sum_{k=1}^{T} P(t|k)\, P(k|c) \tag{7}$$

This is a part of the formula (Eq. 5) of characteristics, which indicates how likely term t occurs under domain c.

4 Experiment Results

In this section, we evaluate DTM on both keyword extraction and content-based tag recommendation. Since we focus on investigating the usefulness of domain-specific rankings, we only compare our methods with other content-based methods, i.e., TextRank and LDA for evaluation.

4.1 Keyword Extraction

The experiments of keyword extraction using DTM are carried out on a dataset of English news articles. However, we should note that the method is language independent. We first introduce the dataset and the training process of DTM.

Dataset. The dataset of news articles is annotated by Wan and Xiao [29], based on 308 news articles in DUC2001 [23]. The news articles are divided into 30 document sets. Each set is on an event or theme, which is regarded as a specific domain in experiments.

The news articles are too few to learn DTM. We construct a corpus consisting of both the news articles and English Wikipedia to learn DTM. Since the articles in Wikipedia are supposed to compile all human knowledge, high quality topics can thus be learned by taking Wikipedia as background. In experiments, Wikipedia articles come from the March 2008 snapshot. After removing non-article pages and removing articles shorter than 100 words, we collected $2,122,618$ articles. After tokenization, stop word removal and word stemming, we build the vocabulary by selecting $20,000$ words with top document frequency value. We learn DTM on the corpus by taking the set of each news article as its domain label, as well as taking the title of each Wikipedia article as its unique domain label. In this paper, we use the learned DTM with the number of topics $T = 1,000$ selected by cross validation.

Results and Evaluation. Keyword is a term which may be a single word or a multi-word phrase. Not all words or phrases in document are possible to be selected as keywords. In order to filter out some noisy words and phrases in advance, we select candidate keywords using some heuristic rules. This step proceeds as follows. Firstly, the document is tokenized for English or segmented into words for Chinese and other languages without word-separators. As reported in [12], most manually assigned keywords turn out to be noun phrases. Therefore, we annotate the document with POS tags using Stanford Log-Linear Tagger [1]. Then we extract the noun phrases

---

[1] The package could be accessed from `http://nlp.stanford.edu/software/tagger.shtml`. In this paper, we select the English tagging model "left3words-distsim-wsj-clean".

Table 1. Comparing TextRank, LDA and DTM when $m = 10$

Methods	Correct No.	Precision	Recall	F-measure
DTM+CHAR	821	0.269	0.331	0.297
DTM+KL	862	0.282	0.348	0.311
DTM+PSC	808	0.264	0.326	0.292
LDA+CHAR	772	0.253	0.311	0.279
LDA+KL	802	0.262	0.324	0.290
LDA+PSC	766	0.251	0.309	0.277
TextRank	744	0.243	0.300	0.269

whose pattern is zero or more adjectives followed by one or more nouns, represented as (adjective)*(noun)+. These noun phrases are regarded as the candidate keywords of the document.

Using DTM, for each candidate keyword, we compute its relatedness with the domain using characteristics, KL-divergence and predictive likelihood. With the relatedness, we carry out domain-specific rankings for keyword extraction. In contrast with DTM, using LDA, we are only able to measure the relatedness between candidate keywords and the document according to their topic distributions. For TextRank, we follow the implementation in [29].

For evaluation, the keywords extracted by different methods are compared with manually labelled keywords. All words in a keyword are first reduced to their base forms for comparison. In this paper, we use Porter Stemmer [2] to complete the process. The precision, recall and F-measure are used as evaluation metrics, which are widely used in keyword extraction task.

The experiment results of TextRank, LDA and DTM when extracting 10 keywords are shown in Table 1, where "CHAR", "KL" and "PSC" indicate characteristics, KL-divergence and predictive likelihood for measuring relatedness, respectively. It is clear that LDA outperforms TextRank and DTM outperforms both TextRank and LDA, which indicates the effect of domain knowledge. We also note that KL-divergence outperforms other measures in both LDA and DTM. In Figure 3, we demonstrate the precision, recall and F-measure with different number of keywords from 1 to 20 for TextRank, LDA and DTM (using KL-divergence). We can see that DTM always outperforms TextRank and LDA especially on precision when the number of keywords are small.

We further demonstrate an example of extracted keywords from a news article by TextRank, LDA and DTM. The title of this article is *Commodities and Agriculture: Investors sought for Zimbabwe diamond mine*. The domain of the article is on *diamond mines and diamond trading*. As shown in Table 2, top five keywords extracted by the three methods is listed in descending order of ranking values. Compared to standard answers, these keywords are identified with + and − marks.

Because TextRank only uses the cooccurrence information within the article for ranking terms, it can not properly measure the relatedness between terms and the article. TextRank thus can not identify most representative terms of the article. As shown in

---

[2] The package could be accessed from http://tartarus.org/~martin/PorterStemmer/

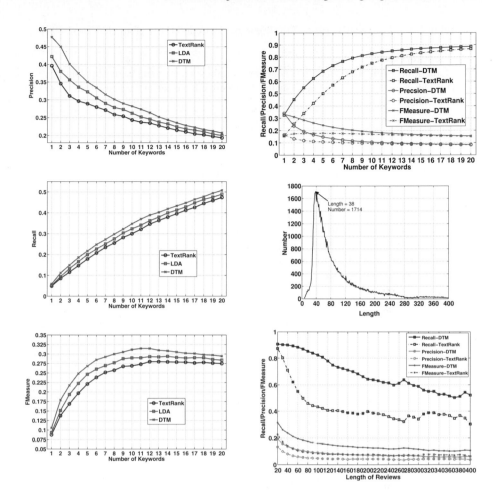

Fig. 3. Comparing TextRank, LDA and DTM for keyword extraction with different number of extracted keywords

Fig. 4. Comparing DTM and TextRank on tag recommendation for restaurant reviews

Table 2, TextRank selects the heavily-connected *de beers* in word graph as a keyword, which in fact does not match the theme of the article. By representing terms and the article using their topic distributions, LDA easily identifies the most theme-relevant terms of the article. Nevertheless, since there are some "noisy" parts in the article which may have nothing to do with the domain of this article, LDA selects *gem quality* as a keyword by mistake. DTM, however, can avoid the mistake by taking the domain knowledge of the article into consideration and make all of top five extracted keywords correct. We also show top five topics of article FT933-8941 and its domain in Table 3 and Table 4 for comparison. These topics are represented by their top three characteristic words. We find that both the domain and the article focus on Topic-1307 on *diamond*. The domain, however, pays more concentration of Topic-1307 with probability 0.1261 compared to 0.0648 of the article on this topic. This makes sure that DTM is more robust against noises.

Table 2. Top 5 keywords extracted by TextRank, LDA and DTM of article FT933-8941

Methods	Keywords
TextRank	de beers official (-), de beers (-), diamond mine (+), mr robin baxter-brown (-)
LDA	diamond business (+), gem quality (-), diamond deposit (+), diamond trade (+), diamond (-)
DTM	diamond mines (+), diamond trade (+), diamond deposit (+), diamond exploration experience (+), diamond mine (+)

Table 3. Top 5 topics of article FT933-8941 and their characteristic words by LDA

Rank	Topic	$P(k|c)$	Characteristic words of k
1	1307	0.0648	diamond, logan, veronica
2	0899	0.0409	company, ceo, acquisition
3	0133	0.0405	fund, money, pay
4	1500	0.0336	zimbabwe, rhodesia, angola
5	0632	0.0302	beer, brewer, brew

Table 4. Top 5 topics of article FT933-8941 and their characteristic words by DTM

Rank	Topic	$P(k|c)$	Characteristic words of k
1	1307	0.1261	diamond, logan, veronica
2	1500	0.0620	zimbabwe, rhodesia, angola
3	0632	0.0544	beer, brewer, brew
4	0378	0.0531	price, cost, demand
5	0379	0.0501	sector, export, econom

From the evaluation results and examples, compared to TextRank and LDA, we show the robust advantages of domain-specific term rankings for keyword extraction using DTM in the news dataset. In the following section, we will further investigate the performance of DTM for content-based tag recommendation.

4.2 Content-Based Tag Recommendation

In this section, we try to recommend tags for restaurant reviews based on their contents. The reviews were crawled from Dianping (http://www.dianping.com), the largest Web review service website in China.

Dataset. The review dataset contains $108,161$ restaurant reviews in Chinese. The dataset itself is also too small to learn DTM. We thus combine more web articles with the review dataset together as the corpus for learning DTM, where the web article dataset contains more than 2 million articles. In this corpus, all restaurant reviews are labeled with domain label *restaurant*, and each web article takes its ID as its unique domain label. After word segmentation and stop word removal, we select $50,000$ words with top document frequency as the vocabulary. We set the number of topics $T = 800$ to learn DTM.

Results and Evaluation. As described in Section 3.3, given the trained DTM, we rank each term in the review given the domain of *restaurant*. In the experiment using TextRank, we follow the approach described by [20] to build a word graph for each review and rank terms using their PageRank values.

Most Dianping reviews have user-labeled tags. For experiments, we only keep the tags that occur in the corresponding reviews. The $108,161$ reviews used here are all selected with one or more tags that occur in the corresponding reviews. Among the reviews, $103,068$ are labeled with one tag, $4,856$ with two keywords and 237 with three or more tags.

We select top-m words from review using DTM and TextRank respectively. Here we do not list the result obtained by LDA due to its poor performance, whose max F-measure value is only 14.2% for m from 1 to 20. This also indicates the importance of modeling domain information for ranking. Similar to the results in Section 4.1, KL-divergence also outperforms other measures in domain-specific term rankings using DTM. In the following results, we only demonstrate the results of DTM using KL-divergence. Figure 4 (Top) compares DTM and TextRank with respect to various number of keywords. From this figure, we can see that DTM outperforms TextRank in all three measures. When m is small, this advantage is especially salient. We also examine the effectiveness of DTM and TextRank with respect to document length. The distribution of document length in Dianping dataset is shown in Figure 4 (Middle), and most reviews have 20 to 100 words. As shown in Figure 4 (Bottom), when $m = 10$, DTM outperforms TextRank completely in range of document length from 20 to 400.

In Table 5, we show top four topics with the highest $P(k|c)$ values in reviews and their characteristic words. Note that we translate original Chinese words in English here. Top 10 characteristic words of reviews computed using Equation 5 are translated as follows: delicious, hot pot, tofu, beef, pepper, snack, taste, flavor, Sichuan-food and wine shop. We can see that using DTM to model domain knowledge for content-based tag recommendation is reasonable.

Comparing the performance of LDA on keyword extraction and tag recommendation, we find that LDA performs better than TextRank on news articles and worse on restaurant reviews. This may be because news articles are better-structured than restaurant reviews. On the other hand, restaurant reviews are generated by millions of users and there are thus more noises. Since LDA ranks terms by comparing their topic distributions with the topic distribution of the document, it is sensitive to the noises in the document. Therefore, LDA performs poorly on the documents with many noises. In contrast, by considering domain information, DTM performs the best on both news articles and restaurant reviews. This indicates that domain information can effectively prevent term rankings from the influence of document noises. In other words, the more

Table 5. Topics with the highest probability in Dianping reviews and most characteristic words

Rank	$P(k|c)$	Characteristic words of k
1	0.079	delicious, hot pot, snack, pepper
2	0.020	egg, potato, Chinese cabbage, tofu
3	0.019	chocolate, bread, fruit, cola
4	0.007	wine shop, customer, waiter, hotel

noises that a document has, the more necessarily we should take domain knowledge into consideration for term rankings.

5   Conclusions and Future Work

In this paper we present a novel method, referred to as Domain-Topic Model (DTM), to model domain knowledge of documents. Using DTM, we further perform domain-specific term rankings. By introducing the domain information as a crucial ranking factor in keyword extraction and content-based tag recommendation, DTM outperforms TextRank and LDA.

In this paper, DTM only considers the importance of a term in a specific domain, without taking the importance of the term in the corresponding document. We plan to combine both measures together for keyword extraction. Considering that in many cases, we do not have explicit domain information, instead, we may have a query. An interesting future work is to extend DTM to query-focused term rankings. In these years, several supervised topic models have been proposed [5,1,2,16,24]. We plan to try these supervised topic models as possible alternatives to DTM for domain-specific term rankings.

Acknowledgments

We want to thank Dr. Yi Wang for helpful discussions and comments. This work is supported by the National Natural Science Foundation of China (NSFC) under Grant No. 60873174.

References

1. Andrzejewski, D., Zhu, X., Craven, M.: Incorporating domain knowledge into topic modeling via dirichlet forest priors. In: Proceedings of ICML, pp. 25–32 (2009)
2. Blei, D.M., McAuliffe, J.: Supervised topic models. In: Proceedings of NIPS, pp. 121–128 (2007)
3. Blei, D.M., Ng, A.Y., Jordan, M.I.: Latent dirichlet allocation. Journal of Machine Learning Research 3, 993–1022 (2003)
4. Brin, S., Page, L.: The anatomy of a large-scale hypertextual web search engine. Computer Networks and ISDN Systems 30, 1–7 (1998)
5. Chemudugunta, C., Holloway, A., Smyth, P., Steyvers, M.: Modeling documents by combining semantic concepts with unsupervised statistical learning. In: Proceedings of ISWC, pp. 229–244 (2010)
6. Cohn, D., Chang, H.: Learning to probabilistically identify authoritative documents. In: Proceedings of ICML, pp. 167–174 (2000)
7. Dean, J., Ghemawat, S.: Mapreduce: Simplified data processing on large clusters. In: Proceedings of OSDI, pp. 137–150 (2004)
8. Frank, E., Paynter, G., Witten, I., Gutwin, C., Nevill-Manning, C.: Domain-specific keyphrase extraction. In: Proceedings of IJCAI, vol. 16, pp. 668–673 (1999)
9. Griffiths, T.L., Steyvers, M.: Finding scientific topics. PNAS 101, 5228–5235 (2004)
10. Grineva, M., Grinev, M., Lizorkin, D.: Extracting key terms from noisy and multitheme documents. In: Proceedings of WWW, pp. 661–670 (2009)

11. Heinrich, G.: Parameter estimation for text analysis. Tech. rep., Vsonix GmbH and University of Leipzig (2008)
12. Hulth, A.: Improved automatic keyword extraction given more linguistic knowledge. In: Proceedings of EMNLP, pp. 216–223 (2003)
13. Hulth, A., Karlgren, J., Jonsson, A., Bostrm, H., Asker, L.: Automatic Keyword Extraction Using Domain Knowledge. In: Gelbukh, A. (ed.) CICLing 2001. LNCS, vol. 2004, pp. 472–482. Springer, Heidelberg (2001)
14. Katakis, I., Tsoumakas, G., Vlahavas, I.: Multilabel text classification for automated tag suggestion. In: ECML/PKDD Discovery Challenge 2008 (2008)
15. Kleinberg, J.: Authoritative sources in a hyperlinked environment. Journal of the ACM 46(5), 604–632 (1999)
16. Lacoste-Julien, S., Sha, F., Jordan, M.: Disclda: Discriminative learning for dimensionality reduction and classification. In: NIPS, pp. 897–904 (2008)
17. Litvak, M., Last, M.: Graph-based keyword extraction for single-document summarization. In: Proceedings of the Workshop Multi-source Multilingual Information Extraction and Summarization, pp. 17–24 (2008)
18. Liu, Z., Huang, W., Zheng, Y., Sun, M.: Extracting keyphrases via topic decomposition. In: Proceedings of EMNLP (2010)
19. Liu, Z., Li, P., Zheng, Y., Sun, M.: Clustering to find exemplar terms for keyphrase extraction. In: Proceedings of EMNLP, pp. 257–266 (2009)
20. Mihalcea, R., Tarau, P.: Textrank: Bringing order into texts. In: Proceedings of EMNLP, pp. 404–411 (2004)
21. Mishne, G.: Autotag: a collaborative approach to automated tag assignment for weblog posts. In: Proceedings of WWW, pp. 953–954 (2006)
22. Newman, D., Asuncion, A., Smyth, P., Welling, M.: Distributed inference for latent Dirichlet allocation. In: Proceedings of NIPS, pp. 1081–1088 (2007)
23. Over, P., Liggett, W., Gilbert, H., Sakharov, A., Thatcher, M.: Introduction to duc-2001: An intrinsic evaluation of generic news text summarization systems. In: Proceedings of DUC 2001 (2001)
24. Ramage, D., Hall, D., Nallapati, R., Manning, C.: Labeled LDA: A supervised topic model for credit attribution in multi-labeled corpora. In: Proceedings of EMNLP, pp. 248–256 (2009)
25. Rosen-Zvi, M., Griffiths, T., Steyvers, M., Smyth, P.: The author-topic model for authors and documents. In: Proceedings of UAI, pp. 487–494 (2004)
26. Tatu, M., Srikanth, M., D'Silva, T.: RSDC 2008: Tag recommendations using bookmark content. ECML/PKDD Discovery Challenge (2008)
27. Turney, P.D.: Learning algorithms for keyphrase extraction. Information Retrieval 2, 303–336 (2000)
28. Wan, X., Xiao, J.: Collabrank: Towards a collaborative approach to single-document keyphrase extraction. In: Proceedings of COLING, pp. 969–976 (2008)
29. Wan, X., Xiao, J.: Single document keyphrase extraction using neighborhood knowledge. In: Proceedings of AAAI, pp. 855–860 (2008)

Learning Chinese Polarity Lexicons by Integration of Graph Models and Morphological Features

Bin Lu[1], Yan Song[1], Xing Zhang[1], and Benjamin K. Tsou[1,2]

[1] Department of Chinese, Translation & Linguistics, City University of Hong Kong
Tat Chee Avenue, Kowloon, Hong Kong
[2] Research Centre on Linguistics and Language Information Sciences,
Hong Kong Institute of Education, Tai Po, New Territories, Hong Kong
lubin2010@gmail.com, {yansong,zxing2}@student.cityu.edu.hk,
btsou@ied.edu.hk

Abstract. This paper presents a novel way to learn Chinese polarity lexicons by using both external relations and internal formation of Chinese words, i.e. by integrating two kinds of different but complementary models: graph models and morphological feature-based models. The polarity detection is first treated as a semi-supervised learning in a graph, and then machine learning is used based on morphological features of Chinese words. The results show that the the the integration of morphological feature-based models and graph models significantly outperforms the baselines.

Keywords: Polarity Lexicon Induction, Graph Models, Chinese Morphology.

1 Introduction

In recent years, sentiment analysis, which mines opinions from large-scale subjective information available on the Web such as news, blogs, reviews and tweets, has attracted much attention [7, 15]. It can be used for a wide variety of applications, such as opinion retrieval, product recommendation, political polling and so on.

In such applications, polarity lexicons consisting of either positive or negative words/phrases are usually important resources for practical systems. They can be constructed by different approaches, including manual construction; using lexical resources such as WordNet to induce positive/negative words [2]; or learning sentiment-bearing words from large-scale corpora, such as news corpora [2] or even the Web [15].

Graph models have been recently used in sentiment analysis for various tasks, such as polarity lexicon induction, ranking the word senses by polarity properties, or document-level sentiment analysis. However, most work has been done based on either on WordNet or English documents. Although these methods can be applied on Chinese, Chinese has its own special characteristics, i.e. Chinese words are composed of characters or morphemes, the smallest meaning blocks. In Chinese, each morpheme has its own meaning, and the polarity of a Chinese word is influenced or even determined by the polarities of its component morphemes. Ku et al. [5, 6] proposed the

P.-J. Cheng et al. (Eds.): AIRS 2010, LNCS 6458, pp. 466–477, 2010.

character-based methods to use sentiment scores of Chinese characters to compute the sentiment scores of Chinese words.

However, either of these two kinds of models, namely graph models and character-based models, is not enough to well tackle the problem by themselves alone. On the other hand, these two kinds of models are complementary to each other, since they models respectively the external relations and internal structures of one Chinese word: word graphs encode the external relations of one word with others in either lexical resources or real texts, while morphological features denote the internal formation or structure of individual Chinese words.

We first build word graphs based on lexical sources, and then induce more positive/negative words from seed words by using semi-supervised graph models. We also propose to use machine learning for polarity classification of Chinese words based on morphological features. Then, we integrate the external relations and internal structures of Chinese words (i.e. graph models and morphological feature-based models) under different strategies. The experiments show that our integrated approach achieves significantly better performance than the baselines.

The rest of the paper is organized as follows. Sec. 2 introduced related work. In Sec. 3, we describe our method for learning Chinese polarity lexicon. Sec. 4 gives the experiments, followed by the discussion in Sec. 5. Finally, we conclude in Sec. 6.

2   Related Work

Some related works have tackled the automated determination of term polarity based on either corpora or lexical resources such as WordNet. Hatzivassiloglou and McKeown [2] learned polarity of adjectives by exploiting co-occurence of conjoined adjectives. Turney and Littman [14] used two statistical methods, namely PMI-IR and LSA, to calculate the polarity of individual terms by calculating mutual information between words and seed words via search engines or corpora. Kamps and Marx [4] proposed the WordNet-based method to compute the word polarity by calculating the semantic distance between words and seed words *good* and *bad*.

2.1   Graph Models for Polarity Lexicon Induction

Recently, graph models have also been tried on polarity lexicon induction. Esuli and Sebastiani [2] presents an application of PageRank to rank WordNet synsets in terms of how strongly they possess a given semantic property, e.g. positivity and negativity. Rao and Ravichandran [8] treated polarity detection as a semi-supervised Label Propagation problem in a graph. Their results indicate that Label Propagation improves significantly over the baseline and other semi-supervised learning methods like Mincuts and Randomized Mincuts for this task.

Velikovich et al. [15] described a new graph propagation framework by constructing large polarity lexicons from lexical graphs built from the web, and they built an English lexicon that is significantly larger than those previously studied. They evaluated the lexicon, both qualitatively and quantitatively, and show that it provides superior performance to previously studied lexicons.

2.2 Chinese Polarity Lexicon Induction

For Chinese, Yuen et al. [16] proposed a method, based on [14], to compute the polarity of Chinese words by using their co-occurrence with Chinese morphemes. It was noted that morphemes are much less numerous than words, and that also a small number of fundamental morphemes may be used to get great advantage. Zhu et al. [18] tried to compute the polarity of Chinese words using the semantic distance or similarity between words and seeds in HowNet[1] based on [14].

Ku et al. [5] measured sentiment degrees of Chinese words by averaging the sentiment scores of the composing characters, called the bag-of-character (BOC) method. The sentiment score of each character is calculated by using the observation probabilities of the character in positive and negative seed words. Ku et al. [6] further considered the internal morphological structures of Chinese words for opinion analysis on words. Chinese words were classified into eight morphological types by the proposed classifiers, and then heuristic scoring rules were manually defined for each morphological type based on the character scores obtained by the BOC method.

2.3 Analysis of the Two Kinds of Models

Graph models and the morpheme-based or character-based models provide different perspectives of Chinese words, and have different characteristics. Word graph encode the external relations of one word with others, while morphological features represent the internal formation or structures of Chinese words. Graph models would need external resources, such as thesauri, lexical resources, or large corpora to construct word graphs, while the character-based methods [5, 6] can assign an opinion score to an arbitrary word without any thesauri or large corpora. However, the character-based methods could have the following problems:

(1) The polarities of many Chinese words cannot directly be derived from its component characters, such as 泡汤 (fail), 仓皇 (in panic), 蓄意 (malicious), etc. For example, 泡汤 (fail) is composed of 泡 (soak) and 汤 (soup), and none of these two characters have salient polarity, but the whole word is negative;

(2) A character may have many possible senses with different polarities, but the character-based methods only compute one polarity score for each character. For instance, the character 动 has many senses in HowNet: a) SelfMoveInManner|方式性自移 or alter|改变, e.g. the 动 in 动荡 (turmoil) and 动乱 (unrest) is negative; b) excite|感动, e.g. the 动 in 动人 (making you feel emotional or sympathetic) and 动听 (pleasant to the ears) is positive; c) use|利用, e.g. the 动 in 动用 (utilize) is neutral;

(3) To cover most Chinese characters, the character-based methods will need a large amount of training data, i.e. Chinese words annotated with polarities.

The problem of graph models could be the need of large-scale lexical resources or corpora to construct the word graphs and to achieve good performance, and even with such large-scale resources it sometimes cannot cover the words concerning. But they could more easily adapt to different domains and compute domain-dependent polarity score based on different corpora. Meanwhile, once the word graphs are constructed, graph models can do semi-supervised learning with a small number of seed words.

---

[1] http://www.keenage.com/html/e_index.html

From the above analysis, we can know that the two kinds of model have different advantages. Thus it would be very attractive to integrate graph models and the morpheme-based or character-based methods to get better performance.

3 Learning Chinese Polarity Lexicons with Graph Models and Morphological Features

3.1 Graph Models for Polarity Lexicon Induction

Let $(x_1, y_1) \ldots (x_l, y_l)$ be labeled words or phrase, where $Y_L = \{y_1 \ldots y_l\}$ are the polarity labels, i.e. positive, negative or neutral. Let $(x_{l+1}, y_{l+1}) \ldots (x_{l+u}, y_{l+u})$ be unlabeled words where $Y_U = \{y_{l+1} \ldots y_{l+u}\}$ are unobserved, usually $l \ll u$. A graph is built where the nodes are all words, both labeled and unlabeled, and the edge between nodes i, j is weighted so that the closer the nodes are, the larger the weights w_{ij}. Intuitively, words that are close should have similar labels, and thus the labels of a node could be propagated to all nodes through the edges. We assume as input an undirected edge weighted graph $G = (V, E)$, where $w_{ij} \in [0, 1]$ is the weight of edge $(v_i, v_j) \in E$. We also assume as input two sets of seed words, denoted P for the positive seed set and N for the negative seed set. After constructing the graph, we can use Label Propagation or PageRank to derive Y_U from X and Y_L based on the graph.

Label Propagation (LP) is an iterative algorithm for classification or regression [17], where each node takes on the weighted average of its neighbor's values from the previous iteration. The result is that nodes with many paths to seeds get high polarities due to the influence from their neighbors. LP is known to have many desirable properties including convergence, a well defined objective function (minimize squared error between values of adjacent nodes), and an equivalence to computing random walks through graphs. We use LP taking a form slightly different from the algorithms in [8] and [15] by adding another sets of seed words, denoted T for the neutral seed sets. The neutral words are manually chosen from the top 200 most frequent words in the LIVAC[2] corpus, and many of them are monosyllabic, include 的 (of), 在 (at), 一 (one), 与 (and), 他 (he), etc. The neutral words are used as *stop* words to prevent polarity propagate into them and also to prevent flow from passing through them into other related words.

PageRank is also a random walk model [1], but used for ranking problem. It allows the random walk to "jump" to its initial state with a nonzero probability. PageRank can be used to get two ranked lists respectively for positive and negative words, and we can normalize the scores for each ranked list, and then use the score in the positive ranking minus that in the negative ranking to get the final score for each word. If the final score is positive, then the word can be classified as positive; otherwise, negative. By this means, we are actually using PageRank for classification. Although Label Propagation and PageRank originally were proposed for different tasks, namely classification and ranking, respectively, they actually are closely related and have theoretical connection [8].

---

[2] http://www.livac.org

3.1.1 Building Word Graphs

The word graph could also be built by different means from a wide variety of resources, such as news corpora [2], WordNet [8], and the Web documents [15]. In this paper, we use Tongyici Cilin (Cilin) [12] and a combined bilingual lexicon to construct word graphs. All the entries in Cilin are organized in a hierarchical tree, and the vocabulary is divided into different categories, i.e. 12 large categories and 1, 400 subcategories. There are some synonym groups within each subcategory, and the words in the same group either have the same or similar meaning or have high relevance. The total number of synonym groups in Tongyici Cilin is 13,440. Following are two synonym group examples:

Ed03A01={好, 优, 精, 良, 帅, 妙, 良好, 优秀, 优异, 精彩, …}

　　{good, excellent, superior, fine, handsome, brilliant, all right, excellent, outstanding, wonderful, …}

Ed03B01={坏, 差, 次, 软, 浅, 破, 不好, 不良, 不行, 差劲, …}

　　{bad, bad, inferior, weak, shallow, rubbishy, not good, not fine, poor, bad, …}

Another lexical resource we used for word graph construction is a combined bilingual lexicon. The idea behind is that a word in one language could be translated into different words in another language. For example, *beautiful* could be translated into 漂亮, 优美, or 美丽 in Chinese, while *ugly* could be translated into 丑, 丑陋 or 难看. In such cases, the different translations of the same word could be seen as synonyms. We combine three bilingual lexicons as the final bilingual lexicon: namely, LDC_CE_DIC2.0[3] constructed by LDC, bilingual terms in HowNet and the bilingual lexicon in Champollion[4]. In total, there are about 251K bilingual entries in the combined dictionary. By using the English words as the pivot, we get 45,448 synonym groups.

In our constructed word graphs, the nodes are all words, the edge between nodes indicates a synonym relation and each edge has a weight w of 1 initially. We assume there are n nodes in the graph which could be represented as a $n{\times}n$ transition matrix T derived by row-normalizing edge weights. Then, Lable Propagation and PageRank can be run on the constructed matrix.

3.2 Polarity Lexicon Induction with Morphological Features

As words are the basic building blocks for texts, most researches on sentiment analysis in English have been done based on words. However, when it comes to Chinese, the situation is rather different. The majority of Chinese words in a corpus are disyllabic or polysyllabic, where each syllable is normally represented by a single logograph, or usually a morpheme. The meaning of the predominant polysyllabic words can be seen as derived from the meanings of its component morphemes, which are considered to be the smallest meaningful linguistic unit[5].

---

[3] http://projects.ldc.upenn.edu/Chinese/LDC_ch.htm
[4] http://sourceforge.net/projects/champollion/
[5] For simplicity, we consider morphemes to be monosyllabic and represented by single character in the following discussion.

In the BOC method [5], the opinion score of a word is determined by the combination of the observation probabilities of its composite characters in positive and negative words. In our implementation of the BOC method, we make a small modification by considering negation markers, such as 无 (no), 不 (no), 没 (no). For the calculation of the sentiment score of a character c, if a negation marker *neg* occurs before some other characters, the characters following the *neg* would be considered as occurring in a word with an opposite polarity. For instance, when computing the frequency of the character 好 (good) as a positive or negative character, our modified method would consider the 好 in the negative word 不好 (not good) as a positive occurrence because of the negation marker 不 before the character 好; while in the original BOC method, it would be considered it as a negative occurrence because it occurs in a negative word. Negation markers are processed with the similar method for calculating sentiment scores of test words by the scores of its component characters.

One problem of the BOC method is that it only assigns a sentiment value for each character without considering character contexts, and cannot easily integrate other possibly useful features, such as bigrams of characters, POS, position information of characters in the word, into the model. Therefore, we propose to learn word polarity using machine learning by integrating more morphological features in addition to its component characters as basic features. The polarity lexicon induction is considered a classification problem and we use machine learning to solve it by using morphological features in Chinese words. The feature templates for the classification model are shown in Table 1.

The POS of each Chinese word is obtained by querying the POS of that word with most senses in HowNet. The features mined for each Chinese word with templates are converted into a vector in which each dimension has the weight of 1.

Table 1. Features used in classification models

Description	Feature Templates	Example Features for 美丽 (beautiful)
Character Unigrams	$\{c_i\}, 1{\leq}i{\leq}l$	{美, 丽}
Character Bigrams	$\{c_{i-1}c_i\}, 2{\leq}i{\leq}l$	{美丽}
Word POS	POS	ADJ
Character Unigrams with Position	$\{i\_c_i\}, 1{\leq}i{\leq}l$	{1_美, 2_丽}

3.3 Integrating Graph Models and Morphological Features

Since graph models and morphological features provide two individual and independent perspectives (i.e. external and internal) of Chinese words, we propose to integrate them to achieve better performance. After obtaining different classifiers based on graph models and morphological features, we could exploit different ensemble methods to combine the results of individual classifiers. According to theoretical analysis [8], the effectiveness of ensemble learning is determined by the diversity of its component classifiers, i.e. each classifier need to be as unique as possible, particularly with respect to misclassified instances. The different classifiers built based on graph models and morphological features could satisfy this diversity requirement.

Let $F=\{f_k(x)|1\leq k\leq p\}$ be the polarity values given by classifiers, where p is the number of classifiers, and $f_k(x) \in [-1, 1]$. We exploit the following ensemble methods for deriving a new value from the individual values:

(1) Average: It is the most intuitive combination method and the new value is the average of the values in F.

(2) Weighted Average: This combination method improves the average method by associating each individual value with a weight, indicating the relative confidence in the value. The weights are experimented to be set in the following two ways:

F1-Weighted Average: The weight of $f_k(x)$ is set to the Micro-F1 of the individual classifier obtained on the development data.

Pre-Weighted Average: The weight of $f_k(x)$ is set to the Micro-Precision of the individual classifier obtained on the development data.

(3) Majority Voting: This combination method relies on the final polarity tags given by each classifier, instead of the exact polarity values. A word can obtain p polarity tags based on the individual analysis results in the p classifiers. The polarity tag receiving more votes is chosen as the final polarity tag of the Chinese word.

(4) SVM Meta-classifier: Motivated by the supervised hierarchical learning, we also propose to use SVM to automatically adjust the weights for each component classifier. It is similar to the re-ranking process with two-layer models: the output values given by the individual low-level classifiers are fed into a machine learning framework (namely SVM) as features, and thus a weight model for individual classifiers is learned from the training and development data. By this strategy, we actually use a two-level classification model with a higher-level meta-classifier to learn the corresponding weights for the individual lower-level classifiers.

4   Experiments and Evaluation

Two manually constructed polarity lexicons are used as gold standard for evaluation: *The Lexicon of Chinese Positive Words* [13] consisting of 5,045 positive words, and *The Lexicon of Chinese Negative Words* [19] consisting of 3,498 negative words. Thus, we have 8,543 words marked with polarity as the gold standard. The entries in the gold standard are randomly split into 6 folds: the first fold as the development set, and the remaining ones for 5-fold cross validation (4 folds for training and 1 fold for testing). The bag-of-character method [5] and Label Propagation [8] are used as baselines.

We use the standard precision (Pre), recall (Rec), and F-measure (F1) to measure the performance of positive and negative class, respectively, and used the MacroF1 and MicroF1 to measure the overall performance. The metrics are defined the same as in general text categorization. The SVM_{light} package is used for training and testing, with all parameters set to their default values. The evaluations are shown as follows.

4.1 Experiments with Graph Models

In this section, we evaluate the performance of PageRank and Label Propagation (LP) on the word graphs built from two resources, namely Tongyici Cilin (Cilin) and the bilingual lexicon (BiLex) introduced in Sec. 3.2.1, and the graph built from their combination (Cilin+BiLex). The residual probability of PageRank is set to 0.85. Since we do not have annotated ranking data of Chinese polarity lexicon to evaluate PageRank, we use the converted classification results introduced in Sec. 3.1 for the evaluation. We run both algorithms for 10 iterations, and show the results in Table 2.

Table 2. Results of graph models (in %)

		Positive			Negative			Total	
		Pre	Rec	F1	Pre	Rec	F1	MacroF1	MicroF1
Cilin	PageRank	92.83	60.37	73.15	92.89	59.89	72.79	72.97	73.24
	LP	93.22	60.47	73.35	93.17	60.23	73.13	73.24	72.99
BiLex	PageRank	84.10	40.73	54.89	93.19	32.57	48.24	51.56	52.30
	LP	84.48	40.62	54.86	92.90	32.91	48.58	51.72	52.40
Cilin+ BiLex	PageRank	89.65	67.86	77.24	95.21	62.66	75.54	76.39	76.55
	LP	89.93	67.60	77.17	94.75	63.04	75.67	76.42	76.56

From Table 2, we can observe that: the graph models show better performance on the word graph built from the combination of Cilin and BiLex than on the graphs built from either of the resources; and the graph models show better performance on Cilin than on BiLex. Meanwhile, PageRank and Label Propagation show similar performance, and the differences are not so remarkable for the word graphs built from Cilin, BiLex or their combination.

4.2 Experiments with Models of Morphological Features

In this section, we investigate the performances of different models with morphological features, including the BOC (Ku) method [5], our modified BOC method with negation processing introduced in Sec. 3.2, and our proposed SVM models with different kinds of features introduced in Sec. 3.2. The SVM-All method uses all the features introduced in Table 1. The results are shown in Table 3.

The SVM models outperform the BOC models. Although the improvement of about 1% from BOC to SVM-ALL seems not remarkable, the t-test shows that the MacroF1 and MicroF1 differences are statistically significant at the 90% level, and the difference between BOC and SVM-Uni+Bi, or between SVM-All and BOC is statistically significant at the 95% level. By adding bigrams of characters, unigrams with position, and POS into SVM, we can improve by about 0.5% compared SVM with only unigrams. Meanwhile, our modified BOC method achieves slightly better result than the original BOC method [5].

We also tried to integrate the features of morphological types in [6] into our morphological feature-based SVM model. Since we do not have the words annotated with morphological types, we just use the unsupervised heuristic rules to compute the morphological type for each Chinese word, and then use the heuristic rules in [6] or integrate it into the SVM model. But it did not improve the performance.

Table 3. Results of models with morphological features (in %)

	Positive			Negative			Total	
	Pre	Rec	F1	Pre	Rec	F1	MacroF1	MicroF1
BOC (Ku)	92.62	89.35	90.95	88.51	83.56	85.96	88.45	88.92
BOC	92.93	89.54	91.20	88.85	83.68	86.18	88.69	89.16
SVM-Unigram	88.13	95.11	91.48	92.01	81.54	86.44	88.96	89.54
SVM-Unigram +Bigram	88.39	95.30	91.70	92.34	81.95	86.82	89.26	89.83
SVM-All	88.69	95.25	91.85	92.32	82.49	87.12	89.48	90.02

4.3   Experiments on Integration

In this section, we investigate the performance of the integration of graph models and morphological features. Different classifier combinations are tried based on the SVM strategy introduced in Sec. 3.3. Since the graph built from the combination of two lexical resources show better performance than the graph built from the individual resources, we use only the combination graph for the graph models in this section. The development data are used to adjust the parameters of each model. The results are shown in Table 4. The LPBOC method denotes the BOC method based on the positive and negative word lists generated by the LP model.

Table 4. Integration results (in %)

	Positive			Negative			Total	
	Pre	Rec	F1	Pre	Rec	F1	MacroF1	MicroF1
BOC+SVM-ALL	92.32	92.90	92.60	89.65	88.88	89.25	90.93	91.25
LP+BOC	93.39	95.94	94.64	93.87	90.20	91.99	93.32	93.58
LP+SVM-ALL	91.49	94.52	92.98	92.16	88.02	90.03	91.50	91.76
LP+BOC+ SVM-ALL	94.43	96.02	95.22	94.07	91.86	92.94	94.08	94.30
LP+ SVM-ALL +BOC+LPBOC	95.17	95.99	95.58	94.11	92.97	93.53	94.56	94.75

All of the ensembles in Table 4 significantly outperform the baselines: the bag-of-character method in Table 3, and Label Propagation in Table 2, which shows that graph models and models with morphological features have their own evidences for polarity classification, and thus the integration of models could significantly improve performance.

The best performance is obtained by the integration of all the four methods: LP, ML-ALL, BOC and LPBOC, i.e. it improves MacroF1 to 94.56% from 88.69% of BOC or 76.42% of LP, and improves MicroF1 to 94.75% from 89.16% of BOC and 76.56% of LP, which are both significant improvements. Even without graph models, we can also significantly improve performance by integrating BOC and SVM-ALL. The integration of LP with BOC shows better performance than that of LP with SVM-ALL, but the integration of these three methods outperforms the integration of any two methods.

We then investigate the other ensemble methods introduced in Sec. 3.3 to integrate LP, BOC, SVM-ALL, and LPBOC. Table 5 gives the comparison results. We can see that all the ensemble methods outperform the constituent individual method, while SVM performs the best, followed by the precision-weighted average. The results further demonstrate that 1) the good effectiveness of the ensemble combination of individual analysis results for Chinese word polarity classification, 2) the SVM strategy seems to be able to find better weights compared with other simpler combination methods.

Table 5. Ensemble results for "**LP+BOC+SVM-ALL+LPBOC**" (in %)

	Positive			Negative			Total	
	Pre	Rec	F1	Pre	Rec	F1	MacroF1	MicroF1
Average	95.91	95.91	95.91	91.04	91.04	91.04	93.48	93.91
F1-Weighted Average	93.87	95.87	94.86	93.84	91.01	92.40	93.63	93.87
Pre-Weighted Average	93.99	95.99	94.97	94.01	91.19	92.58	93.77	94.01
Majority Voting	94.43	93.64	94.03	95.10	86.03	90.34	92.18	92.56
SVM	95.17	95.99	95.58	94.11	92.97	93.53	94.56	94.75

5 Discussion

In this section, we investigate the influence of two factors on the models for Chinese polarity lexicon induction, i.e. the iteration number for graph models and the size of training data. The micro-precision, micro-recall and micro-F1 are reported in this section. Fig. 1 shows the influence of iteration numbers of Label Propagation on the combined graph built from Tongyici Cilin (Cilin) and the combination of Cilin and BiLex (Com). We can observe that the precisions of Label Propagation for Cilin and Com show little difference, both above 90%, but the recalls with Com are much higher with those with Cilin, and thus the F1s are much higher with Com consequently.

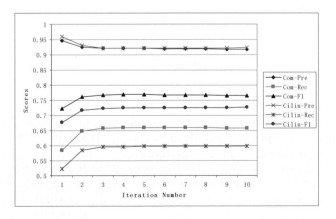

Fig. 1. Influence of iteration numbers on Label Propagation

Fig. 2 and 3 show the influence of the sizes of training data (i.e. the number of training words) on Label Propagation (LP), the BOC method and the SVM Meta-classifier based integration of LP+BOC+SVM-ALL+LPBOC (Integration) introduced in Sec. 4.3. From Fig. 2, we can see that (1) The precision of BOC improves steadily with more training data, from 75% of 100 training words to above 90% of 5K+ words; while the precision of LP remains quite high (i.e. always above 86%), even with only 100 seed words; (2) The recall of BOC improves even much faster the precision when the training data increases, from 23% of 100 training words to above 87% of 5K+ words; while the recall of LP improves much slowly. From Fig. 3, we can observe that the SVM-based integration of the four methods has been always significantly outperforming the individual methods of BOC and LP, and even with only 100 seed/training data, we can achieve 82% MicroF1.

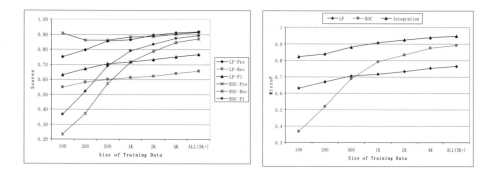

Fig. 2. Influence of training data sizes on LP and BOC   **Fig. 3.** Influence of training data sizes

To summarize Fig. 2 and 3, when the training data is small, LP outperforms BOC, but when the training data becomes large, BOC outperforms LP inversely. However, no matter how much training data, the integration of graph models and morphological features could significantly improve the performance compared to individual methods.

6   Conclusion and Future Work

This paper proposes a novel approach to integrate both internal structures and external relations of Chinese words for polarity lexicon induction via graph models and morphological features. The polarity detection is first treated as a semi-supervised learning in a graph, machine learning, namely Support Vector Machine (SVM), is used based on morphological features, and then we integrate morphological features with the graph models to further improve the performance. The results show that the integration could significantly improve the performance.

In future work, more resources could be explored to further improve the results, especially large-scale corpora or even the Web. Since a word could have different senses with different polarities, we are also interested in classifying the polarity of word senses in Chinese, instead of only the word level. Meanwhile, evaluation of the ranking problem of word polarities could be another direction.

Acknowledgements. We wish to thank Prof. Jingbo Zhu from Northeastern University, China, Dr. Preslav Nakov from National University of Singapore, and anonymous reviewers for their valuable comments, as well as the Harbin Institute of Technology's IR Lab for their sharing of the extended version of Tongyici Cilin.

References

1. Brin, S., Page, L.: The Anatomy of a Large-scale Hypertextual Web Search Engine. Computer Networks and ISDN Systems 30(1-7), 107–117 (1998)
2. Esuli, A., Sebastiani, F.: PageRanking WordNet SynSet: An application to opinion mining. In: Proceedings of ACL, pp. 424–431 (2007)
3. Hatzivassiloglou, V., McKeown, K.: Predicting the Semantic Orientation of Adjectives. In: Proceedings of ACL1997. pp. 174–181 (1997)
4. Kamps, J., Marx, M.: Words with Attitude. In: Proceedings of the First International Conference on Global WordNet, pp. 332–341 (2002)
5. Ku, L.W., Chen, H.H.: Mining Opinions from the Web: Beyond Relevance Retrieval. Journal of American Society for Information Science and Technology, Special Issue on Mining Web Resources for Enhancing Information Retrieval 58(12), 1838–1850 (2007)
6. Ku, L.W., Huang, T.H., Chen, H.H.: Using Morphological and Syntactic Structures for Chinese Opinion Analysis. In: Proceedings of EMNLP, pp. 1260–1269 (2009)
7. Pang, B., Lee, L., Vaithyanathan, S.: Thumbs up? Sentiment classification using machine learning techniques. In: Proceedings of EMNLP, pp. 79–86 (2002)
8. Polikar, R.: Ensemble Based Systems in Decision Making. IEEE Circuits and Systems Magazine 6(3), 21–45 (2006)
9. Rao, D., Ravichandran, D.: Semi-supervised Polarity Lexicon Induction. In: Proceedings of EACL, pp. 675–682 (2009)
10. Rao, D., Yarowsky, D.: Ranking and Semi-supervised Classification on Large Scale Graphs Using Map-Reduce. In: Proceedings of Textgraphs-4, pp. 58–69 (2009)
11. Riloff, E., Wiebe, J.: Learning Extraction Patterns for Subjective Expressions. In: Proceedings of EMNLP, pp. 105–112 (2003)
12. Mei, J., Zhu, Y., Gao, Y., Yin, H.: Tongyici Cilin(2nd version). Shanghai CiShu Press (1996) (in Chinese)
13. Shi, J., Zhu, Y.: The Lexicon of Chinese Positive Words. Sichuan Lexicon Press (2006) (in Chinese)
14. Turney, P.D., Littman, M.L.: Measuring Praise and Criticism: Inference of semantic orientation from association. ACM Trans. On Information Systems 21(4), 315–346 (2003)
15. Velikovich, L., Blair-Goldensohn, S., Hannan, K., McDonald, R.: The Viability of Web-derived Polarity Lexicons. In: Proceedings of NAACL, pp. 777–785 (2010)
16. Yuen, R.W.M., Chan, T.Y.W., Lai, T.B.Y., Kwong, O.Y., Tsou, B.K.Y.: Morpheme-based Derivation of Bipolar Semantic Orientation of Chinese Words. In: Proceedings of COLING, pp. 1008–1014 (2004)
17. Zhu, X., Ghahramani, Z.: Learning from labeled and unlabeled data with Label Propagation. Technical Report CMU-CALD-02-107, CarnegieMellon University (2002)
18. Zhu, Y., Min, J., Zhou, Y., Huang, X., Wu, L.: Semantic Orientation Computing Based on HowNet. Journal of Chinese Information Processing 20(1), 14–20 (2006) (in Chinese)
19. Zhu, L., Zhu, Y.: The Lexicon of Chinese Negative Words. Sichuan Lexicon Press (2006) (in Chinese)

Learning to Rank with Supplementary Data

Wenkui Ding[1,*], Tao Qin[2], and Xu-Dong Zhang[1]

[1] Tsinghua University, Beijing, 100084, P.R. China
dingwenkui@gmail.com, zhangxd@tsinghua.edu.cn
[2] Microsoft Research Asia, No.49, Zhichun Road, Haidian District,
Beijing 100190, P.R.China
taoqin@microsoft.com

Abstract. This paper is concerned with a new task of ranking, referred to as "supplementary data assisted ranking", or "supplementary ranking" for short. Different from conventional ranking, in the new task, each query is associated with two sets of objects: the target objects that are to be ranked, and the supplementary objects whose orders are not of our interest. Existing learning to rank approaches (either supervised or semi-supervised) cannot well handle the new task, because they ignore the supplementary data in either training, test, or both. In this paper, we propose a general approach for the task, in which the ranking model consists of two parts. The first part is based on the matching between a target object and the query (which is similar to that in conventional approaches). The second part depends on the relationship between target objects and supplementary objects. The new ranking model is learned by minimizing a certain loss function on the training data. We call this approach "supplementary learning to rank". As a showcase of the approach, we develop two Boosting-style algorithms. In these algorithms, we leverage the supplementary objects in the definition of weak rankers for the second part of the ranking model, and specify the relationship between target and supplementary objects as pairwise preference. Experimental results on both public and large-scale commercial datasets demonstrate the effectiveness of the proposed algorithms.

Keywords: supplementary ranking, learning to rank.

1 Introduction

Ranking is the central problem for many applications in information retrieval (IR), such as document retrieval, web search, question answering, advertisement, and multimedia retrieval [6]. In the standard setting of ranking, a query is associated with a set of objects to be ranked, and a ranking model is employed to rank these objects in the descending order of their relevance to the query.

In this paper, we study a new task of ranking, called "supplementary data assisted ranking", or "supplementary ranking" for short. Different from the standard setting of ranking, in the new task, two sets of objects are associated with

---

* This work was done when the first author was visiting Microsoft Research Asia.

P.-J. Cheng et al. (Eds.): AIRS 2010, LNCS 6458, pp. 478–489, 2010.
© Springer-Verlag Berlin Heidelberg 2010

a given query. One set contains the target objects to be ranked, and the other set contains some supplementary objects related to the query, whose orders are however not of our interest. For ease of reference, we call these two sets the target set and the supplementary set respectively.

Many real ranking problems are in nature supplementary ranking problems. For example, in multi-lingual search [3], when a user issues an English query, a set of English documents containing the query terms compose the target set, while documents that are relevant to the query but written in other languages compose the supplementary set. In Web image search, the images compose the target set, while the web pages containing these images compose the supplementary set. As can be seen, in some applications, the target objects and the supplementary objects are of the same type (e.g., web pages), while in some other applications, they can be heterogeneous (e.g., images and web pages).

To solve the supplementary ranking task, one can directly apply existing methods developed for standard ranking. However, due to the differences between the two tasks, such a direct application may not be a good choice. For example, while supervised learning to rank techniques have been shown very effective for standard ranking, they completely ignore the supplementary data. Semi-supervised learning to rank methods leverage supplementary data in training, however, the supplementary data is still ignored in test. It is expected that if one can make good use of the supplementary data in both training and test, he/she can do a better job than existing approaches. This is exactly our proposal, and we refer to it as "supplementary learning to rank".

In our proposed approach, the ranking score of a target object is determined by two sub ranking models. The first sub model is similar to the ranking model in previous work, which measures the matching between the target object and the query. The second sub model considers the relationship (e.g., similarity, preference, and parent-child relationship) between the target object and those supplementary objects. Then we learn the two sub models by minimizing a certain loss function (which evaluates whether the ranking of the target objects is correct) on the training data. In the test phase, the learned sub models are applied to rank the target objects associated with a new query, based on the information contained in both the target and supplementary sets. This new ranking mechanism has following advantages. First, the information contained in the supplementary set can be leveraged in a more comprehensive manner (i.e., in both training and test) than supervised and semi-supervised learning to rank. Second, from the machine learning point of view, the training and test processes become more consistent with each other, which ensures the learned model to generalize better than in semi-supervised learning to rank.

As a showcase of the proposed approach, we develop two Boosting-style supplementary learning to rank algorithms. These algorithms address two cases of supplementary ranking, one with homogeneous target and supplementary objects, and the other with heterogeneous objects. In both algorithms, we leverage the supplementary objects in the construction of weak rankers for the second sub ranking model, and specify the relationship between target and supplementary objects as pairwise preference. In this way, the resultant algorithms regard the supplementary data as a reference, and ensure that a target object is ranked high if it is highly relevant to the query by itself, and it is more relevant than many supplementary objects. Experimental results on both public and large-scale commercial datasets show that the proposed algorithms (and thus the "supplementary learning to rank" approach) can make effective use of the supplementary data and outperform previous methods.

The rest of this paper is organized as follows. Section 2 introduces the new task of supplementary ranking and a general approach to tackle the task. In Section 3, we present two Boosting-style algorithms for supplementary ranking. Experimental results are reported in Section 4. Conclusions and future work are given in the last section.

2   Supplementary Ranking

2.1   Supplementary Data Assisted Ranking

In the standard setting of ranking, for each given query, the task is to rank a set of target objects according to their relevance to the query. While this is a general abstraction for ranking tasks, it ignores the fact that in many real applications, one can straightforwardly collect a set of supplementary objects related to the query, in addition to the target objects (for ease of reference, we call the sets containing the target objects and the supplementary objects the target set and the supplementary set respectively). The ranking of the objects in the supplementary set is usually not of our interest, however, these objects can be used to improve the ranking of the target objects.

Here we list several real applications in which supplementary objects naturally exist. Note that this is just an incomplete list, and one can find many other similar applications.

- *Multi-lingual Search*. In the scenario of multilingual search [9], when a user issues an English query, it is supposed to return a ranked list of English documents containing the query terms. Non-English documents that are also related the query can be used to improve the ranking of the English documents, usually by means of machine translation and co-ranking. In this case, the English documents compose the target set, and the non-English documents compose the supplementary set. Gao et al. [3] have shown that the ranking accuracy of target English documents can be greatly boosted by considering supplementary non-English documents.
- *Document Re-ranking*. In the scenario of re-ranking [5], we are given a initial ranked list of n documents, which is produced by a light-weight ranker. Then a complex ranker is applied to re-rank the top k documents in the list. In such a case, the top k documents compose the target set, and the other $n-k$ documents compose the supplementary set.
- *Web Image Retrieval*. Because of the semantic gap between textual queries and visual images, in commercial search engines, the web pages containing

images are usually used to assist the ranking of the images [11]. That is, the images compose the target set and the corresponding web pages compose the supplementary set. Note that in this case, the target set and the supplementary set actually contain heterogeneous objects (i.e., visual objects and textual objects), which is different from the sets in the above examples. Wang et al. [11] have shown that by leveraging the supplementary web pages, the ranking of the target images can be improved.

Given the wide availability of supplementary data as mentioned above, if we can well utilize them to assist the ranking of the target objects, we should be able to achieve better ranking performance in many applications. This is, however, not sufficiently studied in the literature of information retrieval. To emphasize its importance, we formally define the task of "supplementary data assisted ranking" (or "supplementary ranking" for short) in this paper. In the task, it is required that one leverages the supplementary objects to improve the ranking performance of the target objects.

2.2   Supplementary Learning to Rank

In this subsection, we discuss how to solve the problem of supplementary ranking.

One naïve choice is to directly apply existing methods developed for standard ranking, e.g., the learning to rank methods which have been widely used in the literature [6]. However, due to the differences between the two tasks, this might not be a good choice. For example, in most existing learning to rank methods (either supervised or semi-supervised), the ranking score of an object is only determined by the matching between the query and the object. If we use such ranking models, the supplementary data can at most be considered in the training process (e.g., to refine the loss functions as in semi-supervised learning to rank). In the test phase, however, no supplementary data can be leveraged. To tackle the problem, one needs to re-define the ranking model to explicitly incorporate the supplementary data. This is exactly our proposal.

Table 1. Notations

Symbol	Meaning
$q \in Q$	a query
$X^q = \{x_1^q, x_2^q, \cdots\}$	feature vectors of the target objects
$Y^q = \{y_1^q, y_2^q, \cdots\}$	relevance labels of the target objects
$Z^q = \{z_1^q, z_2^q, \cdots\}$	feature vectors of the supplementary objects

For ease of description, we give some notations in Table 1. If without confusion, we will omit the superscript q in the following discussions. With these notations, we can describe our proposed new ranking model as follows.

$$f_Z(x) = f_0(x) + f_1(x; Z), \forall x \in X \tag{1}$$

where $f_Z(x)$ indicates that the ranking score of an object depends not only on itself x but also on the supplementary set Z.

As can be seen, the proposed ranking model consists of two sub models. The first sub model $f_0(x)$ is the same as the ranking model used in traditional learning to rank methods, which is determined by x itself. We refer to it as "individual sub model". The second one $f_1(x; Z)$ is, in contrast, determined by the relationship between x and the supplementary objects in Z. We refer to this sub model as "supplementary sub model". Note that, in some applications like web image retrieval, the target objects and the supplementary objects may be of different types (e.g., one is visual image and the other is textual document). In such a case, x_i and z_i may locate in different feature spaces, and we need to carefully design the supplementary sub model to handle the situation (we will make more discussions on this in Section 3).

Suppose both sub models contain unknown parameters. Then one can use a training set to learn the parameters. We call the approach that automatically learns the parameters in the sub models "supplementary learning to rank". In principle, any loss function can be used for this purpose, such as the hinge loss, the exponential loss, and the cross entropy loss, as long as it can measure whether the target objects in the training set are correctly ranked by the model.

After we learn the sub models f_0 and f_1, we can apply them to rank the target objects associated with a new query. Note that although the ranking model considers the supplementary objects, we only need to compute the ranking scores for the target objects. The supplementary objects contribute to this process, but it is unnecessary to compute their ranking scores, since this is not of our interest.

As compared with supervised learning to rank, supplementary learning to rank can leverage more information contained in the supplementary data. Since the benefit of using supplementary data has been verified by many previous works [3,11], supplementary learning to rank can be expected to achieve better ranking performance than supervised learning to rank. As compared with semi-supervised learning to rank, supplementary learning to rank makes the training and test processes more consistent with each other. According to statistical learning theory [10], the trained model can be expected to generalize better on the test set.

3   Boosting-Based Algorithms

There are two steps to design a supplementary learning to rank algorithm: (1) defining the individual sub model and supplementary sub model, and (2) learning the parameters of the two sub models from the training data.

As mentioned in the previous section, any ranking loss can be used. In this section, we take the exponential loss as example and derive two Boosting-style algorithms for supplementary ranking. The first algorithm, RankBoost-Same, assumes that the target objects and the supplementary objects are of the same type. The second algorithm, RankBoost-Heter, can handle the case where the two sets contain heterogeneous objects.

3.1   RankBoost-Same

In this subsection, we consider a simple case, in which the target set and the supplementary set contain the same type of objects. Here we make discussions on the two sub models separately.

First, following the basic idea of Boosting, it is natural to define the individual sub model as a linear combination of a set of weak rankers. Assume there exist a set of weak rankers $\mathcal{H} = \{h(x)\}$ and each weak ranker is a function of x. Then the individual sub model $f_0(x)$ can be defined as follows,

$$f_0(x) = \sum_t \alpha_t h_t(x), \quad h_t(x) \in \mathcal{H}, \tag{2}$$

where α_t is the combination weight of $h_t(x)$.

Second, we discuss the formulation of the supplementary sub model. We derive a new set of weak rankers from $\mathcal{H}$ using supplementary objects. Specifically, for each weaker ranker $h \in \mathcal{H}$, we can define a new weak ranker as below,

$$h'(x; Z) = \frac{1}{|Z|} \sum_{z \in Z} I(h(x) - h(z)), \tag{3}$$

where $|\cdot|$ is the number of elements in a set, and $I(\cdot)$ is an indicator function.

From Eqn. (3), one can see that here we specify the relationship between target and supplementary objects as pairwise preference. That is, we use h' to count how many supplementary objects the target object x can beat in terms of the weak ranker h. The more supplementary objects a target object beats, the larger score it will get from h'. In this way, the supplementary objects actually serve as a reference, and a target object is ranked high if it is more relevant than many supplementary objects.

Note that all the h' functions compose a new set $\mathcal{H}'$. Again, following the idea of Boosting, we can define the supplementary sub model as the linear combination of the weak rankers in $\mathcal{H}'$,

$$f_1(x; Z) = \sum_t \alpha_t h_t(x; Z), \quad h_t(x; Z) \in \mathcal{H}'. \tag{4}$$

After defining the set of the weak rankers, it is natural to use Boosting techniques to train the sub models. In the training process, we follow two common practices in Boosting-style algorithms: (i) we take each feature of a query-document pair as a weak ranker h in $\mathcal{H}$; (ii) in order to select the best weak ranker, we go through all the weak rankers in the candidate set, compute theirs losses, and choose the one with the minimum loss. The detailed algorithm is shown in Table 2. We refer to the algorithm as RankBoost-Same.

3.2   RankBoost-Heter

In this sub section, we consider another case, in which the target objects and the supplementary objects are of different types. In other words, x_i and z_i have different feature representations. Again, we make discussions on the two sub models separately.

Table 2. RankBoost-Same algorithm

Input: A set of training queries $\{(X^q, Y^q, Z^q)\}, q = 1, 2, \cdots$, and a set of weak rankers $\mathcal{H}$
Training :
1: Generate the set $\mathcal{H}'$ from $\mathcal{H}$ by Eq. (3)
2: Construct the pool P of preference pairs for training: for each pair of query q, if $y_i^q > y_j^q$, add the pair (x_i^q, x_j^q) into P
3: Initialize the weight of each pair in P as $D_0(x_i^q, x_j^q) = \frac{1}{|P|}$
4: Initialize $f_0 = 0$, $f_1 = 0$
5: **For** $t = 1, \cdots, T$
6:   Find the best weak ranker h (together with its weight α) from $\mathcal{H}$ using distribution D_t
7:   Find the best weak ranker h' (together with its weight α') from $\mathcal{H}'$ using distribution D_t
8:   Compare the loss of h and h'. If h corresponds to the smaller loss, set $h_t = h$, $\alpha_t = \alpha$ and $f_0 = f_0 + \alpha_t h_t$; else, set $h_t = h'$, $\alpha_t = \alpha'$ and $f_1 = f_1 + \alpha_t h_t$
9:   Update the weight $D_{t+1}(x_i^q, x_j^q) = e^{\alpha_t (h_t(x_j^q) - h_t(x_i^q))} D_t(x_i^q, x_j^q)$, and normalize it so that the sum of all the weights equals 1
10: **End For**
Output: $f_Z(x) = f_0(x) + f_1(x; Z)$

First, for the individual sub model, the discussions can be very similar to those for RankBoost-Same. That is, we assume that there exists a set $\mathcal{H} = \{h(x)\}$ of weak rankers based on the feature representation of the target objects, and define the individual sub model f_0 as Eqn. (2).

Second, for the supplementary sub model, the situation is a little more complex, since the target objects and the supplementary objects do not share the same feature representation. As a result, weak rankers in $\mathcal{H}$ cannot be applied to the supplementary objects. To tackle the problem, we assume that there is another set of weak rankers $\mathcal{G} = \{g(z)\}$ defined on the supplementary objects. Then for each weaker ranker $h \in \mathcal{H}$ and each weaker ranker $g \in \mathcal{G}$, we define a new weak ranker $h' \in \mathcal{H}'$ as follows,

$$h'(x; Z) = \frac{1}{|Z|} \sum_{z \in Z} I(h(x) - g(z)). \tag{5}$$

The underlying assumption in the above definition is that although the features for x_i and z_i are heterogeneous, the outputs of the weak rankers based on these features can be comparable with each other since they all measure the relevance of an object to the query.

After defining the new weak rankers, the supplementary sub model can be defined as their linear combination in Eqn. (4).

Then we can use Boosting techniques to train the sub models. We call the corresponding algorithm RankBoost-Heter. The relationship between RankBoost-Heter and RankBoost-Same can be summarized as follows.

- RankBoost-Heter can also be used to deal with supplementary ranking with two homogeneous sets if setting $\mathcal{G} = \mathcal{H}$. However, the computational complexity of RankBoost-Heter is significantly higher than that of RankBoost-Same. Actually, $\mathcal{H}'$ contains much more weak rankers than $\mathcal{H}$ and $\mathcal{G}$. Specifically, we have $|\mathcal{H}'| = |\mathcal{H}| \times |\mathcal{G}|$. As a result, RankBoost-Heter is not a good choice for supplementary ranking with homogeneous sets, from the computational point of view.
- For the implementation, RankBoost-Same and RankBoost-Heter can be very similar. The only difference lies in the different ways of constructing the candidate set of new weak rankers. Therefore the algorithm flow of RankBoost-Heter is very similar to that of RankBoost-Same. We omit the details here.

4   Experimental Results

4.1   Settings

Two datasets were used in our experiments: one is from the LETOR benchmark collection [7,8], and the other is from a commercial web search engine. We used the MQ2007-semi dataset in LETOR 4.0 in our experiments, because it contains both labeled and unlabeled data. There are about 1700 queries in this dataset. On average, each query is associated with about 40 labeled documents and about 1000 unlabeled documents. There are three levels of relevance labels. To evaluate the proposed algorithms in the real scenario of web search, we also used a dataset obtained from a commercial search engine. We refer to it as the ComSE dataset. There are 6,600 queries in the dataset. On average, each query is associated with about 20 labeled documents and more than 140 unlabeled documents. There are five levels of relevance labels.

The multi-fold cross validation strategy was used on both datasets. All the results reported in this section are the average results over multiple folds. We used NDCG [4] as the evaluation measure in our experiments, which is a widely-used IR measure for multi-level relevance judgments.

4.2   Supplementary Ranking on Homogeneous Data

Note that in both MQ2007-semi and ComSE, the labeled and unlabeled documents are of the same type, and represented in the same feature space. Therefore it is straightforward to use them to study the supplementary ranking with homogeneous data. In particular, we regard the labeled documents as the target objects and the unlabeled documents as the supplementary objects.

Baselines   In addition to RankBoost-Same, we implemented three baselines.

- **RankBoost.**   RankBoost [2] is a supervised learning to rank algorithm that only uses labeled documents for training.
- **RankBoost-All.**   In this method, we treat unlabeled documents as irrelevant and train a model using RankBoost with all the documents.

– **RankBoost-Prop.** This is the semi-supervised learning to rank method proposed in [1]. In the method, for each labeled training document, the same label is assigned to its nearest unlabeled document. When training with the data, the loss function is defined as the weighted sum of two parts: the loss function on the original labeled documents and the loss function on documents with pseudo labels.

For all these baselines and RankBoost-Same, we set the maximal number of selected weak rankers to 600. All the algorithms have converged within 600 iterations in our experiments. Compared with RankBoost, the computational complexity of RankBoost-Same is increased due to the usage of supplementary data. However, according to [2], the computational complexity of RankBoost-Same is only about twice that of RankBoost since the number of weak rankers is doubled. In our experiments RankBoost-Same took less than two seconds per iteration while RankBoost took one second.

Results. The experimental results on the MQ2007-semi and ComSE dataset are listed in Table 3. Take the results on the MQ2007-semi for example, we have the following observations.

First, RankBoost-All does not perform well. Its performance is even worse than RankBoost. This indicates that improper use of the supplementary data (i.e., simply treating those supplementary objects as irrelevant) may hurt the ranking performance.

Second, RankBoost-Prop slightly outperforms RankBoost. This is also in accordance with the results reported in [1]. This result indicates that appropriately leveraging the supplementary data in the training process can lead to performance gain. However, the improvement of RankBoost-Prop over RankBoost is not statistically significant.

Third, RankBoost-Same outperforms all the baseline algorithms, including both supervised learning to rank methods and semi-supervised learning to rank algorithms. Furthermore, the improvement of RankBoost-Same over RankBoost is statistically significant in terms of NDCG@3, 5, and 10 (we use * to indicate statistical significance in the table). This indicates that further considering the supplementary data in the test process can lead to more performance gain. This is in accordance with our discussions throughout the paper.

Similar conclusions can be drawn from the results on the ComSE dataset.

Table 3. Results of RankBoost-Same

NDCG	on MQ2007-semi				on ComSE			
	@1	@3	@5	@10	@1	@3	@5	@10
RankBoost	0.403	0.406	0.416	0.444	0.504	0.547	0.573	0.632
RankBoost-All	0.395	0.406	0.412	0.439	0.495	0.527	0.557	0.621
RankBoost-Prop	0.405	0.408	0.417	0.444	0.509	0.545	0.573	0.633
RankBoost-Same	0.414	0.419*	0.426*	0.454*	0.512	0.550*	0.577*	0.635*

4.3   Supplementary Ranking on Heterogeneous Data

Note that there is no publicly available heterogeneous dataset that can be used to test our proposed methods. In our experiments, we alternatively simulated such datasets based on MQ2007-semi and ComSE. Specifically, we randomly split the features in each dataset into two subsets A and B, each with half of the original features. We used the features in subset A as the representation of the target objects, and used the features in subset B as the representation of the supplementary objects. In this way, we can guarantee that the target objects and the supplementary objects locate in different feature spaces. For ease of reference, we call the new datasets generated in this way MQ2007-heter and ComSE-heter.

Note that not all the baselines used in Section 4.2 can still work on MQ2007-heter and ComSE-heter, mainly because they assume that the target objects and the supplementary objects share the same feature representation. For example, RankBoost-Prop needs to compute similarity between a target object and a supplementary object. When the target objects and the supplementary objects do not use the same feature representation, the similarity cannot be calculated. As a result, RankBoost becomes the only meaningful baseline on this task. Again, we set the maximal number of selected weak rankers to 600 for RankBoost and RankBoost-Heter.

Table 4 shows the results of RankBoost and RankBoost-Heter on the two heterogeneous datasets. From the table we can see that RankBoost-Heter performs much better than RankBoost. The improvements are statistically significant in terms of NDCG@1, NDCG@3 and NDCG@10 on the MQ2007-heter dataset, and in terms of all the four measures on the ComSE-heter dataset.

To sum up, the experimental results show that our proposed two algorithms perform better than several supervised learning to rank and semi-supervised learning to rank methods. This verifies our claim that by using the supplementary data in both training and test, one can do a better job in supplementary ranking.

4.4   Discussions

In this section, we conduct some further study on our proposed algorithms, in order to understand how supplementary learning to rank leads to performance gains.

As can be seen from Section 3, the supplementary data is mainly used to derive new weak rankers. Therefore, we hypothesize that the good performance

Table 4. Results of RankBoost-Heter

NDCG	on MQ2007-heter				on ComSE-heter			
	@1	@3	@5	@10	@1	@3	@5	@10
RankBoost	0.402	0.404	0.416	0.441	0.461	0.512	0.541	0.606
RankBoost-Heter	0.414*	0.413*	0.419	0.449*	0.469*	0.516*	0.546*	0.610*

of our proposed algorithms should come from these new weak rankers. That is, the new weak rankers h' are on average more effective than the original weak rankers h. To test this hypothesis, we have conducted the following analysis.

First, we looked at the models learned by the proposed algorithms. Note that there is a weight for each selected weak ranker in the models. The larger the weight is, the more important the corresponding weak ranker is. Here we take the MQ2007-semi and MQ2007-heter datasets for example. Given the models learned by RankBoost-Same and RankBoost-Heter from these datasets, we calculated the absolute sum of the weights (denoted as *Sum Of Weight* for ease of reference) for the original weak rankers and that for the new weak rankers, and list them in Table 5. From the table, we can see that for both RankBoost-Same and RankBoost-Heter, the new weak rankers earn much larger weights than the original weak rankers over all the five folds. This clearly shows that the new weak rankers play a major role in the learned models.

Second, we investigated the goodness of each individual weak ranker. Using the exponential loss of RankBoost, we can compute the ranking loss of the original rankers and new rankers as follows.

$$L(h) = \sum_q \sum_{x_i^q \succ x_j^q} e^{-(h(x_i^q) - h(x_j^q))}, \forall h \in \mathcal{H} \tag{6}$$

$$L(h') = \sum_q \sum_{x_i^q \succ x_j^q} e^{-(h'(x_i^q; Z^q) - h'(x_j^q; Z^q))}, \forall h' \in \mathcal{H}' \tag{7}$$

The smaller the loss is, the better the weak ranker is. For the MQ2007-semi dataset, we found that 12 of the top 20 best rankers belong to $\mathcal{H}'$, and the other 8 belong to $\mathcal{H}$. For the MQ2007-heter dataset, we found that 14 of the top 20 best rankers belong to $\mathcal{H}'$ and the other 6 belong to $\mathcal{H}$. In other words, $\mathcal{H}'$ contains more good rankers than $\mathcal{H}$. This verifies our hypothesis: on average, the supplementary data can help enhance the effectiveness of a weak ranker.

Table 5. Weights of the rankers in the models

		Fold1	Fold2	Fold3	Fold4	Fold5
RankBoost-Same	Sum of Weight of h	2.470	2.595	2.604	2.522	2.646
on MQ2007-semi	Sum of Weight of h'	3.631	3.398	3.516	3.693	3.657
RankBoost-Heter	Sum of Weight of h	1.526	1.732	2.033	1.782	1.721
on MQ2007-heter	Sum of Weight of h'	4.871	4.429	4.121	4.292	4.586

However, we would also like to point out that although on average the new weak rankers are more effective, the original weak rankers also play an important role in the models. They occupy a significant part in the top rankers, and their sum of weight is also not negligible. This indicates the necessity of using our proposed two sub models simultaneously.

5   Conclusions and Future Work

In this paper, we have proposed a new task of ranking, named supplementary data assisted ranking, which can cover many important applications. We have proposed a general approach to the task, named supplementary learning to rank, and developed two Boosting-style algorithms. Experimental results have shown that by use of supplementary learning to rank, significantly better ranking performance can be achieved, than using supervised and unsupervised learning to rank techniques.

For future work, we plan to investigate the following issues. (1) We will study other ways of using the supplementary data in the ranking model. (2) We will develop supplementary learning to rank algorithms based on support vector machines and neural networks. (3) We will apply the proposed approach to more real applications. (4) We will study the theoretical properties of supplementary learning to rank, e.g., its generalization ability and statistical consistency.

Acknowledgments

We would like to thank Tie-Yan Liu and Hang Li for their valuable comments and suggestions on this work.

References

1. Amini, M.R., Truong, T.V., Goutte, C.: A boosting algorithm for learning bipartite ranking functions with partially labeled data. In: SIGIR 2008, pp. 99–106. ACM, New York (2008)
2. Freund, Y., Iyer, R., Schapire, R.E., Singer, Y.: An efficient boosting algorithm for combining preferences. JMLR 4, 933–969 (2003)
3. Gao, W., Blitzer, J., Zhou, M., Wong, K.F.: Exploiting bilingual information to improve web search. In: ACL 2009, Singapore, pp. 1075–1083 (2009)
4. Järvelin, K., Kekäläinen, J.: Cumulated gain-based evaluation of IR techniques. ACM TOIS 20(4), 422–446 (2002)
5. Kurland, O., Lee, L.: PageRank without hyperlinks: Structural re-ranking using links induced by language models. In: SIGIR 2005, pp. 306–313. ACM, New York (2005)
6. Liu, T.Y.: Learning to rank for information retrieval. Foundations and Trends in Information Retrieval 3(3), 225–331 (2009)
7. Liu, T.Y., Xu, J., Qin, T., Xiong, W., Li, H.: Letor: Benchmark dataset for research on learning to rank for information retrieval. In: Proceedings of SIGIR 2007 Workshop on Learning to Rank for Information Retrieval, pp. 3–10 (2007)
8. Qin, T., Liu, T.Y., Xu, J., Li, H.: LETOR: A benchmark collection for research on learning to rank for information retrieval. IRJ, 346–374 (2010)
9. Savoy, J.: Comparative study of monolingual and multilingual search models for use with Asian languages. ACM TALIP 4(2), 163–189 (2005)
10. Vapnik, V.N.: Statistical Learning Theory. Wiley, New York (1998)
11. Wang, X.J., Ma, W.Y., Xue, G.R., Li, X.: Multi-model similarity propagation and its application for web image retrieval. In: ACM Multimedia Conference 2004, pp. 944–951. ACM, New York (2004)

Event Recognition from News Webpages through Latent Ingredients Extraction

Rui Yan[1], Yu Li[2], Yan Zhang[1,*], and Xiaoming Li[1]

[1] School of Electronics Engineering and Computer Science,
Peking University, Beijing 100871, P.R. China
[2] School of Computer Science, Beihang University, Beijing 100083, P.R. China
{r-yan,lxm}@pku.edu.cn, carp84@gmail.com, zhy@cis.pku.edu.cn

Abstract. We investigate the novel problem of event recognition from news webpages. "Events" are basic text units containing news elements. We observe that a news article is always constituted by more than one event, namely Latent Ingredients (LIs) which form the whole document. Event recognition aims to mine these Latent Ingredients out. Researchers have tackled related problems before, such as discourse analysis and text segmentation, with different goals and methods. The challenge is to detect event boundaries from plain contexts accurately and the boundary decision is affected by multiple features. Event recognition can be beneficial for topic detection with finer granularity and better accuracy. In this paper, we present two novel event recognition models based on LIs extraction and exploit a set of useful features consisting of context similarity, distance restriction, entity influence from thesaurus and temporal proximity. We conduct thorough experiments with two real datasets and the promising results indicate the effectiveness of these approaches.

Keywords: Event Recognition, Latent Ingredient, Segmentation.

1 Introduction

News webpages increasingly become an essential component of web contents nowadays, and as a result, news flood surges in the Internet. Within the domain of modern information retrieval, news search plays an important role. Contemporary news search is based on document-level retrieval. However, from our observation news documents are not indivisible: they always contain more than one event. An event is defined as "something that happens at a specific time and location"[1]. Events within the same news document are related but to some extent independent from each other. Therefore not all of them are relevant to issued queries. Search engines can instead return fine-grained event-level results to facilitate more accurate search from news webpages and "query-event" match will be more successful than full document in news retrieval. Furthermore, event recognition techniques can stimulate other relevant researches due to its potential use for Topic Detection and Tracking (TDT). The fine granularity of event representation motivates more accurate task results.

---

* Corresponding author.

P.-J. Cheng et al. (Eds.): AIRS 2010, LNCS 6458, pp. 490–501, 2010.

We illustrate a news report from Xinhua News[1] in Fig.1. The article can be divided into several events and we zoom in three of them: new death caused by Swine Flu in Singapore; retrospection of the first infection in Singapore; a confirmed patient in Malaysia. These events are related but independent. By appropriate event recognition, one can find the most relevant event description with less jeopardized noises. If the news report is compared as a "dish" then these constituent events are ingredients to form the dish, but they are latent and need to be mined. Therefore we name them as "Latent Ingredients" (LIs). LIs are atomic for event-level retrieval.

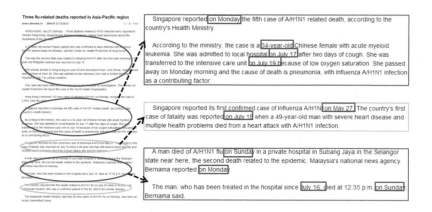

Fig. 1. A news illustration from *Xinhua.net* which consists several Latent Ingredients. Red boxes emphasize temporal information and we tag and use them later in this paper.

The first challenge for event recognition is to distinguish "events" from plain texts. We look into discourse structure and event representation to locate which parts of texts contain events. A more important challenge is to precisely detect event boundaries after we recognize the potential area of events. This is quite different from existed segmentation techniques, e.g. majorly dependent on inter-sentence similarity measurement but ours is event-oriented. Since there are multiple features to affect the procedure, a balance among all features present special difficulties. We manage to decide whether an event shifts or continues with appropriate solutions. We provide two models to address the challenges.

The rest of this paper is organized as follows: in Section 2 we revisit related work. In section 3 we modify the classic TextTiling algorithm into Temporal Textiling Model (TTM). We describe our innovative LIs Growth Model (LGM) based on sentence feature analysis in Section 4. Section 5 presents rich experiments and corresponding results. We draw conclusions in Section 6.

---

[1] http://www.xinhuanet.com/english/sf/

2   Related Work

2.1   Discourse Structure Analysis

We extract atomic events as LIs, similar to key paragraph extraction [6,7]. Discourse analysis in journalism deals with similar problems. Ponte and Croft used a Gaussian Length Model to weight potential segment length with the prior probability defined in [15]:

$$\frac{k}{\sigma\sqrt{2\pi}} exp(-\frac{(x-\mu)^2}{2\sigma^2})$$

(1)

where μ is the estimated mean length, σ is the estimated standard deviation and k is a constant for scaling purpose. Grimes proposed a segmentation standard based on time, space, character and theme [8]. In news this standard can be mapped to temporal expressions, entities (location and person) and semantic contexts. Bestgen et al indicated temporal information was used to signal thematic shift in discourse structures [4,5]. We will use these conclusions as the basic assumptions in this work.

2.2   Segmentation Techniques

Text segmentation techniques have gained emphasis through all these years and kept on progressing. Salton discussed the decomposition of text into segments and themes where a segment is a contiguous block of text discussing a single subtopic [16]. Hearst discussed a method named "TextTiling" to segment expository texts into multi-paragraph subtopics which they call "tiles" [12,10]. The text is initially broken up into blocks of size N and then a similarity curve of adjacent blocks is computed using cosine similarity to identify topic boundaries by calculating relative similarity difference. A great variety of research works [11,9,2,18] furthered deeper on classic TextTiling. Hidden Markov Models (HMMs)[17,13] approaches broke texts using a sequential Markov stochastic decision process which generates text fragments relevant to a particular query. In recent years as topic model proved its importance and researchers connected segmentation techniques with topic analysis [14,3].

Our approaches are different from previous ones. Firstly we cannot use a fixed block size because in our datasets, document length varies significantly due to different representation of news. Yet the comparison between neighboring blocks in fixed size is not enough. Besides, our approach is independent of specific queries, unlike HMMs. Finally, our approaches are more event-centered than topic models. We consider more news elements with the help of lexical thesaurus and deal with the problem of few key terms in common between sentences.

3   Temporal TextTiling Model

Based on Bestgen's conclusion [4] and according to our statistics of human annotated data, 87.23% LIs start from a sentence with temporal information. As illustrated in Fig.1, temporal expressions play a vital part in indicating LIs extraction. We treat the sentence with a timestamp as a head sentence and the LIs extraction starts from it.

3.1   Timestamp Extraction

To identify the head sentences we need to locate temporal expressions. There are specific and non-specific temporal expressions. Specific temporal expressions are meaningful in that they satisfy news elements criterion and indicate events while non-specific ones do not. Specific temporal expressions can be classified as explicit ones, which are simple to recognize, and implicit ones which need semantic inference from reference time point by calculating elapse. Expressions such as "tomorrow" indicate time offsets. Secondly time value can be time points or time intervals. We assign publish time to the whole news article and make references when encounter new time tags during sequential processing within each LI.

Table 1. Categorization of temporal expressions

Meaning	Categorization	Examples
Specific	Explicit expressions	on May 28th
		between 5.9 and 5.11
	Implicit expressions	from Monday to Friday
		after two days
Non-Specific	Useless temporal expressions	34-year-old Chinese
		progress by days of study

We implement a time tagger based on GATE[2] to recognize temporal expressions. The tagger extracts them, discards non-specific ones, makes semantic inference and regulates with uniform format (mm/dd/yyyy). In this work, we use temporal expressions to denote those specific ones.

3.2   Temporal TextTiling

We modified the classic TextTiling algorithm, which uses inter-sentence similarity. Previous TextTiling specifies a fixed size of block as the unit of comparison, and adjacent blocks are compared. However, this measure cannot be directly applied to our scenario due to the character of news representation as mentioned in Section 2. Therefore we regard a sentence as a block.

After extracting and regulating temporal expressions, we locate the first head sentence (s_h) to be the beginning of an LI. All pairs of adjacent sentences from s_h are assigned a similarity value and these values are examined for peaks and valleys. Peak values imply two sentences cohere well whereas valleys indicate potential boundaries. We choose the first boundary from s_h as the end of this

---

[2] http://gate.ac.uk

LI and move on to the next head sentence with temporal expressions. Given two sentences s_1 and s_2, similarity between sentences is calculated by a cosine measurement, where $w(t, s)$ is the weight of term t in sentence s.

$$similarity = \frac{\sum_{t \in s_1 \cap s_2} w(t, s_1)w(t, s_2)}{\sqrt{\sum_{t \in s_1} w(t, s_1)^2} \times \sqrt{\sum_{t \in s_2} w(t, s_2)^2}} \tag{2}$$

Term Weighting. $w(t, s)$ is measured by $tf.idf$ from standard information retrieval in previous TextTiling. In [9] a twist term weighting is introduced: $w(t, s)$ is the tf value (term frequency) of t within the block, and here the block means the sentence. However, only term frequency cannot ensure the terms in common are rare in other parts of the document but the global $tf.idf$ mechanism based on the whole collection would make the vector too sparse. Thus $tf.isf$ (term frequency-inverse sentence frequency) weighting strategy is utilized. Still there may be a problem. tf within a sentence is often too small and successive multiplication of $tf.isf$ weights may cause an underflow. So we implement a novel term weighting strategy $dtf.isf$. dtf is measured within the local document D, and isf in D indicates whether t is a distinguishing term or not. The four term weighting strategies are compared in our experiments to evaluate their performances in the task of LIs extraction.

4   LIs Growth Model

As specified above, we start LIs extraction from a head sentence s_h with temporal expressions, the indicators of topic drifting. Neighboring contexts tend to describe the same event due to the semantic consecutiveness of natural languages: human discourse is consistent. An LI expands by absorbing sentences that stick to the event. We assume there are two factors deciding relevance to the event. Naturally one is the context similarity between the pending sentence (s_p) and every sentence from the expanding LI (s_L). The other factor is the probability for s_L to belong to LI. Here we denote significance to be the probability of being related to LI. Intuitively, if s_p is similar to a more significant sentence, it is more likely to be relevant to LI. These two factors can be formulated in Equation 3 as follows, where $|LI|$ denotes the number of sentences in the expanding LI:

$$relevanceScore = \frac{\sum_{s_p \cup LI} significance \times similarity}{|LI| + 1} \tag{3}$$

4.1   Context Similarity

Similarity is always an important measurement in text processing. We employ pre-process techniques for accuracy, including Part-of-Speech tagging, stemming, stop word removal and named entity recognition. Like the Temporal TextTiling Model, similarity values are measured on sentence level using Equation 2.

We will next move on to the sentence feature analysis according to the news principles. Each of these lexical elements is essential for LIs extraction. We present the symbols that would be mentioned later in Table 2.

Table 2. Symbols used in the following sections

Symbols	Meanings
s_p	The pending sentence to decide whether to add
s_h	The head sentence (with temporal expressions)
$|s|$	The distance (offset) from s_h
e_L	Named entities contained in LI
e_W	Named entities connected by WordNet
e_i	Named entities contained in sentence i
s_e	A sentence in the LI containing relevant entity (entities)
s_t	A sentence in the LI containing temporal expression(s)

4.2 Distance Restriction

According to the Gaussian Length Model, the tendency to agglomerate attenuates as distance becomes larger from head sentence s_h ($|s_h|=0$). The length of LI *Len* follows Gaussian distribution. $P(X \sim O)$ represents the probability for s_p to contain a common event with the expanding LI, which is a decay caused by distance, namely distance restriction $f_d(x)$ ($x = |s_p|$).

$$f_d(x) = P(X \sim O) = P(X < Len) = \int_X^{\infty} \frac{k}{\sigma\sqrt{2\pi}} exp(-\frac{(t-\mu)^2}{2\sigma^2})dt \qquad (4)$$

$f_d(x)$ is illustrated in Fig.2. However, Equation 4 based on statistical distance is incomplete. Considering Grimes' theory, besides theme (semantic context) similarity, space and character (i.e. named entities) and time (i.e. temporal expressions) have influences and should all be taken into consideration. We treat these standards homogeneously and they share similar decay function.

4.3 Named Entity Influence

Named entities, such as person, location or organization names, are usually utilized in text mining problems. They are different from plain terms. Relevant named entities in two sentences indicate a probable common event. Therefore we need to identify such entities, which are either entities from current LI (denoted as e_L) or entities connected to e_L through a path by WordNet(e_W). The structure of WordNet is illustrated in Fig.3. Distance from entity A to entity E is 5 with a path $\{A, B, root, C, D, E\}$. Relevant entities form a dynamically growing set during LI expansion. e_L is initiated from e_{s_h} and iteratively updated by adding e_{s_p} when s_p is added to LI:

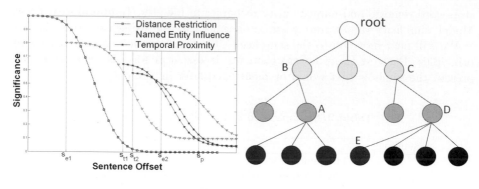

Fig. 2. Decay functions illustration   **Fig. 3.** Hierarchical structure of WordNet

A sentence containing relevant entity(ies) will raise the probability to share the event with LI despite the distance restriction. We use $f_e(x)$ to define the named entity influence and it is illustrated in Fig.2 too.

$$f_e(x) = e^{-\alpha \times dist} \times f_d(x - |s_e|) \qquad (5)$$

$dist$ is the distance between e_{s_p} and e_L, which is measured by the length of the shortest path in WordNet. If entities are exactly matched, $dist$ will be 0, then $f_e(x)$ reduces into $f_d(x - |s_e|)$ and the significance of s_e is equal to s_h. Generally there are various entities in e_L, and $dist$ is the average distance $\overline{dist}$ of all entity pairs. α is a scaling factor between 0 and 1.

4.4   Temporal Proximity

We consider temporal proximity contribute to common events as well. Re-mention of adjacent temporal information might strengthen event continuous-ness, but if two timestamps are too far away, a new event might begin here. When new temporal expressions are identified, we need to decide whether a new LI starts or the original LI still expands. We introduce time decay to measure the temporal proximity in Equation 6 and it is also illustrated in Fig.2:

$$f_t(x) = e^{-\beta \times \frac{\Delta t}{T_d}} \times f_d(x - |s_t|) \qquad (6)$$

Δt means the temporal distance between the new time value t_n and the times-tamp t_0 in s_h. When refers to expressions designating time intervals, Δt means the closest time distance between the two. T_d is the time span of the news doc-ument. β is a also scaling factor between 0 and 1.

We use a significance to measure the probability of being the same event and all features mentioned above impact the significance score. Note that in the expanding LI, there may be more than one s_e or s_t and hence there may be more than one $f_e(x)$ or $f_t(x)$. For the completeness of an LI, we choose the maximum $f_e(x)$ and $f_t(x)$. Equation 7 takes the arithmetic average score of all significance.

$$significance = (f_d(x) + max\{f_e(x)\} + max\{f_t(x)\})/3 \qquad (7)$$

We combine both similarity and significance in Equation 3 and obtain a relevance score from all sentence pairs between s_p and s_L. We add s_p into LI when relevance score exceeds a threshold. This LIs extraction model is like a growing snow ball instead of the parallel process of Temporal TextTiling Model (TTM). Therefore we name it as LIs Growth Model (LGM).

5   Experiments and Evaluation

5.1   Data Description

Since there is no existing standard test set for LIs extraction, we opt to construct our own test sets which consist news datasets and golden standards. We construct two separate datasets manually for LIs extraction. One is based on news documents from Automatic Content Extraction 2004 corpus (ACE04). Considering these news reports are years away from now, we collect recent news pages from Xinhua news website ($Xinhua$). We sample 1000 news documents from the datasets according to their length distribution, 500 from each, all in English.

5.2   Evaluation Metrics

In performance evaluation we use the *Precision* and *Recall* criterion in information retrieval. Firstly we consider the sentence level performance among LIs. Suppose L_1 is an LI given by human with m sentences and L_2 by computer with n sentences. We treat L_1 and L_2 as a pair when L_1 contains the head sentence s_h of L_2. Sentence level precision (p_{sent}) within is calculated by checking how many sentences in L_2 are found in L_1 and the recall (r_{sent}) is to check how many sentences in L_1 are retrieved. We use formalized evaluation metrics as follows:

$$p_{sent} = \frac{|L_1 \cap L_2|}{n}; r_{sent} = \frac{|L_1 \cap L_2|}{m}; F_{sent} = \frac{2 \times p_{sent} \times r_{sent}}{p_{sent} + r_{sent}} \tag{8}$$

Moreover, we also consider the event level performance to measure how many LIs are missed or falsely alarmed. Suppose there are a LIs in document D found by man, b LIs in D by computer and $|L_1 \cap L_2|$ is the number of matched LI pairs. Event level precision (p_{event}) indicates how many LIs are correctly found and the recall (r_{event}) is to measure how many events are found by the algorithms.

$$p_{event} = \frac{|L_1| \cap |L_2|}{b}; r_{event} = \frac{|L_1| \cap |L_2|}{a}; F_{event} = \frac{2 \times p_{event} \times r_{event}}{p_{event} + r_{event}} \tag{9}$$

The final F-score in a document D is calculated by the harmonic mean of $\overline{F_{sent}}$ from all LIs within this document and F_{event}.

$$F = \frac{2 \times \overline{F_{sent}} \times F_{event}}{\overline{F_{sent}} + F_{event}} \tag{10}$$

5.3   Parameter Tuning

There are several free parameters in our LIs extraction models. μ, σ and k are fitted to Formula 1 by the LI length statistics. From our statistics of LIs length from 1000 reports, we choose $k = 15$, $\mu = 7$, $\sigma = 2$ in Formula 1.

Next we examine the influence of scaling factor α and β under a specific threshold. During every "training and testing" process, we vary α from 0 to 1 with the step of 0.1 and make the same move to β. We check the F-score when these two parameters change in Fig.4 and get a best α and β value pair (α_{best} and β_{best}) under each given threshold. In $Xinhua$ we can see that when β exceeds a certain value the F-score improves significantly (β=0.5 in Fig.4) under all α but α shows little and unstable influence of the overall performance. The best F-score in Fig.4 is achieved when α=0.3 and β= 0.6. In ACE04 we observe the best F-score is achieved when α=0.6 and β= 0.5 and the performance varies slightly when α and β are restricted in a particular region. In general the effect of α is weaker than that of β despite of different datasets, but β is more sensitive to datasets than α is.

To the decision of threshold value, we notice $relevanceScore$ sometimes varies significantly from document to document. Therefore, we measure the threshold more locally, within each document. In every news article, we locate all potential head sentences and check the $relevanceScore$ of each sentence following. Hence we obtain all $relevanceScores$ with a range in $[\underline{relScore}, \overline{relScore}]$ and the threshold is computed by $(\underline{relScore} + \gamma \times (\overline{relScore} - \underline{relScore}))$ where γ varies from 0 to 1 at a step of 0.1. Take LGM of Equation 7 as an example, the parameter tuning procedure is listed in Table 3.

5.4   Performance and Discussion

We examine the performance of temporal information extraction. We randomly sample 100 reports and generate timestamps by humans. The time tagger extracted 483 temporal expressions, 441 correctly inferred. The accuracy is 91.30%.

We compare the performance of LIs extraction models. We choose TextTiling as $Baseline$-1, and Temporal TextTiling Model (TTM) as $Baseline$-2. Four

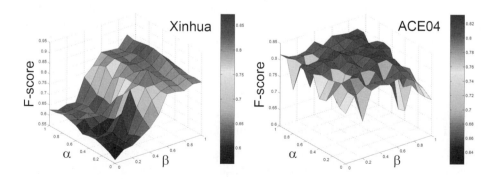

Fig. 4. α, β tuning under a specific γ in $Xinhua$ (left) and ACE04 (right)

Table 3. Parameter tuning in full LGM

	γ	0.0	0.1	0.2	0.3	0.4	0.5	0.6	0.7	0.8	0.9	1.0
Xinhua	α_{best}	0.2	0.3	0.3	0.7	0.5	0.3	0.1	**0.3**	0.8	0.3	0.1
	β_{best}	0.6	0.6	0.7	0.6	0.5	0.6	0.4	**0.6**	0.5	0.5	0.4
	F-score	0.771	0.746	0.681	0.837	0.802	0.794	0.651	**0.879**	0.613	0.765	0.719
ACE04	α_{best}	0.6	0.1	0.4	0.5	0.5	**0.6**	0.1	0.2	0.4	0.7	0.8
	β_{best}	0.5	0.6	0.5	0.4	0.4	**0.5**	0.7	0.4	0.7	0.6	0.6
	F-score	0.814	0.767	0.685	0.600	0.784	**0.823**	0.752	0.571	0.629	0.748	0.791

features are used in LGM extraction: (1) context similarity; (2) distance restriction; (3) named entity influence; (4) temporal proximity. Among them, features (2)(3)(4) influence the significance of a sentence. We tried different combinations of these weights with similarity. *LGM-D* means LIs growth model with only distance restriction, *LGM-DN* denotes LIs growth model with distance restriction and named entity influence, *LGM-DT* includes both distance restriction and temporal proximity and finally the full LGM, *LGM-F*, takes all three features into consideration. Within all these measures, the four term weighting strategies, $tf, tf.idf, tf.isf$ and $dtf.isf$ are utilized to see if they bring any benefits. Due to restricted page limits, we present detail results from *Xinhua* in Table 4 and overall performance for both datasets in Fig.5.

Table 4. Performance Evaluation for different models and term weightings in *Xinhua*

	P_{sent}				r_{sent}				P_{event}				r_{event}			
	tf	tf.idf	tf.isf	dtf.isf	tf	tf.idf	tf.isf	dtf.isf	tf	tf.idf	tf.isf	dtf.isf	tf	tf.idf	tf.isf	dtf.isf
Baseline-1	0.46	0.39	0.48	0.48	0.31	0.27	0.30	0.31	0.20	0.22	0.28	0.29	1.0	1.0	1.0	1.0
Baseline-2	0.53	0.51	0.56	0.54	0.56	0.50	0.52	0.59	0.23	0.22	0.27	0.31	0.89	0.91	0.90	0.93
LGM-D	0.77	0.69	0.73	0.80	0.62	0.61	0.63	0.68	0.68	0.60	0.71	0.70	0.77	0.71	0.74	0.76
LGM-DN	0.85	0.82	0.87	0.87	0.69	0.63	0.65	0.71	0.67	0.64	0.67	0.68	0.69	0.65	0.69	0.70
LGM-DT	0.79	0.77	0.80	0.84	0.84	0.79	0.83	0.83	0.80	0.78	0.81	0.84	0.79	0.78	0.79	0.80
LGM-F	0.85	0.84	0.87	0.89	0.86	0.81	0.87	0.89	0.84	0.82	0.87	0.87	0.81	0.82	0.84	0.87

From Table 4 we can see different behaviors of the two LIs extraction frameworks. *Baseline*-1 and *Baseline*-2 show obvious weakness in LIs extraction. The reason for this phenomenon is most likely that TextTiling is not designed for event-oriented purpose but for expository texts, so it performs especially dreadful in event level precision because most LIs detected by it are not events. However, it discards no sentences and so recall is extremely high. TTM performs better in that it takes temporal expressions into account which are proved to be valuable. Event-level recall for TTM drops slightly. By comparing four varieties of LGM, we find generally considering all features brings the maximum benefits. The distance restriction is reasonable and brings better results compared to two baselines. The entity influence is relatively limited and it hardly improves sentence-level recall. We believe it is due to the incompleteness of WordNet which has not been updated for a long time but news happens anytime. The correlated entities cannot find a path to each other in WordNet and this probably leads to

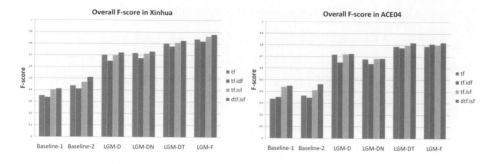

Fig. 5. F-score performance comparison in *Xinhua* and *ACE*04

the failure of relevant entity influence. Recall is greatly enlarged by the effect of temporal proximity and the importance of temporal information is reconfirmed.

The four term weighting strategies have different results as well. Generally *tf.idf* performs worst among all these strategies. The reason may be that our evaluation metrics are based on local contexts so that introduction of global information from the whole collection may cause bias. There do not exist the situation that one always prevails over the others for the rest three weighting methods but at most times our innovative *dtf.isf* beats the other two. We assume this outcome can be ascribed to the local context consideration in document *D* as well as term distinguishing from sentence level pattern, like *tf.isf*. Therefore it is useful to discover uncommon terms and raise their weights.

6   Conclusion

In this paper, we build a framework to address the novel problem of event recognition from news webpages. We implement two models of LIs extraction for event recognition, utilizing multiple features, either semantical or syntactical. We then provide evaluation metrics to measure the effectiveness of event extraction from news articles and conduct the evaluation methods to two real world datasets. According to the results, among all features we used, distance restriction would be helpful compared with only context similarity utilized in baselines. Unexpectedly, relevant entity influence does not benefit much. Temporal information is proved to be quite essential in LIs extraction task and generally the mixture of all four features brings the best performance in balance.

In the future, our research can be directed to find a substitution of WordNet, such as Wikipedia which is more frequently renewed and thus, up to date. What is more, the hierarchical structure of language thesaurus is not yet used. We treat relationships between adjacent entities equally while in fact they should be distinguished. With structural information and a better content organization of the thesaurus, the effect of relevant entities might be improved.

Acknowledgments. This work is partially supported by NSFC Grant No. 60933004, National Key Technology R&D Pillar Program in the 11th Five-year Plan of China (Research No.: 2009BAH47B00) and the Open Fund of the State Key Laboratory of Software Development Environment Grant No. SKLSDE-2010KF-03, Beihang University. We also thank for the discussions with Pan Gu.

References

1. Allan, J., Papka, R., Lavrenko, V.: On-line new event detection and tracking. In: SIGIR 1998, pp. 37–45 (1998)
2. Banerjee, S., Rudnicky, I.A.: A TextTiling based approach to topic boundary detection in meetings. In: Ninth International Conference on Spoken Language Processing, pp. 57–60 (2006)
3. Bestgen, Y.: Improving text segmentation using latent semantic analysis: A reanalysis of choi, wiemer-hastings, and moore (2001). Comput. Linguist. 32(1), 5–12 (2006)
4. Bestgen, Y., Vonk, W.: The role of temporal segmentation markers in discourse processing. Discourse Processes 19(3), 385–406 (1995)
5. Bestgen, Y., Vonk, W.: Temporal adverbials as segmentation markers in discourse comprehension. Journal of Memory and Language 42(1), 74–87 (1999)
6. Fukumoto, F., Suzuki, Y.: Detecting shifts in news stories for paragraph extraction. In: Proceedings of the 19th International Conference on Computational Linguistics, pp. 1–7 (2002)
7. Fukumoto, F., Suzukit, Y., Fukumoto, J.: An automatic extraction of key paragraphs based on context dependency. In: Proceedings of the Fifth Conference on Applied Natural Language Processing, pp. 291–298 (1997)
8. Grimes, J.: The thread of discourse. Mouton De Gruyter (1975)
9. Hearst, M.: A quantitative approach to discourse segmentation. Computational Linguistics 23(1), 33–64 (1997)
10. Hearst, M.A.: Multi-paragraph segmentation of expository text. In: Proceedings of the 32nd Meeting on Association for Computational Linguistics, pp. 9–16 (1994)
11. Hearst, M.A.: Texttiling: segmenting text into multi-paragraph subtopic passages. Comput. Linguist 23(1), 33–64 (1997)
12. Hearst, M.A., Plaunt, C.: Subtopic structuring for full-length document access. In: SIGIR 1993, pp. 59–68 (1993)
13. Jiang, J., Zhai, C.: Extraction of coherent relevant passages using hidden markov models. ACM Trans. Inf. Syst. 24(3), 295–319 (2006)
14. Misra, H., Yvon, F., Jose, J.M., Cappe, O.: Text segmentation via topic modeling: an analytical study. In: CIKM 2009, pp. 1553–1556 (2009)
15. Ponte, J., Croft, W.: Text segmentation by topic. In: Research and Advanced Technology for Digital Libraries, pp. 113–125 (1997)
16. Salton, G., Singhal, A., Buckley, C., Mitra, M.: Automatic text decomposition using text segments and text themes. In: HYPERTEXT 1996, pp. 53–65 (1996)
17. Van Mulbregt, P., Carp, I., Gillick, L., Lowe, S., Yamron, J.: Text segmentation and topic tracking on broadcast news via a hidden Markov model approach. In: Fifth International Conference on Spoken Language Processing, pp. 2519–2522 (1998)
18. Xie, L., Zeng, J., Feng, W.: Multi-scale texttiling for automatic story segmentation in Chinese broadcast news. In: Li, H., Liu, T., Ma, W.-Y., Sakai, T., Wong, K.-F., Zhou, G. (eds.) AIRS 2008. LNCS, vol. 4993, pp. 345–355. Springer, Heidelberg (2008)

Tuning Machine-Learning Algorithms for Battery-Operated Portable Devices

Ziheng Lin[1,*], Yan Gu[2], and Samarjit Chakraborty[3]

[1] Department of Computer Science, National University of Singapore, Singapore
linzihen@comp.nus.edu.sg
[2] Continental Automotive Singapore Pte Ltd, Singapore
Yan.Gu@continental-corporation.com
[3] Institute for Real-time Computer Systems, TU Munich, Germany
samarjit@tum.de

Abstract. Machine learning algorithms in various forms are now increasingly being used on a variety of portable devices, starting from cell phones to PDAs. They often form a part of standard applications (e.g. for grammar-checking in email clients) that run on these devices and occupy a significant fraction of processor and memory bandwidth. However, most of the research within the machine learning community has ignored issues like memory usage and power consumption of processors running these algorithms. In this paper we investigate how machine learned models can be developed in a power-aware manner for deployment on resource-constrained portable devices. We show that by tolerating a small loss in accuracy, it is possible to dramatically improve the energy consumption and data cache behavior of these algorithms. More specifically, we explore a typical sequential labeling problem of *part-of-speech tagging* in natural language processing and show that a power-aware design can achieve up to 50% reduction in power consumption, trading off a minimal decrease in tagging accuracy of 3%.

Keywords: Low-power Machine Learned Models, Part-of-speech Tagging, Mobile Machine Learning Applications, Power-aware Design.

1 Introduction

While mobile devices are already ubiquitous, in the near future such devices are likely to become a dominant computing platform. Since battery-life is a major design concern for these devices, applications currently designed for the desktop need to be redesigned to allow the operating system or human operator to control the application's power consumption. While general methods do exist to regulate the underlying processor's frequency and voltage without detailed knowledge of the applications, we may be able to achieve even better energy savings when we are informed of the specifics of the application domain.

Take the case of email on a portable device. In the near future, portable email clients will gain the capability to correct grammatical errors and recognize names of contacts, products and companies and link them with appropriate information (e.g., address

* This work was partially supported by a National Research Foundation grant "Interactive Media Search" (grant # R-252-000-325-279).

P.-J. Cheng et al. (Eds.): AIRS 2010, LNCS 6458, pp. 502–513, 2010.

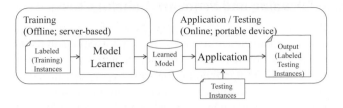

Fig. 1. Machine learning application on portable platforms

book contact information, Wikipedia entries). These nascent functions require the email client to understand the text of emails, requiring the use of natural language processing (NLP) tools. Up to now, applications requiring NLP have been largely restricted to the desktop or server platforms. What software design changes are a consequence of moving to portable, battery-powered platforms?

To answer this question, we explore one such application, namely that of applying a large-scale machine learned model. Diagnosing a patient's illness from symptoms [4], recognizing faces [3], delimiting addresses and place names in an email [8] are all sample problems where an approach of applying machine-learned model is a possible solution. While these applications have traditionally been done solely on desktops, we see a shift where portable devices are also used to perform these tasks: already, web browsers are used on PDAs and digital cameras attempt to recognize faces.

To our knowledge, implementations of such large-scale machine learned models have only concerned themselves with time (and to a much lesser extent, space) efficiency. We introduce the concept of *power-aware machine learning model application*, in which power consumption and prediction accuracy can be traded off, allowing us to choose a suitable performance level based on context. We concretize our investigation on this general model by examining the sample application of *part-of-speech tagging*, a key NLP task that underlies the grammar checking and name recognition functionality (among others) in the email client scenario. We examine how this task can be tackled using a power-sensitive adaptation of the Naïve Bayes machine learning algorithm [6]. We show simulated results using the SimpleScalar instruction set simulator [1] over different hardware configurations that exhibit a power-accuracy tradeoff and confirm this with observed voltage and current measurements on an instrumented PDA. A key contribution of our work is in designing the Naïve Bayes model to trade off accuracy for power conservation by varying the generated learned model size. Such work enables efficient tagging of the parts-of-speech of words in a sentence on mobile platforms.

We first give a general introduction to the machine learning setting and relate how part of speech tagging constitutes an instance of this setting. We discuss how the basic Naïve Bayes algorithm can be designed to make power consumption versus accuracy tradeoffs in Section 3 by selecting a suitable model size. In Section 4, we then further explore how to optimize the algorithm's data access to further reduce power consumption through the use of early termination and batching feature and problem instance computation. We end by discussing both our simulated and real-world experiments and conclude with possible extensions of this work.

2   Machine Learning and Sequence Labeling Tasks

Machine learning is a broad area of research and a subdiscipline in its own right within computer science [6]. The basic task is to predict an output $f(x)$ given inputs x, where x could be a vector of different individual *features*: $\{x_1, x_2, ..., x_n\}$. One method to do this is known as *supervised learning*, in which we are given some *training instances* where the output $f(x)$ is known, which is used as evidence to build a prediction model. While different features may have different utility in predicting the output, in most machine learning scenarios, we typically provide as many potentially useful features as possible, and relegate the task of deciding which features are actually useful to the learning software. Linear regression is an example of a learning method, in which the given examples determine the coefficients (i.e., the model) of the predicted plane. Once a model is computed, new *testing instances* (where the output $f(x)$ is not known) can be run through the model to predict an output.

Building the model (also called *training*) and applying it on unseen instances (or *testing*) are logically distinct steps. As we often want to apply a trained model repeatedly to many sets of unseen instances, we may require that testing is computationally efficient (i.e., fast) to apply, but the computational efficiency of training is not an issue (we could compute the model on a server, for example). In cases where we want to apply a machine learned model on a power-constrained device, we can simply store a precomputed model (often much more compact than the set of training instances itself) on the device and apply it to instances on-line. This scenario is illustrated in Figure 1.

The machine learning paradigm is currently used to obtain state-of-the-art performance on many problems in computer vision and NLP. In this paper, we use the *part-of-speech (POS) tagging* task and the Naïve Bayes (NB) learning algorithm as a motivating running example of how we can adapt the application of machine learned models for a power-aware environment.

Note that our solution is not limited to this task nor to this learning algorithm; we adopt this example as both the task and the learning algorithm are easy to explain. We now explain these two aspects.

Part of speech tagging. The POS tagging task is set as follows: given a text, tag each word with its proper part of speech [7]. For example, given the English sentences "The parachute jump was spectacular" and "IBM and Apple stocks jump", the tagged output would be[1]:

"The/article parachute/noun jump/noun was/verb spectacular/adjective",
"IBM/proper_noun and/conjunction Apple/proper_noun stocks/noun jump/verb".

Note that the word "jump" plays different roles of noun and verb in the two sentences respectively. As many words take on different parts of speech depending on context, it is not trivial to predict the tag of the word. Accurate POS tagging forms the basis

---

[1] English POS taggers generally tag not only for word class but inflections to a word, including number, tense and gender, but we ignore these issues here for a simplified presentation. See [5] for a comprehensive treatment of the standard inventory of tags.

for many NLP applications, including suggesting spelling corrections, grammar checking and locating place and person names in documents, all of which may need to be performed on power-constrained devices.

Determining a word's POS can thus be cast as a machine learning problem, where relevant contextual information are represented as features that help to choose between the possible 45 standard POS tags [5]. Note here that the predicted output is discrete rather than continuous; i.e., $f(x) \in C : \{noun, verb, ...\}$. For example, knowing the word's identity (e.g., "jump" should usually be a verb or noun), the previous word's identity (e.g., words following "the" should be nouns), or whether the word is capitalized (e.g., "Apple" (the company) versus "apple" (the fruit)) are all classes of features that hint at a word's POS tag. Some feature classes may lead to thousands of individual features (e.g., the feature class of word identity needs a feature for every possible English word), where other feature classes may simply be represented by single features (e.g., capitalization). These features are calculated for each word to be tagged, forming the feature matrix in Figure 2. The output of a learning algorithm $f(x)$ is a POS tag, such as noun or verb, selected out of a tag inventory C (where $|C| = 45$).

Naïve Bayes. Naïve Bayes (NB) is a simple machine learning algorithm that uses probability to predict the output function. NB casts the output of calculating $P(f(x)|x)$ as $\frac{P(f(x)) \times P(x|f(x))}{P(x)}$ by Bayes' theorem. As x is given (it is the given testing vector), its probability is constant over all of the $P(f(x)|x)$ calculations and can be dropped, resulting in $P(f(x)|x) = P(f(x)) \times P(x|f(x))$. As x may consist of many (say n) individual features in a feature vector, NB makes a naïve (hence the name) assumption that each feature is independent of others and estimates the true joint probability $P(x|f(x))$ as $\hat{P}(x|f(x)) \approx P(x_1|f(x)) \times P(x_2|f(x)) \times ... \times P(x_n|f(x))$. During testing, NB predicts the output that has the highest estimate over all possible outputs, that is:

$$\hat{c} \approx \underset{f(x)\in C}{\operatorname{argmax}} P(f(x)) \prod_{j=1}^{n} P(x_j|f(x)) \tag{1}$$

NB does its prediction based on the stored probabilities of $P(f(x))$ and $P(x_j|f(x))$. These probabilities form the model that NB computes in training. Note that for POS tagging, storing $P(f(x))$ requires only storing 45 floating point (or fixed precision) probabilities for each of the possible POS tags, but storing $P(x_j|f(x))$ requires storing 45 probabilities for each feature. As typical large-scale machine learning employs tens of thousands of features, the storage of the second part of the model is clearly the bottleneck.

The basic Naïve Bayes classification algorithm is shown as pseudocode in Algorithm 1. For each word to be tagged, we first initialize the scores for each output tag as the unconditional probabilities $P(f(x))$ from the NB model as scores for $P(f(x)|x)$. We process each feature by first calculating the feature value x_j and then updating our score for $P(f(x)|x)$ by multiplying the current score by the conditional probability $P(x_j|f(x))$. We process each of $|x|$ features in turn, where each feature calculation refines the score values for each possible output class.

Output	Feature Classes (as sets of individual features)				
f(x)	fc_1	fc_2	fc_3		fc_n
w_1 Prop_N	"IBM"	\<S\>	Caps	...	
w_2 Conj.	"and"	"IBM"	NoCaps	...	
$\vdots$	FC_1=current word	FC_2=previous word	FC_3=capitalization	$\ddots$	$\vdots$
w_m Verb	"jump"	"stocks"	NoCaps	...	

Words as Instances

Fig. 2. Sample feature matrix for part of speech tagging for training instances

---

Algorithm 1. Standard Naïve Bayes model application for a single problem, where features are applied in ranked order

---

/* Initialize probabilities for each output class $f(x) \in C$ */
  for all $c \in C$ **do**
    $P(f(x) == c) \leftarrow P(c)$
/* Use each of the n features, in turn: */
  for all $j \in \{1, 2, ..., n\}$ **do**
    Calcuate feature x_j
    for all $c \in C$ **do**
      Update $P(f(x) == c) \leftarrow P(f(x) == c) \times f(x_j|c)$
    Assign $f(x) \leftarrow \text{argmax } P(f(x) == c)$

---

3   Impact of Varying the Model Size

In general, the more evidence we provide the learner with, the more accurate the predictions will be. However, we observe that acquiring features can be potentially expensive: given an input text we need to compute these features from an input text, and we also have to allocate space in memory to store the learned model's probabilities and then apply them at runtime. In the standard desktop environment, these space concerns are unimportant; we typically give the learner as many features as possible, as space and power are abundant.

On mobile devices, we have a more constrained environment, in which power and memory limitation creates a more complex scenario. A further complication is that there are usually (implicit) deadlines for when certain processing should be completed by. A user of a mobile device may be willing to wait a few seconds for a background process to highlight names or do grammar checking, but not if it takes over ten seconds and not if it constantly drains the device's batteries.

A key observation is that by using fewer features in the model, we can limit the model size and time and power needed in calculating features at the expense of prediction accuracy. To do this, we need to decide which features to retain and which can be left out. This is the problem of *feature selection* which has attracted much attention in the machine learning community (see [2] for a survey). Work on feature selection is used primarily to filter out features that provide no information or which only add noise. Usually the objective function is to optimize accuracy unconditionally, whereas we wish to optimize accuracy per unit feature, to reduce model size. A simple method for selection uses the *information gain* to rank features by how well they discriminate between the output classes, which we employ here.

$$IG(Ex, f_i) = H(Ex) - H(Ex|f_i). \tag{2}$$

where Ex denotes all the training examples and $H()$ denotes entropy, which is defined as $\sum_{c=1}^{|C|} -P(c) \log P(c)$. Using this selection criteria, we can rank all the features by their information gain and build a pseudo-optimal[2] model of any size using the first k highest-ranking features.

While a smaller model reduces prediction accuracy, it would allow the model to fit in memory and reduce the execution time to compute the output. We can thus compute various models of different sizes in an off-line training (perhaps done on a server) and download the appropriate-sized model on to a portable device.

3.1 Experimental Results

We performed two sets of experiments to verify that our approach works as expected. First, we experimented with different feature set sizes and evaluated how the size of the feature set (i.e., the size of the model) affects the accuracy of the learning algorithm. For each feature set size, we computed the resulting workload using a cycle-accurate instruction set simulator. Towards this, we used the SimpleScalar simulator with the *sim-outorder* configuration [1] for collecting various execution statistics resulting from running our algorithm. As one might expect, the workload increases in an approximately linear fashion with the size of the feature set (see Figure 3(b)). However, the rate at which the accuracy improves, exhibits an exponential decay as the number of features is increased. We can see from Figure 3(a) that beyond 10000 features, the return on accuracy diminishes. Hence, given a battery-operated portable device with a power budget, it would be prudent to settle for a lower-than-optimal accuracy by using less features as input to the learning algorithm. Given that the tagging algorithm has to complete within a pre-specified deadline, settling for a lower accuracy results in a corresponding decrease in the workload (see Figure 3(c)). If we factor in the deadline, the reduced workload can be completed within the same amount of time by operating the processor at a lower frequency. Since most portable devices currently have a voltage/frequency-scalable processor (e.g., an Intel XScale processor), a lower operating frequency (and voltage) immediately translates into lower energy consumption and hence improved battery life.

Our second set of experiments consist of using the SimpleScalar statistics and the power consumption characteristics of a PDAdevelopment board to estimate the energy savings resulting from different choices of the feature set size. We used a PDA development board from iWave Systems[3] and connected it to a National Instruments

---

[2] Optimal given the assumption that features are linearly independent, which is usually not true in general; but useful as a simplifying assumption.

[3] http://www.iwavesystems.com/

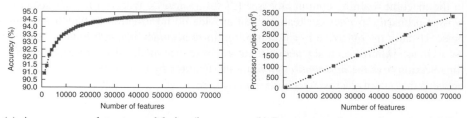

(a) Accuracy correlates to model size (in number of features)

(b) Processor cycles correlate to model size

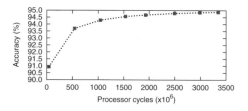

(c) Derived correlation between processor cycles and accuracy

Fig. 3. Processor workload versus model size and accuracy

PXI-4071 $7\frac{1}{2}$-digit Digital Multimeter to measure the power consumption of the CPU core in the iWave board for various operating frequencies. The CPU on the board is an Intel XScale PXA270, a typical commercial CPU found in many off-the-shelf PDAs. The energy consumption estimates obtained using this process accurately reflect those that are obtained by implementing our tagging algorithm on a XScale PXA270 processor.

For our target setup — PDAs, cell phones, etc. running email clients and word-processing applications — it is safe to assume that each screen can display at most 200 words to be tagged for use in downstream applications (i.e., grammar correction). We also assume that once the user triggers such an application, the tagging algorithm for these 200 words should have a 1.5 second latency at most (i.e., an execution deadline of 1.5 seconds).

Why is 1.5 seconds an acceptable deadline? Note that tagging is an intermediate task, a means to an end application such as grammar checking or name recognition. Here we make an assumption that both the tagging and the downstream application are both instances of machine learned model applications and that the models are of approximately the same size. This means that the full NLP pipeline should complete within 3 seconds, which we feel is a reasonable response time that a user is willing to tolerate on a portable device when it is actively being used. In the future we plan to conduct tests with subjects and get Mean Opinion Scores on how delay values affect user perception. Here, we also only examine the tagging execution time; initialization costs in loading the model are not examined, as these are fixed costs that do not vary. The processor frequencies and resulting power consumptions for different feature set sizes that we report in the rest of this section below are based on these assumptions.

Figure 4 gives the CPU-core power consumptions for the six different discrete frequency settings provided by the XScale PXA270 CPU. Note that the power consumption of the CPU-core varies between 0.4 to 0.13 watt, corresponding to the frequency range 520 MHz (maximum) to 104 MHz (minimum). Therefore, the maximum possible reduction in power consumption is upper bound by 68%.

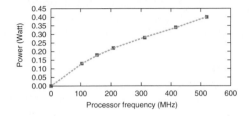

Fig. 4. Processor frequency versus CPU-core power consumption of the PDA

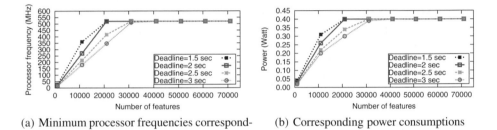

(a) Minimum processor frequencies corresponding specified deadlines

(b) Corresponding power consumptions

Fig. 5. Minimum processor frequencies and power consumptions on the PDA, while tagging 200 words within specified deadlines

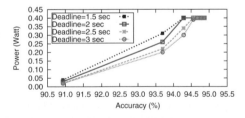

Fig. 6. Power consumption associated with different tagging accuracy values

In our experiments, we designed a simulator where the measured CPU-core power consumption of the iWave board (Figure 4) is used to estimate the power characteristics of the processor. We assume the processor frequency is continuously scalable in the simulator. We set the *deadlines* of the tagging operation to 1.5, 2, 2.5 and 3 seconds respectively, and show the processor frequencies and power consumptions associated with a variable *feature window* size in Figure 5. We investigate these latter, more relaxed deadlines to illustrate additional power savings that can be achieved if the user requirements are relaxed (such as when the tagging task is done concurrently with other processes in the background of a foreground client application).

Note that Figure 5(a) shows that the frequency is scaled within the range of 0 – 520 MHz on the PDA's processor, to match the processing workload with variable model sizes, as specified in number of features. Figure 5(b) shows the corresponding power consumptions estimated by the power characteristics of the PDA. Notice that in the case when the model size is set to 11,000 features, the NB algorithm completes tagging 200 words with 93.6% accuracy in 1.5 seconds and 3 seconds by scaling the processor frequency, thereby achieving a power savings of 23% and 50% respectively (see Figure 6). Note that the accuracy is independent of the delay and depends on the model size.

How does this result compare with typical state-of-the-art taggers? A standard comparison point in the NLP literature is Adwait Ratnaparkhi's tagger [7], which employs a maximum entropy learning technique, similar in spirit to NB, but which is optimizing on conditional probabilities rather than generative ones. This tagger is reported to tag at 96.6% accuracy using over 100K features. In contrast, our tagger adds 3% more absolute error (a very insignificant difference) but reduces the number of features (and power consumption) by a magnitude. This adjustment makes POS tagging plausible on PDA-like devices with realistic deadlines, whereas the original NB and state-of-the-art algorithms would stall, incurring a much longer running time and possibly inducing thrashing, as the memory footprint for the model greatly exceeds the capacity of the cache and onboard memory of the device.

4   Improving Data Caching

Up to now, we have not made any changes to the NB algorithm itself. For prediction, we deal with each problem instance individually (here in POS tagging, each word is a separate problem instance): we calculate features individually in an outer loop and update each conditional probabilities for each possible output prediction in an inner loop, one at a time, as shown in Algorithm 1. While this doubly-nested loop execution pattern may be fine for single problem instances, in POS tagging (and many other NLP tasks) we need to perform testing on many instances. In POS tagging, predicting each word's tag constitutes a separate problem instance.

We can optimize data access to the probabilities stored in the model by batch processing several problem instances in one go (i.e., tagging several words in one go), making better use of parts of the model that have already been loaded in memory while processing one instance. Although this type of processing is typical in the compiler optimization and computer architecture literature, to our knowledge, this type of optimization has not been explored within the machine learning community. We believe this is because such algorithms have (up to now) only been deployed on server computing platforms, where memory is plentiful and bus speeds are fast. With such large memory footprints, optimizing for data access may only result in marginal improvements.

However, on mobile platforms we do not have this luxury as devices need to minimize space, cost and power consumption, resulting in designs with small cache sizes. For example on a cell phone, a typical shared cache size may be only 4 KB. With such small cache sizes, dealing with cache misses become a significant proportion of total

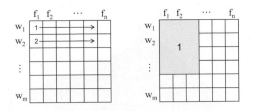

Fig. 7. (1) Naïve Bayes standard computation sequence. (2) Proposed windowed NB computation, where a word window of $WWIN = 4$ and a feature window of $FWIN = 3$ is used.

cycles incurred during the model application. As such, in this scenario, it is worthwhile examining how to lower cache misses by optimizing the use of cached information.

We introduce the notion of batch processing through the introduction of a *word (instance) window*. We predict tags for an entire sequence of words $w_1, w_2, ..., w_m$ rather just for an individual word w_j. In the basic Naïve Bayes algorithm, we loop over all features for each individual instance, computing each feature for a particular instance. In Figure 7(1) this corresponds to calculating values row by row, where each row is a new instance that needs to be tagged. This may be wasteful as the method to compute a feature needs to be reloaded each time a new instance's output class needs to be predicted. Instead, we can compute a feature for a window of words at one time, more effectively utilizing cached information. In our schematic representation, this corresponse to tagging in vertical columns.

We can batch process not only multiple problem instances but also multiple features, computing a set of n features for m words, in one go. In theory, this best utilizes the memory when the necessary memory footprint for computing $m \times n$ is roughly the cache size. This corresponds to processing in vertical tiles, as shown in Figure 7(2). When we finish with one tile, we proceed to the next tile underneath it, looping back to the next set of features. We define this setting through these two parameters: a *feature window* (FWIN) and *word window* (WWIN).

We thus experimented with different cache sizes typical of smaller, portable devices such as cell phones. Note here that such devices are typically more compact and their displays are smaller, allowing an average of 20 words to be displayed. Also, users are used to having significant longer latency on such devices, so we can relax our processing deadline further to 5 seconds. For these devices, we explored different *word* and *feature window* sizes to exploit maximum data cache usage.

The key results we obtained suggest (1) that for any given cache size, there are optimal *word* and *feature window* sizes that maximize data cache reuse, and (2) that not using such windows at all signficantly increases processing load (see Figure 8). The improved data cache reuse immediately translate into fewer cache misses, and hence lower execution time/workload, leading to lower power consumption.

Figure 8 shows the number of cache misses on the 4 KB cache, when tagging 20 words with our optimized algorithm. This plot shows a clear inflection point for the word window axis, illustrating the significance of batching problem instance predictions. Varying the feature window has a much less noticeable effect. We observe that for the cache of 4 KB, when the feature window size is 50 and the word window size is

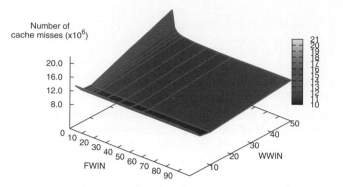

Fig. 8. Cache misses associated with different feature window size and word window size

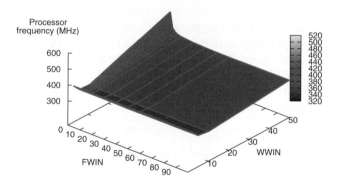

Fig. 9. Processor frequencies to tag 20 words within 5 seconds, associated with different feature window size and word window size

10, the number of cache misses goes down to its minimal point of 10.3×10^6. This is a 48% reduction in cache misses, compared with the case of 20.0×10^6 misses when the feature window and word window are arbitrarily set to 1 and 50 respectively.

We assume that the computational cost to process models (without accounting for cache misses) is linearly proportional to the model size. With a cache penalty of 100 cycles, we derived the total number of processor cycles incurred while tagging 20 words with different feature and word window sizes. With a deadline of 5 sec for tagging 20 words, we then derived the minimum clock frequency at which the processor needs to be clocked to meet this deadline. These results are shown in Figure 9. When the deadline to tag 20 words as 5 seconds, the minimal processor frequency to accomplish tagging is 317.12 MHz, when the feature window is set to 50 and the word window is set to 10; while the maximal processor frequency of the same task goes up to 501.49 MHz, when the feature window is set to 1 and the word window is set to 50. Hence, with the optimal selection of feature window and word window sizes, we were able to reduce the processing frequency required by 36.7%, which immediately translates to significant energy savings on a voltage/frequency-scalable processor.

5   Concluding Remarks

We have introduced the domain of machine learning model applications, where embedded software design methods may be employed to create lightweight, power-sensitive applications. We believe that this domain is critically important in the coming years as portable battery-powered computing becomes a dominant platform, and more applications need to apply machine learning techniques to acquire intelligent behavior.

Towards this, we examined a typical scenario of part-of-speech tagging using the Naïve Bayes algorithm. We showed that with proper use of feature selection, we can tune the model size to fit the memory specifications of a mobile device and reduced the power consumption when applying the model. We also validated these findings with physical voltage and current measurements on an iWave board, as well as via simulation using SimpleScalar.

Further reductions in power consumption can be observed when we redesign how the model application process computes and re-uses the model data. This process is controlled by our newly introduced parameters of *word window* and *feature window*, enabling the batch processing of several words and features together. We showed that the batching of several problems leads to more significant savings, demonstrating a 48% reduction in cache misses when we optimally tune these windows to fit an example cache of 4 KB.

Acknowledgment

We would like to thank Prof. Min-Yen Kan for initiating this work, for numerous discussions, and for his help with the writing of this paper.

References

1. Austin, T., Larson, E., Ernst, D.: SimpleScalar: An infrastructure for computer system modeling. IEEE Computer 35(2), 59–67 (2002)
2. Blum, A.L., Langley, P.: Selection of relevant features and examples in machine learning. Artificial Intelligence 97(1–2), 245–271 (1997)
3. Heisele, B., Ho, P., Poggio, T.: Face recognition with support vector machines: Global versus component-based approach. In: Proceedings of ICCV 2001, Vancouver, Canada, pp. 688–694 (2001)
4. Kononenko, I.: Machine learning for medical diagnosis: History, state of the art and perspective. Artificial Intelligence in Medicine 23(1), 89–109 (2001) (invited paper)
5. Marcus, M.P., Santorini, B., Marcinkiewicz, M.A.: Building a large annotated corpus of english: The Penn Treebank. Computational Linguistics 19(2), 313–330 (1994)
6. Mitchell, T.M.: Machine Learning. McGraw-Hill, New York (1997)
7. Ratnaparkhi, A.: Trainable methods for surface natural language generation. In: Proceedings of ANLP-NAACL 2002, Seattle, Washington, USA, pp. 194–201 (2000)
8. Zhou, G., Su, J.: Named entity recognition using an HMM-based chunk tagger. In: Proceedings of ACL 2002, Philadelphia, PA, USA, pp. 473–480 (2002)

A Unified Iterative Optimization Algorithm for Query Model and Ranking Refinement

Yunping Huang[1], Le Sun[1], and Jian-Yun Nie[2]

[1] Institute of Software, Chinese Academy of Sciences, Beijing, China
{yunping07,sunle}@iscas.ac.cn
[2] Université de Montréal, Montréal, QC, Canada
nie@iro.umontreal.ca

Abstract. Document ranking and query model estimation can be considered as optimization problems. In this paper, we propose an iterative algorithm for optimizing query model and ranking function simultaneously in the context of language model and vector space model, respectively. This algorithm extends the risk minimization framework by incorporating manifold structure of word graph and document graph, and it provides a unified formulation of several existing heuristics for document ranking and query modeling. Moreover, we extend our algorithm by incorporating user's true feedback information, and derive a new ranking model. Experimental results on four TREC collections show that our model is effective.

Keywords: Query Modeling, Document Ranking, Graph-Based Model.

1 Introduction

In order to correctly determine relevant documents for a query, the estimation of query models, the estimation of document models and the definition of document ranking function are three key problems. Document model estimation has been well studied in many studies. In this paper, we address the other two problems together within a unified framework.

Query modeling has attracted much attention in recent years. As the query submitted by a user is usually very short, it needs to be enriched. A commonly used strategy for query modeling is through feedback techniques, such as relevance (pseudo-relevance) feedback [14, 16]. Rocchio feedback formula [14] has been proved to be effective in vector space modeling. In language modeling for information retrieval, two model-based feedback methods have been proposed in [18]: one based on a generative probabilistic model of feedback documents and another on minimization of KL-divergence over feedback documents. Both of them have been proved to be effective. Another commonly used approach to improve query model is to exploit term relations [2]. There are many studies[1,2] that use word relations to improve query models.

Ranking algorithm is another important factor that influences the performance of a retrieval system. In score-based retrieval, a ranking algorithm assigns relevance score

P.-J. Cheng et al. (Eds.): AIRS 2010, LNCS 6458, pp. 514–526, 2010.

to each document with respect to the query. Different methods are defined for estimating relevance scores. Similarity-based methods assume that the relevance is correlated with the similarity/distance between a query and a document [8, 15]. Probabilistic relevance models use a binary random variable to model relevance [7]. Learning to rank is a new family of methods that aims at training a model to rank the document in a supervised learning fashion [5]. However, all the above mentioned models make an assumption that documents are independent. The structure among documents is not taken into consideration. This assumption has been relaxed in several recent studies. [3] utilizes the clustering hypothesis on a graph to smooth the scores and to re-rank the document. Similar studies are described in [10, 12]. These studies demonstrate the advantages of considering the structure among documents. However, query model and ranking function are considered separately in their studies. But in fact, these two elements are strongly dependent. For one thing, query model can be improved with the help of feedback documents. Well ranked documents will be very helpful to refine the query model. For the other thing, query model is a key factor that influences document ranking quality.

In this paper, we propose a unified approach to optimize query model and ranking function simultaneously. We aim to choose the best query model and assign the most appropriate scores to documents. These two elements are optimized together: query model can be improved by well ranked documents, and the ranking function can be improved by a better query model. The previous approaches which fix one of the elements while optimizing another can hit their limit quickly: at some point, it is no longer possible to improve one of the elements (e.g. the ranking function) without also changing the other (query model).

To surpass this limitation, we propose an iterative optimization algorithm: Given a query, a subset D of top-ranked documents in the initial retrieval results and their scores S are used as new evidence to help refine the query model. In turn, the document ranking can be adjusted using the new query model. This process can be done iteratively several times. Different resources, such as word relation, document relation and relevance feedback information, can be incorporated in this process. They are represented as graphs. A constraint onto the smoothness of these graphs will help the optimization algorithm to determine a query model and a ranking function that satisfy the manifold hypothesis: two similar points (terms and documents) in the graph should have similar scores.

In our approach, the above problem is formulated within the risk minimization framework for IR [8]. A unified objective function is defined to integrate multiple criteria: loss function based on risk minimization framework, smoothness of word graphs and document graphs, and fidelity to the original query model. The solution to this optimization problem leads to a new way to define query model and ranking function.

In addition, we extend our approach by incorporating user's true feedback information, which encode the feedback information into a loss function, and combine it with the existing objective function. By minimizing the new objective function, a new ranking method can be derived.

This approach has several potential advantages. First, it can lead to better query model and more appropriate document scores by the unified iterative optimization algorithm which can integrate graph-based optimization into risk minimization framework. Second, the optimization of the query model and document ranking function becomes dependent by systematically incorporating the query term weight and document score as components within the same algorithm. Document scores provide evidence for query model refinement, and query model can influence ranking performance. Once one of them changes, it can be considered as a piece of new evidence for optimizing the other. Finally, it provides a principled general formulation of the query model and ranking function refinement. New resources such as implicit and true relevance feedback information can be flexibly embedded into the approach. Experimental results on four TREC collections show that our model is effective.

The remaining sections are organized as follows. In section 2, we propose a unified iterative optimization algorithm for query model and ranking refinement with graph structure. In section 3, we further integrate user's relevance judgments into our framework. In section 4, we report the experimental results of these methods. We discuss the related work in section 5. We conclude our paper in section 6.

2 Iterative Optimization Algorithm for Query Model and Ranking Refinement

2.1 Risk Minimization Framework

The problem of query model and ranking refinement is essentially an optimization problem. This problem can be formulated within the risk minimization framework for IR [8] by the following loss function:

$$(D^*, S^*, Q^*) = \arg\min_{D,S,Q} \int_{\Theta} L(D, S, Q, \theta) p(\theta \mid q, U, C) d\theta \tag{1}$$

where $D = \{d_1, \ldots d_n\}$ is a subset of the document collection C; q is a query; $S = \{s_1, \ldots s_n\}$ is the scores of documents in D; Q is the query model; U is a user variable; θ is the set of parameters of the document models; $p(\theta \mid q, U, C)$ is the posterior probability distribution of all the parameters; $L(D, S, Q, \theta)$ is a loss function, which can be defined as follows:

$$L(D, S, Q, \theta) = \sum_{d_i \in D} S_i * \Delta(Q, \theta_{di}) \tag{2}$$

where $\Delta(Q, \theta_{di})$ is a distance measure between Q and θ_d, $s(d)$ is the document score of document d. The global risk is defined as a weighted sum of the risk of individual documents. The larger S_i is, the larger the contribution of d_i to the global loss.

In the context of language modeling using KL-divergence, Q and θ_d are usually represented as unigram language model. This leads to

$$\Delta(Q, \theta_d) = \sum_t p(t \mid Q) \log \frac{p(t \mid Q)}{p(t \mid d)} \propto -\sum_t p(t \mid Q) \log p(t \mid d) \tag{3}$$

In the context of vector space modeling, Q and θ_d are represented as vectors. Within this setting, we have:

$$\Delta(Q, \theta d) = -\sum_t tfidf(q, t) * tfidf(d, t) \tag{4}$$

In this paper, we do not change the document model θ, but focus on the optimization of query model and ranking function. We thus define the following loss function. where θ is the document model we selected.

$$r(D, S, Q) = L(D, S, Q, \theta)$$

2.2 Label Smoothness on Data Graph

Manifold hypothesis states that similar points on the graph are likely to have similar scores. Following this hypothesis, we define a cost function: $G(f)$, which penalizes inconsistency between related points, as follows.

$$G(f) = \sum_{i,j} w_{ij} (\frac{f_i}{\sqrt{m_{ii}}} - \frac{f_j}{\sqrt{m_{jj}}})^2 \tag{5}$$

where f_i is the score of point i, W is an affinity matrix, w_{ij} represents the affinity between points i and j and $w_{ii} = 0$, and M is a diagonal normalizing matrix such that $m_{ii} = \sum_j w_{ij}$. This matrix M allows us to normalize the affinity. Such normalization has been shown to result in superior convergence properties than unnormalized affinities for tasks such as spectral clustering [17]. We can use any type of graph to constraint the above function. Points i and j in a graph can be documents, words or users. In this study, we will use word graph and document graph.

2.3 Computing the Optimal Scores

In this section, we introduce our method to refine the query model and ranking function within the context of language modeling and vector space modeling, respectively.

2.3.1 Query Model Refinement

We define the following objective function for query model refinement in the context of language model.

$$\Phi(f) = \frac{1}{2} * (1-\alpha) * \sum_i^n (f_i - y_i)^2 + \alpha * (\frac{\beta}{2} * G(f)) + (1-\beta) * (\frac{r(D, S, f)}{\sum_{d_k \in D} S_k} + \lambda * \sum_i f_i \log P(t_i | C) + \frac{1}{2} * \sum_i f_i^2)) \tag{6}$$

where f and y are query models, $f_i = p(t_i | Q)$, $y_i = p_{ml}(t_i | Q)$; α, β and $\lambda \in [0,1)$ are weighting parameters. The first term guarantees that the refined language model does not deviate too much from its original value; $G(f)$, also known as harmonic function in semi-supervised learning [19], guarantees the consistency of the query model on the graph; $r(D, S, f)$ represent risk function over feedback document, which is defined in section 2.1, where D and S are the feedback documents and the corresponding scores; $p(t|C)$ is the collection language model; $\sum_i f_i \log P(t_i | C)$ measures how different the query model is from the collection language model, and $\sum_i f_i^2$ is a regularization term.

In general, to minimize the objective function in Equation 6, we can compute the first-order partial derivative of it, which is

$$\frac{\partial \Phi(f)}{\partial fi} = (1-\alpha) \times (fi-yi) + \alpha \times (\beta \times \sum_j^n \frac{w_{ij}}{\sqrt{m_{ii}}} (\frac{fi}{\sqrt{m_{ii}}} - \frac{fj}{\sqrt{m_{jj}}}) + (1-\beta) \times (\lambda \times \log p(t_i | C) - \sum_{dj \in D} \frac{Sj}{\sum_{dk \in D} Sk} \times \log P(t_i | \theta_d) + fi))$$

Using the gradient decent method to optimize the objective function, let

$$f_i^{t+1} = fi^t - \frac{\partial \Phi(f)}{\partial fi}$$

we have

$$f_i^{t+1} = (1-\alpha) \times yi + \alpha \times (\beta \times \sum_j^n \frac{w_{ij} \times fj^t}{\sqrt{m_{ii}} \times \sqrt{m_{jj}}} + (1-\beta) \times (\sum_{dj \in D} \frac{Sj}{\sum_{dk \in D} Sk} \times \log P(t_i | \theta_d) - \lambda \times \log P(t_i | C))) \quad (7)$$

From Equation 7, we can see that the new query model f_i has three components, corresponding to the three objective terms in equation 6: The first term is the original query model, the second term is obtained through score regularization on the graph, and the third term is obtained from the document model of feedback documents which is similar to the divergence minimization feedback model in [18]. The difference between the above formulation and that in [18] is that our approach considers the document score Sj as a component.

Similar to the above language model, we define another objective function for vector space model:

$$\Phi(f) = \frac{1}{2} \times (1-\alpha) \times \sum_i^n (fi-yi)^2 + \alpha \times (\frac{\beta}{2} \times G(f) + (1-\beta) \times (\frac{r(D,S,f)}{\sum_{dk \in D} Sk} + \frac{1}{2} \times \sum_i fi^2)) \quad (8)$$

where f and y are two vectors, $yi = tfidf(q, t_i)$ is the *tfidf* weight of the term t_i in query q, and the other parameters are the same as in equation 6. We do not use the collection model in this objective function, because the *idf* value can play a similar role. Using the same manipulation as in language modeling, we have

$$f_i^{t+1} = (1-\alpha) \times yi + \alpha \times (\beta \times \sum_j^n \frac{w_{ij} \times fj^t}{\sqrt{m_{ii}} \times \sqrt{m_{jj}}} + (1-\beta) \times (\sum_{dj \in D} \frac{Sj}{\sum_{dk \in D} Sk} \times tfidf(d, t_i))) \quad (9)$$

2.3.2 Ranking Refinement

In score-based retrieval, the retrieval system assigns each document a relevance score. Document ranking can be considered as a decision problem, which is optimized so as to minimize a loss function within the risk minimization framework. Manifold hypothesis implies that neighbor documents on document graph should have similar scores. So we define the following loss function for ranking refinement as follows:

$$\Phi(S) = a * (r(D,S,Q) + \frac{1}{2} \sum_i Si^2) + \frac{1}{2} * b * G(S) \quad (10)$$

where a and b are two weighting parameters with $a+b=1$; S_i is the score of document d_i. The first term is derived from risk minimization framework, Q is the query model;

$r(D, S, Q)$ is the loss function defined in 2.1; and D is the set of top-ranked documents from the initial retrieval results. The last term guarantees the smoothness of the document scores on the graph; $\sum_i S_i^2$ is a regularization term.

Using the gradient decent method,

$$S_i^{t+1} = S_i^t - \frac{\partial \Phi(S)}{\partial S_i} = a * x_i + b * \sum_j w_{ij} * \frac{S_j^t}{\sqrt{m_{ii}} * \sqrt{m_{jj}}} \qquad (11)$$

$$x_i = -\Delta(Q, \theta_{di})$$

where $\Delta(Q, \theta_{di})$ is defined in Equations 3 or 4 for language model or vector space model respectively.

In order to normalize the value of x_i we replace x_i in Equation 11 by the following normalized value:

$$x_i = \frac{x_i - \min\{x_j, j = 1, \ldots N\}}{\max\{x_j, j = 1, \ldots N\} - \min\{x_j, j = 1, \ldots N\}}$$

2.3.3 The Iterative Optimization Algorithm for Query Model and Ranking Refinement

We observe that the query model Q is a component for refining document scores, and the document scores s_d is also a component for refining query model. We see clearly that these two elements mutually influence each other. The best solution for one element is condition to the other element. A way to solve this problem is to use an iterative algorithm to optimize each of them in turn. This process is expected to improve the query model and ranking iteratively and simultaneously.

We derive two models here: one in the context of language modeling using KL-divergence, denoted by **IOA-KL** (Iterative Optimization Algorithm-KL); another in the context of vector space model using TF-IDF weighting, denoted by **IOA-TFIDF** (Iterative Optimization Algorithm -TFIDF). To obtain a more precise and smoothed query model and document score model, IOA-KL and IOA-TFIDF start with $f = y$, the initial document scores assigned in the initial retrieval step. The algorithm alternates the optimization of query model and ranking model until convergence. The iterative optimization algorithm is defined as follows:

The Iterative Algorithm for Query Model and Ranking Refinement

---

1. Use the initial retrieval model to obtain the top ranked documents and their scores.
2. Use equation 7 (IOA-KL) or 9 (IOA-TFIDF) to compute the new query model.
3. Use equation 11 to compute the new document scores.
4. Compute the change c between two iterations as follows:

    $$c = \sum_i (S_i^{t+1} - S_i^t)^2$$

    If c is smaller than some predefined value or the number of iterations reaches the predefined limit, the algorithm stops. Otherwise, we go to step 2.

For the sake of efficiency, we limit the gradient decent in steps 2 and 3 to only one iteration in our implementation. The above iterative algorithm stops when the change of document scores is smaller than some predefined threshold ((e.g. 10^{-6}). In practice, we do not need to wait till complete convergence. A few iterations can already give an improved query model and ranking. So we set the maximum iteration number to 5.

2.3.4 Construction of the Data Graph

For every query, we construct a k-Nearest-Neighbor (kNN) document graph of all initial documents. The weight of the edge connecting two documents is measured with cosine similarity, which is the same as in [10]. We also construct a word graph for the query model. The weight of an edge is set to be the mutual information between the two words. In order to control the scale of the word graph, in each iteration, the word graph is based on the query model obtained from the last iteration, which only includes the terms in the query model obtained from the last iteration.

3   Considering True Relevance Feedback

The models defined in the previous sections rely on a word graph or a document graph for optimization. The document graph can be constructed using the top N retrieved results. In this section we consider a particular case in which we have true user relevance feedback. True relevance feedback is known to be effective [14, 16]. Previous work using true relevance feedback focuses on query updating such as query term re-weighting and query expansion. Here, we consider such information as encoding preference orders between documents.

When a user provides true relevance judgments for the top N results of the initial retrieval, the relative relevance of each document pair inside the judged set can be obtained. We encode it within a matrix R as follows.

$$R_{ij} = \begin{cases} 1 & d_i \succ d_j \\ 0 & otherwise \end{cases}$$

It is similar to the pairwise relationship in learning to rank approach [5]. In [5], the relative relevance information from the implicit feedback information (clickthrough information) is used to train a model. Previous studies showed that relative relevance preferences can be derived more reliably from implicit feedback than absolute relevance [6].

The matrix R is then normalized as follows to make the sum of each row equal to 1:

$$R_{ij} = \begin{cases} R_{ij} / \sum_{j'} R_{ij}' & \sum_{j'} R_{ij}' \neq 0 \\ 0 & otherwise \end{cases}$$

A cost function F can then be defined as follows:

$$F(S) = \sum_{i} \sum_{j} R_{ij} * exp(S_j - S_i)$$

This cost function is similar to the loss function defined in [4] [13]. The element $\exp(S_j - S_i)$ only contributes when its corresponding R_{ij} is not zero, which means that document i is more relevant than document j. In that case, if document i has a larger score than document j, then the value of the cost function will be small; in contrast, if document i has a smaller score than document j, then the value of the cost function will be large. Approximating $\exp(S_j - S_i)$ using the Taylor expansion, we have:

$$F(S) = \sum_i \sum_j R_{ij}(1 + S_j - S_i + \frac{1}{2}(S_j - S_i)^2)$$ (12)

Appending this cost function to the existing objective function (10) discussed in section 2.3.2 leads to a new objective function.

$$\Phi(S) = a * (r(D, S, Q) + \frac{1}{2}\sum_i S_i^2) + \frac{1}{2} * b * G(S) + c * F(S)$$ (13)

Using the decent gradient algorithm, we have

$$S_i^{t+1} = S_i^{t+1} - \frac{1}{Z_i} * \frac{\partial \Phi(S)}{\partial S_i} = \frac{a}{Z_i} * x_i + \frac{b}{Z_i} * \sum_j w_{ij} * \frac{S_j^t}{\sqrt{m_{ii}} * \sqrt{m_{jj}}}$$ (14)

$$+ \frac{c}{Z_i} * (\sum_j R_{ij}(1 + S_j^t) + \sum_j R_{ji}(S_j^t - 1))$$

$$Z_i = a + b + c * (\sum_j R_{ij} + \sum_j R_{ji})$$

where $a+b+c=1$; x_i is the same as defined in section 2, and it is also normalized. Z_i is used to control the learning rate.

Based on IOA-KL, IOA-TFIDF and the relevance feedback information, we derive two new models: IOA-KL+REL and IOA-TFIDF+REL. The new models only change the method to re-compute the document scores.

4 Experiments

In Section 2, we introduce our algorithm and two instantiations: IOA-KL in language modeling and IOA-TFIDF in vector space modeling. In Section 3, we extend our approach by integrating true relevance feedback information, and derive two further models: IOA-KL+REL and IOA-TFIDF+REL, which incorporate relative relevance feedback information into IOA-KL and IOA-TFIDF respectively. We will evaluate the effectiveness of these methods empirically in this section.

In this study, we fix the document model. Specifically, in IOA-KL, we use a Dirichlet prior (with a setting of 600) to estimate the document language models. In IOA-TFIDF, we use the TFIDF value to weight terms, The TF formula used is the one based on the BM25 retrieval formula as in [18].

4.1 Experimental Setup

We evaluate the proposed method over four TREC data sets: AP (Associated Press news 1988-90), LA (LA Times), SJMN (San Jose Mercury News 1991), and TREC8 (the ad hoc data used in TREC8). They are identical to the data sets used in [10], and are preprocessed in the same way. We used the title field of a query/topic description to simulate short keyword queries.

Because our methods need an initial retrieval document set, the Lemur toolkit[1] is used to retrieval the initial 3000 documents for each query. Our methods will be used to re-rank these documents. For IOA-KL, KL-divergence based on language model using Dirichlet smoothing strategy is selected as our initial retrieval model. For IOA-TFIDF, vector space model using BM25 TF is used as the initial retrieval model. When updating the query model, we set the upper bound of the number of terms to 20, and ignored all terms having a weight less than 0.001.

In all our experiments, the cutoff of relevant documents is set to 1000. The following two performance measures are used in our evaluation: (1) non-interpolated Mean Average Precision (MAP). (2) Precision at 10 documents (P@10).

4.2 Parameter Selection

Our methods for query model and ranking refinement contain a set of parameters: α and β in Equation 7 and 9 to balance the importance of each component; and the parameter b in Equation 11. In order to determine the values of these parameters, we use the AP collection as our training collection. We performed an exhaustive grid search to tune the three parameters on the training set, and then used the parameters on other test collections. The three parameters were swept over [0, 1] with a step size of 0.1. For IOA-KL+REL and IOA-TFIDF+REL, we will have five main parameters: { α, β a, b, c }. When searching for the optimal parameters, α, β were swept over [0, 1] with a step size of 0.1; for a,b,c, the parameter c was swept over [0,1] with a step size of 0.1; since $a+b+c=1$, we set $a = \sigma \times (1-c)$, $b = (1-\sigma) \times (1-c)$, σ was swept over [0,1] with a step of 0.1. We select the parameter values which optimize the MAP. The number of neighbors is set to 60 through the grid search method.

4.3 The Effectiveness of the Iterative Optimization Algorithm

In order to see the effect of our proposed methods, we compare these two methods with other feedback model. IOA-KL is compared with KL-Divergence minimization feedback (DIV-MIN), which is a model-based feedback method used in [18]. IOA-TFIDF is compared with Rocchio feedback method [14] based on vector space model. For DIV-MIN feedback model, we varied the two main parameters: the coefficient that controls the influence of the feedback model and the noise parameter that controls the influence of the collection model. For Rocchio feedback, the TF formula used is the one based on the BM25 retrieval formula, which is the same as the TF formula used in [18]. We vary the coefficient in Rocchio formula to tune the result to its best.

In Table 1, we can see that IOA-KL outperforms DIV-MIN FB consistently and significantly in most cases when using the top 10 documents for pseudo-feedback. The increase in map is between 6% and 10% in most cases. IOA-TFIDF can also outperform Rocchio feedback model in most cases.

---

[1] http://www.lemurproject.org/

Table 1. Basic results. Top 10 documents are selected as feedback documents. ***,**, and * mean significant improvement in paired t-test at the level of p<0.01, p<0.05 and p<0.1, respectively. For IOA-KL, the optimal values of α, β and b are 0.5, 0.8 and 0.3 respectively; for IOA-TFIDF, the optimal values of α, β and b are also the same.

Data		DIV-MIN FB	IOA-KL	Rocchio FB	IOA-TFIDF
AP88~90	MAP	0.2524	0.2763(+9.47%***)	0.2580	0.2741(+6.24%***)
	p@10	0.4525	0.4828(+6.70%**)	0.4303	0.4646 (+7.97%**)
LA	MAP	0.2505	0.2671 (+6.63%)	0.2455	0.2738(+11.53%**)
	p@10	0.2847	0.2888 (+1.44%)	0.2755	0.3061(+11.11**)
SJMN	MAP	0.2310	0.2490(+7.79%***)	0.2497	0.2486 (-0.44%)
	p@10	0.3340	0.3649 (+9.25%**)	0.3734	0.3691(-1.15%)
TREC8	MAP	0.2622	0.2782 (+6.10%*)	0.2609	0.2752 (+5.48%*)
	p@10	0.4600	0.4580(-0.43%)	0.4540	0.4580 (+0.88%)

We also compared IOA-KL with other language models: the basic KL-Divergence model with Dirchlet smoothing (KL Dir), the mixture feedback (Mix FB) model[1] ; FB+QMWG proposed in [10], a graph-based query model smoothing method combined with mixture feedback. In order to evaluate the impact of considering smoothness in word and document graphs, we remove the smoothness constraint from IOA-KL model. This simplified model is denoted by IOA-KL*.

Table 2. Performance (MAP) comparison with related methods. The result of FB+QMWG is from [10]. For the methods need feedback documents, top 5 documents are used as in [10].

	KL Dir	Mix FB	FB+QMWG	IOA-KL*	IOA-KL
AP88~90	0.217	0.266	0.273	0.260	**0.276**
LA	0.247	0.257	0.267	0.266	**0.271**
SJMN	0.204	0.241	0.246	0.241	**0.251**
TREC8	0.257	0.278	0.280	0.271	**0.281**

In Table 2, comparing IOA-KL with KL Dir, we can see that the increase in effectiveness is very large. IOA-KL can also consistently outperform other existing methods. This indicates that unifying multiple resources such as document graph, word graph can help improve the retrieval results. Comparing IOA-KL to IOA-KL*, when the smoothness criterion is removed from the loss function, the retrieval effectiveness decreases. This demonstrates the importance of graph smoothness.

4.4 Effect of Considering Relevance Feedback Information

In section 3, we derive a new optimization algorithm by appending relevance feedback information, and two new document ranking refinement methods **IOA-KL+REL** and **IOA-TFIDF+REL** are derived. We will test the performance of these two models. This experiment simulates a situation where a user accepts to provide relevance judgments for a small set of documents.

In our experiment, we provide true relevance judgments for the top 10 documents. Thus we can get relative relevance between each document pair among the top 10 documents, and encode them in the matrix R described in section 3.

To evaluate the effect of incorporating true relevance feedback information, we compare IOA-KL+REL with DIV-MIN relevance feedback (DIV-MIN+REL) model, which also uses the relevance judgments of the top 10 documents for feedback. In the same way, IOA-TFIDF+REL is compared with the Rocchio relevance feedback (Rocchio REL) model. For KL+REL and DIV-MIN REL model, we use the same initial retrieval method to obtain a document set for each query, and then provide relevance judgments for the top 10 documents. The same processing method is used by IOA-TFIDF+REL and Rocchio REL method.

Table 3. Comparing IOA-KL+Rel and IOA-TFIDF+Rel with other relevance feedback model. For IOA-KL+REL and IOA-TFIDF+REL, the optimal parameters are $\alpha =0.6$, $\beta = 0.8$, c=0.7, and a:b=7:3 respectively.

Data		DIV-MIN+REL	IOA-KL+REL	Rocchio+REL	IOA-TFIDF+REL
AP88~90	MAP	0.2672	0.3107(+16.28%***)	0.2973	0.3053(+2.69%)
	p@10	0.5010	0.5970(+19.16%***)	0.5526	0.5788(+4.74%**)
LA	MAP	0.3356	0.3873(+15.41%***)	0.3741	0.3855 (+3.05%**)
	p@10	0.3561	0.3837 (+7.75%**)	0.3714	0.3929 (+5.79%*)
SJMN	MAP	0.2768	0.3097(+11.89%***)	0.3087	0.3120(+1.07%***)
	p@10	0.4160	0.4766(+14.57%***)	0.4617	0.4743(+2.73%***)
TREC8	MAP	0.2974	0.3375(+13.48%***)	0.3170	0.3409 (+7.54%**)
	p@10	0.5400	0.6280(+16.30%***)	0.5920	0.6140(+3.72%**)

Table 3 shows that our IOA-KL+REL model can outperform DIV-MIN REL consistently and significantly on all the four datasets. The IOA-TFIDF+REL method can also outperform Rocchio REL. A possible explanation to this comparison is that, in traditional relevance feedback model, the relevance feedback information is used only to update query model, and then the updated query model is used to re-rank the documents. When re-ranking the documents, the same ranking function is used, i.e. the relevance judgments did not affect the general ranking function. However, in our model, we interpret the relevance feedback information as relative relevance of document pair. It can be used as a constraint when re-ranking the documents. Thus our method can makes thorough use of the relevance feedback information.

5   Related Work

Risk minimization [8] provides a general framework to further improve a retrieval model. Formally, it treats the task of information retrieval as a statistical decision problem. It can unify several existing retrieval models such as KL-divergence language model and vector space model. KL-Divergence minimization feedback model described in [18] can be considered as one of its instantiation. Our approach is based on risk minimization framework. However, we take the graph structure into consideration, also, our approach can contain document scores as a component, making it possible to use the document score as evidence to help update query model. This allows us to unify query model and document ranking refinement within the same framework.

Graph-based learning has attracted much attention in recent years [3, 9, 19]. Manifold ranking method is proposed in [19]. Our cost function on graph structure is similar to the objective function proposed in [19]. In information retrieval, there are also some investigations using graph structures [3, 10]. These studies focused on the following aspects, however, separately - document score regularization or query model. In contrast, our approach combines graph structure into the risk minimization framework. This makes it easy to unify the refinements of query model and ranking function. We combined both word graph and document graph in our approach, which can lead to a smoothed query model and ranking function. Through the iterative process, we can make use of the mutual influence between the query model and the document ranking in order to optimize both of them.

One of the concrete instantiations of our algorithm is proposed in section 3, which is related to some learning to rank approaches [4, 13]. [4] uses user feedback information to refine ranking. [13] utilizes document relations to obtain a ranking function. Our method also encodes user feedback into document preference relations, and combines them with other cost function to form a unified objective function. It is also related to the problem of relational object ranking. Our method takes the label smoothness on the graph into consideration. This enables user's relevance judgments to propagate in the graph. In addition, the iterative optimization process further enables the relevance information to propagate between query model and document ranking.

6   Conclusions

In this paper, we proposed a unified iterative optimization algorithm which provided a principled way to refine both the query model and the document ranking. It combines the risk minimization framework and the manifold structure of both the word graph and the document graph. The combination of these multiple criteria forms a new optimization problem. The solution to the optimization problem leads to some new methods. We derived two methods in the context of language model and vector space model respectively. Moreover, we extended the algorithm by combining user's true relevance judgments.

The approach has several potential advantages. First, this approach can lead to better query model and more appropriate document scores by our proposed unified iterative optimization algorithm. Second, the optimization of the query model and document ranking function becomes dependent by systematically incorporating the query model and document score as components within the same framework. Finally, it provides a principled formulation of the query model and ranking refinement, which can serve as a general framework for systematically exploring other methods.

The evaluated results on four test collections show that these methods are more effective than the existing ones in the literature. In our future work, we will consider the problem of parameter optimization as well as the problem of document model refinement. Moreover, we can use extend the optimization algorithm by exploring other kind of retrieval model such as dependent ranking model.

Acknowledgements

This work was supported by the National Science Foundation of China (Grants No.60736044, 60773027, 90920010), as well as 863 Hi-Tech Research and Development Program of China (Grants No. 2008AA01Z145, 2006AA010108).

References

1. Bai, J., Nie, J., Bouchard, H., Cao, G.: Using Query Contexts in Information Retrieval. In: Proceedings of SIGIR, pp. 15–22 (2007)
2. Cao, G., Nie, J., Bai, J.: Integrating word relationships into language models. In: Proceedings of SIGIR, pp. 298–305 (2005)
3. Diaz, F.: Regularizing ad hoc retrieval scores. In: CIKM, pp. 672–679 (2005)
4. Jin, R., Valizadegan, H., Li, H.: Ranking refinement and its application to information retrieval. In: Proceedings of WWW, pp. 397–406 (2008)
5. Joachims, T.: Optimizing search engines using clickthrough data. In: KDD, pp. 133–142 (2002)
6. Joachims, T., Granka, L., Pan, B., Hembrooke, H., Gay, G.: Accurately interpreting clickthrough data as implicit feedback. In: Proceedings of SIGIR, pp. 154–161 (2005)
7. Sparck Jones, K., Walker, S., Robertson, S.E.: A probabilistic model of information retrieval: development and comparative experiments—part 1and part 2. Information Processing and Management, 36(6), 779–808 (2000)
8. Lafferty, J., Zhai, C.: Document language models, query models, and risk minimization for information retrieval. In: Proceedings of SIGIR, pp. 111–119 (2001)
9. Mihalcea, R., Radev, D.R.: TextRank – bringing order into texts. In: EMNLP. pp. 404–411 (2004)
10. Mei, Q., Zhang, D., Zhai, C.: A General Optimization Framework for Smoothing Language Models on Graph Structures. In: Proceedings of SIGIR, pp. 611–618 (2008)
11. Ponte, J.M., Croft, W.B.: A language modeling approach to information retrieval. In: Proceedings of SIGIR 1998, pp. 275–281 (1998)
12. Qin, T., Liu, T.-Y., et al.: A study of relevance propagation for web search. In: Proceedings of SIGIR, pp. 408–415 (2005)
13. Qin, T., Liu, T.-Y., et al.: Learning to Rank Relational Objects and Its Application to Web Search. In: Proceedings of WWW 2008, pp. 407–416 (2008)
14. Rocchio, J.J.: Relevance feedback in information retrieval. In: The SMART Retrieval System: Experiments in Automatic Document Processing, pp. 313–323 (1971)
15. Salton, G., Buckley, C.: Term-weighting approaches in automatic text retrieval. Information Processing and Management 24, 513–523 (1988)
16. Salton, G., Buckley, C.: Improving retrieval performance by relevance feedback. Journal of the American Society for Information Science 41(4), 288–297 (1990)
17. Von Luxburg, U., Bousquet, O., Belkin, M.: On the convergence of spectral clustering on random samples: The normalized case. In: Shawe-Taylor, J., Singer, Y. (eds.) COLT 2004. LNCS (LNAI), vol. 3120, pp. 457–471. Springer, Heidelberg (2004)
18. Zhai, C., Lafferty, J.: Model-based feedback in the language modeling approach to information retrieval. In: Proceedings of ACM CIKM, pp. 403–410 (2001)
19. Zhou, D., Weston, J., Gretton, A., Bousquet, O., Scholkopf, B.: Ranking on data manifolds. In: Proceedings of NIPS, pp. 169–176 (2003)

A Study of Document Weight Smoothness in Pseudo Relevance Feedback

Peng Zhang[1], Dawei Song[1], Xiaochao Zhao[2], and Yuexian Hou[2]

[1] School of Computing, The Robert Gordon University, United Kingdom
[2] School of Computer Sci & Tec, Tianjin University, China
{p.zhang1,d.song}@rgu.ac.uk,{0.25eye,krete1941}@gmail.com

Abstract. In pseudo relevance feedback (PRF), the document weight which indicates how important a document is for the PRF model, plays a key role. In this paper, we investigate the smoothness issue of the document weights in PRF. The term *smoothness* means that the document weights decrease smoothly (i.e. gradually) along the document ranking list, and the weights are smooth (i.e. similar) within topically similar documents. We postulate that a reasonably smooth document-weighting function can benefit the PRF performance. This hypothesis is tested under a typical PRF model, namely the Relevance Model (RM). We propose a two-step document weight smoothing method, the different instantiations of which have different effects on weight smoothing. Experiments on three TREC collections show that the instantiated methods with better smoothing effects generally lead to better PRF performance. In addition, the proposed method can significantly improve the RM's performance and outperform various alternative methods which can also be used to smooth the document weights.

Keywords: Pseudo relevance feedback, Document weight smoothness, Query language model, Relevance Model.

1 Introduction

Pseudo relevance feedback (PRF) assumes that the top n (e.g., 30) documents in the first-round retrieval are all relevant to the query. Due to its automatic manner and effective performance, PRF has been widely applied in information retrieval (IR), where the PRF (i.e., top n) documents are often used to derive a new query model that expands the original query [5,8]. The document weight, which represents the weight of a PRF document in the query expansion (QE) model, is a key factor for the QE performance [8].

In this paper, we investigate the smoothness issue of document weights in QE. The term *smoothness* in this paper does not refer to the smoothness of document language models [11,14,9]. Instead, it is with respect to the PRF document weights used in QE and means that, firstly, the document weights decrease smoothly (i.e. gradually or slowly) from the top-ranked document to the subsequent ones along the rank list, and secondly, the document weights are smooth within the topically similar documents, i.e., the topically similar documents should have similar weights. We postulate that a reasonably smooth document weighting function

P.-J. Cheng et al. (Eds.): AIRS 2010, LNCS 6458, pp. 527–538, 2010.

(weighting function for short) can benefit the QE performance. First, it can reduce the risk when some topmost-ranked documents with very high weights are not truly relevant. Second, considering the inter-document similarity can make smoother the conventional weighting functions which often take into account the query-document similarity only.

We test the above hypothesis under the Relevance Model (RM) [5], which is a typical language model based QE approach [8]. In RM, effectively the document weight consists of two components: the document relevance score and the document prior. The former represents the initial document relevance probability, while the latter is the prior probability of selecting the corresponding document to estimate the RM. In implementation (e.g. in the RM1 [5]), the document prior is set to be uniform, and the document relevance score is the query-likelihood (QL) [11,14,8]. Empirical evidence (see Section 2) shows that the QL scores decrease rapidly along the topmost-ranked $k(k < n)$ documents, where the truly relevant ones, however, are often quite randomly distributed. Moreover, the QL scoring function only considers the query-document similarity but ignores the inter-document similarity.

In the literature, various methods have been proposed to smooth the document relevance score or revise the document prior, thereby adjusting the document weights. Based on the clustering hypothesis [12], the score regulation method [2,3,4] forces the topically related documents to have similar relevance scores. In a similar manner, the graph-based smoothing framework proposed in [9] can also smooth the document relevance scores. To the best of our knowledge, neither of the above methods has been used to smooth the relevance scores for query expansion. Moreover, they do not explicitly consider the score smoothness along the document rank list. As for revising the document prior, the rank-related prior was proposed in [6] by utilizing the document rank and document length. This method, however, does not consider the inter-document similarity.

In this paper, we propose a two-step document weight smoothing method to obtain smoother weighting functions. The first step is to smooth the weights of the topmost documents in order to prevent the document weights from dropping sharply along the rank list. The second step aims to further smooth the document weights of all the PRF documents, by considering the inter-document similarity. Specifically, we allocate the weights of topmost-ranked documents to the lower-ranked documents which are statistically similar to the topmost ones. In this step, different weight allocation strategies as well as different similarity measures are considered and analyzed in terms of their effects on document weight smoothness, thus instantiating several smoothing methods each with different smoothing effect. Experiments on three TREC collections show that the methods with better smoothing effects generally give better QE performance. In addition, the proposed smoothing method can significantly improve the performance of the RM, and outperform three comparative methods, i.e., the score regulation approach [2,3], the graph-based smoothing approach [9] and the rank-related prior approach [6], for revising the document weights in the RM.

2 Document Weight and Its Smoothness

In this section, we start with a description of the Relevance Model (RM) and a re-formulation of the model for explicitly applying revised (e.g. smoothed) weighting functions in it. We then provide empirical evidence, showing that the query-likehood scores (as RM's document weights) are not reasonably smooth along the rank list.

2.1 The Relevance Model (RM)

For each given query $q = (q_1, q_2, \cdots, q_m)$, based on the corresponding PRF document set M ($|M| = n$), the Relevance Model (RM) [5] estimates an expanded query model:

$$p(w|\theta_R) = \sum_{d \in M} p(w|\theta_d) \frac{p(q|\theta_d)p(\theta_d)}{\sum_{d' \in M} p(q|\theta_{d'})p(\theta_{d'})} \qquad (1)$$

where $p(w|\theta_R)$ is the estimated relevance model[1]. A number of terms with top probabilities in $p(w|\theta_R)$ will be used to estimate the query expansion (QE) model (i.e. the expanded query model). In Equation 1, $p(w|\theta_d)$ is the probability of a term w in the language model θ_d for a document d, $p(\theta_d)$ is d's prior probability, and $p(q|\theta_d)$ is the query likelihood (QL) [11,14]:

$$p(q|\theta_d) = \prod_{i=1}^{m} p(q_i|\theta_d) \qquad (2)$$

In RM, the weighting function is:

$$f(d, q) = \frac{p(q|\theta_d)p(\theta_d)}{\sum_{d' \in M} p(q|\theta_{d'})p(\theta_{d'})} \qquad (3)$$

where the QL relevance score $p(q|\theta_d)$ and document prior $p(\theta_d)$ are integrated to form the document weight. The $f(d, q)$ plays a key role in RM since it distinguishes the RM from a mixture of document language model (say $\sum_{d \in M} p(w|\theta_d)$).

To apply revised weighting functions under the RM framework, we re-formulate the RM as:

$$p(w|\tilde{\theta}_R) = \sum_{d \in M} p(w|\theta_d)\tilde{f}(d, q) \qquad (4)$$

where $\tilde{f}(d, q)$ denotes any revised document-weighting function that satisfies $\sum_{d \in M} \tilde{f}(d, q) = 1$, and different $\tilde{f}(d, q)$ will derive different QE models.

2.2 Smoothness of QL as the Document Weight

In the RM [5,8], since the document prior $p(\theta_d)$ is assumed to be uniform, it turns out that the weighting function is the normalized query likelihood (QL):

$$f(d, q) = f_{QL}(d, q) = \frac{p(q|\theta_d)}{\sum_{d' \in M} p(q|\theta_{d'})} \qquad (5)$$

---

[1] This formulation is equivalent to RM1 in [5], but some notations are slightly different. We adopt the similar notations used in the recent work [8,2] related to RM.

Table 1. Topmost 4 documents' QL weights (f_{QL}) and relevance judgements (r)

query id	$f_{QL}(d_1)/r$	$f_{QL}(d_2)/r$	$f_{QL}(d_3)/r$	$f_{QL}(d_4)/r$
#151	0.206/0	0.167/1	0.106/1	0.064/0
#152	0.153/0	0.097/1	0.085/0	0.075/1
#153	0.232/0	0.185/1	0.103/1	0.090/1

Table 2. Topmost 4 documents' mean QL weights (Mf_{QL}) and mean relevance judgements (Mr)

Data	Queries	$Mf_{QL}(d_1)/Mr$	$Mf_{QL}(d_2)/Mr$	$Mf_{QL}(d_3)/Mr$	$Mf_{QL}(d_4)/Mr$
WSJ8792	151-200	0.256/0.600	0.123/0.580	0.084/0.560	0.063/0.440
AP8889	151-200	0.235/0.580	0.104/0.560	0.075/0.560	0.057/0.480
ROBUST2004	601-700	0.252/0.650	0.125/0.490	0.085/0.500	0.063/0.480

The normalized QL scores are called as QL weights in this paper. From Equation 5, it turns out that the QL weights do not take into account the inter-document similarity. Therefore, we just present the empirical evidence showing that the QL weights are not reasonably smooth along the PRF rank list. We start with a small example on one TREC collection, and then present more statistical data on three TREC collections. In both cases, for each query, the top $n = 30$ documents are selected for the PRF documents. Note that the following data correspond to the topmost $k(k < n)$ documents. Therefore, the sum of QL weights of these topmost documents for each query will not necessary be 1.

The data in Table 1 are from the WSJ8792 collection and three queries. For each query, the QL weights of the topmost $k = 4$ documents are listed. As shown in Table 1, the QL weights decrease rapidly along the rank list, e.g., for all three queries, the weights of d_1 are about twice the d_3's weights and three times the d_4's weights. All the d_1s, however, are non-relevant.

Next, we provide more statistical data about the topmost 4 documents, denoted as d_i ($1 \leq i \leq 4$) for different sets of queries from three TREC collections. First, we define two statistics:

$$Mf_{QL}(d_i) = \frac{1}{|Q|} \sum_{q \in Q} f_{QL}(d_i, q) \quad and \quad Mr(d_i) = \frac{1}{|Q|} \sum_{q \in Q} r(d_i, q) \qquad (6)$$

where Q denotes the set of all involved queries, $|Q|$ is the number of queries, and $r(d_i, q) = 1$ if d_i is truly relevant to q, and 0 otherwise. The $Mf_{QL}(d_i)$ computes the d_i's mean QL weight, and the $Mr(d_i)$ denotes d_i's mean relevance judgement. The values of these two statistics are summarized in Table 2, which shows that the mean QL weights drop rapidly along the topmost 4 documents. The truly relevant documents, however, are rather randomly distributed, since the mean relevance judgements decrease quite slowly. This indicates that the QL weights are not reasonably smooth on these collections and queries.

3   Two-Step Weight Smoothing

Now, we propose a two-step weight smoothing method, in which the first step is to smooth the sharply dropping weights within the topmost-ranked documents, and the second step is to allocate the weights in the topmost-ranked documents to the lower-ranked documents, based on the similarity between these two parts.

3.1   Smoothing Topmost Weights

Recall that in Section 2.2, we presented the initial evidence that document weights drop rapidly along the topmost-ranked $k(k < n)$ documents. To solve this problem, our basic idea is to smooth every adjacently-ranked document pair subsequently, along the rank list. Specifically, given the topmost document list $d_1 d_2 \cdots d_k$, set $\tilde{f}(d_1, q) = f(d_1, q)$, and then from the document index $i = 1$ to $k-1$, smooth $\tilde{f}(d_i, q)$ and $f(d_{i+1}, q)$ as follows:

$$\tilde{f}(d_i, q) \leftarrow \tilde{f}(d_{i+1}, q) \leftarrow avg(\tilde{f}(d_i, q), f(d_{i+1}, q)) \tag{7}$$

The average operation (i.e. avg) can reduce the difference between d_i's weight and d_{i+1}'s weight subsequently. For example, consider the document weights of the query 151 in Table 1. The strategy is to first change $\tilde{f}(d_1, q)$ (0.2060) and $f(d_2, q)$ (0.1670) to their average weight 0.1865, then set the $\tilde{f}(d_2, q)$ (0.1865) and $f(d_3, q)$ (0.1060) to the average weight 0.1462, finally revise the $\tilde{f}(d_3, q)$ (0.1462) and $f(d_3, q)$ (0.0640) as the average weight 0.1051. The revised weights for these four documents are 0.1865, 0.1462, 0.1051 and 0.1051, which are smoother than the original weights, in the sense that the d_1's weight has been reduced, while the weights of d_2 and d_3 have been relatively improved.

The above strategy can retain the weight sum of topmost k documents, making the weight sum of all PRF documents to be always 1. Actually, we also considered smoothing the original weighting function by interpolating it with a uniform weighting function which assigns the same weight for every document. However, one more parameter (i.e., the interpolation coefficient) was required to control the smoothing, and according to our prior study the experimental results were not so good.

3.2   Improving Lower Weights

In this step, we aim to allocate the weights of topmost-ranked $k(k<n)$ documents to the lower-ranked documents, according to the similarity between these two parts of documents. This is not only to further smooth the document weights, but also to improve the ranks[2] of those documents which are truly relevant but have lower weights. Recall that usually the topmost-ranked documents (e.g, the first 5 documents) are more likely to be truly relevant, since the corresponding retrieval precision (e.g., P@5) is often relatively higher compared with the average precision of all the PRF documents. According to the clustering hypothesis [12], the weight allocation methods, in which the allocation is actually based on the similarity value with respect to the topmost-ranked documents, could

---

[2] Here, we assume that the higher rank corresponds to the higher weight.

boost the weights of the truly relevant documents which may have lower initial weights. In the following, we present two weight allocation methods (WAs) with different smoothing effects. Note that in the formulation of WAs, $\tilde{f}(d, q)$ is the weighing function obtained from the previous step (see Section 3.1).

Linear Weight Allocation (LWA). To see the basic idea, let us consider one topmost-ranked document d_t, and a lower-ranked document d_l. Our basic idea is to keep d_t's weight unchanged, and meanwhile improve d_l's weight based on the similarity between d_t and d_l, which is measured by $sim(d_l, d_t)^3$. Specifically, LWA lets d_l have $(1 - sim(d_l, d_t))$ proportion of its own weight and $sim(d_l, d_t)$ proportion of d_t's weight, and the allocation can be formulated as:

$$\tilde{f}_{LWA}(d_l, q) = (1 - sim(d_l, d_t))\tilde{f}(d_l, q) + sim(d_l, d_t)\tilde{f}(d_t, q) \tag{8}$$

where $\tilde{f}_{LWA}(d_l, q)$ is the LWA weight for the d_l. For the d_t, LWA retains its own weight, meaning that $\tilde{f}_{LWA}(d_t, q) = \tilde{f}(d_t, q)$. Therefore, the Equation 8 can also represent the LWA weight of d_t due to the fact that $sim(d_t, d_t) = 1$.

Next, if considering all the k topmost documents, for any PRF document d, we have

$$\tilde{f}_{LWA}(d, q) = \frac{1}{Z} \times \sum_{d_t \in M_t} (1 - sim(d, d_t))\tilde{f}(d, q) + sim(d, d_t)\tilde{f}(d_t, q) \tag{9}$$

where $\tilde{f}_{LWA}(d, q)$ denotes the LWA weighting function, Z is the normalization factor, and the M_t is the set of the topmost k documents.

Nonlinear Weight Allocation (NLWA). In addition to LWA, we propose a nonlinear version of weight allocation, called NLWA, which has the same basic idea as LWA. The difference between NLWA and LWA is the specific allocation strategy. For a topmost document d_t and a lower one d_l, the NLWA weights are formulated as:

$$\tilde{f}_{NLWA}(d, q) = \sqrt{\tilde{f}(d, q)}\sqrt{\tilde{f}(d_t, q)}sim(d, d_t) \tag{10}$$

where d can be d_t or d_l. In a similar manner as for the LWA, if considering all the topmost documents, for any PRF document d, the NLWA weighting function is:

$$\tilde{f}_{NLWA}(d, q) = \frac{1}{Z} \times \sum_{d_t \in M_t} \sqrt{\tilde{f}(d, q)}\sqrt{\tilde{f}(d_t, q)}sim(d, d_t) \tag{11}$$

Analyzing WAs' Effects on Smoothing. Generally, the LWA weights are smoother than the NLWA weights. For simplicity, our analysis on WAs' smoothing effects is only based on any two documents d_t and d_l, where d_t is ranked higher than d_l. Let $s = sim(d_t, d_l)$, $\tilde{f}(l) = \tilde{f}(d_l, q)$ and $\tilde{f}(t) = \tilde{f}(d_t, q)$, where $0 < \tilde{f}(l) < \tilde{f}(t)$. According to Equation 8, we have $\tilde{f}_{LWA}(l) = (1 - s)\tilde{f}(l) + s\tilde{f}(t)$, and from the Equation 10, we can obtain $\tilde{f}_{NLWA}(l) = s\sqrt{\tilde{f}(l)\tilde{f}(t)}$. Then, the quotient of d_l's LWA weight and d_l's NLWA weight is:

$$\frac{\tilde{f}_{LWA}(l)}{\tilde{f}_{NLWA}(l)} = \frac{1 - s}{s}\sqrt{\frac{\tilde{f}(l)}{\tilde{f}(t)}} + \sqrt{\frac{\tilde{f}(t)}{\tilde{f}(l)}} \tag{12}$$

---

[3] Generally, sim can be any similarity metric with values on $[0, 1]$.

Since $\frac{1-s}{s}\sqrt{\frac{\tilde{f}(l)}{\tilde{f}(t)}} > 0$ and $\sqrt{\frac{\tilde{f}(t)}{\tilde{f}(l)}} > 1$, we can get:

$$\frac{\tilde{f}_{LWA}(l)}{\tilde{f}_{NLWA}(l)} > 1 \qquad (13)$$

It turns out that d_l's LWA weight is larger than its NLWA weight. Since d_t's weight is unchanged in both LWA and NLWA, we can conclude that LWA makes the weight difference between d_t and d_l smaller than NLWA.

Similarity Measurements with Different Smoothing Effects. The similarity metric that we adopt is the Cosine similarity between the $tf \times idf$ vectors of two documents. Here, we set two specific options for the Cosine similarity: the first option (S1) is the similarity based on the document vectors with all the terms, while the second option (S2) is the similarity based on the document vectors with query terms removed. Since query terms often have high term frequency in the PRF documents, the similarity values in S1 are generally larger than those in S2. If similarity values are larger, the lower-ranked documents can have more weights allocated by the WAs. Therefore, the S1 can lead to smoother document weights than the S2.

Overall Smoothing Effect Analysis. Since different similarity measurement options have different smoothing effects, it is necessary to investigate different combinations of the weight allocation method (LWA or NLWA) and the similarity measurement option (S1 or S2) for the PRF. Accordingly, we denote the four resulting methods as LWA_S1, LWA_S2, NLWA_S1 and NLWA_S2. With the same similarity option, LWAs' weights are generally more smooth than NLWAs' weights. On the other hand, the similarity option S1 can give smoother weighting function than the S2 if we use the same weight allocation (WA) method.

4   Experiment Evaluation

4.1   Evaluation Configuration

Collections. The evaluation involves topics 151-200 on WSJ87-92 (173,252 documents) and AP88-89 (164,597 documents) in TREC disks 1 and 2, as well as topics 601-700 on ROBUST 2004 (528,155 documents) in TREC disks 4 and 5. The *title* filed of the topics are used as queries. The documents involved are related to a variety of texts, e.g., newswire and journal articles. Lemur toolkit 4.7 [10] is used for indexing and retrieval. All collections are stemmed using the Porter stemmer and a standard stop words list is removed during the indexing.

Evaluation Set-Up. The first-round retrieval is carried out by a standard language model (LM), i.e., the query-likelihood (QL) model [14,11]. LM is set as one of the baseline methods. The smoothing method for the document language model is the Dirichlet prior [14] with the fixed value 700. After the first-round retrieval, the top n ranked documents are selected as the pseudo relevance feedback (PRF) documents. Due to the limited space, only the results with respect to $n = 30$ PRF documents will be reported. Nevertheless, we have similar observations on other n (e.g., 50, 70, 90). Relevance Model (RM) in Equation 1, is selected as the second baseline method, where the document prior is set as uniform. For all the involved query expansion (QE) models, The top 100 terms are selected for the QE terms.

Evaluation Procedure. The aim is to test the query expansion performance of different weighting functions. Recall that different weighting functions in Equation 4 have different QE models. First, we evaluate the first-step of the proposed weight smoothing method, i.e., the smoothing topmost weights (STW) described in Section 3.1. Next, we compare different combinations of the weight allocation method (LWA or NLWA) and the similarity option (with query (S1) or without query (S1)).

We then compare the proposed approach with other three methods which can be used to adjust the document weights. They are: the score regulation (SR) approach [2,3,4], the graph-based smoothing framework [9], and the rank-related priors (RRP) [6]. The score regulation method is formulated as:

$$f^* = (I_n - \alpha D^{-1/2} W D^{-1/2})^{-1} y \tag{14}$$

where f^* is the optimal relevance score and y is the original relevance score (i.e., QL score). We use the normalized f^* (i.e., the sum is 1) as the weighting function for Equation 4. Under the smoothing framework [9], the DSDG method (i.e., smoothing relevance score with document graph) is formulated as:

$$s(q, d_u) = (1 - \lambda)\tilde{s}(q, d_u) + \lambda \sum_{v \in V} \frac{w(u, v)}{Deg(u)} s(q, d_v) \tag{15}$$

where $s(q, d_u)$ is the smoothed score for document d_u and $\tilde{s}(q, d_u)$ is d_u's original score. We use the normalized s as the corresponding weighting function for Equation 4. The rank-related priors [6] can be formulated as:

$$p(\theta_d) = \frac{1}{Z} \times \frac{\alpha + |d|}{\beta + Rank(d)} \tag{16}$$

where $|d|$ is the d's document length and $Rank(d)$ is d's rank. This prior $p(\theta_d)$ and the QL scores are integrated as the document weights in Equation 3.

Parameter Configuration. For the proposed smoothing methods (i.e., STW and WAs), we tested different k in [2, 10] with the increment 1. For the SR, we tuned three parameters: the α in [0.1, 0.9] with the increment 0.1, the t^{-1} in [0.1, 0.9] with the step 0.1, and the number of nearest neighbor kNN in [5, 10] with the step 1. For the DSDG, we tuned two parameters: the λ in [0.1, 0.9] with the increment 0.1 and the nearest neighbor kNN in [5, 10] with the step 1. The iteration number is fixed to 3. Basically, the above parameter settings for both SR and DSDG are consistent with those in the original papers [2,9]. The values of kNN are smaller than values in [2,9], since we focus on the PRF task. As for the RRP, the α is set as 140 and the β is set as 50, where both values are the optimal values reported in [6].

Evaluation Metrics. The Mean Average Precision (MAP), which reflects the overall ranking performance, is adopted as the primary evaluation metric. The

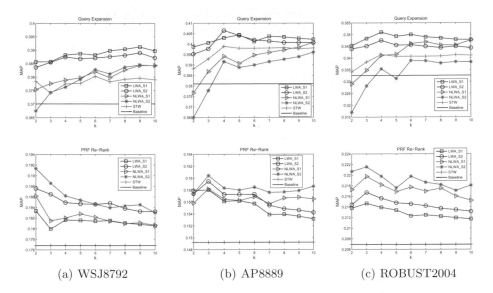

(a) WSJ8792   (b) AP8889   (c) ROBUST2004

Fig. 1. The query expansion and re-ranking performance of different weight smoothing methods on three TREC collections. The baseline for the query expansion is the RM, while the baseline for the re-ranking is the PRF document rank by the LM. Note that only PRF documents are involved in the re-ranking performance evaluation.

Wilcoxon signed rank test is the measure of the statistical significance of the improvement over baseline methods. For the original and the expanded query models, 1000 documents retrieved by the KL-divergence language model [10] are used for the performance evaluation.

4.2 Evaluation on Smoothing Topmost Weights

The aim is to test the performance of the smoothing topmost weights (STW) method described in Section 3.1. The results are reported in Figure 1, from which we can come up with the following observations. Firstly, the STW's performance increases before the k reaches a value ($k = 6$ on WSJ8792 and $k = 4$ on other collections), and then performance stabilizes. Secondly, for every k, STW outperforms the baseline (RM) on every collection. The best performance of STW is reported in Table 3, from which we can observe that STW outperforms RM by about 2.8%, 4.7%, and 2.7% on three collections, respectively.

4.3 Evaluation on Weight Allocation Methods

This set of experiments evaluates different combinations of the weight allocation method (LWA or NLWA) and the similarity measurement (S1 or S2) (see Section 3.2). The QE results of the four methods are summarized in Figure 1.

Generally, the results show that the smoother weighing functions generally give better results. Firstly, for every k, LWAs outperform the STW. This supports the effectiveness of the second step of the proposed smoothing framework. Secondly, in most cases, the LWA_S1, the most smooth method, gives the best performance, and LWAs generally outperform the NLWAs. Thirdly, each WA method with the S1 performs better than the WA with the S2. Specifically, the LWA_S1 outperforms the LWA_S2, and the NLWA_S1 outperforms the NLWA_S2. Finally, as for the parameter sensitivity of WAs , we can observe that NLWAs are more sensitive to different k values than LWAs.

Interesting observations can be made after we evaluate the re-ranking performance of the different WAs. The re-ranking performance is reported in the Figure 1, from which we can observe that all WAs outperform the baseline. This empirically demonstrates that WAs can improve the ranks of the truly relevant documents with lower initial weights (see the analysis in Section 3.2). In addition, we can see that the least smooth method (i.e. NLWA_S2) gives the best re-ranking performance. Moreover, the LWA_S2 performs much better than the LWA_S1, although the LWA_S1 is a smoother method. This indicates that the improved QE performance might be more due to the better smoothness of document weights than due to a better PRF rank list, which in turn emphasises the importance of the smoothness of document weights for the QE.

4.4   Comparison with Other Weight Smoothing Methods

Now, we compare the performance of LWA (i.e., LWA_S1) with those of other document weight revision methods, i.e., the score regulation (SR) [2,3], the DSDG method [9] and the rank-related priors (RRP) [6]. The formulation and parameters configuration of SR, DSDG and PPR are described in Section 4.1. We report the best performance of the above three methods in Table 3.

Both SR and DSDG can outperform the RM, but not significantly on some collections. On the other hand, the LWA outperforms SR and DSDG, and improves the RM significantly on all three collections. It is probably because neither SR nor DSDG considers the document weight smoothness along the rank list. The main aim of SR and DSDG is to re-rank the documents. However, as discussed in the previous experiments (see Figure 1), a better PRF rank list may not guarantee a better QE performance.

For the RRP, we found that its performance (using $\alpha = 140$ and $\beta = 50$) is not so good. We think that this approach can help the RM become robust if a large number (e.g., 500) of PRF documents are involved, since it effectively depress the weights of lower-ranked documents. However, if the number of PRF documents is relatively small (e.g., 30), we can observe that it can make the document weights less smoother, and hence possibly hurt QE retrieval performance.

4.5   Discussion

In the above experiments, we did not interpolate the expanded query model with the original query model, since we wanted to focus on the document weight smoothness issue. As observed from our experiments and also in [7], the QE performance is very sensitive to interpolation coefficient α. Actually, using a

Table 3. Overall query expansion results of different weight smoothing methods

MAP% (chg% over LM)	WSJ8792	AP8889	ROBUST2004
LM	31.25	30.43	29.15
RM	37.01 (+18.4$^\alpha$)	38.10 (+25.2$^\alpha$)	33.26 (+14.1$^\alpha$)
RRP	36.76 (+17.6$^\alpha$)	37.54 (+23.4$^\alpha$)	31.56 (+8.2$^\alpha$)
SR	38.51 (+23.2$^{\alpha\beta}$)	38.70 (+27.1$^\alpha$)	34.29 (+17.6$^\alpha$)
DSDG	38.26(+22.4$^\alpha$)	39.44(+29.6$^{\alpha\beta}$)	34.37(+17.9$^\alpha$)
STW	38.03 (+21.7$^\alpha$)	39.89 (+31.0$^{\alpha\beta}$)	34.15(+17.1$^\alpha$)
LWA	39.12 (+25.2$^{\alpha\beta}$)	40.44 (+32.9$^{\alpha\beta}$)	35.10 (+20.4$^{\alpha\beta}$)

Statistically significant improvements over LM and RM are marked with "α" and "β", respectively. Note that here LWA is actually the LWA_S1.

well-tuned α for the RM3[4], the proposed weight smoothing method LWA can improve the RM3 by 4%-5% on the three TREC collections. However, the smoother weight smoothing methods (e.g., LWA) can not always have better QE performance. This also raises an important research question: how to define and control the weight smoothness degree for different queries? It is reasonable that different queries may need different degrees of the document weight smoothness for an optimal QE performance.

On the other hand, the score regulation method [2,3] and the DSDG method under the graph-based smoothing framework [9] both target at re-ranking the documents. Recently, the portfolio theory has been adopted in [13] to derive an optimal document rank, by considering the document dependency into the probability ranking principle (PRP). However, for the query expansion task, as we have stressed before, a better PRF rank list may not guarantee a better QE performance. Therefore, how to further smooth the document weight after a good document rank has been obtained by a re-ranking method, becomes an important problem. We will investigate this issue in-depth in the future.

5   Conclusions and Future Work

We have proposed to study the document weight smoothness issue in query expansion (QE) based on PRF documents. We have also proposed a two-step document weight smoothing method, in which the first step is to smooth the sharply dropping weights along a small number of topmost-ranked documents, and the second step is to allocate the weights of the topmost-ranked documents to the lower-ranked ones, based on the inter-document similarity. Under the framework of the Relevance Model (RM), different document-weighting functions have been tested. The experiments on three TREC collections show that the smoother weighting functions derived by the proposed method have better QE performance. The proposed method, in particular the LWA, can significantly

---

[4] The expanded query model by the RM1 can be interpolated by a original query model and then derive the RM3 [1].

improve the RM's performance. Compared with other methods that can be used to revise the document weights, LWA also gives a better QE performance. We also would like to mention that LWA's good performance is because that it has better effect on weight smoothing than NLWA, although its re-ranking performance is not better than that of NLWA (see Figure 1). This also suggests the importance of the smoothness of document weights for the QE.

In the future, we will investigate how to adapt the smoothness degrees of document weights to individual queries, in order to obtain an optimal QE performance. We are also planning to derive methods to further smooth the document weights after a good document rank has been obtained by re-ranking methods. Furthermore, we will study the connection between the smoothness of document weights and the smoothness of document language models. Our goal is to build a formal and effective method for smoothing document weights not only under the RM framework but also for other QE models [8], to improve their performance.

Acknowledgments. We would like to thank Jun Wang, Leszek Kaliciak and anonymous reviewers for their constructive comments. This work is supported in part by the UK's EPSRC grant (No.: EP/F014708/2).

References

1. Abdul-Jaleel, N., Allan, J., Croft, W.B., Diaz, F., Larkey, L., Li, X., Metzler, D., Smucker, M.D., Strohman, T., Turtle, H., Wade, C.: Umass at TREC 2004: Novelty and hard. In: TREC 2004 (2004)
2. Diaz, F.: Regularizing ad hoc retrieval scores. In: CIKM. pp. 672–679 (2005)
3. Diaz, F.: Regularizing query-based retrieval scores. Inf. Retr. 10(6), 531–562 (2007)
4. Diaz, F.: Improving relevance feedback in language modeling with score regularization. In: SIGIR, pp. 807–808 (2008)
5. Lavrenko, V., Croft, W.B.: Relevance-based language models. In: SIGIR, pp. 120–127 (2001)
6. Li, X.: A new robust relevance model in the language model framework. Inf. Process. Manage. 44(3), 991–1007 (2008)
7. Lv, Y., Zhai, C.: Adaptive relevance feedback in information retrieval. In: CIKM, pp. 255–264 (2009)
8. Lv, Y., Zhai, C.: A comparative study of methods for estimating query language models with pseudo feedback. In: CIKM, pp. 1895–1898 (2009)
9. Mei, Q., Zhang, D., Zhai, C.: A general optimization framework for smoothing language models on graph structures. In: SIGIR, pp. 611–618 (2008)
10. Ogilvie, P., Callan, J.: Experiments using the lemur toolkit. In: TREC-10, pp. 103–108 (2002)
11. Ponte, J.M., Croft, W.B.: A language modeling approach to information retrieval. In: SIGIR, pp. 275–281 (1998)
12. Tombros, A., van Rijsbergen, C.J.: Query-sensitive similarity measures for information retrieval. Knowl. Inf. Syst. 6(5) (2004)
13. Wang, J., Zhu, J.: Portfolio theory of information retrieval. In: SIGIR, pp. 115–122 (2009)
14. Zhai, C., Lafferty, J.D.: A study of smoothing methods for language models applied to ad hoc information retrieval. In: SIGIR, pp. 334–342 (2001)

Modeling Variable Dependencies between Characters in Chinese Information Retrieval

Lixin Shi and Jian-Yun Nie

DIRO, University of Montreal
CP. 6128, succursale Centre-ville, Montreal, H3C 3J7 Quebec, Canada
{shilixin,nie}@iro.umontral.ca

Abstract. Chinese IR can work on words and/or character n-grams. In previous studies, when several types of index are used, independence is usually assumed between them, which obviously is not true in reality. In this paper, we propose a model for Chinese IR that integrates different types of dependency between Chinese characters. The role of a pair of dependent characters in the matching process is variable, depending on the pair's ability to describe the underlying meaning and to retrieve relevant documents. The weight of the pair is learnt using SVM. Our experiments on TREC and NTCIR Chinese collections show that our model can significantly outperform most existing approaches. The results confirm the necessity to integrate dependent pairs of characters in Chinese IR and to use them according to their possible contribution to IR.

Keywords: Term dependency, Dependency weight, Dependency language model, Discriminative model, Chinese IR.

1 Introduction

A crucial problem in Chinese Information Retrieval (IR) is to determine the appropriate elements to serve as index. Two general families of approaches have been proposed in the literature: using characters (mainly character unigrams and bigrams) and using words. It has been found in several studies that it is beneficial to combine different types of index [5, 6, 11]. Indeed, while a word can represent precisely a meaning, the meaning can also be expressed by other words and characters. In Chinese, related words often share some characters. Therefore, character unigrams and bigrams can be used as a means to perform partial matching between them.

However, the previous approaches usually assumed that different types of index are independent. Typically, each type of index is considered as forming a distinct representation space from other types. The typical approach to Chinese IR determines a matching score according to each type of representation, and the final score is an interpolation of these scores. It is obvious that the assumption of independence between different indexes does not hold in reality. For example, the word or bigram 植树 (tree planting, forestation) is strongly dependent on the characters 植 (planting) and 树 (tree). Some studies have tried to deal with the relationships between different indexes. For example, Shi et al. [13] considers that longer and shorter words, as well as the constituent characters, are strongly

P.-J. Cheng et al. (Eds.): AIRS 2010, LNCS 6458, pp. 539–551, 2010.
© Springer-Verlag Berlin Heidelberg 2010

dependent due to their overlapping. However, the relationship between them is simply determined by the scale of the overlap, which does not necessarily reflect the true strength of relationship. In general IR, several models have also been proposed to capture dependencies between terms [4, 8, 9]. Usually, a dependence model is defined in addition to the traditional bag-of-words or word unigram model. Each of these models is assigned a fixed weight in the final combination. However, in reality, term dependencies do not have equal importance in IR. Some dependencies (or word groups) are mandatory to consider because the constituent words without their dependency could mean different things (e.g. "hot dog") and they would retrieve off-topic documents; while some other dependencies are moderately useful (e.g. "text printing") because the constituent words separately can represent the same meaning equally well and they can retrieve a similar set of documents.

The necessity to consider dependencies in Chinese IR is even higher. Indeed, a Chinese sentence is basically constructed from characters, which act as words or part of words. Characters can be strongly dependent. The dependencies between characters can be more or less useful for IR, depending on whether the meaning can be expressed by separate characters. If the meaning can be expressed well by separate characters, then the need to consider the dependency between the characters is low. This is the case for 房屋 (house). Indeed, the characters 房 and 屋 alone can also express the same meaning. The dependency between them does not provide much additional information to IR. On the other hand, in an expression such as 京九铁路 (Beijing-Kowloon Railroad), it is important to capture the dependency between 京 (Beijing, capital) and 九 (nine) because these characters are very ambiguous and they would not mean Beijing-Kowloon when considered separately. The dependency between them in this expression helps determine a specific meaning and retrieve documents on a specific topic. Therefore, this dependency is important to capture.

The above examples illustrate the variable necessity to take into account the dependency between a pair of Chinese characters according to how strong the dependency is and how useful it is for IR. In the first example, even if there is some dependency between 房 and 屋, the dependency should play a limited role. On the other hand, the dependency between 京 and 九 in the second example should be assigned a much higher importance. This aspect has not been considered in the previous IR models. In this paper, we will define a model capable of coping with this problem. We will consider characters as forming the basic index for Chinese IR. Then dependencies between pairs of characters are incorporated with variable weights depending on the usefulness of considering the dependency. Several types of dependency will be considered: dependency between adjacent characters and dependency between co-occurring characters at different distances. For example, the characters in the word 铁路 (railway) form a dependency between adjacent characters. Co-occurring characters within a sentence at some distance such as 世 (world, age, era) and 贸 (trade) in 世界贸易 (world trade) is also important to capture. In particular, this helps account for the many abbreviations often used in Chinese, which are usually formed by co-occurring, non-adjacent, characters.

In this paper, we use SVM to determine the appropriate weight of a pair of characters according to a set of features. The experiments on several TREC and NTCIR collections show that our model can significantly outperform the previous independent models and dependency models using fixed weights for types of index.

The remaining of the paper is organized as follows. In the next section, we review some related studies on Chinese IR and term dependency models. Then, we will describe our character-based dependency model and our parameter learning method. In Section 4, we present the experiments on TREC and NTCIR collections, and finally conclude our work in Section 5.

2 Related Work

A number of studies have investigated the effectiveness of Chinese IR using either or both characters and words. It is found that approaches using either characters (bigrams) or words can lead to comparable retrieval effectiveness [6, 11, 12]. In [14], it is further found that the retrieval effectiveness using a character-based language model is highly competitive to, and on several collections, is even higher than that using words and bigrams. This result motivates our use of characters as our basic index units in this study.

Within the language modeling framework, given a vocabulary V, the score of a document D to a query Q can be determined according to the following equation [2]:

$$Score(D, Q) = \sum_{w \in V} P(w|\theta_Q) \log P(w|\theta_D)$$

where θ_Q and θ_D are respectively the language model for the query Q and the document D. The vocabulary V in the model can be unigrams (U), bigrams (B), words (W), or a mixture of them. A general way to combine different types of index is to determine a score according to each type of index and then to combine the scores as follows:

$$Score(D, Q) = \sum_{R} \lambda_R Score_R(D, Q)$$

where R denote a type of index, which could be U, B and W.

We notice that in such a combination, no relationship between different types of index is considered. In addition, a fixed global weight is assigned to each type of index regardless to the strength of dependency between a pair of characters. As we argued earlier, this is counterintuitive: some dependencies should be attributed a higher weight than others in the matching process because of their ability to express unambiguously a meaning and to retrieve the required documents, in comparison to characters.

Term dependency is a general phenomenon present in all the languages. Several attempts have been made to define IR models capable of capturing term dependencies. Gao et al. [4] proposed a dependency model in which term dependency is captured by a biterm model. The final model combines the unigram model and the biterm model. Metzler and Croft [8] proposed Markov Random Field (MRF) models for IR, in which dependencies between terms in the same clique (a set of fully connected nodes) are considered. In the full dependence model (MRF-FD), all the terms in a sentence (query) are assumed to be dependent. This will lead quickly to the problem of complexity when the number of terms in a clique becomes large. To limit the complexity, a sequential dependence model (MRF-SD) is used, in which only dependencies between adjacent terms are considered. In addition to unigrams, two types of dependence are considered: ordered and un-ordered. These types of dependence are assigned fixed weights $(\lambda_U, \lambda_O, \lambda_U)$ in the final score function.

As we mentioned earlier, dependencies between non adjacent characters are also important in Chinese IR, and the role of each pair of dependent characters in the matching process varies. To deal with the last problem, Bendersky et al. [1] extended recently the MRF-SD model to a weighted MRF-SD model (which we denote by WSD), in which the weight of a term and a pair of terms becomes dependent on the individual term and pair of terms. The scoring function is as follows:

$$P(D|Q) \overset{rank}{=} \sum_{q_i \in Q} \lambda(q_i) f_T(q_i, D) + \sum_{q_i q_{i+1} \in Q} \lambda(q_i q_{i+1})[f_O(q_i q_{i+1}|D) + f_U(q_i q_{i+1}|D)]$$

in which $\lambda(q_i) = \sum_{j=1}^{k_{uni}} w_j^{uni} g_j^{uni}(q_i)$ and $\lambda(q_i q_{i+1}) = \sum_{j=1}^{k_{bi}} w_j^{bi} g_j^{bi}(q_i q_{i+1})$ are the importance of the unigram q_i and bigram $q_i q_{i+1}$ respectively, the function $g_j(\cdot)$ is a feature defined over unigrams or bigrams, and w_j is its weight, a free parameter to be estimated. This goes in the same direction as our model, i.e. to assign variable weights to unigrams and pairs of terms. However, the relationship between non-adjacent query terms is still ignored in [1] and the ordered and un-ordered pairs of terms are treated in the same way. Our model will go a step further: we will consider dependencies between non-adjacent characters as between 世 and 贸 in 世界贸易 (world trade). We will also separate ordered and unordered pairs of characters.

3   Our Method

3.1   Variable Dependency Model

MRF models are limited due to its high complexity. It is difficult to extend them to cover dependencies between distant characters. On the other hand, discriminative models have the advantage that one can selectively use a subset of useful dependencies as features rather than all the dependencies [10]. Discriminative models have been successfully used in IR [3]. A typical discriminative model corresponds to the following equation:

$$score(D, Q) = P(Rel|D, Q) = \frac{1}{Z} \exp\left(\sum_{i}^{n} \lambda_i f_i(Q, D)\right) \quad (1)$$

where $f_i(Q, D)$ is a feature function with weight λ_i and Z a normalization constant. The model we propose is a discriminative model. We limit the dependencies to pairwise dependencies, which often correspond to the strongest dependencies that we want to capture. The flexibility of discriminative models allows us to consider dependencies between more distant characters, without having to increase the complexity of the model to account for more complex and less useful dependencies.

The previous experiments show that the LM based on character unigrams works well [14]. Therefore, we use Chinese characters as our basic index units. In addition, we consider the following types of dependencies: (1) bigram, (2) unordered co-occurring characters within some distance. Let us use C_w to denote the character co-occurrence within a window of size w in documents. To express the proximity of co-occurring characters in documents, we use a set of window sizes W (in our implementation, we use 3 window sizes: 2, 4, and 8) when we construct document models. The idea of using windows of different sizes for documents is to try to capture the strength of proximity between characters: intuitively, a pair of closer characters has a stronger relationship. The ranking function is extended from Equation (1) to the following one:

$$P(Rel|D,Q) \stackrel{rank}{=} \sum_{q_i \in Q} \lambda_U(q_i|Q) f_U(q_i, D)$$
$$+ \sum_{q_i q_{i+1} \in Q} \lambda_B(q_i, q_{i+1}|Q) f_B(q_i q_{i+1}, D)$$
$$+ \sum_{w \in W} \sum_{q_i, q_j \in Q, i \neq j} \lambda_{C_w}(q_i, q_j|Q) f_{C_w}(q_i, q_j, D)$$

This model contains three classes of features: unigram features $f_U(q_i, D)$, bigram features $f_B(q_i q_{i+1}, D)$ and co-occurrence features $f_{C_w}(q_i, q_j, D)$ where w is the document window size. The characters q_i and q_j used in the above ranking function are any pair of (not necessarily adjacent) characters in a query. Each feature is associated with a function λ denoting the importance of the feature for the query Q. This function allows us to take into account the variable dependencies between bigrams and co-occurring characters according to their strength and utility. The discriminative feature functions we use are simply the language model features defined as follows:

$$f_U(q_i, D) = P_U(q_i|Q) \log P_U(q_i|D)$$
$$f_B(q_i q_{i+1}, D) = P_B(q_i q_{i+1}|Q) \log P_B(q_i q_{i+1}|D)$$
$$f_{C_w}(q_i, q_j, D) = P_{C_w}(\{q_i.q_j\}_w|Q) \log P_{C_w}(\{q_i.q_j\}_w|D)$$

where $\{q_i.q_j\}_w$ denote a pair of co-occurring characters q_i and q_j in document within a window of size w. The features are defined in this way in order to make it easier to compare our model with other approaches using language modeling. However, tone can well define other features.

For the ranking purpose, we will simply fix $\lambda_U(q_i|Q)$ at the constant 1, and try to vary the other λ functions for bigrams and co-occurring terms. Putting all together, we have the following final model:

$$P(Rel|D,Q) \stackrel{rank}{=} \sum_{q_i \in Q} P_U^{ml}(q_i|Q) \log P_U(q_i|D)$$
$$+ \sum_{q_i q_{i+1} \in Q} \lambda_B(q_i, q_{i+1}|Q) P_B^{ml}(q_i q_{i+1}|Q) \log P_B(q_i q_{i+1}|D) \qquad (2)$$
$$+ \sum_{w \in W} \sum_{\substack{q_i, q_j \in Q \\ i \neq j}} \lambda_{C_w}(q_i, q_j|Q) P_C^{ml}(\{q_i.q_j\}|Q) \log P_{C_w}(\{q_i.q_j\}_w|D)$$

This model will be called Variable Dependency Model (VDM). The fundamental difference of our model with most of previous models is that the λ functions are now dependent on the specific pair of characters. For example, for 世界贸易 (world trade), the model will capture the relations between the following character pairs: 世界, 世贸, 世易, 界贸, …, 贸易 The importance of each pair varies depending on the usefulness to consider it in IR. The weight will be learnt using SVM (see Section 3.2).

For the query models in Equation (2), we will simply use Maximum Likelihood estimation as follows, where t_R is a unigram, a bigram or a pair of co-occurring terms and $c(t_R; Q)$ its count in the query:

$$P_R^{ml}(t_R|Q) = \frac{c(t_R; Q)}{|Q|_R}, \quad R \in \{U, B, C_2, C_4, C_8\}$$

For the document model, Dirichlet smoothing is used:

$$P_R(t_R|D) = \frac{c(t_R; D) + \mu_R \cdot P_R(t_R|C)}{|D|_R + \mu_R}$$

where $c(t_R; D)$ is the count of term t_R in document D (within a window for C_w); $P_R(t_R|C) = \frac{\sum_{D \in C} c(t_R; D)}{\sum_{D \in C} |D|_R}$ is the collection language model; μ_R is a Dirichlet prior for the corresponding type of model; and $|D|_R$ is the document length in the expression of R, i.e. the total number of unigrams, bigrams or co-occurring terms within the corresponding window size.

3.2 Parameter Estimation

The λ functions are determined according to the strength and utility of bigrams or co-occurring terms in IR, in comparison to characters. We will use the epsilon Support Vector Machine Regression (ϵ-SVR) [15] method to train $\lambda_R(\cdot)$. The toolkit LIBSVM[1] is used for this purpose.

The training examples are obtained as follows. For each training query, we first find the best weights (z_i) for each bigram or pair of co-occurring characters within different windows (x_i). We use a coordinate-level ascent search algorithm [7] to find the best weight for each x_i. A set $\mathbf{x}_i$ of features is used to characterize x_i. This defines a learning example ($\mathbf{x}_i, z_i$).

In our experiment, we use 10-fold cross-validation method, i.e., 1/10 of the data ($\mathbf{x}_i, z_i$) will be used in turn as the test data for IR while the remaining 9/10 will be used as the training data for parameter learning. In this study, we use the following features (where x is a bigram or a co-occurring character pair, and q_i, q_j are characters in x):

- Point-wise mutual information in an independent text collection: PMI_all(x). We use the concatenation of all test collections as the independent collection.

---

[1] http://www.csie.ntu.edu.tw/~cjlin/libsvm/

- PMI in the current test collection: $PMI\_coll(x)$
- A binary value according to the test: $PMI\_all(x) >$ Threshold? (we set the[2] threshold to 0 in our experiments)
- Binary test value: $PMI\_coll(x) >$ Threshold?
- $idf(x) - idf(q_i) - idf(q_j)$
- $(idf(x) - idf(q_i) - idf(q_j))/(idf(q_i) + idf(q_j))$
- $count(x, coll)/min(count(q_i, coll), count(q_j, coll))$
- $count(x, coll)/max(count(q_i, coll), count(q_j, coll))$
- A binary value according to whether x appears in a Wikipedia Chinese title?
- The distance between q_i and q_j in the query (for co-occurring character pair)

In addition, for a bigram b_i, we also use the following additional feature, which determines the proportion of document in which one of the characters only appears in the bigram:

$$\frac{|\{D|c(b_i; D) > 1 \; \& \; c(b_i; D) = min(c(q_i; D), c(q_{i+1}; D))\}|}{|\{D|c(b_i; D) > 1\}|}$$

We have not defined a large set of features because our primary goal of this study is to show the importance to incorporate dependencies between characters at variable degrees. The set of features could be easily extended in the future.

4 Experiments

4.1 Test Collections

We use the collections from TREC and NTCIR. The characteristics of the collections are summarized in Table 1.

Table 1. Characteristics of collections

Collection	Name	#Document	Size (MB)	Avg. Doc Length
TR56	Peoples Daily	164,788	173	158
TR9	Xinhua news agency	127,938	86	205
NT34	CIRB011&CIRB020	381,681	543	226
NT56	CIRB040r	901,446	1106	207

In our experiments, we use topic titles as our queries (see Table 2). This choice is made to better correspond to real queries on search engines.

---

[2] http://download.wikimedia.org/chwiki/, which includes 338,164 titles.

Table 2. Characteristics of queries

Query Set	Collection	Queries	#Query	Avg. len. (in character)
TREC5	TR56	CH1-28	28	4.7
TREC6	TR56	CH29-54	26	4.7
TREC9	TR9	CH55-79	25	3.7
NTCIR4	NT34	001-060	59	4.3
NTCIR5	NT56	001-050	50	4.6
NTCIR6	NT56	003-110	50	3.9

4.2 Pre-processing and Indexing

As the collections are in different coding schemas, we converted all the characters into GB codes. To compare to the word-based method, we use a word segmentation tool ICTCLAS[2] to segment Chinese texts to words, and use another segmentation program from LDC[3] to further segment long words into short words. For example, the long word 世界贸易组织 (World Trade Organization) will be further segmented in the second step into its constituent short words: 世界 (World), 贸易 (Trade), 组织 (Organization). The previous experiments showed that short words perform better than long words [5].

We use Indri[4] to build the index for our model. The basic index units are Chinese characters (which we denote by U). To compare to the baseline models, we also build the indexes for other index units: words (W), bigrams (B), words and bigrams combined with unigrams (WU, W+U, BU and B+U). In the combinations WU and BU, all types of index are indexed together, while in W+U and B+U, they are indexed separately and the scores from each index are combined linearly.

4.3 Experimental Results

We first provide the retrieval results of the baseline methods in Table 3. The combination parameters in W+U and B+U are tuned to their best. For a Chinese query $q_1 q_2 ... q_n$, we assume the word segmentation result to be $w_1, w_2, ... w_m$. The baseline models are listed below:

- U: We use unigrams of character, and the query is "$q_1 q_2 ... q_n$".
- B: We use bigrams of characters. The corresponding Indri query is "#1(q_1 q_2) ... #1($q_{n-1}q_n$)".
- BU: We use both bigrams and unigrams mixed up in a single query. The Indri query is "#1(q_1 q_2) ... #1($q_{n-1}q_n$) q_1 q_2 ... q_n".
- B+U: of the scores using B and U are interpolated.
- W: We use segmented words. The query is "w_1 w_2 ... w_m".
- WU: The segmented words are mixed up with character unigrams. The Indri query is "w_1 w_2 ... w_m q_{i1}, q_{i2} ...".
- W+U: The scores using W and U are interpolated.

[2] http://ictclas.org/
[3] http://www.ldc.upenn.edu/Projects/Chinese/seg.zip
[4] http://www.lemurproject.org/indri/

Table 3. The baselines (MAP) of traditional Chinese IR models

Query	U	B	BU	B+U	W	WU	W+U
Trec5	0.3013	0.2696	0.3184	**0.3269**	0.2802	0.3265	0.3173
Trec6	0.3601	0.3610	0.3875	0.3878	0.3881	0.3983	**0.3998**
Trec9	0.2381	0.2119	0.2469	**0.2543**	0.1905	0.2283	0.2381
Ntcir4	0.2371	0.1995	0.2243	**0.2489**	0.2237	0.2396	0.2469
Ntcir5	0.3587	0.3151	0.3563	0.3681	0.3840	0.3817	**0.3998**
Ntcir6	0.2695	0.2448	0.2931	**0.3064**	0.2739	0.2863	0.3012

To see the importance of different type of index, we plot the results of the methods B+U and W+U on Trec6 and Ntcir6 collections in Figure 2. We can see that a reasonable interpolation usually leads to a higher effectiveness than using only one type of index (the two extremities of the curves). This shows that different types of index are complementary and it is useful to combine them. However, the best weight for each type of index depends on the collection and on the types of index combined. Indeed, the usefulness of different words and bigrams varies largely. The weight we assign to a type of index corresponds to a compromise among all the words and bigrams. As we will see in the experiment with our proposed model, it is better to assign a different weight to a word or a bigram depending on its usefulness.

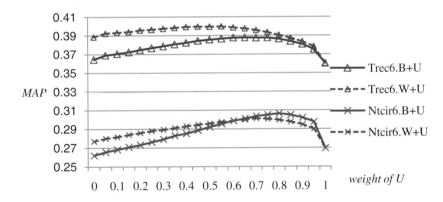

Fig. 1. Compare the MAP of B, U, W, and their interpolations on Trec6 and Ntcir6 Collections

In Table 4, we show the effectiveness with other baselines - MRF-SD and Weighted MRF-SD (WSD). For MRF-SD, we use a grid search to find the best parameters $\lambda_T, \lambda_O, \lambda_U$ so as to maximize MAP for each collection. Therefore, the effectiveness of this model is tuned to its best. The results with MRF-SD are slightly better than B+U. Indeed, if we remove the unordered part, the MRF-SD becomes identical to B+U. The difference between MRF-SD and B+U corresponds to the contribution of unordered unigram pairs. The WSD model is slight better than MRF-SD except on Trec6. However, the differences between the two models are not statistically significant.

Table 4. The baselines of dependency models: MRF-SD and WSD. † and ‡ means statistically significant difference at the level of p<0.05 and p<0.01.

Query	MRF-SD				Weighted-SD		
	MAP	%U	%B+U	%W+U	MAP	%U	%SD
Trec5	0.3271	+8.6‡	+3.1	+3.1	0.3279	+8.8‡	+0.2
Trec6	0.3899	+8.3‡	+0.6	-2.5	0.3780	+5.0	-3.1
Trec9	0.2576	+8.2	+1.3	+8.2	0.2732	+14.8†	+6.0
Ntcir4	0.2490	+5.0†	+0.0	+0.8	0.2514	+6.0‡	+1.0
Ntcir5	0.3846	+7.2 ‡	+4.5	-3.8	0.3909	+9.0†	+1.6
Ntcir6	0.3066	+13.8‡	+0.0	+1.8	0.3088	+14.6‡	+0.7

Table 5. The results (MAP) with Variable Dependency Model (VDM)

Query	VDM (best fixed)			VDM (10-fold cross-validation)							VDM (ideal)
	MAP	%U	%SD	MAP	%U	%B+U	%W+U	%SD	%WSD	%fixed	MAP
Trec5	0.3278	+8.8‡	+0.2	0.3501	+16.2‡	+7.1‡	+10.4‡	+7.1‡	+6.8†	+6.8‡	0.4414
Trec6	0.3916	+8.7‡	+0.4	0.4159	+15.5‡	+7.3‡	+4.0†	+6.7‡	+10.0†	+6.2‡	0.5272
Trec9	0.2627	+10.4	+2.0	0.2713	+14.0	+6.7	+14.0	+5.3	-0.7	+3.3	0.3896
Ntcir4	0.2503	+5.5‡	+0.5	0.2613	+10.2‡	+5.0†	+5.8‡	+4.9†	+3.9‡	+4.4‡	0.3494
Ntcir5	0.3851	+7.4‡	+0.1	0.3949	+10.1‡	+7.3†	-1.2	+2.7	+1.0	+2.5	0.5261
Ntcir6	0.3070	+13.9‡	+0.1	0.3142	+16.6‡	+2.5†	4.3†	+2.5†	+1.7	+2.3†	0.4126

The results with our variable dependency model (VDM) are shown in Table 5. The results show that the VDM model with fixed weights is slightly better than MRF-SD. This is due to the fact that we added non-adjacent co-occurring characters.

When we vary the weights of the bigram and the pair of co-occurring characters, the result becomes much better. In general, our model outperforms all the baseline methods except in two cases. Many of the improvements are statistically significant. In comparison to B+U, W+U, MRF-SD and VDM with fixed weights, this result shows the benefit of assigning variable importance to pairs of characters. The result clearly validates the general approach we used in our model.

Notice that in the above comparison, we gave considerable advantage to the baseline models, as their parameters are tuned to their best, which is not the case for our model. In order to have an idea of the potential of our model, we also show (in the last column) the effectiveness of our model using the best parameters (best weights for each bigram and pair of characters). We can see that our model with the ideal parameters can largely outperform the existing models. This shows that the assignment of variable weights to individual pairs of characters is indeed an important aspect in Chinese IR, which our model captures. The large difference between the ideal VDM and VDM using parameters set by cross-validation also shows that the parameter learning process can be much improved. This is part of our future work.

4.4 Analysis and Discussion

In this section, we analyze the experimental results in order to understand why our model can outperform the other models. We have observed two categories of cases in which our model can increase the retrieval effectiveness.

1. By setting proper weights to character pairs (high weights to useful pairs, low weights to noisy pairs), our model can benefit from the strengths of unigram model and dependency model, and avoid the disadvantages of them.

 – Unigrams (characters) are useful for matching synonyms, near-synonyms or various forms of transliterations due to the characters they share. For example, the two variants of AIDS 爱滋病 and 艾滋病 can be partly matched because they share two characters 滋 (grow, multiply) and 病 (disease). In our experiments, for the query Ch73 in Trec9: "中国的艾滋病" (AIDS in China), the average precision (AP) using words is close to 0 because the documents use a different variant of AIDS - 爱滋病. On the other hand, using unigrams, we obtain an AP of 0.3344. Using VDM, we obtain an AP of 0.4070. In VDM, we observe that except for the bigrams 艾滋 and 滋病, the weights of other bigrams and co-occurring character pairs are close to 0. This means that our model heavily relies on unigrams for this query. However, as some of the bigrams (in particular, the bigram 滋病) have a non-zero weight, they help enhance the connections between these characters. This explains the improved effectiveness of VDM over unigram model.
 – On the other hand, characters that are highly ambiguous should be combined and our model can successfully make use of dependencies in these cases. For example, in the query Ch27 of Trec5 "中国 (China) 在 (in) 机器人 (robotics) 方面 (area) 的 (of) 研制 (research)", if we use unigrams, both the terms 中国 (China) and 机器人 (robot) are decomposed into very common characters 中 (China, middle), 国 (country), 机 (machine, engine), 器 (machine, utensil), 人 (human, person). These latter lead to a low effectiveness of 0.1057. When words are used the average precision is increased to 0.4079. Although our VDM model is unable to decide to rely entirely on words in this case, it still assigns a quite strong relative importance to the words, leading to an average precision of 0.3030. The highly ambiguous characters are indeed put into dependencies as follows: 中国 (with a weight of 0.64), 器人 (0.59). These strong weights help solve the ambiguity problem of separate characters.

2. Our model can capture the dependencies between non-adjacent characters.

 – For the query 003 of Ntcir4 "胚胎 (embryonic) 干细胞 (stem cells)", we obtain an AP of 0.1891 using unigrams, 0.2174 using MRF-SD, and 0.2410 using WSD, while our VDM model results in an AP of 0.4096. The good performance of VDM is due to the fact that strong dependencies between non-adjacent characters are captured. In this case, we observe strong weights for the co-occurring characters 胎 and 干 (with a weight of 0.22), 胚 and 干 (0.54), 胎 and 胞 (0.27). These pairs do not correspond to legitimate words in this query, but their combinations tend to enhance the relationship between the words 胚胎 and 干细胞. We can see that co-occurring characters can also successfully capture relationships between different words.

The above analyses show that our model has the potential of taking advantage of both groups of characters and individual characters and determine their importance in the matching process according to how useful they are. This is the very goal of our model.

5 Conclusion

Chinese is a language basically constructed from characters. Even though words can be recognized from sentences, they are not unique and invariable in form. The high flexibility in Chinese to express the meaning using different combinations of characters makes it challenging to match a query against documents using similar but different words. This characteristic of the language is the very reason why a combination of words with characters in Chinese IR has been successful. However, words and characters are not independent. The previous approaches that assume their independence fail to capture the inherent relationships between them. In this paper, we propose a model to take into account the relationships between different types of index. Pairs of characters become dependent to different degrees, and they can be useful for IR to different degrees. In our model, a pair of characters is used in the retrieval model according to its strength and usefulness for IR. The assignment of variable weights to pairs of characters has not been investigated in previous studies. It turns out that this is highly beneficial in our experiments. The model we propose in this paper points to an interesting direction for future research – the integration of dependencies according to their usefulness in IR.

The study reported in this paper has not exploited all the potential of the model. Several aspects could be further improved. For example, we have considered dependencies only between pairs of characters. It would be possible to extend them to more characters. We have used a limited set of features to train the importance of dependencies between characters. This set could be extended in the future.

References

1. Bendersky, M., Metzler, D., Croft, W.B.: Learning Concept Importance Using a Weighted Dependence Model. In: Proc. of the Third International Conference on Web Search and Web Data Mining, pp. 31–40 (2010)
2. Croft, W.B.: Language Models for Information Retrieval. In: Proc. of the 19th International Conference on Data Engineering, pp. 3–7 (2003)
3. Gao, J., Qi, H., Xia, X., Nie, J.-Y.: Linear Discriminant Model for Information Retrieval. In: Proc. of the 28th Annual International ACM SIGIR Conference, pp. 290–297 (2005)
4. Gao, J., Nie, J.-Y., Wu, G., Cao, G.: Dependence language model for information retrieval. In: Proc. of the 22nd Annual International ACM SIGIR Conference, pp. 170–177 (1999)
5. Kwok, K.L.: Comparing representations in Chinese information retrieval. In: Proc. of the 20th Annual International ACM SIGIR Conference, pp. 34–41 (1997)

6. Luk, R.W.P., Wong, K.F., Kwok, K.L.: A comparison of Chinese document indexing strategies and retrieval models. ACM Transactions on Asian Language Information Processing 1(3), 225–268 (2002)
7. Metzler, D., Croft, W.B.: Linear feature-based models for information retrieval. Information Retrieval 10(3), 257–274 (2007)
8. Metzler, D., Croft, W.B.: A Markov random field model for term dependencies. In: Proc. of the 28th Annual International ACM SIGIR Conference, pp. 472–479 (2005)
9. Nallapati, R., Allan, J.: Capturing Term Dependencies using a Sentence Tree based Language Model. In: Proc. of the 2002 ACM CIKM, pp. 383–390 (2002)
10. Nallapati, R.: Discriminative Models for Information retrieval. In: Proc. of the 27th Annual International ACM SIGIR Conference, pp. 64–71 (2004)
11. Nie, J.-Y., Gao, J., Zhang, J., Zhou, M.: On the use of words and n-grams for Chinese information retrieval. In: Proc. of the Fifth International Workshop on Information Retrieval with Asian Languages, pp. 141–148 (2000)
12. Nie, J.-Y., Brisebois, M., Ren, X.: On Chinese text retrieval. In: Proc. of the 19th Annual International ACM SIGIR Conference, pp. 225–233 (1996)
13. Shi, L., Nie, J.-Y., Cao, G.: Relating Dependent Indexes using Dempster-Shafer Theory. In: Proc. of the 2008 ACM CIKM, pp. 429–438 (2008)
14. Shi, L., Nie, J.-Y., Bai, J.: Comparing different units for query translation for Chinese cross-language information retrieval. In: Proc. of the 2nd International Conference on Scalable Information Systems, Article, No. 63 (2007)
15. Vapnik, V.N.: Statistical Learning Theory. Wiley, New York (1998)

Mining Parallel Documents across Web Sites

Pham Ngoc Khanh and Ho Tu Bao

Japan Advanced Institute of Science and Technology,
923-1292 Japan, Ishikawa, Nomi, Asahidai 1-1
{khanh,bao}@jaist.ac.jp
http://www.jaist.ac.jp

Abstract. Most methods on building parallel corpora often start from
large scale bilingual websites that are not always an available resource for
many language pairs. In this paper we present a novel method to mine
parallel documents between English and other non-popular languages
which are situated on different locations on the Internet. Our method
is motivated by the observation that many non-popular language news
are translated from popular English news websites. Given a news in a
non-popular language, a method is proposed to search for its original
English version located on another website using search engines. Experiments with English-Vietnamese show that our method can provide
bilingual document pairs in science domain with precision around 90%.
Our method is more flexible and scalable than traditional approaches
that collect parallel texts from multilingual websites as its starting point
is only a set of monolingual news. Furthermore, this method can be applied to mine parallel documents between non-popular languages pairs
with scarce resources.

Keywords: Parallel Corpus, Web Information Retrieval.

1   Introduction

Parallel corpora are sets of texts in one language together with their translation
in another language. Parallel corpora are indispensable resources for many areas
of text and web mining research including statistical machine translation [1],
cross-lingual information retrieval [2], automatic bilingual lexical building [3].

While manually complied parallel corpora is costly and time consuming, methods to automatically build the parallel corpora have gained substantial attention
in the field of NLP. There are a number of good Web mining systems such as
STRAND [4], BITS [5] and PTMiner [6] that automatically acquire parallel documents from bilingual web sites. Those systems first crawl bilingual web sites
exhaustedly to collect two sets of web pages in different languages. Then bilingual dictionary and HTML structure information are used to align translation
equivalent web pages. Beginning with two sets of large scale monolingual documents, cross-lingual information retrieval models can also be applied to search
for noisy parallel documents [7,8]. Using search engine to search for parallel texts
is introduced recently in the work of Achim Ruopp and Fei Xia [9].

P.-J. Cheng et al. (Eds.): AIRS 2010, LNCS 6458, pp. 552–563, 2010.

With the help of above-mentioned methods, many parallel corpora with various language pairs [10,11,12] have been built and publicly available for researchers. Unfortunately, parallel corpora are only available for a limited number of popular language pairs like English-French, English-Japanese. For many non popular language pairs like English-Vietnamese, English-Thai such resources are not available for researchers in these countries to conduct their research.

Moreover, the task to build parallel corpora for popular language pairs is much easier than that for non-popular language pairs. Popular language pairs have abundance of online texts database that were well-organized and thus is easy to collect. For instance, in Europarl project[1], authors could easily collect more than one million parallel sentence pairs by just crawling the European parliament website which provides law documents and discussions in 11 European languages[2]. Documents in these websites are well-organized. For example, in Europarl website, documents referring to the same content have the same name and stored in different directories in accordance with their languages.

These above facts are not true for non-popular language pairs. Resources to build parallel texts for those language pairs are very scarce and building parallel corpora for such language pairs is a really tough challenge for NLP researchers. To our knowledge, research conducted to build bilingual resources for non-popular language pairs until now just focused on only word-level. Sources for extracting bilingual lexicons are either from comparable corpora [13] or via a third pivot language [14].

In this paper, we propose a new method that can be applied to mine parallel documents located on different web sites on the Internet, which can be applied to collect parallel texts for resource scarce language pairs. Our method is based on the observation that many news of non popular languages in domains such as outside world, technology, science, health are collected and translated from other popular English news' websites on the Internet like BBC, VOA and so on. An illustrated example was shown in Figure 1 between a Vietnamese news[3] posted in http://www.vnexpress.net website and an English news[4] posted in http://www.dailymail.co.uk website. The source websites are cited within the content of translated news due to copyright law. We also noted that between two translated documents there exists contents that do not change during translation process. We defined those data as *Translation Independent Data (TID)*. Given a source news in non popular language, we formulated queries based on TIDs, posted date and news source. By sending those queries to search engines, we obtain some English candidates. Then a document matching process which combines both lexical and length features is implemented to find out the target English news.

---

[1] http://www.statmt.org/europarl/
[2] http://www.europarl.europa.eu/
[3] http://www.vnexpress.net/GL/Khoa-hoc/2008/11/3BA086BE/
[4] http://www.dailymail.co.uk/sciencetech/article-1085059/Pictured-The-robot-pull-faces-just-like-human-being.html

Fig. 1. An example of English-Vietnamese cross-website parallel documents

The main contribution of this work includes the followings. First, we identify new clues from the Internet to extract parallel documents. Second, a new method have been proposed to build a set of parallel documents from those clues.

The rest of the paper is organized as follows. In the next section, we introduce our method in details. The experiment and discussion on results are presented in Section 3, 4. In Section 5, we conclude our work and give some directions for future research

Table 1. Steps in the proposed framework

Steps	Description
Clue extraction	Extract clues from t_S that guide the process to find t_E.
Query generation and ranking	Use extracted clues to generate a set of queries combining extracted information with several search constraints. After that queries are sent to search engines with order from high rank to the low rank until we get candidates. The rank of a query is defined based on the constraints put on this query. The more constraints put on a query, the higher the rank it is evaluated.
Filtering	Look for the original English news t_E from the list of candidates. A method that combines both length-based and TID-based features is proposed.

2 Proposed Method

Given a potential news t_S in non popular and resource scarce language S that is likely to be translated from an English news, our task is to determine its original English version t_E on the Web. To determine whether t_S is a potential news or

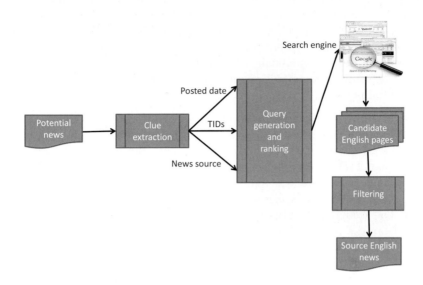

Fig. 2. Framework to find original English news of a potential translated news in non popular language

not, we check its citation. If t_S is cited to an English news website, it is regarded as potential news. Otherwise, t_S is not a potential news. Given a potential news in language S, we propose a framework with 3 main steps to discover its original English news as described in Table 1 and Fig. 2.

2.1   Clues Extraction

Given a potential news t_S, we extract three following clues:

- *Posted date*: the date that the news was put online and available for Internet users to access.
- *URL of news source*: To get the URL of news source, we first extract the name of the cited source which if often put in the bottom of the news using regular expression technique. We then will create a query by appending the word *"news"* to the name and send its to Google search engine. We use language restriction feature (*lr* parameter) to search for only pages in English. The domain name of first URL returned by Google will be chosen as the URL of news website.
- *Translational independent data (TID)*: TID is defined as data that is unchanged during translation process. TIDs can be viewed as common texts in the writing system between two languages. For example, given an English sentence "60 people were killed in Republic of Congo Train Crash" and its equivalent Vietnamese translation "60 người chết trong tai nạn xe lửa ở CHDC Congo", 60 and Congo are considered as numeric and textual TIDs

respectively. TIDs that are close together will be grouped into phrases. The task to extract TIDs can be regarded as a sequence labeling problem and can be solved using well-known techniques such as HMM, CRF. Nevertheless, this approach suffers from a major drawback that we need to build a training data set manually, which is a time-consuming process. We propose two simple unsupervised methods to extract TIDs from the content of potential news t_S.

- The first method is dictionary-based approach. Assuming we have a monolingual dictionary containing all of words that are originated in S. All words that does not appear in this dictionary will be considered as an TID word. We assume that texts that are not originated from language S are kept the same as their appearance in English but not be transliterated into writing system of language S.
- The second method is machine translation-based. This approach comes from the nature of TID. Texts in t_S are translated into English using a translation system. Tokens and phrases that appears in both t_S and its English translated news will be considered as TIDs.

2.2   Query Generation and Ranking

Next step in our method is to create a set of queries from data extracted from previous step. We generate not a single query but a bunch of queries with the different levels of search restriction. Intuitively, the more restriction we set on the query, the smaller number and more accurate the candidates we can get. On the other hand, if we put too strict restriction, it is likely that search engines return no candidates. For those reasons, instead of one query, we generate a set of queries, rank the queries from high to low orders and send them to the search engine until we get some candidates.

We use only *text* TIDs to generate queries. Numeric TIDs are not included in this step. Regarding to search constraints, we define several kinds of search constraints as follows:

- *Phrase constraint*: Only web pages that contain extract phrase in the query are retrieved.
- *Date constraints*: Only web pages within a range of date will be returned.
- *Site constraint*: Only web pages belonging to a specific web site are returned.
- *Language constraint*: As we want to search for source articles written in English, the language of retrieved pages should be in English.
- *n-gram constraint*: With n-gram constraint, the query will be built from TIDs that have at least n tokens.

After being created, queries are ranked and sent to the search engine from high to low orders. There are many methods proposed to rank words and phrases in a document based on their frequency and co-occurrence statistics [15] that can be applied to rank the queries. In this work, we propose a much more simpler heuristic approach that ranks the query based on the types of constraints put into the query. We apply language, date constraint and site constraint to all queries. For the remaining constraints including phrase, site and n-gram constraints, we will define their corresponding rank in the following ways:

- The query with more constraints will be rank higher than query with less constraints.
- The rank of site constraint is highest while the rank of the phrase constraint is lowest. That is

$$\text{rank(n-gram constraint)} > \text{rank(phrase constraint)}$$

- Within n-gram constraints, the n-gram with lower n will be assigned higher rank as n-gram constraint with lower n provides query with more specific information .

$$\text{rank(1-gram constraint)} > \text{rank(2-gram constraint)} > \cdots > \text{rank(N-gram)}$$

Queries that contains too few and short TIDs are not dispatched to the search engine. Only query created from at least two words and the total length of words larger than a threshold of, says 10 characters, is qualified.

2.3   Filtering

In this step, after getting a list of candidate web pages returned by Google, we have to select among them the original English news t_E of the given potential news t_S.

First, web pages are preprocessed. Noisy texts in web pages like boilerplates, advertisement and HTML scripts are removed because they are proved to have bad impacts on many text processing tasks. Cleaning web page is a challenging problem. There are many works that employ sophisticated features set and advanced supervised machine learning techniques such as SVM, CRF . In this paper we choose to apply method developed by Jing Li and C. I. Ezeife [16]. This work applied n-gram language models to distinguish between main texts and noisy texts which produces comparable performance in shared task competition of 3rd Web as Corpus workshop in summer 2007 and has been released as the open source project NCleaner[5].

After web pages are preprocessed, we implement a process to determine whether the original English news is among the list of N-best candidates. In common approaches, bilingual lexicons are often used to measure the similarity between two documents in two languages. In this research we develop a simple approach by incorporating length and TID features together. The length-based filtering is based on assumption that a long text should have a long translation and vice versa. The length-based constraint is defined as follows

$$\frac{1}{3} \times \text{length}(t_S) < \text{length(EN-text)} < 3 \times \text{length}(t_S)$$

---

while TID-based matching score is computed by the following formula

$$matchingScore = \frac{\text{Number of TIDs found within English text}}{\text{Total number of TIDs in } t_S}$$

The best matched English document is one that satisfies length-based constraint and have the highest TID-based matching score higher than a pre-defined threshold δ. In our experiment, we choose δ as 0.33 empirically.

3   Evaluation

The main objective of this section is to evaluate effectiveness of our proposed method. The language pair used in our experiment is English-Vietnamese. The finally obtained English documents were checked manually as we do not have any gold data sets for this problem.

3.1   Evaluation Measures

In order to evaluate how good our proposed approach is, we use popular measures: recall, precision and f-measures. In our research, those measures are shortly described as below

$$Precision = \frac{\text{Number of correct English news}}{\text{Number of English news found by our approach}}$$

$$Recall = \frac{\text{Number of correct English news}}{\text{Number of Vietnamese news}}$$

$$F - Score = \frac{2 \times Recall \times Precision}{(Recall + Precision)}$$

3.2   Experiment Setup

To conduct the experiments for parallel documents searching, Vietnamese articles are collected from VNExpress web site[6], which is a very popular news website in Vietnam. We focused on two domains i.e. world and science. In our observation, many articles from those two domains are likely to be gathered and translated from other English web sites. We collected articles in science domain that was posted within the first 4 months of 2009 and articles in world domain in posted within April 2009. We extract only main texts from those news using Java-based HTML Parser[7] library. We compile a list of URLs of more than 20 Vietnamese news agency that are often cited by other news website. We selected only Vietnamese news that is cited to an website that is not in the above list. Totally, we have 211 science articles and 108 world articles for our experiments.

---

[6] http://www.vnexpress.net
[7] http://htmlparser.sourceforge.net/

The dictionary for Vietnamese are taken from training corpus for word segmentation task compiled by Lê Hồng Phương et al, a Vietnamese group doing research on word segmentation. This Vietnamese dictionary data was provided together with their open source Vietnamese word segmentation tools namely vntokenizer[8]. However, we do not need all data in the dictionary. We only need a list of Vietnamese words that are composed from English alphabet. Words that contain special Vietnamese characters such as 'á', 'â', 'ê', 'ố' are considered to be Vietnamese and are filtered out from the original dictionary. We then revised the list by hand and finally get a list of our Vietnamese words contains only 420 words.

To translate texts from Vietnamese into English, we use Google translation system.

3.3   Experiment Results and Discussion

We conducted three experiments. The first experiments is to evaluate the effectiveness of the proposed method and to compare the performance in two cases: dictionary-based and machine translation-based TID extractions. In this experiment, we set the threshold δ for document matching score is 0.33 and only top 8 web pages are examined. Due to the different nature of world and science news (world news need to be updated at a short time while science news is not required to be delivered to audience in a short time), we set the date range for them as 90 and 1 respectively. Experiment results are shown in Table 2. In this table, DIC and MT are represented for dictionary-based and machine-translation-based methods respectively. Experimental results show that the machine translation based TID extraction has better performance in comparison with dictionary-based method. However, the difference is not too big. With language pairs that a machine translation is not available, simple dictionary-based approach can be a good alternative choice.

Table 2. Performance with world and science data

Settings	Docs	Found	True	Precision	Recall	F-Score
Science						
MT	211	136	124	**91.18%**	58.77%	71.47%
DIC	211	129	117	**90.76%**	55.45%	68.82%
World						
MT	108	77	55	71.43%	50.93%	59.46%
DIC	108	67	43	64.17%	39.81%	49.14%

The experimental results show that our method has promising performance with precision approximately 90% on science news while that with world news is around 70%. This indicates that TIDs extracted from science news has more discriminative power than TIDs extracted from world news. In a world news,

---

[8] http://www.loria.fr/~lehong/tools/vnTokenizer.php

many of the TIDs extracted are popular names and have their appearance in many other news. News in world domain can have many developments, which are different phases of a same story. Moreover, a Vietnamese news in world domain is often translated and integrated not only from one news source but multiple news agencies. This fact makes the task of finding the original news in English become much more difficult for world domain data.

We also do further investigation and figure out some reasons why English news could not be found as follows: (1) The English news are not posted within the date range we set. This often happens with Vietnamese news in science domain which has its original English news posted later than 90 days. (2) Wrong typings: There are terms and named entities that are mis-spelled. As a result, our method could not find the right original English news. (3) News that are integrated from many news sources. In world domain, there are many news that are integrated from not only one news website but some news websites to provide different developments of a hot news to readers. For those news, the search engine often returns no candidates. (4) The news do not contain text TIDs. There is a fact that not all data has TIDs within its contents. For such kind of data, our method fails to gather enough and reliable clues to construct the queries and consequently fails to find the original English news.

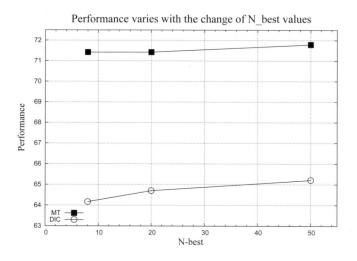

Fig. 3. Performance with different values of N

Moreover, we also implemented the other two experiments with an aim to see how performance of our approach varies when we change the value of matching threshold parameter δ and the number of documents N need to be checked. We did experiments with various values of δ and N. In these experiments, we did the test on world data only. We can see from Fig. 4 that δ having values around 0.375-0.4 produced the highest F-score while still achieving high precision. We also noted that increase the value δ does not always lead to the increase of precision. This may be due to the fact that the TID-based matching score is

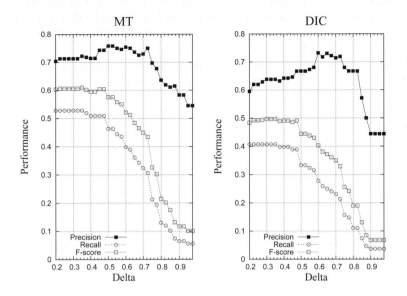

Fig. 4. Performance varies with different values of δ

not strong enough to distinguish between relevant English news and the original English news as their contents often contain the same set of TIDs. This weakness need to be overcome in future research. Meanwhile, increasing the number of examined candidates N from 8 to 20 or 50 does not lead to much improvements of precision as seen in Fig. 3. This suggests that the best candidates can be found in the top 8 candidates. We thus need to consider only first 8 pages returned by the search engine, which helps to reduce a lot of processing time.

4   Discussion

Our method is more flexible than previous works that relied only on collecting data from large scale bilingual websites [4,6,17] or collection of domain data [18]. Our starting point is monolingual data that is abundant and straightforward to collect.

Munteanu et al. [8] built a system to extract parallel sentences from two sets of millions monolingual documents that refer to some common topics. However, their focus is recall rather than precision. Besides, their approach suffer from high computational cost that requires an expensive clustering system to implement. Whereas, this proposed method has inexpensive computational cost by using Google's powerful system to conduct the search process.

The work closely related to this study is that of Achim Ruopp and Fei Xia [9]. This work also use commercial search engines to find translated document pairs. Author applies query expansion techniques to form sampling queries in both languages using a set of bilingual lexicons. However, their approach suffers a very large search spaces because for each query pair there are substantial amount of web pages returned by search engines in both languages. In this work, as we only search for documents in target languages with time and domain restriction, the search space is greatly reduced.

The proposed method allows people to incrementally mine parallel documents which is not easy to implement with approaches starting from a bilingual source [4,5]. One can build a system to collect updates from news websites using XML-based RSS feed technology. Whenever there are new contents available, they will be input into monolingual news database. Accordingly, the system will search for new pairs of parallel documents and add them to current database. Therefore, it is possible to incrementally upgrade the scale of the corpus.

5   Conclusion and Future Work

We have presented a novel and flexible way to discover parallel documents from the Internet. Different from other approaches that often focus on only one large scale bilingual website or collection, our method can identify parallel documents that are located separately on two different websites using available search engines. Clues to identify those parallel pairs are TID data, date information and the news source cited within the content of source news. Based on those clues, we propose a method to generate and rank the queries, which is based on search restrictions put on them. We develop a parallel document matching algorithm that combines both TID and length features. Our method performs well with data in science domain (precision around 90%) while the precision for data in world domain is still not high but acceptable (around 70%). This method can be applied to collect parallel resources for non-popular languages.

This work is just our initial investigation and there are still room for improvements. Our future works will explore the following directions: (1) Develop a new method to extract and rank TIDs more efficiently. (2) Develop a new method to find source English news corresponding to potential news that does not share any TIDs. (3) Develop a new method to extract the parallel sentences or sub-sentences from obtained parallel documents.

Acknowledgments

This work is supported by KC.01.01.05/06-10 national project. The first author has been supported by Japanese Government Scholarship (Monbukagakusho) to study in Japan. We also want to thank the four anonymous reviewers for their invaluable comments.

References

1. Brown, P.F., Cocke, J., Pietra, S.A.D., Pietra, V.J.D., Jelinek, F., Lafferty, J.D., Mercer, R.L., Roossin, P.S.: A statistical approach to machine translation. Computational Linguistics 16(2), 79–85 (1990)

2. Gey, F.C., Kando, N., Peters, C.: Cross-language information retrieval: the way ahead. Inf. Process. Manage 41(3), 415–431 (2005)
3. Kumano, A. and Hirakawa, H.: Building an MT dictionary from parallel texts based on linguistic and statistical information. In: Proceedings of the 15th conference on Computational Linguistics, pp. 76–81 (1994).
4. Philip, R., Smith, N.A.: The web as a parallel corpus. Computational Linguistics 29(3), 349–380 (2003)
5. Ma, X., Liberman, D.Y.: BITS: A method for bilingual text search over the web. In: Proceedings of Machine Translation Summit VII, pp. 538–542 (1999)
6. Chen, J., Nie, J.Y.: Automatic construction of parallel English-Chinese corpus for cross-language information retrieval. In: Proceedings of the Sixth Conference on Applied Natural Language Processing, pp. 21–28 (2000)
7. Colleier, N., Hirakawa, H., Kumano, A.: Creating a noisy parallel corpus from newswire articles using cross-language information retrieval. Transactions of Information Procession Society of Japan 40(1), 351–361 (1999)
8. Munteanu, D.S., Marcu, D.: Improving machine translation performance by exploiting non-parallel corpora. Computational Linguistics 31(4), 477–504 (2005)
9. Ruopp, A., Xia, F.: Finding parallel texts on the web using cross-language information retrieval. In: Proceedings of the Second International Workshop On Cross Lingual Information Access Addressing the Information Need of Multilingual Societies, pp. 18–25 (2008)
10. Jorg, T., Nygaard, L.: The OPUS corpus - parallel and free. In: Proceedings of LREC 2004, pp. 1183–1186 (2004)
11. Koehn, P.: Europarl: A parallel corpus for statistical machine translation. In: Proceedings of MT Summit, pp. 79–86 (2005)
12. Ralf, S., Pouliquen, B., Widiger, A., Ignat, C., Erjavec, T., Tufis, D., Varga, D.: The JRC-Acquis: A multilingual aligned parallel corpus with 20+ languages. In: Proceedings of the 5th International Conference on Language Resources and Evaluation, pp. 2142–2147 (2006)
13. Yu, K., Tsujii, J.: Extracting bilingual dictionary from comparable corpora with dependency heterogeneity. In: Proceedings of Human Language Technologies: The 2009 Annual Conference of the North American Chapter of the Association for Computational Linguistics, Companion Volume: Short Papers, pp. 121–124 (2009)
14. István, V., Shoichi, Y.: Bilingual dictionary generation for low-resourced language pairs. In: Proceedings of the 2009 Conference on Empirical Methods in Natural Language Processing, pp. 862–870 (2009)
15. Matsuo, Y., Ishizuka, M.: Keyword extraction from a single document using word co-occurrence statistical information. International Journal on Artificial Intelligence Tools 13, 157–170 (2004)
16. Li, J., Ezeife, C.I.: Cleaning web pages for effective web content mining. In: Bressan, S., Küng, J., Wagner, R. (eds.) DEXA 2006. LNCS, vol. 4080, pp. 560–571. Springer, Heidelberg (2006)
17. Zhang, Y., Wu, K., Gao, J., Vines, P.: Automatic acquisition of Chinese-English parallel corpus from the web. In: Proceedings of the 28th European Conference on Information Retrieval, pp. 420–431 (2006)
18. Utiyama, M., Isahara, H.: A Japanese-English patent parallel corpus. In: Proceedings of Machine Translation Summit XI, pp. 475–482 (2007)

A Revised SimRank Approach for Query Expansion

Yunlong Ma, Hongfei Lin, and Song Jin

Information Retrieval Laboratory, School of Computer Science and Engineering,
Dalian University of Technology, Dalian 116023, China
kevinma@mail.dlut.edu.cn, hflin@dlut.edu.cn,
jinsong@mail.dlut.edu.cn

Abstract. Query expansion technologies based on pseudo-relevance documents have been proven to be effective in many information retrieval tasks. One problem with these methods is that some of the expansion terms extracted from feedback documents are irrelevant to the query, which may hurt the retrieval performance. In this paper, we proposed a normalized weight SimRank (NWS) approach for query expansion, with query logs collected by a practical search engine. Analyzing the relationship between queries and URLs, we create a query-click graph, and a term-relationship graph is constructed by several transformations. In order to reduce the computational complexity of NWS, strategies of pruning and radius limit were used to optimize the algorithm. Experimental results on two TREC test collections show that our approach can discover the qualified terms effectively and improve queries' accuracy.

Keywords: Search Engine, Query Expansion, Query Logs, SimRank.

1 Introduction

In general, most web search engines discover relevance documents for a query by term matching. Unfortunately, in most cases, the original query can't express user's information need accurately, and people often use different words to describe concepts in their queries from authors use to describe the same concepts in their documents. In order to help a user in such a case, the query expansion approach becomes very important which focus on generating new queries by adding words to the original query.

Query expansion is the approach of adding words to the original query to improve retrieval performance in information retrieval operations. It can discover some related property between words and original query automatically by analyzing a collection of documents or some resources. There are two main challenges in the query expansion process. One is where should the additional words be found. As an external resource, a query log is a rich information source [1], which including billions of submitted queries, viewed search results, and clicked URLs. Thus the huge amount of search engine log data offers excellent opportunities for additional words mining. The other one is what types of association are useful to help improve the queries quality. In the paper [2], we look into association and similar patterns at the level of terms through analyzing the relations of terms inside a query log in a real search engine, and use them as candidate terms.

P.-J. Cheng et al. (Eds.): AIRS 2010, LNCS 6458, pp. 564–575, 2010.
© Springer-Verlag Berlin Heidelberg 2010

In this paper, we focus on query expansion base on the recent history of queries. We try to generate a historical query-click graph that records the clicks that were generated by URLs when a user inputs a query. The query-click graph is a weighted bi-partite graph [3], with queries on one side and URLs on the other. Then, the term-relationship graph which was obtained by several transformations from the query-click graph could reflect the direct connections of the terms in query logs. And our approach is based on the notion of SimRank [4], which can compute term similarity based on not only directly connections but also indirectly relationships in the term-relationship graph. However, in our case we need to extend SimRank to take into account the weights of the edges in the term-relationship graph, and we call the revised algorithm normalized weight SimRank (NWS). Term pairs with high similarity scores are with high confidence and then used for query expansion.

In the next section, we discuss the related work of query expansion and query logs analysis. Section 3 we describe how we construct the query-click graph and term-relationship graph from query logs. Section 4 describes the original SimRank algorithm and our normalized weight SimRank algorithm. Section 5 shows the candidate terms section and our query expansion strategy. Section 6 contains the experimental results based on the AOL query log, as well as a discussion of those results and the last section is conclusion.

2 Related Work

2.1 Query Expansion

In query expansion, the query is expanded using words or phrases with similar meaning to those in the query and the chances of matching words in relevant documents are therefore increased. One of the earliest studies of query expansion was carried out by [5] who clustered words based on co-occurrence in documents and used those clusters to expand the queries. The techniques that have been used recently can be described as being based on either global or local analysis of the documents in the corpus being searched.

The global analysis technique we describe here is one of the first techniques to produce consistent effectiveness improvements through automatic expansion. Other researchers have developed similar approaches, i.e., using LSI (Latent semantic indexing) or LDA (Latent Dirichlet allocation), and have also reported good results [6]. Among all the local analysis approaches, pseudo-relevance feedback (PRF) exploiting the retrieval result has been the most effective [7]. It has been implemented in different retrieval models: vector space model [8], probabilistic model [9], and so on. Recently, the PRF principle has also been implemented within the language modeling framework [10]. In these works, the top ranked documents were assumed to be relevant as a special case of relevance feedback.

Compare with PRF approaches a crucial question is the expansion terms determined in traditional ways from the pseudo-relevant documents are not all useful [1]. So, some studies focus on using an external resource for query expansion. Several external collection enrichment approaches have been proposed, such as search engine query logs [2], WordNet [12], Wikipedia [13] etc. Our work follows this strategy of a query expansion approach using query logs as a resource of query expansion terms.

2.2   Query Graphs

Baeza-Yates [14] identifies five different types of query graphs based on query logs. In all cases, the nodes are queries, a link is introduced between two nodes respectively if: (1) the queries contain the same word(s) (word graph), (2) the queries belong to the same session (session graph), (3) users clicked on the same URLs in the list of their results (URL cover graph), (4) there is a link between the two clicked URLs (URL link graph), (5) there are l common terms in the content of the two URLs (link graph). Baeza-Yates and Tiberi [15] study a weighted version of the cover graph. Their analysis provides information not only about how people query but also about how they behave after a query and the content distribution of what they look at. Moreover the authors study several characteristics of click graphs, i.e., Query-click graphs (also known as query-document graph) are introduced by [3][11], are bipartite graphs of queries and URLs, where a query and a URL are connected if a user clicked on the URL that was an answer for the query. This framework is used to infer semantic relations among queries and to detect multi-topical URLs, i.e., URLs that cover either several topics or a single very general topic. Query-click graphs are presenting more in detail in Section 3.

3   Basic Graph Model

3.1   Query-Click Graph

Query-click graph (also known as query-document graph) is introduced by [3]. It is a weighted bi-partite graph which the nodes in the one set are queries and the nodes in the other set are URLs which appears in query logs. An edge appears between a query q and a URL u if the user that issued the query, clicked on the URL in the list of results. Let $G_{QC} = \{V_{QC}, E_{QC}\}$ be a bi-partite graph such that $V_{QC} = \{v_q, v_u\} = Q \cap U$ and $E_{QC} = \{e_{qu}\} \subseteq Q \times U$, where Q a set of all queries in query logs and U a set of URLs clicked for those queries, v_q is a node of query and v_u is a node of URL in the graph. Let $\omega(e_{qu})$ be a weighting function for an edge $e_{qu} \in E_{QU}$, for this instance it is the number of clicks there are for a query q on a URL u.

Specifically, the query-click graph constructed by the following four steps:

1. Remove all noisy records and stopwords from the query logs (details in Section 6.1).
2. Add a new query node to the query-click graph for every unique query in the query logs.
3. In the same way, add a new URL node to the graph for every unique URL in the query logs.
4. Make a directly connection edge form every query-URL node, if they appear in the same record, and the weight of edge is assigned 1. If the edge already exists, add 1 to the weight.

3.2 Term-Relationship Graph

A term-relationship graph is a weighted and directed graph. We model terms and relationships as a graph $G_T = \{V_T, E_T\}$ where nodes in $V_T = \{v_t\}$ represent terms inside query logs and edges in $E_T = \{e_t\}$ represent relationships between terms. A directed edge which appears between two term nodes, represent a kind of direct relationship, if the user input them in different queries, and clicked the same URL in their list of results. The weight of edge $\omega(e_{ij})$ is the number of co-occurrence represent associated degree between two terms i and j.

The term-relationship graph can be obtained by two transformations from the query-click graph.

3.2.1 Query Nodes Substitution

Although the query-click graph can reflect all queries, URLs and the connections between them completely, then we can discover knowledge at the level of queries. But in this paper, we propose to mine query logs for query expansion at the level of terms through analyzing the relations inside queries. Thus we must substitute term nodes for query nodes by following four steps:

1. For every query node v_q in the query-click graph, replace it with all term nodes inside the query of v_q.
2. If the node does not exist, build this node.
3. Copy all adjacency edges from every query node to all terms nodes include in it.
4. Delete all query nodes and their adjacency edges.

Then we obtain a graph composed by term nodes, URL nodes and directed edges between them.

3.2.2 URL Nodes Elimination

Query expansion technique needs the relations at the level of terms, so the URL nodes are unnecessary, and what's more, it will cause lots of extra cost. For this reason, we decide to eliminate them by following steps:

1. For every term node pair (v_{t1}, v_{t2}) and every URL node v_u, if there are two edges from v_{t1} to v_u and from v_{t2} to v_u concurrently, then add two edges in the graph, one is from v_{t1} to v_{t2} and the other is from v_{t1} to v_{t2}, that both have weight as $c(v_{t1}, v_{t2}, v_u)$, or add the weight of edge to $c(v_{t1}, v_{t2}, v_u)$.
2. Delete all URL nodes and their adjacency edges.

Besides, $c(v_{t1}, v_{t2}, v_u)$ represents the value of crossover frequency which can be compute by following formula:

$$c(v_{t1}, v_{t2}, v_u) = \min\left(\omega(v_{t1} \to v_u), \omega(v_{t2} \to v_u)\right) \cdot \qquad (1)$$

To sum up, after these steps in Subsection 3.2.1 and Subsection 3.2.2, we can transform query-click graph into term-relationship graph, and the transformation has many practical significance:

1. The term-relationship graph is conducive to mine the association between terms in query logs.
2. The analysis is at the level of terms rather than at the level of queries, and it is useful to help to reformulation an effective query.
3. Compared to the number of queries and URLs, the number of terms is quite small, so the space which the term-relationship graph takes in the memory is smaller.
4. Compared to the bi-partite graph model, the process of SimRank and optimization based on one type node graph will be more convenient.

4 Computing SimRank

4.1 Naïve Method

SimRank [4] is a method for computing object similarities, applicable in any domain with object-to-object relationships, that measures similarity of the structural context in which objects occur, based on their relationships with other objects. The intuition behind it is that, in many domains, similar objects are related to similar objects. More precisely, objects a and b are similar if they are related to objects c and d, respectively, c and d are themselves similar. The base case is that objects are similar to themselves.

Moreover, SimRank is an iterative technique to compute the similarity score for each pair of objects. In our case, we can consider the terms as one type of objects and use SimRank to compute similarity scores for each term-term pair.

For a node v_t in the term-relationship graph, we denote by $I(v_t)$ the set of in-neighbors, and individual in-neighbors are denoted as $I_i(v_t)$, for $1 \le i \le I(v_t)$. Let $Sim(v_a, v_b)$ denote the similarity between term v_a and v_b. For $v_a \ne v_b$, we write the naive equation:

$$Sim(v_a, v_b) = \frac{C}{|I(v_a)||I(v_b)|} \sum_{i}^{|I(v_a)|} \sum_{j}^{|I(v_b)|} Sim(I_i(v_a), I_j(v_b)) \tag{2}$$

If $v_a = v_b$, then $Sim(v_a, v_b)$ is defined to be 1. Otherwise, where C is a constant between 0 and 1, gives the rate of decay as similarity flows across edges. In the SimRank paper [4], it is shown that a simultaneous solution $Sim(*,*) \in [0,1]$ to the above equations always exists and is unique. Also notice that the SimRank scores are symmetric, i.e. $Sim(v_a, v_b) = Sim(v_b, v_a)$.

According to the Equation (2), we can use the SimRank score as the association for query expansion instead of co-occurrence degree and probability of translating.

4.2 Normalized Weight SimRank

In the term-relationship graph, there may be many "unpopular" terms, i.e., term nodes with very few in-degree. Although the scarcity of contextual information makes them difficult to analyze, these terms are often the most useful, since they tend to be harder to find. Unlike the simple co-occurrence scheme, SimRank can effectively analyze terms with little contextual information in sparse graph.

Unfortunately, because of the weight on graph edges, the naive SimRank fails to properly identify term similarities in our application. In the naive form SimRank, the information of weights is neglected and we tried to derive similarity scores for term pairs by just using the term-relationship graph's structure.

In general, in order to utilize the edge weights in the computation of similarity scores. We first normalize the in-edge weights for every node v_t in the term-relationship graph by following the next equation:

$$\sum_i^{|I(v_t)|} \omega\big(I_i(v_t) \to v_t\big) = 1 \tag{3}$$

And now, we can incorporate the normalized weight into the SimRank equations. In the new form SimRank, named normalized weight SimRank (NWS), we modify the Equation (2) as follows:

$$NWS\left(v_a,v_b\right) = \begin{cases} C \displaystyle\sum_i^{|I(v_a)|}\sum_j^{|I(v_b)|} NWST\big(I_i(v_a),I_j(v_b)\big) & v_a \neq v_b \\ 1 & v_a = v_b \end{cases} \tag{4}$$

$$NWST\big(I_i(v_a),I_j(v_b)\big) = \omega\big(I_i(v_a)\to v_a\big)\omega\big(I_j(v_b)\to v_b\big)NWS\big(I_i(v_a),I_j(v_b)\big) \tag{5}$$

The value $\omega(v_a \to v_b)$ corresponds to the normalized weights of the edge that start from v_a to v_b.

4.3 Pruning

Let us analyze the time and space requirements for this method of computing Sim-Rank. Let d be the average of $I(v_t)$, and K be the number of iterations of SimRank computing. The space required is simply $O(n^2)$ to store the results. The time required is $O(Kn^2d^2)$, since on each iteration, the score of every node-pair (n^2 of these) is updated with values from its in-neighbor pairs (d^2 of these on average). We mentioned that typically $K \approx 5$ [4], n^2 can be prohibitively large in some cases, such as the query logs. Thus, in this subsection we do briefly consider pruning techniques that reduce both the time and space requirements.

Our way to reduce the resource requirements is to prune the term-relationship graph. So far we have assumed that all n^2 node-pairs graph are considered, and a similarity score is computed for every node-pair. In the SimRank paper [4], it is shown that if n is significantly large, it is very likely that the neighborhood (say, nodes within a radius of 2 or 3) of a typical node will be a very small percentage of the entire domain. Nodes far from a node v, whose neighborhood has little overlap with that of v, they will tend to have lower similarity scores with v than nodes near it. Thus one pruning technique is to set the similarity between two nodes far apart to be 0, and consider node-pairs only for nodes which are near each other. So, in our works, we consider only node-pairs within a radius r of n from each other, and there are on average d_r such neighbors for a node, then the time and space complexities become $O(Knd_r d^2)$ and $O(nd_r)$ respectively.

Moreover, in most cases we also expect the average in-degree to be relatively small. According to the Equation (4) and (5), it is very likely that the in-edge with a very small weight will tend to have smaller contribution to the $NWS(v_t, *)$ score than edges with large weight. So another pruning technique is to limit the maximum in-degree to a fixed value of d_m, consider only the top d_m edges sorted by their weight, and then the time complexities become $O(Knd_r d_m^2)$.

Of course, the quality of the approximation needs to be verified experimentally for the actual datasets. For the case of scientific papers, our empirical results suggest that this is a good approximation strategy, and allows the computation to be carried out entirely in several days for a query-log of $n = 413,013$ terms. More details can be found in Section 6.

5   Query Expansion

For any given query $q = w_1 \ldots w_{i-1} w_i w_{i+1} \ldots w_n$, our approach will iterate through all terms w_i and try to find similar terms in the query logs for each of them. For each w_i, the approach select candidate terms and do query expansion by following three steps:

1.   If there is a node of t_i in the term-relationship graph, then consider every terms t_j with $NWS(v_i, v_j) \neq 0$ as a candidate term.

2.   Remain only the top M expansion candidate terms t_j sorted by their $NWS(v_i, v_j)$.

3.   Join all remaining candidate terms in the original query, and then retrieval using the new query.

In the follow sections, the method above is called NWSE (Normalized Weight Sim-Rank based Expansion).

6 Experiments

6.1 Dataset

Our experiments are based on the query logs distributed by AOL, containing 36,389,567 records, 10,154,742 distinct queries and 657,426 users. Most of them are in English and sampled during three month and including an anonymous user-id, a query, a timestamp, and the results (for each result, the position on the result page is also provided).

All evaluation is done using three standard TREC collections: Robust04 and Gov-2, containing 528,155 documents and 25,205,179 documents respectively. It should be noted that the two collections are quite different: Robust04 is a newswire collection, while the Gov-2 is a web collections.

We used 150 queries associated with each collection for evaluation (No.301-450 queries for Robust04 and No.701-850 queries for GOV-2 respectively). In particular, we treat all topic titles as queries and neglect their description.

6.2 Design of Experiments

6.2.1 Baseline
In order to evaluating the effectiveness of our method, we use two methods as the baseline for comparison. One is the language model implemented by Indri toolkit and the Dirichlet smoothing prior μ was set to 1500 empirically. This method is denoted by LM-Dir. The other one, we implemented a Relevance-Based Language Model, one of the PRF expansion approaches, based on the method by Lavrenko and Croft [10], denoted by RM.

We used precision at 10 (P@10), precision at 20 (P@20) and MAP to measure retrieval effectiveness for all experiments.

6.2.2 Query Expansion with NWSE
In order to remove noisy records, we remove all index queries and meaningless queries from AOL query logs, i.e., queries such as "fidelity.com" and "wu 20v 20-----". And stopword removal was done in this process. Moreover, there are also a large number of adult queries, and we did not use it in our experiments, though. For creating the term-relationship graph, we creating the query-click graph first, that contains approximately 4 million query nodes and 2 million clicked URL nodes. After several transformations have been described in Subsection 3.2, the term-relationship is obtained finally, containing 413,013 term nodes.

Before computing the similarity scores, let's discuss the parameter for pruning. Table 1 shows that how the d_m (the maximum number of in-edges considered by the NWS) influences the NWS scores, When M (the number of candidate terms remained) is set to 5 empirically. We find that the NWS scores nearly no longer grow, if the value of d_m is bigger than 500, so the d_m is set to 500 in all experiments.

Table 1. Examples of NWS similarity when d_m takes different values

d_m :	100	300	500	700	900
NWS("history", "record")	0.0031	0.0067	0.0083	0.0086	0.0088
NWS("diamond", "gold")	0.0047	0.0069	0.0079	0.0081	0.0081
NWS("state", "country")	0.0078	0.0094	0.0105	0.0107	0.0107

Similarly, we set r (the radius of similarity transmission) and K (the number of iterations) to 2 and 5 respectively.

According to the description in section 5, we can expand the original query weight candidate terms. The candidate terms and the original query terms are combined using "#weight" operator and "#combine" operator implemented in Indri, and Equation 6 is implemented by creating an Indri query of the form:

$$\#weight(\, \lambda\, Q_{ori}\, (1.0-\lambda)\, Q_{exp}\,) \tag{6}$$

Where Q_{ori} is the original query and λ is free parameter determining the weight given to the original query. Specifically, we work out two different strategies for creating the final query. One is all candidate terms are considered equally good in the Q_{exp}, named NWSE-Unweighted. The other one is adding their NWS scores in the final query as weights, named NWSE-Weighted.

6.3   Results

Figure 1 shows the results of assigning different λ on two TREC collections, when the M is set to 30 empirically. As can be seen in Figure 1, the RM method perform well when $\lambda = 0.3$ and $\lambda = 0.6$. On the other hand, the MAP of the NWSE-Weighted method and NWSE-Unweighted method is higher than the RM method's. The NWSE-Weighted method and NWSE-Unweighted method performed the best when λ is set to 0.5 for Robust 04, 0.9 and 0.8 respectively for Gov-2. Finally, we set the parameter λ to optimal values for each of methods.

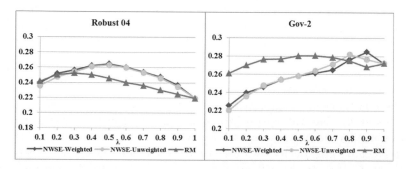

Fig. 1. MAP performance of all query expansion approach when M=30

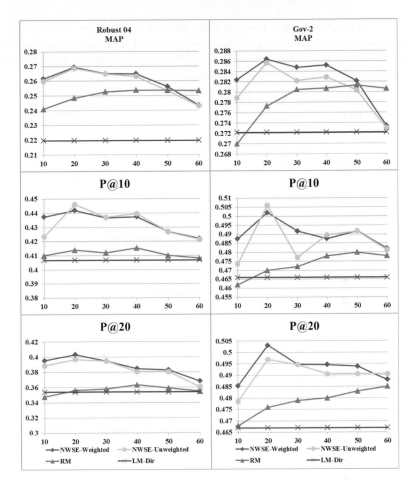

Fig. 2. MAP, @10 and P@20 score curves for all query expansion results

The Figure above show the results of assigning different value to M for all methods on three TREC collections. The MAP of our methods are 6.19% and 1.81% higher than the query expansion based on pseudo relevance feedback, 7.49% and 5.44% higher on P@10, and 10.96% and 3.73% higher on P@20 for Robust 04 and Gov-2 respectively.

According to Figure 2, we can see the NWSE-Weighted and NWSE-Unweighted methods preform as well as the RM model does in the MAP evaluation. We also can see that the methods we proposed outperform the RM method, it shows that the expansion terms selected from query logs by NWSE is more relevance than them extracted from pseudo-relevance documents.

Figure 2 shows the trend of MAP, P@10 and P@20 for all methods. Comparing to the LM-Dir method, we can see all of the three query expansion methods have the very great scope enhancement in the evaluating metrics. The NWSE-Weighted and NWSE-Unweighted methods perform well when $20 < M < 40$, but RM method does the same when the expansion scale is bigger. It means that the effective retrieval process can be finish in a short time by using the NWSE methods, just because more terms in query cause more time and space cost. Specially, we notice that the NWSE-Weighted works better and more stable than NWSE-Unweighted, and it proves that the weights provide by NWS scores is quality.

7   Conclusion

In this paper, we have explored the AOL query logs as a new resource for query expansion. We generated a weighted bi-partite query-click graph, with queries on one side and URLs on the other, and then, obtained the term-relationship graph by several transformations from it. We also proposed new methods for mining expansion terms from AOL query logs. Our methods named normalized weight SimRank are based on a revised SimRank algorithm, and we measure the importance of expansion terms according to their NWS with the original query terms. Our experiments show that the expansion terms extracted from AOL query logs are better than those from the feedback documents, using a simple statistical method, on the different TREC collections.

There are a few limitations of our work. First, all the experiments are based on click-throughs instead of real relevance judgments, so a future work would be to test the proposed methods with real relevance data. Second, query logs have more meaningful information of sessions was neglected in our experiments. The last, because of the great capacity for query log, we do not have enough time and equipment for pruning radius optimization. So we will pay more attention on this in our future work.

Acknowledgements

This work was supported in part by grant from the Natural Science Foundation of China (No. 60673039 and 60973068), the National High Tech Research and Development Plan of China (2006AA01Z151), the Doctoral Fund of Ministry of Education of China 20090041110002.

References

1. Dang, V., Croft, W.B.: Query Reformulation Using Anchor Text. In: Proceedings of WSDM 2010, New York City, New York, USA, pp. 41–50 (2010)
2. Wang, X., Zhai, C.: Mining Term Association Patterns from Search Logs for Effective Query Reformulation. In: Proceedings of CIKM 2008, Napa Valley, California, USA, pp. 479–488 (2008)
3. Boldi, P., Bonchi, F., Castillo, C.: Query Suggestions Using Query-Flow Graphs. In: Proceedings of WSCD 2009, Barcelona, Spain, pp. 51–58 (2009)
4. Jeh, G., Widom, J.: SimRank: A Measure of Structural-Context Similarity. In: Proceedings of SIGKDD 2002, Edmonton, Alberta, Canada, pp. 538–543 (2002)
5. Sparck, J.K.: Automatic Keyword Classification for Information Retrieval. Butterworth, London (1971)
6. Croft, W.B., Xu, J.X.: Query Expansion Using Local and Global Document Analysis. In: Proceedings of SIGIR 1996, Zurich, Switzerland, pp. 4–11 (1996)

7. Diaz, F., Metzler, D.: Improving the Estimation of Relevance Models Using Large External Corpora. In: Proceedings of SIGIR 2006, Seattle, Washington, USA, pp. 154–161 (2006)
8. Rocchio, J.: Relevance Feedback in Information Retrieval. J. The SMART Retrieval System: Experiments in Automatic Document Processing 21, 313–323 (1971)
9. Robertson, S., Sparck, J.K.: Relevance Weighting of Search Terms. J. The American Society for Information Science 27, 129–146 (1976)
10. Lavrenko, V., Croft, W.B.: Relevance Based Language Models. In: Proceedings of SIGIR 2001, New Orleans, Louisiana, United States, pp. 120–127 (2001)
11. Antonellis, I., Molina, H.G., Chang, C.C.: Simrank++: Query Rewriting through Link Analysis of the Click Graph. In: Proceedings of VLDB 2008, Auckland, New Zealand, pp. 408–421 (2008)
12. Collins-Thompson, K., Callan, J.: Query Expansion Using Random Walk Models. In: Proceedings of SIGIR 2005, Bremen, Germany, pp. 704–711 (2005)
13. Xu, Y., Jones, J.F., Wang, B.: Query Dependent Pseudo-Relevance Feedback Based on Wikipedia. In: Proceedings of SIGIR 2009, Boston, Massachusetts, USA, pp. 59–66 (2009)
14. Baeza-Yates, R.: Graphs from Search Engine Queries. In: van Leeuwen, J., Italiano, G.F., van der Hoek, W., Meinel, C., Sack, H., Plášil, F. (eds.) SOFSEM 2007. LNCS, vol. 4362, pp. 1–8. Springer, Heidelberg (2007)
15. Baeza-Yates, R., Tiberi, A.: Extracting Semantic Relations from Query Logs. In: Proceedings of SIGKDD 2007, New York, NY, USA, pp. 76–85 (2007)
16. Beeferman, D., Berger, A.: Agglomerative Clustering of A Search Engine Query Log. In: Proceedings of SIGKDD 2000, Boston, Massachusetts, USA, pp. 407–416 (2000)
17. Silverstein, C., Marais, H., Henzinger, M.: Analysis of A Very Large Web Search Engine Query Log. ACM SIGIR Forum 33(1), 6–12 (1999)

Improving Web-Based OOV Translation Mining for Query Translation

Yun Dong Ge, Yu Hong, Jian Min Yao, and Qiao Ming Zhu

Provincial Key Laboratory of Computer Information Processing Technology,
Soochow University, Suzhou, China, 215006
geyundong@gmail.com, {hongy,jyao,qmzhu}@suda.edu.cn

Abstract. Query translation is the most widely used approach for cross-language information retrieval (CLIR). The major challenge of query translation is translating Out-Of-Vocabulary (OOV) terms. This paper proposes three methods to improve OOV translation mining for query translation. Firstly, Co-occurrence information is utilized to extract topic words and to expand the source language query with the translations of topic words for collecting relevant bilingual snippets. Secondly, an improved frequency change measurement method which combines context dependency is utilized to extract valid OOV translation candidates from noisy, small-sized bilingual snippets. Thirdly, for choosing the proper translation, a combination model considering frequency-distance, surface patterns matching and phonetic features is proposed to pick out the appropriate translation(s). Experimental results show that this OOV translation mining approach for query translation has substantial CLIR performance improvement.

Keywords: Out Of Vocabulary, OOV, Translation Mining, Query Translation.

1 Introduction

CLIR enables people to retrieve documents written in one language by another language query. Although CLIR has been advancing rapidly, a major bottleneck remains for translating OOV in queries. Because OOVs are translated incorrectly, irrelevant documents may rank highly, which will cause worse performance (precision, recall etc.) of CLIR.

Conventional CLIR uses a bilingual dictionary to translate queries. Pirkola & al. [12] analyzed the shortcomings of dictionary-based approaches and proposed the possible resolutions. As real queries are usually short, dynamic and diverse, even using the state-of-the-art dictionary cannot avoid the OOV problem.

As increasing number of bilingual resource is available on Internet, exploiting the web to translate OOV is feasible and reliable. For bilingual resource collecting, if directly send the source language OOV to search engine, the returned snippets (contain titles and summaries) are usually monolingual, which cannot be used to extract the target language translation of OOV. That is to say, OOV without expansion usually cannot extract effective snippets. Besides, mostly existing query expansion methods for

P.-J. Cheng et al. (Eds.): AIRS 2010, LNCS 6458, pp. 576–587, 2010.
© Springer-Verlag Berlin Heidelberg 2010

collecting snippets need to segment the OOV. This segment will introduce extra errors and lower the quality of snippets.

Extracting MLUs (Multi-Lexical Unit) as candidates from the gathered snippets is the second main problem. If the candidate of OOV is not extracted correctly, the substantial translation of OOV cannot be mined. The most common method for candidate extraction is taking continuous characters after removing stop words as candidates. However, most of these continuous strings are invalid lexical units.

How to select the most appropriate translation from the large candidate set is the third challenge. The intuitive frequency feature of candidate is mostly adopted in existing methods. More effective features (distance, surface patterns and phonetic etc.) can be used for OOV translation selection.

For the above problems, this paper proposes a novel solution to mine high quality translation of OOV for query translation. Briefly, OOV translation mining method consists of three main parts:

1. Bilingual snippets collection. Gather the bilingual snippets containing the OOV in English and its translation in Chinese from a search engine.
2. Candidate extraction. Extract MLUs from snippets as OOV translation candidates.
3. Appropriate translation selection. Rank candidates generated in 2 for picking out the correct OOV translation.

The Co-occurrence information is used to extract the topic words of the OOV. The OOV expanded with translations of the topic words are sent to search engine to collect relevant bilingual web snippets. The translation of topic words based cross-language expansion method can get more relevant bilingual snippets. To enhance the quality of candidates, a variation of frequency change measurement term extraction method is adopted. Features such as frequency, distance, surface patterns and transliteration are exploited for better translation selection.

The remainder of this paper is organized as follows. Section 2 presents the related work. Section 3 proposes the solution to bilingual resource collection. In section 4, we present the OOV translation candidates extraction method. Candidates ranking for choosing the OOV translation and experiments are presented in section 5 and section 6 respectively. Finally, conclude the paper in the last section.

2   Related Work

Nagata & al. [11] firstly attempted to use the web for translating Japanese OOV. They downloaded the top 100 full web pages as resource. Lu & al. [9] extracted translations of terms through mining of web anchor texts and link structures. For the dependence on full web pages, these two methods need big network bandwidth, large storage capacity and long computing time.

Cheng & al. [3] and Lu & al. [8] utilized the top 100 snippets to mine the OOV translation. Thus the complexity of collecting bilingual resource by these two approaches is sharply reduced. The main shortcoming, however, is the snippets seldom contain corresponding translations since the source query is not expanded with cross-language words; and most of the snippets returned are usually monolingual, which cannot be used to extract the target language translations.

Fang & al. [4] segmented the source OOV, and then expanded the terms with cross-language words to collect web resource. Sun & al. [15] used forward-backward maximum matching method to segment the source term and looked up the target language translations of segmented units to expand the source term for collecting bilingual snippets. These approaches all exploited cross-language query expansion to collect more relevant bilingual snippets and needed to segment the source term, unfortunately, the meaning of a source term is not always the simple combination of the component words meanings. Thus segmenting source term will introduce extra noise in query expansion and further lead to translation mining errors.

Zhang & al. [18] used all substrings of twenty Chinese characters immediately before OOV and twenty Chinese characters immediately after OOV as candidates. Huang & al. [6] and Sun & al. [15] exploited punctuations to segment the snippets and continuous English strings were taken as candidates. Taking the continuous string as candidate or taking substrings of strings before and after OOV as candidates has a drawback because this kind of candidate set often contains lots of invalid lexical units. If the valid candidate of OOV can not be extracted, then correct translation of OOV can hardly be mined. Chien & al. [2] proposed a variant method of mutual information called Significance Estimation (SE). Silva & al. [13] extracted MLUs from large corpora with Local Maxima algorithm, the formula used in the algorithm is symmetric conditional probability (SCP). Cheng & al. [3] introduced Context Dependency (CD) to improve SCP for Chinese MLUs extraction. SE, SCP and SCPCD achieved good performance in large corpora situation.

3   Bilingual Snippets Collection

Unfortunately, not all the snippets gathered from a search engine with the source OOV contain both the OOV and the translation. Take Kim Dae-Jung as an example(Kim Dae-Jung is translated as "金大中" in Chinese), only 1 snippet in the top 10 returned snippets contains target language information since most of the snippets are in English which cannot be used to extract Chinese translations. Ballesteros & al. [1] proposed that query expansion lays a substantial basis for translation extraction. The most expansion methods in previous researches must segment the source OOV, but the meaning of a source term usually is not the combination of individual word meaning in the source term. For example in "风凉话", which means sarcastic remarks, the meanings of the component characters are "wind", "cool" and "talk" respectively. The component characters meanings are irrelevant to the meaning of "风凉话". So an expansion method based on co-occurrence information is utilized in our study which doesn't need segmentation. We first take the OOV as a whole unit with quotation marks and submit it to a search engine. And then extract the topic words from the returned snippets in the source language. Topic words are that with high relevant relation to the source OOV in the same topic or domain. After that, we send the OOV together with the translations of the topic words in the target language respectively to a search engine to collect bilingual resource.

We filter out the non-noun words and English stop words from the bilingual resource, and then we can get an English noun word list. TF*IDF metric is used to extract topic words from the noun English word list. Then we select the top 5 of the list as the topic words.

In the previous example of "Kim Dae-Jung", the topic words extracted from top 20 snippets are "Korea", "president", "winner", "peace" and "prize". Their corresponding translations (if they have several meanings, we choose the first meaning in order to simplify the procedure) are then used as the cross-language expansion words. In this example, the cross-language expansion words are "韩国(Korea)", "总统(president)", "胜利者(winner)", "和平(peace)", and "奖品(prize)". Then we send the source OOV "Kim Dae-Jung" together with translations of topic words respectively to retrieve bilingual snippets. The quality of these bilingual snippets is greatly improved than using only the source OOV.

4 Candidates Extraction

The translation of the OOV may be either a MLU or a single word. As the scale and domain of the dictionary, conventional dictionary-based segmentation approaches are not able to identify the OOV in the snippets, thus the translation of the OOV can hardly be obtained by these approaches.

The approaches for extracting MLUs from large corpus (SE, SCP, SCPCD) are not satisfactory in search engine based candidates extraction, as the size of snippets is quite small. One snippet usually just contains 2 or 3 sentences. Moreover, the snippets are usually fragments of sentences.

We use Frequency Change Measurement together with Context Dependency (FCMCD) to extract MLUs from the bilingual collection. It combines the Frequency Change Measurement (FCM) [8] and Context Dependency (CD). FCM is based on two observations as follows: the first observation is that the component characters of the term have similar frequencies in a collection returned from a search engine. Such as "金(Kim)", "大(Dae)"and "中(Jung)" have similar frequency in the mixed language snippets gathered by "Kim Dae-Jung" with cross-language expansion; the second is that when a valid MLU is extended with an extra character; the frequency of extended term drops apparently. The frequency of "金大中几"is quite lower than that of "金大中" in the snippets. In the FCM method, the following equation is used to evaluate the probability of string S being a MLU.

$$R(S) = \frac{f(S)}{1 + \sqrt{\frac{1}{n}\sum_{i=1}^{n}(x_i - \bar{x})^2}} \tag{1}$$

where S is a Chinese string; f(S) is the frequency of S; x_i is the frequency of each character in S and $\bar{x}$ is the average frequency of all the characters in S.

The candidates extracted by FCM still contain some invalid fragments which are sub-sequences of the valid MLUs. Thus some correct candidates will not be extracted by FCM only. In order to deal with this problem, we combine the Context Dependency (CD) to improve the quality of candidates since we discovered that valid candidates usually have diverse adjacent characters while their sub-terms have relative less and fixed adjacent characters. The CD reflects the degree of a string stands alone as a word. In FCMCD method, Equation (1) is modified as follows.

$$R'(S) = \frac{LN(S) \times f(S) \times RN(S)}{1 + \sqrt{\frac{1}{n} \sum_{i=1}^{n} (x_i - \bar{x})^2}}$$

(2)

where LN(S) is the number of unique left neighboring characters of S; RN(S) is the number of unique right neighboring characters of S. Virtual sentence start mark "B" and sentence end mark "E" were inserted into each sentence at the sentence boundary. If S occurs at the start of the sentence, LN(S) is one. If S occurs at the end of the sentence, RN(S) is one.

We do not simply remove the Chinese stop words from a snippet directly. That will lead to the possibility that the left neighboring character of the stop word and the right neighboring character are extracted as MLU and thus introduce extra noise. Take the sentence "前总统慰问金大中的妻子以及他们的三个儿子" (viz. Former president condoled to the wife of Kim Dae-Jung and their three sons.) as an example. If we directly remove the stop word "的", "中妻" may be extracted as MLU, but "中妻" is an invalid lexical unit in Chinese.

5 Translation Selection

A method that combines frequency-distance, surface patterns matching and phonetic features of the Chinese candidates is used in choosing the correct translation(s).

5.1 Frequency Distance Model

We consider the intuitive features: the frequency of the candidate, the distance between the candidate and the OOV. Intuitively, the authentic translation of the OOV usually co-occurs with the OOV frequently in the snippets. The nearer the candidate to the OOV, the more probable it is the final translation. The measurement between one candidate and the OOV is calculated as:

$$FD(s,t) = \frac{\sum_J \sum_k \frac{1}{d_k(s,t)}}{\max_{fre-dis}}$$

(3)

where s is the OOV, t is one candidate. $d_k(s,t)$ is the k-th distance between s and t in one snippet, for s and t might co-occur more than once in a snippet. J is the number of the snippets and K is the number of co-occurrence between s and t. The denominator is the max reciprocal of the distance among all the candidates. We adopt the count of words between s and t as the distance other than the byte distance, for the snippets may contain several kinds of symbols such as Chinese characters, English characters and punctuation marks etc., which are encoded differently. Thus it reflects more linguistic information to take word count as the distance measure. If there are no character between s and t, the distance is one and so forth.

5.2 Surface Patterns Matching Model

Some Asian languages users usually annotate terms with their translations in English inside a pair of parentheses. These punctuation marks can be used to enhance the precision of the final OOV translation(s). In our solution, some English-Chinese pairs are submitted to a search engine to learn the surface patterns automatically [16], [7]. Some surface patterns obtained by this procedure are listed in table 1. E is one English term; C is the Chinese translation of E.

Table 1. Surface patterns example

No.	Surface patterns
1	C(E, E(C, C (E, E (C
2	C[E, E[C, C [E, E [C
3	C.E, E.C, C,E E,C
4	C>>(E, C|E, C-E

If one candidate matches most of surface patterns in a bilingual snippet set, its probability of being the right translation will increase greatly. The cost of the surface patterns matching is formulated as:

$$SP(s,t) = \frac{N_{matching}}{\max_{num}} \tag{4}$$

where s is the OOV, t is one candidate. The numerator is the number of times that s and t matches the surface patterns. The denominator is the maximum number of matching patterns among all the candidates.

5.3 Transliteration Model

Many OOVs are translated based on phonetic pronunciations, which we called transliteration. Firstly, our transliteration model resolves a sort of matching problem, computing the phonetic similarity between the English OOV and Chinese candidates. We already have the Chinese candidates and thus we don't need to generate the Chinese transliterations. Secondly, to avoid the double errors from English phonetic representation to pin-yin and from pin-yin to Chinese characters, we use a method proposed by [14], [10] to segment an English name into a sequence of syllables, computing the probability between an English syllable and a Chinese character to estimate the possibility. The aim is to compute the phonetic similarity for selecting the right translation. First of all, we segment the English OOV into a sequence of syllables based on heuristic rules and then compute the transliteration cost using the following equation.

$$Trl(s,t) = \frac{P(s,t)}{D(s,t)} \tag{5}$$

where P(s,t) is the co-occurrence probability of s and t which is defined as:

$$P(s,t) \approx \prod_{i=1}^{\min(m,n)} (1-\gamma_1)prob(e_i,c_i) \tag{6}$$

where γ_i is the smoothing weight. $prob(e_i,c_i)$ is the probability between an English syllable e_i and a Chinese character c_i and is computed based dynamic programming from the training corpus contains 37,665 proper name pairs. $D(s,t)$ is the number of syllable difference between an English OOV s and a Chinese candidate t, which is defined as:

$$D(s,t) = \varepsilon + |m-n| \tag{7}$$

here ε is a decaying parameter, m is the total number of English term syllables and n is the total number of Chinese characters.

In order to improve incorrect transliteration mapping between English syllables and Chinese characters, we combine the forward and backward mapping. The final transliteration cost is defined as the average of forward value and backward value.

5.4 Model Combination

We use the frequency-distance model as the baseline model, and re-rank the results by the surface pattern matching model. Not all the OOVs are transliteration terms, directly combing with the transliteration model value decreases the whole performance. If one source term is transliteration word, the transliteration model value of it is much higher than values of those are not transliteration words. The threshold of the transliteration model is computed. If the transliteration value of one candidate is greater than the threshold, then we re-rank the candidate by the transliteration value. Otherwise the rank of the candidate stays the same.

6   Experiments and Analysis

TDT4 corpora were used in our CLIR experiment. TDT4 contains topics, documents and relevance judgments. This document set contains the complete set of English, Arabic and Chinese news text used in the 2002 and 2003 Topic Detection and Tracking technology evaluations. TDT4 have 80 topics. Each topic has four parts: topic number and Title, Seminal Event, Topic Explication Rule of Interpretation. There are 27,142 Chinese documents in TDT4 corpora. We use the title of the topic as our English query, that is to say we have 80 source language queries. There are 4 queries in all the source queries have no OOV; the other 76 queries have 82 OOVs.

6.1 Snippets Collection Experiment

We sent the 82 English OOV terms (without cross-language expansion) to search engine to gather snippets and also used our expansion method to gather snippets. We used top 50 snippets returned by search engine for each OOV. Each method gathered 4,100 snippets. If one snippet contains the target language information of the OOV, we consider this snippet is effective.

Without expansion method collected 545 effective snippets. With our expansion method collected 2,636 effective snippets. Our proposed snippets collection method can get more 2,091 effective snippets than the no expansion method, the result shows our method is valid in resource collection stage. High quality of snippets is a key fundamental resource for MLUs extraction and translation selection.

6.2 Candidates Extraction Experiment

50 OOV terms were randomly selected from OOV set. Our expansion method was used to collect snippets for each selected OOV. MLUs were extracted from the 2,500 of 4,200 snippets by SE, SCP, SCPCD, FCM and FCMCD respectively. If one candidate is extracted with valid lexical boundary, this candidate is regarded as correct. Precision is used to evaluate candidate extraction. The precision is defined as the percentage of correct candidates in all candidates. As we do not know the exact number of valid candidates in the specific snippets in advance, so the number of candidates extracted by each methods is used to measure how close to the exact number. That is to say the number of extracted candidates works as an indirect measure of recall. Table 2 contains the results of MLUs extraction.

Table 2. The quality of MLUs extraction

Methods	Precision	Total
SE	55.30%	38,573
SCP	61.32%	47,904
SCPCD	68.54%	48,397
FCM	84.28%	37,355
FCMCD	91.84%	36,006

SE, SCP and SCPCD do not work well on this small size snippets resource. These methods extracted more MLUs, but the precisions are very low. FCM alone achieves better performance than SCPCD, the precision increases 15.74%. FCM together with CD achieves the best performance 91.84% which increases 7.56% precision compared to FCM, but the number of MLUs is lower than that of FCM. Using CD can filter more invalid candidates, although it reduces the recall. As for query translation, precision is more important than recall, the high quality of candidate set is the primary element.

6.3 OOV Translation Selection Experiments

The top n inclusion rate [3] is used as evaluation metric for translation selection, which is defined as the percentage of terms whose translations are included in the top n returned translations and we implemented the Chi-square and Context Vector (Chi+CV) translation selection method which was proposed in [3]. Each OOV was expanded by our method and then 100 snippets were gathered for candidate extraction. Different translation selection models were combined in turn for evaluating the power of each model.

Table 3. Translation mining result

	TOP1	TOP3	TOP5	TOP10
Chi+CV	30.50%	45.12%	56.10%	60.98%
FD	54.88%	71.95%	79.27%	87.80%
FD+SP	60.98%	72.17%	82.93%	92.68%
FD+SP+Trl	65.85%	75.61%	84.15%	93.90%

FD is frequency-distance model. SP is surface patterns matching model. Trl is transliteration model. FD achieves better performance than that of Chi+CV. Chi+CV doesn't use the cross-language expansion and the CV sometimes misguides the selection when the distribution of the incorrect translation is confirmed with the distribution of the OOV. FD together with SP get further improvement. Top 1 inclusion rate increased 6.1% compared to FD. FD+SP+Trl get the best performance, improving the Top 1 inclusion rate with 4.87% increase compared to FD+SP. This indicates three models are complementary for each other.

In order to examine the influence of the number of snippets, we use 50 snippets, 100 snippets and 150 snippets to mine translation with FD+SP+Trl for each OOV respectively. The mining result is shown in table 4.

Table 4. OOV translation mining results with different numbers of snippets

	TOP1	TOP3	TOP5	TOP10
50	52.44%	63.41%	69.51%	85.37%
100	65.85%	75.61%	84.15%	93.90%
150	67.07%	80.49%	85.37%	95.12%

Using 100 snippets improves the Top 1 inclusion rate by 13.41% compared to using 50 snippets. Using 150 snippets slightly improves Top 1 inclusion rate by 1.22% compared to using 100 snippets. The performance improves when the number of snippets increases. The number of relevant snippets increases when use more snippets; the correct OOV translation co-occurs more often and matches more surface patterns with the OOV when using more snippets. However, the main drawback of using more snippets is needs more bandwidth and time for extracting candidates and selecting translation.

6.4 CLIR Experiments

TDT4 English titles are used to retrieve Chinese documents. The retrieval system is constructed with Lucene. Documents were indexed using 2-gram based inverted file index. Mean Average Precision (MAP) values were used to evaluate the performance of retrieval system. Five runs are compared to investigate the performance of different query translation methods. Query disambiguation and relevance feedback [5] were not applied in retrieval because our main aim is to evaluate the improvement of our web based OOV translation mining for query translation.

RUN 1: Monolingual retrieval. English titles were translated into Chinese by professional translators and the translated titles are used to retrieve the Chinese documents. This run provides a comparison of "ideal" retrieval case.

RUN 2: English Queries were translated using a dictionary (containing 286,932 single word pairs) ignoring the OOV.

RUN 3: Translation equivalents were extracted from parallel corpus. This parallel corpus was constructed using the method proposed in [17]. There are 760,000 sentences in this corpus. English queries were translated using the same dictionary in RUN2, and then the translation of OOV was looked up from the translation equivalents.

RUN 4: English queries were translated using the same dictionary in RUN2, and then the translation of OOV was mined using our proposed web based method.

RUN 5: English queries were translated with dictionary, translation equivalents and the translations of OOV which mined by our web based method.

Table 5. MAP values obtained by different query translation methods

	MAP	Per. of RUN 1 （%）
RUN 1	0.4945	-
RUN 2	0.0975	19.72
RUN 3	0.1496	30.25
RUN 4	0.3850	77.86
RUN 5	0.4070	82.31

Two main reasons account for the poor performance of RUN 2 .First, our dictionary only contains common words, such compound words and proper names in the queries cannot be found in this dictionary. Second, some terms have several translations and we just select the first entity as their translation which introduces extra error. RUN 3 gets the performance of 30.25% percentage of RUN 1. The improvement is not remarkable because most of the translation equivalents are common words, thus most OOV cannot be translated. RUN 4 improves the performance greatly with 77.86% percentage of RUN 1. RUN 5 achieves the best performance. That is because the high quality translation equivalents of common words obtained from parallel corpus and the power of OOV translation mining using web are all benefit to the query translation.

Our web based OOV translation mining method returns 10 translations for every OOV. We found that some returned translations are full names or abbreviations of the correct translations; some are the different transliterations using different Chinese characters of the correct translations; although some results are not the correct translations, they have high relation with the source OOV. All these kinds of OOV translations can be used as natural query expansion for OOV. Whether using more translations of OOV improves the performance of CLIR or not? We investigate this problem using the method of RUN4. The result of web method is shown in table 6 using top 1, top3, top5 and top 10 translations of OOV respectively.

Table 6. MAP values obtained by RUN 4 with different number of translations

	TOP1	TOP3	TOP5	TOP10
MAP	0.3850	0.3901	0.3921	0.3853
Per. of RUN 1 （%）	77.86	78.89	79.30	77.91

Using top 5 translations achieves the top performance. However, while using top 10 translations the performance drops slightly. The reason is the last 5 translations are usually incorrect and decrease the whole performance.

7   Conclusion

This paper proposes a web-based OOV translation mining for query translation. The topic words based method was used to expand the OOV for collecting relevant bilingual snippets. Then an improved Frequency Change Measurement method which combines Context Dependency (FCMCD) is used to extract valid MLUs from noisy, small bilingual snippets. A method using frequency-distance, surface patterns and transliteration modeling is proposed to select the correct translation. Experimental results show that this method has impressive improvement in English-Chinese CLIR on TDT4 test set.

For further work, we will combine our candidate extraction method with POS tagging to extract more reliable candidates. Semantic relation between OOV and candidates will be used to improve Top 1 inclusion rate of translation selection. Our experiment will be conducted on other CLIR test set (CLEF, NTCIR etc.). For better CLIR performance, query disambiguation and relevance feedback will be integrated into our CLIR architecture.

Acknowledgments

The work is supported by the National Natural Science Foundation of China under Grant No 60970057.

References

1. Ballesteros, L. and Croft, W. B.: Phrasal Translation and Query Expansion Techniques for Cross-Language Information Retrieval. In: Proc. of 20th International ACM SIGIR Conference on Research and Development in Information Retrieval, pp. 84-91. Philadelphia, USA (1997)
2. Chien, L.-F.: PAT-tree-based Keyword Extraction for Chinese Information Retrieval. In: Proceedings of the 20th annual international ACM SIGIR conference on Research and development in information retrieval, ACM Press, Philadelphia (1997)
3. Cheng, P.–J., Teng, J.-W., Chen, R.-C., Wang, J.-H., Lu, W.-H., Chien, L.-F.: Translating Unknown Queries with Web Corpora for Cross-language Information Retrieval. In: The Proceedings of 27th ACM SIGIR, pp. 146–153. ACM Press, New York (2004)

4. Fang, G., Yu, H., Nishino, F.: Chinese-English Term Translation Mining Based on Semantic Prediction. In: Proceedings of the 21th International Conference on Computational Linguistics and the 44th Annual Meeting of the Association for Computational Linguistics Main Conference Poster Session, pp. 199–206 (2006)

5. He, D., Wu, D.: Enhancing query translation with relevance feedback in translingual information retrieval. Information Processing and Management, In Press, Corrected Proof, Available online (2009)

6. Huang, F., Zhang, Y., Vogel, S.: Mining Key Phrase Translation from Web Corpora. In: Proceedings of Human Language Technology Conference and Conference on Empirical Methods in Natural Language Processing, pp. 483–490 (2005)

7. Lin, D., Zhao, S., Derme, B.V., Pasca, M.: Mining Parenthetical Translations from the Web by Word Alignment. In: Proceedings of 46th Meeting of the Association for Computational Linguistics: Human Language Technology, pp. 994–1002 (2008)

8. Lu, C., Xu, Y., Geva, S.: Web-Based Query Translation for English-Chinese CLIR. Computational Linguistics and Chinese Language Processing 13(1), 61–90 (2008)

9. Lu, W.-H., Chien, L.-F., Lee, H.-J.: Translation of Web Queries Using Anchor Text Mining. Asian Language Information Processing 1(2), 159–172 (2002)

10. Lu, W.-H., Lin, J.-H., Chang, Y.-S.: Improving Translation of Queries with Infrequent Unknown Abbreviations and Proper Names. Computational Linguistics and Chinese Language Processing 13(1), 91–120 (2008)

11. Nagata, M., Saito, T., Suzuki, K.: Using The Web as a Bilingual Dictionary. In: 39th Meeting of the Association for Computational Linguistics 2001 Workshop Data-Driven Methods in Machine Translation, pp. 95–102 (2001)

12. Pirkola, A., Hedlund, T., Keskustalo, H., Järvelin, K.: Dictionary-based Cross-language Information Retrieval: Problems, Methods, and Research Findings. Information Retrieval 4(3/4), 209–230 (2001)

13. Silva, J.F.d., Dias, G., Guilloré, S., Pereira, J.G.: Using LocalMaxs Algorithm for the Extraction of Contiguous and Non-contiguous Multiword Lexical Units. In: Progress in Artificial Intelligence: 9th Portuguese Conference on Artificial Intelligence, pp. 113–132 (1999)

14. Wan, S., Verspoor, C.M.: Automatic English-Chinese Name Transliteration for Development of Multilingual Resources. In: Proceedings of 36th Annual Meeting of the Association for Computational Linguistics, Montreal, Quebec, Canada, pp. 1352–1357 (1998)

15. Sun, J., Yao, J.-M., Zhang, J., Zhu, Q.-M.: Web Mining of OOV Translations. Journal of Information & Computational Science 5(1), 1–6 (2008)

16. Wu, J.-C., Lin, T., Chang, J.S.: Learning Source-Target Surface Patterns for Web-based Terminology Translation. In: Proceedings of the 43th Annual Meeting of the Association for Computational Linguistics Interactive Poster and Demonstration Sessions, Ann Arbor, pp. 37–40 (2005)

17. Yan, Z.-X., Feng, Y.-H., Hong, Y., Yao, J.-M.: Parallel Resources Mining From Bilingual Web Pages. In: Conference of China Information Retrieval (CCIR), pp. 513–524 (2009)

18. Zhang, Y., Vines, P.: Using the Web for Automated Translation Extraction in Cross-Language Information Retrieval. In: Proceedings of SIGIR Conference, pp. 162–169 (2004)

On a Combination of Probabilistic and Boolean IR Models for Question Answering

Masaharu Yoshioka

Graduate School of Information Science and Technology, Hokkaido University
N-14 W-9, Kita-ku, Sapporo 060-0814, Japan
yoshioka@ist.hokudai.ac.jp

Abstract. To make a good question answering (QA) system based on a text database, it is preferable to have a good information retrieval (IR) system that can find appropriately relevant document sets for a given query. To make a good IR system for QA about particular named entities (NEs), it is preferable to use a Boolean IR model that uses appropriate Boolean queries with the NE information. In this paper, we propose to use appropriate Boolean query reformulation for information retrieval (ABRIR) for this problem. In this system, an appropriate list of synonyms and variations of Japanese katakana descriptions of a given query are used to construct the Boolean query. Evaluation results show that ABRIR works effectively for the IR task in QA.

Keywords: Information Retrieval, Boolean IR model, Probabilistic IR model, Question Answering.

1 Introduction

QA is a task concerned with finding answers to natural language (NL) questions (e.g., "How tall is the Tokyo Tower?" and "Who is George Bush?") from large text collections. To construct a good QA system, it is preferable to have an appropriate IR system for retrieving documents that have descriptions relevant to providing answers. IR for QA (IR4QA) is a task that evaluates IR modules from the viewpoint of QA system construction [1–3].

There are several approaches to IR4QA, but most of the systems discussed use partial-match IR models, such as the probabilistic IR model, the language model, and the vector-space model [1–3].

In contrast, we assume that one of the significant differences between document retrieval in general and QA about particular NEs is that documents that do not contain any information about the given NEs must be irrelevant. Therefore, it is preferable to use a Boolean IR model. However, because of variations in the description of NEs and synonyms of other related terms, it is not straightforward to make an appropriate Boolean query at the initial retrieval stage.

ABRIR [4] is an IR system that combines probabilistic and Boolean IR models for handling this type of problem. The system constructs an appropriate

P.-J. Cheng et al. (Eds.): AIRS 2010, LNCS 6458, pp. 588–598, 2010.
© Springer-Verlag Berlin Heidelberg 2010

Boolean query based on the comparison between the initial query and pseudo-relevant documents. It then calculates a penalty for retrieved documents that do not satisfy the Boolean query.

In this paper, we briefly review ABRIR and then discuss how to adapt ABRIR for Web documents to become suited to the QA task. Experimental results show that our approach is better than one that uses a probabilistic IR system model alone.

2   The ABRIR Approach

ABRIR is an IR system that has the following combination of features from the probabilistic and Boolean IR models.

1. Reformulation of a Boolean query
   The system compares an initial Boolean query and pseudo-relevant documents and modifies the query, aiming to satisfy most of these documents.
2. Calculating a score based on the results of the probabilistic and IR model
   Basic document scores are calculated by using the probabilistic IR model. A penalty is used in scoring documents that do not satisfy the given Boolean query.

2.1   Reformulation of the Boolean Query

The following procedure is used to reformulate a Boolean query. Figure 1 shows an example of this process.

1. Selection of Boolean candidate words
   We select all terms used in the original query that also exist in all relevant documents. We reformulate the Boolean query by using the selected words with the AND operator. In this example, "A" and "C" exist in all relevant documents, so "A and C" is selected as a candidate query.
2. Reformulation of the Boolean query based on the initial query
   When we have created an original Boolean query, we relax it. When there are one or more words in the initial query that are used with an OR operator, we expand the generated query by using this OR-operator information. In this example, because "C or D" exists in the original query, we extend the generated query to "A and (C or D)."

2.2   Modification of the Score Based on the Boolean Query

The probabilistic IR model in ABRIR is almost equivalent to Okapi BM25 [5] with pseudo-relevance feedback and query expansion, and is implemented by using the generic engine for transposable association (GETA) tool [1].

---

[1] http://geta.ex.nii.ac.jp/

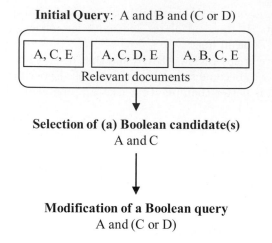

Initial Query: A and B and (C or D)

A, C, E   A, C, D, E   A, B, C, E

Relevant documents

Selection of (a) Boolean candidate(s)
A and C

Modification of a Boolean query
A and (C or D)

Fig. 1. Boolean query construction. [4]

The probabilistic IR model in ABRIR used the BM25 weighting formula to calculate the score for each document:

$$\sum_{T \in Q} w^{(1)} \frac{(k_1 + 1)tf}{K + tf} \frac{(k_3 + 1)qtf}{k_3 + qtf}. \tag{1}$$

Here, $w^{(1)}$ is the weight of a (phrasal) term T, which is a term or a phrasal term in query Q, and is calculated using Robertson-Sparck Jones weights [5]:

$$w^{(1)} = log \frac{(r + 0.5)/(R - r + 0.5)}{(n - r + 0.5)/(N - n - R + r + 0.5)}, \tag{2}$$

where N is the count of all documents in the database, n is the count of all documents containing T, R is the given number of relevant documents, and r is the count of all relevant documents containing T. In addition, tf and qtf are the number of occurrences of T in a document and in a query, respectively, and k_1, k_3, and K are control parameters.

For handling phrasal terms, we introduced a parameter c ($0 \leq c \leq 1$), which is used to count the phrasal terms in a query, such that qtf is incremented by c rather than 1 when a phrasal term is found.

For the query expansion, we used Rocchio-type feedback [6]:

$$qtf = \alpha qtf_0 + (1 - \alpha) \frac{\sum_{i=1}^{R} qtf_i}{R}, \tag{3}$$

where qtf_0 and qtf_i are the number of times T appears in the query and in relevant document i, respectively.

The system used the following procedures to extract word and phrase indexes from the text.

1. Morphological analysis

   We converted ASCII text characters into two-byte extended Unix codes (EUC) by using KAKASI [2] as a code converter, and ChaSen [7] as a morphological analyzer.

2. Extraction of index terms

   We extracted noun words (nouns, unknowns, and symbols) as index terms. We excluded numbers, prefixes, postfixes, and pronouns from the index terms. We removed "—" from the end of a term when the length of the term was longer than two katakana characters. All alphabets were then normalized to one-byte ASCII codes and stored in lower-case format.

3. Extraction of phrasal terms

   Aiming to use compound nouns as phrasal terms, we extracted phrasal terms from pairs of adjacent noun terms. We also used prefixes, postfixes, and numbers in extracting phrasal terms.

ABRIR used the five top-ranked documents for pseudo-relevance feedback and selected 300 different terms having the highest mutual information content between a relevant document set and a term.

Because we assume that documents that do not satisfy the Boolean query may be less appropriate than documents that do satisfy the query, we give a penalty score to documents that do not satisfy the Boolean query.

We apply the penalty based on the importance of the word. For the probabilistic IR model, we used the BM25 weighting formula to calculate the score of each document (Equation 1). In this equation, $w^{(1)} \frac{(k_3+1)qtf}{k_3+qtf}$ indicates the importance of the word in the query. We used a control parameter β to calculate the penalty score:

$$Penalty(T) = \beta * w^{(1)} \frac{(k_3 + 1)qtf}{k_3 + qtf}. \tag{4}$$

For the OR operator, we used the highest penalty among the OR terms as the overall penalty.

We now describe how to calculate the penalty, using the example Boolean query ("A" and ("C" or "D")) shown in Figure 1. First, we calculate the penalty score for all individual words ("A," "C," and "D"). We assume $Penalty(C) \geq Penalty(D)$ in this case. Documents possessing none of "A," "C," or "D" receive the penalty $Penalty(A) + Penalty(C)$. Documents possessing only the "C" term receive $Penalty(A)$.

3   ABRIR for QA

3.1   Differences between WWW Document Retrieval and QA Retrieval

ABRIR, as discussed in the previous section, was developed for WWW document retrieval. Because the characteristics of document retrieval in WWW documents

---

[2] http://kakasi.namazu.org/

and those of QA for particular NEs are different, it is necessary to modify some parameters when applying ABRIR to QA.

The following significant differences should be considered.

1. Use of verbs as index terms
   It is necessary to include verbs as index terms for handling queries containing verbs. In addition, because verbs have various synonyms, it is preferable to have a mechanism for dealing with synonyms.
2. Handling NEs
   Because keywords about NEs are important for this type of query, it is preferable to identify the NE information. In addition, because various NE representations exist, particularly for Japanese katakana NEs (mostly derived from foreign NEs), it is preferable to have a mechanism for dealing with such variations.
3. Number of relevant documents
   Because there are relatively few articles reporting the same events, it is preferable to modify the number of pseudo-relevant documents.
4. Number of query expansion terms
   For QA, precision is more important than recall, and it is therefore preferable to reduce the number of query expansion terms.

3.2   Query Construction Using Synonyms and Variation Lists

To make a good Boolean query, it is preferable to have an appropriate list of synonyms and variations of Japanese katakana descriptions.

For the verbs, the EDR electronic dictionary, developed by Japan Electronic Dictionary Research (EDR) Institute, Ltd., [8] is used for finding synonyms. In this dictionary, each verb has one or more semantic ids. All verbs that share a semantic id with the original verb are candidate synonyms.

For NEs written in Japanese katakana, the following rules are used for generating varieties of description[3].

1. Remove "ー" from the original keyword.
2. Remove small katakana (e.g., "ァィゥェォャュョヮヵヶッ") from the original keyword.
3. Replace small katakana (e.g., "ァィゥェォャュョヮヵヶッ") by large katakana (e.g., "アイウエオヤユヨワカケツ").

By applying this generation rule to the keyword "ヘップバーン" (Hepburn), three candidates ("ヘップバン", "ヘプバーン", and "ヘツプバーン") are generated.

Figure 2 shows the procedures for query construction and retrieval in ABRIR, which can be described as follows.

---

[3] Our NE Variation generation rule is simple. It is better to use more sophisticated method [9, 10] for our future works

0. Initial Query

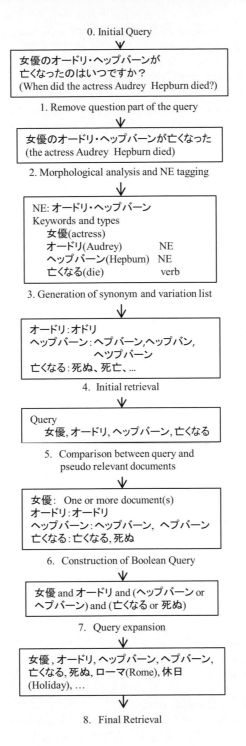

女優のオードリ・ヘップバーンが
亡くなったのはいつですか？
(When did the actress Audrey Hepburn died?)

1. Remove question part of the query

女優のオードリ・ヘップバーンが亡くなった
(the actress Audrey Hepburn died)

2. Morphological analysis and NE tagging

NE: オードリ・ヘップバーン
Keywords and types
　女優(actress)
　オードリ(Audrey)　　　　　NE
　ヘップバーン(Hepburn)　NE
　亡くなる(die)　　　　　　　verb

3. Generation of synonym and variation list

オードリ：オドリ
ヘップバーン：ヘプバーン,ヘップバン,
　　　　　　　　ヘツプバーン
亡くなる：死ぬ、死亡、…

4. Initial retrieval

Query
　女優, オードリ, ヘップバーン, 亡くなる

5. Comparison between query and
　　pseudo relevant documents

女優： One or more document(s)
オードリ：オードリ
ヘップバーン：ヘップバーン, ヘプバーン
亡くなる：亡くなる,死ぬ

6. Construction of Boolean Query

女優 and オードリ and (ヘップバーン or
ヘプバーン) and (亡くなる or 死ぬ)

7. Query expansion

女優, オードリ, ヘップバーン, ヘプバーン,
亡くなる, 死ぬ, ローマ(Rome), 休日
(Holiday), …

8. Final Retrieval

Fig. 2. Procedures for query construction and retrieval in ABRIR

1. Remove the question element from the query
   The question part of the query (e.g., "のはいつですか?" (when)) is trimmed from the original query.
2. Morphological analysis and NE tagging
   Almost the same index-term-extraction system is used to extract initial keywords, except for two differences:
   – extraction of verbs, and
   – identification of NEs, where Cabocha [11] is used to identify NEs.
3. Generation of the synonym and variation lists
   The system generates a synonym list for verbs and a variation list for NEs.
4. Initial retrieval
   The probabilistic IR model is used to find pseudo-relevant documents. Based on the discussion in section 3.1, we use only the top-three-ranked documents for this purpose.
5. Construction of a Boolean query
   There are three types of keyword in the query, namely, NEs, verbs, and other keywords. The system compares query keywords and pseudo-relevant documents in the following manner.
   – NEs.
     Because the system generates a variation list for a given NE automatically, most of the keywords are meaningless. Therefore, the system compares the variation list and keywords in the documents, removing keywords that do not exist in the documents. For example, when there are two documents containing "ヘップバーン" and one document containing "ヘプバーン", the system constructs an OR description ("ヘップバーン" or "ヘプバーン") for "ヘップバーン".
   – Verbs.
     When all pseudo-relevant documents contain one or more synonyms of the verb, these documents are sufficient to generate a synonym list for the final Boolean query. In this case, synonyms that exist in the documents are used for the Boolean query. For example, when there are two documents that contain "亡くなる" (die) and one document that contains "死ぬ" (die), the AND elements are modified to give ("亡くなる" or "死ぬ").
     When at least one document does not contain any synonyms, the system generates a new query by replacing the verb by the synonym list and conducting a secondary retrieval. By using three new pseudo-relevant documents, the system selects synonyms that exist in the documents for the Boolean query.
   – Other keywords.
     When other keywords in the initial query exist in one or more pseudo-relevant documents, these keywords are used as AND elements of the final query.
6. Construction of the Boolean query
   The set of synonyms, NE variation lists, and keywords from all pseudo-relevant documents are joined by the AND operator to construct the Boolean query.

7. Query expansion using pseudo-relevant documents
   The system selects the five different terms with the highest mutual-information content between a relevant document set and a term. The system also adds keywords in the Boolean query as expansion terms.
8. Final retrieval
   Based on the final query, final retrieval is conducted using the probabilistic IR model. We apply a penalty based on the importance of the word by using equation 4. In this formalization, we assume that a Boolean query element for NE is more important than the others, and we therefore give a higher value to β_n than to β for NE.

4 Experimental Results and Discussion

4.1 Experimental Setup

The NTCIR-8 GeoTime Japanese monolingual task data [12] was used to evaluate the proposed system. There are 24 QA topics about geographic and temporal information in Japanese for Mainichi newspapers over the period 2002-2005, which comprises 377,941 documents. Submitted results are evaluated based on the view point of document based relevance judgement. They uses the same techniques used for analyzing IR4QA runs [3].

The parameter values used for the experiments were as follows. Most of the values are common in WWW retrieval. We used $k_1 = 1, k_3 = 7, K = \frac{dl}{avdl}, c = 0.3, and a = 0.7$ for the probabilistic IR model. Here, dl is the length of a document (the number of terms and phrasal terms) and $avdl$ is the average length of all documents.

In addition, we used $\beta = 3, and \beta_n = 1000000$ for the penalty calculations. Using this formalization, many documents had minus scores. Therefore, we simply recalculated the score values to retain the ordering of all document scores.

These are descriptions of the versions of the system tested for comparison:

NE-filter-Verb-penalty (NfVp). Boolean operators on NEs are used for filtering the results, instead of using penalty calculations. Boolean operators on verbs are used for penalty calculations.

NE-penalty-Verb-penalty (NpVp). Boolean operators only are used for penalty calculations.

Baseline-Okapi (BO). No Boolean operators are used. Query expansion terms and term weighting is same as our proposed system. This system is equivalent to the baseline Okapi BM25 system.

4.2 Discussion of the Experimental Results

Table 1 shows evaluation measures for each version of the system and Figure shows normalized Discounted Cumulative Gain (nDCG) of each system per topic. NpVp, using descriptions only in the query, is the best-performed system for the NTCIR-8 GeoTime Japanese monolingual task.

Table 1. Evaluation measures for each version of the system

	NfVp	NpVp	BO
AP	0.3697	0.3719	0.2881
nDCG	0.4117	0.4162	0.3282
Q	0.5710	0.5881	0.4993

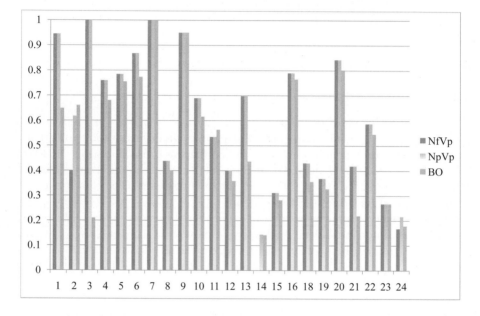

Fig. 3. Normalized Discounted Cumulative Gain (nDCG) of each System per Topic

Comparing NfVp and NpVp enables us to discuss the effectiveness of the Boolean query for the filter. For 14 of the topics (4, 5, 7, 8, 10, 11, 12, 15, 16, 18, 21, 22, 23, and 24), the system could not make a strict Boolean query for selecting small numbers of documents , and the results for NfVp were the same as for NpVp. For seven of the topics (Topic:Boolean_matched_documents 1:772, 3:1, 6:275, 9:6, 13:105, 19:329, and 20:945), the system did make an appropriate Boolean query, retrieving all relevant documents using fewer documents. For the remaining three topics (Topic:filter_out/total_rel 2:26/48, 14:2/2, and 25:1/3), the constructed Boolean queries were too strict, and some relevant documents were filtered out. For example, topic 2, "ハリケーン・カトリーナ" (hurricane Katrina) is recognized as an NE. Therefore, articles with "カトリーナ" (Katrina) and without "ハリケーン" (hurricane) were filtered out. The quality of Boolean query filter for NE is highly depends on the one of NE tagging system. The topic 14 includes an NE keyword "アフリカ" (Africa). However, the relevant documents have the name of the African country "コンゴ民主共和国"

(Democratic Republic of the Congo) instead of "アフリカ". To deal with such relations, it is necessary to have a good query analyzer and a mechanism to deal with the part-whole relationship when generating the related keyword list for the Boolean query. Topic 25 has an NE keyword "スマトラ沖" (off the coast of Smatra) but a relevant document that has exculded with Boolean filter has "スマトラ島沖" (off the coast of Smatra island) and does not have "スマトラ沖" (off the coast of Smatra). Because of this problem, the system performance for NfVp was worse than for NpVp.

Because NpVp performs better than NfVp, we use the comparison between NpVp and BO (base line) to analyze the effectiveness of using a Boolean query. The t test and Wilcoxon Signed Rank test were used to compare the AP, the normalized Discounted Cumulative Gain (nDCG), and the Q measure (Q). From the results of the t test at a significance level of 0.05 for two-sided tests, the differences for nDCG (0.018) and Q (0.040) are statistically significant and that for AP(0.055) is not significant. For the Wilcoxon Signed Rank tests at a significance level of 0.01 for two-sided tests, the AP (0.0015), nDCG (0.0006), and Q (0.0024) results are statistically significant.

There were three topics (2 (AP, nDCG, Q), 11 (AP, nDCG, Q), and 21 (AP)) where the results for NpVp were worse than for BO.

For topic 2, "ハリケーン" (hurricane) is recognized as an NE and articles about "ハリケーン" (hurricane) without "カトリーナ" (Katrina) get a similar score to "カトリーナ" (Katrina) without "ハリケーン" (hurricane).

For topics 11 and 21, these topics do not contain NE information. In such cases, it is difficult to assure the quality of the generated query.

Based on the comparison of the relevant documents and queries generated by our system, we found there are many relevant documents that do not have keywords of each query. It is necessary to have such Boolean query modification mechanism for constructing IR4QA system. In addition, it is very difficult to construct a perfect Boolean query from given query and pseudo-relevant documents, Boolean penalty type system performs well especially for the survey type question.

5 Conclusion

In this paper, we propose to use ABRIR as an IR system for QA about particular NEs. From an evaluation experiment using the NTCIR-8 GeoTime Japanese monolingual task, we confirm that ABRIR can be used in a system that uses appropriate Boolean queries and penalties to outperform a baseline system (the probabilistic IR model, Okapi BM25).

Acknowledgment

This research was partially supported by a Grant-in-Aid for Scientific Research (B) 21300029, from the Japan Society for the Promotion of Science. I would also like to thank organizers of the NTCIR-8 GeoTime task and the reviewer of the paper for their fruitful contribution.

References

1. Greenwood, M.A. (ed.): Proceedings of the 2nd workshop on Information Retrieval for Question Answering (2008)
2. Sakai, T., Kando, N., Lin, C.J., Mitamura, T., Shima, H., Ji, D., Chen, K.H., Nyberg, E.: Overview of NTCIR-7 ACLIA IR4QA task. In: Proceedings of the 7th NTCIR Workshop Meeting on Evaluation of Information Access Technologies: Information Retrieval, Quesiton Answering, And Cross-Lingual Information Access, pp. 63–93 (2010)
3. Sakai, T., Shima, H., Kando, N., Song, R., Lin, C.J., Mitamura, T., Sugimoto, M., Lee, C.W.: Overview of NTCIR-8 ACLIA IR4QA. In: Proceedings of the 8th NTCIR Workshop Meeting on Evaluation of Information Access Technologies: Information Retrieval, Quesiton Answering, And Cross-Lingual Information Access, pp. 63–93 (2010)
4. Yoshioka, M., Haraguchi, M.: On a combination of probabilistic and boolean IR models for WWW document retrieval. ACM Transactions on Asian Language Information Processing (TALIP) 4, 340–356 (2005)
5. Robertson, S.E., Walker, S.: Okapi/Keenbow at TREC-8. In: Proceedings of TREC-8, pp. 151–162 (2000)
6. Uchiyama, M., Isahara, H.: Implementation of an IR package. In: IPSJ SIGNotes, 2001-FI-63, 57–64 (2001) (in Japanese)
7. Matsumoto, Y., Kitauchi, A., Yamashita, T., Hirano, Y., Matsuda, H., Takaoka, K., Asahara, M.: Morphological Analysis System ChaSen version 2.2.1 Manual. Nara Institute of Science and Technology (2000)
8. Japan Electronic Dictionary Research Institute, Ltd (EDR): EDR Electronic Dictionary Version 2.0 Technical Guide TR2-007 (1998)
9. Masuyama, T., Sekine, S., Nakagawa, H.: Automatic construction of Japanese katakana variant list from large corpus. In: COLING 2004: Proceedings of the 20th international onference on Computational Linguistics, Association for Computational Linguistics,Morristown, NJ, USA, pp. 1214–1219 (2004)
10. Goto, I., Kato, N., Ehara, T., Tanaka, H.: Back transliteration from Japanese to English using target English context. In: COLING 2004: Proceedings of the 20th international Conference on Computational Linguistics, Association for Computational Linguistics, Morristown, NJ, USA, pp. 827–833 (2004)
11. Kudo, T., Matsumoto, Y.: Japanese dependency analysis using cascaded chunking. In: CoNLL 2002: Proceedings of the 6th Conference on Natural Language Learning 2002 (COLING 2002 Post-Conference Workshops), pp. 63–69 (2002)
12. Gey, F., Larson, R., Kando, N., Machado-Fisher, J., Sakai, T.: NTCIR-GeoTime overview: Evaluating geographic and temporal search. In: Proceedings of the 8th NTCIR Workshop Meeting on Evaluation of Information Access Technologies: Information Retrieval, Quesiton Answering, And Cross-Lingual Information Access, pp. 147–153 (2010)

Emotion Tag Based Music Retrieval Algorithm

Jing Li, Hongfei Lin, and Lijuan Zhou

Information Retrieval Laboratory, School of Computer Science and Technology,
Dalian University of Technology
Dalian, P.R. China, 116024
lijing1009@126.com, hflin@dlut.edu.cn,
zhoulijuan@mail.dlut.edu.cn

Abstract. Music is to express emotions and interpreted by tags. Different emotion tags describe the same piece of music in different perspectives. This paper proposes a music retrieval algorithm which is based on the users' emotion tags. First, we build a bi-partite graph, with tags on one side and music on the other, to compute the semantic similarity between the tags by T_SimRank. Second, we use the T_PageRank algorithm to get the music-popularity. Last, by taking the advantage of learning to rank, we combine many methods to get the final ranking results. Experimental results show that our method is better than the traditional cosine similarity and the Co_Tags similarity, and the fused method performs better than the single method.

Keywords: music retrieval, music emotion, semantic similarity, music popularity, learning to rank.

1 Introduction

With the boom of digital music on the Internet, music consumption grows to an unprecedented volume for its least cost and easily availability, the activity of music retrieval is now the heavy traffic on the Internet [1]. Traditional MIR (music information retrieval) system cannot meet people's various needs. As there is a close connection between music and emotion, the idea of emotion based music retrieval is proposed. For example, when someone is sad for some reason, she or he wants to listen to a piece of music that can cheer her or him up, at this moment she or he will search music by mood no matter what the melody sounds or whom the artist is.

As the prevalence of Web 2.0, web users are bestowed more freedom of motion to define music tags according to their own understanding of music, which denote users' distinguishing comprehension of music. Music is to express emotions and interpreted by tags, so the tags annotated by users inevitably involve emotion tags that reflect joviality or sorrow. Emotion based MIR system allows users to search music via imputing emotional words, which satisfies the individual needs.

This paper proposes an emotion tag based music retrieval algorithm to assist in improving user experience. We focus on two aspects of music retrieval: Similarity and Popularity.

P.-J. Cheng et al. (Eds.): AIRS 2010, LNCS 6458, pp. 599–609, 2010.

Similarity: it means the estimated emotion similarity between a query and a song. Emotion tags, provided by listeners from different perspectives, are usually good emotional summaries of the corresponding music. For example, the emotion tags of the music *"Take Me To Your Heart"* are *"sad", "heartbroken", "grieved", "suffering", "lost"* etc. These emotion tags provide a new metadata for the similarity calculation between a query and a piece of music. We propose a new similarity estimation algorithm, T_SimRank to compute latent semantic similarity between tags and music.

Popularity: Through the analysis of users' behavior, we discover that most people tend to choose the music with higher popularity. The more popular the music is, the more people tend to pick it while browsing the music list, and the more tags will be annotated. In Web2.0, many people like clicking the tags to search the music, and they tend to click the popular the tags. Considering the above intuitions, we propose a novel algorithm, T_PageRank to measure the popularity of music using tags.

In this paper, we will show the detailed algorithm and evaluate on a music corpus which consists of 169 emotion tags and 35421 corresponding songs. All tags are Chinese emotion tags, and most songs are Chinese. Preliminary experimental results show that T_SimRank can calculate the emotion tags similarities semantically, and after adding T_PageRank to similarity algorithms with SVM^{light} tool, we achieve a satisfactory performance. By incorporating different methods (cosine, Co_Tags will be introduced below), it reaches a best performance.

The rest of this paper is organized as follows. Section 2 discusses the related work. Section 3 presents the semantic similarity algorithms, especially, T_SimRank algorithm in detail. Section 4 proposes the popularity ranking algorithm, T_PageRank. Section 5 describes the learning to rank model - Ranking SVM. In Section 6, our experimental methods and corpus are presented together with results analysis. The last section concludes the paper with a brief outlook on future work.

2   Related Work

Nowadays, much research work on music emotion chiefly is emphasized on the analysis of audio information such as tempo, rhythm, timbre, strength, etc [2-6]. In the field of psychology of music, Hevner's adjective circle [7] and Thayer's 2-dimensional model [8] are two most popular ways to demonstrate the relationship between music and emotions. In Hevner's adjective circle, eight groups of adjectives are formulated, in particular, all groups are arranged on a circle and neighbored groups are consisting of related expressions. The variety of adjectives in each group gives a better representation of the meaning of each group and depicts the different user perceptions. Thayer's model describes mood as a product of the dimensions energy and stress: dimensions energy, measured from *"calm"* to *"be energized"*, is related to individual's physiological activity and cognition; stress reflects people's psychological emotion from *"happy"* to *"anxious"*. In traditional MIR system, music mood is annotated by audio experts, but professionally created labels have been criticized for not capturing the users' perspectives on mood. Emotion tags were imported to analyze the music mood to avoid the discrepancies between the general human and the audio experts in Xiao Hu's experiments [9]. Kerstin collected music tags from *last.fm* and found that the number of emotion tags is second only to genre tags [10], and users' emotional cognition to the same music is similar, from this perspective, emotional tags can enhance music information retrieval.

3   Tags Semantic Similarity

Tags denote the users' understanding and annotation to music. Different tags, that express music sentiment from various views, can be attached to the same music. Emotion tags defined in this article includes not only conventional emotion terms such as *"joyful"* and *"sorrowful"*, but also *"heartbroken"*, *"summer"*, *"sunshine"*, *"love"* and so forth, since these terms hold some sentimental information when looked at from a certain level. For example, Jay Chou's song *"simple love"* goes with many emotion tags including *"graceful"*, *"leisure"*, *"first love"*, *"summer"*, *"quietness"*, *"happy"*, *"tenderness"*; likewise, *"sorrowful"* is added to Fish Leong's *"breathing pain"*, *"unfortunately not you"* and A-sang's *"quite all the time"*. Hence, there is many-to-many relationship between tags and songs. Figure 1 depicts a bipartite graph of tags and songs.

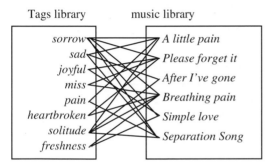

Tags library   music library

sorrow	A little pain
sad	Please forget it
joyful	After I've gone
miss	Breathing pain
pain	Simple love
heartbroken	Separation Song
solitude	
freshness	

Sim(sad，sorrow)=0.2
Sim(sad，joyful)=0.1
Sim(sad，miss)=0.2
Sim(sad，pain)=0.2
Sim(sad，heartbroken)=0.2
Sim(sad，solitude)=0.2
Sim(sad，freshness)=0.1

Fig. 1. Bipartite graph of tags and music

Fig. 2. Similarity between "sad" and other tags after 1st iteration

Tags *"sad"* and *"sorrow"* are both added to *"A little pain"*, *"After I've gone"* and *"Separation song"*, which denotes that the two tags are semantically similar; as such, songs *"A little pain"* and *"After I've gone"* are semantically similar to some extent because of the same tags attached to them. Music information retrieval based on tags similarity aims to retrieve songs that do not have just tags but are highly similar. Taking the tag *"sad"* for example, the song *"Breathing pain"* attached with those tags similar to *"sad"* except the tag itself may be ranked in front of those songs that exactly have the tag.

3.1   Co_Tags Semantic Similarity

Each piece of music is related to some tags, which reveal attribution of the music from different perspectives, e.g. emotion, theme, genre and so on. Semantic similarity computing method based on tag concurrence is defined with respect to use tag concurrence frequency [11].

$$Co\_Sim(t_i, t_j) = \frac{|t_i \cap t_j|}{|t_i \cup t_j|} \qquad (1)$$

Here, $|t_i \cap t_j|$ shows the number of songs attached both with tags t_i and t_j, while the value of $|t_i \cup t_j|$ expresses the number of songs attached with either t_i or t_j.

3.2 T_SimRank Semantic Similarity

Proposed by G. Jeh and J. Widom in 2002, SimRank attempts to compute similarity between two arbitrary vertices by using global information of a graph [12]. The main idea of it lies in the assumption that the two objects are similar when the neighbors of them are similar. Meriting our reference to it, we propose T_SimRank algorithm, the idea of T_SimRank can be described as following:

(1) Similar tags are usually assigned to similar music.
(2) Similar music usually has similar tags.
(3) A tag has highest similarity with itself.
(4) A piece of music has highest similarity with itself.

Table 1. T_SimRank Algorithm

T_SimRank Algorithm

Input: N_{tag}, N_{music}, $P_{t \to s}$, $P_{s \to t}$, attenuation coefficient c_1, c_2, convergence threshold ε_1 and ε_2.

Step 1. initialization:

$$S_{tag}(t_i, t_j) = \begin{cases} 1, i = j \\ 0, i \neq j \end{cases}, \quad S_{music}(s_i, s_j) = \begin{cases} 1, i = j \\ 0, i \neq j \end{cases}$$

Step 2. Do{

$$S_{tag}^{k+1}(t_i, t_j) = c_1 \cdot \sum_{m=1}^{|N_{music}|} \sum_{n=1}^{|N_{music}|} P_{t \to s}(t_i, s_m) \cdot P_{t \to s}(t_j, s_n) \cdot S_{music}^{k}(s_m, s_n)$$

$$S_{music}^{k+1}(s_i, s_j) = c_2 \cdot \sum_{m=1}^{|N_{tag}|} \sum_{n=1}^{|N_{tag}|} P_{s \to t}(s_i, t_m) \cdot P_{s \to t}(s_j, t_n) \cdot S_{tag}^{k}(t_m, t_n)$$

}Until(

$$\left| S_{tag}^{k}(t_i, t_j) - S_{tag}^{k-1}(t_i, t_j) \right| \leq \varepsilon_1 \; \&\& \; \left| S_{music}^{k}(s_i, s_j) - S_{music}^{k-1}(s_i, s_j) \right| \leq \varepsilon_2)$$

Output: S_{tag}, S_{music}

T_SimRank is a iterative procedure as described in Table 1 where N_{tag} denotes the number of tags, N_{music} is the number of music, S_{tag} stands for the similarity matrix of tags, $S_{tag}(t_i, t_j)$ is the semantic similarity between t_i and t_j. S_{music} is similarity matrix of music, $S_{music}(s_i, s_j)$ means the similarity between s_i and s_j. $P_{t \to s}$ represents transition probability matrix of $N_{tag} \times N_{music}$ with $P_{t \to s}(t_i, s_j)$ denoting the transition probability of t_i to s_j, $P_{s \to t}$ is transition probability matrix of $N_{music} \times N_{tag}$ showing the transition probability of s_i to t_j. In this paper, if tag t_i is assigned to N songs, the transition probability from t_i to each assigned song is $1/N$. Similarly, if a song s_i has N tags, the transition probability from s_i to its tag is $1/N$.

The convergence of the algorithm can be proved in a similar way as SimRank. For each iteration, the time complexity is $O(N_{tag}{}^2 N_{music}{}^2)$. Taking advantage of many improved methods such as BlockSimRank[13], we can reduce the complexity. Figure 2 shows the first iteration's T_SimRank results of the sample data in Figure 1, where c_1 and c_2 are set to 1.

Tags are used as query in tags based information retrieval systems, in this situation, we make $q=\{q_1,q_2,q_3,...,q_n\}$ denote the query string q, $T(s)=\{t_1,t_2,t_3,...t_m\}$ represents the tags set of music s, the similarity between q and s can be computed by:

$$sim(q,s) = \sum_{i=1}^{n} \sum_{t \in T(s)} S_{tag}(q_i,t) \tag{2}$$

By taking the contribution of tags to music into consideration and referring to the short text semantic similarity computing method described in [14], we add **idf** value to the formula:

$$sim(q,s) = \frac{1}{2}(\frac{\sum_{i=1}^{n} \max S_{tag}(q_i,s) \times idf(q_i)}{\sum_{i=1}^{n} idf(q_i)} + \frac{\sum_{j=1}^{m} \max S_{tag}(t_j,q) \times idf(t_j)}{\sum_{j=1}^{m} idf(t_j)}) \tag{3}$$

4   T_PageRank Popularity

Music popularity is defined by users' attention degree to it. People usually like to choose a song with higher popularity. The more popular the music is, the more people tend to pick it while browsing the music list, and the more tags will be annotated to it. In this paper, we suppose that all tags are annotated by the users to express their ideas. In Web2.0, many people like clicking the tags to search the music. The more popular the tag is, the more people tend to click it. When people is browsing the music pages, he or she is easy to jump from one music to another by clicking the tags, so we can connect the different music with tags, the more same tags two songs have, the higher probability of jumping from one music to another. Taking advantage of PageRank [15], we construct a graph with vertices presenting music and edges estimating by concurrence similarity between the tags. In consideration of people's behavior that they are apt to select music by clicking popular tags, we propose T_PageRank algorithm which can be elaborated as:

(1) Music is more popular if it is linked by more music.
(2) Music is more popular if it is linked by popular music.
(3) Music is more popular if it has more popular tags.

Here, tag popularity, in general, refers to the number of usage of the tags, and can be computed by the number of correlative music, which means that the more music are attached, the more popular the tag is. *Hot(t_i)* is the popularity of the tag t_i, $N(t_i)$ is the number of annotated music, then $Hot(t_i) = N(t_i)$.

$$w_{ij} = \frac{\sum_{m=1}^{|T_i \cap T_j|} Hot(t_m)}{\sum_{n=1}^{|T_i \cup T_j|} Hot(t_n)} \tag{4}$$

Weights of the music graph are computed by formula (4) above. Where w_{ij} is the assigned weight of the edge between v_i and v_j, T_i and T_j represents the tag sets of v_i and v_j respectively. $|T_i \cap T_j|$ is the intersection of T_i and T_j, $|T_i \cup T_j|$ is the union of T_i and T_j.

Figure 3 shows the subgraph of music graph.

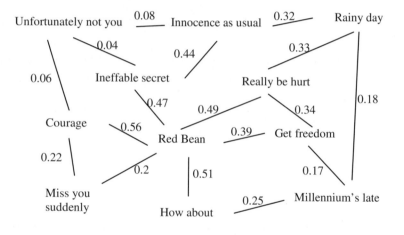

Fig. 3. Subgraph of music graph

Similar to PageRank, T_PageRank is iterative, the key point of it can be described by the formula (5), after convergence, we use *Hot(v_i)* to represent final popularity of music v_i. d is the damping coefficient with a value of 0.85. $In(v_i)$ is the set of vertices that point to v_i, $Out(v_i)$ is the set of vertices that point from v_i, in our experiments, we can see that $In(v_i) = Out(v_i)$.

$$Hot(v_i)^{p+1} = (1-d) + d \sum_{v_j \in In(v_i)} Hot(v_j)^p \frac{w_{ij}}{\sum_{v_k \in Out(v_j)} w_{jk}} \tag{5}$$

By assuming that the algorithm reaches its convergence after k steps of iteration, the time complexity is $O(N_{music}N_{average}k)$. Here, N_{music} is the number of music; $N_{average}$ is the average number of neighbor nodes for each song. We can use some improved methods such as the idea of block to reduce the complexity.

5 Learning to Rank Model

Ranking is the key step in information retrieval system and ranking algorithm includes traditional cosine similarity measurement, T_SimRank, T_PageRank and so on. Learning to rank takes the advantage of theories in machine learning to solve ranking problem, the goal of it is to optimize loss function through fusing all ranking algorithms into one algorithm.

The data necessitated in learning to rank comprises the following three parts: query, query related documents and manually annotated relatedness between query and documents. In this paper, users' emotion tags are taken as query, songs are represented as documents. Similarly, relatedness between query and documents are tagged by members in our lab. Ranking SVM model [16] employed here adopts partial ordered documents to train, and the optimization function of it can be expressed with the following formula:

$$\min \frac{1}{2} \vec{w} \cdot \vec{w} + C \sum \varepsilon_{i,j,k}, \forall (d_k^i, d_k^j) \in d_i \times d_j : \vec{w}\Phi(q_k, d_k^i) > \vec{w}\Phi(q_k, d_k^j) + 1 - \varepsilon_{i,j,k} \quad (6)$$

$\vec{w}$ is the weight vector and needs to be gradually adjusted during the learning procedure, C is used to balance the complexity and training deviation of the model, $\varepsilon_{i,j,k}$ is the nonzero slack variable, and $\Phi(q_k, d_k^j)$ denotes the mapping from query q_k and document d_k^j to eigenvector X_j^j.

6 Experiments

6.1 Datasets and Evaluation Measure

There are myriad music emotion tags on the Web. We collect the data from *zhangmen.baidu* (http://zhangmen.baidu.com), which consists of 169 emotion tags and 35421 corresponding songs. All tags are Chinese emotion tags, and most songs are Chinese. These data are processed by following steps: (1) judgmental tags such as *"pleasant to hear"*, *"favorite"* and *"love"* are removed. (2) Tags with ambiguous meanings are filtered out. For example, we cannot determine whether the tag *"like"* means the song is about love or the user loves the song. To ensure the quality of the emotion tags, these ambiguous words are removed. (3) Obviously synonymous tags like *"sorrow"*, *"sorrowful"*, *"sorrowful music"* are merged. (4) A song without an emotion tag is not selected. At last, we get 140 emotion tags and 35418 songs.

We build 20 query sets which involves 10 positive queries and 10 opposite. There are 1 to 5 tags in each query. Ten students are asked to select the top100 songs for each query, according to the times recommended, each music is set as one of the five levels: *Irrelevant* (score 1, recommended by 0 times), *Weakly Relevant* (score 2, recommended by 1-2 times), *Partially Relevant* (score 3, recommended by 3-5 times), *Relevant* (score 4, recommended by 6-8 times), and *Most Relevant* (score 5, recommended by 9-10 times). We use P@N and NDCG@N (Normalized Discounted Cumulative Gain) [17] as the performance evaluation measure.

P@N: In this paper, P@N is defined as the ratio of *Most Relevant* (score 5) music in the TopN returned results.

$$P @ N = \frac{|music_{rel=5}|}{|N|} \qquad (7)$$

NDCG@N: NDCG is well suited to MIR evaluation as it returns relevant music that is top-ranked more heavily than those ranked lower. NDCG@N is computed as:

$$N_n = Z_n \sum_{i=1}^{n} (2^{r(i)} - 1) / \log(1+i) \qquad (8)$$

Where Z_n is a specially calculated normalization constant for making a perfect ordering obtain an NDCG value of 1; and each $r(i)$ is an integer relevance level of the i_{th} music returned.

6.2   Experiment Result

In our experiment, the *"cosine Similarity"* and *"Co_Tags Similarity"* are taken as the baseline. In cosine Similarity, tags assigned to music are considered as the short text, each tag is a feature term whose weight is computed by TFIDF. The songs are ranked by the cosine score. Co_Tags Similarity has been introduced in section 3.1.

In this paper, Ranking SVM [16], a typical method of learning to rank, is used to learn weights for all the features. All parameters are default in SVM^{light} tool.

6.2.1   Ranking Using Similarity
Figure 4 shows the comparison of P@N of the cosine, Co_Tags and T_SimRank. We can easily find that both Co_Tags and T_SimRank perform much better than cosine, T_SimRank performs best. In the top5 or top10 results returned by T_SimRank, more than 70% songs are *Most Relevant* (score 5).

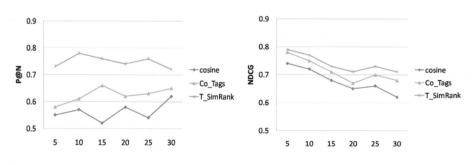

Fig. 4. Average P@N of single method   **Fig. 5.** Average NDCG@N of single method

The average NDCG@N results with different methods are illustrated in Figure 5, and the results demonstrate that T_SimRank can achieve better performance than others.

6.2.2 Ranking Using Similarity and Popularity

To verify the importance of popularity in music information retrieval, we integrate T_PageRank algorithm with cosine, Co_Tags and T_SimRank respectively.

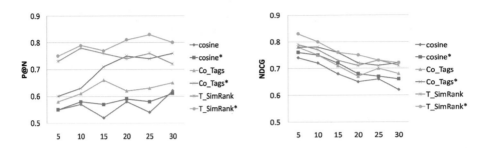

Fig. 6. Average P@N of cosine[*], Co_Tags[*], T_SimRank[*]

Fig. 7. Average NDCG@N of cosine[*], Co_Tags[*], T_SimRank[*]

Figure 6 and Figure 7 show the P@N and NDCG@N results of "cosine+T_PageRank", "Co_Tags+T_PageRank" and "T_SimRank+T_PageRank" (we use cosine*, Co_Tags*, T_SimRank* instead below) respectively. In the experiment, both 6 positive and 6 negative results are selected as the training sets, and the remaining 8 results are test sets. With the music popularity added, we can clearly see that all methods perform better than before, T_SimRank* is significantly best.

6.2.3 Ranking Using Fused Methods

After analyzing the ranking results in section 5.2.1, we find that 18 of them are in harmony with the average results, but for the two queries *"natural fresh enjoyment"* and *"aesthetic relax soul life"*, T_SimRank does not perform as good as cosine method. By analyzing the data, we figure out that there are many unwell-known songs retrieved as inputting the two queries mentioned above. When computing the similarity between two tags, T_SimRank considers the average similarity of songs related by tags which is superior in songs with less tags.

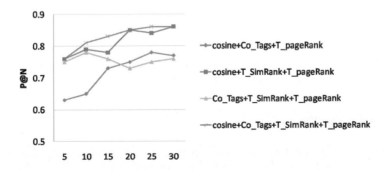

Fig. 8. Average P@N of fused methods

We also choose 6 positive and 6 negative results as the training sets, and the remaining 8 results are test sets. Figure 8 and Figure 9 show that the fused methods are better than single method and by incorporating the three all methods, we can achieve the best search result, and both P@N and NDCG@N show statistically significant improvements.

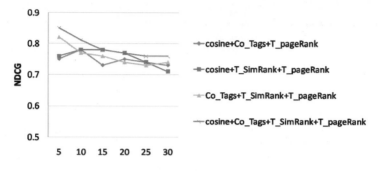

Fig. 9. Average NDCG@N of fused methods

7   Conclusions

Music is to express emotions; emotion tags based MIR allows users to search music by describing one's mood. In this paper, we study the novel problem of integrating emotion tags into music retrieval. Two novel iterative algorithms are proposed to improve the performance on MIR. The experimental results show that T_SimRank can successfully find the latent semantic relations among tags and T_PageRank can provide the music popularity effectually. With the tool of Ranking SVM, we find that the fused method is better than single method; by incorporating all methods, we can achieve the best search result. The main contributions can be concluded in three aspects:

(1)   The proposal of the T_SimRank algorithm to measure the association among various emotion tags;
(2)   The proposal of the T_PageRank algorithm to measure the music popularity;
(3)   The proposal to incorporate different methods with Ranking SVM to get a better performance.

In the future, our mainly work will focus on optimizing the proposed algorithms and exploring more sophisticated features to improve the search quality. We will also take advantage of other related researches such as audio music mood and so on.

Acknowledgements

We are grateful to the annotators in these experiments, and particularly, we also thank three anonymous reviewers for their valuable comments. This work was funded by NSFC under award #60673039 and #60973068.

References

1. Feng, Y.-Z., Zhuang, Y.-T., Pan, Y.-H.: Music Information Retrieval by Detecting Mood via Computational Media Aesthetics. In: The 2003 IEEE/WIC International Conference on Web Intelligence, Halifax, Canada, pp. 235–241 (2003)
2. Yang, Y.-H., Liu, C.-C., Chen, H.-H.: Music Emotion Classification: A Fuzzy Approach. In: The ACM Multimedia 2006 (MM 2006), SantaBarbara, CA, USA, pp. 81–84 (2006)
3. Lu, L., Liu, D., Zhang, H.-J.: Automatic mood detection and tracking of music audio signals. J. IEEE Trans. Audio. Speech. Lang. Processing, 5–18 (2006)
4. Li, T., Ogihara, M.: Content-Based Music Similarity Search And Emotion Detection. In: The 2004 IEEE International Conference on Acoustics, Speech, and Signal Processing, pp. 705–708. IEEE Press, Montreal (2004)
5. Yang, Y.-H., Chen, H.-H.: Music Emotion Ranking. In: The 2009 IEEE International Conference on Acoustics, Speech and Signal Processing, pp. 1657–1660. IEEE Press, Taipei (2009)
6. Kuo, F.-F., Chiang, M.-F., Shan, M.-K., Lee, S.-Y.: Emotion-based Music Recommendation By Association Discovery from Film Music. In: The 13th Annual ACM International Conference on Multimedia, Hilton, Singapore, pp. 507–510 (2005)
7. Hevner, K.: Expression in music: a discussion of experimental studies and theories. J. Am. J. Psychiatry 48, 246–268 (1936)
8. Thayer, R.E.: The biopsychology of mood and arousal. Oxford University Press, Oxford (1989)
9. Hu, X., Downie, J.S., Ehman, A.F.: Lyric Text Mining in Music Mood Classification. In: The 10th International Symposium on Music Information Retrieval (ISMIR), Kobe, Japan, pp. 411–416 (2009)
10. Bischoff, K., Firan, C.S., Nejdl, W., Paiu, R.: Can All Tags Be Used For Search? In: The 17th ACM onference on Information and Knowledge Management, Napa Valley, California, USA, pp. 193–202 (2008)
11. Wu, L., Yang, L.-J., Yu, N.-H.: Learning To Tag. In: The 18th international conference on World Wide Web, Madrid, Spain, pp. 361–370 (2009)
12. Jeh, G., Widom, J.: SimRank: A Measure of Structural Context Similarity. In: The 8th ACM SIGKDD International Conference on Knowledge Discovery and Data Mining, Edmonton, Alberta, Canada, pp. 538–543 (2002)
13. Li, P., Cai, Y.-Z., Liu, H.-Y., He, J., Du, X.-Y.: Exploiting the Block Structure of Link Graph for Efficient Similarity Computation. In: Theeramunkong, T., Kijsirikul, B., Cercone, N., Ho, T.-B. (eds.) PAKDD 2009. LNCS, vol. 5476, pp. 389–400. Springer, Heidelberg (2009)
14. Mihalcea, R., Corley, C., Strapparava, C.: Corpus-based and Knowledge-based Measures of Text Semantic Similarity. In: The 21st National conference on Artificial intelligence, Boston, USA, pp. 775–780 (2006)
15. Page, L., Brin, S., Motwani, R., Winograd, T.: The PageRank citation ranking: Bringing order to the web. Technical report, Stanford Digital Library Technologies Project (1998)
16. Joachims, T.: Optimizing Search Engines Using Click-through Data. In: The 8th ACM SIGKDD International Conference on Knowledge Discovery and Data Mining, New York, USA, pp. 133–142 (2002)
17. Jarvelin, K., Kekalainen, J.: IR evaluation methods for retrieving highly relevant documents. In: The 23rd Annual International ACM SIGIR Conference on Research and Development in Information Retrieval, Athens, Greece, pp. 41–48 (2000)

An Aesthetic-Based Approach
to Re-ranking Web Images

Shao-Hang Kao, Wei-Yen Day, and Pu-Jen Cheng

Dept. of Computer Science and Information Engineering,
National Taiwan University, 100 Taipei, Taiwan
{denehs,wydays}@gmail.com
pjcheng@csie.ntu.edu.tw

Abstract. We propose an approach to re-ranking images retrieved from existing image search engines based on image quality in aesthetic view. Previous works ranked images based mainly on their relevance to queries. However, it happens that often the top-ranked images cannot satisfy users due to their low visual quality. To present quality images to users, our approach learns a regression model, which combines both conventional and novel image features according to a given quality-image collection. We conducted several experiments on the datasets sampled from INRIA Holiday datasets, Photo.net, DPChallenge, Google Image, and Flickr. The experimental results show the feasibility of the proposed approach in searching aesthetically-pleasing Web-image search results for users.

Keywords: Image Search, Image Quality, Image Ranking.

1   Introduction

Previous works on Web image search focused mainly on retrieving relevant images to users' queries. Most of them used textual information associated with the images such as filenames, anchor texts, tags and surrounding texts. A few exploited image content to filter out noisy images in search results. [7] presented a reliable measure of image similarity to re-rank image search results returned from Google Image. Despite the continuous improvement of relevance in image search, users are still not fully satisfied with the top-ranked Web images in terms of image quality[1]. For example, Fig. 1 shows the top-3 image results returned from Google Image[2] with respect to the query "*Statue of Liberty*". It could be observed that the left image is under exposure; the middle one is slightly overexposed so the detail of sky is missing; the right one has good exposure but does not set the tone well. Although the three images are all relevant to the query topic, they are not good enough in image quality.

---

[1]   Different from compression quality, which is used to efficiently store or transmit images, in this paper, we focus on the aesthetic quality of an image, which is often determined by the photographic process.
[2]   Google Image provides Web-image search (http://images.google.com)

P.-J. Cheng et al. (Eds.): AIRS 2010, LNCS 6458, pp. 610–623, 2010.

Fig. 1. Top 3 images returned by Google Image for "Statue of Liberty" in March, 2010

To recommend users images with both high relevancy and quality, a popular solution adopted by current search engines is to provide some simple filters, which utilize information such as image resolutions or sizes, types of image content (e.g., news, faces, photos, clip arts, line drawings, etc), image colors (e.g., full color or black and white) and types of image-file formats (e.g., jpeg and png). Such options indeed prevent users from reaching certain types of low-quality images. Unfortunately, many low-quality Web images will still be returned like those in Fig. 1 due to the simplicity of the options provided.

Searching relevant images with high quality is not only helpful for users in satisfaction in perception, but also useful for them in personal and commercial usage. In this paper, instead of pursuing more relevant images, we shift to investigate how to re-rank the images returned from search engines based on their visual quality. We assume the images returned are all relevant to users' queries. Our goal is to re-rank the images with better quality higher in the search-result lists. To do this, we cannot use textual information associated with a Web image because it often gives no description about image quality. We turn our attention to image content itself. In this paper, we propose an approach to re-rank the images, which learns a regression model. A set of novel image features are presented. Together with conventional ones, our features could significantly improve the ranking accuracy in five real data sets; includes images from Google Image, Flickr[3], INRIA Holiday datasets[4], Photo.net[5], and DPChallenge[6]. The experimental results show the feasibility of the proposed approach in searching aesthetically-pleasing Web-image search results for users.

The contributions of this work are as follows. We not only adopt conventional image features such as color and texture in our approach, but also introduce a set of new features, which have been shown their effectiveness in extensive experiments. Moreover, we apply our approach to re-ranking Web images according to their quality. Different from previous work on image-quality classification or assessment that conducted experiments in a small scale, we evaluated our approach on Web images, whose topics are more diverse and whose content is more dynamic. The experimental results show that our approach is robust across different image categories.

---

[3] Flickr provides online photo management and sharing (http://www. flickr.com)
[4] INRIA Holiday collects some personal photos taken on holidays
(http://lear.inrialpes.fr/~jegou/data.php)
[5] Photo.net allows photographers to upload their own photos and give ratings
(http://www. flickr.com)
[6] DPChallenge offers different challenges to train users to be good photographers
(http://www.dpchallenge.com)

2   Related Work

There existed many studies that used image content to improve the performance of Web image retrieval. [7] presented a reliable measure of image similarity to re-rank image search results returned from Google Image. Although image content has shown its usability in improving Web image search, most of previous work only concerned the relevance issue, instead of the quality issue.

Regarding image quality, most of previous work paid attention to image-quality classification, which identifies whether an image has good or bad quality [8,10,11,15]. [8] aimed at distinguishing high quality professional photos from low quality snapshots. [10] extracted the subject region from a photo, and then formulated various high-level semantic features based on this subject and background division. [11] proposed a fusion method integrating query relevance and image aesthetics at the same time. [15] developed several discriminative features to classify images according to whether they are taken by experienced photographers. Although the problem of image quality classification can be applied to image quality ranking, previous work focused mainly on image low-level features and evaluated in a specific dataset. Our work also presents new features, which are extracted based on closest training examples given by experts and have been proven their effectiveness in determining image quality in extensive experiments. Moreover, we attempt to re-rank images on the Web with diverse topics and dynamic content. We not only manually generate quality training data by ourselves but also use the ratings given by real websites as labeled data. The experimental results show the feasibility of the proposed approach under various datasets.

There are some works tending to make images look better by image processing techniques. [3] presented a useful method that enhances the harmony among the colors of a given image, while remaining faithful, as much as possible, to the original colors. [12] presented an algorithm for removing motion blur from a single image. These works all tried to enhance the quality of images. Some features measuring image quality are related to our work. However, in this paper, our goal is not to enhance the quality of given images. We want to improve the ranking list of Web images according to their aesthetic quality.

3   The Proposed Approach

3.1   Image Re-ranking Based on Quality

Given a ranking list $L = \{I_1, I_2, I_3, ..., I_k\}$ with top-k image search results returned from an image search engine, the goal of this paper is to learn a regression function $r: L \rightarrow R$, mapping each image in L to a real value. The regressed value stands for the quality an image I_i has. With the permutation π given by the function r, the original ranking list L can be re-ranked as $L' = \{I_{\pi(1)}, I_{\pi(2)}, I_{\pi(3)}, ..., I_{\pi(k)}\}$. We develop the regression function r by learning examples in the form of $\{f(I_i), q(I_i)\}$, where $f(I_i)$ is the set of features for I_i, which will be described in Section 0, and $q(I_i)$ denotes the quality of the image, which is manually labeled by experienced photographers. The values of $q(I_i)$ varies between -2 and 2; -2 means the worst quality while 2 means the best quality.

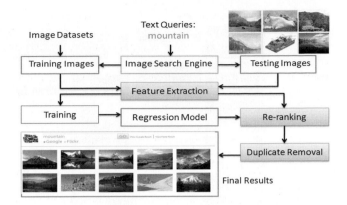

Fig. 2. System Architecture

Fig. 2 shows our system architecture. In the training phase, our training images $\{I_i\}$ coming from image search engines and some photography community sites are labeled as $\{q(I_i)\}$ manually (some web sites provide such $\{q(I_i)\}$). These training images' features $\{f(I_i)\}$ are then extracted and a regression model r is learned according to $\{f(I_i), q(I_i)\}$. In the testing phase, we first extract features $f(I_j)$ for each (testing) image I_j returned from a search engine in the initial ranking list L and then apply the regression model r to predict the quality of each image $q(I_j)$, which will be used to re-rank L as L'. As some images in L' are probably very similar, to maximize the diversity of L', we remove duplicated images. Specifically, if the similarity between two images in L' exceeds a certain threshold, we will remove the one inferior in L'. Finally, the topmost images in L' are shown to users. In this paper, we apply support vector regression (SVR) to learn r; other alternatives can also be adopted for calculation.

3.2 Image Features

Two sets of factors affecting image quality are considered in this paper. One set is *objective*. The factors of this set are about basic photographic techniques such as focus (Q1) and exposure (Q2). For example, photographers should take care of shutter speed, aperture and lighting to make an appropriate exposure. Inappropriate exposure will lower the contrast of images and looks awful. Tripod is needed during long exposure shots; otherwise, the images would have high blurriness caused by handshake. The other set is *subjective*. The factors of this set are about visual arts. Although art and taste are quite different from one to another, four major common rules that have been accepted by experienced photographers are adopted here, including simplicity (Q3), realism (Q4), color harmonization (Q5), and composition (Q6). For simplicity, professional photographers usually make their photos simple, so that the objects from images are obviously presented to people. A high quality image should make its subject clear, as shown in Fig. 3(a). For realism [8], experienced photographers use a wide range of techniques to make their photos 'surreal' like adjusting camera settings, taking shots from a different view angle, and choosing specific times of the day, e.g. morning or dusk. However, non-photographers usually let their photos 'real'. That is, they take photos as they see. Figure 3(b) gives an example of realism.

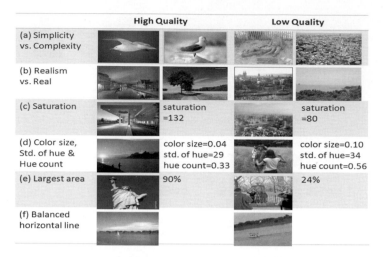

Fig. 3. Effect of various image features on image quality

We propose four types of image features: basic photography (measuring Q1 and Q2), color distribution (measuring Q2~Q5), composition (measuring Q3 and Q6), and retrieval features (measuring Q1~Q6). Some of them have been used in the literature; The features of "retrieval", "standard deviation of hue" and "horizontal balance" features are novel.

3.2.1 Basic Photography Features
The features are designed to detect if a photo is taken with accurate focus and appropriate exposure.

Blurriness: If an image is out-of-focus, it becomes more blur. We employ the blurriness features proposed in [14]. First, the image I_i is converted from spatial domain to frequency domain by Fast Fourier Transform (FFT). Then we have:

$$C(I_i) = \{ p_j | FFT(p_j) > \theta, p_j \in I_i \} \tag{1}$$

where p_j is the pixel j in I_i and θ is a given threshold. We count the number of elements in $C(I_i)$ and divide it by the image size $|I_i|$, i.e., the number of pixels in I_i, to obtain blurriness value, in which lower means more blur.

$$blurriness(I_i) = \frac{|C(I_i)|}{|I_i|} \tag{2}$$

Contrast: This is a measurement of appropriate exposure, i.e., whether an image is taken with wrong shutter time or diaphragm. The photometric exposure is given by:

$$H = Et \tag{3}$$

where E is the image-plane luminance and t is the exposure time. Exposure affects contrast. If an image is over-exposure or under-exposure, then its contrast will often be too low. There are many ways to define an image's contrast. We obtain an image's

contrast by computing the entropy of its histogram under grey scale with the following formula:

$$contrast(I_i) = -\sum p_j \log p_j \tag{4}$$

$$p_j = \frac{\#(pixels\ in\ j\text{-}th\ bin)}{|I_i|}, 0 \le j \le 255 \tag{5}$$

Noise: We observe some images contain noises, which is caused by CCD (Charge-
Coupled Device) in digital cameras with high ISO configuration and low environment
luminance. The other possibility is caused by the jpeg artifact [5]. Here we apply a
simple noise detector to detect noises from camera CCD or jpeg artifacts. Bilateral
filtering [13] is well-known for its ability of removing noises. We, therefore, compare
the images before and after performing bilateral filtering (BF) to get the noise area in
an image.

$$noise(I_i) = \frac{\#(|p_j - BF(p_j)| > \theta)}{|I_i|}, p_j \in I_i \tag{6}$$

where p_j is the pixel j in I_i and θ is a given threshold. In our experiment, we adopt a
5x5 bilateral filter and set threshold θ to 1.

3.2.2 Color Distribution Features

This set of features is designed to detect how well the color distribution or toning an
image is.

Color Harmonization: Color harmonization is used to measure the quality of color
distribution of an image. [3] presented seven good harmonic templates for image I_i,
which is calculated by:

$$harmonic(\boldsymbol{I_i}) = F_{min(I_i,(m,\alpha))} \tag{7}$$

$$F(\boldsymbol{I_i},(m,\alpha)) = \sum_{p_j \in I_i} \|H(p_j) - E_{T_m(\alpha)}\| \times S(p_j) \tag{8}$$

where H is the hue channel and S is the saturation channel. p_j denotes j-th pixel in I_i.
$T_m(\alpha)$ is the harmonic template given in [3], where m stands for one of the seven
harmonic templates and α is the orientation for m. Based on this feature, we can detect
how harmonious an image is.

Hue, Saturation and Value (HSV): For each pixel of an image, we can convert it
from RGB color space to HSV color space[7]. Given hue (h), saturation (s) and value
(v) for each pixel j in image I_i, we compute their average for I_i :

$$hue(I_i) = \frac{\sum_j h(p_j)}{} |I_i| \tag{9}$$

saturation(I_i) and *value*(I_i) can be easily obtained by replacing $h(p_j)$ with $s((p_j)$ and
$v(p_j)$, respectively. HSV is related to the exposure. If a photo taker controls the exposure well, the hue of sky will be close to blue instead of white or gray. Under or over
exposure makes the saturation of an image become lower. And exposure also effects

---

[7] HSV color space: http://en.wikipedia.org/wiki/HSL_and_HSV

value. Hue and saturation are all about the realism issue for image quality. Figure 3(c) gives some examples.

Color Size: The feature is to calculate how many different colors (in RGB color space) appearing in an image and to measure the image's simplicity. Only the colors with frequency more than θ are counted ($\theta=3$ in our experiment). If an image is full of noise, then its color size grows significantly. Sometimes users cannot easily find main objects if an image has too many different colors.

Standard Deviation of Hue: The feature detecting the changing of colors is to measure the simplicity of an image, and can be computed by:

$$huestd(I_i) = STDVAR(\{h(p_j)|p_j \in I_i\}) \tag{10}$$

Hue Count: This feature captures the simplicity of an image. We cluster hues of an image to 18 bins and count the number of different bins:

$$huecnt(I_i) = \frac{COUNT\ (apperance\ of\ hue\ bins)}{\#\ hue\ bins=18} \tag{11}$$

Figure 3(d) shows the effect of color size, standard deviation of hue, and hue count on image quality.

Largest Area: Images with a large area having the same color (hue) have more probability to achieve high quality. This is because the subject of such image is quite clear. This is also why photographers sometimes convert their photos into mono color space to avoid noises caused by colors. Figure 3(e) gives an example. We calculate largest area by:

$$hue_{largest}(I_i) = \frac{\#\ of\ pixels\ with\ hue=max\ COUNT(h(p_i)),0\leq h(p_i)\leq360}{|I_i|} \tag{12}$$

3.2.3 Composition

The features are used to detect whether objects within an image have appropriate sizes and locations.

Region of Interest (ROI): The size of the main object for an image should not be too large or too small. The size of ROIs can help us detect it. We adopt the attention model developed by Itti et al. [6] to find the areas with higher visual attention, where we combine two Gaussian functions whose centers are at 1/3 and 2/3, respectively, to simulate the influence of the rule of thirds in photograph composition. An object should avoid to appear at center or the border. The best position is 1/3.

Horizontal Balance: We can take the absolute arctangent between the longest line in an image and the horizon to see if an image is horizontal balanced.

$$horizon(I_i) = 1 - \frac{2\theta_{hl}}{\pi} \tag{13}$$

Horizontal balance is important for high-quality images since not-balanced horizon lines usually make viewers feel uncomfortable. Figure 3(f) gives an example.

Edge Distributions: [8] computed the spatial distribution of the high frequency edges of an image to capture its simplicity. We implement this feature by Canny's approach to edge detection [1] and count the 2D stand deviation of edges in an image:

$$edge(I_i) = STDVAR \ (location \ of \ edges) \tag{14}$$

3.2.4 Image Retrieval Features

In this section, we introduce our new retrieval features. We apply the content-based image retrieval (CBIR) technique to extract so-called retrieval features. Our idea is quite simple: an image visually-similar to high-quality images has more chance to be a high-quality image. More specifically, the quality of a given image is determined by a majority vote of its closest training examples, whose quality has been manually labeled already. Since our regression function r tries to analyze how image quality changes when each adopted feature is varied. Such r is very sensitive to the details of the distribution for each feature. In practice, it is very difficult to fetch perfect distribution for the features discussed previously except the retrieval features. Empirically, the retrieval features are quite robust and reasonably effective for training and prediction.

Suppose I is the set of the top ranked images visually similar to a given image I_i. The retrieval features can be calculated as:

$$CBIR_X(I_i) = \frac{\Sigma_j \ \text{quality}(I_j)}{|I|} \tag{15}$$

where quality(I_j) denotes the quality value varied from -2 (low quality) to 2 (high quality) and X is the way to compute the image similarity. Because we can apply any similarity measure to the retrieval features, four different measurements, including conventional color-texture, basic photography, composition and tone (i.e., color distribution), are defined here, i.e., $X \in \{$ color-texture, basic, composition, tone $\}$. The color-texture-based retrieval feature makes use of HSV color histograms and Gabor filters with various orientations and scales as its feature space. The basic-based, composition-based, and tone-based retrieval features adopt the features described in Section 3.2.1, 3.2.2, and 3.2.3, respectively, as their feature spaces for similarity computation. In our experiment, we use top 10 ranked images, i.e., 10-nearest neighbors, to predict image quality.

4 Experiments

4.1 Datasets

There is no existing benchmark for this work, so we collect 5 image datasets from some photo community web sites and image search engines. For each dataset, 70% of the images are used for training, and the remaining 30% are for testing. The 5 datasets are introduced below. Table 1 shows the statistical information about the 5 datasets. Photo.net is a web community for photographers. Photographers can upload their own photos and give ratings (scaled from 1 to 7) to others' photos. There are two types of ratings for each image: aesthetics and originality. We take their aesthetic ratings and randomly choose photos with $\geq$20 ratings and their standard deviation is less than 1.0. The original idea behind DPChallenge is to teach users to be better photographers by giving each other different 'challenges'. For example, one challenge is about "church", which asks people to photograph a church from any religion and show its beauty, grandeur or simplicity. Similar to photo.net, photographers in DPChallenge can upload their photos and rate others' photos with a rating scale from 1 to 10. DPChallenge doesn't limit the types of ratings. Sometimes users may not rate photos from the aesthetic viewpoint. To relieve this problem, we only take 750 top-ranked images and 750 bottom-ranked images from the total 3682 images as our data. The INRIA Holidays dataset is designed for the evaluation of image search. The dataset contains a set of personal photos taken on holidays. There are also some other images taken on purpose to test the robustness to various attacks: rotations, viewpoint and illumination changes, blurring, etc. Hence, the dataset covers different image quality. In our experiment, 3 experienced photographers are asked to rate these photos with the rating scale from -2 to 2. For Web images, we collect them from Google Image and Flickr by 30 manually-constructed queries like apple, building, cat, Tokyo Tower, and summer. For each query, top 100 images returned from each are collected. Dead links are discarded. Type filters provided by Google Image are applied to prevent from some noise like clip art images.

Table 1. Numbers of images for each data set

Source	Training	Testing	Total
Photo.net	1939	875	2814
DPChallenge	1038	462	1500
INRIA	1043	448	1491
	# of ratings:(2:49, 1:103, 0:1107, 1:171, 2:61)		
Google Image	1456	608	2064
	# of ratings:(-2:92, -1:824, 0:899, 1:453, 2:38)		
Flickr	1908	784	2692
	# of ratings:(2:72, 1:800, 0:1232, 1:796, 2:73)		

4.2   Evaluation Metrics

There evaluation metrics are adopted in this paper, including NDCG, Kendall's tau, and ERR. We slightly modify it to measure the performance of image ranking based on quality, instead of relevance. Kendall's tau coefficient [9] is used to measure the association between two rankings. Its value will be 1 if two rankings are exactly the same and -1 if one is the reverse of the other. Here we compare our rankings to ideal rankings by Kendall's tau. ERR (Expected Reciprocal Rank) [2] is defined as the expected reciprocal length of time that a user needs to find a relevant document (or a high quality image for our purpose). $ERR = \sum_{r=1}^{n} \frac{1}{r} P(user\ stops\ at\ position\ r)$.

4.3   Ranking Performance

In this experiment, we rank all of the images for each dataset. Since the quality score for each image in the datasets has been labeled by either the website or our experienced photographers (the scores are varied from -2 to 2 for INRIA Holidays, Google

Image and Flickr datasets, 1 to 7 for Photo.net, and 1 to 10 for DPChallenge), we can use NDCG, Kendall's tau, and ERR to examine the performance of our ranking results. Table 2 shows the experimental results, where the Web datasets are those collected through Google Image and Flickr. In Table 2, six feature sets are adopted. Basic (Section 3.2.1), color (Section 3.2.2), composition (Section 3.2.3), image retrieval (Section 3.2.4), basic+color+composition (Sections 3.2.1~3.2.3), and basic+color+composition+retrieval (all) represent the proposed approach based on individual features, the combination of conventional image features (basic+color+composition, which is adopted by previous work) and all of the features (including the proposed new features).

Table 2. Performance of using different methods and datasets.(+x%) means performance improvement (compared to method Basic+Color+Composition)

Method	Dataset	NDGC@3	NDGC@5	NDGC@10	NDGC@20	Kendall's tau	ERR
Basic	Web	0.166	0.223	0.367	0.237	0.060	0.203
	INRIA	0.707	0.788	0.804	0.801	0.438	0.490
	Photo.net	0.737	0.654	0.646	0.627	0.200	0.398
	DPChallenge	0.168	0.338	0.446	0.501	0.280	0.118
Color	Web	0.776	0.653	0.576	0.574	0.301	0.503
	INRIA	0.776	0.795	0.742	0.713	0.255	0.513
	Photo.net	0.646	0.654	0.567	0.599	0.213	0.641
	DPChallenge	0.739	0.648	0.609	0.563	0.127	0.198
Composition	Web	0.000	0.103	0.122	0.131	0.050	0.126
	INRIA	0.776	0.653	0.578	0.629	0.241	0.504
	Photo.net	0.472	0.543	0.488	0.529	0.239	0.293
	DPChallenge	0.215	0.368	0.415	0.449	0.136	0.120
Image Retrieval	Web	0.628	0.650	0.589	0.717	0.320	0.563
	INRIA	0.776	0.757	0.802	0.799	0.443	0.511
	Photo.net	0.650	0.655	0.621	0.600	0.245	0.270
	DPChallenge	0.253	0.427	0.443	0.497	0.274	0.188
Basic + Color + Composition	Web	0.776	0.692	0.548	0.669	0.428	0.510
	INRIA	0.863	0.858	0.713	0.683	0.318	0.587
	Photo.net	0.719	0.642	0.517	0.666	0.285	0.444
	DPChallenge	0.394	0.492	0.610	0.594	0.317	0.150
Basic + Color + Composition + Image Retrieval	Web	0.845 (+8.86%)	0.806 (+16.55%)	0.795 (+12.18%)	0.751 (+12.18%)	0.441 (+2.97%)	0.823 (+61.49%)
	INRIA	0.913 (+5.88%)	0.895 (+4.27%)	0.829 (+19.59%)	0.816 (+19.59%)	0.459 (+44.29%)	0.837 (+42.57%)
	Photo.net	0.662 (-7.98%)	0.713 (+11.16%)	0.725 (+7.96%)	0.719 (-7.96%)	0.296 (+3.83%)	0.338 (-23.84%)
	DPChallenge	0.740 (+87.55%)	0.764 (+55.34%)	0.780 (+27.87%)	0.731 (+23.09%)	0.325 (+2.70%)	0.227 (+51.53%)

From the result, we find that basic and composition features do not work on web dataset, and the performances of color features are better than composition features. The composition features cannot deal with complicated images well (e.g., photos with complicated backgrounds) because it is difficult for us to correctly detect ROIs. Such errors will propagate in the following processes of image-quality prediction and final ranking. That's the reason why the composition features have bad performance in the Web, Photo.net and DPChallenge datasets. Most of the features are, therefore, effective in quality prediction. With the assistance of image retrieval features, the performance can be further improved especially for the ERR in Web dataset. This implies that the image retrieval features are useful for promoting high-quality images to satisfy users. The concept of the retrieval features is close to that of the k-nearest neighbor (k-NN) algorithm. Because such features are only sensitive to the local structure of the distribution, if an image has a few visually-similar high-quality images, it often tends to have good quality. From Kendall's tau, we can see our rankings are slightly correlated with the ideal ranking, but achieve higher NDCG. It means even our approach can't produce perfect rankings but still rank high-quality images in the top.

4.4 Feature Analysis

This section analyzes the effectiveness of different features on image-quality prediction. We use F-score [4], which is a simple metric measuring the discrimination of two sets of real numbers. Given a set of training vectors $x_k, k = 1, \dots, m$, if the number of positive and negative instances are n_+ and n_-, respectively, then the F-score of the ith feature is defined as:

$$F(i) = \frac{\left(\bar{x}_i^{(+)} - \bar{x}_i\right)^2 + \left(\bar{x}_i^{(-)} - \bar{x}_i\right)^2}{\frac{1}{n_+ - 1}\sum_{k=1}^{n_+}\left(x_{k,i}^{(+)} - \bar{x}_i^{(+)}\right)^2 + \frac{1}{n_- - 1}\sum_{k=1}^{n_-}\left(x_{k,i}^{(-)} - \bar{x}_i^{(-)}\right)^2} \tag{16}$$

where $\bar{x}_i, \bar{x}_i^{(+)}, \bar{x}_i^{(-)}$ are the averages of the ith feature of the whole, positive and negative data sets, respectively; $x_{k,i}^{(+)}$ is the ith feature of the kth positive instance, and $x_{k,i}^{(-)}$ is the ith feature of the kth negative instance. The larger the F-score is, the more likely this feature is more discriminative.

The F-score of each individual feature for different datasets is listed in Fig. 4 (a). To examine if different features have different impacts on image-quality prediction for different types of images, we manually classify our image datasets into five categories, including landscape, building, night, object and indoor.

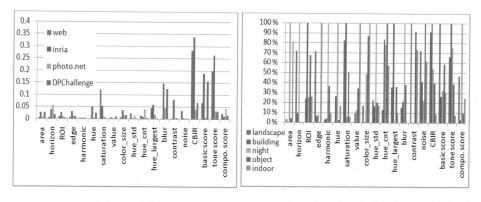

(a) **Different datasets**   (b) **Different image types**

Fig. 4. F-score for each feature under different image collections

To calculate the F-score, we need to separate an entire dataset into two sets, called positive and negative. For the Web and INRIA dataset, we can use the sign of the average ratings to separate them. But for the others, it is not easy to pick a threshold as these ratings are all positive numbers (photo.net: 1~7, DPChallenge: 1~10). We cut these data by the average of average ratings but it still seems not a very good choice. That is also why our features on the Photo.net dataset have low F-scores in Fig. 4(a). Figure 4(a) shows the most discriminative features are $CBIR_{color+texture}$, $CBIR_{tone}$, and $CBIR_{basic}$. Also some of the basic and tone features have relative high F-score like blur, contrast, and saturation. The composition features seem not so discriminative. The possible reason is that these features depends on the accuracy of ROI and edge detection. Unlike the composition features, the methods of calculating the basic or tone features are quite simple and robust, so these features perform well here. Although the image retrieval features can help to achieve high performance, but these features have limitations in computation and insufficient training data. Finding nearest neighbors often has high time complexity. The retrieval features require sufficient training data.

From Fig. 4(b), the features of "noise" and "hue count" work for most of the types. The result is reasonable since the possibility of noise appearance is independent to image types. And hue count is a naïve way to capture the simplicity of an image. Consider different image types. We find the most discriminative features for the landscape images are horizontal balance, edge distribution, saturation and contrast. For the building images, the most useful features are location of ROI, saturation, and largest area. For the night images, the most effective features are size of ROI, horizontal balance, color harmonization, hue, std. of hue, and blur. For the object images, they are color size, saturation and contrast. For the indoor images, they are size of ROI, edge distributions, value, color size and contrast. Blurriness is especially good for the night images because lots of these images are taken under long exposure and would cause motion blur when no tripod is used.

Table 3. Averaged result for comparison to original rankings

(*: pass the t-test with α=0.05, **: with α=0.01)

	Google (Baseline)	Google	Flickr (Baseline)	Flickr
NDCG@3	0.224	0.523**	0.296	0.561**
NDCG@5	0.249	0.502**	0.286	0.580**
NDCG@10	0.270	0.521**	0.294	0.575**
NDCG@20	0.313	0.539**	0.316	0.557**
Kendall's tau	0.044	0.283**	0.033	0.330**
ERR	0.211	0.341**	0.270	0.435**

Fig. 5. Top 5 image-search results w.r.t query 'building'

4.5   Comparison to Web-Image Search Engines

To compare the re-ranked results and the original ranking lists given by Google Image and Flickr, we test our method on each query of the 30 queries that we manually construct (as mentioned in Section 4.1). In the experiment, we use Google Image and Flickr as our base search engines, and re-rank top 100 images returned from Google Image and Flickr. Table 3 shows that after re-ranking, high-quality images are ranked higher. Only top 100 images retrieved from Google Image and Flickr are re-ranked, and in most case these images are all relevant to queries. Figure 5 gives an example of using "building" as a query to re-rank the images returned from Google Image and Flickr in June, 2010, where high-quality images are re-ranked higher.

5   Conclusion

We have proposed an approach to re-ranking images based on quality with supervised learning and its feasibility in Web-image search. Our approach can also be adapted to other applications, including photo album management systems, personalized photo recommendations, etc. For future work, it is possible to include more image features in the ranking algorithm as to improve upon the results and to integrate our approach to the video domain.

References

1. Canny, J.: A computational approach to edge detection. IEEE Transactions on PAMI 8(6), 679–698 (1986)
2. Chapelle, O., Metlzer, D., Zhang, Y., Grinspan, P.: Proc. of CIKM, pp. 621–630 (2009)
3. Cohen-Or., D., Sorkine, O., Gal, R., Leyvand, T., Xu, Y.-Q.: Color harmonization. In: Proc. of SIGGRAPH, pp. 624–630 (2006)
4. Chen, Y.W., Lin, C.J.: Combining SVMs with various feature selection strategies. In: Feature extraction, foundations and applications, pp. 315–324 (2006)
5. Dinh, P., Patry, J.: Video compression artifacts and MPEG noise reduction. In: Video Imaging DesignLine, Febuary 24, pp. 1–1 (2006)
6. Itti, L., Koch, C., Niebur, E.: A model of saliency-based visual attention for rapid scene analysis. IEEE Transactions on PAMI 20(11), 1254–1259 (1998)
7. Jing, Y., Baluja, S.: PageRank for product image search. In: Prof. of World Wide Web Conference, pp. 307–316 (2008)
8. Ke, Y., Tang, X., Jing, F.: The design of high-level features for photo quality assessment. In: Proc. of IEEE CVPR, pp. 419–426 (2006)
9. Kendall, M.: A new measure of rank correlation. Biometrika 30(1-2), 81–93 (1938)
10. Luo, Y., Tang, X.: Photo and video quality evaluation: Focusing on the subject. In: Forsyth, D., Torr, P., Zisserman, A. (eds.) ECCV 2008, Part III. LNCS, vol. 5304, pp. 386–399. Springer, Heidelberg (2008)
11. Obrador, P., Anguera, X., Oliveira, R., de Oliver, N.: The role of tags and image aesthetics in social image search. In: Proc. of SIGMM Workshop on Social Media, pp. 65–72 (2009)

12. Shan, Q., Jia, J., Agarwala, A.: High-quality motion deblurring from a single image. In: Proc. of SIGGRAPH, pp. 1–1 (2008)
13. Tomasi, C., Manduchi, R.: Bilateral filtering for gray and color images. In: Proc. of ICCV, pp. 839–846 (1998)
14. Tong, H., Li, M., Zhang, H.-J., Zhang, C.: Blur detection for digital images using wavelet transform. In: Proc. of IEEE ICME, pp. 17–20 (2004)
15. Yeh, C.-H., Ng, W.-S., Barsky, B.A., Ouhyoung, M.: An esthetics rule-based ranking system for amateur photos. In: Proc. of SIGGRAPH ASIA, pp. 1–1 (2009)

Author Index

Printing: Mercedes-Druck, Berlin
Binding: Stein+Lehmann, Berlin